QUANTIFICATION RULES

Let *u* represent any variable, *x*, *y*, etc., and *i* represent any individual symbol, either names, *a*, *b*, etc. or variables, *x*, *y*, etc.

Universal Instantiation (U.I.)

(u)ϕu entails ϕi

(*provided that* [Chapter 11] if *i* is a variable, then it must òccur free in ϕi in all places that *u* occurs free in ϕu)

Existential Generalization (E.G.)

ϕi entails ($\exists u$)ϕu

(*provided that* [Chapter 11] if *i* is a variable, then for every *u* free in ϕu, the same *i* is free in ϕi)

Existential Instantiation (E.I.)

($\exists u$)ϕu entails ϕw

provided that (1) *w* is a variable which does not occur free in any previous line (and (2) [Chapter 11] *w* occurs free in ϕw in all places that *u* occurs free in ϕu)

Universal Generalization (U.G.)

ϕw entails (u)ϕu

provided that (1) *w* is a free variable, (2) *w* is not flagged in any previous line, (3) *w* is not free in an assumed premise within whose scope ϕw occurs, and (4) [Chapter 11], *w* is not free in a line obtained by E.I.)

QUANTIFICATION EQUIVALENCES

I $\sim(\exists x)\phi x \equiv (x) \sim \phi x$

II $\sim(x)\phi x \equiv (\exists x) \sim \phi x$

III $(x)\phi x \equiv \sim(\exists x) \sim \phi x$

IV $(\exists x)\phi x \equiv \sim(x) \sim \phi x$

D1597313

LOGIC

THE ESSENTIALS

LOGIC

THE ESSENTIALS

Peter T. Manicas
Professor of Philosophy
Queens College

Arthur N. Kruger
Professor of Speech
C. W. Post College

McGRAW-HILL BOOK COMPANY

New York St. Louis San Francisco Auckland Düsseldorf Johannesburg Kuala Lumpur
London Mexico Montreal New Delhi Panama Paris São Paulo Singapore
Sydney Tokyo Toronto

This book was set in Optima by Ruttle, Shaw & Wetherill, Inc.
The editors were James F. Mirrielees and Barry Benjamin;
the designer was J. E. O'Connor;
the production supervisor was Sam Ratkewitch.
The drawings were done by Danmark & Michaels, Inc.
Kingsport Press, Inc., was printer and binder.

LOGIC: THE ESSENTIALS

1234567890 KPKP 7832109876

Library of Congress Cataloging in Publication Data

Manicas, Peter T
    Logic: the essentials.

    Revision of the authors' Essentials of logic
published in 1968.
      Bibliography: p.
      Includes index.
      1. Logic. I. Kruger, Arthur N., joint author.
II. Title.
BC108.M34 1976   160   75-34267
ISBN 0-07-039893-3

To
Theodore Manicas
and
Eleanor Kruger

If a man can play the true logician, and have as well judgment as invention, he may do great matters.

Francis Bacon

CONTENTS

PREFACE

Logic: The Essentials is a basic text for an undergraduate course in logic. It aims to offer a clear and modern treatment of logic as it bears upon reasoning, argument, rational inquiry, and rational decision making. Those familiar with the previous edition will note that we have retained all of the features which have appealed to the users of that edition and have added several other features which we believe will enhance the pedagogical value of the book.

In Part One we have added two new chapters, Language and Meaning and Definition, which explore some of the relationships between language and logic as well as some current issues in the philosophy of language.

As before, although the topics in Part Two, Formal Logic, are essentially the same as those treated in other standard texts, the discussion here seeks to avoid the impression that a command of the syllogism or other formal methods equips one to be preeminently logical. Consequently, the emphasis is not upon symbol manipulation but rather upon *understanding* the key concepts of deductive argument, such as entailment, proof, and inconsistency. Much attention is also paid to translating ordinary English into the symbolism of formal logic. In this way, we are able not only to keep formal logic in close touch with reality but also to make the student aware of the subtleties and problems of ordinary English.

The book departs from most introductory treatments, though not from the more advanced texts, in treating the logic of truth-functions before the syllogism. Experience in the classroom indicates that this order is both pedagogically and logically sounder than the traditional one. There is undoubtedly more material in Part Two than can be covered in a one-semester course, that is, if other subjects are to be dealt with as well. Besides treating the logic of truth-functions, categorical statements, and the syllogism, we have amplified and, hopefully, improved the material on the predicate calculus. Users of the previous edition will note that there are now three chapters on quantification instead of one. Instructors will find ample material in this section to choose from to enable them to achieve their particular objectives or desired orientation.

In keeping with the practical aim of the book, induction is treated extensively. Because so many arguments encountered in everyday experience are inductions, much attention is paid to clarifying the differences between inductive and deductive modes and to underscoring those features which bear on the appraisal of inductions. This material and the chapters on probability and scientific method, both of which have been revised, are, hopefully, enhanced by the use of the most recent discussions of these concepts. In the chapters on fallacies, the emphasis is upon developing a sensitivity to the ways in which arguments can go wrong. Illustrations are not confined to schoolroom stereotypes. Paradigm fallacies are presented in order to provide some rough criteria for judging fallacies, and the bulk of the discussion, as well as the exercises, includes arguments which require close analysis. Some may prefer to treat informal fallacies immediately after the discussion of basic concepts, Chapter 3. This is easily done, depending upon the instructor's individual preferences.

The material in Part Four, Applied Logic, seeks to show how logic is applied, first in scientific inquiry and then in decision making. Concepts and methods previously discussed are reintroduced in order to show some of the logical features of scientific method. The chapter on decision making contains material rarely found in a book of this type. Included here are rather detailed discussions of means and ends, facts and values, and the meaning of rational choice.

Besides the new chapters on language and quantification, we have also added many new exercises. The answers to every third exercise are contained in a special section at the end of the book. In addition, we have provided a complete set of progress tests that will allow the students to gauge their understanding while working on their own.

We are indebted, directly and indirectly, to many colleagues for their valuable comments and suggestions. Among these are Professors William T. Parry, George Dickie, P. R. Edwards, Chung-Ying Cheng, Robert S. Kruger, Edward Hacker, Andrej Zabludowski, and Robert S. Gurland. Special thanks are also due the publisher's reviewers, Professors S. Jack Odell and Stephen Braude, whose perceptive comments led to our restructuring and rewriting two chapters.

Peter T. Manicas
Arthur N. Kruger

INTRODUCTION

*The sleep of reason brings forth
monsters.*

F. Goya

Why Logic?

The question "Why logic?" would be far more interesting if anyone could really
get along without logic. Of course, this does not mean that one could not get
along without a *course* in logic, for apparently many do—and some even rather
well. But these people, too, need logic.

In the course of an ordinary day we do many things: we turn off the alarm
clock, dress, eat, catch a bus, study, work, go to a movie—we make decisions.
On some days we have more important decisions to make than on others: should
we apply to a graduate school, get married, buy a house, join the Army? Now
all of these activities and decisions involve *beliefs*. We believe that the alarm
is ringing, that the bus is due at 10:10, that the boy or girl we intend to marry
will make the perfect mate. It is hard to imagine anyone who had no beliefs and
harder still to envision anyone who did absolutely nothing. Indeed, to suppose
the existence of such a person is somewhat paradoxical; for if a person *could*
have *no* beliefs, we would be tempted to say that person wasn't a person at all or
that the person *believed* that he or she could believe nothing. But all beliefs
are subject to rational scrutiny, even the belief that one should believe nothing!
That is, there are *reasons* for our beliefs.

To be sure, some of our beliefs are unexamined or have not been subjected
to rational scrutiny. But even though we may not always be aware of the
reasons for holding them, still, if we *never* had reasons for them, then we would
hardly be considered human. We might be a vegetable or an automaton but
not a *thinking* human being. This is the crux of the matter: whenever there are
"reasons" for a belief—and most of us do *want* reasons—then we are involved

with logic, for logic, generally speaking, is primarily concerned with the *relation* between "reasons" and "beliefs"—more specifically with the relation between "evidence" and a "conclusion." For a belief basically is the psychological acceptance of a statement as being true or probably true. A statement is called a *conclusion* when it is justified by other statements, which in turn are called *evidence* or *reasons*. So try as we may, there is no escaping reason. As J. M. Robertson astutely observed, ". . . all discussion, all criticism, whether wise or unwise, is reasoning. The blunderers who warn you against reason are simply bad or temporarily confused reasoners. There is no getting away from reasoning, save by way of insanity. . . ."

Of course there are many different kinds of beliefs, ranging from the commonsensical to the esoteric. We believe, for example, that the alarm clock will ring if we set it, that it will stop ringing if we turn it off, that graduate school is a good thing, that God exists. Notice that in each case reasons could be produced in support of these beliefs. For example, we might believe that the alarm clock will ring if we set it *because* it has done so in the past. We might believe that graduate school is a good thing because we want to teach in a college and having advanced degrees is a prerequisite to such a career. As the the nature of the belief varies, so accordingly do the kinds of reasons. Different beliefs require different kinds of "evidence." The evidence for believing that the alarm is ringing might simply be that you hear it. The evidence for believing that graduate school is a good thing might include documents, statistics, and the like. The evidence that God exists might be the design which the universe seems to have.

Not all reasons, however, are *equally* "good" reasons, and some reasons are not good at all. Seeing the sun set or hearing a symphony is, in most circumstances, an excellent reason for believing that the sun *is* setting or that a symphony *is* being played. The "in most circumstances" added here is important because there might be *other* reasons for believing that seeing or hearing are *not* good reasons. One might be intoxicated and imagining such events or one might be dreaming. And, of course, there could be reasons other than our direct sense experience which might lead us to believe in their occurrence. We might, for example, believe that the alarm is ringing even though we are not in the room to hear it, for we might remember setting it to ring at say 7:00 o'clock and we see that it is now 7:00 o'clock. Most of us would want to say that in this case these are good reasons but quite probably not *as good* as actually hearing it. Put more generally, the strength of a logical relationship between reasons and belief varies, and sometimes there may be *no* logical relationship at all. Wishing that the alarm would stop ringing is *no* reason for believing that it has stopped.

When we say that there are "good" reasons for a belief, we are using terms of logical appraisal. More specifically, we are evaluating the *argument* which is produced in support of the belief—and this is the main task of logic. Actions presuppose beliefs, beliefs need reasons, and most of us want *good* reasons. A course in logic should help us to clarify what is involved in having "good reasons." Clear thinking and correct arguments, however, involve language. In Part One, therefore, we begin with an examination of language, giving special attention to those aspects of language which bear on the appraisal of argument.

PART ONE

FIRST PRINCIPLES

ONE

LANGUAGE AND MEANING

*. . . the ill and unfit choice of words
wonderfully obstructs the understanding.*

Francis Bacon

Since language is the primary medium of thought, logicians have long been concerned with the nature of language, both with its assets and its liabilities. But the writers in this long tradition—a tradition which begins at least with the systematic inquiries of Aristotle—have not always agreed with one another in their approach to language. Moreover, in our century, much attention has been paid to various questions regarding language and meaning so that the present is characterized by both progress and, unfortunately, unresolved controversy. This chapter and the one which follows are not the place for an exhaustive discussion of the various issues which have been raised. Still, it is important for our purposes that at least some of the central ideas concerning language be elucidated and some of the advances in this area indicated, especially as they bear on clear thinking and argument.

Speech Acts

Speaking (and writing) are things *we do,* just as getting married, buying food, and voting in an election are things we do. And, like these actions, speaking (and writing) are *social* acts. They involve other persons in a complex fabric of relationships. To characterize speaking as a social act leads directly to certain conclusions. First, we may say that *language is a system of symbols,* of words and sentences, *with which* we speak and write. A certain pattern of sounds or string of marks becomes symbols insofar as they are meaningful to members of a linguistic community. These sounds and marks, *as* words and sentences, are the vehicles employed by members of a community in performing linguistic acts. We may say that these symbols are conventional in the sense that they have meaning by virtue of the fact that they are used in particular ways by the members of a linguistic community. Thus, the word "dog"[1] has the same meaning as *chien* in French, *hund* in German, and *perro* in Spanish.

Second, given that speaking and writing are things we do, if we look at the *purpose* or *uses* of our verbal and written acts, we may then get some insight into both meaning and language. As we shall see, this is a much more complicated matter than might seem at first blush. Finally, given that these acts are social acts, we must always recognize that there is a *social context* in which they are performed. Just as getting married, buying food, and voting in an election take place in a context which involves circumstances, conventions, and implicit understandings, so too are speech acts social acts which involve circumstances, conventions, and various understandings. And, as with all social acts, in the case of linguistic acts, there is a *transaction* between speaker (or writer) and an audience.

These considerations suggest that we should look (at least) at the following three important aspects of linguistic acts:

1 What was said. This includes examination of the content of our utterances, of the particular words and expressions employed.
2 What was the force of what was said. Here we can consider both the intentions of the speaker and the context.
3 Whether what was said produced certain kinds of consequences or effects upon the thoughts, attitudes, feelings, or actions of the hearer or reader.

These points are easily illustrated. Suppose that Sam says, "Close the door." First, in this sentence "door" refers to some door and "close" means close. Second, in saying "Close the door," we may suppose that (generally) the context includes some door which is open (or at least a door which Sam believes is open), that someone else is present to hear Sam, and that Sam would like that person to close the door.[2]

---

[1] In what follows, when we mention a word we will put it within quotation marks or sometimes in italics. Thus, in the sentence *"Boston" has six letters,* we mention a word and say something about it. In mentioning the word we use its name. In *Boston is a city in Massachusetts,* we *use* a word to say something about a city.

[2] Instead of saying that there is an open door or that Sam believes that there is, etc., we might say that Sam *takes responsibility* for these conditions holding. In other words, Sam would be prepared to "take back" his utterances if any of them fail to obtain. See William P. Alston, *Philosophy*

Given these circumstances, then, we might say that "Close the door" is a request or command: It has this force or function. (Whether it is a request or a command will in large measure depend upon *how* Sam says, "Close the door," and this, too, is part of context.) Third, Sam's saying "Close the door" may bring the person addressed to close the door which Sam referred to, or it might only get the person angry or affect him or her in various other ways.

The points illustrated here are quite elementary (even if, surprisingly perhaps, they are often forgotten). But in the remainder of this chapter we may develop each of them somewhat more systematically. In the section which immediately follows, the idea of the *force* of an utterance is examined. The section concludes with some considerations regarding the effects or consequences of saying something. In the sections which follow, we look more closely at problems of reference and meaning.

The Force and Effects of Speech Acts

In saying something, we perform a linguistic act, but our linguistic acts may be seen to have different uses, functions, or purposes: they differ in *force*. Since a sentence is the smallest linguistic unit which can be used to say something, each of the following sentences might be employed in the performance of a (complete) speech act[3]:

1　Close the door.
2　It is raining.
3　I shall pay you the money tomorrow.
4　Is he in Detroit or Chicago?
5　The apples are good.

In particular linguistic actions, each of the five sentences could be used to say something, but there is no necessity that on particular occasions of their use, they have the same *force* or *function*. For example, sentence 1 might be used to make a request, to command, or, in appropriate circumstances, to plead, entreat, or beg. Sentence 2 might be used to make a report, to make an announcement, to state an opinion or belief, to express disgust, to inform, or to answer. Sentence 3 might be used to promise, to declare one's intentions, to express impatience or hostility, or to contract. Sentence 4 might be used to

---

of *Language* (Englewood Cliffs, N.J.: Prentice-Hall, 1964). Alston's book has been most helpful in this discussion.

[3] We are proceeding here both roughly and perhaps somewhat dogmatically. Remember that context is crucial. Although shouting "Fire!" in a theater would count as saying something, in the absence of some such particular linguistic context, the single word "fire" could not be used to perform a complete speech act. In expressing the view that sentences are the smallest units available to say something, Alston states: "To perform a complete linguistic action we must utter a sentence or some expression which in that context is elliptical for a sentence" (ibid., p. 33 n.).

question, to ask, or to interrogate, and sentence 5 might be used to recommend, to espouse, to affirm, to assess, or to approve.[4]

There are of course similarities between various functions, e.g., between requesting and ordering or between announcing and informing. But it is as important to notice that there are also differences. Moreover, quite evidently, it will be *context* which will generally determine the particular force of a speech act. Our list of five sentences is, of course, but a paltry sample, and the various functions which we have identified also represent but a few of the possible functions of language. Others which readily come to mind are naming, pronouncing, adopting, praying, making a bet, and ascribing or recognizing a right or a responsibility.

What further complicates matters is that these functions are not entirely exclusive. On any one given occasion, an utterance may function in several ways at once. "I am sorry," for example, generally functions as an apology, but it may also shade over into a statement or description of the speaker's feelings. "This is good" may be an assessment (in the sense that "The painting is valuable" might be an assessment) *as well as* a recommendation — in which case, the hearer is being urged to try it, buy it, etc. "The stoplight is red," uttered by a passenger in a car moving toward an intersection, might be both reportive and prescriptive; that is, it may be intended to be factual *and* to have the force of "Stop!"

Notice, next, that the *form,* syntax, grammatical structure, or punctuation of a sentence do not necessarily indicate its function, even if at times such factors do provide a clue to it. Declarative sentences, like "It is raining" or "The stoplight is red," may function as reports, announcements, or prescriptions. Imperatives, like "Close the door," may function as demands, requests, suggestions, or even warnings. Finally, a sentence with an interrogative form, like "Do you like *that* painting?" or "Didn't you close the window?" might function as a criticism, an expression of disapproval or reproach, or a request. It has been said that when Stanislavsky was directing the Moscow Art Theater, he would require his pupils to convey fifty different senses of the word "tonight" to a special audience that recorded what they thought was being communicated.

The preceding considerations suggest that the older classifications of the functions of discourse — consisting of two or three categories, such as "informative," "expressive," and "directive" — though perhaps pedagogically useful, do not adequately deal with the diversity, flexibility, and complexity of our linguistic acts. This is particularly true when the so-called "descriptive" or "informative" function is given special status — when it is assumed, for example, that the primary aim of language is to communicate factual information or that "descrip-

---

[4] J. L. Austin called the act *of* saying something "the locutionary act," and the function which was served *in* saying something, "the illocutionary act." Thus in saying anything at all, we utter certain noises which have some "meaning." But in saying something, we also either request, state, ask, recommend, assess, etc. See Austin's informative book *How to Do Things with Words,* J. O. Urmson (ed.) (New York: Oxford University Press, 1962).

tive" sentences constitute a special class which somehow stands apart from the actions and intentions of speakers.[5]

While it is undoubtedly true that we usually do discern and grasp the differences in the various kinds of speech acts being performed—for otherwise we could scarcely communicate with each other at all—it is also true that we often fail to grasp subtle, and sometimes not so subtle, differences in the force of utterances. Such failure is an important source of *mis*understanding, of controversy, and of ill feeling. Since communication is a transaction, either or both parties may contribute to its breakdown. To anticipate one aspect of our subsequent discussion of verbal disputes, the failure of a speaker to make clear, or of a hearer to grasp, that an utterance in some context is advice and *not* an order leads to misunderstanding, often to fruitless argument, and possibly to anger or some other unfortunate consequence. One can only speculate on how often breakdowns in communication do occur.

These considerations lead us naturally to a final pair of distinctions. Consider first the distinction between speech acts and their effects or consequences. Saying something with a certain force will generally have effects on the hearer. When we say anything at all, we aim, at the very least, to be understood. When we succeed, the "effect" of saying something is that the hearer is brought to an understanding of the meaning and force of the utterance. But there may be other "effects" as well. The hearer may, in consequence, become irritated, aroused, confused, deceived, convinced, or, as in our early example, perform some overt act like closing the door.

By distinguishing between speech acts and their effects, we can also discriminate between effects which are intended and those which are not. To be sure, we always intend at least to be understood, but we may or may not intend to arouse or to anger, to deceive, or even to inform. You may mention something to me, for example, without intending anything in particular, but your utterance might nonetheless convince me that someone is a liar or that someone is my friend.

As the example suggests, some speech acts are such that their effects go beyond "understanding," in the sense that certain *other* effects are brought about by saying something. Following J. L. Austin's terminology, we may call these effects the *perlocutionary effects* of an utterance. Thus, *getting someone to close the door* by saying "Close the door" is a perlocutionary effect of the speech act. *Persuading someone to do something* by saying something or *irritating someone* by saying something is a perlocutionary effect. In general, then, a perlocutionary effect is what we bring about by saying something, as when we distract, prevent, confuse, or even deceive by our words. Notice that such effects may be intended or not.

There are several important applications of the idea of perlocutionary ef-

---

[5] The issue is too large to pursue here. The idea that the descriptive, informative, or, sometimes, cognitive, function is fundamental apparently underlies the *verification theory of meaning,* a fundamental tenet of what is known as logical positivism, or logical empiricism. For some introductory discussion of this issue, see Alston, op. cit., chap. 4.

fects. First, we should not confuse informing, expressing, exhorting, or requesting with convincing, persuading, encouraging, and getting someone to do something. One can inform and not convince or one can express and not persuade. There is a difference between what we *intend* in saying something, what we *do* in saying something, and what the effects are of our saying something. I may *intend* to give you advice, my utterance *may be taken as* an order, and you may *become* irritated. I may intend to convince you by telling you something, but instead I may only confuse you.

Second, the distinction shows that "successful communication" is a more complex matter than may be supposed. There is a sense in which successful communication means being understood, but there is another or extended sense in which it involves getting persons to change their minds, attitudes, beliefs, or mode of behavior. Words may "fall on deaf ears" in just the sense that the intended perlocutionary effects do not obtain.

EXERCISES

A Suppose that you aim to advise Sam that he ought to stay in school by saying: "Sam, you ought to stay in school." If so, then (at least) the following conditions in the context of your utterance must obtain for you to advise meaningfully:

1 There is some person named "Sam" who is the addressee of the utterance.
2 The context makes clear that "Sam" refers to Sam.
3 Sam is considering leaving school.
4 It is possible for Sam to leave school.
5 You believe that it would be good for Sam to stay in school.

For the following speech acts, fill out as many conditions as you can which would seem to hold:

1 Informing Sam that it is raining by saying: "It is raining."
2 Ordering Sam to dismiss Debbie by saying: "Fire her."
3 Warning Sam of impending danger by saying: "Watch out."
4 Expressing happiness at Sam's winning a scholarship by saying: "What great news!"

B Each of the following sentences might be used to perform speech acts with a different force. Provide at least three and give the special conditions which might obtain so as to discriminate them. For example, "The stoplight is turning red" might be a report, a warning, a command, or an answer to a question if . . . .

5 I am sorry.
6 The cheese is mushy.

7   Didn't you do your homework?
8   Please listen.
9   Shut it, if you can.
10 The play was good.

Terms

Part of the problem of determining "what was said" or in determining the linguistic content of a speech act is the problem of determining to what, if anything, linguistic expressions *refer*. In our initial illustration of this chapter, we noted that in saying "Close the door," "door" is used to refer to some door. Similarly, in saying "She is at home," "she" refers to some person and "home" presumably to her place of residence. We can say that generally in speaking (and writing), some linguistic expressions are often used to refer to something or other. In "It is raining" we refer to the condition of the weather. In "The apples are good" we refer to some apples and say something about them. For reasons which are perhaps already evident, philosophers have long been interested in what we may call the *referring* function of linguistic expressions, a function which is often ancillary to, but essentially involved in, the performance of many various linguistic acts. Thus, while "Close the door" is a request or order, the speaker evidently is referring to some door.

We may begin our discussion with an account of terms. *Term* may be defined as follows: An expression is a term if it makes sense to apply it to a thing. As we shall see, it is this feature of terms which allows us to use them referentially. Thus, "dog" is a term, but "and" is not. We couldn't say "This thing is an and." Not all words, accordingly, are terms and, as we shall see, some phrases, such as "the little brown dog" or "dogs with blue-ribbon pedigrees who have consistently won prizes," will also count as terms. Terms may be usefully classified in the following categories, though the categories given here are by no means exhaustive.

General and Singular Terms General terms may be used to refer to, or may be said to be true of, many different objects, examples being "horse" (or "horses"), "automobile," "school," "cocker spaniel," and "little brown cocker spaniel." As we noted, phrases may count as terms, e.g., "little brown cocker spaniel." General terms are sometimes also called *class terms* because they are indifferently true of any member of the class defined by the term. General terms, or class terms, may be arranged in decreasing (or increasing) generality; thus "living being," "animal," "dog," "poodle," and "miniature poodle" are true of increasingly smaller classes of objects and, accordingly, they are increasingly less general.

Singular terms are used to refer to a single person, place, thing, or event, any one of which, though individual, may be very complex. Singular terms, in contrast to general terms, are true of but one thing. Singular terms thus play a central role in the mechanism of reference. All proper nouns ("Golden Gate Bridge," "Pike's Peak," and "Pegasus"), expressions called *definite descriptions* (such as "the winged horse of Bellerophon," "the author of *Waverly*," and "the Battle of Bunker Hill"), as well as demonstratives and possessives followed by general terms (such as "this chair," "that house," and "my dog") are singular terms. Indeed, general terms may and do play an important role in the construction of singular terms, which we can get by prefixing the former with demonstrative particles and articles. Then, instead of requiring that everything which we choose to refer to have a name, we can speak of *this* chair or *that* house.

Demonstratives and pronouns ("this," "he," "you," "it," etc.) can also function as singular terms, as in "This is Sam's," "He is at home," and "It is red." To fix the reference or intended application of "this," "he," and "it" in such sentences, context is, of course, all important; for apart from context, the reference of such terms is undeterminable. The same may be said of what are called *singular descriptions,* such as "the President of the United States" or "the woman who led the march." These are distinguishable from definite descriptions — e.g., "the first President of the United States" — precisely because, while definite descriptions pick out one object without special conditions of context, singular descriptions do not.

The distinction between singular and general terms, it should be noted, turns on their respective roles in sentences, e.g., on whether they are subjects or predicates, and not on their grammatical components. Thus, in the sentence "The agile center of the Braves was voted to the All-Star team," "agile" and "All-Star" are adjectives, "center," "team," and "Braves" are substantives, and "was voted" is a verb. But the whole phrase "The agile center of the Braves" is a singular term, since it is true of a single individual; and the whole phrase "was voted to the All-Star team" is a general term, since it is true of all the players who were voted to the All-Star team.

The contrast between singular terms and general terms is logical and plays an important role in what logicians call *predication.* In predicating, a general term is joined to a singular term to form a sentence which is true or false depending upon whether the general term is true of or false of the object referred to by the singular term. Predication is illustrated in each of the following sentences:

1 My daughter is a hockey player.
2 My daughter is tall.
3 My daughter studies.

Apart from some unimportant subtleties of idiom, 2 is interchangeable with "My daughter is a tall person," and 3 is interchangeable with "My daughter is a studier."

Absolute and Relative Terms Strictly speaking, our discussion thus far of singular and general terms has been of *absolute* singular terms and absolute general terms, and we have not yet considered relative terms. *Relative* terms are those which refer to things that are involved in, or are an integral part of, some relationship. Thus, while "Pike's Peak" applies to, or is true of, only Pike's Peak and the general term "athlete" is true of Billie Jean King, Henry Aaron, and Joe Namath, a relative term like "brother of" is true of Jesse James *with respect to* Frank James and vice versa. Similarly, "bigger than," "part of," "indebted to," and "gives to" are relative terms. "Bigger than" is true of Tokyo with respect to Rome or of Wilt Chamberlain with respect to Calvin Murphy.

Collective Terms and Mass Terms *Collective* terms are those which can be used to refer to a number of things grouped together as a unit, such as "jury," "ball team," "union," "army," and "crowd." *Mass* terms by contrast have the property of referring cumulatively. Good examples are "water" and "red." Thus, any sum of parts which are water is water, and any sum of parts which are red are red. Some general terms may also double as mass terms. For example, take the sentence "Put some oil in the salad." We may assume that this does not mean "Put a particular oil in the salad" but that it means "Put some portion of the stuff called 'oil' in the salad." Some sentences tend to be ambiguous because the context does not always make clear whether a given term is being used in a general or a mass sense. For example, in the sentence "Mary had a little lamb," "lamb" might be taken in either of two senses (which we leave to the reader to determine).

When employing both collective and general terms, one must be aware that they have two very different uses, which we may call the *collective* and the *distributive* use. Such terms are used distributively when something is predicated of each of the several members of a unit (or class); they are used collectively when something is predicated of the unit (or class) taken as a whole. Thus, in "The jury were all white, middle-class," "jury," a collective term, is being used distributively. That is, something is predicated of each person in the jury. In "The jury was deadlocked for two days before it came in with a verdict of not guilty," "jury" is being used collectively. Sometimes a collective term is used both collectively and distributively, as in "All juries are carefully selected." Here "jury" is used collectively as regards each jury taken as a unit, and it is used distributively as regards different juries — something is predicated of each taken severally.

Similar considerations apply to general terms. In "Whales are mammals," "whales" is used distributively; in "Whales are rapidly disappearing," it is used collectively. Failure to grasp these differences leads to a host of confusions and misunderstandings. For example, if one treats "whales" distributively in "Whales are rapidly disappearing," one may reach the nonsensical conclusion that the creature now swimming off the coast of Long Island is rapidly disappearing because it is a whale.

Abstract and Concrete Terms This distinction is commonly drawn by saying that a concrete term refers to a *thing,* while an abstract term refers to an *attribute,* where "thing" means roughly anything capable of possessing attributes.

Terms, such as proper names and singular descriptions, which can be used to refer to particular entities — particular persons, things, objects, operations, processes, places, etc. — are thus concrete. By contrast, terms such as "fatherhood," "humanity," "triangularity," and "virtue" are abstract because they are used to refer to the attribute of being a father, or a human, etc.

There is an important difference between "father" and "fatherhood" and between "red" and "redness." "Father" is a concrete term since it is used to refer to individual fathers. "Fatherhood" by contrast refers to the attribute of being a father. Thus when "fatherhood" is used referentially it would seem to require the existence of *abstract objects,* as in "Fatherhood is a virtue." Here we are not referring to fathers but apparently to the attribute. Similarly, "red" is easily thought of as a general term used to refer to red *things,* while "redness" evidently refers to the attribute *red.* Unfortunately, pursuing the difficulties raised by these considerations would be out of place in this introductory discussion.[6]

Polar-Opposite Terms These are terms which refer to a quality which may vary from one extreme to another, such as hot-cold, rich-poor, black-white, fast-slow, and smart-dumb. Such terms are called *polar opposites* because the two extreme conditions or characteristics to which they refer may be thought of as being at the opposite ends or poles of an axis. Polar terms are by nature vague, or lack precision, since the quality or class which they refer to cannot be precisely delineated. That is, they overlap adjoining qualities, as do qualities like cold, cool, tepid, lukewarm, hot, and very hot. The fact that such terms refer to characteristics which are imprecise is often a source of misunderstanding and confusion, as we shall see shortly.

EXERCISES

Classify the following terms, using one or more of the following categories: general, singular, absolute, relative, collective, mass, abstract, concrete, and polar. Keep in mind that a given term may fall into more than one category.

1	class	2	government
3	salad oil	4	immoral
5	the federal government	6	regiment
7	teacher of	8	Judge John Sirica
9	motherhood	10	sand
11	New York Jets	12	dark-complexioned
13	cousin of	14	ointment
15	chewy	16	brightness
17	aptitude	18	clear
19	perseverance	20	leadership

[6] For further discussion see W. V. O. Quine, *Word and Object* (Cambridge, Mass.: M.I.T. Press, 1960), pp. 118ff.

Connotation (Intension) and Denotation (Extension)

Our discussion of terms gave us some important insight into the mechanisms of reference and the referring function of language. In determining "what was said" we saw that linguistic expressions may be used to refer to things in the world. Indeed, it is hard to imagine a language which did not provide some means to allow us to talk about the world we live in. But this account needs to be further expanded to include what philosophers have variously called the **connotation, intension,** or **sense** of terms. In one of its many meanings, connotation, intension, or sense — three words which we shall use interchangeably — is the **meaning** of a term.

Our discussion will begin with what we called general terms, or those terms which may be said to be true or false of more than one object. Regarding general terms, logicians have customarily drawn an important distinction between the connotation (intension, or sense) and the denotation (extension, or reference) of a term. Let us first define denotation. The **denotation** of a term consists of all those objects of which the term is true. The denotation of "tiger," for example, includes all the tigers that ever were, are, or will be. The denotation (reference, or extension) of "satellite of Jupiter" includes just twelve objects, since "satellite of Jupiter" is true of only Jupiter's twelve moons. And "unicorn" or "centaur" denotes the empty class, for in fact there are no unicorns or centaurs. This is not to say that "unicorn" and "centaur" have *no* meaning, for, as we shall see, both terms have sense, or connotative meaning.

As we shall use the term here, the sense or connotation of a term is the conventional criterion for applying a term. That is, the connotation is the set of characteristics or features which something must have if the term is correctly to apply to it. In the strictest sense, the connotation or sense is the *meaning* of a term and tells us how the term is used by speakers of the language. It is the *conventional* criterion of application or use in that speakers of the language normally, or in ordinary circumstances, employ the criterion to determine correct use. For example, the connotation of the word "bachelor" is "unmarried male." This is what speakers of English *mean* by "bachelor." In this case the criterion, unmarried male, provides the necessary and sufficient conditions for applying the word "bachelor." In other words, "bachelor" applies correctly to anyone who is an unmarried male and does not apply to persons who are not unmarried males.

For many ordinary words, however, no characteristic seems to be pervasive in all of its proper uses. That is, the criteria which may correctly determine usage may vary. Consider Ludwig Wittgenstein's well-known example of the word "game." "Game" connotes a diversion, a contest, an activity played according to rules, and an activity whose outcome is decided by superior skill, strength, or good fortune. Although these are all senses of the word "game," there are activities properly called "games" which lack one or another of these characteristics. Thus, some games are not diversions, some are not contests, some are not played according to rules, and some have no outcome decided by superior skill, luck, etc. Consider as examples the Olympic games, a variety of children's games, and the ritualistic games which so frequently appear in anthropological literature.[7]

A diagram will be helpful in illustrating this situation. In the diagram the letters A, B, etc., represent various activities, and P_1, P_2, etc., represent properties or features of these activities.[8]

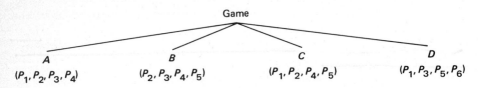

Game

| A | B | C | D |
| (P_1, P_2, P_3, P_4) | (P_2, P_3, P_4, P_5) | (P_1, P_2, P_4, P_5) | (P_1, P_3, P_5, P_6) |

As the diagram suggests, there is no feature common to all those activities which we call games. Indeed, even if we select some number of those activities, for example, A, B, and C, which have some feature in common—in this case P_2—it is not necessarily in virtue of having P_2 that they are called games. Nor will we always be able to say whether some features are more important than others or how many a thing should have (or lack) before we would say that some activity is a game.

Wittgenstein called the network of overlapping and crisscrossing similarities a *family resemblance,* and said that games form a "family." This idea is extremely helpful to an understanding of the structure of language, for it shows *how* a term may properly apply to things in the world, even when the latter do not have certain necessary and sufficient conditions for properly applying the term.

EXERCISES

A Illustrate the difference between the connotation and the denotation of the following terms: athlete, United States senator, college, widow, solar system, religion, liberal, wise man.

B Comment on the views expressed in the following opinions:

1   The word "good" applies equally to actions, persons, societies, tools, food, houses, and many other things. But if so, then there must be some characteristic which all these various things share. That characteristic must be goodness itself.

2   "Religion" is a term void of meaningful application, since, as far as I

---

[7] Compare Johan Huizinga, *Homo Ludens* (Boston: Beacon Press, 1955).

[8] A similar diagram was used by Renford Bambrough in his "Universals and Family Resemblances," reprinted in George Pitcher (ed.), *Wittgenstein: The Philosophical Investigations* (New York: Doubleday Anchor, 1966).

can tell, there is nothing in common in all the different things which people call "religion."

Problems in Meaning

Several errors stem from the confusion of connotation and denotation. One such error is to suppose that expressions which have different senses or connotations necessarily have different references or denotations. But it is quite possible that two expressions have different senses — i.e., their meaning is different — and yet denote the same thing. Frege's well-known example of "the Evening Star" and "the Morning Star" is a good illustration.[9] While these two expressions have different senses, they nonetheless denote the same object, namely Venus. Similarly, "rational animal" and "featherless biped" have different meanings, but in most contexts they would likely have the same denotation or extension.

More interesting, consider the following two descriptions of a political meeting:

1 Mr. M's audience was made up chiefly of older schoolboys, housewives, local labor bosses, the rank and file of the Garment Workers' Union, and a few Socialist academics.
2 Mr. M's audience was made up chiefly of a number of male college students, nonsalaried working women, local labor leaders, the members of the Garment Workers' Union, and some professors who favor industrial democracy.

Although the denotations of the key terms in both accounts might very well be identical, the accumulated differences in the connotative meanings suggest two entirely different conclusions about the audience.

As this example indicates, efforts to persuade, influence, and convince often depend as much upon the choice of words with differing connotations as upon the facts. Thus, "rank and file" has a meaning or connotation which is quite different than "members," although the two terms would likely apply to the same persons. "Members" is more neutral in the sense that it is less pejorative than "rank and file" in the context in which it appears. Similarly, "a few Socialist academics" and "some professors who favor industrial democracy" are used to apply to the same persons, but the first is pejorative and the second honorific. In short, the first version attempts to persuade the reader that Mr. M is not deserving of support because of the kind of people who support him, whereas the second attempts to do just the opposite. Both convey the same facts but use words which convey entirely different meanings.

Often, of course, replacing a word with another having a slightly different sense will also result in an important shift in denotation. Compare, for example,

[9] Gottlob Frege (1848–1925) was an important logician and philosopher of language.

"gourmet," "gourmand," and "glutton." "Gourmet" applies to one who is a connoisseur in eating and drinking; "gourmand" applies to one who is less fastidious than a gourmet; and "glutton" applies to one who eats voraciously or to excess. "Gourmet" is complimentary and "glutton" is pejorative. But here it is because the terms apply to quite different sorts of persons and behavior. A person who is a gourmet is by no means the same as one who is a glutton. The former is praised in our society and the latter is condemned. Other examples are easy to find: "brave" and "foolhardy"; "administrator" and "ruler"; "one who is generous" and "squanderer"; "educate" and "indoctrinate." Foolhardiness is *un-reasoned,* bravery is not; a ruler dominates or controls, an administrator does not; a squanderer spends foolishly, one who is generous does not; indoctrination is propagandistic slanting, education is not.

Obviously, settling questions of meaning does not settle questions about the facts. That is, there may be ample room for argument as to whether some act was brave or foolhardy, whether some person is an administrator or a ruler, whether someone is generous or a squanderer, and whether what goes on in schools, newspapers, etc., is education or indoctrination. Again, there is much room here for controversy and confusion.

In considering such differences, some writers speak of "the emotive force" or the "emotive meaning" of terms. Different words surely do have a different emotive force if by this one means that they can be used to express different attitudes. But this would seem to be less a difference in *kind* of meaning than a difference either in *meaning* or in the *force* of our speech acts. And these latter differences may indeed be subtle. Here both intention and context are important. The two sentences "He is a stool pigeon" and "He is an informant of the police" are clearly different, but it is not clear whether there is a difference in the denotation of "stool pigeon" and "informant of the police," or whether there is a difference in connotation. For example, is a stool pigeon one who betrays his friends? Finally, it is not clear whether, in the statement "He is a stool pigeon," one is *primarily* expressing one's contempt for the person or, say, simply reporting or describing.

It is evident that for practical purposes, settling on which is the correct answer to these questions is less important than grasping the moral of the story, which is quite clear: The critical writer and reader must be alert to differences, especially subtle ones, in the *meaning* and *force* of discourse. And when the function is primarily informative, we must be careful to choose words which accurately characterize what we are trying to talk about.

A final point relating to this discussion of meaning and to the difference between connotation and denotation pertains to what literary critics (in contrast to logicians!) call connotation. Such critics point out, rightly, that people tend to associate various personal experiences with certain words. Thus, because of their actual experiences with, say, cows, the word "cow" to some people is associated with gentleness while to others it may be associated with peevishness. Rather than call such associations the "subjective connotation" or simply "connotation" of a word, as most literary critics do, it makes more sense—and certainly reduces confusion—to call such associations what they are, namely, **asso-ciations.** The associations of a word differ from the sense meaning in that they are not part of the meaning in the normal use of the word, even though in appropriate contexts the word may evoke a variety of different ideas in the mind of the reader or writer. Consider, e.g., Keats's lines "Oh, for a draught of vintage that hath cooled a long age in the deep-delved earth" rewritten as "Oh, for a drink of wine that has been reduced in temperature over a long period in ground with deep furrows in it."[10] While the key words and phrases in both versions are roughly synonymous in sense meaning and denotation, the difference in associations is quite marked.

EXERCISES

A The following collections of words are close, but not exactly the same, in meaning. Explain the differences in their connotations. Which are complimentary and which are pejorative?

1 Firm, obstinate, pigheaded, determined, stubborn
2 Bold, rash, foolhardy, brave, daring
3 Frank, candid, naive, honest, ingenuous, sincere
4 Self-reliant, self-centered, independent, resolute, know-it-all
5 Energetic, hyperactive, frenetic, vigorous, hard-working

B Translate the following passage into language whose terms denote (roughly) the same things or persons but whose connotative meaning suggests a difference in attitude or evaluation of what is being talked about. Write two versions, one pejorative and one honorific. The key terms are within parentheses.

The (program, which was not clear in all of its aspects), marked (an important departure from the status quo). It appealed mainly to (those who believe that the United States should pay exclusive attention to domestic programs) and to (those who defend the legitimacy of governments of left-wing persuasion). A key feature of the program involved (restraints) against funding programs which provide countries with (the instruments of war).

Vagueness and Ambiguity

To achieve absolute precision in language is an unattainable ideal, since most words exhibit varying degrees of vagueness. This is probably an inevitable consequence of the basic ways language is learned and of the fact that meanings

[10] The paraphrase of Keats is borrowed from Alston, op. cit., whose discussion of these matters is highly recommended.

are not fixed by explicit rules. For most purposes, however, one does not have to be overly precise. Failure to express ourselves clearly is due often to our careless use of language rather than to the nature of language itself. Instead of being specific and saying "sombrero," e.g., we say "hat"; instead of "cocker spaniel," we say "dog"; instead of "shuffled," we say "walked." In some cases, of course, there is no need to be more specific; in others, we are too lazy or our vocabulary is limited.

At other times vagueness results from the inherent lack of precise boundaries in the extension of certain terms. We saw this to be true of polar-opposite words, like "warm," "crowded," and "heavy." But it is an error to suppose that a sharp line must be drawn before such terms can be meaningfully or usefully applied. Even certain singular terms which seem to be fairly precise may upon inspection prove to be vague. Who is to say, e.g., precisely how much of the surrounding terrain is included in what we call "Mt. Everest"?

Failure to recognize that it is not logically possible to draw absolute boundaries between overlapping or contiguous categories often leads to unwarranted assumptions and erroneous conclusions, such as, "All differences in degree or all small differences are insignificant," or "Overlapping categories are basically the same," or even "Polar opposites, like hot-cold, are the same because they are connected on a continuum."

In addition to the kind of vagueness which results from our inability to fix once and for all the boundaries of the extension of some terms, there are two other kinds of vagueness inherent in terms. One results from a feature of some words noted earlier, namely, that it is impossible to provide the necessary and sufficient conditions for the application of a term, as with "game," "religion," or "romantic literature." Here the situation seems to be as follows: We usually have some "paradigm" case or cases regarding which there is general agreement as to the application of the term. Thus, baseball and chess are surely games, Episcopalianism and Roman Catholicism are surely religions, and Keats's and Shelley's poetry is surely romantic literature. But it is less clear, perhaps, whether some of the informal rituals described by social psychologists are games, whether Humanism is a religion, or whether Swinburne's poetry is romantic literature.

Finally, there is what Friedrich Waismann has called "open texture."[11] The point of open texture is that we cannot *foresee* all the possible conditions in which a term *might* be used. "Gold," for example, would seem to be defined with absolute precision in terms familiar to scientists. But, Waismann asks, what would we say if we discovered a substance which satisfied all the known tests for gold but which emitted a new sort of radiation? Should we call it "gold" or not? Waismann argues—and rightly it seems—that this *possibility of vagueness* characterizes all the terms which we use to talk about the things in our experience; for as experience remains open-ended, so, too, are the terms which we use to apply to it.

[11] Compare Friedrich Waismann, "Verifiability," in A. Flew (ed.), *Logic and Language,* 1st series (Oxford: Basil Blackwell, 1952).

There is a vagueness, then, which is to be distinguished from the vagueness which results from carelessness and lack of specificity. This vagueness which is inherent in many of our terms may serve useful purposes, however. It enables us to communicate without being overly wordy; it facilitates communication across the boundaries of inherently open-ended experience; and, if need be, we can conjoin several vague terms and use additional words or nonverbal signs — such as gestures and facial expressions when speaking — to give greater precision to our meanings.

Where vagueness is sometimes useful, ambiguity, except for its important uses in imaginative literature and poetry, is harmful — i.e., it is an obstacle to communication. We may distinguish two kinds of ambiguity: (1) ambiguity which results when a word or expression can be readily interpreted in two or more different ways, and (2) ambiguity of reference, where a term may refer to more than one thing but where the context does not indicate which one. Let us consider the first type of ambiguity first.

While many words have several very different meanings — e.g., "air," "round," "light," "case," and "means" — by themselves they are not ambiguous. They only become so when used in contexts in which there could be doubt over which meaning is the appropriate or intended one. Consider these sentences in which "means" occurs unambiguously:

1 "Since there were no survivors in the plane crash, it means that the ambassador, who was a passenger, perished." Here "means" means "implies."
2 "Maintaining a high scholastic average means much to him." Here "means" means "has value or importance."
3 "Those heavy clouds mean that it's probably going to rain." Here "mean" means "are a sign of."
4 " 'Stag' means 'an adult male deer.' " Here "means" means "is defined as."

Even in the artificial context of textbook illustrations, the meaning of "means" is generally clear in these sentences.

Ambiguity, however, does occur in sentences like these: "Our mothers bore us" or "Kojak cracked the case." The ambiguities would likely be resolved by locating each sentence in a wider context. Thus, regarding the first sentence, were there contiguous remarks about birth or boredom? In the second sentence, while reference to "Kojak" might suggest that the case referred to is a crime under investigation, context might show that "case" means a twelve-bottle carton of whiskey or a plaster form used for making molds. Ambiguity is used humorously in making puns. For example, in the introduction of a speech given at a Thanksgiving Day dinner, William M. Evarts, Secretary of State under Hayes, noted: "You have been giving your attention to turkey stuffed with sage; you are now about to consider a sage stuffed with turkey." Or consider Mae West's famous remark, "When women go wrong, men go right after them."

Ambiguity of reference occurs where, as with the use of pronouns in some contexts, there is unclarity regarding the antecedent of the pronoun. In addition, faulty syntax, misplaced modifiers, dangling modifiers, certain elliptical constructions, and the blurring of the collective/distributive use of certain terms are often sources of such ambiguity. Here are some examples:

1. "Those who come late often miss some good opportunities." Here it is impossible to tell if "often" modifies "come late" or "miss." Logicians generally call this type of ambiguity *amphiboly*, or ambiguity due to faulty grammatical construction. (Grammarians call the error a *squinting modifier*.)
2. "Jane told Bob that she didn't like his checkered suit, which was in bad taste." Here "which" may refer to Jane's remark or to Bob's suit.
3. "A jar of preserved peaches fell off the shelf and struck Mary in the pantry." Here the phrase "in the pantry" is apparently misplaced. The humor may be intentional or not.
4. "Walking down the street, the trees swayed in the breeze." Here it is not clear as to who was walking down the street. Literally, the sentence says that the trees were.
5. "When a young man, my father bought me a camera." Here we are not sure whether the speaker was a young man when he received the camera or whether the father was a young man when he bought it.
6. "He is closer to his mother than his father." This may mean "He is closer to his mother than he is to his father," or "He is closer than his father is to his mother."
7. "All the dogs in the window cost $100." Here one can't be sure whether all the dogs taken together as a group cost $100 or whether each dog in the window costs $100.

EXERCISES

A   Comment on the views expressed in the following:

1. A debater: "What's the use of arguing about who is wealthy or who is powerful or who is free? 'Wealthy,' 'powerful,' and 'free' are hopelessly vague terms."
2. A student: "My English teacher wrote in the margin of my paper 'vague,' but I tried to explain to him that vagueness is an inherent feature of language."
3. Every term directs a beam of light onto the screen of experience, but whatever it is we wish to illuminate, something else must be left in the shadow.

Abraham Kaplan, *The Conduct of Inquiry*[12]

[12] (Scranton, Pa.: Chandler Publishing, 1964), p. 66.

4 A philosopher: "The terms employed in the natural sciences — terms like 'gold,' 'mass,' 'energy,' etc. — are scientific because they are not vague. On the other hand, because the terms of the social sciences are vague — e.g., 'class,' 'status,' and 'power' — it shows that the social sciences are not really scientific."

B Identify the ambiguity in each of the following:

5 All alcoholics — who are emotionally disturbed — should receive psychiatric care.
6 The issue remained unsettled despite controversy and ill feeling. It was something nobody wanted.
7 Mr. Rukeyser will present more valuable advice on the stock market next week.
8 Does a tree which falls in a forest with nobody around make a sound?
9 Although the item was light, it was inappropriate for our purposes.
10 The only proof that a sound is audible is that people actually hear it. In like manner, the sole evidence that anything is desirable is that people actually desire it.

John Stuart Mill

TWO

DEFINITION

*For any language to be a language, one
has to understand what he is saying.*

George H. Mead

We have seen that the opportunities for misunderstanding are numerous, that
what is intended is often taken in unintended ways, and that there are many
different sources of controversy which stem from confusions over meaning and
language. In the first part of this chapter, therefore, we shall summarize some
of the main failures; and in the remainder of the chapter, we shall examine definition and its uses. As we shall see, definition can be a help, at least sometimes,
in resolving disputes.

Misunderstanding and Verbal Disputes

All too often there is a failure to communicate in the sense that there is a gap
between what a speaker is thinking (and intending) and the hearer is interpreting. Consider the following exchanges:

I

A: These apples are quite good.
B: I'd rather have a pear any day.

A: Look, they're uniformly large and ripe; they are not mealy and have practically no blemishes or russeting.[1]

B: So what, if you don't like apples, you don't like apples.

Here the disagreement would seem to result from a misunderstanding of the force of A's initial utterance. Although we cannot provide a detailed context, A seems to be *grading* or characterizing the apples referred to in accordance with some fairly standardized criteria which define "good apples." B, however, apparently takes A's utterance to be a recommendation to him—perhaps to try an apple or to like them. Of course, in A's sense the apples could be "good apples" and B might agree, even if he doesn't particularly like apples. In this case, however, we may suppose that A and B are simply talking past one another.

II

A: Sam is a bigot.

B: I wouldn't say that.

A: What else can you call him? He didn't pick me for the team.

B: But why should he have picked you anyhow?

A: Because I can play just as well as Louie.

B: But that doesn't make him a bigot.

This sort of disagreement is more complex than the preceding one, and we would need to know much more before we could say wherein the disagreement lies. Perhaps A is simply venting his anger or expressing his dislike of Sam, in which case there is no question of whether "bigot" applies to Sam. Or possibly, there is a disagreement over the *meaning* of "bigot"; i.e., A possibly *misuses* the word to refer to anyone who selects on the basis of criteria with which he disagrees. Or perhaps there is a disagreement over the "facts." That is, A may be reporting or describing; both A and B may have a correct understanding of the meaning of "bigot" but are disagreeing as to whether the word properly applies to Sam. Or perhaps some combination of these factors is involved.

III

A: The professor asked the class to write a substantial essay on Plato's discussion of justice, and I did.

B: The one I wrote was twice as long as yours. Perhaps that's why you received a "C."

A: She did write on the back of my paper "Too sketchy."

The difficulty here is quite plain. How substantial is substantial? With

---

[1] Russeting in apples refers to the reddish-brown and rough texture of the skin or parts of the skin of some apples. The example is suggested by J. O. Urmson, "On Grading," in A. Flew (ed.), *Logic and Language,* 2d series (Oxford: Basil Blackwell, 1961).

vague terms, as we noted, there is always the problem of "drawing the line," for where one draws the line will depend upon context and purpose. If all the teacher said was "Write a substantial essay," then A's puzzlement would be justified; but we may wonder whether A thought that his four pages constituted "a substantial essay."

IV

A: In America there are just two classes, a working class and a capitalist class.

B: That's just not true. What, for example, do you call the people Galbraith refers to as "the technostructure"? Are they working class or capitalist?

A: They're capitalists.

B: But they're salaried employees; so why not call them "working class"?

Here we have two terms, "working class" and "capitalist class," which are fraught with difficulties, particularly since they have very different meanings in different contexts. Each term probably derives its central meaning from the clearer paradigms of nineteenth-century capitalist society, and the difficulty is that of applying the term in a twentieth-century context. Moreover, like many other terms, such as "religion," their extension may be regarded as imprecise. Thus, even if A and B could come to agree on some groups as being *clearly* capitalist class, there might still be room for disagreement on certain borderline groups. Indeed, what is the extension of "technostructure"? Ultimately, theoretical considerations and those of explanatory usefulness would be required to resolve such disputes.

V

A: The Warriors certainly play a smart game of basketball.

B: That's silly. They have a rookie in the back court who makes a lot more mistakes than does Walt Frazier.

C: I wouldn't call their game "smart basketball."

In this brief exchange possibly three different failures of communication may be involved. A is likely using "Warriors" collectively and means that as a unit they play smartly, that they hit the open man, that they take advantage of mistakes by their opponents, etc. B seems to understand the term distributively, for what he says may surely be true and yet not be relevant to A's claim. Second, "smart" is a polar term, and perhaps A and C are drawing the line between "smart basketball' and "dumb basketball" in a different place. Finally, A and C may have different ideas about what counts as "smart basketball."

VI

A: It's surprising how little progress man has made in the last 2,000 years. Man's inhumanity to man is as evident today as it was then — if not more so, or at least with more devastating effects. We still fight wars regularly, only now we kill millions instead of thousands, including defenseless civilians, innocent women, and children.

B: I really think you're unduly pessimistic. I believe man has made remarkable progress—particularly in the twentieth century. Can you imagine what the people of George Washington's day—if they were alive today—would think of our automobiles, our supersonic jets, and our atomic-powered subs? And how would they react to our rockets, which take pictures of Mars and put a man on the moon? If that's not progress, I don't know what is.

In this exchange A and B are apparently speaking about two different things, even though they call both "progress." A is speaking about moral or spiritual progress, whereas B is speaking about technological or scientific progress. There is really no dispute over the facts. The disagreement is apparent rather than real, since A and B are discussing different subjects.

VII

A: I would say that literacy is a mark of an educated man—that a man who was not literate could not be called educated.

B: I don't agree. I know individuals whom I would consider literate but not educated—at least, not in the broad sense of that term.

In this exchange A and B are again speaking at cross purposes. Though B says he disagrees with A, his comment is irrelevant to A's; for he apparently fails to understand what A is saying. A has stated that literacy is a necessary condition of education—that it is *one* of the required ingredients. B replies that literacy is not a sufficient condition of education—that it is *not all* of the required ingredients. Since A never claimed it was *all* but only *one,* B has addressed himself to something A has never said.

Many disagreements, of course, involve no misunderstanding, or difficulties of language and meaning, and in the strictest sense they are disagreements over the facts. If, for example, A claims that the primary reason why so many people in America neglect their health is that they make medical decisions on economic grounds and B counters that the reasons why people do or do not seek medical care have little to do with the cost of such care or with an individual's income, the dispute need involve no confusions or misunderstandings of what is being said or argued for. Such controversy can be resolved by ascertaining the facts, however difficult it may be to get the relevant facts.

EXERCISES

Indicate the probable grounds of disagreement, factual, verbal, or otherwise, in the following exchanges:

1   Lida: Francis C. Lowell built the first cotton mill in New England and thus may be credited with making New England an industrial area.

Ted: Wrong. Sam Slater built a cotton mill in New England in 1790, twenty-four years before Lowell built his mill.

Lida: But Lowell's mill was the first to use power looms. Though Slater's mill may have been the first to have spinning machinery, it still used hand looms.

2   Bea: The United States treated Ezra Pound unjustly by putting him into St. Elizabeth's Hospital for the Criminally Insane, for they deprived him of his right to be tried in a court of law.

Al: Ridiculous. The United States actually treated Pound very justly, for by putting him into St. Elizabeth's, they prevented him from being convicted of treason — for which the evidence was overwhelming — and possibly shot.

3   Steve: Considering its fanaticism and devotion to Marxist philosophy, communism is really a religion.

Jo Ann: I disagree completely. Communists don't worship in churches or believe in the supernatural. If anything, communism is antireligious.

4   Sylvia: It looks as though we're over the worst. The latest figures from the Bureau of Labor Statistics show that the rate of unemployment has slowed down and that currently about 8 million are unemployed — just about the same as last month.

Ben: Yes, but what the Labor Bureau doesn't report is that in the past month about a million of the unemployed have become so discouraged that they have dropped out of the labor force altogether and are no longer counted as unemployed. So the rate of unemployment really has significantly increased during the past month.

5   Marigold: We're often told that we ought to legalize gambling because so many people refuse to obey the law and gamble illegally. I say, rather than make it legal, simply *enforce* the law.

Larry: But the law isn't enforceable. In New York City alone there are 17,000 collecting policy bets, and the jails of the entire state of New York can accommodate only 3,500.

6   Gloria: Babe Ruth holds the record for most home runs in a season — 60.

Irv: Wrong. Roger Maris hit 61 in one season.

Gloria: Yes, but that was over a period of 162 games. Ruth's was over a period of 154 games.

7   Don: Modern abstract expressionist art is inferior art. It doesn't portray recognizable subjects. Much of it consists of dots, lines, or circles, which any draughtsman can produce. And many of the paintings are done in simply one or two colors. The impact and subtlety of the French impressionists are completely lacking.

Marilyn: I don't see how you can call modern art inferior. First of all, most of the paintings are not done in simply one or two colors. Besides, you fail to consider the tension between the parts, the interesting treatment of space, the striking design, and the unusual forms found in many of the paintings.

Definition

The subject of definition has long been a concern of philosophers and of special interest and importance to the study of logic. Since clarity of meaning is central to clarity of argument, logicians have given much thought to the problem of clarifying, through definition, the meanings of the words we use. Unfortunately, in the long history of the discussion of definition—from at least Aristotle—there has been considerable controversy regarding the theory of definition. Indeed, in some ways the theory of definition takes one to the center of important philosophical differences. Accordingly, any treatment of this question will be, to some extent, controversial. In what follows, the effort is made to minimize these differences, to give conflicting points of view a hearing and to provide a classification which aims at clarity, usefulness, and completeness.

We shall distinguish three main kinds or types of definitions with some subspecies of each. Although each main kind differs in fundamental ways from other kinds, there will be some inevitable overlapping and imprecision in applying the three categories to particular instances. Each of the three types of definitions will be seen to serve different and important purposes.

Lexical Definitions

As the phrase is intended to suggest, **lexical definitions** are of words or symbols in some language, and, broadly, they are reports or descriptions of how a word is actually used in the language. For example, "table" means "an article of furniture, consisting of a smooth flat slab, board or the like, fixed horizontally on legs or other support and used variously in eating, writing, etc." This is the definition (roughly) as found in Webster's dictionary. This definition provides the meaning of "table" in English. Two terms frequently encountered in the theory of definition may be conveniently introduced at this point. As is customary, we shall use the word *definiendum* for the word or expression being defined and *definiens* for the phrase which defines the definiendum. In our example, the definiendum, or word defined, is "table" and the definiens is the whole phrase which follows the word "means."

Obviously, lexical definitions are used to increase our vocabulary, as when we use a dictionary to look up unfamiliar words. They also serve to clarify the meanings of words of which we are unsure and may be used to settle disputes over meaning. When lexical definitions are formulated as sentences, as in our example, we can also say that they are either true or false: true if the definition is an accurate report of established usage and false otherwise.[2]

There are several *methods* of providing lexical definitions, and these methods give rise to some subspecies. One might, as in the foregoing example, provide what are called **connotative definitions,** sometimes called **analytic definitions.** In connotative definitions the definiens is simply a report of the connotation of the definiendum. It selects those features of a thing which users of the language accept as criterion of use or application. Dictionaries often give connotative definitions, and often such definitions are not **exact definitions** of the word. That is, the definiens does not include the necessary and sufficient characteristics for correct application of the term. The definition of "table" (above), for example, does not seem to rule out any of several sorts of shelves or even benches. While it might be desirable to have exact definitions of ordinary words, such definitions might not always be possible since, as noted, many words in natural languages apply to things sharing only a "family resemblance."

Traditionally, certain "rules" for framing good definitions have been given. When construed as standards or criteria, they may be applied to connotative definitions.

Rule 1:   The definiens should be equivalent to the definiendum.

That is, the definiens should be *synonymous* with the definiendum in the sense that the definiens and definiendum should be interchangeable in contexts without a change of meaning. Exact definitions (by definition) satisfy this rule, but, again, for some words it may not be possible to frame an exact definition.

From Rule 1 follows a corollary, Rule 2:

Rule 2:   The definiens should be neither broader nor narrower than the definiendum.

Thus, in the definition " 'House' means 'dwelling used for shelter,' " the definiens is *too broad;* for we could apply it to things which are *not* houses, e.g., caves. In " 'House' means 'wooden structure used for shelter,' " the definiens is *too narrow;* for we cannot apply it to things which rightly are called "houses," e.g., brick houses. It should be noted that a definition may be *both* too broad and too narrow at the same time—i.e., too broad in one respect and too narrow in another. An example of such a definition would be "A hat is an article of clothing made of felt." This is too broad, for it is applicable to things which are not

---

[2] The lexicographer is in this sense an empirical scientist, whose task is the recording of the "facts" of usage. The matter, unfortunately, is not that simple and there is controversy among lexicographers regarding the function of a modern dictionary. Some argue that it merely records usage, while others argue that it should assume the role of *arbiter linguae* and determine what is "correct" or at least preferred. For some discussion of this issue see Mario Pei, *The Many Hues of English* (New York: Knopf, 1973), part 3.

hats, e.g., vests made of felt. And it is also too narrow, for it is inapplicable to things which are rightly called "hats," e.g., straw hats.

A third rule is this:

Rule 3: The definition should not be circular.

That is, it should not contain the definiendum in the definiens. Evidently, if it did, it would fail of its purpose, which, as we have seen, is to explain the meaning of the definiendum. An example of a circular definition would be: " 'Inexpensive' means 'that which is not expensive' " or " 'Socialism' means 'doctrine which advocates socialistic ideas.' "

The next rule also bears on the purpose of definition.

Rule 4: The definiens should not be expressed in obscure or figurative language.

Since what is obscure often varies with the knowledge of the person, this rule must be applied contextually. In any case, the following definition of "network" by Samuel Johnson would hardly be very illuminating: "anything reticulated or decussated, at equal distances, with interstices within the intersections." (Johnson very likely was being facetious.) The use of figurative language in the definiens raises different problems. To define "politics," e.g., as "the science of the possible" is informative but, like most definitions of this type, does not help one grasp the meaning of the definiendum.

Finally, we have Rule 5:

Rule 5: The definiens should not be expressed negatively unless the definiendum is negative.

This rule also follows from the purpose of connotative definition. Generally we cannot learn what a term means by being told what it does not mean. Defining "spinster," however, as "an unmarried woman" is entirely appropriate.

Closely related to connotative definition is **definition by synonym.** This consists simply in giving synonyms for the definiendum, such as " 'Injudicious' means 'imprudent' "; or " 'Chicanery' means 'trickery.' " Dictionaries often use this method, which serves, as above, to introduce unfamiliar words. Evidently, success presupposes familiarity with the word being offered as a synonym. But an inherent difficulty is that of discerning the subtle, and sometimes not so subtle, differences in the meanings of words offered as putative synonyms. *Roget's Thesaurus* lists some of the following as synonyms for "obstinate": tenacious, inflexible, mulish, pigheaded, perverse, dogmatic, hidebound, bigoted, stiff-backed, impervious, incorrigible, and crotchety. All these words do not have the same meaning; some are colloquial, some are not, some pejorative, and some are complimentary. In short, they have different connotations.

Another method of introducing unfamiliar terms—one which at least partially circumvents the limitations of the foregoing methods—is by ostension. **Ostensive definition** consists in pointing to physical referents of the definiendum. Young children, of course, learn part of their vocabulary in this way, as when a book is pointed to and Mother says "book." Though obviously useful—indeed, it is indispensable in avoiding the ultimate circularity of connotative definition—the method has obvious shortcomings. For one thing, it is limited to words with denotation, or to words which can be pictured. For another, one or two examples can't delimit the extension of the definiendum or exhibit its connotation. Such definitions are lexical in the sense that their purpose is to teach one the correct use of words in a language. And dictionaries commonly use a variation of this method by showing pictures of various referents—a squirrel, a gear, a heptagon, etc.

Closely related to definition by pointing is **definition by examples.** Using this method to define "suspension bridge," one might mention the Brooklyn Bridge, the George Washington Bridge, and the Narrows-Verranzano Bridge. However informative this might be, examples cannot be depended upon as infallible guides to the meaning of terms. In this case, is it part of the connotation of "suspension bridge" to be located in New York City?[3] On the other hand, logicians have tended to be overly hard on the method of defining by example. For some words, at least, this method may be the most useful. Thus, as Robinson has noted, "romanticism" (in the literary context) has an obscure and controversial meaning, but writers do agree in contrasting the writings of Shelley, Wordsworth, Keats, and Scott with those of Dryden and Pope.[4]

A variation of definition by example is **definition by enumeration of subclasses.** In defining "citrus fruit" by this method, one might mention lemons, oranges, tangerines, and grapefruits. What was said about the previous two methods also applies to this one.

Clarifying the meanings of important terms can also be philosophically important, and philosophers—in contrast to lexicographers—have engaged in a related but variant definitional activity. This activity is sometimes called **explication** or **analysis.** Explication (or analysis) differs from the lexicographer's definition in the following important way: The philosopher begins his analysis by examining typical uses of an important word, but his aim is to unravel perplexities in its ordinary use or to reveal the "logic" of the sentences in which it occurs.[5]

---

[3] It has often been held that Socrates criticized definition by example on the grounds that it could not yield connotations. Compare, for example, Plato's dialogue *Euthyphro*. But it is not entirely clear that this is the thrust of Plato's criticism. Socrates was not concerned with the meaning of words like "piety" but with the *nature* of pious acts. (Compare below, p. 34.)

[4] Richard Robinson, *Definition* (Oxford: Clarendon Press, 1954), pp. 113ff.

[5] Efforts at explication in this sense are an important part of what is called *analytic philosophy* and sometimes *ordinary-language* philosophy. For some excellent illustrations, see the writings of Gilbert Ryle, e.g., almost any of the essays in his *Dilemmas* (Cambridge: Cambridge University Press, 1956). Instead of speaking of the analysis of the meaning of a word, philosophers often speak of the analysis of a concept. The two expressions are practically interchangeable, since the concept, characteristically, is the meaning.

For example, a philosopher might be concerned with an analysis of the meaning of "motive" so as to glean a clearer understanding of its role in the explanation of human actions. Thus, R. S. Peters begins a chapter of *The Concept of Motivation* with a discussion of "the ordinary use of the term 'motive.'" Peters argues that "Motives . . . are reasons for action which are asked for when there is an issue of justification as of explanation."[6] This is a philosophical explication of the use of "motive" in ordinary language. It might be noted here that there is considerable disagreement among philosophers on the importance and use of analysis so conceived. But this book is not the place to discuss the important issues involved.

EXERCISES

   A   Give connotative definitions for each of the following, and state which, if any, of the definitions which you give are exact:

1	chair	**2**	work	**3**	propaganda
4	democracy	**5**	gnome	**6**	palaver
7	rummy	**8**	seraglio		

   B   Give definitions by synonym for the following:

9	buffoon	**10**	abode	**11**	friend
12	doctor	**13**	intellectual	**14**	statesman

Are the examinations of your pairs identical? Quite different?

   C   Indicate which rules, if any, the following definitions violate:

15   Watch: an instrument used for telling time and worn on the wrist.
16   Mirror: anything which gives off one's reflection.
17   Overwork: a dangerous disorder afflicting high public functionaries who want to go fishing.

Ambrose Bierce

18   Mammal: a creature that generally does not fly, live in the water, or lay eggs.
19   Faith: the substance of things hoped for, the evidence of things not seen.

St. Paul

20   Laughter: a synchronized coordination of neuro-physiological reflexes with a semi-automatic impulse of mass-inherited suggestivism.

George Robey

21   Fishing pole: a rod with bait at one end and a fool at the other.

Samuel Johnson

---

[6] R. S. Peters, *The Concept of Motivation* (London: Routledge and Kegan Paul, 1958). See pp. 28, 31, and 35ff. for an expanded definition.

22 Square: a four-sided plane figure with parallel sides.
23 Communist: one who belongs to the Communist party.
24 Evolution: a continuous change from indefinite, incoherent homogeneity to definite coherent heterogeneity of structure and function, through successive differentiations and integrations.

Herbert Spencer

25 Patriotism: the last refuge of a scoundrel.
26 Coed: female college student.
27 Good: that which the good man approves.

Aristotle

28 Equilateral triangle: a triangle with equal sides.
29 Poetry: the impish attempt to paint the color of the wind.

Maxwell Bodenheim

30 Parallel lines: lines which do not intersect.

Stipulative Definitions

Stipulative definitions comprise the second important family of definitions to be discussed, and, as we shall see, there are various degrees to which definitions can be stipulative. The clearest and perhaps best example occurs when a brand-new word is first introduced into the language by means of an explicit definition. For example, Alexander Fleming introduced the word "penicillin" to refer to a specific mold broth filtrate. Up to that time this word was not in the language and hence had no meaning. It was *given* meaning by means of definition. We might say, then, a **stipulative definition** is a proposal to use a word in a specific sort of way. As the example shows, however, the proposal may eventually be so widely accepted by users of the language that it *becomes* established usage. At that point it becomes a lexical or dictionary definition.[7] This, of course, is one reason why the boundary between stipulative and lexical definition is often unclear.

Stipulative definitions, in contrast to lexcial definitions, are not reports or descriptions of usage, and partly for this reason they serve different purposes. They might, as in the case of "penicillin" when it was first introduced, serve the purpose of convenience. Instead of using the longer phrase "mold broth filtrate," Fleming chose the more convenient term "penicillin." Stipulative definitions which are explicit abbreviations also serve this purpose. Thus, the symbol < is used for "is included in." Or exponents in algebra may be introduced as follows: $a^3 = a \times a \times a$, where a^3 is defined as equal to the longer $a \times a \times a$.

Stipulative definitions occur in contexts like the following: "In this book, we shall use the term 'valid' to mean . . . ." In such contexts, it is intended that the reader will accept the proposal and that, when the term is used in subsequent

[7] In the case of penicillin, the language already contained the word "penicillium," which referred to a genus of fungi. It often is the case that new words are etymologically related to words in current use. Regarding stipulations, of course, this is deliberate.

discussion, the reader will understand the meaning of the definiendum to be that which was proposed. Of course, such stipulations should be justified. In this case, the word "valid" is used with various meanings both in ordinary English and by writers in logic. The stipulation thus serves the purposes of clarity and, we may hope, of technical adequacy. Parenthetically, it should be noted that in stipulating new meanings for familiar words, one should not depart too radically from the old meanings. One would not be justified, for example, in stipulating, "For the purposes of this paper, we shall define 'fascism' as any attempt by big business to influence the political process" or " 'Communism' is defined here as any program which I disapprove of." To assign such unusual meanings to fairly common terms can only lead to confusion.

Closely related is the **precising definition,** which serves to set limits as precisely as necessary to the boundaries of the extension of a familiar term. One might, e.g., define "wealthy American" as any American whose income exceeds $50,000 per year. This definition has important descriptive elements in the sense that the definiens does denote those who are commonly thought of as wealthy. On the other hand, the definition has clear elements of being a proposal as well as a description. As before, such definitions should be justified or at least not depart too radically from common usage.

Another type of definition which has elements of both description and stipulation is the so-called **operational definition.** In discussing this concept, C. G. Hempel stated:

> An operational definition of a term is conceived as a rule to the effect that the term is to apply to a particular case if the performance of specified operations in that case yields a certain characteristic result.[8]

A good illustration of an operational definition is provided by the behaviorist psychologist E. C. Tolman in defining "expectancy of food" in rats:

> When we assert that a rat expects food at L, what we assert is that if (1) he is deprived of food, (2) he has been trained on path P, (3) he is now put on path P, (4) path P is now blocked, and (5) there are other paths which lead away from path P, one of which points directly to location L, then he will run down the path which points directly to location L.[9]

---

[8] "A Logical Appraisal of Operationism," in *Aspects of Scientific Explanation* (New York: The Free Press, 1965), p. 123. Hempel's discussion is extremely useful, both as an account of the relation of operationism to logical empiricism and as a critique of the limitations of operational definition. By now the central theses of logical empiricism (or logical positivism) have been largely abandoned by those who were its formulators and early defenders. Thus, P. W. Bridgman, who first introduced the idea of operational definition (in *Logic of Modern Physics,* published in 1927), and Rudolph Carnap, who at about the same time introduced the parallel idea of "reduction sentences," have both repudiated their earlier views on the subject. For discussion, see Hempel, "The Theoretician's Dilemma," op. cit., chapter 8.

[9] Quoted by Hempel in "The Theoretician's Dilemma," from E. C. Tolman, B. F. Ritchie, and D. Kalish, "Studies in Spatial Learning, I, Orientation and the Short-Cut," *Journal of Experimental Psychology,* 36 (1946).

Many terms, especially some of the most important ones in psychology and the social sciences, lack precise meanings. Moreover, many—such as "expects," "hopes," "intends," "is anxious," and "is sublimating"—seem to lack an objective criterion of application. As the nature of operational definition and the accompanying example suggest, an operational definition seeks to give clear, precise, and objective meaning. Thus, there is an element of stipulation and description in such definitions.[10]

Operational definitions resemble another type of definition called **contextual definition,** which defines a word by putting it into a context. Thus, instead of defining "hard" as a certain condition or quality or "under" as a certain relationship, such words would be defined contextually as "X is hard when it is solid and firm to the touch" and "X is under Y when X is beneath and covered by Y." Such definitions are especially useful when defining concepts expressed by parts of speech other than nouns, as may be seen in the two examples given, which define, respectively, an adjective and a preposition.

EXERCISE

The text argued that the distinction between lexical definitions and stipulative definitions was a significant one even though in particular instances the boundaries between the two may be unclear. Explain why.

Real Definitions

The idea of real definition is certainly the most controversial one in the controversial literature on definition. Writers have characterized real definition in several very different ways, and many have asserted that there is no such thing as real definition. In what follows we shall offer a formulation which seems in keeping with the historical rationale of real definition but which is also compatible with current views in the philosophy of language.[11]

Real definition may be defined as follows: The **real definition of an object is an unequivocal characterization of that object.** By this is meant that it is a true statement about some object which serves to distinguish and uniquely identify it. For example, we may say, "Common salt is the body having the chemical composition NaCl" or "A triangle is a three-sided plane figure." Notice that

[10] We have noted several times that stipulative definitions may be justified or not, depending upon the purposes they intend to serve. Although extended discussion is inappropriate here, it might be noted that in the case of operational definition, the criticism is precisely in these terms. That is, critics have maintained that operational definitions too severely restrict the use of key terms in the construction of explanatory scientific theories. (See the previous note.) Indeed, in a review of his own work published in 1959, Tolman himself expressed serious doubts regarding the validity and utility of the "standard defining experiment." Compare his "Principles of Purposive Behavior," in S. Koch (ed.), *Psychology: A Study of a Science* (New York: McGraw-Hill, 1959), esp. pp. 147ff.

[11] Compare Kazimierz Ajdukiewicz, "Three Concepts of Definition," reprinted in T. M. Olshewsky (ed.), *Problems in the Philosophy of Language* (New York: Holt, Rinehart and Winston, 1969).

real definitions are of things, not words.[12]   Indeed, it is this which distinguishes real definition from all the forms of lexical definition.   The first example brings out this distinction clearly: The chemical composition NaCl can hardly be considered part of the "meaning" of the words "common salt."   That is, one may very well correctly use the words "common salt" and yet not know that *in fact* common salt *is* NaCl.   The second (and perhaps more typical) example is ambiguous and might be taken as a connotative definition of the word "triangle" or as a real definition of triangles.   But the difference may nevertheless be brought out.   A lexical definition of the word "triangle" is a definition which tells us something about the use of a word in the English language; a real definition of triangles tells us something about the nature of triangles.   While lexical definitions are always related to some language or other, real definitions need not be.   To be sure, there will often be a close relation between language and reality, between meaning and the things which language applies to.   Indeed, the usage of a word — its conventional connotation — may be determined by those characteristics of things which people want to talk about, and this fact no doubt accounts for the tendency to blur or erase the distinction between real definition and connotative (lexical) definition.

And thus it is also that connotative definitions often do two things: They tell us what a word *means and,* at the same time, they provide us with an *analysis* of the thing denoted by the word.   Still, the distinction is worth preserving — for reasons especially important to the study of logic.   First, those who ask questions like "What is justice?" or "What is religion?" or "What is heat?" are not really concerned with the words "justice," "religion," or "heat," or with descriptions of their meaning or use in English (or whatever the language).   Nor are they generally seeking to refine or enlarge upon the ordinary meaning of words.   Rather, they are concerned with what these words denote, with the *nature* or *structure* or *properties* of the things — objects, institutions, practices — being defined.   Such definitions are thus syntheses of our knowledge of the things characterized.   Second, and consequently, controversies over the nature of justice or religion or law, or disputes over whether some offense is a crime or some state is a democracy are not verbal disputes or disputes over words; for if they were, they could easily be settled by appeal to standard usage.   Rather, such controversies are concerned primarily with existent realities and are attempts to locate and delineate the fundamental nature of these realities.

Historically, the most important method of providing real definitions is **definition by genus and differentia** (or difference).   For Aristotle, a definition was "a phrase signifying a thing's essence," where the "essence of a thing" was given by identifying its genus and its differentia.   No doubt the Aristotelian doctrine of "essences" is what many of the friends and enemies of real definition have in mind when defending or criticizing the latter.   But we may interpret "essence"

[12] Some readers may balk at this and insist that definitions (properly) are of words, not things. Perhaps there are advantages to restricting "definition" in this way, although there is ample historical precedent for not doing so.   Moreover, if we do, we shall need another name for what is here called real definition.

in various ways or we may totally reject the notion of essence and still acknowledge the importance of definition by genus and differentia. Accordingly, rather than beg unnecessary questions by attempting a definition of genus and differentia,[13] let us simply offer some examples of definition by genus and differentia.

			Genus	Differentia
1	A square	is	a four-sided plane figure	with all of its sides equal and all of its angles right angles.
2	Brass	is	a yellow metal	made up of copper and zinc in variable proportions.
3	A clause	is	a group of words	containing a subject and a finite verb.
4	A submarine is		a naval vessel	which can operate both on and beneath the surface of the sea.

Genus and differentia may be analyzed in different ways. In Examples 1, 2, and 4, the genus is a kind of thing. In Example 3, it is a collection of things. In 2, the kind is "a natural kind"; in 4, it is an artifact. In the first three examples, the differentia consist of parts or characteristics. In the last example, it pertains to the function of the thing characterized. Some call this type of definition **functional;** a better illustration of this kind of example is as follows: "A blowpipe is a tube through which a stream of air or gas is forced into a flame to concentrate and increase its heating action." Sometimes, the differentia may set forth the origin of the thing or explain how it is produced. A definition with this type of differentia is sometimes called a **genetic definition** and may be illustrated as follows: "A mound is an elevation formed by the piling up of earth, sand, etc."

Worth distinguishing as a kind of real definition is **theoretical definition.** This type of definition often has the form of definition by genus and differentia. Nonetheless, it has some important distinguishing features. As the name suggests, in a theoretical definition, the definiens makes reference to terms in a theory; e.g., "Water is a substance composed of molecules consisting of two

---

[13] Aristotle's distinction between genus and differentia was based on his metaphysics, which we need not here either accept or reject. One widely held version of the distinction is that a genus is a *class* in the sense of a collection of members and the differentia is the characteristic which distinguishes the species from other species in the same genus. This is very dubious Aristotle but conforms neatly to a modern extensional analysis of real definition. Thus, the extension (denotation) of the term "triangle" includes all possible triangles. But triangles are members of the class *plane figure* and are differentiated from others of the class by being three-sided. Further, we can also say that "triangle" (in English) denotes all and only those things denoted by "three-sided plane figure," or that the two terms "triangle" and "three-sided plane figure" are *extensionally* equivalent; i.e., they have identical extensions or denotations. Similarly, the terms "common salt" and "NaCl" are extensionally equivalent. Notice, however, that extensional equivalence is *not* synonymy or sameness of meaning; hence connotative definition is not the same as real definition.

As a *method* of definition, definition by genus and differentia is also common and appropriate regarding connotative definition. Thus, "triangle" means (in the sense of *connotes*) "three-sided plane figure."

hydrogen atoms and one oxygen atom." To evaluate such a definition is tantamount to evaluating the theory in terms of which the definition is couched; for only if the theory is accepted does one accept the definitions which derive from it.

Similar considerations apply to traditional and contemporary efforts to propound definitions of law, religion, justice, and the like. As already suggested, when in the course of a book or essay, a writer asserts "Religion is . . . ." he is not usually making a claim about the meaning of the word "religion." Rather, he is offering a theory of religion in an effort to make intelligible to the reader some of the aspects of religion with which he proposes to deal. Typically, of course, there will often be conflicting theories regarding the nature of law, religion, government, and the like, and, typically, the issue will be over making one, rather than another, aspect of the concrete phenomena central or fundamental. Thus, e.g., is religion to be understood in terms of its functional role in society, in terms of beliefs and doctrines, or in terms of some particular type of emotional experience? It should be noted that the interpretation, or theory, which is chosen, will bear directly on the conclusions which are drawn. Thus, if religion is regarded as a system of beliefs and doctrines, certain logical criteria will be applicable to it. If it is regarded primarily as an emotional experience, conclusions of a psychological nature will probably be derived. Such conclusions, of course, could not be drawn if the definition in question was simply one of word usage.

As before, evaluating a theoretical definition is tantamount to evaluating the theory; and, of course, this will be difficult. Obviously, the emotional associations and overtones, the special interests, prejudices, and biases, as well as the differing practical consequences which flow from the conflicting theories further complicate the matter and make evaluation doubly difficult. Still, there is nothing easy or unproblematic in the critical evaluation of theories in the natural sciences either. (See Chapter 14.)

Theoretical definitions suggest still another type of definition, namely, **persuasive definition,** whose predominant purpose is to persuade — i.e., to influence attitudes, beliefs, and actions — rather than to inform. On this view, such definitions are only partially or not at all informative or descriptive. They are offered to win approval, to stir the emotions, or to prescribe what ought to be. Some examples are: "A liberal is one who is right-thinking and right-acting" and "Religion is fanaticism with a soul." While it may be hard to see what purpose other than persuasion these definitions could serve, the fact is that some are also partly informative. Depending upon the context, some evidently true definitions may function persuasively. As noted earlier, we should not confuse the force and the effect of our speech utterances. In any case, it would be a mistake to suppose that a definition or a theory which, in some contexts, did persuade is impervious to rational evaluation and criticism. Thus, our two examples might be rejected as false — even if they did succeed in persuading someone.

In conclusion, definitions can be helpful in a variety of ways, but it is important to keep in mind both the differences in kinds of definitions and the different purposes they serve. Finally, definitions should not be expected to do more than they can do. Stanley Baldwin, a former Prime Minister of Great Britain, once denigrated definitions, saying: "Don't let us be too keen on definition. . . . If we try to define the Constitution too much, we may split the Empire into fragments. . . . 'The letter killeth, and the spirit giveth life.'" Commenting on this, L. Susan Stebbing wrote:

> He supposes that the logician must demand a definition, and that the definition must set forth precisely determinable characteristics. But whosoever demands such a definition of that which lacks precisely determinable characteristics is being illogical. . . . The mistake consists in demanding that a sharp line be drawn concerning characteristics which are not in fact sharply distinguishable.[14]

Aristotle long ago expressed the point well when he said, ". . . it is the mark of an educated man to look for precision in each class of things just so far as the nature of the subject admits. . . ."[15]

EXERCISES

A Consider the following statement: "A polygon is a plane figure having many sides." Explain why this statement is ambiguous with respect to being either a connotative definition or a real definition.

B Provide definitions by genus and differentia for the following:

1 vixen   2 brother   3 mare
4 carburetor   5 axe   6 excavation
7 typewriter   8 flagpole   9 wrench
10 political party

C Bring to class 3 examples of a theoretical definition.

D Classify each of the following definitions, using the appropriate letters from the following list. Each will have at least two numbers; e.g., every definition by synonym (d) is also a lexical definition (a). Where there is ambiguity regarding the type of definition, indicate this by giving both alternative classifications.

a Lexical	**b** Stipulative	**c** Real	**d** By synonym
e By example	**f** By subclass	**g** By ostension	**h** Operational
i Contextual	**j** Precising	**k** Theoretical	**l** Persuasive
m Connotative	**n** Genetic	**o** Functional	**p** Genus and difference

[14] *Thinking to Some Purpose* (Penguin Books, 1951), p. 31.

[15] *Nichomachean Ethics*, book I, chap. 3.

1 A stalactite is a deposit, usually made of calcium carbonate shaped _____
like an icicle, hanging from the roof of a cave and formed by the
dripping of percolating calcareous water.

2 "And that," said my friend as he pointed to a gray furry marsupial, _____
"is a koala."

3 Poetry is what Auden, Browning, Milton, and Shakespeare wrote. _____

4 "Fortuitous" means accidental. _____

5 A knife is a thin blade attached to a handle and used for cutting. _____

6 Let us define "deviant behavior" as "behavior which violates insti- _____
tutionalized expectations."

7 An enzyme is a biological catalyst, that is, an agent which accel- _____
erates some chemical change; but while it participates in the reaction it influences, it is regenerated and so can be used again and
again.

8 The expression "soluble in water" means "if anything x is put into _____
water at any time t, then if x is soluble in water, x dissolves at the
time t, and if x is not soluble in water, it does not."

9 The term "dog" denotes poodles, collies, fox terriers, schnauzers, _____
and pomeranians.

10 The Social Security Administration in 1969 defined "poverty" as an _____
income below $3,700 per annum for a nonfarm family of four.

THREE

BASIC CONCEPTS
OF LOGIC

*It is not . . . the object of logic to
determine whether conclusions be true
or false; but whether what are asserted
to be conclusions are conclusions.*

Augustus DeMorgan

One of the most difficult things to learn about a new subject matter is its specialized vocabulary, or "jargon." In economics, for example, such terms as "propensity to consume" and "multiplier" are used. Logic also has its special terminology. Unfortunately much of it has been appropriated from ordinary language but given special meaning—thus it is potentially ambiguous and subject to misinterpretation. Sometimes the meanings of certain terms are quite close to those of ordinary language, but in other instances they are very much different. In this chapter we shall try to clarify and explain certain terms which are basic to our logical vocabulary—terms like "statement," "premise," "conclusion," "inference," "reasoning," "proof," "argument," "correct argument," "sound argument," "valid argument," "deduction," and "induction."

Statements

While there is a great variety of linguistic acts, it is important to notice that some of the sentences used in such acts may be said to be either true or false. If someone says, "It is snowing" in the snow, or if in the course of speaking or writing about the history of the United States, someone says, "Thomas Jefferson was the first Vice President of the United States," we can say that what is said is either true or false. This feature characterizes an indefinite number of sentences which can be used in a wide variety of linguistic acts. In traditional discussions, such sentences are conveniently called **statements** (and sometimes **propositions**).

Strictly speaking, insofar as particular utterances on particular occasions of their use are true or are false, the idea of a statement is an abstraction. For example, "She is tall" is true if said of some particular woman who is tall, while on some other occasion, if said of some woman who is *not* tall, it is false. And sometimes it is neither true nor false, as, e.g., when it is used as the password of the week to gain entrance into a floating crap game.

In what follows, it will be convenient to employ the idea of a statement, even while recognizing that it is an abstraction. We shall define a statement as any sentence which on a particular occasion of its use *could* be either true or false. Thus, "It is snowing," "Thomas Jefferson was the first Vice President of the United States," "Sugar is water-soluble," and "Aluminum is heavier than lead" would in most contexts be statements, while "Close the door," and "Who was the first Vice President of the United States?" are not statements.

Notice that a statement does not have to be true, nor indeed do we need to *know* whether some particular sentence is true (or false) for it to be a statement. "Sugar is water-soluble" happens to be true, and "Aluminum is heavier than lead" happens to be false. "There is life on Mars" is a statement, even though we don't know *whether* it is true or false.

By contrast, "Close the door" is not a statement because it is hard to see how, on any particular occasion of its use, it *could* be either true or false. One might comply or not, but it wouldn't make sense to say to the speaker "That's true" or "That's false."

Grammar is helpful in identifying statements, but, as we have seen, it is not an infallible guide. The sentence "How can we be expected to *support* such a program?" though phrased as an interrogative, in many contexts might have the force of "We should not be expected to support such a program." Here context would be the determining factor.

In short, given any sentence, a useful test to determine if it is a statement is to ask yourself, "Is it being used in its particular context to say something which can be either true or false?

EXERCISES

Determine which of the following (in most contexts) are statements. Can you find a context in which some sentences not ordinarily construed as statements might be considered statements?

1 Should we continue to fight?
2 Send your contribution to National Educational Television now!
3 The European "common market" countries have experienced much economic growth since World War II.
4 Why should *Americans* be taxed to support slavery in Saudi Arabia?
5 The United States expects to be self-sufficient in oil by 1985.
6 Does severing relations with Cuba promote the best interests of the United States?

7   Suppose we assume that the economy will grow at a rate of 6 percent each year.

8   But for a lucrative scholarship, Jane would not have attended graduate school.

9   I'm suspicious of anyone who doesn't look you in the eye.

10 The cost of the space program for the fiscal year 1966 was approximately $15 billion.

11 Some historians attribute Hitler's rise to power largely to the Versailles Treaty.

12 The union shop is a form of compulsory unionism.

13 How can we ever expect to get *peace* with such a program?

14 For the purpose of this discussion let us take "liberal" to mean "favorably inclined to change" and "conservative" to mean "opposed to change."

15 Do you call *that* a painting?

Arguments

It was necessary to clarify the difference between statements (propositions) and sentences so that we could proceed to see what constitutes an argument. In ordinary language usage the term "argument" suggests a heated disagreement, usually characterized by shouting, rising blood pressure, and, if anything, *il*logic. However, logicians do not use the word "argument" in this sense. What, then, is an argument as construed here? An **argument** is a set of statements in which one, called a **conclusion,** is claimed to be either the consequence of or to be justified by the others, called variously **evidence, reasons, grounds,** or **premises.** Thus every argument consists of two parts: (1) one or more statements, or propositions, called the premises or evidence, and (2) a proposition called the conclusion, which is claimed either to follow from the premises or to be supported by the evidence. This construction is regarded by logicians as the basic unit of reasoning. The mental process of moving from premises to conclusion is called **inference,** although this term is sometimes confused with the result of that process, namely, the conclusion. Constructing an argument is sometimes called **reasoning.**

Before illustrating some of these concepts, it should be noted that the terms "inference," "reasoning," "argument," and "proof," though closely related, are not identical in meaning. "Inference" refers to the activity or process of drawing a conclusion from accepted premises. "Reasoning" likewise refers to an activity or process, that of adducing or collecting reasons, weighing them, and drawing conclusions. In drawing conclusions we move from given premises to a conclusion; in reasoning we must *find* premises or evidence which support our conclusions. "Argument" refers to a construction of words or other symbols consisting of premises and a conclusion drawn or inferred from them. "Proof" in a broad sense refers to a sound argument, that is, one which establishes the truth of its conclusion. Mathematicians and formal logicians generally use the term in a more restricted sense to refer to any demonstration that a given conclusion *necessarily* follows from certain premises, without regard to whether or not the premises or conclusion is true. However, as we shall see, only the conclusions of deductive arguments are capable of proof in this latter sense.

To take some simple arguments, consider the following: "Nobody's perfect; so, surely, you can't expect him to be"; or, "He probably knows how to drive, since he took driver education in school." In the first, the statement "Nobody's perfect" constitutes evidence, or provides a "reason," for asserting: "You can't expect him to be (perfect)." Similarly, the statement "He took driver education in school" constitutes "grounds," "evidence," or a "reason" for saying: "He probably knows how to drive."

Some arguments, however, are considerably more complex, and in subsequent chapters we shall investigate many different types. But, in general, every argument, no matter how complex, can be put into this simple schema:

This is true; *therefore,* that is true.

or

That is true *since* this is true.

Translated into logical terms:

Premises (evidence, grounds, or reasons); therefore, conclusion.

or

Conclusion because of premises.

Even complicated proofs in mathematics fit this schema. For, as noted, a proof is simply a species of argument. In plane geometry you may recall the distinction made between axioms and theorems. The axioms were not proved; they were taken as assumptions. Indeed, they are the initial premises of the arguments of geometry. The theorems were proved, and this proof was accomplished by showing that they followed logically from the premises. Schematically:

Axioms (the initial premises); therefore, theorem
(the statement "supported" by the premises).

Unfortunately, arguments are not always easy to detect. In the first place, they are very rarely presented as in the rarefied and usually simplified atmosphere of a logic book. More often we find them submerged in complex and intricate patterns of discourse — disguised by rhetoric, irrelevancies, redundancies, and subtle connections with other arguments. A premise may be compounded with an exhortation, or a description, or an aside which has no bearing on the point at issue. Then, too, rarely do we find premises arranged in a neat logical order, all leading to some crystal-clear conclusion which is the last statement of the discourse. Sometimes the conclusion is offered first, sometimes last; sometimes it is somewhere in the middle, and sometimes it is not even stated but implied.

The same may be said of premises. Oftentimes they are only suggested or elliptically expressed rather than clearly stated. Finally, there is the matter of language itself. As we noted in discussing statements and sentences, it is sometimes hard to distinguish statements from nonstatements, and the problem is heightened in any sort of relatively complex context.

Word Clues in Argument Before we can begin to appraise or evaluate arguments, we must first be able to detect them and to dissect them. This is our first problem. In the exercises which follow this section, you can begin your practice. While there are some clues and guides, there is no substitute for practice. This means that in your reading and discussion, whether in connection with newspapers, textbooks, or conversations in and out of class, you should try to be consciously aware of the elements of argument. Try to find the conclusion, the point being argued for. Try to find the evidence offered in its support. Try not to be misled by asides and irrelevancies. By following these simple rules, you will be surprised at how much you can improve your ability to see arguments.

Here are some additional clues to finding and dissecting an argument. First, consider linguistic clues. Generally, terms like the following indicate that the statement which follows is a *conclusion:* "thus," "hence," "so," "therefore," "accordingly," "consequently," "proves that," "it follows that," and "indicates that." Similarly, expressions like the following generally indicate that the statement which follows is a *premise:* "because," "for," "since," "in view of," "as shown by," "may be inferred from," and "is substantiated by." But one should not expect that these expressions always mark premises or conclusions. Sometimes they do not. Nor should one always expect to find such expressions marking a premise or a conclusion. Indeed, there are many different and more subtle signs which are used, including punctuation, pauses (in oral discourse), and sentence and paragraph construction. For these signs, no rules are available; experience is the best and possibly only guide.

Some people, you may have discovered, seem to be more adept at spotting arguments than others. They "see the point" more quickly, and are not easily put off by irrelevancies. This, no doubt, is part of what we usually mean when we say that someone is "logical." But again, it must be emphasized that this is an ability which almost everyone—at least every college student—can acquire with practice. The following steps, some of which we have already alluded to, may prove helpful:

1 Read (or listen) with an eye (or ear) to "getting the point." That is, find the main conclusion first. Always ask yourself, "What is being argued for?" If nothing, then there is no argument. Or if it is impossible to tell, the chances are that the argument is too confused to worry about further.
2 Once you have established the main thesis, seek out the statements which are being offered in its support. Frequently you will find subsidiary arguments or arguments within the main argument. In this case, a statement may be the conclusion of one argument and simultaneously the premise of another.

3 See if there are any implicit premises. Frequently a premise may be so obvious that it is left unstated. For example, in the little argument, "It must be cold. Everybody is shivering," the conclusion, "It must be cold," is supported by one explicit premise, "Everybody is shivering." But the premise "People shiver when it is cold" is undoubtedly implied. It is always possible to add premises, and in many contexts it is not at all clear whether a premise is implied or if it is, exactly what the premise is.

4 Finally, check to be sure that you have not omitted anything relevant to the conclusion. The question of relevance is an important one in evaluating arguments, and much more will be said on this matter subsequently.

To illustrate some of these difficulties we shall thoroughly dissect an argument from one of Bertrand Russell's works:

> I think there ought to be no rules whatever prohibiting improper publications. . . . I think prohibitions immensely increase people's interest in pornography, as in anything else. I used often to go to America during Prohibition, and there was far more drunkenness than there was before, far more, and I think that prohibition of pornography has much the same effect. Now, I'll give you an illustration of what I mean about prohibitions. The philosopher Empedocles thought it was very, very wicked to munch laurel leaves, and he laments that he will have to spend ten thousand years in outer darkness because he munched laurel leaves. Now nobody's ever told me not to munch laurel leaves and I've never done it, but Empedocles who was told not to, did it. And I think the same applies to pornography.[1]

First, what is the point of this paragraph? The first sentence states it quite clearly: *There ought to be no rules whatever prohibiting improper publications.* To see clearly how the argument is organized, let us separate and number each of the main statements.

1 There should be no prohibitions on publishing improper publications (that is, pornographic writing).

2 Prohibitions on publishing pornography would stimulate an interest in it.

3 Prohibitions on anything lead to an interest in that which is prohibited. (Stated elliptically in the original as "as in anything else.")

4 Prohibition (of alcoholic beverages) in America led to more drunkenness than before prohibition.

5 Empedocles ate laurel leaves because he was prohibited from doing so. (Literally, because he thought it was wicked to do so.)

6 Empedocles lamented his eating of laurel leaves.

7 Russell never ate laurel leaves.

8 Russell was never prohibited from eating laurel leaves (that is, he was never told not to eat laurel leaves).

[1] *Bertrand Russell Speaks His Mind* (New York: Bard Books, 1960), p. 56.

9 Prohibiting the publication of pornography would stimulate an interest in pornography ("the same applies to pornography").

Finally, we diagram the argument by rearranging the statements; we also put into words all implicit assumptions and use appropriate connectives between statements, such as "therefore" before all conclusions or "for" before all premises. Depending on which seems easier, either one may begin with the reasons and work downward to the conclusion; or conversely, one may begin with the conclusion and work downward to the reasons which are given to substantiate it. Or one may put the conclusion in the middle of the page and show reasons converging to it. Here we use the first alternative:

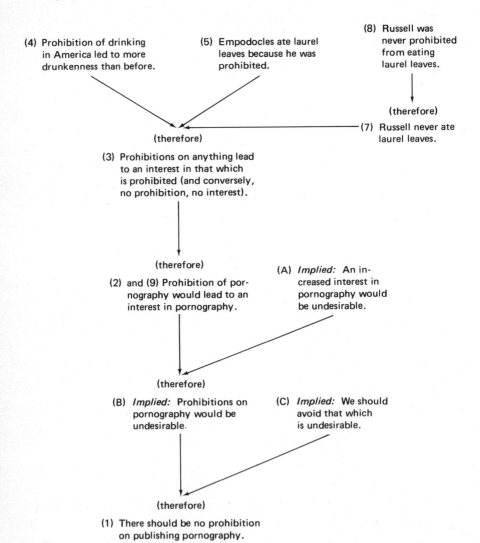

(4) Prohibition of drinking in America led to more drunkenness than before.

(5) Empodocles ate laurel leaves because he was prohibited.

(8) Russell was never prohibited from eating laurel leaves.

(therefore)

(7) Russell never ate laurel leaves.

(therefore)

(3) Prohibitions on anything lead to an interest in that which is prohibited (and conversely, no prohibition, no interest).

(therefore)

(2) and (9) Prohibition of pornography would lead to an interest in pornography.

(A) *Implied:* An increased interest in pornography would be undesirable.

(therefore)

(B) *Implied:* Prohibitions on pornography would be undesirable.

(C) *Implied:* We should avoid that which is undesirable.

(therefore)

(1) There should be no prohibition on publishing pornography.

Note that proposition 6 of the original ("Empedocles lamented his eating of laurel leaves") does not appear in the diagram, for it is a side remark and irrelevant to the overall argument. Note also that propositions 2 and 9 say the same thing, being repeated for emphasis. Propositions A, B, and C did not appear at all in the original but are clearly presupposed—connecting links considered obvious perhaps and thus unstated. Although the connective "therefore" doesn't appear at all in the original, putting it in clearly indicates the direction of the argument, the relationship between various premises and conclusions. Note, finally, that conclusions are in turn used as premises for other conclusions. Thus, proposition 8 is used as a premise for conclusion 7, which in turn becomes one of the premises for conclusion 3, which in turn becomes a premise for conclusion 2–9, which in turn becomes one of the premises for conclusion B, which in turn becomes one of the premises for conclusion 1.

Taken in reverse, the diagram of Russell's argument would appear as follows:

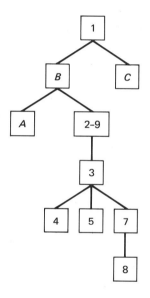

This should give the reader a clearer idea of how many links a serial argument may contain. Sometimes, an entire book is devoted to the development of a single conclusion.

Though we have not yet explicated the criteria involved in *evaluating* an argument, would you say that Russell's argument is a good one? How would you defend your position?

Motives, Causes, and Arguments We noted that certain words, e.g., "for," "since," and "because," are often helpful clues in finding and dissecting arguments. But these words also have other uses. Consider this example:

I shut the door because it was cold.

In this sentence, "it was cold" is a reason for shutting the door, but it is not a reason offered in support of the truth of the sentence, "I shut the door." Thus, this is not an argument. In this context, "it was cold" is a motive and the sentence is an explanation.

Now consider this example:

The window fell because the catch broke.

Here "the catch broke" is offered as a *cause* of the falling window, and the sentence is best construed as above, as an explanation. Unfortunately, not all cases will be easy to distinguish, for there is a close relation between providing a reason in the sense of a cause or motive and providing a reason in the sense of providing evidence to support some conclusion.

The Conditional Statement   One last word of caution: there is a difference between an argument and a conditional statement, though the two are frequently confused. A conditional statement is an "if-then" statement. For example "If it rains, then you will get wet." This is not an argument, for no conclusion is asserted, no premise has been offered. The confusion arises because this type of statement is easily put into an argument: "It is raining; *so* you will get wet." Notice that the conditional statement doesn't assert that you will get wet or that it is raining. It says only that *if* it rains, *then* you will get wet. In the argument, on the other hand, *evidence* is offered for the assertion that you will get wet, namely, that it *is* raining. What we are saying here essentially is that every argument actually makes two claims: (1) that if certain statements or premises are true, then a certain conclusion is justified; and (2) that the statements or premises are indeed true and that, therefore, the conclusion is justified. The first claim, as we shall see, pertains to the *relationship* between statements, the second to the *truth* of the statements. In the case of a hypothetical statement, we have only the first claim — not both — and this is why such a statement is not an argument, though as we have just seen, it can readily be made the basis for one.

EXERCISES

Determine which of the following are arguments. Identify the conclusion, the premises (or reasons given in support), and the expression, if any, which suggests that the selection is an argument.

1   In the provinces where Italian per capita income is the highest, the Communists received 52 percent of the total vote in the 1951–1952 elections.

2   You ask me, why, though ill at ease,
Within this region I subsist,
Whose spirits falter in the mist,
And languish for the purple seas.
It is the land that freemen till,

That sober-suited Freedom chose,
The land where, girt with friends or foes,
A man may speak the thing he will.

Alfred, Lord Tennyson, "You Ask Me, Why, Though Ill at Ease"

3 If we have faith in democracy and in the ability of our students to make sound judgments, we should not fear that an occasional Communist teacher will subvert the student body.

4 Attempts to legislate discrimination by means of an FEPC law are bound to fail, for as the failure of Prohibition proves you simply can't legislate mores and attitudes.

5 [F]rom the time that Athens was the university of the world, what has philosophy taught men, but to promise without practicing, and to aspire without attaining? What has the deep and lofty thought of its disciples ended in but words? . . . Did philosophy support Cicero under the disfavor of the fickle populace, or nerve Seneca to oppose an imperial tyrant? It abandoned Brutus, as he sorrowfully confessed, in his greatest need, and it forced Cato, as his panegyrist strangely boasts, into the false position of defying heaven.

John Henry Newman, "The Idea of a University"

6 As an example of how lobbies affect legislation, in 1946, $2,500 was spent to promote a public housing law, while $197,460 was spent to kill it. It was killed. $29,000 was spent to promote medical care, $260,000 to kill it. It was killed. $134,000 was spent in an effort to remove the oleomargarine tax, $3 million to retain it. It was retained. Do such facts indicate that Congress is concerned with the public interest?

7 A great proportion of United States military and economic aid goes to a handful of countries.

8 Since all matter is subject to the law of gravity, it stands to reason that when someone steps out of a window, he is not going to fall up.

9 An aged man is but a paltry thing,
A tattered coat upon a stick, unless
Soul clap its hands and sing, and louder sing
For every tatter in its mortal dress,
Nor is there singing school but studying
Monuments of its own magnificence;
And therefore I have sailed the seas and come
To the holy city of Byzantium.

W. B. Yeats, "Sailing to Byzantium"

10 Our imports last year amounted to little more than 3 percent of our gross national product. So, if we lowered our trade barriers so that imports could amount to 5 percent of our gross national product, as they did from 1925 to 1929, there would be no "dollar gap."

11 Alexander VI never did, nor thought of, anything but cheating, and never wanted matter to work upon; and though no man promised a

thing with greater asseveration, nor confirmed it with more oaths and imprecations, and observed them less, yet understanding the world well he never miscarried.

A prince, therefore, is not obliged to have all the forementioned good qualities in reality, but it is necessary that he have them in appearance. . . .

Niccoló Machiavelli, *The Prince*

12 According to the terms of the will, money is to be provided for the education of the deceased's nephew. Since "education" can be defined as a never-ending process, the boy should be paid for the rest of his life.

13 On Monday Mr. Blumenthal came out strongly in favor of a very liberal abortion law and the next day he was removed as chairman of the Legislative Advisory Committee. The conclusion seems obvious.

14 It is often argued that having a *chargé d'affaires* in Peiping would be advantageous to the United States. But, remember, a United States *chargé d'affaires* in China with his finger on the pulse of Chinese affairs would mean Chinese representatives in this country with their fingers on our throat.

15 We must know what perfection is. One thing which can surely be affirmed about it is that those forms or natures which are not susceptible of it to the highest degree, say the nature of numbers or of figures, do not permit of perfection. This is because the number which is the greatest of all (that is, the sum of all numbers), and likewise the greatest of all figures, imply contradictions. The greatest knowledge, however, and omnipotence contain no impossibility. Consequently power and knowledge do admit of perfection, and insofar as they pertain to God they have no limits.

Whence it follows that God who possesses supreme and infinite wisdom acts in the most perfect manner not only metaphysically, but also from the moral standpoint.

Gottfried Wilhelm Leibniz, "Concerning Divine Perfection"

16 The latest available returns filed by labor unions with the Bureau of Internal Revenue show that the total receipts for all American labor unions in 1946 amounted to only $477,701,000. Contrasted with this, receipts for one corporation — General Motors — in 1948 amounted to $4,700,000,000.

Truth and Correctness

Up to this point we have been concerned mainly with understanding what arguments are and how to recognize them. We must now turn to some crucial preliminary distinctions bearing on the problem of appraising, or evaluating, arguments. In every argument, we have suggested, there are two quite different questions which could be asked:

1 Are the statements in the argument true or are they false?
2 Do the statements making up the premises constitute grounds, or evidence, or reasons, for asserting the conclusion?

The first question is factual and scientific; the second one, properly, is the *logical* question because it is concerned with the *relation* between evidence and conclusion. For example, whether or not it is the case that mammals are carnivores is a problem of biology, not of logic. But it is a problem of logic to determine if the *argument* "Whales are mammals; mammals are carnivores; so, whales are carnivores" is *correct*. Logic, strictly speaking, is not concerned with truth. When appraising an argument, the logician need only ask, "*If* the premises *were* true (whether they are or not is another problem), then *would* they constitute sufficient grounds for asserting the conclusion?" If they would, the argument is said to be correct. Thus, for example, the following argument has nothing but false statements, but the argument is nonetheless *correct:*

> France is in Asia.
> Denver is in France.
> _____
> Therefore, Denver is in Asia.

In this case the premises constitute excellent grounds for the conclusion; that is, *if* France were in Asia and *if* Denver were in France, then inescapably, Denver would be in Asia. As logicians, we will be prepared to see exactly why the argument is correct — indeed, it is formally valid; and as geographers, we are prepared to say that each of the statements making up the argument is in fact false. Generally, of course, we don't think of ourselves exclusively as logicians or geographers. Ordinarily, in arguments we are interested in *both* truth and correctness; so we must ask both questions: Are the statements true? *And* do they constitute grounds for asserting the conclusion? When an argument satisfies *both* of these conditions, that is, when it has true premises *and* is correct, we shall call the argument *sound.*

To summarize: only statements are properly called either true or false; arguments are either correct or incorrect, or sound or unsound. We shall never say that an argument is true, and to avoid confusion, we shall *not* call a statement correct or sound.

The terms "correct," "incorrect," "sound," and "unsound" are evaluative terms which apply to arguments. Parts Two and Three of this book are largely directed at determining when and why these terms should be applied. But before we directly examine these "whens" and "whys," one final *descriptive* distinction is necessary. For the kinds of criteria which we can apply to arguments will depend, in a large measure, on the sorts of arguments which we are examining. The relevant distinction here is the one between deduction, or deductive arguments, and induction, or inductive arguments. But before moving onward, here is a summary of the new terms which you should master:

1 *Sentence:*   a grammatically constructed expression in some language. *a thought*

2	*Statement:*	a sentence which may be used to assert or to deny something; a sentence which could be either true or false.
3	*Proposition:*	same as *statement.*
4	*Premise:*	a statement asserting grounds, reasons, or evidence used in support of a conclusion.
5	*Conclusion:*	a statement which is either supported by premises or is claimed to be the consequence of them.
6	*Inference:*	the mental act of moving from premises to conclusion.
7	*Reasoning:*	the act of marshaling evidence, weighing it, and drawing conclusions from it.
8	*Argument:*	a set of statements in which some are used as premises to justify some conclusion.
9	*Correct Argument:*	an argument in which the premises constitute sufficient grounds for asserting the conclusion.
10	*Sound Argument:*	a correct argument with true premises.

Deduction and Induction

The distinction between deduction and induction is a fundamental one for logic, but here again the ordinary language use of these words has tended to obscure and confuse the distinction. Sir Arthur Conan Doyle's famous tales of the master detective, Sherlock Holmes, are fairly typical in this respect. You probably remember how Holmes would look for clues, gather evidence, and formulate a hypothesis as to who was the guilty party. Watson, his faithful colleague, would then explain, "Brilliant deduction!" For Holmes, of course, all this was quite "elementary." Unfortunately, however, most of Holmes's "brilliant deductions" were in reality *inductions.* Let us see why.

Customarily in logic *all* arguments may be classified as either deductive or inductive. Some logicians prefer to use the expressions "deductive" and "nondeductive" so as to clearly indicate that the classification is both *exhaustive* (it covers all arguments) and *exclusive* (no argument can be both deductive and inductive). We shall use the terms "deductive" and "inductive" in this exhaustive and exclusive, or mutually exclusive, sense.

There are several different criteria which can be employed in making this distinction.

A **deductive argument** is one in which the premises *necessarily* imply or entail the conclusion; or alternatively, the premises constitute *conclusive* evidence for the conclusion.

An **inductive argument,** on the other hand, is one in which the premises *do not* necessarily imply the conclusion, or, stated positively, the premises provide *some* evidence (though *not* conclusive evidence) for the conclusion.

Here are two examples on which you can test your logical intuition:

> All hasapika are folk-dances.
> All folk-dances are enjoyable.
> _____
> All hasapika are enjoyable.

> Ignatz smoked Chesterton filters.
> Chesterton filters were found at the scene of the
> crime.
> _____
> Ignatz is the guilty party.

In the first, which is the deduction, if we accept the two premises regarding has-apika and folk-dances, we must accept the conclusion; it follows *necessarily*. But given the premises of the second argument we are not forced (logically speaking) to accept the conclusion[2] — it is an example of induction. Indeed, the most we can say is that on the basis of the evidence Ignatz should be considered as one of the suspects. The evidence does not necessarily imply the conclusion; it is *not* conclusive proof of it. This difference in the two arguments could be brought out by rewriting them in this way:

> All hasapika are folk-dances.
> All folk-dances are enjoyable.
> _____
> Hence, NECESSARILY, all hasapika are enjoyable.

> Ignatz smoked Chesterton filters.
> Chesterton filters were found at the scene of the
> crime.
> _____
> So, POSSIBLY, Ignatz is the guilty party.

Notice that in inductions the relation between premises and conclusion is one of *probability,* while in deductions the relation is one of *necessity.* In deductions the premises *logically imply* or *entail* the conclusion. In inductions the premises at best support or to some degree confirm the conclusion. Thus we say that in inductive arguments the probability relation varies with the evidence, whereas in deductive arguments it does not because the evidence is conclusive. For example, we could add a premise to the induction concerning Ignatz:

> Ignatz had a motive for the crime. (Added premise.)
> Ignatz smoked Chesterton filters.
> Chesterton filters were found at the scene of the
> crime.
> _____
> So, quite possibly, Ignatz is the guilty party.

---

[2] Remember, we are not concerned at this time with the truth—or, indeed, even with the meaning —of the statements. Our sole interest, now, in this distinction is the *relation* of the premise set to the conclusion.

As evidence mounts, or becomes more relevant, the probability increases, but still it is not conclusive. If we now added the premise "None of the other persons with a motive for the crime smoke Chesterton filters," we *still* would not have conclusive evidence, although, to be sure, poor Ignatz would be in a bit of trouble. Before you read on, you might stop here and try to determine why, even on the revised evidence, it is not *necessarily* the case that Ignatz is guilty.

If we were to introduce the notion of truth into the discussion, another criterion for distinguishing deductions from inductions could be employed:

A **deductive argument** is one in which it is *impossible* for the premises to be true and the conclusion false.[3]

An **inductive argument,** on the other hand, is one in which it is possible for the premises to be true and the conclusion false.

In dealing with these criteria it is important to see that we need not *know* whether or not the premises are true or, indeed, that it makes no difference whether or not they are *in fact* true (independent of our knowledge). We need only to ask ourselves, if they *were* true, *could* the conclusion be false? So, for example, it is *impossible* for it to be true that all hasapika (whatever they are) are folk-dances and all folk-dances are enjoyable and at the same time for it to be *false* that all hasapika are enjoyable. One could not assert the two premises and at the same time deny the conclusion—without contradicting himself. The argument is correct (though it may not be sound). Whenever premises and conclusion are so related, we have a correct deductive argument. Another way to describe the argument is to call it valid, which is another of those terms that are important in the vocabulary of every logician and to the further clarification of which we shall now turn.

Validity

Like several of the other terms previously discussed, the word "valid" is one which seems to cause confusion. Not only is it used in a variety of ways in ordinary discourse but even logicians are not unanimous as to its technical meaning. In ordinary language "valid" is frequently used as a close synonym for "true" and applied indiscriminately to statements, to the process of drawing in-

---

[3] It might be objected here, as with the previous criterion of deduction, that we have defined not a deductive argument but a *valid* deductive argument. There is, however, a very good reason for putting it the way it is stated in the text. Although many arguments—indeed, most arguments which we normally encounter—are *in*valid, they are sometimes correct. Hence, it seems more sensible to reserve the term "deductive" for *only* valid arguments. If an argument is invalid, then it must be evaluated in accordance with the criteria of an induction, and may be either correct or incorrect. See the discussion below, Chapter 10.

ferences, and to arguments.   During the course of a discussion, for example, we might hear, "His point was valid," in which case the term was probably being used to describe a statement or a premise.   In the study of logic, however, the word "valid" is restricted in meaning and applied only to *arguments*.   On this point almost all logicians agree; on deciding *what* arguments to call "valid," however, they do not.   Some logicians apply it only to what we shall call *formally* valid arguments (see p. 58); some apply it to what have here been called *correct* arguments; and some apply it to any correct *deductive* argument.   In this book we shall use it in the last sense; that is, <u>whenever an argument satisfies our criteria as a deduction, then it is, by definition, valid</u>.   Thus, if it is impossible for the premises to be true and the conclusion false, the argument is a deduction — and valid.   If it does not satisfy this criterion, then it is an induction — and nonvalid.   Remember, however, being nonvalid is not synonymous with being incorrect.   Many inductions are *correct* arguments, though they are not deductively valid.   For example, the argument "Most Frenchmen are Roman Catholics; Henri is a Frenchman; therefore, he is probably a Roman Catholic" is correct but not deductively valid.

Much unnecessary anguish has been caused by the failure to see exactly to what one is committed in calling an argument *valid*.   Consider an argument with just one premise.   Now with respect to truth and falsity, there are just four combinations possible.   They are:

1	T	2	T	3	F	4	F
so,	T	so,	F	so,	T	so,	F

Both the premise and the conclusion could be true; the premise true and the conclusion false, etc.   The pertinent question then is, "If the argument is *valid*, which combination *cannot* occur?"   If you said 2, true premise and false conclusion, you were right; for *only* this cannot occur.   It is quite possible to have a false premise and a true conclusion in a valid argument, or a false premise and a false conclusion.   (The true-true combination doesn't usually present any difficulty.)   This can be illustrated by some examples.   In these examples we have safely assumed that if someone is a bachelor, then he is an unmarried male. That is, being a bachelor *necessarily implies* or entails being an unmarried person and being a male; or, it is impossible for anyone to be a bachelor and at the same time to be married or be a female.   These are all ways of saying that these argument schemata are valid:

X is a bachelor (where *X* may be filled in with
  someone's name);

so, *X* is unmarried.

X is a bachelor;

so, *X* is a male.

Here, now, are the arguments:

1	(Plato) was a bachelor.	**T**
	(Plato) was unmarried.	**T**

2	(Plato) was a bachelor.	**T**
	(Plato) was married (?)	How is this possible?

3	(Senator Muskie) is a bachelor.	**F**
	(Senator Muskie) is a male.	**T**

4	(Senator Muskie) is a bachelor.	**F**
	(Senator Muskie) is unmarried.	**F**

In Case 1, there is no problem. It was in fact true that Plato was a bachelor, from which we can deduce the true statement that Plato was unmarried. But in Case 2, if it is true that Plato was a bachelor, then it is *impossible* to deduce the false statement that he was married (just as it is impossible to deduce the false statement that he was a female). We are, as it were, stuck. In Case 3, although the premise is *false,* we can still deduce the true statement concerning Senator Muskie's masculinity. And in Case 4, the false premise necessarily implies the false conclusion. The point may be summarized by saying that in deductions (i.e., valid arguments) false premises may imply either true *or* false conclusions, but true premises can imply *only* true conclusions. And this is a significant feature to notice.

Now contrast a valid argument with the argument concerning Ignatz's guilt. When we do, we see that the situation is quite different. Surely it is possible for it to be true that Ignatz smokes Chesterton filters and that Chesterton filters were found at the scene of the crime and *at the same time* for it to be false that Ignatz is the guilty party. Quite possibly, Horatio, who also smokes Chestertons, did the job! This argument, then, is *not* a deduction; it is an induction. But is the argument correct? Do the premises support the conclusion? If the conclusion was "Ignatz *possibly* is guilty," then it would seem to be correct, for the premises do constitute sufficient evidence for this claim. If the conclusion was "Ignatz *certainly* is guilty," then the argument would be incorrect, for the premises do not support such a strong conclusion. In the terminology used by logicians the argument would be called a *non sequitur,* meaning literally "it does not follow," which is an elliptical expression whose full meaning simply is "the conclusion does not follow from the premises."

The descriptive distinction between deduction and induction forces us to find different sets of criteria for evaluating the two types. In Part Two, we shall be able to develop quite explicit and conclusive criteria for calling an argument *valid* or *invalid.* But the task of providing comparable criteria for evaluating inductive arguments, which are all invalid though not necessarily incorrect, will be much harder. Part Three deals with this problem.

But before moving on, here are some more terms to master:

1 *Deductive Argument:* an argument in which the premise set necessarily implies the conclusion; it is impossible for the premise set to be true and the conclusion false.
2 *Inductive Argument:* a nondeductive argument.
3 *Valid Argument:* a deductive argument.
4 *A Nonvalid or Invalid Argument:* an inductive argument.

EXERCISES

Although we have only touched upon the methods used to test arguments, try to determine which of the following arguments are deductions and which are inductions. Also, try to judge which of the inductions seem to be correct. (It might be noted that intuition, though sometimes helpful, is usually not a good guide for making these distinctions. Because of your relative lack of experience up to this point, we have deliberately presented fairly simple arguments.)

1 The carton is a cube; therefore it has six sides.
2 Most bouzouki players are right-handed, so since Stavros is a bouzouki player, he is probably right-handed.
3 The lights were out and the car was gone, so we concluded that nobody was home.
4 Mr. Hummingbird said that he was going to Toronto or to Stratford. He didn't go to Stratford, so he must have gone to Toronto.
5 If he bypasses the city, he will arrive at least one hour sooner. He arrived almost two hours sooner, so he must have bypassed the city.
6 If he catches a plane instead of a train, he will be in Detroit tonight. He caught a plane so he must be in Detroit tonight.
7 Statistics show that 86 percent of the people treated with penicillin recover from throat infections. Theodore had a throat infection and was treated with penicillin, so he probably will recover.
8 Since everybody loves somebody sometime, John either has loved somebody, loves somebody now, or will love somebody.
9 Everybody interested in being on the team was at the meeting yesterday. Phil was at the meeting yesterday, so he probably is interested in being on the team.
10 On my vacation to Cap Cod, I noticed that no fish were caught at low tide. I concluded that one cannot catch fish at low tide on the Eastern seaboard.
11 Since $a^2 + b^2 = c^2$ for all right triangles and since $a = 2$ and $b = 4$, $c^2 = 20$ and $c = \sqrt{20}$.

12   The last six sirloin steaks we bought at Foodville were delicious, so this steak, which was also bought at Foodville, is bound to be good.

13   Our problem was determining what caused the fuse to blow. Four hypotheses were proposed and for various reasons three of them were eliminated. This left us with the hypothesis that there was a short circuit in the terminal connection of the dryer. We therefore concluded that this must be the cause of the blown fuse.

14   Given that Sam is taller than Harry and that Harry is taller than Ignatz, it follows that Sam is taller than Ignatz.

15   Since all horses are animals, we may conclude that the head of a horse is the head of an animal.

Logical Form

In reading the "hasapika" example, you probably noticed that the conclusion followed necessarily even if you didn't know what a hasapika was. (As it happens, a hasapika is a Greek circle dance, which you may have seen done in the films *Never on Sunday* and *Zorba the Greek*.) In this example there was a strict logical relationship between the premise set and the conclusion—one which was independent of the empirical or material *content* of the statements. That is, this argument could have been evaluated for its correctness simply by virtue of its form. This feature is true of many deductions, and *formal* logic takes it as its point of departure.

Consider the statement "All hasapika are folk-dances." What is *the form* of this statement? In answering the question, what we must try to do is to discover what this specific statement has in common with all other statements of the *same* sort. We must abstract out its reference to a particular subject matter and state it in a more generalized way. There are, in fact, two quite different approaches we might take here. We might say that this statement has the form "All *S* are *P*." The letters *S* and *P* could then be filled in to make particular statements. It would then be clear that the statement "All hasapika are folk-dances" has the *same form* as the statement "All kielbasa are Polish sausages." The two statements differ not in *form* but in (subject) *matter*.

The letters *S* and *P* in the above may be thought of as *variables*; in this mode of analysis they are variables for terms, which are expressions like "hasapika," "enjoyable," "great white whale," etc. These letters are merely place markers which serve in lieu of blank spaces. It is convenient to use a capital letter for our term variables to keep things straight. But any sort of symbol might serve equally well. We might, for example, have said that the form of the statement is "All $ are %." Notice also that once we take the content out of the statement, we no longer have a statement, since, by definition, the result could not be used to affirm anything. The expression "All *S* are *P*" or "All $ are %" doesn't say anything; hence it can't affirm anything, or it cannot be said to be either true or false. When we substitute some content for the variable, we have a statement again. Expressions like "All S are P" will be called, understandably, **statement forms** or **formulas.** The analysis of statements in this way, which Aristotle initiated, is the heart of so-called Aristotelian or traditional logic. Arguments are then handled in a similar fashion. The form of the argument:

> All hasapika are folk-dances.
> All folk-dances are enjoyable.
> _____
> So, all hasapika are enjoyable.

would be this:

> All H are F.
> All F are E.
> _____
> So, all H are E.

Because we are now considering the argument *as a whole* (rather than the statements taken individually), it matters that we keep the order of the terms straight. The first H was put in place of "hasapika"; so where "hasapika" appears again, we must use H. (What particular symbol we use doesn't matter; it only matters that we use the same one throughout a given argument.)

It is now clear why this argument is correct, regardless of its content. For *whatever* we substitute for H, F, and E, if the premises are true, then the conclusion must be true. Hence this argument is a (*correct*) *deductive argument,* or a *valid* argument.

Earlier we observed that there were two quite different approaches to getting at form and that the problem was to discover what some specific statement had in common with other statements of the same sort. Consider this example: "If there is a change in the interest rate, then there is a change in aggregate saving." What is the form of this statement? Apparently it doesn't fit our earlier analysis — it doesn't seem amenable to the "All S is P" form, yet it has some form. We might, however, abstract from it in a different way. While it doesn't have the word "all" followed by a term, it has the word "if" followed by a statement and the word "then" followed by another statement. Indeed, this statement might be called a compound statement in which two statements are joined by the logical words "if" and "then." Now if we introduce another sort of symbol to serve as place markers for such statements, we get this:

> If p, then q.

The letters p and q accordingly may be thought of as variables for statements. So, the compound statement "If (p) there is a change in the interest rate, then (q) there is a change in aggregate saving" has the same form as "If (p) it rains, then (q) you will get wet." This way of getting at logical form is employed in usual developments of what is called in modern logic the *statement calculus.*

Someone might object at this point: Why consider form at all? And why have two *different* ways of analyzing the form of a statement? Since this is a book on logic, let us do the logical thing and answer the first question first. In doing so, we find two main answers to this question. First, there is the matter of generality. As was probably apparent, there is an infinite number of possible statements which all have the same form. Hence there is an infinite number of possible arguments which have the same form. Once we know that one form of an argument is correct, then we know that all particular instances of this form are correct. And thus we have considerably simplified the task of logical appraisal. It is also interesting to note that, with respect to form, language too is irrelevant. Every natural language—French, Greek, Chinese, or what have you —has in its syntax forms of the same logical type. To take a somewhat extreme illustration, in Greek this statement has the form of "If *p*, then *q*": εἰ ὁ ποταμὸς ἦν διαβατος, ἤθελον αὐτὸν διαβαίνειν. ("If the river is crossable, they wish to cross it.")

Sometimes this fact is not apparent, but then it isn't even always apparent in English. The statement "He is eligible only if he is a citizen" also has the form "If *p*, then *q*," but the statement "He is eligible" is the component *p*, and the statement "He is a citizen" is the *q*. For, as we shall see when we fully discuss such syntactical transformations, the compound statement here means "If he is eligible, then he is a citizen." Secondly, there is the matter of being able to formulate exact criteria for evaluating arguments by virtue of their form. But to adequately explain this topic, we shall need to consider the contents of the next several chapters.

As to the second question—Why have two different ways of analyzing the form of a statement?—a brief answer may be given here. In essence it is that not all the statements occurring in argument can be analyzed by one method or the other. Subsequently it will be shown how the two modes can be combined to give us a more powerful apparatus; but even then, we are going to have some statements which are not covered.

PART TWO
FORMAL LOGIC

FOUR

TRUTH FUNCTIONS

*It seems that the human mind has
first to construct forms independently
before we can find them in things.*

Albert Einstein

Deductions

Part Two of this book is concerned with those quite special kinds of arguments which are called *deductions*. Though deductions are by no means the only important species of arguments, they are absolutely basic to any understanding of logic. In the first place, many arguments which we do encounter are deductions. In the second place, many of the key concepts of deduction enter into almost all arguments, both deductive and inductive. Thus it is that we must command an understanding of the features of deduction. To accomplish this, it would not be possible, even if it were helpful, to list all possible deductions, for they are infinite in number. Nor will it do to learn some typical examples, the syllogism, for example, since unless we understood what made them deductions, we could not judge unfamiliar cases, nor could we see how the concepts of deductions enter into reasoning and argument. Fortunately, the path to understanding has been well marked out by logicians from Aristotle to Bertrand Russell. And what they all tell us is, *look to form*.

We noted in Chapter 3 that there was no one way to analyze form. While one mode of analysis may reveal some key features of deduction, it may obscure others. We will be content, therefore, with *ways* to analyze form. In Chapters 4 to 6 we will use one approach, in Chapters 7 and 8 we will use another, and in Chapters 9 to 11 we will combine these methods to produce a more power-ful analytical device. Each of these analyses of form will generate "a skeleton language," which is simply a system of symbols by means of which we can il-luminate the essential features of deductive reasoning. These "formal," "arti-ficial," or "constructed" languages (in contrast to a "natural" language like English or French) must be such that they can effectively reveal the logical struc-ture of natural languages or more simply, the underlying logic of language. By doing so, they will serve several immediate purposes. First, by ignoring those aspects of a natural language which are *not* part of its prominent underlying logical features, we can achieve great generality and economy. We can con-centrate, as it were, on those characteristics which are shared by a countless number of various deductions. Secondly, we can bring precision and rigor to our analysis. A natural language is a rich and subtle instrument, but this has its disadvantages as well as its advantages. While we can use it for many purposes and express ourselves with nuance, elegance, and variety, if we are not careful its richness can also produce confusion and illogic. Hence we want an artificial language to achieve these two main goals: (1) to reveal the prominent logical features of deduction; (2) to be precise but at the same time useful in analyzing a subtle natural language like English. In this chapter we shall undertake the task of describing such a language.

The Statement Calculus

The mode of analysis with which we begin is rather imposingly called the **state-ment calculus** or alternatively, the **sentential calculus,** or the **logic of truth func-tions.** All of these designations are revealing, as we shall see, but none of them should give cause for concern. Sodium chloride is, after all, nothing more than common table salt.

The statement calculus analyzes the form of an argument by taking simple affirmative statements as the primary unit and then determining the logical *re-lations* asserted between the statements. Consider this argument:

Either scallopini has green peppers or cacciatore has
green peppers; but there are no green peppers in
scallopini; so cacciatore has green peppers.

Our analysis reveals that it contains only two simple affirmative statements: (1) "Scallopini has green peppers" and (2) "Cacciatore has green peppers." But these are linked together and altered by means of the logical words, "either . . . or," "not" and "so." If we represented statement (1) by the letter *p,* and state-ment (2) by the letter *q,* we could put the argument into this form:[1]

---

[1] Strictly speaking, the letters "p" and "q" in this sentence should be within quotation marks since we are mentioning rather than using them. However, because they are in italics and no confusion is likely to result, we will omit quotation marks.

either *p* or *q*	or more simply	*p* or *q*
but not *p*		not *p*
so, *q*		so, *q*

The "language" of the statement calculus has two different sorts of symbols:

1 It uses letters, such as *p, q, r,* etc., to represent simple affirmative statements. These letters may be thought of as blanks which stand in place of any simple affirmative statement, or they may be thought of as statement variables.

2 It uses special symbols, such as ~, ·, v, ⊃, and ≡ for the important "logical words," "not," "and," "or," "if . . . then," and "if and only if." These are called **logical connectives** because they "connect" statements, **logical operators** because they "operate" on statements, or simply the **constants** in contrast to the variables of our primitive artificial language. The five connectives may be summarized in a table with their corresponding English words:

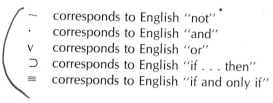

~ corresponds to English "not"
· corresponds to English "and"
v corresponds to English "or"
⊃ corresponds to English "if . . . then"
≡ corresponds to English "if and only if"

It is important to remember that the logical connectives are *not identical* to or merely alternative symbols for the English. If they were, there would be no point in having them, for we would lose the precision that English lacks and that our formal language is supposed to have. At the same time they must correspond to some degree to the English words, for if they did not, they could not be used to analyze arguments expressed in English.

We now must define what is meant by a *simple affirmative statement.* A simple affirmative statement is a statement (that is, a sentence which is either true or false) which contains *none* of the five logical connectives. The following are all simple affirmative statements, and each can be represented by the letter variable *p* or *q* or *r,* etc.

1 Today is Tuesday.
2 My name is Harriet.
3 Scallopini is made with red wine.
4 Sugar is water-soluble.
5 A natural language, like English, is a subtle instrument.

A **compound,** or **complex, statement** is one which contains one or more of the logical connectives. For example, each of the following is a compound statement:

1 Either scallopini has green peppers or cacciatore has green peppers.
2 There are no green peppers in scallopini.
3 If the interest rate falls, then aggregate investment increases.
4 A natural language, like English, is a rich instrument and it has many uses.

But before we can put these statements into symbolic form, we must understand the symbols for the various connectives. We will begin with "not."

~ and English "Not" The symbol ~ (the "curl" or "tilde") is read as "not," or, more specifically, "it is not the case that" or "it is false that." Thus ~p may be read as "not-p," "it is not the case that p," or "it is false that p." The function of ~ is clear. It serves to contradict or deny and may be called the symbol for *negation*. Notice that ~ is an odd "connective" in that it really doesn't connect two statements. For this reason it is sometimes called a uniary or unitary connective, in contrast to a *binary* connective, which does connect two statements. Calling it an "operator," however, causes no difficulties, since it does "operate" on affirmative statements: it contradicts them. In English, there are many different ways to express negation. For example:

1 It is not the case that Marx was a Russian.
2 It is false that logic is difficult.
3 Today is not Tuesday.
4 There are no green peppers in scallopini.
5 He never puts catsup on ice cream.

Each of these statements should be expressed as ~p, where p stands for the affirmative statement. So, "Today is not Tuesday" becomes "It is not the case that today is Tuesday," or simply "not-p," and thence ~p. In some contexts the negation is less clear. For example:

1 He is illogical.
2 This will be inconvenient.
3 The gas is unstable.

Prefixes like *il-*, *in-*, and *un-* usually function to deny, and in the context of an argument it is best to make this meaning explicit. "He is illogical," becomes "It is not the case that he is logical," and hence ~p.
Sometimes, however, prefixes like *un-*, *il-*, etc., do not function as ~. Consider, for example, (1) "Doing what you request is not inconvenient." Here, if the prefix *in-* is functioning as negation, then (1) would be exactly equivalent to (2), "Doing what you request is convenient." But in many contexts this would not be true. In other words, (1) might mean that doing what was requested was neither convenient *nor* inconvenient, but somewhere in between. Accordingly, one must be wary in handling such prefixes.
An expression like ~p is called a **statement form** or a **formula.** In this case ~p is the logical form of all of the examples listed in this section for each ex-

hibits the same essential feature: each is a simple affirmative statement being denied. (Similarly *p* is the form of all the simple affirmative statements.) Notice the generality and economy which this device has produced. Notice also that while *statements* are either true or false, *statement forms* cannot be said to be either true or false, for they say *nothing*. Before we can know whether *p* is true or false, we must know what *p* stands for; that is, we must substitute a statement for the statement form. Similarly, the formula ~*p* is neither true nor false; it too must await a substitution for *p*.

Although neither *p* nor ~*p* can be said to be true or false until a substitution for *p* is made, a *relation* between the two in terms of truth and falsity can be precisely determined, or defined. This relationship is: if *p* is true, then ~*p* is false; if *p* is false, then ~*p* is true. In short, both *p* and ~*p* cannot be true simultaneously. If one is true, the other must be false; and if one is false, the other must be true. This definition, which is very important and very exact, can be represented graphically thus:

	p	~*p*
1	T	F
2	F	T

Such a graphic representation is known as a **truth table,** which is simply a device for representing all the possible truth values of a statement form. Since any statement is either true or false, it has two possible truth values. For simple affirmative statements of the form *p*, the truth table representing its possible truth value is simply:

p
T
F

When we begin employing our connectives, however, and begin compounding statements in various ways, determining the truth value is easily accomplished by means of truth tables. The use of such tables will also give us great generality. Thus the formula ~*p* contains only one statement variable, namely *p*. Since any statement is either true or false, the truth table for negation or ~ determines the truth value of the compound ~*p* under all possible substitutions of *p*. For example, if we substitute for *p* in the formula ~*p* the true statement "Rust is ferrous oxide," we can see from line 1 of the table for negation that ~*p* would be false. If we substitute for *p* in the formula ~*p* the false statement "Martinis are made with Scotch," line 2 tells us that ~*p* would be true. Accordingly, *whatever* true statement is replaced for *p*, ~*p* is false (line 1); *whatever* false statement is replaced for *p*, ~*p* is true (line 2).

It is worth noticing here that the symbol ~ corresponds very closely to most English variants of "not." That it does not conform exactly may be brought out by noticing that ~ *always* has the force of contradiction, while "not" does not.

For example, the "not" in the statement "Some coeds do not smoke cigarettes" does *not* deny that some coeds *do* smoke cigarettes, for the two statements: "Some coeds smoke cigarettes," and "Some coeds do not smoke cigarettes" may both be true. Hence they cannot be contradictories, and "not" is not functioning to contradict. Chapter 7 further discusses this sort of statement.

EXERCISES

Which of the following are accurately symbolized as $\sim p$? What is the statement which p represents?

1 Rome was not built in a day.
2 Hegel's philosophy is unintelligible.
3 Wars will never end.
4 He is not unwise.
5 A noncommittal attitude is not desirable.
6 Inconceivable ideas cannot be conceived.
7 A bat is not a bird.
8 He bothered me unnecessarily.
9 It seems impossible.
10 Some athletes are not well paid.

· and English "And" The symbol · ("dot") is used for logical conjunction and may be read as the English "and." Again the function of · is quite clear; it serves to make a conjunction of two statements and is, therefore, a binary connective. The statements conjoined are called **conjuncts.** Just as there are many ways in English to express negation, so are there many ways to express conjunction. For example:

1 Bentham was a utilitarian and he was a hedonist.
2 Myrtle studied, but Sam watched TV.
3 The revolution of 1688 was peaceful; the revolution of 1776 was violent.

In these cases, "and," "but," and ";" function to express the conjunction of two statements. In terms of the relationship between truth and falsity, this sense of conjunction may be defined as follows: if both p is true and q is true, $p \cdot q$ is true. If either p or q is false or if both are false, $p \cdot q$ is false. Again, these relationships may be graphically illustrated by means of the truth table:

	p	·	q
1	T	T	T
2	T	F	F
3	F	F	T
4	F	F	F

To simplify our tables, we put the truth value of the *compound* under the connective, in this case ·, which conjoins the statements.

Notice that in the construction of the truth table for $p \cdot q$, there are *four* lines. Why this is so can readily be seen. Since the truth table is to represent all the possible truth values of the compound $p \cdot q$ and since there are two alternatives each for p (true or false) and two for q (true or false), the total possible combinations for both are four: (1) both p and q could be true; (2) p could be true and q could be false; (3) p could be false and q could be true; and (4) p could be false and q could be false. Thus, we have four lines, one for each possible combination. Turning now to the truth table, we see that on line 1, if p is true and if q is true, then the compound (under ·) is true; that on line 2, if p is true and q is false, then the compound is false; that on line 3, if p is false and q is true, then the compound is false; and that on line 4, if p is false and q is false, then the compound is false.

When conjunction is intended in ordinary English (in any of its variant forms), our definition (and the corresponding truth table) accurately represents its sense. Intuitively, we would agree that the conjunction of two statements is true only when both statements are true. If someone says, "Bentham was a utilitarian and he was a hedonist," he has spoken the truth only if it is true that Bentham was *both* a utilitarian and a hedonist. As with negation (the curl), the truth table unequivocally determines the truth value of any conjunction; for no matter which two statements we choose, there will be a place for them on the truth table. For example, if we substitute for p the false statement "Napoleon Bonaparte was born in Bordeaux," and for q the true statement, "Robespierre was a member of the 2d Committee on Public Safety," the substitutions would be represented by line 3 of the truth table, which tells us that the resulting compound is false.

In general, since the truth table gives the full meaning of all our statement connectives, the latter are called **truth-functional connectives** or more simply, **truth-functions.** The name for this mode of analysis is the **logic of truth-functions.**

By way of contrast, consider a connective which is not truth-functional in our sense. For example, "He had indigestion because he ate beef stew." Here, "because" connects the statements "He had indigestion" and "he ate beef stew." But the truth value of the compound, "He had indigestion because he ate beef stew" can*not* be determined by knowing the truth values of the two constituents of the compound.

It is important to see that the meaning of the connectives is *fully* given by the truth table. Failure to see this causes certain problems and may lead to serious confusion, which may be illustrated by considering English expressions as candidates for · (dot). What shall we do with statements like these:

1 A natural language is rich and subtle.
2 Goethe and Hegel were contemporaries.

In sentence 1 "and" conjoins two adjectives and *not* two statements; hence at a first glance, it doesn't appear to fit our schema. We might say, however, that in this case (and in similar ones) the conjunction of two statements is being expressed elliptically. Thus, to take the first example, "A natural language is rich and subtle" is equivalent in meaning to "A natural language is rich, and a natural language is subtle." Whether or not the original statement is elliptical, it would appear that *in this case,* no harm is done by thinking of it as elliptical, for the logical force remains the same.[2] The statement "A natural language is rich and subtle" is true if and only if "A natural language is both rich and it is subtle." But in many contexts this approach will not do.

The statement "Goethe and Hegel were contemporaries" does *not* expand to mean "Goethe was a contemporary and Hegel was a contemporary." Still, by a suitable (if rather strained) rendering we can get our sense of logical conjunction. Thus "Goethe lived from 1749 to 1832, and Hegel lived from 1770 to 1831." Now it is simply false that the original statement and our rendering mean the same thing. Still, in this context our interpretation might be justified. Though they are unusual, there are other contexts in which such verbal manipulations would capture the sense of · (dot). Hopefully, it is becoming clear that English is, indeed, a rich and subtle language and that our artificial language, the language of truth-functions, while quite precise, *is not* a perfect mirror of English.

These next examples make the point more emphatically:

1 Napoleon and his army marched into Russia.
2 Two and two make four.
3 They got married and had two children.
4 He was good and ready.

Statement 1 could be rendered as "Napoleon marched into Russia, and Napoleon's army marched into Russia," which for convenience we will call 1'. This looks fine at first, for it would appear that 1 and 1' would be true under the same conditions, namely if both Napoleon and his army marched into Russia. But, 1 *also* implies that they did this *together* or at the same time. Hence 1 could be false and 1', true. The truth-table definition of ·, however, cannot account for this. $p \cdot q$ is true whenever p is true and q is true — togetherness notwithstanding.

Statement 2 raises an interesting problem. Two and two *when taken together* make four, and there is no way to express this in our artificial language. "And" in this context is not the sense of "·," but rather represents an arithmetical operation.

Nor can the truth-functional connective "·" express *temporal order*. The "and" of statement 3 does not simply express conjunction in our sense since, if it did, the order of p and q would make no difference. Remember, as defined, $p \cdot q$ is true only when p is true and q is true or when q is true and p is true. That is, two conjuncts may be interchanged in position without affecting their

---

[2] We might argue that the formulations are logically equivalent.

truth relationship. But surely this doesn't apply in example 3, at least as most people would interpret this statement.

Finally, 4 does not mean, "He was good and he was ready." Here the "and" serves an entirely different function from that of conjoining, for the statement means something like, "He was quite ready."

All of this, however, should not be discouraging, for the formal logician is not attempting to *represent* ordinary language. To do this adequately he would need an artificial language as complex as English, and this would be self-defeating. What he wants, as we indicated earlier, is a tool whereby he can display and analyze some of the most *prominent* logical features of language. The dot (·) effectively does this for him, for it gives the minimum content of the sense of logical conjunction.

EXERCISES

Some of the following may be formalized as $p \cdot q$ without any loss of meaning; others may be formalized as $p \cdot q$ with some loss of meaning; and still others may not be formalized as $p \cdot q$ at all. Discriminate among them.

   1 William James wrote *Pragmatism* and *The Principles of Psychology.*
   2 A yellow canary is a yellow bird, but a small elephant is hardly a small animal.
   3 He made a mess and cleaned it.
   4 Richard and Elizabeth got married.
   5 Birds do it; bees do it.
   6 John took arsenic and died.
   7 Two and three make five.
   8 Lenin and Trotsky were enemies.
   9 Her hair was golden-brown and her eyes were deep purple.
  10 Even though he approved, he dissented vigorously.

v and English "Or" We come next to v (the "wedge"), which reads as "or." Some languages — though English is not one of them — have two different words for two different senses of "or." These senses are the *inclusive* sense of "or" and the *exclusive* sense of "or." The inclusive sense means "either . . . or *and possibly both.*" The exclusive sense — the "stronger" of the two — means "either . . . or *but not both.*" The following two statements illustrate the difference:

   1 The door to the cafeteria is locked on windy or on cold days.
   2 Willy is in class or he is at the ball game.

In statement 1 the use of "or" strongly suggests the inclusive sense. That is, 1 suggests that the door is closed on windy days, that it is closed on cold days, *and* that it is closed on windy *and* cold days. This, however, is not perfectly clear and illustrates the sort of ambiguity to which "or" is vulnerable. In 2,

"Willy is in class or he is at the ball game," however, there is no mistaking the sense of "or"; Willy cannot be in both places at once. The truth tables for these two senses of "or" graphically reveal the difference.

	p	inclusive-or	q		p	exclusive-or	q
1	T	[T]	T		T	[F]	T
2	T	T	F		T	T	F
3	F	T	T		F	T	T
4	F	F	F		F	F	F

At first it would appear that in order to account for the two different senses of "or" we should have two different symbols. But this is unnecessary. In formal logic, it is preferable to define v as the *inclusive*, or *weaker, sense* of "or" for two reasons: (1) When the context is ambiguous, the weaker sense makes fewer assumptions and gives, as it were, the benefit of the doubt; and (2) when it is clear that the stronger sense is intended, this can be easily handled without introducing a new symbol. In terms of the relationship between truth and falsity, the definition of $p \lor q$, then, is as follows: if either p or q or both are true, $p \lor q$ is true; if both p and q are false, $p \lor q$ is false. Again, this is graphically illustrated by the truth table for $p \lor q$:

	p	v	q
1	T	T	T
2	T	T	F
3	F	T	T
4	F	F	F

Statements joined by the wedge are called **alternations** and sometimes **disjunctions;** the constituent statements are called the **alternatives.** Using the wedge for "or" will generally cause little difficulty if you bear in mind that v is the *inclusive* "or." Sometimes negation makes matters confusing, especially with words like "neither . . . nor." For example, "It was neither safe to drive nor were we able to catch a train" means "It was not safe to drive *and* we were not able to catch a train," which is not an alternation but a *conjunction* of the two statements.

Like "and," "or" is frequently used to join words and clauses; but these can usually be expanded into statements connected with v.

EXERCISES

Which of the following can be formalized as $p \lor q$? Which of these *clearly* indicate the *exclusive* or?

1 You have a headache from lack of sleep or from nervous tension.

2   He smokes a pipe or a cigar.
3   Either road leads to Rome.
4   He used his savings to buy stock or to buy his house.
5   The sole owner of the car is Harry or Louie.
6   The fourth President of the United States was Adams or Jackson.
7   The dress was light purple or chartreuse.
8   Gold may be tested for purity by either test.
9   He was married or a bachelor.
10   The last man to finish was Ignatz or Wilberforce.
11   The children love ice cream with peanuts or with chocolate sauce.
12   Heartburn can be caused by overeating or nerves.
13   Fertilizer or rain increases growth.
14   The cat was a female or a male.

⊃ and English "If . . . Then"   The symbol ⊃ (the "horseshoe") is to be read as "if . . . then." Statements of the form $p \supset q$ are called **material conditionals,** a term which indicates that they are conditionals but of a *special* sort.[3]   As was emphasized earlier, the truth table gives the full meaning of all the statement connectives.   Noticing this is especially important with respect to ⊃.   It is defined in our truth-functional logic as: if p is true and q is false, $p \supset q$ is false; for all other substitutions of p and q, $p \supset q$ is true.   As illustrated by the truth table for $p \supset q$:

	p	⊃	q
1	T	T	T
2	T	F	F
3	F	T	T
4	F	T	F

Thus $p \supset q$ is tantamount to saying, "it is not the case that p can be true and q can be false," for the only time when $p \supset q$ is false is when the statement replacing p is *true* and the one replacing q is *false*.   That is, $p \supset q$ is false only on line 2.

There are many instances in English where the sense of the horseshoe (as defined by the truth table) only partially, at best, corresponds to the English "if . . . then."   And, as we shall see, there are senses of "if . . . then" which bear *no* correspondence to our truth-functional version.

Let us consider first a set of cases where ⊃ only partially corresponds to "if . . . then":

---

[3] As we shall see, finding an appropriate English reading for $p \supset q$ is not easy.   Strictly we should read it as "p materially implies q."   This would emphasize the fact that ⊃ is a special sort of conditional, namely, the material conditional.   However, as we shall show, $p \supset q$ does approximate many important senses of "if p, then q" and we shall, therefore, use this reading.

1 If Louie gets his check, then he will pay his debts.
2 If water in the pipes freezes, then it will expand.
3 If Bing Crosby is a father, then he has children.
4 If Barry Goldwater is a liberal, then I'm a monkey's uncle.

Although each of these could and will be formalized as $p \supset q$, the resulting formula eliminates significant features of each. In Example 1 there is a fairly clear temporal, or chronological, relation between the antecedent (i.e., the "if" clause, or the statement which precedes the horseshoe) and the consequent (i.e., the "then" clause, or the statement which follows the horseshoe). In this example the order in which things happen is clearly significant: Louie must *first* get his check and *then* he will pay his debts. But the $\supset$ does not express this sense. Indeed, it only says that 1 is false if and only if the antecedent is true and the consequent false—the chronological order is not taken into account. Notice also that according to the truth table, if the antecedent is in fact false (Louie *doesn't* get his check), the conditional statement taken as a whole is still *true*, which again, in certain contexts, is contrary to the ordinary sense of "if . . . then." Most people would say that if the antecedent of a conditional is not fulfilled (i.e., if it turns out to be false or is false), then, because the condition was not met, the whole conditional statement could not be considered either true or false. In what follows, we will try to justify this deliberate departure from ordinary usage.[4]

Example 2 suggests that there is a *causal* relationship between the events expressed in the antecedent and the events expressed in the consequent. Lowering the temperature of water *causes* it to expand. But this causal sense is also lost in the formalization $p \supset q$. The $\supset$ simply asserts a truth relation and *not* a causal relation. Hence, when we substitute for p and q in the statement form $p \supset q$, the resulting statement is true whenever p and q are both true (line 1 of the truth table), whenever p and q are both false (line 4), and whenever p is false and q is true (line 3)—*no matter what the subject matter of p or q*. To put it another way: there need be no chronological relation, no causal relation, no existential or no logical relation between p and q. All we are interested in is the *truth relation* as defined by our truth table.

At this juncture the problem posed regarding $\cdot$ may be raised again. How can the symbol $\supset$ aid us in a formal analysis of the logic of ordinary discourse? Again, the answer is that the formal logician is not claiming to mirror the subtlety of English with his symbols. His basic concern is: Does $\supset$ capture the most significant logical features of most conditional sentences, even if it does ignore very much? To this question, the answer is "yes"—an answer which we shall subsequently substantiate.

Example 3, "If Bing Crosby is a father, then he has children," illustrates

---

[4] Example 1 also could be construed as a provisional announcement, in the sense of, "If the weather is good, then we shall go." In this sense, however, it would not even be a statement and hence neither true nor false. Promises, too, are often phrased as "if . . . then" sentences. For example, "If I win the election, I promise to build new roads."

an extremely important sense of "if . . . then." It is the sense of **entailment,** or of **logical implication.** Entailment is the fundamental concept of all deduction and much more will be said about it in the chapters which follow. In general, however, to say that "p entails q," or that "p logically implies q" is to say that "q is deductible from p." Knowing that Bing Crosby is a father enables us to deduce that he has children. But this sense of "if . . . then" is not *to be identified* with ⊃. The confusion between the two is a common one and must be guarded against at all costs. One reason for such a confusion is that "if . . . then" is *sometimes* synonymous with "implies." Indeed, even some logic texts interpret ⊃ as "implies." But ordinarily "implies" suggests "logically implies" or "entails," and this results in confusion. To circumvent this pitfall, we shall read ⊃ as "if . . . then"; and whenever we mean "implies" in the sense of "entails," we shall say either "entails" or "logically implies."

That ⊃ is not synonymous with "entails" or "implies" is easily seen by remembering that the meaning of ⊃ is fully given by the truth table and that the relation which it represents is simply a truth relation. Thus if the antecedent of a conditional is false, the truth table for ⊃ shows that the conditional is true. For example, the conditional statement, "If sparrows are mammals, then the sun is the center of the solar system," is *true because the antecedent as a matter of fact is false.* But it would be rather preposterous to believe that one could deduce the position of the sun and planets from the statement that sparrows are mammals. Thus one cannot say that "Sparrows are mammals" implies or entails "The sun is in the center of the solar system."

Consider finally Example 4, "If Barry Goldwater is a liberal, then I'm a monkey's uncle." This use of "if . . . then" here differs from that in the three former examples. Indeed, it might be argued that 4 is not a conditional statement at all, for it appears to say, "Barry Goldwater is not a liberal." Now while this may be its effect, it is accomplished by having as the consequent of a conditional a statement which is patently false. That is, the only relation between antecedent and consequent is that they are *both* false. But construed in this way, we can say that 4 is a *pure* truth-function; that is, its truth value is determined *exclusively* by the truth values of its component statements.

Before we examine some uses of "if . . . then" which are not amenable to the sense of ⊃, let us try to justify somewhat further our adoption of the truth-table definition. In the first place, though each of the four examples differs in certain interesting respects, they all share what may be termed the *minimum content* of "if . . . then." That is, if we are prepared to accept as true a statement of the form "if p then q," then to be consistent we must accept the weaker corresponding statement of the form $p ⊃ q$. Thus, if we accept as true the statement "If Louie gets his check, then he will pay his debts," then we must accept "Louie gets his check ⊃ he will pay his debts," which only says: "It is not the case that Louie gets his check and doesn't pay his debts." Granted that this latter formulation leaves something out, it does at least capture a significant part of the sense of the original. Similarly, if we accept as true the statement "If the water in the pipes freezes, then it expands," we must accept the statement, "The water in the pipes freezes $\supset$ it expands," which says, "It is not the case that the water in the pipes freezes and doesn't expand." The same explication applies to the other two examples in this section.

By way of review, notice that although we will accept the form $p \supset q$ if we accept the "if . . . then" statement from which it is taken, the converse does not hold. That is, if we accept as true a statement of the form $p \supset q$, we need not accept the corresponding "if . . . then" statement. For example, by our definition $p \supset q$ would be true if p were the false statement "Sparrows are mammals" and q were the true statement "Sugar is water-soluble."[5] But when "if . . . then" carries the sense of chronological order, causal connection, or logical implication, the resulting "if . . . then" statement breaks down. For example, we would not accept as true the statement "If sparrows are mammals, then sugar is water-soluble," if this meant, "Sugar is water-soluble *because* sparrows are mammals."[6]

But again, this need not cause any concern. For when we put the statements and arguments of ordinary discourse into logical form, we want a symbolism (with its precise meanings) which gets at the crucial common features of most uses of "if . . . then." Though $\supset$ may leave out something important, we can still accomplish much with it in terms of logic.

There are, however, two kinds of conditional statements which cannot be adequately handled by our truth-functional connective. They are the **generalized conditional** and the **contrary-to-fact conditional.** Each is illustrated below:

1 If a number is prime, then it is not divisible by two.
2 If Napoleon had not invaded Russia, then he could have maintained the Empire.

Example 1, which is a generalized conditional, cannot be adequately handled with our present symbolism because, strictly speaking, the "if . . . then" does not connect two statements. That is, the clause "a number is prime" is neither true nor false. Its function, however, is clear; it refers to an indefinite set of numbers which are prime. The force of the whole conditional may be brought out with this rendering:

1′ If x is a prime number, then x is not divisible by two.

This sentence is held to be true for any substitution of x. A more thorough treatment of this type of sentence must wait until Chapter 9. On the other hand, if we are willing to accept 1 or 1′, then, as before, we must be willing to accept, "x is a prime number $\supset x$ is not divisible by two," since this means "It is not the case that x is a prime number and is divisible by two." The difficulty, however, remains. Until some number is substituted for the variable x, we do not have a statement.

[5] Note that given a false p, $p \supset q$ remains true whether q is true *or* false.

[6] In general, statements of the form "if p, then q" entail corresponding statements of the form $p \supset q$, but not conversely.

Example 2, however, cannot be treated at all. The conditional is in the subjunctive mood and the antecedent is contrary-to-fact. Hence, we are faced with this perplexing situation: Since the antecedent is always false (in such conditions), the conditional must always be true. For example:

2 If Napoleon had not invaded Russia, then he would have maintained the Empire.

2' If Napoleon had not invaded Russia, then he would *not* have maintained the Empire.

Interpreting the "if . . . then" of 2 and 2' as truth-functions would force us to say that they are *both true;* but this is certainly counter-intuitive and implausible. Ordinary usage of "if . . . then" in contrary-to-fact conditionals demands that some contrary-to-fact conditionals with false antecedents and false consequents be true, while others with false antecedents and false consequents be false. Any adequate analysis of contrary-to-fact conditionals must, therefore, go beyond any attempt to explicate them by appeal only to the truth values of the constituent statements.[7]

In the following chapter we shall begin to see the power which $\supset$ as well as the other connectives introduced offers in the analysis of deductive arguments. But before moving on to these matters, let us briefly discuss the English variants of "if . . . then." Each of the following may be symbolized as $p \supset q$:

1 if p then q **2** q, if p
3 p only if q **4** not p unless q

Notice that "if" determines the antecedent *regardless of sentence order.* Thus, for example, each of the following expresses the same statement:

a If you study hard, then you will graduate.
b You will graduate if you study hard.

But while "if" is the sign of the antecedent, the presence of "only" *reverses the order; "only if" is the sign of the consequent.*[8] Thus, for example, these two statements say the same thing:

c If the paper burns, then there is oxygen present.
d The paper burns only if oxygen is present.

Although "if" and "only if" are frequently confused, they are clearly not the

---

[7] Notice the relevance of this point from the standpoint of the logic of historical inquiry.

[8] Compare, for example, the statement "only men are priests," which means that "all priests are men" but *not* that "all men are priests." Just as the subject and predicate terms must be reversed for proper understanding when "only" is used in simple affirmative statements, so must the clauses be reversed when it is used in compound statements of the form "If p, then q."

same. "The paper burns only if oxygen is present" *does not mean* "If oxygen is present, then the paper burns." Consider what this latter statement means. If it is true, the paper you are now reading should be in flames! On the other hand, the correct version ("If the paper burns, then oxygen is present"), if true (and it is true), does not say this at all. Clearly oxygen is present (or you would be unconscious) and the paper is not burning. The statement means that the presence of oxygen is one of the *necessary conditions* for burning but not that it is sufficient, which the misinterpretation of "only if" states. In general, the "if" clause *always* asserts a sufficient condition, whereas the "then" clause or the clause following "only if" always asserts a necessary condition.[9]

Notice, however, that whether something is or is not a sufficient or a necessary condition is not a matter of logic. All we are saying here is that $p \supset q$ asserts that p is a sufficient condition for q or that q is a necessary condition for p. In other words, logic cannot decide whether any statement of the form $p \supset q$ is true or if it is false, since we need to know what the truth values of p and of q are.

Item 4 above, "not p unless q," is an interesting idiomatic variation of "if p, then q." For example:

   e   Harriet will not go to the party unless Edith does

has the same meaning as:

   f   If Harriet goes to the party, then Edith will go.

In other words, Harriet's attendance is a sufficient condition for Edith's attendance, *but not conversely*. That is, if we accept statement e as true and then discover Harriet at the party, then we have the right to expect Edith. But if we see Edith at the party, we may *not* assume that Harriet is there. Statement f does *not* say that if Edith goes, Harriet will also go; it only says that if Edith *doesn't* go, then neither will Harriet. A good intuitive example is: "Paper won't burn unless oxygen is present," which says: "If paper burns, then oxygen is present."

---

[9] With some rather extreme verbal manipulation, the following could be thought of as two additional formulations of "if p then q":

   5 p is sufficient for q
   6 q is necessary for p

Thus,

   g   Burning paper is sufficient for oxygen being present.
   h   The presence of oxygen is necessary for burning paper.

The difficulty with these formulations is that neither g nor h is a compound joined with a logical connective. Again, however, one might argue that they are elliptical ways of expressing "if p then q." (Compare above, p. 77.) But this seems farfetched. To be sure, however, for all practical purposes they are equivalent to "If paper burns, then oxygen is present."

EXERCISES

A   Which of the following can be formalized as $p \supset q$? Take the first affirmative statement as p, the second as q.

1   The iron rusted because it was exposed to salt water.
2   If sugar is sweet, then so are you.
3   If Roosevelt had not gone to Yalta, the cold war would not have begun.
4   If x is a square, then x has four sides.
5   If Edith is a vixen, then she is a female fox.

B   Express each of the following as $p \supset q$. Take the first affirmative statement as p, the second as q.

6   If it rains, it pours.
7   You will be inducted if you are 1A.
8   On condition that the election is free, the people have some choice.
9   Assuming he comes, we will have things ready for him.
10   You may leave the country only if you have a passport.
11   You will be rested if you nap now.
12   Sam won't graduate unless he pulls his average up.
13   Only if Sam goes will Joe go.
14   Unless she pays me, I won't pay you.
15   Harriet will be at the party if she can get a lift.

$\equiv$ and English "If and Only If"   The last of our five connectives is $\equiv$ ("triple bar"), which in English reads "if and only if." Statements of the form $p \equiv q$ are called **material biconditionals.** In our truth-functional logic, $p \equiv q$ is defined as follows: If p and q have *the same truth value* (i.e., if both are true or both are false), then $p \equiv q$ is true; if p and q do not have the same truth value (i.e., if one is true and one is false), then $p \equiv q$ is false. As illustrated by the truth table for $p \equiv q$:

	p	$\equiv$	q
1	T	T	T
2	T	F	F
3	F	F	T
4	F	T	F

Almost all of the same points made concerning the difficulties of $p \supset q$ apply to $p \equiv q$, for, as its name suggests, "if and only if" is a way of asserting *two* conditionals and could be eliminated in favor of the conjunction of the conditionals $q \supset p$ and $p \supset q$. That is, "p if and only if q" is a conjunction of "p, if q" *and* "p only if q." Although expressions of the form "p if and only if q"

do not occur frequently in ordinary language, one must be on guard against confusing them with either "*p*, if *q*" or with "*p* only if *q*," both of which are much weaker claims. Thus, while "Oxygen was present if the paper burned" and "The paper burned only if oxygen was present" are both true, "The paper burned if and only if oxygen was present" is *false*. The biconditional asserts that if the paper burned, then oxygen was present, which is true; but it also asserts that if oxygen is present, then the paper burns, which is false.[10]

To review the relationships conveyed by the five connectives:

1	not *p*	$\sim p$	always has the opposite truth value of *p*.
2	*p* and *q*	$p \cdot q$	is true if and only if *p* is true and *q* is true.
3	*p* or *q*	$p \vee q$	is false if and only if both *p* is false and *q* is false.
4	if *p* then *q*	$p \supset q$	is false if and only if *p* is true and *q* is false.
5	*p* if and only if *q*	$p \equiv q$	is true if and only if *p* and *q* have the same truth value.

If you have not already learned the truth tables for the connectives, memorize this summary, for you will need to know it to understand the next chapter.

EXERCISES

Which of the following may be expressed as material biconditionals?

1 If you are 1A and only if you are 1A, will you be inducted.
2 If you go, I'll go and if I go, you go.
3 Only if Sam is reelected will he serve another term.
4 The figure is a trapezoid if it has four sides.
5 Only if Edith goes to the party will Harriet go to the party.

Logical Punctuation

As we have seen, the artificial language which has been developed in this chapter contains dummy letters (the statement variables), *p*, *q*, *r*, . . . , which stand for simple affirmative statements, and it contains the logical connectives (the logical constants) $\sim$, $\cdot$, $\vee$, $\supset$, $\equiv$, which "operate" on the dummy letters. Like any other language, this language also needs punctuation in order to express complicated arrangements of the symbols. In English, for example, we might say: "John will leave the company or he will get a raise and be promoted." Let us put this state-

---

[10] As with the statement form $p \supset q$, which can be read as "*p* is sufficient for *q*," $p \equiv q$ may be read as "*p* is necessary and sufficient for *q*."

ment into form. If we write:

1 $p \lor q \cdot r$

the formulation is ambiguous, for it might mean:

1' $p \lor (q \cdot r)$ John will leave the company, or he will both get
                       a raise and be promoted.

                    or

1" $(p \lor q) \cdot r$ John will leave the company or he will get a raise,
                       and he will be promoted.

Note that these two interpretations are not at all alike. The first one says that
if John doesn't leave the company, then he will get a raise and be promoted,
but the second one says that regardless of whether or not he leaves the company,
he will be promoted. Thus, it is not clear whether Example 1 is an alternation
with a conjunction as one of its alternatives, or whether it is a conjunction with
an alternation as one of its conjuncts. Only *one* of the two captures the sense
of the original. They both cannot, for they are not logically equivalent formulations. This can be shown by making the *same* substitution of the variables in
each and getting conflicting results — getting one as true and the other as false.
For example, if p and q are true and r is false, then 1' is true and 1" is false (because the truth of p makes 1' true and the falsity of r makes 1" false). To eliminate such ambiguity and to indicate clearly the *scope* of the connectives, we have
a system of parentheses, brackets, and braces. These punctuation marks enable
us to build up immensely complex expressions which are not ambiguous. For
example, in 1' the scope of the dot is limited by the parentheses; in 1" the scope
of the wedge is limited by the parentheses. In general, parentheses, brackets,
and braces will be employed to *group* the constituents of complex formulas.
    Consider these examples:

2 $\sim(p \lor q)$

In 2 the curl is operating on the compound statement $p \lor q$, which has been
grouped by the parentheses. Without the parentheses we would have this:

3 $\sim p \lor q$

in which the curl denies *only* the p.

4 $[(p \supset q) \lor r] \equiv p$

Example 4 uses a bracket in order to group together the compound, $(p \supset q) \lor r$,
which has been grouped internally by means of the parentheses.

5 $\{[\sim(p \cdot q) \supset p] \supset (p \cdot q)\} \vee (p \supset q)$

Highly involved, Example 5 must further employ a brace to unambiguously group the lengthy alternative, $[\sim(p \cdot q) \supset p] \supset (p \cdot q)$. If the expression is so complex that additional markings are needed, we shall begin a new series of parentheses, brackets, and braces. For example:

6 $\sim(\{[(p \equiv q) \cdot (p \vee q)] \vee p\} \supset \{[\sim(p \vee q)] \cdot r\})$

Example 6 is simply a very complex formula being denied.

Although the notations which we have introduced here may appear cumbersome, they are extremely advantageous by comparison with ordinary language. Complex statements in English are often very hard—if not impossible—to interpret. Consider this example:

7 The Stars will win the pennant and the Bulls will take second place if Goover begins to hit.

The trouble with Example 7 is that we don't know whether Goover's beginning to hit is the condition for the Stars' winning the pennant *or* for the Bulls' taking second place. In other words, does 7 say

7' If Goover begins to hit, then the Stars will win the pennant and the Bulls will take second place;

or does it say,

7″ The Stars will get the pennant; and if Goover begins to hit, then the Bulls will take second place.

In the absence of additional information 7 cannot be resolved unambiguously into 7' or 7″.[11] Again, the moral is this: Sometimes we say things in our natural language which *appear* to be clear but which upon analysis prove to be unclear. Forcing ourselves to move from a natural language to an unambiguous formal language gives us practice in being clear about what we are saying and some insight into the problems involved. Finally, it might be noted in passing that the ability to use symbols is a uniquely human achievement. Thinking and communication, not to mention formal logic, mathematics, and science, would be practically impossible without symbols. Imagine multiplying without a symbolism for numbers. Indeed, imagine multiplying using Roman numerals! We will now simplify our notation by adopting three conventions.

[11] Compare: 8 "The Yankees will win the pennant and Baltimore will take second place if Munson begins to hit!" Since we know that Munson plays for the Yankees, we should assume that 8 means: 8'. If Munson begins to hit, then the Yankees will win the pennant and Baltimore will take second place.

A Conjunction will be expressed by simply juxtaposing the component statements.

This convention, coupled with our use of parentheses, etc., allows us to dispense altogether with the dot. For example, $p \cdot q$ becomes simply pq; $(p \lor q) \cdot (p \supset q)$ becomes $(p \lor q)(p \supset q)$.

B The connectives $\lor$, $\supset$, and $\equiv$ are understood to mark a greater break than conjunction.

Thus, for example, $(pq) \lor r$ becomes $pq \lor r$; $p \supset (qr)$ becomes $p \supset qr$; and $[(p \supset q)p] \supset q$ becomes $(p \supset q)p \supset q$.

C The negation sign ($\sim$) will govern as little as possible.

For example, $[\sim(pq)]r$ becomes simply $\sim(pq)r$; $[\sim(p)] \supset q$ becomes simply $\sim p \supset q$.

With these three conventions, Example 6 becomes the simpler

6′ $\sim\{[(p \equiv q)(p \lor q) \lor p] \supset \sim(p \lor q)r\}$

Notice that in each of our formulas there is what is called the *main connective*, or a connective which indicates the greatest break. In 2 the main connective is $\sim$; in 3 it is $\lor$; in 4 it is $\equiv$; in 5 it is $\lor$; and in 6 it is $\sim$.

Some formulas will not require a main connective though one can always be provided. Such formulas occur only with conjunction and alternation. For example, the compounds pqr and $p \lor q \lor r$ are unambiguous as they stand and no further grouping is necessary. This is so because conjunction and alternation are **associative.** That is, the truth value of $(pq)r$ is the same as that of $p(qr)$, which is the same as pqr. Similarly, the truth value of $(p \lor q) \lor r$ is the same as that of $p \lor (q \lor r)$ and of $p \lor q \lor r$. Consider why this is so: $p(qr)$ is true if and only if p is true and qr is true. But qr is true if and only if both q and r are true. Hence, $p(qr)$ is true if and only if p, q, and r are each true, which is to say that $p(qr)$ is true when pqr is true. The same explanation (which the reader can provide) applies to $p \lor q \lor r$. As was indicated earlier, conjunction is also **commutative;** that is, the conjuncts may be interchanged without affecting their relationship. This is also true of alternation. That is, the *order* in which the simple affirmative statements, or alternatives, are placed has no bearing on their relationship. Thus, just as pq has the same truth value of qp, so does $p \lor q$ have the same truth value as $q \lor p$.[12]

---

[12] In arithmetic, which symbols are both associative and commutative? Is $\supset$ or $\equiv$ associative and commutative? In the next chapter a simple proof procedure as an answer to this question will be provided.

EXERCISES

A Only some of the following are ambiguous. Resolve each ambiguity by means of parentheses, brackets, etc. Show several versions. Which are not ambiguous? Why?

   1 $p \supset q \supset r$
   2 $\sim p \vee q$
   3 $(p \supset q)(q \supset r) \vee p$
   4 $p \equiv q \vee r$
   5 $p \vee q \vee r$
   6 $\sim pq \supset q \vee p \supset r$
   7 $(\sim q \supset \sim p) \sim q \supset \sim p$
   8 $pq \vee r$
   9 $pq \vee r(p \supset q)$
  10 $(pq \vee r)(p \supset q)$

B Put the following into form. If the English is ambiguous, indicate how it is ambiguous. Take the first simple affirmative statement as p, the second as q, etc.

  11 Either Louie failed and Harriet passed or Louie wasn't in the class.
  12 Harriet passed and either Louie failed or he wasn't in the class.
  13 Louie failed and Harriet passed or Edith was in the class.
  14 If Louie was in the class and if he didn't fail, then Harriet helped him out.
  15 If it doesn't continue to rain and the dam holds up, then the city will be safe and rescue will not be needed.

FIVE

TRUTH TABLES

*The paradox is now fully established
that the utmost abstractions are the
true weapon with which to control
our thought of concrete fact.*

Alfred North Whitehead

Formal Analysis

Up to this point we have been concentrating on developing an artificial language whereby we can put the statements of ordinary English into logical form. Our "artificial language" is now complete. To be sure, you must practice in order to become proficient in translating English into our new symbolism.[1] The purpose of such a formal analysis is to enable us to lay bare some key concepts of deductions and to generate some procedures by which we can test for the validity of arguments. Thus, we have two distinct kinds of problems: (1) we must be able to go from English into our symbolism and to formalize the arguments of English, and (2) we must develop some logical criteria for using the symbols. In this chapter we shall concentrate on the second problem, which in turn will necessitate our having to understand such concepts as "validity," "tautology," "contradiction," "contingency," and "entailment"; we will also provide several procedures for determining validity.

[1] We might call our symbolism the language of "PMese," since it is the "language" which Russell and Whitehead used in their classic of modern logic, *Principia Mathematica,* the first volume of which was published in 1910.

The Nature and Use of Truth Tables

In Chapter 4, we noted that a compound was a truth-function of its components when its full meaning was determined by the truth table. We also noted that expressions like $p \lor q$, $p \supset qr$, and $(p \lor q)r \equiv p$ are not *statements* since they say nothing and thus can be neither true nor false. We called such expressions *statement forms* or *formulas*. Strictly speaking, we should call them *truth-functional formulas*, because, as we shall see, there are other types of statement forms (formulas) which are not truth-functional in our sense.

But truth-functional formulas[2] do have this very important characteristic: We can "interpret" the dummy letters (that is, the statement variables). Now interpretation might mean substituting an actual statement for the dummy letter; or, since statements are either true or false, it might mean specifying a truth value for the dummy letter. Once interpretation in either sense is achieved, the resulting sentence becomes a statement. Given the formula $\sim p \lor q$, for example, we might "interpret" p as true and q as false. This would be tantamount to substituting some true statement for p and some false statement for q, as for example, "France is in Europe" for p and "Ethiopia is in Asia" for q. But when p *is* true, $\sim p$ is false (by the truth table for negation) and since "**F** v **F**" is false (by the truth table for alternation), the resulting statement is false.

Not only do truth tables enable us to *define* the connectives, but given these definitions, they also enable us to graphically represent the truth values of *all possible truth-functional compounds under all possible interpretations*. This device makes possible great generality and economy. For example, the truth-functional compound, "it was not safe to drive and we did not catch the train" becomes $\sim p \sim q$. This compound will have a determined truth value for each interpretation (in either sense) of its constituent parts. It can be represented thus:

	p	q	$\sim p$	$\cdot$	$\sim q$[3]
1	T	T	F	F	F
2	T	F	F	F	T
3	F	T	T	F	F
4	F	F	T	T	T

Building the Truth Table   Let us see how we arrive at such a table. Since the compound $\sim p \sim q$ contains two variables (p and q), the truth table must have four lines in order to represent all the possible combinations. Notice that if the formula had *three* variables, we would need *eight* lines in order to have all the combinations. Thus:

---

[2] In the remainder of this chapter we shall drop the adjective "truth-functional" with the understanding that it applies to the sort of formulas about which we are talking.

[3] Strictly the dot ($\cdot$) is superfluous, but for ease of exposition we shall sometimes employ superfluous notation.

	p	q	r
1	T	T	T
2	T	T	F
3	T	F	T
4	T	F	F
5	F	T	T
6	F	T	F
7	F	F	T
8	F	F	F

Each combination is different. In general the number of lines in our truth table will be determined by the algebraic expression 2^n, where n represents the number of variables.[4]

The left side of the table for $\sim p \sim q$ enumerates the four possible truth combinations for the variables (in this case p and q). Since this is the first step we must take in constructing a truth table, we shall place the number 1 under these combinations to indicate this. Thus:

	p	q	$\sim p$	·	$\sim q$
1	T	T			
2	T	F			
3	F	T			
4	F	F			
	(1)				

Substituting Truth Values   Now we wish to determine the truth values of $\sim p$ and $\sim q$ for each combination of p and q, and this we can do by recalling the table for negation. Thus, on line 1, where p is true and q is true, we know that $\sim p$ must be false and $\sim q$ must be false. So we write in **F** under each of these on that same line. Thus, up to this point we have the following:

	p	q	$\sim p$	·	$\sim q$
1	T	T	F		F
2	T	F			
3	F	T			
4	F	F			
	(1)				

Still using the table for negation, we now complete this step for the remaining three combinations of p and q, and the table fills out to this:

[4] Note also that constructing all the possible combinations can be done systematically. First, determine the number of lines and divide by two. Begin the first column with the resulting number of **T**'s and follow with the same number of **F**'s. For the second column, start with half the number of **T**'s which began the first column and alternate with the same number of **F**'s until the column is complete. Follow the same procedure for any remaining columns.

	p	q	$\sim p$	$\cdot$	$\sim q$
1	T	T	F		F
2	T	F	F		T
3	F	T	T		F
4	F	F	T		T
	(1)		(2)		(2)

We place the number (2) under $\sim p$ and $\sim q$ to indicate that this has been the second step of the procedure. Now there only remains the task of determining the truth values of the conjunction of $\sim p$ and $\sim q$ for the four resulting combinations of $\sim p$ and $\sim q$, a task which is accomplished by using the truth table for conjunction. Thus, on line 1, where we have a false statement conjoined to a false statement, we know that the resulting compound is false, and thus we write an **F** between $\sim p$ and $\sim q$. On line 2, where we have a false statement conjoined to a true statement, again the resulting compound is false and we write an **F** between the two. On line 3, we get the same result. And on line 4, where we have a true statement conjoined to a true statement, we know that the resulting compound is true, and so we write a **T** between the two. This third (and last step) is accordingly numbered (3), and we now have the completed truth table, thus:

	p	q	$\sim p$	$\cdot$	$\sim q$
1	T	T	F	F	F
2	T	F	F	F	T
3	F	T	T	F	F
4	F	F	T	T	T
	(1)		(2)	(3)	(2)

To recapitulate, in order to construct a truth table for any compound so as to determine its truth value, the following steps are taken:

1 Enumerate all of the combinations of truth and falsity for its variables, using the formula 2^n, where n represents the number of variables.
2 Determine the truth values for the smallest subordinate compound by applying the results obtained in Step 1.
3 Apply the results obtained in Step 2 to the next largest constituent of the compound.
4 Repeat the procedure of Step 3 until the main connective is reached.

At first, it probably will be helpful if you number each step as you proceed.

Consider next a more complex example: "If linguine is a noodle, then either clams are not nourishing or parsley makes you fat." This becomes the formula, $p \supset (\sim q \vee r)$. Here we have three variables, so our table requires eight lines.

We construct them first:

	p	q	r	p	⊃	(~q	v	r)
1	T	T	T		T	F		T
2	T	T	F		T	F		F
3	T	F	T		T	T		T
4	T	F	F		T	T		F
5	F	T	T		F	F		T
6	F	T	F		F	F		F
7	F	F	T		F	T		T
8	F	F	F		F	T		F
		(1)			(2)	(3)		(2)

The values for p and for r can be carried directly over for Step 2 or they may be omitted since we already have them; then we can fill in the compound ~q as Step 3. Before we can determine the value of the conditional p ⊃ (~q v r), we must determine the value of the consequent (~q v r). This may be accomplished as Step 4 and involves appealing to the table for alternation. Once this is done, appeal to the table for ⊃ gives us the value of the full compound under all possible substitutions of its variables. Thus:

	p	q	r	p	⊃	(~q	v	r)
1	T	T	T	T	T	F	T	T
2	T	T	F	T	F	F	F	F
3	T	F	T	T	T	T	T	T
4	T	F	F	T	T	T	T	F
5	F	T	T	F	T	F	T	T
6	F	T	F	F	T	F	F	F
7	F	F	T	F	T	T	T	T
8	F	F	F	F	T	T	T	F
		(1)			(2) (5)	(3)	(4)	(2)

One final example may answer some remaining questions. "Either Sam will go only if Mike goes and if Mike doesn't go then Sam won't, or Sam will go if and only if Mike goes." If we read "Sam goes" as p and "Mike goes" as q, then we have: [(p ⊃ q)(~q ⊃ ~p)] v (p ≡ q), which results in the following truth table:

	p	q	[(p	⊃	q) ·	(~q	⊃	~p)]	v	(p	≡	q)
1	T	T		T	T F	T	F	T		T		T
2	T	F		F	F T	F	F	F		F		F
3	F	T		T	T F	T	T	T		F		F
4	F	F		T	T T	T	T	T		T		T
		(1)		(5)	(6) (3)	(4)	(3)		(7)		(2)	

The left side of the table [numbered (1)] indicates fulfillment of Step 1. Since there are two variables, there are four truth combinations.

Next, we ask, what is the smallest subordinate compound? Since the main connective is the wedge, we look to the two alternatives. Noting that the right-hand alternative is a biconditional of p and q, we can immediately fill in its truth value under all four interpretations. They are shown as Step 2. Now to determine the truth values of the left-hand alternative, we need to determine the truth values of the conjunction. But to do this we need the truth values of two conditionals. Moreover, to determine the values of the right-hand conditional, we need to determine the values of the negated variables. Since these, then, are the smallest subordinate compounds, we determine them first. The results are shown as Step 3.

We can now proceed to build up the table. Step 4 gives the values of the right-hand conditional. Step 5 gives the values of the left-hand conditional. In Step 6 we determine the values of the conjunction, which are a function of the values of the two conditionals; that is, we use the results of Steps 4 and 5. In Step 7 we get the values of the main connective, which are a function of the results of Steps 6 and 2.

Now that this is done, what have we accomplished? The truth values under the wedge tell us the truth value of the entire expression under all possible substitutions. For example, if p is true and q is false, then the formula is false (line 2). Notice that it doesn't matter what true statement is represented by p and what false statement is represented by q. Similarly, if p is false and q is true, then the formula is true (line 3); and so on for the remaining two possibilities. This same procedure can be followed for an *infinite* set of formulas, *each* of which represents the logical form of an *infinite* set of statements in English.

EXERCISES

Construct truth tables for each of the following formulas:

1 $(p \lor q)(pq)$
2 $(\sim p \supset q)p$
3 $p \equiv \sim q$
4 $\sim (p \lor q)$
5 $\sim (pq) \lor (p \supset q)$
6 $p \lor qr$
7 $pq \supset \sim (pq)$
8 $(p \supset q)(q \supset r)$
9 $\sim [(pq) \lor (p \supset \sim q)]$
10 $pq \lor [\sim p \supset (p \equiv \sim q)]$

First Test for Validity

The apparatus presently at our disposal immediately gives us our first test for validity. A valid argument, you will recall, is one in which it is *impossible* for the premises to be true and the conclusion false. (Remember, in valid arguments, or deductions, it *is* possible for the premises to be false and the conclusion true.) Consider this argument:

1   If Nikos is a Greek, then he drinks ouzo.
         Nikos is a Greek.
   _____
   So,   Nikos drinks ouzo.

If we use the symbol ∴ to represent "so," "hence," "therefore," and their synonyms, we can put this argument into full symbolic form.
   It becomes:

1′ $p \supset q$
        p
   _____
        $\therefore q$

Now, is it possible for the premises to be true and the conclusion false? Let us see if it is by constructing a truth table for *all the possible* truth values. We then can indicate the premises and the conclusion and determine by inspection if it ever *could* happen that the premises were true and the conclusion, false. Thus:

	Premise 2 p	Conclusion q	Premise 1 $p \supset q$
1	T	T	T
2	T	F	F
3	F	T	T
4	F	F	T

The only time that *both* the premises are true occurs on line 1; but when this occurs, the conclusion, too, *must* be true. Therefore, the argument is *valid*. Strictly speaking, we should say that Argument 1 is *formally* valid because the form of Argument 1′ is valid.[5] This means that *any* argument which has this form is valid—no matter what its subject matter is; for, as the truth table indicates,

_____

[5] More strictly, we should say it is truth-functionally valid, because we analyzed its form in terms of truth-functions.
   The form of this argument is so important that it has a name, *modus ponens*, first given to it by medieval logicians.

regardless of what statements we substitute for p and for q, it will be impossible to make the premises true and the conclusion false.

Consider next an invalid argument:

2   If Nikos is a Communist, then he reads *The Daily Worker.*
            Nikos reads *The Daily Worker.*
   So, Nikos is a Communist.

which becomes:

2' $p \supset q$
    q
   $\therefore p$

Again, we construct a truth table, indicate the premises and the conclusion and determine by inspection if it could ever happen that the premises could be true and the conclusion, false. (In this case the elements of the table are the same as for Argument 1, but the premises and conclusions are different.)

	Conclusion p	Premise 2 q	Premise 1 $p \supset q$
1	T	T	T
2	T	F	F
3	F	T	T
4	F	F	T

We notice that on line 1 the premises are true and the conclusion is true. But this proves nothing, since in invalid arguments as well as valid arguments this can happen. What we are looking for is a case where the premises are true and the conclusion, false. There is such a case on line 3 where p is false and q and $p \supset q$ are true. Hence the argument is formally invalid; the conclusion does not necessarily follow from the premises. As before, we can say that *any* argument of this form — no matter what its subject matter — is invalid.[6]

Notice that we are not saying that Argument 2 is necessarily incorrect, for incorrectness cannot be evaluated on grounds of form alone. Indeed, if in Argument 2 the conclusion were weakened to read, "So, with some probability Nikos is a Communist," we would say that the argument is correct. That is, since it is a matter of *fact* that a high percentage of readers of *The Daily Worker* are Communists, there is some *inductive* warrant for believing that there is some probability that Nikos is a Communist. However, to assert the conclusion as probable requires going beyond the *form* of the argument. In this case it involved know-

---

[6] The argument commits a formal fallacy, which is to say that it is not formally valid. This fallacy is so pervasive that it, too, has a name: "the fallacy of affirming the consequent."

ing that many, though certainly not all, of the readers of *The Daily Worker* are Communists. By comparison, the argument "If bananas are horses, then bananas are fruits; bananas are fruits; so, bananas are horses," which has the same form as Argument 2, is neither valid *nor* correct. That is, its *form* shows that the conclusion doesn't follow necessarily; its *content* shows that its conclusion doesn't even follow probably. Evaluating correctness will be the problem of Part Three of this book.

Validity in Complex Arguments   The truth-table technique which has been introduced in this section can be employed to determine the validity (or invalidity) of much more complex arguments, though, to be sure, when the number of variables gets beyond three, the truth table becomes extremely cumbersome to use. Let us check for validity in a more complex argument.

> **3**   Liliuokalani is a Queen only if she is a Hawaiian.
> She is not a Hawaiian if she is a haoli.
> She is not haoli but is a Queen.

Hence,   She is Hawaiian.

which becomes:

3' $p \supset q$
$\quad r \supset \sim q$
$\quad \underline{\sim r \cdot p}$
$\quad \therefore q$

Let $p =$ "Liliuokalani is a Queen"; $q =$ "She is a Hawaiian"; and $r =$ "She is a haoli."
   We construct the truth table as follows:

	Conc.			Premise 1			Premise 2			Premise 3		
	p	q	r	p	$\supset$	q	r	$\supset$	$\sim q$	$\sim r$	$\cdot$	p
1	T	T	T		T		T	F	F	F	F	T
2	T	T	F		T		F	T	F	T	T	T
3	T	F	T		F		T	T	T	F	F	T
4	T	F	F		F		F	T	T	T	T	T
5	F	T	T		T		T	F	F	F	F	F
6	F	T	F		T		F	T	F	T	F	F
7	F	F	T		T		T	T	T	F	F	F
8	F	F	F		T		F	T	T	T	F	F
	(1)				(2)		(5)	(7)	(3)	(4)	(6)	(5)

(It should be noted that the order in which the steps are numbered may vary from person to person but that getting the correct result is what counts.)

The full array of truth values tells us by inspection that it could never happen that the premises of this argument could be true and the conclusion, false; for the only time that all three premises are true, the conclusion, too, is true (line 2). Hence the argument is valid.

EXERCISES

Check the following argument forms for validity:

1 $p \vee q$
$\underline{p}$
$\therefore q$

2 $p \vee {\sim}q$
$\underline{q}$
$\therefore p$

3 $p \supset q$
$\underline{p}$
$\therefore q$

4 $p \supset q$
$\underline{{\sim}q}$
$\therefore {\sim}p$

5 $p \supset q$
$\underline{q \supset p}$
$\therefore p \equiv q$

6 $pq \supset r$
$\underline{p \vee {\sim}r}$
$\therefore q$

7 $p \equiv qr$
$\underline{{\sim}p}$
$\therefore {\sim}q \vee {\sim}r$

8 $p \vee qr$
$\underline{{\sim}p}$
$\therefore q$

9 ${\sim}q \supset {\sim}p$
$\underline{{\sim}p \supset {\sim}r}$
$\therefore {\sim}q \supset {\sim}r$

10 $(p \vee q) \sim (pq)$
$\underline{p}$
$\therefore q$

Tautologies, Contradictions, and Contingencies

Truth tables may also be used to place statement forms into one of three exhaustive and exclusive categories: **tautologies, contradictions,** and **contingencies.**

Tautologies   A statement form is a tautology *if it is true under all possible interpretations of its variables.*[7]   Thus, for example $p \supset p$, $p \vee {\sim}p$, $(p \supset q)p \supset q$ are tautologies, as can be seen by their truth tables:

---

[7] This definition, it should be noted, does not claim to characterize *all* tautologies.   It covers only statement *forms*.

1 $p \supset p$

T	T	T
F	T	F

2 $p \quad \vee \quad \sim p$

T	T	F
F	T	T

3 $p \quad q \qquad [(p \supset q) \cdot p] \supset q$

p	q					
T	T	T	T T	T	T
T	F	F	F T	T	F
F	T	T	F F	T	T
F	F	T	F F	T	F
(1)		(3)	(4) (2)	(6)	(5)

The truth values of each of these expressions is read, as before, under the main connective; in the third example, it is the $\supset$ (Step 6). Inspecting the tables shows that no matter what the truth value of the variables may be, each of these expressions comes out true. Hence we may call them *necessarily true* or *logically true*.

There are several interesting features of such tautologies. First, not all logical truths may be analyzed as tautologies in our sense. For example, "If Harry W. is a bachelor, then he is an unmarried male" is necessarily or logically true. But showing this is *not* a matter of its logical form, for its form is simply $p \supset q$, and, as we know, there is a substitution of $p \supset q$ (line 2 of the truth table) which makes it *false*. The tautological character of the statement, then, must reside in something external to its form. In this case we would say that it is a matter of *meaning*. That is, the meaning of "bachelor" in English "contains" or implies "unmarried male." Thus, in this case *semantic* considerations are crucial. The statements of arithmetic, too, are frequently called necessarily or logically true, as for example, $2 + 2 = 4$. Here we might argue that, as above, the "meaning" of the symbols 2, +, 4, and = makes the statement necessarily true; that is, the truth of the statement resides in the fact that we use these symbols in such a way that it is impossible for $2 + 2 = 4$ to be false.[8] Whether or not this is the correct explication of the tautological character of the statements of arithmetic, the fact remains that the truth-functional analysis of tautologies discussed here is not adequate to the task of displaying their tautological character. This is not to say that the definition of a tautology which was presented above is either useless or unimportant. On the contrary, a great many very important tautologies may be seen as tautologies in our formal sense.

The second important feature of tautologies applies to all tautologies (including those which cannot be analyzed by truth-functions). Because they are logically true, they can tell us nothing about the universe we live in. The most that

[8] In courses in advanced logic and in the foundations of mathematics, more powerful logical tools than we have presented are employed in the discussion of this point. The classic treatment is Russell and Whitehead's *Principia Mathematica,* in which their aim was to show that by means of suitable definitions and axioms, arithmetic could be deduced from the truth-functional logic which has been discussed in these pages.

they reveal is the structure of the language which we use to talk about our universe and everything in it. This is perhaps rather startling but nonetheless correct. If someone says to you, for example, "It is raining or it is not raining," he has certainly said something which is true; indeed, the statement is necessarily true. But he has said nothing whatever about the weather. No matter what is happening with the elements, the statement is true. If it is in fact raining, then the statement is true; if it is in fact not raining, it is still true; but either it is or it isn't raining. To put it another way: If you were told that it was raining or that it wasn't, would you know whether to carry an umbrella, to have a picnic, etc.? All tautologies have this property: they are *necessarily* true but *factually* empty! Similarly, the statement "If Harry W. is a bachelor, then he is an unmarried male" tells us nothing about Harry W. The most that it tells us is how the word "bachelor" is used in English. (You might call this a linguistic fact, if you remember that "facts" of this sort are immensely different from facts about the weather, the planets, the origin of species, and the like.)

The third important feature of all tautologies is that we determine their truth value a priori or independently of the evidence of our senses. In short, we need have no factual knowledge (except for the knowledge of how we are using our symbols) in order to know that a tautology is true. Why this is so is best seen with respect to truth-functional tautologies. Consider formula 3 above: $(p \supset q)p \supset q$. As was demonstrated, 3 comes out true under all possible substitutions. But what does this mean? It means that the truth values of p and of q are *totally irrelevant* to determining 3's truth value. We need not know whether p stands for "Today is Monday," or whether it is in fact the case that today is Monday. Such considerations play no role whatever in our knowing that formula 3 is true. Indeed, because their truth value is *only* a matter of pure logic, tautologies have a special status. In the next section we will examine some of their very special roles.

Contradictions   A statement form is a contradiction *if it is false under all possible interpretations of its variables.* So, for example, $p\sim p$, $\sim(p \lor \sim p)$, $(p \supset q)p \sim q$ are contradictions, which can be seen by their truth tables:

1	p	$\cdot$	$\sim$	p
	T	F	F	
	F	F	T	

2	$\sim$	$(p$	$\lor$	$\sim p)$
	F	T	T	F
	F	F	T	T

3	p	q		$(p$	$\supset$	$q)$	$\cdot$	$(p$	$\cdot$	$\sim q)$
	T	T		T		F	T	F	F	
	T	F		F		F	T	T	T	
	F	T		T		F	F	F	F	
	F	F		T		F	F	F	T	

Again, inspection of the truth tables shows that no matter what truth values the variables have, these formulas always come out false. They may be called *necessarily* false or *logically* false; that is, their falsity is only a matter of logic. As with tautologies, not all contradictions are analyzable by means of truth tables. For example, "Harry W. is a bachelor, but he has a wife," is a contradiction; it is necessarily false, since if it is true that he is a bachelor, then by definition he can't have a wife. On the other hand, if it is true that he has a wife, then by definition he can't be a bachelor. But again, the contradictory character of the statement is not a function of its form, which is simply, $p \sim q$ and which comes out *true* under some substitutions.

The other two features of all tautologies are also characteristic of all contradictions with but a slight variation. Contradictions, because they are *logically false*, can tell us nothing about the world. We are given no information about the weather if we are told, "It is not true that it is either raining or not raining." Indeed, the contradictory character of this remark makes it quite unintelligible. Similarly, the truth value of a contradiction is determined a priori, since if the formula is always false, then the truth values of the constituent parts are totally irrelevant.

It is worth noting here that sometimes expressions in English may look like contradictions or tautologies, but may be functioning quite differently. For example, someone might say in some context: "If it rains, it rains," meaning something like "Whatever happens we cannot control," which is not a tautology. Or someone in some context might say, "It's raining but it's not," which looks like a contradiction but might mean something like, "What is falling is something between rain and snow." If this is what it means, then it is quite intelligible and not a contradiction. Also, certain paradoxical expressions look like contradictions but are not. Take, for example, an expression like "He's a man, I suppose, but he's not really a man." Here the context makes it rather clear that "man" is being used in two different senses, referring to physical attributes in the first part of the statement and to character attributes in the second part. Another figure of speech, known as *oxymoron*, also deliberately uses an apparent contradiction for humorous effect. Thus, a statement like "He spoke with a calculated spontaneity," though it appears to embody contradictory concepts (speaking with calculation and speaking without calculation), is not really contradictory, for the reader is expected to recognize the apparent contradiction and to be amused at the clever way in which the real meaning is expressed. This real, or intended, meaning is that the speaker made a great effort to appear natural but that in making the effort he appeared unnatural. All of these examples point up the richness and subtlety of language, which at the same time make matters difficult for logicians as well as for inexperienced readers.

Contingencies   A statement form is a contingency *if it is true under some substitutions of its variables and false under others.* So, for example, each of the following are contingencies: $p \vee q$, $\sim pq$, $[(p \supset q)q] \supset p$, as can be seen by their truth tables:

1	p	v	q
	T	T	T
	T	T	F
	F	T	T
	F	F	F

2	p	q	~p	·	q
	T	T	F	F	T
	T	F	F	F	F
	F	T	T	T	T
	F	F	T	F	F

3	p	q	[(p	⊃	q)	·	q]	⊃	p
	T	T		T		T	T	T	T
	T	F		F		F	F	T	T
	F	T		T		T	T	F	F
	F	F		T		F	F	T	F

Formula 1 comes out false only when p and q are false; formula 2 comes out true only when p is false and q is true; formula 3 comes out false when p is false and q is true. Hence all three are contingencies. The single most important feature of contingencies is that when we put statements into a contingent statement form, we get a statement which is *neither* logically true *nor* logically false. But this means that it is *factually significant;* that is, it *does* tell us something about the world. What it says, of course, might be true or it might be false, but whether it is true or false is *not a matter of logic.* In other words, to know if a contingency is true or false, we must know which line on the truth table is the relevant line, for unlike tautologies and contradictions we cannot tell in advance whether on any particular line the interpretation makes the formula come out true or false. To know which line to look at, however, we must know whether the statements being substituted for the variables are true or false, and to know this we must appeal to the facts. Suppose that someone asserted a statement of the form p v q. We know that statements of this form are usually true, but they are not always true. Suppose that you were then told that p represented "It is raining," and q represented "It is snowing." Do these interpretations put us on line 1? Line 2? Line 3? Line 4? Which? We must look outside or call the weather bureau or ask somebody who has just come in. No amount of pure logic will help. With tautologies and contradictions, none of this labor was necessary, and herein resides both their certainty and their factual emptiness.[9] From the point of view of imparting something about the world, the statements which result from substitution into contingent statement forms are the only interesting ones; but from the point of view of pure logic, the statements which result from substitution into tautologies and contradictions are the only interesting ones.

[9] Statements (not statement forms or formulas) which are either logically true or logically false are frequently called *analytic* statements, since they share the feature of being factually vacuous. Statements which are *not* logically true or logically false are called *synthetic* because they add to knowledge, or *empirical* because their truth value is determined by appeal to experience.

In the sections which follow and in the discussion of science and scientific method, we shall see how important these distinctions are.

EXERCISES

Determine which of the following are tautologies, contradictions, contingencies:

1 $p \supset \sim p$
2 $p \vee \sim q$
3 $\sim (p \supset p)$
4 $p \supset (p \vee q)$
5 $p \equiv \sim p$
6 $pq \vee \sim p \sim q$
7 $pq \supset (p \vee \sim q)$
8 $(p \supset q)(q \supset r) \supset (p \supset r)$
9 $(p \vee q)(pq) \supset p$
10 $(p \vee q) \sim p \supset \sim q$

$\supset$ and "Entails": The Second Test for Validity

In Chapter 4, we saw that $\supset$ could not be taken to mean "implies" or "entails" if these expressions are to mean the converse of deducibility. That is, if "p entails (or implies) q" means that "q is deducible from p,"[10] then $p \supset q$ does not capture this sense. For example, when we say: "The paper is red" *implies* "the paper is colored," we have *not* expressed this relation by $p \supset q$. $p \supset q$ is *only* a truth relation and is defined by its truth table. This truth relation does not express the sense of logical implication or entailment. But we are now in a better position to see how $\supset$ can be employed to shed some light on "entails." Consider this valid argument form:

$$p \vee q$$
$$\underline{\sim p}$$
$$\therefore q$$

The truth-table test shows this to be valid. Because it is valid, however, we can say that the premises entail or logically imply the conclusion. That is, the conclusion is deducible from the premises. This, however, is tantamount to saying, "If the premises are both true, then the conclusion must be true," or

---

[10] Since p entails q asserts a relation between p and q, entailment is the converse of deducibility: p entails q if and only if q is deducible from p.

IF $p \lor q$
AND $\sim p$ are true,

THEN q is true.

Thus, the argument form shown above is easily transformed into a statement form which will look like this:

$(p \lor q)\sim p \supset q$

The argument becomes a conditional statement in which the premises $p \lor q$ and $\sim p$ are *conjoined* and become the antecedent, and the conclusion q becomes the *consequent*. This resulting form, however, can now be seen to be a tautology:

p	q	$(p$	$\lor$	$q)$	$\cdot$	$\sim p$	$\supset$	q
T	T		T		F	F T	T	T
T	F		T		F	F T	T	F
F	T		T		T	T F	T	T
F	F		F		F	T F	T	F

In general, if P (where capital *P* represents any truth-functional statement form, simple or complex) *entails Q* (where capital *Q* represents any truth-functional statement form), then *P* $\supset$ *Q is a tautology*.[11]   Thus, there is a great deal of difference between the horseshoes ($\supset$'s) in

1 $p \supset q$

and

2 $(p \lor q)\sim p \supset q$

The horseshoe of Formula 1 is simply the material conditional, which at best approximates the sense of "if . . . then." The horseshoe of Formula 2, although it is the same symbol, is a very close approximation of "entails," because, unlike the horseshoe of 1, it represents a logical truth. This means that there is a logical relation between $(p \lor q)\sim p$ and q, whereas in 1 there is *no* logical relation between p and q. For example, if "It is raining or it is snowing" *and* "It is not snowing" are true, then "It is raining" *must* be true. By contrast, "If it is raining, then today is Monday" is true, "Today is Monday" may or may not be

---

[11] Although we have stated this rule so that it applies only to truth-functional formulas, it applies to all other types of formulas and to statements as well. Thus, if "All *S* is *P*" entails "No *S* is non-*P*," then "All *S* is *P* $\supset$ No *S* is non-*P*" is a tautology. Similarly, if "Harry W. is a bachelor" entails "Harry W. is unmarried," then, "Harry W. is a bachelor $\supset$ Harry W. is unmarried" is a tautology. The difficulty is that neither of these examples may be analyzed as tautologies with our present methods.

true. To express this another way: in valid arguments the logical relation between premises and conclusion holds whatever may be the truth values of the statements which comprise the premises, or the conclusion is *deducible* from the premises regardless of whether or not the premises are true. This is what the corresponding conditional says. Since it is a *tautology*, the relation between the antecedent and consequent holds or obtains, irrespective of the truth values of the constituent statements. The truth table graphically shows this.

This knowledge gives us another test for validity. To test for the validity of any argument, construct a conditional statement with the conjoined premises as antecedent and the conclusion as consequent. If the resulting conditional is a tautology, the corresponding argument is valid; if the conditional is not a tautology, the argument is not valid. Thus there is an intimate relationship between deductive arguments and logical truths.[12] Indeed, deduction *depends* upon the condition that the *relation* between premise set and conclusion is a logical truth. That is, Q is deducible from P only if P entails Q, and P entails Q only if $P \supset Q$ is a tautology.

With truth-functionally valid arguments this new insight also enables us to generate a greatly shortened procedure for evaluating validity.

The Shortened Truth Table

Making arguments into conditional statements does not conserve time or energy if we must construct a full truth table. But we need not construct a full truth table. Since a statement form is a tautology *only* if it comes out true under *all* possible substitutions, we can shorten our procedure considerably by looking only for those cases which might possibly make our statement form *false*. With conditionals, the only way they can ever come out false is if the antecedent is true and the consequent is false. These observations are utilized in the shortened truth-table method. Consider this example:

$$p \lor q$$
$$\underline{p }$$
$$q$$

which becomes

$$(p \lor q)p \supset q$$

The only way this formula could come out false would be if q is false and the antecedent $(p \lor q)p$ could be made true. So this is what we try to do:

[12] This relation holds for all possible deductions whether or not they are truth-functionally valid. Thus, the argument form "x is red; therefore x is colored," is valid and has as its corresponding logical truth the conditional, "if x is red, then x is colored."

$(p \lor q) p \supset q$
T T F T   F
    T
        F

We first make q false throughout the expression. In order to make $(p \lor q)p$ true, we need to make both conjuncts true, which means we must make p and $p \lor q$ true. But if p is true, then $p \lor q$ is true and the antecedent is true. Hence, we have found a substitution which makes the whole conditional false; hence, the statement form is *not* a tautology; and hence, the original argument is *not* valid. The point is to find the *one* line of the full truth table which makes the conditional false. In this case, it turns out to be line 2 of a full table.

With this technique at our disposal, we can easily treat arguments with many variables. Consider next this argument form which contains four variables:

$p \supset q$
$r \supset s$
qs _____

$\therefore ps$

which becomes

1 $(p \supset q)(r \supset s)(qs) \supset ps$

Notice that in this case there are three interpretations of the consequent which make it false: p true and s false; p false and s true; or p and s both false; hence we might be forced to try all three substitutions. This is so because we prove nothing by finding a line in which the consequent is false *and* the antecedent is false. What we are looking for is some substitution in which the consequent is false and the antecedent is *true*. To be sure, if there is *no such* substitution, then we have proved that the formula is a tautology, but to prove this we might in this case find it necessary to try all three possiblities. This is not too discouraging, however, when we consider that the *full* truth table would involve us with sixteen possibilities!

We begin by trying p as true and s as false. (See formula 1' below.) This doesn't help much, however, since if s is false, then conjunct C is also false. But if any of the conjuncts are false, then the whole conjunction is false; hence the antecedent is false.

         A   B   C
1' $(p \supset q)(r \supset s)(qs) \supset ps$
     T   F F   TF
                F   F
                  T

We then try making p false and s true. (See 1″ below.) Making s true and p false automatically makes both conjuncts A and B true; so we can forget about them. To make conjunct C true, q must be true. We are able to do this. We have found a substitution in which ps (the consequent) is false *and* (p ⊃ q)(r ⊃ s)(qs) is true. Hence, the formula is not a tautology, and hence the argument is not valid. Notice that we need not continue on to the final possibility, for we have already found what we are looking for.

$$
\begin{array}{cccc}
& A & B & C \\
\mathbf{1''} & (p \supset q) & (r \supset s)(qs) & \supset & ps \\
& F \quad T & T \ TT & & FT \\
& T & T \quad T & & F \\
& & T & & F \\
& & F & &
\end{array}
$$

Finally, let us consider what happens with a valid argument form:

$p \supset q$
$r \supset s$
$p \vee r$
∴ $q \vee s$

which becomes

$$
\begin{array}{cccc}
& A & B & C \\
\mathbf{2'} & (p \supset q)(r \supset s)(p \vee r) & \supset & (q \vee s) \\
& F \quad F \ F \quad F \ F \quad F & & F \ F
\end{array}
$$

To make the consequent false, we must make both q and s false. We do this throughout. To make conjunct A true, given q as false, we must make p false; and this makes p in conjunct C false. To make the second conjunct true, because s is false, we must make r false; but if we do this, then the third conjunct is false. And there is no escape. If we decide to make r true to make C true, then B would be false; if to avoid this, we make p true instead, then A is false. Hence it is impossible to make the consequent false and the antecedent true; hence the formula is a tautology; and hence the argument is valid.

EXERCISES

A Check the following for validity by the shortened truth-table method:

1 $p \supset q$
$q \supset r$
$r \supset s$
∴ $p \supset s$

2 $(p \supset \sim q)r$
$\sim p \vee \sim r$
$q \supset s$
∴ $q \vee s$

3 $pq \vee r$
  $\sim(pq)(r \supset t)$
  ─────────
  $\therefore u$

4 $p \vee q \vee r$
  $\sim(pr)$
  $r \supset (s \vee t)$
  ─────────
  $\therefore \sim s \supset t$

5 $(p \vee q) \sim (pq)$
  $p(r \equiv \sim s)$
  $q \supset (r \supset s)$
  s
  ─────────
  $\therefore r$

6 $p \supset (q \supset r)$
  $r \supset (s \supset t)$
  $p \vee r$
  ─────────
  $\therefore s \vee t$

7 $(p \vee q) \sim r$
  $(q \vee r) \sim p$
  $(q \supset s)(s \supset t)$
  ─────────
  $\therefore t$

8 $p \supset q$
  $r \supset p$
  $s \vee r$
  ─────────
  $\therefore q \sim s$

9 $pqr \vee pq \sim r$
  $p \supset q$
  $q \supset s$
  ─────────
  $\therefore ps$

10 $p \equiv q$
  $q \equiv r$
  $p \vee s$
  ─────────
  $\therefore p \equiv s$

B The shortened truth-table method may also be used to determine whether any statement form is a tautology, a contradiction, or a contingency. First see if the formula can come out true. If so, it is *not* a contradiction. Then see if the formula can come out false. If so, it is *not* a tautology. Note that showing that a formula comes out true once does not establish it to be a tautology, for tautologies *always* come out true. Similarly with regard to contradictions. They must *always* be false. Accordingly, you will need to make at least two substitutions in order to determine whether a formula is a contradiction, contingency, or tautology.

Use the shortened method to determine the character of the following:

11 $pq \vee (p \sim q) \vee pr$
12 $\sim\{[(p \supset q)p] \supset q\}$
13 $(p \vee r)(\sim p \supset q) \supset \sim r$
14 $[p(r \equiv q)(s \vee p)] \equiv (p \supset s)$
15 $\{[(p \vee q)p] \sim (q \supset s)(st \supset q)\} \supset (pq \vee r)$

Consistency and Validity

To call an argument "valid" is to say that the premises entail the conclusion, which in turn is to say that it is impossible for the premise set to be true and the conclusion false. But this is tantamount to saying that the *conjunction* of the premise set with the *negation* of the conclusion is a contradiction. That is, one cannot consistently (without self-contradiction) affirm the premises *and* deny the conclusion; or, one cannot simultaneously hold the premises to be true *and* the conclusion false. Consider this argument:

> If Sam is just, then he acts virtuously.
> He acts virtuously only if he enjoys what he does.
> He does not enjoy what he does unless he is happy.
> ———————————————
> Hence, Sam is just only if he is happy.

The point here is that one could not accept the three premises as true and yet insist that Sam is just and *not* happy. If, indeed, it is the case that Sam is just and not happy, then one or more of the premises must be rejected as false, since the three premises when taken together do entail the conclusion as stated. Let us demonstrate this by developing an inconsistency. We first put the argument into form:

A	$p \supset q$	p = Sam is just
B	$q \supset r$	q = he acts virtuously
C	$r \supset s$	r = he enjoys what he does
∴	$p \supset s$	s = he is happy

We then conjoin the premises with the contradiction of the conclusion, thus:

Contradiction of original

   A   B   C   conclusion

1 $(p \supset q)(q \supset r)(r \supset s) \sim (p \supset s)$

Formula 1 has the effect of saying that we accept as true Premises A to C, *and* we *deny* the conclusion $p \supset s$. But if the premises entail the conclusion, then 1 is a contradiction: it *never* comes out *true*. Let us see if this is the case. To make a conjunction true, each of the conjuncts must be true; so we try to do this:

   A   B   C   D

1' $(p \supset q)(q \supset r)(r \supset s) \sim (p \supset s)$
     F   F   F   F F T

The easiest way to do this is to make p, q, and r each false. This makes the premises (conjuncts A to C) all true. But under this substitution, conjunct D comes out false. Can we avoid this? If we make p true and s false, then conjunct D comes out true:

1″ $(p \supset q)(q \supset r)(r \supset s) \sim (p \supset s)$
     T   T T   T T $\left(\dfrac{F}{T}\right)$T T F
                                  F

But if p is true, then q must be true (to make A true); if q is true, then r must be true (to make B true); if r is true, then s must be true; but this is impossible since we have already assumed that it must be false. Hence there is *no* way to make 1 come out true; hence it is a contradiction; and hence the original argument is valid: the conclusion p ⊃ s follows from the premises. *In general, then, if P entails Q, then P · ~Q is a contradiction!*

This observation immediately gives us another test of validity. We conjoin the premises with the denial of the conclusion and check if the resulting conjunction is a contradiction. If it is, then the argument is valid; if it is not, then the argument is invalid. Consider this invalid argument form:

2   pq ⊃ r
     r v s
     ―――――
    ∴ p

which becomes, when we negate the conclusion:

```
                        Contra-
                        diction
                        of con-
            A      B    clusion
2    (pq  ⊃ r)(r v s)~p
     F  T        T F
```

We make p false, making ~p true; but if p is false, then pq ⊃ r is immediately true. We then make either r or s true, which makes the conjunction true. Thus, it is possible to affirm the premises and simultaneously to deny the conclusion. Hence, the premises do *not* entail the conclusion; hence the argument form is invalid. So we see there is an intimate relation between validity and logical falsity.[13]

EXERCISES

Check the validity of the exercises of the previous section by conjoining the premises with the denial of the conclusion and determining if a contradiction results.

Consistency of Premises

Inconsistency, logically speaking, is always bad, for as we have noted, it is the same as asserting (believing, etc.) a contradiction; and contradictions are not only false but also logically or necessarily false. Thus, if someone is caught in

---

[13] As before, this relation holds for all possible valid arguments whether or not they are truth-functionally valid. Thus, for example, the valid argument "x is red; therefore x is colored" has as its corresponding logical falsehood the conjunction "x is red *and* x is *not* colored."

a contradiction, it is *impossible* to accept what he says as true. One need not "check the facts" to know that the following statement is false:

> Although Marx wrote *Das Kapital,* if he did, then he's crazy and Marx wasn't crazy,

for that claim is logically false.[14] That is why, we may suppose, *factual* mistakes —making false statements—may be forgiven more easily than making the logical mistake of holding to a contradiction. There is a world of difference between saying something which is *necessarily* false and saying something which can be termed *factually* false. The second sort of error reveals inadequate research or command of the subject matter; the first sort of error is one of muddled thinking. Inconsistency, therefore, should be avoided at all costs.

Inconsistency causes other difficulties as well. Frequently we want to offer grounds for a decision, a belief, a scientific hypothesis, or a mathematical theorem. But if the premises we offer in support of our claim are themselves inconsistent, then we can be sure that we have proved *nothing whatever.* Why this is so can be seen quite easily. Consider the following argument form:

$$\frac{p{\sim}p}{\therefore q}$$

Now clearly the premise $p{\sim}p$ is a contradiction. But does the conclusion "follow"? If this means, can we *deduce* q from the premise, we would surely be puzzled. To illustrate: to the request, "Produce evidence that sugar is water-soluble" the evidence offered is "Because today is Monday and today is not Monday." This "evidence" is not, we may assume, very convincing. Hence, how could we deduce the fact that sugar is water-soluble from the assertion that today is Monday and today is not Monday? Yet the conditional $p{\sim}p \supset q$ is a tautology and the conjunction $p{\sim}p{\sim}q$ is a contradiction. But notice why. The conditional is a tautology because the antecedent is *necessarily false,* and hence there is no way to make the conditional false. The conjunction, to be sure, is a contradiction, but it is because the premise *itself* is a contradiction. The conclusion to be drawn from this little example is this: If we begin with inconsistent premises, then we can prove *anything whatever.* But if everything "follows from" inconsistent premises, then *nothing* is proved. The moral is evident: Don't use inconsistent premises.[15]

In theory construction in science and in mathematics, the problem indicated

---

[14] "If Marx wrote *Das Kapital,* then he is crazy; Marx wrote *Das Kapital;* but Marx is not crazy" becomes $(p \supset q)p{\sim}q$. Try to make that true!

[15] The perceptive reader has noted perhaps that the difficulty seems to arise because of the peculiar nature of $\supset$. But there is more at issue. It would be agreed that where P entails Q, one cannot consistently affirm P and deny Q. Yet where P is itself inconsistent (either truth-functionally or otherwise), the inconsistency arises not from affirming P and denying Q, but from affirming P alone.

here is an absolutely fundamental one. Scientists, in seeking explanations, and mathematicians, in producing mathematical systems, must constantly be on guard against introducing implicit and explicit contradictions into their theories and axiom sets. For if they do, all the conclusions which they draw are entirely worthless. Indeed, an important part of the task of the logician and pure mathematician is the developing of various tests for consistency of their premise sets. Some of the most important discoveries in mathematics, including non-Euclidean geometries, Gödel's theorem and theorems by Lowenheim, Skolem, and others, stem from various difficulties associated with the problem of consistency. Discussion of these matters is beyond the scope of this book, but it is worth noting that inconsistent premise sets are not always easily seen. Our example is quite atypical in this respect. Inconsistencies, or contradictions, are frequently implicit; that is, they rarely take the form $p\sim p$. Fortunately, if we confine our attention to truth-functions, we need never be caught in a contradiction, for the methods already introduced are entirely adequate to find them. All we need do is to conjoin the *premises* and see if we can make them true. If we can, then we know that the set is consistent. Once this is accomplished, we can then check for validity either by forming a conditional with the premises as antecedent and the conclusion as consequent, or by conjoining the negation of the conclusion with the premise set and checking for a contradiction.

In the chapter which follows we shall turn to a discussion of the notion of logical equivalence. We then will introduce another method for testing for the validity of truth-functional arguments. This new method, unlike the method of truth tables, will require ingenuity.

EXERCISES

Determine if the following sets of statements are consistent. Put each statement into symbols, conjoin them, and try to make the conjunction come out true. If there is an interpretation (i.e., some substitution of **T**'s and **F**'s) which make the conjunction true, then the set of statements is consistent. Remember, these are *not* arguments, so there is no conclusion.

1 I will attend the meeting only if my work is finished on time. If I attend the meeting, then I will have had my supper. If I finished my work on time, then I will not have had my supper. I'll attend the meeting. ($p =$ I will attend the meeting; $q =$ my work is finished on time; $r =$ I will have had my supper.)

2 If she loves me, then she wouldn't date other boys. If she doesn't date other boys, she will think that I'm jealous and inconsiderate. If she thinks that I'm jealous and inconsiderate, she doesn't love me. She wouldn't date other boys unless she loves me. ($p =$ she loves me; $q =$ she would date other boys; $r =$ she does date other boys; $s =$ she thinks that I'm jealous; $t =$ she thinks that I'm inconsiderate.) Be careful of that last statement, "She wouldn't date other boys unless she loves me."

3 If God's existence cannot be demonstrated, then if Christianity presupposes belief in God, we must believe on faith alone. But either God's existence cannot be demonstrated or we must believe on faith alone. Christianity does presuppose belief in God, but we must not believe on faith alone. (p = God's existence can be demonstrated; q = Christianity presupposes belief in God; r = we must believe on faith alone.)

4 Democracy is misunderstood by many people. But either both socialism and capitalism are democratic or democracy and socialism are misunderstood by many people. If socialism is misunderstood, then democcracy is understood. But socialism is not democratic. (p = democracy is understood; q = socialism is democratic; r = capitalism is democratic; s = socialism is understood.)

SIX

TESTING
TRUTH-FUNCTIONAL
ARGUMENTS

*The prejudice against careful analytic
procedure is part of the human
impatience with technique which arises
from the fact that men are interested in
results and would like to attain them
without the painful toil which is the
essence of our moral finitude.*

Morris R. Cohen

≡ and Equivalence

In the last chapter we considered some important relationships which may exist
between propositions, namely, contradiction and entailment. Still another important relationship in the study of logic is that of equivalence, which may be
partially explicated as follows: If P is equivalent to Q, then $P \equiv Q$ is a tautology.[1]
What this means with regard to truth-functional formulas is that two truth-functional formulas are equivalent if their truth values are identical under all possible
substitutions. For example:

p q	1 $p \supset q$	2 $\sim p \vee q$
T T	T	F T T
T F	F	F F F
F T	T	T T T
F F	T	T T F
	*	*

---

[1] Again P and Q refer to truth-functional formulas though the rule holds also for non-truth-functional
formulas. Compare note, p. 100.

3	$\sim (p \cdot \sim q)$	4	$\sim p \lor pq$
T TF F		F T T
F TT T		F F F
T FF F		T T F
T FF T		T T F
*		*

Since the four statement forms illustrated here agree in truth value under all four interpretations of their variables, they are equivalent to one another. This means that any biconditional composed of two of these forms is a tautology. Take, for example, the biconditional composed of forms 1 and 2:

$(p \supset q) \equiv (\sim p \lor q)$
T   T   T
F   T   F
T   T   T
T   T   T

This principle immediately gives us several tests for equivalence. First, we form a biconditional of the two statement forms in question and see if there is some interpretation which makes the biconditional false. Although we can do this with a full truth table, we can also take a short cut by using the knowledge that biconditionals are false only when the two sides are opposite in truth value. For example, suppose we wish to determine if $pq \lor r$ is equivalent to $p(q \lor r)$. Making the two statement forms into a biconditional, we get:

1 $(pq \lor r) \equiv p(q \lor r)$

Now we try to make one side of the biconditional true and the other false. If we can do this, then we will show that the two formulas are not equivalent; if we cannot, we will know that they are equivalent. In this case the proof is expeditious. We make r true, which makes the left side true, and we make p false, which makes the right side false. Thus the statement forms are not equivalent.

Consider next this case: Is p equivalent to $pq \lor p\sim q$?

2 $p \equiv (pq \lor p\sim q)$

If we make p false, then both sides of the biconditional are false. If we make p true, however, we can't make the right side false because for whatever value we choose for q one of the alternatives will be true. Hence, p is equivalent to $pq \lor p\sim q$.

As these examples have already illustrated, there are many ways "to say the very same thing," ways which are sometimes deceptively simple or extremely complex. Formula 2 proves that "March 17 is St. Patrick's Day" says the same

thing as "Either March 17 is St. Patrick's day and March 21 is Greek Independence day or March 17 is St. Patrick's Day and March 21 is not Greek Independence Day." Similarly, to say "It is not true that Sam is here or that Millie is
here" says the same thing as "Sam is not here and Millie is not here."[2]

However, the notion of equivalence here presented and the expression "says
the same thing as" is subject to considerations exactly analogous to those given
to the notion of "entailment," which were discussed in the previous chapter.
First, regarding truth-functional formulas, the expression "says the same thing as"
means *only* that the two statement forms agree with respect to truth and falsehood. To say that they are equivalent in our sense is *not* to say that they are
semantically identical or synonymous. Semantic identity cannot be determined
on formal grounds, for it raises questions of *meanings* in a natural language. For
example, it may be true that in English the words "vixen" and "female fox" are
synonymous. But if they are, this is not a question that can be decided by appeal
to truth tables, or indeed, by any *formal* analysis.[3] Secondly, many schema are
formally equivalent but not truth-functionally equivalent; e.g., "All *S* is *P*" is
equivalent to "No *S* is non-*P*," but truth tables cannot show this. Finally, since
contradictory formulas are always false, they are each formally equivalent to one
another. Similarly, since tautologies are always true, they are each formally
equivalent to one another.

EXERCISES

A Determine which of the following pairs are truth-functionally equivalent:

1	$\sim(pq)$	p
2	$p \lor \sim q$	$p \supset q$
3	$\sim(p \lor q)$	$p \sim q$
4	$pq \lor r$	p
5	$p \equiv \sim q$	$(p \lor q) \sim (pq)$
6	$\sim q \supset \sim p$	q
7	$p \supset (q \supset r)$	$pq \supset r$
8	$p \equiv (pq)$	$p \supset q$
9	$p \lor q \lor r$	$(p \lor \sim p)r$
10	$(p \supset q)q \supset p$	$\sim p \supset (\sim pq \lor q)$

B Why is the notion of "equivalence" only partially explicated when construed in terms of truth-functions?

[2] This is an instance of what is called *DeMorgan's theorem.* See the next section.

[3] On the other hand, if "vixen" is (semantically) equivalent to "female fox," then the expression,
"x is a vixen $\equiv$ x is a female fox" is a tautology. But again, the tautologous character of this expression appeals to extraformal considerations which lie beyond the scope of our analysis.

Some Important Logical Equivalences

It is interesting to notice that among the universe of actual and possible statement forms there is an *infinite* number of them which are equivalent to one another. For, as we have seen, whenever any two statement forms have the same truth values under all possible substitutions, they are truth-functionally equivalent to one another. Some of these are of special interest, however, and we shall now take notice of them.

In Chapter 4, it was observed that the five statement connectives introduced were more than we actually needed. We can now determine why this is so. Consider first the definition of v, which on the truth table was this:

p	v	q
T	T	T
T	T	F
F	T	T
F	F	F

But now we see that any formula constituted of p and of q which has the same table as the one for alternation will give us an equivalent statement form. Assume that we had only the connectives ~ and ·. Could we, with just these two connectives, construct a formula which had a truth table identical to the one for v? Indeed, we can. For example:

p	q	1	~ (~p · ~q)		
T	T		T	F F F
T	F		T	F F T
F	T		T	T F F
F	F		F	T T T

Formula 1 perfectly satisfies our request, for it comes out false only when both p and q are false, and that exactly captures the sense of v. Therefore, whenever we want to say p v q we could just as well say ~(~p·~q). Hence the v can be completely eliminated. Could we do the same for the ⊃?

p	q	2	~(p · ~q)		
T	T		T	TF F
T	F		F	TT T
F	T		T	FF F
F	F		T	FF T

Formula 2 comes out false only when p is true and q is false, and that fully captures the sense of p ⊃ q. Accordingly, it too is expendable.

The reader has perhaps inductively arrived at a general method for constructing a formula for any contingent truth-function. Given the truth table for the desired truth-function, we explicitly reject (deny) those interpretations which make the compound false; if there is more than one, we conjoin them. For example, we describe some truth-function so that it has this truth table:

p	q	p	?	q
T	T		T	
T	F		F	
F	T		F	
F	F		T	

The function in question is to come out false only when p is true and q false and when p is false and q true. We explicitly deny these two cases and conjoin them. This yields:

3 $\sim(p\sim q)\cdot\sim(\sim pq)$[4]

This function, of course, is the material biconditional, so we have eliminated it also. Conclusion: Anything which can be said in the logic of truth-functions can be said with *only* the curl and the dot.[5] To be sure, it would be inconvenient to restrict ourselves in this way, but the fact remains, it could be done.

The method of constructing a formula by means of negation and conjunction suggests another interesting set of equivalences. These employ negation, conjunction, *and* alternation. Again, consider the truth table for alternation:

p	v	q
T	T	T
T	T	F
F	T	T
F	F	F

[4] The reader should verify this with a truth table.

[5] Conjunction, however, might also have been eliminated in favor of alternation and negation. *pq* is translatable as $\sim(\sim p \vee \sim q)$; $p \supset q$ is equivalent to $\sim p \vee q$, and $p \equiv q$ is equivalent to $\sim[\sim(\sim p \vee q) \vee \sim(\sim q \vee p)]$. Readers should attempt to establish these equivalences for themselves.

Finally, it has been shown (by Sheffer, 1913) that a *single* connective will suffice. This connective | ("stroke") comes out true *except* when p and q are *both* true. Its table, therefore, is:

p	q	p	|	q
T	T		F	
T	F		T	
F	T		T	
F	F		T	

If we start with stroke as basic, then negation can be expressed as $p|p$; and conjunction as $(p|q) | (p|q)$. Similarly, alternation, the material conditional, and the material biconditional admit of definition exclusively in terms of |. How *is* alternation, etc., expressed in terms of stroke?

The function $p \vee q$ comes out true when pq is true *or* when $p{\sim}q$ is true *or* when ${\sim}pq$ is true; that is, it comes out true on lines 1, 2, and 3. So instead of denying the case in which it comes out false, as we did before, why not affirm all the cases in which the function comes out true?

Thus,

4 $pq \vee p{\sim}q \vee {\sim}pq$

Notice that we *alternate,* not conjoin, the *true* cases, because we are saying that the function comes out true when pq is true *or* when $p{\sim}q$ is true, etc. Expressions of this sort are sometimes called **normal forms.** They have the interesting feature of explicitly stating which lines on the truth table for the formula in question are true.[6]

The following include some other interesting and important equivalences:

5 ${\sim}(p \vee q) \equiv {\sim}p{\cdot}{\sim}q$
6 ${\sim}(pq) \equiv {\sim}p \vee {\sim}q$

Formulas 5 and 6 are known as *DeMorgan's laws* and are important insofar as they show us we need never apply negation across a whole conjunction or alternation. They are interesting since the negated alternation becomes a conjunction and the negated conjunction becomes an alternation. Although this is perhaps surprising at first blush, consideration of the properties of alternation and conjunction disposes of any qualms. Conjunction and alternation are *duals* of one another. That is, their truth tables are throughout the opposite in truth value. Consider the tables for both:

p	q	$p{\cdot}q$		p	q	$p \vee q$
T	T	T		F	F	F
T	F	F		F	T	T
F	T	F		T	F	T
F	F	F		T	T	T

Note that in the table for conjunction when every **T** is replaced with **F** and every **F** with **T**, we get the table for alternation. Similarly, in any formula, if each letter variable is negated and also the whole, a dual is generated. This is so since negating each letter has the effect of reversing the truth values on the table, and

---

[6] All truth-functional formulas may be "reduced" to normal form. For example, given the formula $(p \supset q)r$, we first eliminate the horseshoe by using the equivalence ${\sim}p \vee q$. This yields $({\sim}p \vee q)r$. By means of equivalence, 11 below, this in turn yields ${\sim}pr \vee qr$, which is a normal form; it tells us that the function comes out true whenever p is false and r is true or when q and r are true. Notice, however, that this occurs four times: when ${\sim}prq$, or ${\sim}pr{\sim}q$, or ${\sim}pqr$, or pqr is true. Notice why this is so. The first alternative ${\sim}pr$ is equivalent to ${\sim}pr(q \vee {\sim}q)$ since conjoining a tautology cannot alter the truth value of ${\sim}pr$. But by 11 this yields ${\sim}prq \vee {\sim}pr{\sim}q$. Hence it is equivalent to ${\sim}pr$. Similarly, the second alternative qr is equivalent to $qr(p \vee {\sim}p)$, which in turn is equivalent to $qrp \vee qr{\sim}p$.

negating the whole reverses the truth of the outcome. But since pq is the dual of $p \lor q$ and $\sim(\sim p \cdot \sim q)$ is the dual of pq, $p \lor q$ must be equivalent to $\sim(\sim p \cdot \sim q)$.

> 7 $\quad pq \equiv qp$
> 8 $\quad (p \lor q) \equiv (q \lor p)$

These show that conjunction and alternation are commutative.

> 9 $\quad p(qr) \equiv (pq)r$
> 10 $\quad [p \lor (q \lor r)] \equiv [(p \lor q) \lor r]$

Conjunction and alternation according to formulas 9 and 10 are associative.

> 11 $\quad p(q \lor r) \equiv (pq \lor pr)$

This formula is called *distribution* and is analogous to "multiplying out."

> 12 $\quad (p \supset q) \equiv (\sim q \supset \sim p)$

Formula 12 is called **transposition** or **contraposition.** $p \supset q$ and $\sim q \supset \sim p$ are frequently called the **contrapositives** of one another.

The Ingenuity Problem

Up to this point we have utilized only mechanical procedures for determining the validity of arguments. That is, it was sufficient to determine validity to render the argument into its form and then to apply either a full truth table or one of the shortcut versions of the truth table. These methods provide a type of proof which is frequently called a **decision procedure.** Decision procedures for determining validity (and the logical character of formulas) are methods which do not require ingenuity since by mechanically following certain steps we can unequivocally decide if any given argument is valid or invalid. Moreover, this can always be accomplished in a finite number of steps. In addition to the obvious advantage that such procedures require no ingenuity, their greater advantage is that they therefore can be completely mechanized and employed in computers. That is, one can design "logic machines" which can be programed to do validity tests.

However, many important types of deductions and correspondingly many important types of proofs do not admit of full decision procedures. These include many of those deductions which lie beyond the scope of the present analysis, for example, proofs in mathematics. In geometry, you probably remember that proofs involved showing that the theorems were a logical consequence of the axioms, definitions, and rules of geometry. To construct a proof required ingenuity, for there were no prescribed steps to be followed in deducing the theorem. One either saw how to put the proof together or one didn't. Once it was put together, to be sure, no ingenuity was needed to follow it, but putting it together was another matter. In what follows we shall offer a small logical system, comparable in some ways to geometry, though considerably simpler. Our system will contain only a set of inference rules and a set of logical equivalences. The problem will be to determine if a conclusion logically follows from given sets of premises by means of the inference rules and equivalences. Every step in the proof will require ingenuity and every step will need to be justified by appeal to one of the rules or equivalences.

To begin with, the inference rules are as follows:

1 P and $P \supset Q$ entails Q (Modus Ponens)
2 $\sim Q$ and $P \supset Q$ entails $\sim P$ (Modus Tollens)
3 $\sim P$ and $P \vee Q$ entails Q (Disjunctive Syllogism)
4 PQ entails P (Simplification)
5 P and Q entails PQ (Conjunction)
6 $P \supset Q$ and $Q \supset R$ entails $P \supset R$ (Hypothetical Syllogism)
7 P entails $P \vee Q$ (Addition)
8 $(P \supset Q)(R \supset S)$ and $P \vee R$ entails $Q \vee S$ (Constructive Dilemma)[7]

These eight rules may be considered as valid *elementary argument forms*. Thus Rule 1 says in effect that the following argument form is valid:

$$p \supset q$$
$$\underline{p \hspace{3cm}}$$
$$\therefore q$$

But it says more than this, for the capital letters in each of the rules will represent not only single variables, p, q, r, etc., but also all possible truth-functional formulas. Suppose, for example, that we have as a premise the formula pq and as another premise the formula $pq \supset \sim r$. Then capital letter P represents pq and capital letter Q represents $\sim r$. $P \supset Q$ then represents $pq \supset \sim r$. Accordingly, Rule 1 tells us that the following argument is also valid:

$$pq \supset \sim r$$
$$\underline{pq \hspace{3cm}}$$
$$\therefore \sim r$$

The point is perfectly general. Whenever a formula has as its main connective $\supset$, it may be represented as $P \supset Q$. Thus, $(p \vee q) \supset r$ is an *instance of* $P \supset Q$ with $p \vee q$ as P and r as Q. Similarly, the very complex $\sim(p \equiv q) \supset$

---

[7] Notice that each of the inference rules may be justified by translating them into tautologous conditionals. Hence Rule 1 is $P(P \supset Q) \supset Q$, which is a tautology. Similarly, each of the equivalences on p. 121 is translatable into a tautologous biconditional.

$[(s \lor t) \lor (\sim pr)]$ is an instance of $P \supset Q$ with $\sim(p \equiv q)$ as P and $[(s \lor t) \lor (\sim pr)]$ as Q. Accordingly, the rule says that the following is valid:

$$\sim(p \equiv q) \supset [(s \lor t) \lor (\sim pr)]$$
$$\underline{\sim(p \equiv q)}$$
$$\therefore (s \lor t) \lor (\sim pr)$$

Similar considerations apply to each of the rules. Thus, Rule 2 tells us that the following argument is valid:

$$(p \lor \sim q) \supset st$$
$$\underline{\sim(st)}$$
$$\therefore \sim(p \lor \sim q)$$

for P represents $p \lor \sim q$ and Q represents st. Hence, $\sim Q$ is $\sim(st)$ and $P \supset Q$ is $(p \lor q) \supset st$. Finally, then, $\sim P$ is $\sim(p \lor \sim q)$. Be careful with the parentheses. If Q represents st, then $\sim Q$ is $\sim(st)$, *not* $\sim st$.

Similarly, inference Rule 3 tells us that we may deduce Q from the premises $\sim P$ and $P \lor Q$, or that

$$\sim(p \supset q)$$
$$\underline{(p \supset q) \lor r}$$
$$\therefore r$$

is valid. Here P is $p \supset q$ and Q is simply r; so $\sim P$ is $\sim(p \supset q)$.

Now let us illustrate the method, using only the first eight rules. Assume that we are given as premises of an argument the two statement forms $(p \lor q)r \supset qr$ and $(p \lor q)r$ and as conclusion the formula qr. The question is, "Do the premises entail the conclusion in accordance with the rules?" We list (and number) the premises and label them with an asterisk (*) to mark them as our original assumptions. They are, as it were, what is given. Alongside the premises we write the (putative) conclusion. Thus:

$$* \begin{cases} 1 & (p \lor q)r \supset qr \\ 2 & (p \lor q)r \qquad /\therefore qr \end{cases}$$

Can qr be justified by appealing to one or more of the rules? We see that it can, for Rule 1 says that we may deduce Q from the premises P and $P \supset Q$. That is, if we have a line of the form P and a line of the form $P \supset Q$, we may deduce as a line Q. In this case, Q is the compound qr, P is the compound $(p \lor q)r$. Hence, $P \supset Q$ is the compound $(p \lor q)r \supset qr$. Notice that once we fix on a substitution instance of P we must use that *same* instance in $P \supset Q$. The deduction is complete with line 3:

* **3**   *qr*   **1 and 2, Rule 1, Modus Ponens**

Alongside line 3, we write the numbers of the lines from which 3 was derived. We also note the rule which we employed; this justifies the move from 1 and 2 to 3. Line 3 also carries an asterisk, for the asterisk tell us that the truth of line 3 depends upon the truth of the original assumptions (the premises). That is, the proof shows that the conclusion is deducible from the premises and thus *if* the premises are interpreted as true, then the conclusion must be true.

Consider next this more complex argument:

   1   *pq ⊃ r*
   2   *r ⊃ s*
   3   ~*s*
   4   *pq* v *t*
     ∴ *t*

Can this argument be proved valid by means of our rules? From premises 1 and 2 we can infer *pq ⊃ s* by means of Rule 6, Hypothetical Syllogism. But *pq ⊃ s* *and line 3, ~s*, entail ~*(pq)* by means of Rule 2, Modus Tollens. Finally, ~*(pq)* and premise 4 entail *t* by means of Rule 3, Disjunctive Syllogism. The full proof looks like this:

     ⎧**1**   *pq ⊃ r*
     ⎪**2**   *r ⊃ s*
   *⎨
     ⎪**3**   ~*s*
     ⎩**4**   *pq* v *t*   / ∴ *t*
 * **5**   *pq ⊃ s*   **1 and 2**, Rule 6, Hypothetical Syllogism
 * **6**   ~*(pq)*   **3 and 5**, Rule 2, Modus Tollens
 * **7**   *t*   **6 and 4**, Rule 3, Disjunctive Syllogism

EXERCISES

A For each of the following formal proofs of validity, provide the justification for each line which is not a premise. (Identify the line or lines used and the appropriate rule of inference.)

1   ⎧**1**   *p ⊃ (q ⊃ r)*
   *⎨**2**   *s* v *p*
   ⎩**3**   ~*st*   / ∴ *q ⊃ r*
   * **4**   ~*s*
   * **5**   *p*
   * **6**   *q ⊃ r*

2   ⎧**1**   *p ⊃ q*
   *⎨**2**   *r ⊃ s*
   ⎩**3**   *(p* v *r) ~q*   / ∴ *q* v *s*
   * **4**   *(p ⊃ q)(r ⊃ s)*
   * **5**   *p* v *r*
   * **6**   *q* v *s*

3
$$\ast \begin{cases} 1 & pq \\ 2 & (p \lor r) \supset (s \lor t) \end{cases} \quad /\therefore p(s \lor t)$$
* 3 p
* 4 $p \lor r$
* 5 $s \lor t$
* 6 $p(s \lor t)$

4
$$\ast \begin{cases} 1 & (p \lor g) \supset r \\ 2 & (r \lor q) \supset [p \supset (s \supset t)] \\ 3 & ps \end{cases} \quad /\therefore s \supset t$$
* 4 p
* 5 $p \lor q$
* 6 r
* 7 $r \lor q$
* 8 $p \supset (s \supset t)$
* 9 $s \supset t$

5
$$\ast \begin{cases} 1 & p \supset {\sim}q \\ 2 & {\sim}q \supset {\sim}r \\ 3 & {\sim}{\sim}r \end{cases} \quad /\therefore {\sim}p$$
* 4 ${\sim}{\sim}q$
* 5 ${\sim}p$

6
$$\ast \begin{cases} 1 & p \supset {\sim}q \\ 2 & {\sim}p \supset (r \equiv {\sim}q) \\ 3 & ({\sim}s \lor {\sim}r) \supset {\sim}{\sim}q \\ 4 & {\sim}s \lor {\sim}r \end{cases} \quad /\therefore r \equiv {\sim}q$$
* 5 ${\sim}{\sim}q$
* 6 ${\sim}p$
* 7 $r \equiv {\sim}q$

B Construct a proof for each of the following valid argument forms.

7
$$\ast \begin{cases} 1 & p \lor (q \supset r) \\ 2 & {\sim}pq \\ 3 & q \sim s \end{cases} \quad /\therefore r$$

8
$$\ast \begin{cases} 1 & (p \supset q) \supset rs \\ 2 & rs \supset (t \equiv u) \\ 3 & {\sim}(t \equiv u) \end{cases} \quad /\therefore {\sim}(p \supset q)$$

9
$$\ast \begin{cases} 1 & (p \supset qr)(r \supset st) \\ 2 & p \end{cases} \quad /\therefore qr \lor st$$

10
$$\ast \begin{cases} 1 & p \supset qr \\ 2 & s \supset t \\ 3 & p \lor s \\ 4 & {\sim}(qr) \end{cases} \quad /\therefore t$$

C Construct a formal proof of validity for each of the following valid arguments.

11 If Sam gets an A in Spanish, he must have studied hard and paid attention in class. But it is false that he studied hard and paid attention in class, so he didn't get an A in Spanish. (p = Sam gets an A; q = Sam must have studied hard; r = Sam paid attention in class.)

12 If Sally won the prize, then Jane didn't. But if Jane didn't, then Harry lost his bet. Harry lost his bet only if Sam tricked him, and Sam didn't trick him, unless Harry lost his head. But Harry didn't lose his head. Therefore, Sally didn't win the prize. (p = Sally won the prize; q = Jane won the prize; r = Harry lost his bet; s = Sam tricked Harry; t = Harry lost his head.)

13 If either Edith went to Detroit or took Sally with her on the trip, she took the train. If she took the train, she didn't fly. But if she didn't fly, she must have left Tuesday. Edith went to Detroit and had a nice time. So she must have left Tuesday. (p = Edith went to Detroit; q = Edith took Sally; r = Edith took the train; s = Edith flew; t = Edith must have left Tuesday; u = Edith had a nice time.)

14 If universities charge no tuition, everyone will enter. If universities charge tuition, there is not equality of opportunity unless deserving students get scholarships. But universities must either not charge tuition or charge tuition. Moreover, it is false that everyone will enter universities. Accordingly, if there is equality of opportunity, then deserving students get scholarships. (p = universities charge tuition; q = everyone will enter; r = there is equality of opportunity; s = deserving students get scholarships.)

15 If the world is chaos, then it cannot be reformed unless a sage appears. But no sage can appear if the world is chaos. The world surely is chaos; hence it cannot be reformed. (p = the world is chaos; q = the world can be reformed; r = a sage appears.)

Completion of the Method

Very many valid arguments cannot be proved using only the eight inference rules so far introduced. In this section, accordingly, we introduce eleven more rules. These eleven are different from the foregoing set of eight rules in that they allow us to replace a line or any part of a line with a formula which is logically equivalent to what was replaced. For example, Rule 13, double negation, tells us that we may replace any formula with the form $\sim\sim P$ with (simply) P. Thus, $\sim\sim p$ is equivalent to p; $\sim\sim p \vee q)$ is equivalent to $p \vee q$; and $p \supset \sim\sim q$ is equivalent to $p \supset q$. Notice that in the last instance, we replaced *part* of a formula with its equivalent. Similarly, Rule 14, DeMorgan's laws, tells us that $\sim (P \vee Q)$ is equivalent to $\sim P \cdot \sim Q$ and so $\sim (p \vee q)$ becomes $\sim p \cdot \sim q$ and $\sim (pq \vee st)$ becomes $\sim (pq) \cdot \sim (st)$. Again, we may replace part of a formula: $\sim (p \vee q) \supset (r \equiv s)$ becomes, by Rule 14, $\sim p \cdot \sim q \supset (r \equiv s)$.

The equivalences are as follows:

   9 $P \supset Q$ is equivalent to $P \supset (PQ)$ (Absorption)

10 $P \vee Q$ is equivalent to $Q \vee P$
      PQ is equivalent to QP (Commutation)

11 $P \vee (Q \vee R)$ is equivalent to $(P \vee Q) \vee R$
      $P(QR)$ is equivalent to $(PQ)R$ (Association)

12 $P(Q \vee R)$ is equivalent to $PQ \vee PR$ (Distribution)

13 $\sim\sim P$ is equivalent to P (Double negation)

14 $\sim (P \vee Q)$ is equivalent to $\sim P \cdot \sim Q$
      $\sim (PQ)$ is equivalent to $\sim P \vee \sim Q$ (DeMorgan's Laws)

15 $P \supset Q$ is equivalent to $\sim Q \supset \sim P$ (Transposition)

16 $P \supset Q$ is equivalent to $\sim P \vee Q$ (Implication)

17 $PQ \supset R$ is equivalent to $P \supset (Q \supset R)$ (Exportation)

18 PP is equivalent to P
      $P \vee P$ is equivalent to P (Tautology)

19 $P \equiv Q$ is equivalent to $(P \supset Q)(Q \supset P)$
      $P \equiv Q$ is equivalent to $PQ \vee \sim P \cdot \sim Q$ (Equivalence)

Consider now an argument which requires use of the equivalence rules:

* $\begin{cases} \mathbf{1} & (p \vee q) \supset r \\ \mathbf{2} & \sim(\sim p \sim q) \qquad /\therefore r \end{cases}$

Do these premises entail *r*? No mechanical procedure is available here. We must consider what rules we have at our disposal and what consequences may be deduced which might lead to *r*.

* $\begin{cases} \mathbf{1} & (p \vee q) \supset r \\ \mathbf{2} & \sim(\sim p \sim q) \qquad /\therefore r \end{cases}$
* $\quad \mathbf{3} \quad \sim\sim p \vee \sim\sim q \qquad$ 2, Rule 14, DeMorgan's Law

We deduced line 3 from line 2 by means of DeMorgan's Law. The use of DeMorgan's Law is explained as follows: It says that $\sim(PQ)$ is equivalent to $\sim P \vee \sim Q$. In this case *P* is the compound $\sim p$, and *Q* is the compound $\sim q$. Hence $\sim(\sim p \sim q)$ becomes $\sim\sim p \vee \sim\sim q$. This can be thought of as a straight substitution (or replacement) of the compounds $\sim p$ and $\sim q$ for *P* and for *Q*, respectively.

But it doesn't appear that we are any closer to our goal, which is *r*. We are, however, for we next use Rule 13, double negation, and infer line 4 from line 3.

* $\begin{cases} \mathbf{1} & (p \vee q) \supset r \\ \mathbf{2} & \sim(\sim p \sim q) \qquad /\therefore r \end{cases}$
* $\quad \mathbf{3} \quad \sim\sim p \vee \sim\sim q \qquad$ 2, DeMorgan's Law
* $\quad \mathbf{4} \quad p \vee q \qquad\qquad$ 3, Double Negation

But now we see that we can use Modus Ponens. We finish the proof with line 5:

* $\mathbf{5} \quad r \qquad$ **1** and **4**, Modus Ponens

In this example, then, we have a chain of inferences. From line 2 we inferred line 3, from 3 we derived 4, and from 1 and 4 we derived 5. The asterisk on line 5 indicates that its truth depends upon the truth of 1 and 2. Since each inference was in accordance with a valid inference rule, the chain of inferences proves that the premises do entail the conclusion. That is, *if* lines 1 and 2 are interpreted as true, then 3 is true. But if 3 is true, then 4 is true, and if 1 *and* 4 are true, then 5 *must* be true. The entire deduction could be rounded off with a last *un*asterisked line. As we noted, *r* is not true absolutely; it is true only on condition that the premises $(p \vee q) \supset r$ and $\sim(\sim p \sim q)$ are true. But this says that *if* $p \vee q \supset r$ *and* $\sim(\sim p \sim q)$ are true, *then r* is true, which is the tautology $[(p \vee q) \supset r][\sim(\sim p \sim q)] \supset r$. This could be asserted as line 6 *without* an asterisk since its truth does *not* depend upon *any* assumption: it is true absolutely.

$\quad \mathbf{6} \quad [(p \vee q) \supset r][\sim(\sim p \sim q)] \supset r$

EXERCISES

In each of the following proofs provide the justification for each step. (All nineteen rules may be used.)

1 ∗{1 $p \supset q$
    {2 $\sim (q \vee r)$ /∴ $\sim p$
  ∗ 3 $\sim q \sim r$
  ∗ 4 $\sim q$
  ∗ 5 $\sim p$

2 ∗{1 $\sim (pq) \supset (rs)$
    {2 $p \supset (\sim p \vee \sim q)$ /∴ r
  ∗ 3 $\sim p \vee (\sim p \vee \sim q)$
  ∗ 4 $(\sim p \vee \sim p) \vee \sim q$
  ∗ 5 $(\sim p) \vee \sim q$
  ∗ 6 $\sim (pq)$
  ∗ 7 rs
  ∗ 8 r

3 {1 $p \vee \sim q$
∗{2 $\sim p(r \supset s)$
 {3 $q \vee r$ /∴ s
  ∗ 4 $\sim p$
  ∗ 5 $\sim q$
  ∗ 6 r
  ∗ 7 $(r \supset s) \sim p$
  ∗ 8 $r \supset s$
  ∗ 9 s

4 {1 $p \equiv q$
∗{2 $q \supset (rs)$
 {3 $\sim r$ /∴ $\sim p$
  ∗ 4 $\sim r \vee \sim s$
  ∗ 5 $\sim (rs)$
  ∗ 6 $\sim q$
  ∗ 7 $(p \supset q)(q \supset p)$
  ∗ 8 $p \supset q$
  ∗ 9 $\sim p$

5   {1 $(\sim q \supset \sim p)(\sim s \supset \sim r)$
∗{2 $(\sim t \supset \sim q)(\sim u \supset \sim s)$
 {3 $\sim t \vee \sim u$
 {4 $p \supset r$ /∴ $\sim p$
  ∗ 5 $\sim q \vee \sim s$
  ∗ 6 $\sim p \vee \sim r$
  ∗ 7 $\sim r \vee \sim p$
  ∗ 8 $r \supset \sim p$
  ∗ 9 $p \supset \sim p$
 ∗10 $\sim p \vee \sim p$
 ∗11 $\sim p$

Implications of the Ingenuity Problem

The method introduced in these pages is analogous to proof procedures in mathematics, except that in mathematics the inference rules are not usually made explicit.[8] Still, the "logic" of such proofs is the same. What we try to do is to draw out the implications of our premises.

---

[8] In this century, mathematicians have been interested in making explicit their inference rules, and an important part of mathematics is the theory of proof.

While this method does give some insight into what has here been called the *ingenuity problem,* we must emphasize that ingenuity is not a problem if we confine ourselves to truth-functional formulas. Since we have a decision procedure for truth-functions (truth tables), we need never concern ourselves with proof according to rules. Moreover, the list of nineteen rules which was offered is redundant. That is, many of them might be dropped from the list with no loss of power for our proofs. For example, Rule 2, modus tollens, is unnecessary, since by means of transposition, Rule 15, every requirement for modus tollens can be treated by Rule 15 and modus ponens. Thus, since $P \supset Q$ is equivalent to $\sim Q \supset \sim P$, if we have $\sim Q$ we can infer $\sim P$ by modus ponens. Similarly, the disjunctive syllogism, Rule 3, may be eliminated in favor of modus ponens, implication (Rule 16), and double negation. However, since the proofs are considerably easier with these extra rules, they will be employed.

Finally, it should be noticed that the method discussed in this section is a method of *proof,* but not a method of *dis*proof. That is, if you can demonstrate that a conclusion is entailed by a chain of inferences from the premises, you have proved validity. But if you can*not,* it does not follow that the argument is invalid (that the conclusion does not follow), since it may simply be that you have not yet stumbled on the right sequence. From this point of view you can easily see how valuable truth tables really are.

EXERCISES

Construct a proof for each of the following. Any of the rules may be employed and there are *no* invalid arguments. Supposing the premises are *inconsistent,* what problems does this raise? Check for consistency of the premises.

1.
1 $(p \vee q) \supset (r \cdot s)$
*2 $r \supset t$
3 $\sim ts$ /∴ $\sim p$

2.
*1 $(p \supset q) \supset s$
2 $\sim (r \vee s)$ /∴ p

3.
*1 $(pq) \vee (rs)$
2 $p \supset \sim p$ /∴ r

4.
1 $(p \supset q) \supset r$
*2 $(s \vee t) \supset (pq)$
3 s /∴ r

5.
*1 $(p \supset q)(r \supset s)$
2 $p(r \vee \sim t)$ /∴ $q \vee s$

6.
*1 $p \equiv q$
2 $p \vee q$ /∴ p

7.
1 $(p \supset q)(r \supset s)$
*2 $(q \supset t)(s \supset u)$
3 $t \supset \sim u$
4 $p \supset r$ /∴ $\sim p$

8.
*1 $(pq \supset r)p$
2 $p \sim q \supset \sim r$ /∴ $q \equiv r$

9.
1 $\sim pq \supset r$
*2 $\sim (q \supset p)$
3 $(r \supset s)(r \supset q)$ /∴ $s \vee q$

10.
1 $p \supset (q \supset r)$
*2 $\sim s \vee p$
3 $(q \supset r) \supset tu$
4 s /∴ $u \vee m$

Conditional Proof

The technique called the **conditional proof** is one which we frequently encounter or employ in reasoning, proof, and argument. Before introducing it, however, let us reconsider the "logic" of deductive argument. Assume that we have a two-premise deductive valid argument. We mark the first premise as P_1, the second premise as P_2, and the conclusion as C. It looks like this:

$$P_1$$
$$\frac{P_2}{}$$

So, necessarily, C

Since, ex *hypothesi*, this argument is valid, we are entitled to say: (1) *if P_1 is true and if P_2 is true, then C is true.* But notice that this is tantamount to saying, (2) *if P_1 is true, then if P_2 is true, C is true.* That is, P_1 and P_2 are still stated as *conditions* for asserting that C is true. But (2) can be retranslated into a corresponding argument which looks like this:

$$\frac{P_1}{}$$

So, necessarily, $P_2 \supset C$

Thus, it is the case that we can always construct a conditional conclusion with a premise as the antecedent and the original conclusion as the consequent.[9] This feature is more explicitly seen by observing that (1) and (2) are logically equivalent. That is, $[(P_1 \cdot P_2) \supset C] \equiv [P_1 \supset (P_2 \supset C)]$ is a tautology. Indeed, this is the equivalence we earlier called **exportation**. In conditional proofs we utilize this feature in the following way: We are given a set of premises which can be conjoined and called P_1. We are asked if P_1 entails $P_2 \supset C$. But this is tantamount to asking if P_1 *and* P_2 entail C. Let us illustrate the important use of this technique by means of an example:

*1 $p \supset q$ $/\therefore p \supset pq$

The conclusion $p \supset pq$ does follow from the premise since it is impossible for the premise to be true and the conclusion false. This can be demonstrated by means of a truth table, but how can we construct a proof by the methods discussed in this chapter? There is an easy way. We assume that $p \supset q$ (the premise) is true. Again, we note this by putting an asterisk alongside the premise. Let us *in addition* assume that p is true. This is an additional assumption, for

---

[9] Notice that the argument $\dfrac{P_1}{\therefore P_2 \supset Q}$ is "weaker" than the original since in the original both P_1 and P_2 are asserted as true, whereas in the translated case only P_1 is asserted as true.

it cannot be deduced from the one premise which has been offered. Hence it needs a double asterisk. That is, $p \supset q$ could be true and p false (if q is also false—which it might very well be). We are saying, in effect, assuming that $p \supset q$ is true, if p *were* true what could be deduced? The added asterisk is a convenient way to indicate that p is an additional premise.

> *1 $p \supset q$ /∴ $p \supset pq$
> **2 p

Now we can make some inferences. As line 3 we deduce q by modus ponens:

> *1 $p \supset q$ /∴ $p \supset pq$
> **2 p
> **3 q 1 and 2, Modus Ponens

The truth of q, however, depends upon both $p \supset q$ being true and p being true; hence it carries two asterisks. As line 4, by means of Rule 5, we deduce pq. Again, this assertion depends upon the double assumption, so it too carries two asterisks.

> **4 pq 2 and 3, Conjunction

But what have we said? We have said that if $p \supset q$ is true (the original premise) *and* if p is true (the added premise), then pq is true. But this is equivalent to saying that if $p \supset q$ is true, *then* if p is true, pq is true (by the exportation equivalence). That is, $p \supset q$ *entails* $p \supset pq$, which is what we wanted to prove. We show this by writing line 5, which carries only one asterisk:

> *5 $p \supset pq$

What we have done, in effect, is to make the second assumption (the assumption that p was true) an explicit *condition* for the truth of pq by making it the antecedent of a conditional with pq as the consequent. Notice that line 5 still carries one asterisk since its truth depends upon the condition that $p \supset q$ is true. As before, we can write a last *un*asterisked line by making *this* assumption explicit. That is, since $p \supset q$ entails $p \supset pq$, $(p \supset q) \supset (p \supset pq)$ is a tautology.

> 6 $(p \supset q) \supset (p \supset pq)$

The device of the conditional proof has obvious advantages when we are trying to prove conditional conclusions, since we may always assume as an extra premise the antecedent of the conditional and seek to prove the consequent. For example, we prove that the following argument form is valid:

$$p \supset (qr \lor s)$$
$$qr \supset \sim p$$
$$t \supset \sim s$$
$$\overline{\therefore p \supset \sim t}$$

*	1	$p \supset (qr \lor s)$	
	2	$qr \supset \sim p$	
	3	$t \supset \sim s$	$/\therefore p \supset \sim t$
**	4	p	
**	5	$qr \lor s$	**1** and **4**, Modus Ponens
**	6	$\sim (qr)$	**2** and **4**, Modus Tollens and Double Negation
**	7	s	**5** and **6**, Disjunctive Syllogism
**	8	$\sim t$	**3** and **7**, Modus Tollens and Double Negation
*	9	$p \supset \sim t$	**4** and **8**, Conditionalization

Unlike the example with which we illustrated conditional proof, this particular case can be proved with the present methods *without* conditionalization. But the speed, ease, and intuitive obviousness of the proof are greatly diminished. Consider the proof *without* conditionalization:

*	1	$p \supset (qr \lor s)$	
	2	$qr \supset \sim p$	
	3	$t \supset \sim s$	$/\therefore p \supset \sim t$
*	4	$\sim p \lor (qr \lor s)$	**1**, Implication
*	5	$(\sim p \lor qr) \lor s$	**4**, Association
*	6	$(p \supset qr) \lor s$	**5**, Implication
*	7	$s \lor (p \supset qr)$	**6**, Commutation
*	8	$\sim s \supset (p \supset qr)$	**7**, Implication
*	9	$t \supset (p \supset qr)$	**8** and **3**, Hypothetical Syllogism
*	10	$\sim t \lor (\sim p \lor qr)$	**9**, Implication (twice)
*	11	$(\sim p \lor \sim t) \lor qr$	**10**, Association and Commutation
*	12	$\sim(\sim p \lor \sim t) \supset qr$	**11**, Implication
*	13	$\sim(\sim p \lor \sim t) \supset \sim p$	**12** and **2**, Hypothetical Syllogism
*	14	$p \supset (\sim p \lor \sim t)$	**13**, Transposition
*	15	$p \supset (p \supset \sim t)$	**14**, Implication
*	16	$pp \supset \sim t$	**15**, Exportation
*	17	$p \supset \sim t$	**16**, Tautology

Not only was the proof eight lines longer, but what is worse, it was difficult to see how it was to be developed. In proofs of this sort, many of the moves lead to blind alleys, and frustration follows confusion. By using conditional proof in this example, however, the use of modus ponens and modus tollens very nearly comes to mind at once.

But conditional proof has other, perhaps more important, advantages. Notice first that we need *not* assume the antecedent of a conditional conclusion (though if we are given such a conclusion, this is usually advantageous). Indeed, we may assume anything we want in a deduction, *if* before we finish the deduction, we construct a conditional with the added premise as antecedent and whatever was deduced with its help as the consequent. For example, suppose that you were asked to deduce the consequences from this set of premises:

1 $\sim p \supset \sim q$
2 $rs \supset t$
3 $(r \lor q)s$

It is not at all clear what could be deduced from this set.[10] But we might, in a realistic situation, make some *additional* assumptions. We might, for example, further assume that $\sim p$ is true. The logic of the situation is this: We assume, or have been told, that the premises are each true, but we want to know what this commits us to. In order to find out we make the further assumption and begin the deduction. Thus:

*	1	$\sim p \supset \sim q$	
	2	$rs \supset t$	
	3	$(r \lor q)s$	
**	4	$\sim p$	
**	5	$\sim q$	1 and **4**, Modus Ponens
**	6	$\sim q \lor \sim s$	5, Addition
**	7	$\sim (qs)$	6, DeMorgan's Law
**	8	$rs \lor qs$	3, Distribution
**	9	$qs \lor rs$	8, Commutation
**	10	rs	7 and **9**, Disjunctive Syllogism
**	11	t	2 and **10**, Modus Ponens
*	12	$\sim p \supset t$	4 and **11**, Conditionalization

The added assumption that $\sim p$ was true enabled us to readily deduce t. Hence, we conclude that the premises do commit us to the conditional $p \supset t$. This sort of reasoning is very characteristic of problem solving, in which we are given some "facts" and seek solutions. The facts in this case tell us that *if* $\sim p$ is true, then *so* is t. For example, the three premises given might be:

1 If there is no change in aggregate investment ($\sim p$), there is no change in aggregate saving ($\sim q$), or ($\sim p \supset \sim q$).
2 The rate of investment increases (r) and opportunities for investment are used up (s) only if the marginal efficiency of capital diminishes (t), or ($rs \supset t$).

[10] There are several interesting consequences which the reader can explore.

3 Either the rate of interest increases (*r*) or there is a change in aggregate savings (*q*) and opportunities for investment are used up (*s*), or (*r* v *q*)*s*.

Given the truth of the premises, our proof has shown that if there is no change in aggregate investment, then the marginal efficiency of capital diminishes, a conclusion which was by no means obvious.[11]

But we could have made some other assumption to see what happens. Suppose as an additional premise we assume that there is no decrease in the marginal efficiency of capital, that is, we assume ~*t*:

$$
\begin{array}{lll}
* & \begin{cases} \mathbf{1} & \sim p \supset \sim q \\ \mathbf{2} & rs \supset t \\ \mathbf{3} & (r \lor q)s \end{cases} & \\
** & \mathbf{4} & \sim t & \\
** & \mathbf{5} & \sim(rs) & \text{2 and 4, Modus Tollens} \\
** & \mathbf{6} & rs \lor qs & \text{3, Distribution} \\
** & \mathbf{7} & qs & \text{5 and 6, Disjunctive Syllogism} \\
** & \mathbf{8} & s & \text{7, Simplification and Commutation} \\
* & \mathbf{9} & \sim t \supset s & \text{4 and 8, Conditionalization}
\end{array}
$$

Thus, if there is no decrease in the marginal efficiency of capital, then opportunities are used up. Also, since *q* follows from *qs* (line 7), and hence if there is no decrease in the marginal efficiency of capital, then there is a change in aggregate saving (~*t* ⊃ *q*); and, by modus tollens from line 1 and *q* we get *p*. Thus, if there is no decrease in the marginal utility of capital, then there *is* a change in aggregate investment.

Although in everyday reasoning we do not ordinarily employ the formal techniques discussed in this chapter, we frequently utilize the "logic" of such techniques. We are constantly faced with the problem of deductively developing our beliefs, hypotheses, and given facts. In doing so we frequently implicitly appeal to this mode of reasoning.

EXERCISES

Construct conditional proofs for each of the following:

$$
\begin{array}{lll}
\mathbf{1} & * \begin{cases} \mathbf{1} & p \supset q \\ \mathbf{2} & \sim r \supset \sim q \end{cases} & / \therefore p \supset r \\
\mathbf{2} & * \begin{cases} \mathbf{1} & (p \lor q) \supset rs \\ \mathbf{2} & (s \lor t) \supset u \end{cases} & / \therefore p \supset u
\end{array}
$$

[11] Since this is not a text in Keynesian economics, no claim is made that the statements offered as premises are in fact true or that they have been held to be true by Keynes. But it should be evident from this deduction that the device of formalization gives us considerable power and clarity. In our discussion of scientific method, particularly with reference to theory construction, we shall return to this feature.

3   * **1** $p \supset q$ $/\therefore \sim(qr) \supset \sim(rp)$

4   *$\begin{cases} \textbf{1} & p \supset (q \supset r) \\ \textbf{2} & q \supset (r \supset s) \end{cases}$ $/\therefore p \supset (q \supset s)$

       (Use Conditionalization twice.)

5   *$\begin{cases} \textbf{1} & pq \equiv r \\ \textbf{2} & \sim r \supset (\sim p \vee s) \\ \textbf{3} & p \end{cases}$ $/\therefore \sim s \supset pq$

6   If the cost of living rises, then interest rates increase and there are fewer housing starts. There are fewer housing starts or savings decrease only if investment opportunities are used up. Hence, if the cost of living rises, investment opportunities are used up. (p = the cost of living rises; q = interest rates increase; r = there are fewer housing starts; s = savings decrease; t = investment opportunities are used up.)

7   If the test subject asks for food, then he is hungry and if he is deprived of food for twenty-four hours, he is hungry. Analysis of the test subject's blood will indicate an absence of significant amounts of glucose only if he is deprived of food or asks for food. Hence, if the analysis of the subject's blood shows an absence of significant amounts of glucose, he is hungry. (p = subject asks for food; q = he is hungry; r = he is deprived of food; s = analysis shows an absence of glucose.)

8   If Jones carries Erie County, he must carry South Buffalo and the West Side. He'll carry South Buffalo only if there is a strong Irish vote for him. But if the Flanigan vote is strong and the voters don't turn out, then there won't be a strong Irish vote for Jones. Accordingly, if Jones carries Erie County, then if the Flanigan vote is strong, the voters turned out. (p = Jones carries Erie County; q = Jones carries South Buffalo; r = Jones carries the West Side; s = there is a strong Irish vote for Jones; t = the Flanigan vote is strong; u = the voters turn out.)

9   If sugar is put in water, then if it is water-soluble, it dissolves. If it dissolves, then other conditions are under experimental control. But it is false that either other conditions are under experimental control or that the moon is made of green cheese. But if so, we must conclude that if sugar is water-soluble then it isn't put in water and it doesn't dissolve! (p = sugar is put in water; q = sugar is water-soluble; r = sugar dissolves; s = other conditions are under control; t = the moon is made of green cheese.)

10   Alphonse is the sort of guy who if he marries a beautiful woman, will be jealous and if he marries a rich woman, will be discontented. But if he is either jealous or discontented, he is not liberated. Moreover, if he marries a liberated woman, he'll be happy. Alphonse will marry either a beautiful woman, a rich woman, or a liberated woman. Hence, if he is liberated, he will be happy. (p = Alphonse marries a beautiful woman; q = he is jealous; r = he marries a rich woman; s = he is discontented; t = he is liberated; w = he marries a liberated woman; h = he is happy.)

The *Reductio ad Absurdum*

The technique called the **reductio ad absurdum** (to reduce to absurdity) is another mode of proof which we frequently encounter. The technique may be described as follows: Assume the contradictory of the conclusion as an added premise and try to deduce a contradiction. If you can, then the premises entail the conclusion. The logic of such a proof involves a feature of entailment which we earlier noted. That is, if *P* entails *Q*, then $P \cdot \sim Q$ is a contradiction. If there is an entailment relation between the premise set and the conclusion, and if the premises are true, the conclusion must be true. But if the conclusion is true, then its contradictory must be false; so, we are contradicting ourselves if we assume the premises to be true and add as a premise the contradictory of the conclusion. Let us illustrate the method:

*	1	$\sim (pq) \supset r$	
	2	$q \vee \sim r$	$/\therefore q$
**	3	$\sim q$	
**	4	$\sim r$	2 and 3, Disjunctive Syllogism
**	5	pq	1 and 4, Modus Tollens and Double Negation
**	6	qp	5, Commutation
**	7	q	6, Simplification
**	8	$\sim qq$	3 and 7, Conjunction; *Reductio ad Absurdum*

As before, we double asterisk the added premise and begin the deduction. However, with the *reductio* mode of proof, we maintain the double asterisks to the last line to indicate that the explicit contradiction was generated *because* we assumed as true both the original premises *and* the added premise which was the contradictory of the conclusion. Strictly speaking, the *reductio* method of proof is simply a species of the conditional proof, which could be justified by the same logic as the conditional proof discussed above. For example, our deduction might have proceeded thus:

*	1	$\sim (pq) \supset r$	
	2	$q \vee \sim r$	$/\therefore q$
**	3	$\sim q$	
**	4	$\sim r$	3 and 2, Disjunctive Syllogism
**	5	pq	1 and 4, Modus Tollens
**	6	qp	5, Commutation
**	7	q	6, Simplification
*	8	$\sim q \supset q$	7, Conditionalization
*	9	$q \vee q$	8, Implication
*	10	q	9, Tautology

The *reductio* mode of proof is especially important in mathematics. Indeed, the discovery of non-Euclidean geometries stems from attempts by this method to prove that the famous parallel postulate of Euclidean geometry could be deduced from the remaining axioms.   The parallel postulate, as you may remember, asserts that in a space there is one and only one line through a given point parallel to a given line.   Mathematicians had long been bothered about the status of the parallel postulate.   Did it need to be assumed as an axiom without proof or could it be deduced from the remainder of the set and hence proved?[12]   The logic of the attempt is quite straightforward and may be schematized as follows: Assume that A_j comprises the conjoined set of axioms *exclusive* of the parallel postulate which we label P.   If A_j entails P, then $A_j \cdot \sim P$ should be a contradiction.   Hence by assuming $\sim P$[13] as *one* of the axiom set, we should be able to deduce the contradiction in much the same way as it has been done in this section.   But much to the surprise of everybody, *no* contradiction results.   To be sure, many of the theorems (the logical consequences) of the revised axiom set are different from Euclid's theorems, but *no explicit contradiction* could be deduced.   By the last half of the last century, it became increasingly clear that, indeed, the parallel postulate could *not* be deduced from the other axioms.   The axiom is, therefore, **independent**.   In general, given a set of statements, P_1, P_2, . . . , P_n, P_i (any arbitrary statement of the set) is independent if it cannot be deduced from the others.

The implications of this discovery are monumental, for it has forced us to revise our ideas about the entire status of geometry.   In a book of this sort, we cannot properly say very much on this large issue.   But this much seems clear and can perhaps be mentioned here: As in all deduction we must distinguish the two questions: (1) Are the premises (axioms) true?   (2) Are the conclusions entailed by the premises?   In Euclidean *and* non-Euclidean geometries the answer to question (2) is "yes."   Both systems are valid.   But if geometry is thought of as a description of space, which system has *true* premises?   That question, we now see, cannot be answered by mathematics or logic alone.   The failure to deduce a contradiction by denying the parallel postulate shows us that there are alternative geometries whose truth must be tested not by mathematics but by observation.   Indeed, work by Riemann and Einstein suggests that non-Euclidean geometries might be *better* suited to describe the far-out regions of space than Euclidean geometry.

[12] Euclid himself was apparently a little hesitant about its status, for in his formulation of geometry, he avoided using it in his first twenty-eight propositions.   Early in the eighteenth century, a Jesuit named Saccheri (1667–1733) sought to prove Euclid's original postulate by the *reductio ad absurdum* method here discussed.   But Saccheri mistakenly thought that he had achieved his aim and proved it to be true.

Early in the nineteenth century, Lobatschewsky (1840) and Gauss (1846), through a rigorous examination of the foundations of geometry, showed that the non-Euclidean geometries were as *logically* tenable as Euclid's.   This work was generalized and extended by Riemann and Helmholtz.

[13] Strictly, all that is necessary is that a *contrary* to P is assumed instead of P.   If we assume that *no* line is parallel to the given line, then we have elliptic geometry.   If we assume an *infinite* number parallel, then we have hyperbolic geometry.

EXERCISES

A Give *reductio ad absurdum* proofs of the following:

1. $_*\begin{cases} 1 & p \supset q \\ 2 & \sim(q \lor r) \end{cases}$ $/\therefore \sim p$

2. $_*\begin{cases} 1 & (p \supset q)(r \supset q) \\ 2 & s \supset (p \lor r) \end{cases}$ $/\therefore s \supset q$

3. $* \quad 1 \quad p$ $/\therefore qr \supset p$

4. $_*\begin{cases} 1 & p \supset (q \supset r) \\ 2 & p \supset q \\ 3 & \sim s \supset (r \lor p) \end{cases}$ $/\therefore s \lor r$

5. $_*\begin{cases} 1 & (p \supset q) \supset rs \\ 2 & (r \lor t) \supset (s \supset p) \end{cases}$ $/\therefore p$

B Construct a proof for each of the following:

6. If Sam tries again, then neither George nor Ronald will cooperate. Ronald will cooperate. So Sam will try again only if George doesn't cooperate. ($p =$ Sam tries again; $q =$ George will cooperate; $r =$ Ronald will cooperate.)

7. Sam will try again only if he is drafted at the convention. He won't be drafted at the convention unless the party supports him and not Ronald. If the party supports Sam, then it will support Ronald. Therefore, Sam will not try again. ($p =$ Sam tries again; $q =$ Sam is drafted at the convention; $r =$ the party supports Sam; $s =$ the party supports Ronald.)

8. If Gloria goes, then Sam will go. Sam will go only if Louie doesn't go; and if Red doesn't go, then Louie will. But either Gloria is going or Red isn't; so Gloria is going if and only if Louie isn't. ($p =$ Gloria goes; $q =$ Sam goes; $r =$ Louie goes; $s =$ Red goes.)

9. If either Jennifer or Harriet have dates, then if Julie is working, I won't be able to get a date. Julie is working; but if I am not able to get a date, I might as well go home for the weekend. So, if Jennifer has a date, I might as well go home for the weekend. ($p =$ Jennifer has a date; $q =$ Harriet has a date; $r =$ Julie is working; $s =$ I am able to get a date; $t =$ I might as well go home for the weekend.)

10. If we are a rich nation, then we can help the poor. If we can help the poor, then surely we should. On the other hand, if the poor could help themselves, then we shouldn't help them. But if the poor can't help themselves, then there are not sufficient jobs. If there are not sufficient jobs, then we can't help the poor. But either the poor can help themselves or they cannot. Hence, either way, it seems that we are not a rich nation! ($p =$ we are a rich nation; $q =$ we can help the poor;

r = we should help the poor; s = the poor can help themselves; t = there are sufficient jobs.)

11　If liquidity preference remains constant and the supply of money increases, then the rate of interest falls.　Either the marginal efficiency of capital does not decrease or best opportunities for investment are used up.　During the period from July 1 to September 1, liquidity preference has remained constant.　If the rate of interest falls, then the marginal efficiency of capital decreases.　Hence, if the supply of money has increased from July 1 to September 1, then during that period, the best opportunities for investment were used up.　(p = liquidity preference remained constant; q = the supply of money increased; r = the rate of interest falls; t = marginal efficiency of capital decreases; u = best opportunities for investment are used up.)

12　The right of free speech is a natural right if and only if each person in some sense possesses it and it is not a privilege given by a sovereign power.　But if the right to free speech is a natural right, then the right to employment is also a natural right.　If the right to employment is a natural right, then the right to free speech is not a privilege in the sense indicated.　Still, free speech is a natural right only if every person possesses it equally.　Hence if all persons possess the right to free speech then persons possess the right to free speech equally, or the right to employment is not a natural right.　(p = the right to free speech is a natural right; q = each person possesses the right to free speech; r = the right to free speech is a privilege; s = the right to employment is a natural right; t = every person possesses the right to free speech equally.)

13　Either Marx was a Marxist or Lenin was a Bolshevik and Kautsky was Lenin's best friend.　If Marx was a Marxist, then if Locke was a natural law theorist, Mill was a utilitarian.　But if Marx was not a Marxist, then nobody was.　Locke was a natural law theorist and Kautsky was anything but Lenin's best friend.　Hence, either Mill was a utilitarian or nobody was a Marxist.　(p = Marx was a Marxist; q = Lenin was a Bolshevik; r = Kautsky was Lenin's best friend; s = Locke was a natural law theorist; t = Mill was a utilitarian; u = nobody was a Marxist.)

SEVEN

CATEGORICAL STATEMENTS

Civilization advances by extending the number of important operations which we can perform without thinking about them.

Alfred North Whitehead

Despite the great value of the statement calculus, there are still certain types of valid arguments which do not readily lend themselves to this mode of analysis. In order to cope with such arguments, we turn now to the more traditional logic, known also — if somewhat ambiguously — as *classical logic* or *Aristotelian logic*. Aristotelian logic properly is the schema presented by Aristotle in his *Organon*. In the development and evolution of this doctrine, stoic, medieval, renaissance, and modern logicians have introduced several variations. Since our concern here is not historical,[1] we need not be bothered by the details of these interesting developments. In our discussion, however, we will acknowledge certain important divergencies from Aristotle. We begin this discussion with a consideration of what are called **categorical statements.**

The Form of Categorical Statements

Consider the statement, "All hasapika are folk-dances." As we saw in Chapter 3, this statement may be formalized by eliminating its material content — which gives us this: "All *H* are *F*." As before, "All *H* are *F*" is no longer a statement

---

[1] Some writers of logic books have argued that the treatment of "classical logic" is only of historical interest, a view which this text explicitly rejects.

since it is neither true nor false. It is, rather, a statement form or formula, which can become a statement if we interpret the letters *H* and *F*. But the letters in this case do not stand for *statements*. What, then, do they stand for? We shall say that they are dummy letters (or variables) for **terms**. In what follows we shall give considerable latitude to what constitutes a term. It could be simply a common noun, such as "hasapika," "folk-dance," or "philosopher." Or it could be a noun phrase, such as "Greek folk-dance," "fat, unhappy clown," or "philosopher who drank the hemlock." In the same way, we can treat adjectives as terms, such as "unhappy," "green," "large and round," since their function will be largely a matter of phrasing. If *F* is the adjective "unhappy" in the statement "All dictators are unhappy," we could rewrite the statement as "All dictators are unhappy people." Similarly, we can admit as terms intransitive verbs, construing, for example, "All living things grow" as "All living things are things which grow." In the same way we can treat complex verb phrases as terms. For example, "All mammals bear their young alive" is renderable as "All mammals are animals which bear their young alive." Nor need we concern ourselves with whether a term is singular or plural, for number, too, is a matter of phrasing. Thus the statements "No Spartans are cowards" and "No Spartan is a coward" need not be differentiated.

All terms, however, share this feature: they are *true* of everything, something, or nothing. Notice that this way of putting the matter is analogous to that which enables us to say that statements are true or false. The term "dictator" is *true of* Hitler; it is false of Pericles, a petunia, and a thumb. The term "things which grow" is true of Socrates, a petunia, and an elephant. The term "round square" is true of nothing, since there are no round squares. In order to maintain the distinction between statements and terms, we shall use only capital letters as variables for terms.

But notice that the statement "All hasapika are folk-dances" also contains words like "all" and "are," which are not terms. Words like "all" are appropriately called **quantifiers**, since they indicate how many or what quantity of a given term is involved, and verbs like "are" are appropriately called the **copula**, since they link or indicate some relationship between terms.

In English there are many expressions besides "all" which function as quantifiers, for example, "every," "each," "none," "no," "some," "most," "a few," "many," "quite a few," and "a great many." Similarly, in English the verb "to be" has many tenses and numbers, for example, "is," "were," "was," "will be," "has been," "will have been," etc., each of which counts as a form of the copula. Finally, one other feature must be noted. As before, each statement is either affirmative or negative. If it asserts, it is affirmative; if it denies, it is negative. Thus, for example, "Some Greeks are not good dancers" and "No spiders are friendly" are negative. "Every whale is a mammal" and "A few coeds smoke" are affirmative.

We are now ready to discuss the four traditional forms of the categorical statement. Known as **A, E, I,** and **O,** respectively, these forms may be illustrated by the following expressions:

A: All *F* is *G*
E: No *F* is *G*
I: Some *F* is *G*
O: Some *F* is not *G*

Briefly, each may be described as follows: **A** represents a universal affirmative statement; **E** represents a universal negative statement; **I** represents a particular affirmative statement; and **O** represents a particular negative statement.[2]

In Chapter 4 we emphasized that the mode of analysis and the symbolism introduced were designed to capture significant logical features of a wide range of statements. Just as it was not our intention then to represent ordinary English precisely or to provide a substitute symbolism for the words of English, so is it not our intention now to do so. The four categorical forms presented here will enable us to analyze a wide range of quantified statements. Indeed, it is a sign of Aristotle's genius that he saw how important these four simple forms are. Let us now see how they can be used to shed light on certain kinds of statements in English.

First, let us take the **A** form, "All *F* is *G*." Each of the following statements has this form:

1 All sugar is water-soluble.
2 All Romans were patriots.
3 All Greeks dance.
4 All the mail arrived on time.
5 Every book he has is here.
6 Each person is liable.
7 A whale is a mammal.
8 Whales are mammals.
9 Whatever is a vegetable is organic.
10 Anything that is beautiful is rare.
11 Whoever comes will be welcomed.
12 Wherever he goes, I go.
13 He always arrives late.
14 When it rains, it pours.
15 He who hesitates is lost.
16 Whales are all mammals.
17 None but the brave deserve the fair.
18 Only visitors will be admitted.

At first sight this list may seem a little astounding. Notice that we are *not* saying that each of these statements is alike in every respect, for clearly there are considerable differences among them, which the richness of language makes it

---

[2] As a mnemonic aid, the affirmative and negative forms can be differentiated by remembering that **A** and **I** derive from the first two vowels in the Latin word *AffIrmo* (affirm) and **E** and **O** from the two vowels in *nEgO* (deny).

possible to express in different contexts. But still, they do share in these three important logical features: each is a *quantified universal* and *affirmative* statement, which can be expressed as a substitution instance of "All *F* is *G*." Let us see why. In doing so, we will translate each into standard form and italicize the terms.

Statement 1 constitutes no problems. All *sugar* is a *water-soluble substance*. Statement 2 has a past-tense form of "to be." But this is no problem, for we may simply say that the copula "is" should be taken in a tenseless sense. This may be explained by noting that the tensed expression can always be made part of a term. Thus: "All *Romans* are *those who were patriots*." Hence, for purposes of logical study, tense is irrelevant. Since we have noted that we need not concern ourselves with whether a term is singular or plural, the word "Romans" is as acceptable a term as the word "sugar." Therefore, "All *Romans* were *patriots*" would be appropriate as stated.

Statement 3 is easily translated as "All *Greeks* are *dancers*." Statement 4 has no copula, but with some linguistic manipulation the sense is captured with "All *the mail* is *mail which arrived on time*." Statement 5 has the word "every" as a quantifier, but "every" carries the sense of "all," which can be seen with this rendering: "All *books that he has* are *books which are here*."[3] Similar considerations apply to 6, which becomes "All *persons* are *persons who are liable*." Statement 7 undoubtedly means "All *whales* are *mammals*." This construction, however, must be treated gingerly. For example, "A bird flew in the window" does *not* mean "All birds are birds who flew in the window."

Statement 8 has its quantifier suppressed. In practice this sometimes leads to a fallacy, but in this case it is quite clear that "all" is intended.[4] Thus, "All *whales* are *mammals*." Statement 9 becomes, "All *things which are vegetables* are *organic things*." Statement 10 becomes, "All *things which are beautiful* are *rare things*."[5] Statement 11 can be rendered as "All *persons who come* are *persons who will be welcomed*." Statement 12, like 9, 10, and 11, requires what may be called a **parameter,** or an additional word or phrase. It becomes, "All *places where he goes* are *places where I go*." Statement 13 is subject to similar considerations. It becomes, "All *times* are *times in which he arrives late*." Statement 14 is treated in much the same way as 13. "All *times when it rains* are *times when it pours*."

Statement 15 becomes "All *those who hesitate* are *those who are lost*." Statement 16 needs to have its quantifier rearranged. Though the sense of 16 is not crystal clear, it seems to mean "All *whales* are *mammals*." Statements 17 and 18 are fairly common **A** constructions, and the confusion which surrounds them is comparable to those surrounding "if," "only if," and "if and only if."

---

[3] The use of "every" as the quantifier is much closer to the medieval treatment and is preferable in many respects. But since "all" has become so ingrained in contemporary logic, we will stay with it.

[4] See below, Chapter 14.

[5] One must be on guard with a term like "rare," especially when it suggests "becoming rare," "becoming scarce," or "diminishing in number." See discussion of collective and distributive use of terms, p. 11.

Generally, "only" and "none but" reverse order.[6]   That is, "only F is G and "none but F is G" become "All G is F."   So 17 means "All *who deserve the fair are brave."*   Similarly, 18 becomes "All *those who will be admitted* are *visitors."*

Now let us consider the **E** form of the categorical statement, which is illustrated by the following examples:

1   No sugar is sour.
2   No Spartans were cowards.
3   No birds swim.
4   None of the mail arrived on time.
5   Not any of the books are here.
6   Each person is not liable.
7   A bat is not a bird.
8   Reptiles are not mammals.
9   Nothing that is a vegetable is mineral.
10   Not anything which is pleasurable is free.
11   No one who comes will be welcomed.
12   Nowhere that he goes, will I go.
13   He never arrives late.
14   There are no innocent coeds.
15   He who doesn't hesitate is foolish.

These become (with their terms in italics):

1'   No *sugar* is a *sour substance.*
2'   No *Spartans* were *cowards.*
3'   No *birds* are *swimmers.*
4'   No *mail* is *mail which arrived on time.*
5'   No *books* are *books which are here.*
6'   No *person* is a *liable person.*
7'   No *bats* are *birds.*
8'   No *reptiles* are *mammals.*
9'   No *vegetables* are *minerals.*
10'   No *pleasurable thing* is a *free thing.*
11'   No *person who comes* are *persons who will be welcomed.*
12'   No *place that he goes* is a *place that I go.*
13'   No *time* is a *time that he arrives late.*
14'   No *coeds* are *innocent coeds.*
15'   No *person who hesitates* is a *person who is foolish.*

It may be noticed that the linguistic distortions, which sometimes become extreme, may be minimized if we are more tolerant in formulating the terms.   For example, "person who is foolish" might simply be "foolish" in Statement 15. Strictly speaking, no linguistic transformation is necessary if we are clear about

[6]Which is how "only" functioned earlier.   (See above, p. 77.)

the form of the statement.   At the beginning, however, it is usually better to provide an exact categorical form.   As we shall see, before we can engage in some
formal logic with these forms we will need to explore the forms.   But making
these translations into forms has the added advantage of forcing us to be clear
about what we are saying, which is itself worthwhile.

Next we consider the I form of categorical statement, "Some F is G."   As
we noted earlier, there are many different words and phrases which function as
quantifiers in English.   But it is convenient in logical studies to restrict the number
of quantifiers we use.   We have already employed the universal quantifier not
only in its affirmative forms but also in many of its linguistic variants.   The other
quantifier we will use is "some," which will be interpreted to mean *at least one
and possibly all*.   This interpretation, it must be emphasized, is a departure from
the ordinary one.   In English "some" frequently means "at least one and possibly more" and sometimes it means what we have taken it to mean, "at least
one and possibly all," but in some contexts it also means "at least one but not
all."   Our rendering takes the minimum content and admits vagueness in
"some."[7]   It might mean only one; it might mean a few, many, or most.   Here,
at least, the English is also vague.   If someone asserts: "Some students failed," it
is not clear how many failed.   Perhaps only one, and perhaps more.   But our use
of "some" does not close the possibility that all failed.   It only says (perhaps
cryptically) at least one person failed (and possibly even all).   With this understanding, each of the following will be translated as "some": "a few," "quite a
few," "many," "most," "almost all."   That is, everything short of "all" is "some."

Consider now some instances of "Some F is G:

1   Some coeds are innocent.
2   A few coeds are innocent.
3   Many coeds are innocent.
4   Most coeds are innocent.
5   There are innocent coeds.
6   Some things are both free and pleasurable.
7   A bird flew in the window.
8   We saw the opera and had a good time.
9   I liked him before he got rich.
10   Man-eating whales exist.

Statements 1 through 5 each asserts (at a minimum) that at least one coed is innocent, so each becomes "Some *coeds* are *innocent*."   Statement 6 is "Some *free
things are pleasurable things*."   Statement 7 is best rendered as "Some *bird is a
creature who flew in the window*."[8]   Statement 8 is troublesome, but the inflec-

---

[7] It should be noted that rendering quasi-numerical quantifiers such as "the majority" or "most"
indiscriminately as "some" can sometimes turn a valid argument into an invalid argument.   Thus,
"If the majority vote for a candidate, he will be elected; the majority voted for Jones; hence Jones
was elected" is valid.   But if the second premise is rendered "Some of the voters voted for Jones,"
it doesn't follow that Jones was elected.

[8] Compare "A whale is a mammal," p. 138.

tion of the verb suggests that time considerations are relevant. It becomes, "Some *times we went to the opera* are *times we had a good time.*" In 9 the "before" appears to be a statement connective, but the statement is best construed as an **I** form in this way: "Some *times in which I liked him* are *times before he was rich.*" Statement 10 simply asserts that there is at least one man-eating whale, or "Some *whales* are *maneaters.*"

Finally, we have the **O** categorical statement, "Some *F* are not *G.*" The "some" of the **O** statement is subject to the same considerations as those of the **I** statement. The following are instances of the **O** form:

1 Some Russians are not Bolsheviks.
2 A few Russians are not Bolsheviks.
3 Many Russians are not Bolsheviks.
4 Most Russians are not Bolsheviks.
5 There are things which are not free.
6 We saw the opera and didn't have a good time.
7 All that glitters is not gold.
8 Not everything which is expensive is well made.
9 Not all coeds are innocent.
10 Smart alecks aren't always around.

As before, 1 through 4 need no comment. Statement 5 says "Some things are not free things." Statement 6 becomes "Some *times that we saw the opera* are not *times that we had a good time.*" Statement 7 is another misleading construction in English. Because of the presence of "all" it is easy to suppose that 7 is an **A** statement. But the "not" does peculiar things. Statement 7 almost surely means "It is not the case that all glittering things are gold," which is the contradictory of the **A** statement "All glittering things are gold." But as we shall see, the contradictory of the **A** statement is the **O**. Hence 7 becomes "Some *things which glitter* are not *gold.*" Generally, statements of the (odd) form "All *F* is not *G*" become "Some *F* is not *G.*" But not always; "All birds are not reptiles" might mean "No birds are reptiles." For clarity, the form "All *F* are not *G*" should be avoided. Similar considerations apply to 8 and 9, which quite clearly are contradictories of **A** statements. They become, respectively, "Some *things which are expensive* are not *well made,*" and "Some *coeds* are not *innocent.*" Statement 10 could use a parameter. "Some *places* are not *places where there are smark alecks.*"

There are several additional sorts of statements which deserve special attention. These include statements which contain quasi-numerical quantifiers such as "almost all," "not quite all," and "almost everyone," etc., and expressions containing the quantifiers, "all except" and "all but." For example, what does the statement "Almost all Communists are Bolsheviks" assert? Some writers claim that it asserts *two* statements, namely "Some Communists are Bolsheviks" *and* "Some Communists are not Bolsheviks." Other writers say that it asserts *only* the former even though it may suggest (though not logically imply) the latter. Unfortunately, neither point of view is free of difficulties. In some contexts, the speaker may be quite sure that some (at least one) Communists are Bolsheviks, but wish to leave it open whether all are. In such a context, his claim commits him to the thesis that some Communists are Bolsheviks, but it doesn't commit him to the thesis that some are not. On the other hand, he may be responding to the assertion that all Communists are Bolsheviks; and the force of his assertion is that while some are, some are not. It would seem that the original expression is not perfectly clear. In practical contexts, we should be wary of this difficulty and insist upon a clarification. For classroom work, however, we shall say that expressions like "almost all" and "not quite all" assert one statement, either the **I** or the **O**, but not both.

Similar considerations apply to statements with "all except" and "all but." Consider the statement, "All except nonresidents are taxed." In most contexts, this would be taken to mean, "All residents are taxed" *and* "No nonresidents are taxed." But again it is not clear whether the original statement asserts both, asserts only the first, or asserts only the second. Again, in practical contexts, a clarification is in order. However, since in most contexts "exceptive" statements do seem to mean both, for uniformity of classwork we shall treat them as asserting the conjunction of two categorical statements. Thus, for example, "All but sinners are among the saved" will be taken to mean "All nonsinners are among the saved" and "No sinners are among the saved."

The discussion of this section has served several purposes. First, it has indicated the wide range of English sentences which can be rendered into one of the four categorical forms. Other types might have been included, but those offered here are fairly typical. Secondly, by forcing ourselves to analyze various sorts of sentences in English we can come to a clearer grasp of the meanings of statements in ordinary language. Finally, to the extent to which we can reduce English to one of the four categorical forms, to that extent we can employ formal logic to see how they function in argument.

One last word about translating into form: The examples offered should not be taken slavishly. Good sense rather than unthinking application of our paradigms should be the rule. English is a rich and subtle language, and developing a sensitivity to it requires both patience and practice.

EXERCISES

Translate the following into standard-form categorical propositions:

1 Smith hates us all.
2 Sinners are always wretched.
3 If you don't study philosophy, you aren't too smart.
4 All who miss this question deserve to flunk the course.
5 Only he is skinny who eats not.
6 I kid you not.
7 None but the brave loves only glory.
8 He does what he wants.

9 Blessed is he that giveth.
10 Not all dancing is vulgar.
11 Man is the measure of all things.
12 Sheep only produce wool.
13 To know her is to love her.
14 John always eats too much.
15 Somebody loves a skunk, Hebsebeth by name.
16 The only good flea is a dead flea.
17 The desire of the wicked will perish.
18 His praise stands fast forever.
19 Not on bread alone is man to live.
20 Boors wear hob-nailed boots and sing in the bath.
21 Not one aardvark is callipygian.
22 Many brave hearts are asleep in the deep.
23 Parrots love to talk.
24 A man came to see mother.
25 Nothing that is a callipygian aardvark is frigorific.

Quality, Quantity, and Distribution

We have already employed the notions of quality and quantity. The **quality** of a categorical statement refers to its affirmative or negative character. Thus the **A** and the **I** are affirmative; the **E** and **O** are negative. The **quantity** refers to the quantifier which precedes the first term. The **A** and **E** are universal; the **I** and **O** are particular. These facts can be summed up in a diagram:

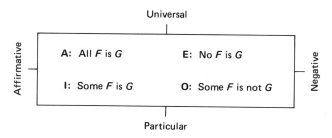

For convenience, let us call the first term of a categorical statement the **subject term** or simply the **subject,** and the second term the **predicate term** or simply the **predicate**.[9] Thus in the formula "No F is G," represents the subject term and G, the predicate term. Again, for purposes of clarity we will use the letter S for the subject term and P for the predicate term.

[9] Naming the terms this way is done only for purposes of exposition. Though these designations suggest the grammatical distinction between subject and predicate, they are not the same. The grammatical predicate, for example, contains everything which follows the subject. But that is not true of our distinction. From our point of view, moreover, all terms are on a logical par.

The analysis of categorical statements also requires that we understand what is meant by the **distribution of terms,** a concept which relates to quantifiers. Each of the terms in a categorical statement will be either distributed or undistributed. Since there are but two types of quantifiers, either universal or particular, we may say that a term is *distributed* if it is preceded by a universal quantifier, and *undistributed* if it is preceded by a particular quantifier. Thus, for example, the expression "all men" refers to each and every man, or "man" is distributed. By contrast, the expression "some men" refers only to at least one man, and thus "man" in this context is undistributed.

With respect to distribution, determining the subject terms of each of the four categoricals presents no problem, for each contains an *explicit* quantifier, "all," "no," and "some." The predicate terms, however, contain an *implicit* quantifier, which must be determined. This can be done by formulating the four categoricals in the following way:

A: *Every S* is (identical with) *some P,* or
Every S is a P, or All S is P.

E: *Every S* is distinct from *every P,* or
No S is any P, or No S is P.

I: *Some S* is (identical with) *some P,* or
Some S is a P, or Some S is P.

O: *Some S* is distinct from *every P,* or
Some S is not any P, or Some S is not P.

In the **A**-statement form, for example, "Every" (or "all," etc.) quantifies S and "some" quantifies P. While we do not ordinarily explicitly quantify predicate terms, the *sense* of the four standard form categoricals is best captured by recognizing their implicit quantifiers.[10]

---

[10] The device of quantifying predicates also enables us to clearly distinguish four types of *nontraditional* categorical forms. Designated with corresponding Greek letter names, they are:

α: *Every S* is identical with *every P.*
η: *Every S* is distinct from *some P.*
ι: *Some S* is identical with *every P.*
ω: *Some S* is distinct from *some P.*

Some of these four forms were explored by Aristotle and the scholastic logicians.

For this way of explaining distribution we are indebted to William T. Parry.

The obscurities in most modern explanations of distribution have been pointed out by both Professor Parry and P. T. Geach in his *Reference and Generality* (Ithaca, N.Y.: Cornell University Press, 1962), chap. I. These formulations usually involve an unclear distinction between what a term "refers to" and what it "denotes." Additional confusions are introduced by talking about wholes and parts of classes or about the "information" conveyed in statements. Geach concludes that the notion of distribution is useless. The present text, however, follows Parry in maintaining that it is useful and can be rehabilitated in a clear and unambiguous way.

We may summarize our results with a table:

A: All *S* is *P*   The subject term *S* is distributed; the predicate term *P* is *un*distributed.

E: No *S* is *P*   Both *S* and *P* are distributed.
I: Some *S* is *P*   Both *S* and *P* are *un*distributed.

O: Some *S* is not *P*   The subject term *S* is *un*distributed; the predicate term *P* is distributed.

Before we can proceed to the "logic" of the categoricals, one last bit of terminological terrain needs to be explored, namely the notion of **complementary terms.** For example, the term "those who are married" has as its complement (or complementary term) "those who are not married." Thus a complement of a term is the negation or denial of a term. If we designate "those who are married" as *F*, then its complement is clearly designated non-*F*. Instead of "not" we use "non-" as a prefix and attach it to "*F*," so as to make clear that the negation is *part* of the *term*. Hence, "All *S* is non-*P*" is still an **A** form: it affirms, but in this case it affirms that "every *S* is identical with some non-*P*." Every term will have its complement. The complement of the term "men" is simply "non-men." As the term "men" is true of all objects which are men and false of all objects which are non-men, so the term "non-men" is true of all non-men, for example, a chair, a vegetable, the sun, etc. It is false of all men, for example, Socrates, Pico della Mirandola, etc.

EXERCISES

For each of the following, state its quality and quantity and the distribution of its terms. If necessary translate into standard form. Label each statement form as an **A, E, I,** or **O.**

1   All non-*S* are *P*.
2   Some *S* are non-*P*.
3   No non-*S* are non-*P*.
4   Every *S* is *P*.
5   Some *S* is not non-*P*.
6   Each non-*S* is distinct from every *P*.
7   Some *S* is identical with some *P*.
8   Some non-*S* is distinct from every *P*.
9   Every *S* is distinct from every *P*.
10 Not all *S* is *P*.
11 Only *S* is non-*P*.

12 There are no *S* which are non-*P*.
13 A few non-*S* are non-*P*.
14 None but *S* are *P*.
15 Many non-*S* are not *P*.

The Square of Opposition

If we had four categorical forms which had the same subject and predicate terms, what logical relations would hold between them? The **square of opposition** is a medieval device for graphically representing these relations and looks like this:

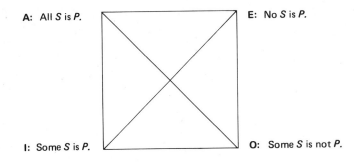

A: All *S* is *P*.   **E:** No *S* is *P*.

I: Some *S* is *P*.   **O:** Some *S* is not *P*.

Inspection of the square suggests that there are certain *truth* relations which hold between the various statement forms. Consider first the **A** and the **O**. Assume that either one of them is true. Take, for example, the **A** as true. On this interpretation of *S* and *P*, what must be the value of **O**? Apparently it must be false. So if **A** is "All whiskey is alcoholic," and this is true, then it *must* be false that "Some whiskey is not alcoholic." Indeed, it is easy to see that under no interpretation of *S* and *P* is it possible for **A** and **O** to have the same truth value. If one is true, the other must be false, and conversely. **A** and **O** are therefore *contradictories*.

The same line of reasoning applies to **E** and **I**. If "No coeds are innocent" is false, then "Some coeds are innocent" *must* be true. Similarly, if "Some birds are mammals" is false, then "No birds are mammals" must be true.

> In general, two statements are **contradictory** if both cannot be true and both cannot be false at the same time. Two statement forms are contradictory if there is no interpretation of their variables which makes them both true or both false.[11]

Consider next **A** and **E**. It is easy to suppose that **A** and **E**, like **A** and **O**, are contradictories, but a moment's reflection will prove that they are not. Indeed, the difference lies in this fact: It is possible for *both* **A** and **E** to be *false* under the

---

[11] This holds for *all* formulas, including the truth-functional formulas of the previous chapters. Thus $\sim(pq)$ and pq are contradictories. No interpretation of p and q makes them both true or both false.

same interpretation. How is this possible? It is possible if "Some S is P" is true *and* "Some S is not P" is true; but this surely can occur. For example, read S as "coeds" and P as "innocent." Though it may be bad sociology, it is probably *false* that "All coeds are innocent" and that "No coeds are innocent." It is probably true that "Some coeds are innocent" and "Some coeds are not innocent." But if the **O** and the **I** are both true, then their contradictories, the **A** and the **E,** respectively, must both be false! Hopefully, the logical point has not been obscured by the sociological point. If it has, then read S as "mammals" and P as "whales." (This is a safe biological point.) The confusion arises because the **A** and the **E** cannot both be *true*. If "All birds are oviparous" is true, then "No birds are oviparous" must be false, and conversely. The **A** and the **E** are called contraries and must be distinguished from contradictories.

> In general, two statements are **contraries** *(of one another)* if both cannot be true at the same time, but both can be false. Two statement forms are contrary if there is an interpretation of the variables which makes them both false, and if there is no interpretation which makes them both true.[12]

But it would be a mistake to call **I** and **O** contraries, for they display different logical features. While both **A** and **E** can be false but not true simultaneously, both **I** and **O** can be *true* but *not* false simultaneously. We have already seen that both can be true, but why is it that both cannot be false? Suppose it is false that "Some football players are professionals." What can be inferred? Intuitively, it must be the case that some football players are *not* professionals. But this is, of course, the **O** statement. Another approach, however, is possible. For the statement "Some football players are professionals" is the **I,** and by assumption it is false. But if it is false, its contradictory the **E,** "No football players are professionals," must be true. But surely, if it is true that *no* football players are professionals, it *must* be true that the weaker statement "Some football players are not professionals" is true. Hence we cannot simultaneously hold that the **I** and the **O** are both false. We shall call the **I** and **O** subcontraries to distinguish them from contradictories and contraries.

> In general, two statements are **subcontraries** if both cannot be false, but both can be true. Two statement forms are subcontraries if there is an interpretation of their variables which makes them both true, and if no interpretation makes them both false.[13]

We have already discussed the last of the relationships, namely that of implication (or entailment): **A** implies **I,** and **E** implies **O**; that is, if **A** is true, then **I** must be true; similarly if **E** is true, then **O** must be true.

---

[12] This holds for all formulas, including truth-functional formulas. For example, pq and $\sim(p \equiv q)$ are contraries. These relations do not hold, however, for statements or formulas which are either necessarily true or necessarily false.

[13] Again, this holds for all truth-functional formulas as well. For example, $p \vee q$ and $p \equiv q$ are subcontraries.

In general, the statement form S_1 **entails** S_2 if no substitution of the variables of S_1 and S_2 makes S_1 true and S_2 false.[14]

Notice also by the very logic of "entails," if **I** is *false,* then **A** must be false, and if **O** is *false,* then **E** must be false. This is seen by putting **A** and **I,** and **E** and **O** in the form of arguments:

All *S* is *P*   No *S* is *P*
∴ Some *S* is *P*   ∴ Some *S* is not *P*

If the premise is true, the conclusion must be true (**A** entails **I**). But since **A** entails **I,** if the conclusion is false, then the premise must be false.

These relationships may be efficiently summarized as valid conditionals or biconditionals as follows:

1	**A ≡ ~O**	**O ≡ ~A**}	Contradictories
2	**E ≡ ~I**	**I ≡ ~E**	
3	**A ⊃ ~E**	**E ⊃ ~A**}	Contraries
4	**~I ⊃ O**	**~O ⊃ I**}	Subcontraries
5	**A ⊃ I**	**~I ⊃ ~A**	Implication
6	**E ⊃ O**	**~O ⊃ ~E**	

These relationships may now be filled in on our square:

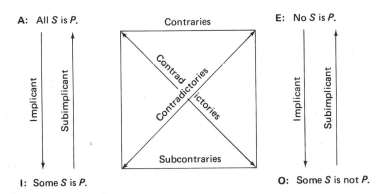

Notice that if we now interpret any of the four as either true or false, certain inferences can be made. For example, assume "All *S* is *P*" is true. Since this is the **A, O** must be false (by contradictory), **E** must be false (by contrary), and **I** must be true (by implication). Or, if you will, if **O** is false (by contradictory), then **I** must be true (by subcontrary) and **E** false (by contradictory). One can go round and round, over and across, and back and forth. What happens, however, if

[14] If S_1 entails S_2, then $S_1 \supset S_2$ is a tautology.

we assume that **A** is false? All we can infer is that **O** is true. Since **E** could also be false, though it might be true, no inference is possible there. Since **I** could be true or false, no inference is possible there. Remember "some" means *at least one;* hence knowing that the **I** is true is not sufficient to infer the truth of the **A** or the falsehood of the **O.**

Summary of Relations among the Four Categorical Forms

Given		Inferred					
A	true	E	false	I	true	O	false
E	true	A	false	I	false	O	true
I	true	A	unknown	E	false	O	unknown
O	true	A	false	E	unknown	I	unknown
A	false	E	unknown	I	unknown	O	true
E	false	A	unknown	I	true	O	unknown
I	false	A	false	E	true	O	true
O	false	A	true	E	false	I	true

EXERCISES

What can be inferred about the truth or falsehood of the remaining propositions in each of the following sets if we assume the first to be true? If we assume it to be false?

1 a All sugars are organic compounds.
   b No sugars are organic compounds.
   c Some sugars are organic compounds.
   d Some sugars are not organic compounds.
2 a No reptiles are warm-blooded animals.
   b Some reptiles are warm-blooded animals.
   c Some reptiles are not warm-blooded animals.
   d All reptiles are warm-blooded animals.
3 a Some former college presidents have been successful candidates for the Presidency of the United States.
   b Some former college presidents have not been succcessful candidates for the Presidency of the United States.
   c All former college presidents have been successful candidates for the Presidency of the United States.
   d No former college presidents have been successful candidates for the Presidency of the United States.
4 a Some alcohols are not radioactive substances.
   b All alcohols are radioactive substances.
   c No alcohols are radioactive substances.
   d Some alcohols are radioactive substances.

The Immediate Inferences

The following inferences have traditionally been called the **immediate inferences,** because they may be construed as simple one-premise arguments in which the conclusion follows immediately from the premise.[15]

Conversion   Suppose that we are given an **E** statement form, "No S is P." What can be immediately inferred? Well, if we simply "convert" the S and the P, we get "No P is S." Does this follow from "No S is P"? Obviously it does, since if every S is distinct from every P, then every P is distinct from every S. In general, **conversion** involves interchanging terms. Consider next the **I** form. Does "Some S is P" entail "Some P is S"? Since "Some S is P" asserts that there is at least one S which is P, it follows thaa there is one P which is an S. Indeed, "Some S is P" is equivalent to "Some **P** is S" just as "No S is P" is equivalent to "No P is S." As before, this means that there is *no* interpretation of S and P which would make the two statements have different truth values. Hence converting the terms of **E** and **I** forms yields logically equivalent formulas. This procedure will be called **simple conversion.**

Consider next the **A** form. From "All S is P" can we infer "All P is S"? We cannot, for there are interpretations of S and P which would make one true and the other false. For example, "All Frenchmen are Europeans" (which is true) does not entail "All Europeans are Frenchmen." Hence we cannot simply convert the **A** form. But the statement "All Frenchmen are Europeans" does entail "Some Frenchmen are Europeans," which can be converted to "Some Europeans are Frenchmen." Thus if we convert the **A** form, we must weaken the quantifier to "some." We call this **conversion by limitation** (or **per accidens,** its Latin name).

What then of the **O** statement? To answer this question, consider first an example: Does "Some Europeans are not Frenchmen" (which is true) entail "Some Frenchmen are not Europeans" (which is false)? No, it does not and there is no way out of this.

People are sometimes misled into thinking that the **O** statement is convertible because *sometimes* "Some S is not P" and "Some P is not S" are both true. For example, "Some college graduates are not successful" and "Some successful people are not college graduates." But because they are both *true,* that is not sufficient grounds to assert that one *entails* the other. As we have seen from the beginning, a true premise and a true conclusion prove nothing, for it is easy to construct invalid arguments with them. Secondly, we are here concerned with what can be inferred on grounds of *form* alone. But this means that if there are

---

[15] Strictly speaking, the inferences from the square of opposition are also immediate inferences, for the same reason. Later we shall discuss syllogisms, which involve more than one premise. They are sometimes called *mediate inferences.*

any interpretations of "*S*" and "*P*" which make "Some *S* is not *P*" true and "Some *P* is not *S*" false, then the first does not *formally* entail the second.

Schema of Conversion

Original Form		Converse
A: All *S* is *P*	⊃	**I:** Some *P* is *S*
E: No *S* is *P*	≡	**E:** No *P* is *S*
I: Some *S* is *P*	≡	**I:** Some *P* is *S*
O: Some *S* is not *P*		None

Obversion   The inference called **obversion** is one which Aristotle did not allow. We shall introduce it here, however, though later we shall see that when used in combination with conversion, its use must be restricted.   In obversion we do two things: we change the quality of the form and replace the predicate term with its complement.   All four forms have obverses, and each of them is equivalent to the original.   We begin with the **A:** "All *S* is *P*."   Since it is universal *affirmative,* it becomes universal *negative,* or an **E,** "No *S.* . . ."   But we also replace the predicate with its complement, thus, "No *S* is non-*P*."   The **E** form, "No *S* is *P*," since it is universal *negative,* becomes *affirmative,* or an **A,** "All *S.* . . ."   We then replace the predicate with its complement and get "All *S* is non-*P*."   The **I,** "Some *S* is *P*," becomes the **O,** "Some *S* is not non-*P*."   And similarly, the **O,** "Some *S* is not *P*," becomes the corresponding **I,** "Some *S* is non-*P*."

To summarize obversion, **A** becomes **E, E** becomes **A, I** becomes **O,** and **O** becomes **I.**   In each case the predicate is replaced by its complement.

Schema of Obversion

Original Form		Obverse
A: All *S* is *P*	≡	**E:** No *S* is non-*P*
E: No *S* is *P*	≡	**A:** All *S* is non-*P*
I: Some *S* is *P*	≡	**O:** Some *S* is not non-*P*
O: Some *S* is not *P*	≡	**I:** Some *S* is non-*P*

Other inferences   By combining conversion and obversion in different ways, it is possible to generate new implications and equivalences.   Thus, for example, we can infer an obverse, then convert, and obvert again.   If our inferences are valid and if we begin with a true premise, we should finish with a true conclusion.   Use of obversion, conversion, and obversion in that order yields what is generally called the **contrapositive.**   Let us see what it looks like:

A: All *S* is *P* by obversion becomes
No *S* is non-*P*, which by conversion becomes
No non-*P* is *S*, which by obversion again becomes
All non-*P* is non-*S*.

Since each move yields an equivalent statement, we may say that "All S is P" is equivalent to "All non-P is non-S." The contrapositive of an **A** can be arrived at directly by converting terms and replacing both with their complements:

E: No S is P by obversion becomes
All S is non-P, which by conversion by limitation becomes
Some non-P is S, which by obversion again becomes
Some non-P is not non-S.

Since the move from the **A** to the **I** was not an equivalence, "No S is P" is *not* equivalent to "Some non-P is not non-S" but implies it. The contrapositive of an **E** may be arrived at directly by stating an **O,** converting each term, and replacing with complements.

The **I** statement form has no contrapositive. Let us see why.

I: Some S is P by obversion becomes
Some S is not non-P, which is not convertible.

The **O** presents no special problems and should be worked out by the reader.

A Problem Besides contrapositives, other inferences are possible. (Most of these have names, which can be ignored here.) Earlier we noted, however, that the use of obversion along with conversion can lead to difficulties. One example will suffice to show this. Consider an **A** categorical form:

A: All S is P, which becomes by contrapositive
All non-P is non-S, which becomes by conversion *per accidens*
Some non-S is non-P, which becomes by obversion
Some non-S is not P.

Apparently all our inferences have been valid; hence "All S is P" *should* entail "Some non-S is not P," but unfortunately it does *not*. One interpretation will show this. We read S so that it is true of something in the universe (it doesn't matter what) and we read P so that it is true of everything in the universe. Then "All S is P" is true, since whatever S is true of, P will be true of it also. But "Some non-S is not P" will be false simply because P is true of everything, *even the non-S's*.[16] The reader has undoubtedly seen that the counterexample here employed is a rather special case. Indeed, *most* interpretations of S and P will *not* cause this difficulty. So for all practical purposes we can ignore it. Indeed, the practical purpose of obversion, as we shall see, is to *eliminate* the occurrences of both a term and its complement so that we can put arguments into standard form. This purpose is wholly unaffected by the sort of argument which has been

[16] Notice that this difficulty is independent of the question of existential import, to be discussed later.

produced here. Hence, we will continue to use obversion and conversion, recognizing that strictly speaking, there will be some lines of argument which will lead to invalid inferences.[17]

Finally, we should emphasize that the use of obversion *without* conversion is always valid. Likewise, contrapositives are always valid. Indeed, they are very important and useful forms of inferences. To remember how to get a contrapositive, just remember *OCO*, that is, Obvert, Convert, and Obvert.

Schema of Contraposition

Original Form		Contrapositive
A: All S is P	$\equiv$	**A:** All non-P is non-S
E: No S is P	$\supset$	**O:** Some non-P is not non-S
I: Some S is P		None
O: Some S is not P	$\equiv$	**O:** Some non-P is not non-S

EXERCISES

A Take the converse (either simple or *per accidens*, if possible) of the following:

1 Some sitar players are Indian.
2 All foolish people will go astray on this one.
3 Visitors who overstay their leaves are unwelcome.
4 No one indifferent to the well-being of humanity is humane.
5 A few books of indifferent merit are not bestsellers.

B Take the obverse of the following:

6 No Quakers are combatants.
7 Some beverages are intoxicants.
8 Acids are corrosive.
9 Many educators are teachers.
10 No visitor is unwelcome.

C Assuming that "All S is P" is true, what can be inferred about the truth value of each of the following? Use the immediate inferences *and* the square of the opposition. Be prepared to defend your answer:

11 All non-P is non-S.
12 No S is non-P.

---

[17] Though the point has minimum practical interest—so little, indeed, that many books do not even mention it—it does have great logical and historical interest. From a logical point of view, the counterexample does show that any analysis of the relation of terms which admits both conversion and obversion as valid inferences must somehow resolve this difficulty. Several alternative solutions have been proposed, but the one which seems best is Aristotle's—not to allow obversion in the formal system.

This does not mean, it must be emphasized, that all uses of conversion with obversion lead to difficulties. On the contrary, every use in the text up to the counterexample offered is *absolutely valid*.

13 Some non-*P* is non-*S*.
14 Some *P* is not *S*.
15 No non-*S* is *P*.
16 All *S* is non-*P*.
17 Some *S* is *P*.
18 Some *S* is non-*P*.
19 Some non-*P* is not non-*S*.
20 No *S* is *P*.

EIGHT

THE SYLLOGISM

*We know well that a fallacy that would
be obvious to all in a three-line
syllogism may deceive the elect in 400
pages of crowded fact and argument. . . .*

Josiah Stamp

Standard-Form Categorical Syllogisms

In the previous chapter we considered a wide range of inferences made possible from one categorical statement form. In this chapter we turn our attention to two-premise arguments, or syllogisms. Strictly speaking, *all* two-premise arguments are syllogisms, but the high point of traditional logic is the doctrine of the *categorical* syllogism—that which contains only categorical statements. Such syllogisms occur frequently in ordinary discourse, though generally in disguised ways; hence their importance cannot be underestimated. One further qualification, however, must be noted. Our analysis requires the concept of a **standard-form categorical syllogism.**

Standard-form categorical syllogisms have the following defining features:

1 They contain three and only three terms. One is called the **major term** and is the predicate term of the conclusion; another is called the **minor term** and is the subject term of the conclusion; and the third is called the **middle term** and appears in *both* premises.

2 A syllogism is not in standard form until the premise containing the major term is listed first. This premise is called the **major premise.** The premise containing the minor term, not surprisingly called the **minor premise,** is listed second, and the conclusion is listed last. For example:

No *P* is *M*.

Some *S* is *M*.

∴ Some *S* is not *P*.

This syllogism is in standard form. *P* is the major term, *S* is the minor term, and *M* is the middle term.

Though the syllogisms of ordinary discourse are not always offered in standard form, we shall find this concept useful, for all categorical syllogisms can be put into standard form. In what immediately follows we shall confine our attention to standard-form categorical syllogisms; hence we shall drop the qualifying adjectives standard-form categorical and refer only to syllogisms.

A scheme for coding syllogisms introduced by medieval logicians involves naming in consecutive order the form of statements in a standard-form syllogism. This naming gives what is called the **mood** of the syllogism. In our example, the major premise is an **E** form of statement, the minor is an **I** form, and the conclusion is an **O** form; hence its mood is **EIO**. Since there are four possible statement forms and three statements in every syllogism, there are altogether 4^3 combinations, or 64 moods. Many of these forms, however, are invalid and in this chapter we shall determine which ones are and why. Given only the mood of a syllogism, we can generate many different argument forms by locating the middle term in different positions. There are four possible arrangements of the middle term. These are called **figures**[1] and can be represented as follows:

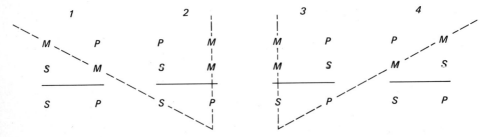

These are easy to remember because of their symmetry. As has been noticed by more than one teacher of logic, the middle terms form the front of a shirt collar. Since we have 64 possible moods and 4 possible figures for each mood, the total number of standard-form categorical syllogisms is 264! By specifying the mood and the figure of a syllogism, its form is *fully* given. Thus, for example, **AEE**-4 means that the major premise is an **A**, the minor premise is an **E**, the conclusion is an **E**, and the syllogism is in the fourth figure. Thus:

A: All *P* is *M*.

E: No *M* is *S*.

∴ **E:** No *S* is *P*.

---

[1] Aristotle did not admit the fourth figure in his system.

EXERCISES

Put the following syllogisms into standard form and determine the mood and figure of each. (The first step is to translate each statement into its categorical form. Next find the conclusion and locate the subject and predicate terms so that the major and minor premises can be found. List the major premise first, then the minor. Then the figure can be determined.)

1 Everyone loves a lover, but pugilists don't have lovers, so pugilists aren't people.
2 Some fish smell and some cheese smells, so some cheese is fish.
3 Since all northern industrialists are Republicans, and no Republicans are supporters of states' rights, no northern industrialists are supporters of states' rights.
4 Every barbiturate is a narcotic, so a few narcotics are not habit forming, since some barbiturates aren't habit forming.
5 Atheists are men who do not believe in God, but men who believe in God are wise men; hence, there are no wise atheists.

Some Ways to Determine Validity:
(1) Refutation by Logical Analogy

There are countless syllogisms which can be constructed out of the 264 different forms.[2] But surely not all of these arguments are valid. In what follows, we shall introduce several methods whereby validity can be tested. We begin with what is called **refutation by logical analogy.** Although this method is by no means the easiest of the several which are available, from a logical point of view, it is perhaps the most revealing.

In all deductions we know that it is impossible for the premises to be true and the conclusion false. Refutation by logical analogy uses this feature in a straightforward way. Consider this argument:

> Some societies which had taboos against incest were not among those cultures which were under the domination of a priestly caste. So there are ancient civilizations of notable achievements which were not societies having incest taboos. This is so because not all ancient civilizations of achievement were cultures dominated by priestly castes.

In this argument, it is a bit hard to see what is going on. But suppose we eliminate the excess verbiage and get down to the "bare bones" of the argument. What then would we have? By examining its *form* we could see if there were

[2] Again, for each form there is an *infinite* number of possible syllogisms. We just continue interpreting the term variables to generate new syllogisms.

any interpretations of its term variables which yielded obviously true premises and an obviously false conclusion. If there were, then we would know that the *form* is invalid. But if the form is invalid, then all arguments — including the original — which share this form are invalid. What, then, is the form of the argument?

Let us work it out in steps:

Some (societies which had taboos against incest)
    are not (cultures dominated by a priestly caste).
Some (ancient civilizations of achievement) are not
    (cultures dominated by a priestly caste).
_____

Some (ancient civilizations of achievement) are not
    (societies which had taboos against incest).

This becomes

Some *P* are not *M*.
Some *S* are not *M*.
_____

Some *S* are not *P*.

The form of the argument is **OOO**-2. The problem then is: Can we interpret *S*, *P*, and *M* so that the premises are obviously true and the conclusion is obviously false? If we read *S* as "whales," *P* as "mammals," and *M* as "gorillas," we get:

Some mammals are not gorillas.
Some whales are not gorillas.
_____

Some whales are not mammals.

Since the premises are quite certainly true and the conclusion is quite certainly false, the argument is invalid; and hence, since the original argument is invalid, all arguments of this form are invalid.[3]

Refutation by logical analogy not only is a useful method of disproof but also has excellent rhetorical possibilities. If in a debate someone introduced the argument about incest taboos, an effective response would simply be to point out that if we accept this argument, then we must also accept the conclusion that some whales are not mammals!

Interestingly enough, although refutation by logical analogy is a method of disproof, it is not a method of proof. That is, if we *fail* to find an interpretation of the variables which makes the premises true and the conclusion false, it does not follow that the argument is *valid*. For we may have simply not come up yet with the right interpretation. Such proofs require imagination and ingenuity.

[3] Note that this test requires outside knowledge.

To be sure, if the form is invalid, there will be *some* interpretation which will show this. But finding it may be another matter.[4]

In constructing refutations by logical analogy (which, incidentally, can be used for any argument which is formally analyzable) it is usually best to start with the conclusion and make it false, then keep juggling to make true premises.

EXERCISES

Show that the following arguments are invalid by the method of constructing logical analogies.

1 Employers are not advocates of prolabor legislation, but the advocates of prolabor laws are friends of labor; hence we may conclude that no employer is a friend of labor.
2 Every drink containing alcohol is an intoxicant and each drink which contains alcohol is a stimulant. So intoxicants are stimulants.
3 Not any outspoken radicals are State Department officials, so a few State Department officials are subversive since some subversives are not outspoken radicals.
4 All veterans support bonus legislation, for all those who support bonus legislation are Legionnaires and all Legionnaires are veterans.
5 Many foods are not protein and chocolate bars are all food; hence, chocolate bars are not protein.

Some Ways to Determine Validity:
(2) Rules for the Syllogism

Refutation by logical analogy, though a useful and illuminating device, is not the most practical of procedures. Indeed, we might systematically begin refutations of each of the possible forms of syllogisms. In this way we could eliminate quite a few. But even if we did absolutely eliminate all the invalid forms, we would then need to memorize all those which were valid. Memorizing the valid forms would certainly be possible, but it is hardly desirable nor, indeed, necessary.[5]

---

[4] Compare this with the "ingenuity problem" of Chapter 6. Refutation by logical analogy is not a full decision procedure.

Compare also the refutation in Chapter 7, p. 152, which is a refutation by logical analogy.

[5] It is interesting, however, to notice that this is one of the medieval methods. Indeed, the substance of the doctrine of the syllogism is contained in a set of memory lines which stem from at least the thirteenth century and appear in the writings of Peter of Spain (Pope John XXI; d. 1277), though Peter does not claim to have authored them. They are:

Barbara, *Celerant, Darii, Ferioque,* prioris:
Cesare, Camestres, Festino, Baroco, secundae:
Tertia, *Darapti, Disamis, Datisi, Felapton, Bocardo, Ferison,* habet:
Quarta insuper addit *Bramantip, Camenes, Dimares, Fesapo, Fresison.*

The words "prioris," "secundae," "tertia," and "quarta" refer to the four figures. The *vowels* in each of the italicized words give the *mood* of the valid syllogisms in that figure. Thus *Barbara* is **AAA**-1; *Baroco* is **AOO**-2; etc. The consonants in each of these words also have a function, which need not be explained here.

A convenient approach would be to generate some *rules* which could be applied to test for validity. These rules could be generated inductively by determining what goes wrong in all the invalid forms (assuming, as we may, that we could get such a list) or by seeing what features all the valid forms have in common. We will not attempt such a process here. Rather we shall simply list four such rules. Each of the four states a necessary condition for the validity of any syllogism. Taken together they constitute a sufficient condition for the validity of any syllogism.[6] But since the rules are not self-evident, they will need some justification, which will be provided. The rules for any valid syllogism are as follows:

1 The middle term must be distributed at least once.
2 No term can be distributed in the conclusion which is not distributed in the premises.
3 It is impossible to have two negative premises.
4 There is a negative premise if and only if there is a negative conclusion. (That is, if one premise is negative, the conclusion must be negative and if the conclusion is negative, one premise must be negative.)[7]

Justification of Rule 1 Consider the form of an argument with an undistributed middle term:

All P is M.
All S is M.
———————
All S is P.

To help see that M is undistributed let us rewrite the argument as

Every P is identical with some M.
Every S is identical with some M.
———————————————————
Every S is identical with some P.

But consider what is being asserted. The major premise says that some M can be provided for every P, namely those M's which are P's. Similarly, the minor says that some M can be provided for every S, namely those M's which are also S's. But there can be no assurance that the M's in question in the major premise

---

[6] Throughout the discussion up to this point (and until later in the chapter), we have been making what may be called the *existential presupposition;* that is, we assume that S, P, and M are true of something. This will be discussed later along with the implications of rejecting that presupposition. One of these implications will be that we must add a fifth rule.

[7] Rules 3 and 4 can readily be combined by stating them this way: There may be two and only two negative statements, one of which must be the conclusion. Indeed, it has been shown, by J. M. Keynes for one, that two wholly independent rules can be formulated which will suffice. The four selected here, however, are customary and convenient, especially for pedagogical purposes.

and in the minor premise are the *same M's*. Accordingly, there is no assurance that the *S's* have *anything whatever to do with the P's*.[8]

Now compare an argument in which the middle term is distributed at least once:

No *P* is *M*.
Some *S* is *M*.
_____
Some *S* is not *P*.

Or

Every *P* is distinct from every *M*.
Some *S* is identical with some *M*.
_____
Some *S* is distinct from every *P*.

In this case the middle term, being distributed, does provide the missing link. It does "unite" *S* and *P*, because whichever *S* is *M*, every *M* is distinct from *every P*; hence every *P* must be distinct from *that S*.

Whenever a rule of the syllogism is broken, a formal fallacy is committed. Breaking Rule 1 is understandably called the **fallacy of the undistributed middle.**

Justification of Rule 2   Consider the form of an argument with a term distributed in the conclusion and undistributed in the premise:

All *M* is *P*.
No *S* is *M*.
_____
No *S* is *P*.

Or

Every *M* is identical with *some P*.
Every *S* is distinct from every *M*.
_____
Every *S* is distinct from *every P*.

In this case, the major term, *P*, is distributed in the conclusion and undistributed in the major premise. Why must this be fallacious? Essentially, the difficulty is that we asserted that what is true of *some P* (in the premises) is true of *every P* (in the conclusion). Let us see how this works in the syllogism. The major premise asserts that every *M* is identical with some *P*, for example, that for every Frenchman (*M*), some European (*P*) is identical with him. This is true of all and *only* those Europeans who are French. The minor then says that every *S* (say,

---

[8] The form considered in the discussion, **AAA**-2, should be thought of as *any arbitrary* form with an undistributed middle term. Hence, what is true of it will be true of all such syllogisms in whatever mood and figure they may be. And so for the remainder of the test cases.

Greek) is distinct from every Frenchman. Taken together the two premises do imply that every *French* European is distinct from every *Greek* European, but the conclusion of the syllogism says too much; for it claims that *every* Greek (*S*) is distinct from *every* European — including, therefore, both the non-Greek Europeans (of which it is true) *and* the Greek Europeans (of which it is patently false). In summary, what is true of *some* — the *non*-Greek Europeans — is not true of *every* European.

Breaking the second rule is called **the fallacy of illicit process.** If the major is undistributed in the premise and distributed in the conclusion, it is called **the fallacy of illicit process of the major,** or more simply, **illicit major.** Similarly, if the illicit process occurs with regard to the minor term, it is called **illicit minor.**

Justification of Rule 3 Rule 3 says that in a valid syllogism it is impossible to have two negative premises. Consider this form:

> No *P* is *M*.
> No *S* is *M*.
> ─────────
> No *S* is *P*.

Notice first that this syllogism does not break either of the first two rules. The middle term is distributed twice and no illicit process occurs with either the major or the minor.[9] Yet it is invalid, and it is easy to see why.

Knowing that every *P* is distinct from every *M* and that every *S* is distinct from every *M* is *no* reason to suppose that the *S*'s are distinct from the *P*'s, since it is perfectly possible that every *S* is a *P*, that some *S* is a *P*, or that some *S* is not *P*. But this means that *no* conclusion is entailed by the two negative premises. The truth of the two **E** statements is compatible with the **A**, "All *S* is *P*," with the **I**, "Some *S* is *P*," with the **E**, "No *S* is *P*," and with the **O**, "Some *S* is not *P*." The point is that if *S* and *P* are distinct from *M*, they may or may not be distinct from each other.

Similar considerations apply to arguments with two **O** premises or with any combination of **E** and **O** premises.

Justification of Rule 4 Rule 4 asserts that any valid syllogism has a negative conclusion if and only if it has one negative premise. This means that if a syllogism is to be valid and have a negative premise, then its conclusion must be negative; and if its conclusion is negative, then it must have a negative premise.

We shall consider two species, the first of which follows:

> No *M* are *P*.
> Some *S* are *M*.
> ─────────
> Some *S* are *P*.

[9] Notice also that with respect to the invalidity of the previous example, it did not break Rules 1 or 3. The same can be said for the last example to be discussed. It will be invalid, but not because it breaks Rules 1, 2, or 3.

If we assume the truth of the premises, there is no contradiction in asserting the contradictory of the given conclusion, namely "No S is P." This is so because, while the major excludes all the M's from the P's, the minor asserts only that some S's are M's. But if all the S's are M's (which is possible), then none of the S's are P's. Therefore, "Some S is P" is not entailed by the premises.

Consider, finally, a form with affirmative premises and a negative conclusion. For example:

All *P* is *M*.
All *M* is *S*.
_____
Some *S* is not *P*.

Inspection of this argument form shows that the premises do entail "All *P* is *S*." Thus, while the truth of the premises assures us that "All *P* is *S*," it might be the case that "All *S* is *P*" as well (if *S* is true of the same objects as *P*). But "All *S* is *P*" is the contradictory of "Some *S* is not *P*"; so the premises cannot entail it. It is interesting to observe here that this form, **AAO**-4, is the only one which requires that Rule 4 be stated as a biconditional. That is, all other possible syllogisms with affirmative premises and a negative conclusion will break either Rules 1 or 2.[10]

EXERCISES

A Test for the validity of the arguments on p. 157 by applying the four rules. Indicate what rule, if any, is broken.

B Determine the validity of the following:
1 He who finds war ennobling forgets its horrors. He who forgets war's horrors has never seen them; therefore, he who finds war ennobling has never seen its horrors.
2 When there is an inclination to war, there is no peace. The inclination to war is always present; hence no times are times of peace. (*Hint:* Premise 1 becomes "No times when there is an inclination to war are times when there is peace.")
3 Whenever there is a need to break an order, one may justifiably do so. Sometimes occasions arise when there is a need; hence, breaking orders is sometimes justified. (*Hint:* Premise 1 becomes "All times when there is a need to break an order are times when breaking orders is justified.")
4 There are no just wars and there are no humane wars; hence no just wars are humane.
5 A war is just only if fighting the war is morally better than not fighting it. A war against nations with whom we disagree is a war that is morally better to fight than not to fight; therefore, wars against nations with whom

[10] Later on we shall discuss "seeming" violations of Rules 3 and 4, which disappear when statements are obverted.

we disagree are just wars. (*Hint:* Premise 1 becomes "All just wars are wars in which fighting the war is morally better than not fighting it.")

Existential Import and Venn Diagrams

The traditional analysis of categorical statements examined in the last two chapters has been much criticized by many modern symbolic logicians on the grounds that it makes certain unwarranted assumptions about the existential import of statements. Such assumptions, they claim, should be carefully examined if we wish to be clear in our thinking, for, as we have seen, different assumptions result in different valid inferences. Thus, the question is asked: "Do we or should we commit ourselves to the *existence* of anything when using a statement of one of the four categorical forms?" Let us try to answer this question now. We noticed earlier that terms may be said to be true of or false of certain objects, but suppose in some given statement there are *no* objects of which a term is true. How does this affect the *truth value* of the statements which contain such terms? Consider, for example, the statement "Some students who took the exam failed." Now suppose there were no students who took the exam; what would we say of the statement? Undoubtedly we would want to say it is false. But is it false because no students failed or because no students took the exam at all? From this example it would appear that "some" carries an existential commitment, which is to say that a term like "Some students who took the exam" presupposes that there *actually* were some students who took it. In other words, in asserting that at least one S is P, we are saying *there are S's and* they are P's. Similar considerations apply to the **O** form. To say "Some S is not P" is to assert that there *is* at least one S and that it is not a P.

What now do we say of this statement: "All infractions will be penalized"? Suppose there are no infractions. Then what? Would we want to say that the statement is false? Probably not. Indeed, the modern view would maintain that "All S is P" really means, "If there are any S's then they are P's," a formulation which makes no existential commitment. Similarly, with regard to the **E** form of statement: "No S is P" becomes "If there are any S's, then they are not P's," which again makes no existential commitment regarding the S's. Thus, on this view, we conclude that "some" makes an existential commitment, or has existential import, while "all" (and "no") do not. This view, also called the *hypothetical viewpoint* and held by most modern logicians (though not all), interprets "all" and "some" in a way which fits quite naturally with what is known as the *predicate calculus*, which will be introduced in the next chapter.

Venn Diagrams The foregoing interpretation also fits perfectly with a system of diagrams devised by John Venn in the nineteenth century. To bring out clearly the meaning of the four categoricals from the hypothetical viewpoint, we introduce these diagrams. Overlapping circles are used to represent the two terms of any categorical statement; thus:

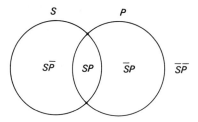

The region in which the two circles overlap will include all and only those possible objects which are both *S* and *P*. The "bar" over a term indicates a complement. Hence $S\bar{P}$ will include all and only those possible objects which are both *S* and non-*P*. Similarly, the $\bar{S}P$ area will include all and only those possible objects which are both non-*S* and *P*. The area outside the circles will include those possible objects which are *neither S nor P*. We will use an asterisk (*) to designate existential commitment. That is, when we wish to indicate that there are objects in some area, we put an asterisk in that area.

Thus in this diagram:

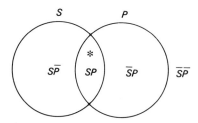

the asterisk indicates that *there is* at least one *S* which is a *P*. This fully captures the sense of the **I** statement, "Some *S* is *P*." But how can we represent the **A** and the **E** forms which make no such commitment? We shall shade in a region to indicate that there can be no objects in that region. In other words, shading represents emptiness. The **E** statement then becomes

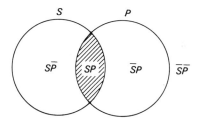

This diagram explicitly rules out the possibility of there being any *S*'s which are *P*'s and thus perfectly captures the sense of "If there are any *S*'s, then they are not *P*'s," or "No *S* is *P*." Notice that it does not assert that there are any *S*'s or that there are any *P*'s, since no * appears anywhere.

We can diagram each of the four categoricals as follows:

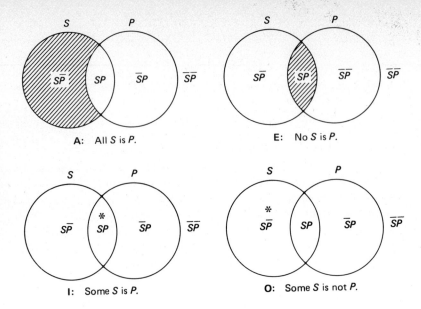

A: All S is P.

E: No S is P.

I: Some S is P.

O: Some S is not P.

From the hypothetical viewpoint, the **A** form asserts, "If there are any S's, then they are P's." Thus it explicitly rules out the possibility of there being S's and non-P's. The shading shows this. Notice that the SP area is blank. Blankness indicates lack of information. We do not know if there are S's or not. But *if* there are S's, then surely they must be P's, which is all that the **A** asserts.

The system of circles allows us directly to diagram statements with the terms reversed and with complements. For example, "All P is S" says that the area $P\bar{S}$ is empty; "Some non-S is P" says that there is at least one non-S which is a P, which becomes, respectively:

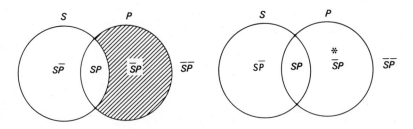

But before we accept the hypothetical point of view, let us be clear on what we have done.

Implications of Adopting the Hypothetical Point of View   If we interpret *only* the **I** and **O** forms as having existential import, then the inferences on the square of opposition are reduced to two; conversion by limitation is eliminated and many valid syllogisms become invalid. This is indeed drastic. But why must it be so?

Suppose that we know that some statement of form **I,** "Some *S* is *P*," is false. Under the traditional view when we knew this, we knew that the corresponding **A** *must* be false. But under the new interpretation, this is not so. To say that "Some *S* is *P*" is false says that there are no *S*'s which are *P*'s, but it *may* be the case that "All *S* is *P*" is *true*. Under the new interpretation, "All *S* is *P*" means, "If there are *S*'s, they are *P*'s," *or* "There are no *S*'s which are not *P*'s." But of course if there are no *S*'s, then "All *S* is *P*" must be true! Similarly, to know that "All *S* is *P*" is true does *not* entitle us to infer that there are *S*'s which are *P*'s, since "All *S* is *P*" only says that *if* there are *S*'s, then they will be *P*'s.

A and **E** will no longer be contraries either, since from the hypothetical point of view, they could both be true. They could both be true if there were no *S*'s. For, again, when there are no *S*'s, there surely are no *S*'s which are not *P*'s (the **A** form) *and* there are no *S*'s that *are* *P*'s (the **E** form). Similarly, **I** and **O** are no longer subcontraries, since if there are no *S*'s, they will both be false. Indeed, the only relation on the square which continues to hold are the *contradictories*. The Venn diagrams clearly indicate this. The Venn diagram of an **A** form is shaded where, and only where, **O** has an asterisk; **E** is shaded where, and only where, **I** has an asterisk.

Of the immediate inferences, simple conversion still holds and so does obversion, but conversion by limitation (*per accidens*) fails. Again, the Venn diagrams clearly show the equivalence of "No *S* is *P*" to "No *P* is *S*" and of "Some *S* is *P*" to "Some *P* is *S*." Similarly, "All *S* is *P*" is still equivalent to "No *S* is non-*P*," and the diagrams make this quite vivid. But we cannot infer from "All *S* is *P*" that "Some *P* is *S*" since if there are no *S*'s, interpretations of the **A** form would be true and of the **I** form, false.

For similar reasons, all of the so-called *strengthened* moods and all of the so-called *weakened* (or subaltern) moods fail. The strengthened moods include **AAI**-3, **EAO**-3, **AAI**-4, and **EAO**-4. (These four are called "strengthened" because the same conclusion would follow if we replaced *one* of the premises with its corresponding particular.) The weakened moods (so called because in each case a particular conclusion is obtained where the premises warrant a universal), **AAI**-1, **EAO**-1, **EAO**-2, **AEO**-2, and **AEO**-4, also fail. In each of these nine syllogisms, a *particular* conclusion is drawn from only universal premises; hence the premises could be true and the conclusions false, even though none of the four rules of the syllogism is broken.[11] Valid syllogisms with universal conclusions are unaffected by the problem of existential import, since as their universal premises are hypotheticals, so, too, are their conclusions. If we accept the hypothetical viewpoint, however, then we must add a *fifth syllogistic rule*, namely: *no particular conclusion is entailed by two universal premises*.

These limitations are drastic and should cause us to ponder on some way to avoid them. For *practical* purposes, indeed, we would insist on maintaining the inferences which have been eliminated. Paying close attention to the way

[11] Specifically, in the weakened moods, the minor term is the problem; in **AAI**-3, **EAO**-3, and **EAO**-4 the middle is the problem; and in **AAI**-4, the major is.

in which we normally use words like "all" and "some" is, as we shall see, the way out.

Rehabilitation of the Traditional View[12]

The most obvious route to take would be to simply assume that universal propositions always do make an existential commitment, that is, that their terms have existential import. This would save all the inferences which we are forced to abandon by taking the hypothetical viewpoint. But such a tack raises certain problems. In the first place, it would be hard to defend this approach for such statements as "All infractions will be penalized" or "All bodies freely falling near the earth fall at 32 feet per second squared." We would want to say that "All infractions will be penalized" is true even if there were no infractions and that the Galilean law is true even though there are no free-falling bodies. Secondly, making such a blanket assumption leads to logical difficulties. Take, for example, this (by now classic) true statement: "No mathematician has squared the circle," or "No mathematician is a circle-squarer," which by simple conversion entails "No circle-squarer is a mathematician." This in turn entails, by obversion, "All circle-squarers are non-mathematicians." Though the difficulty is already quite apparent, this in turn entails, by conversion *per accidens,* "Some nonmathematician is a circle-squarer." This however is patently false, since it is logically impossible for anyone to square a circle![13] Here the difficulty arises because the term "circle-squarer" is not true of anything and we cannot give it existential import without generating problems. What then are we to do?

We might make the following distinction: *some* sentences in their normal use *presuppose* existence before they can be said to be *either true or false.* That is, some *sentences* become statements only if we presuppose existence of the objects represented by their terms. Let us illustrate this. The sentence "All John's children are asleep" could be *used* on certain occasions to make a statement, and those occasions *presuppose* that John has children. If John has no children, and someone says, "All John's children are asleep," we would justifiably be puzzled because the sentence simply does not *apply.* We might think: How could they be either asleep or not asleep; John has no children. The sentence has meaning, but in this context it is not appropriate and hence neither true nor false. The ordinary use of "true" and "false" might allow that the statement in question is false. But even then, notice that its "falsity" is of a highly peculiar

---

[12] The line of argument which follows was advanced by P. F. Strawson in his *Introduction to Logical Theory* (London: Methuen, 1952), pp. 173–194. Alterations have been made of his point of view.

   Whether or not Strawson's approach should be adopted in *formal* systems is not the point of concern here. Nor is it being maintained that this approach solves certain perplexing problems in logical theory. We are interested only in rehabilitating traditional logic as a consistent and practical method of evaluating arguments. To be sure, for more philosophically inclined readers, the problem is worth pursuing in all of its ramifications.

[13] This problem is not to be confused with the one involving distribution and obversion discussed in Chapter 7. In that case the predicate term was undistributed, but we assumed existential import (it was true of something). In that case obversion with conversion led to the undistributed predicate being distributed, which commits the fallacy of illicit process.

sort. In normal uses, to say that the statement is false would imply that some of them, at least, are awake. But obviously this presupposes that John has children.

Notice that the presupposition of John's having children does not make the sentence true; nor does it make it false. Rather it is a *necessary* condition for its being a statement. This device preserves the ordinary sense of "all" in the sentence in question and at the same time is effective in preserving the inferences eliminated by the hypothetical view. The four traditional categorical forms may each be interpreted as sentences of this sort. We may imagine each use of the four forms to be preceded by the qualifying phrase, "Assuming that the sentence formed is either true or false, then . . . ." In this view, certain "all" and "no" sentences will *not* be statements (either true or false) *unless* we presuppose existence; others will not need such a presupposition; they can be understood as true hypotheticals. Unfortunately, this means that there is no way on *formal* grounds to decide whether or not statements of the form "All *S* is *P*" and "No *S* is *P*" have existential import. Some statements of universal form *do* carry existential commitment and some do not. The decision must be made by considering the particular statement in its particular context. This, to be sure, is an undesirable feature of our analysis, and is, without doubt, one of the reasons why formal logicians have preferred to assume that an existential commitment is never made in universal propositions. On the other hand, we are here primarily concerned with deductions in the context of reasoning, argument, and problem-solving as they occur in ordinary life and language. Thus, we must be aware of the fact that on this issue, context does make a difference.

In order to handle the existential commitment in our Venn diagrams, we shall simply need to add an asterisk to the two universal forms. Here are the diagrams for them *with* existential import:

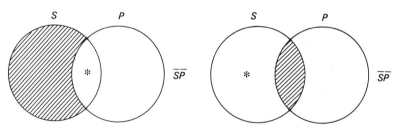

A: All *S*'s are *P*'s *and* there are *S*'s.   E: No *S*'s are *P*'s *and* there are *S*'s.

EXERCISES

A Represent each of the following with Venn diagrams. Assume that the universally quantified statements are true hypotheticals and hence make no existential commitment. (It is convenient to use the first letter of each term instead of *S* and *P*.)

   1 All visitors will be welcomed.
   2 No mathematician has squared the circle.
   3 There are irascible landlords.

4 At least one student did not fail.

5 Sugar is always water-soluble.

B Represent each of the following with Venn diagrams. Assume that the universally quantified statements presuppose existence.

6 All of Harry's uncles are wealthy.

7 None of the bait in this can is fresh.

8 Only money is needed.

9 Many houses are not needed.

10 There were no cowardly Spartans.

Some Ways to Determine Validity:
(3) Venn Diagrams

Venn diagrams afford a quick and easy method for testing the validity of syllogisms. Since a syllogism contains three terms totally, we will need three overlapping circles. Any two circles will adequately represent one statement. But since the circles overlap, we can handle the three statements of any syllogism. The diagram looks like this:

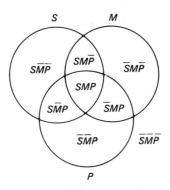

Each section of the diagram can be used to represent possible objects. For example, there are those possible objects which are SMP, $S\overline{M}\overline{P}$, and $SM\overline{P}$. When we include those possible objects which are neither S, nor M, nor P (that is, those objects falling *outside* the three circles), then there are eight total combinations.

In testing for validity, we diagram *only* the premises. We then see if in so doing we have automatically diagramed the conclusion. The reason for this displays an important feature of *all* valid arguments. If by diagraming only the premises, we *also* diagram the conclusion, then that proves that the conclusion is *entailed* by the premises. That is, the "information" contained in the premises also "contains" the conclusion. The point is that in all valid arguments (deductions) the conclusion can assert nothing that has not been *implicitly* asserted by the premises. Indeed, that is what we mean when we say that the premises *necessarily imply* (entail) the conclusion. Let us see how this works. Consider the argument:

No *M* is *P*.
Some *S* is *M*.
___
Some *S* is not *P*.

Assume that the universal has no existential import. We first diagram the universal premise. We shall always diagram the universal premise first, since that premise will tell us what possible objects are ruled out. In this case, the universal is made up of the *M* and *P* circles. Thus,

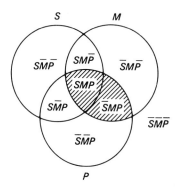

We then diagram the particular premise, which is made up of the *S* and *M* circles. Notice that the *SMP* area has been ruled out by the major premise. Hence the * can *only* go in the *SMP̄* area.

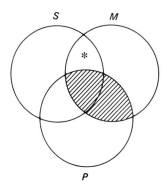

But the conclusion, "Some *S* is not *P*," has automatically been diagramed, for we find an *S* which is not a *P*. Hence, the argument is valid.
Consider next an invalid argument:

Some *P* is *M*.
All *S* is *M*.
___
Some *S* is *P*.

Again, we assume that the universal premise has no existential import and we diagram it first. (In this case, it is the minor premise.) We get:

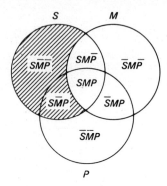

This tells us that there can be no S's which are not M's. However, it leaves open the question of whether or not there are any S's, and it leaves open the question of whether if there are S's, they are P's or not P's. That is, the $SM\overline{P}$ and the SMP areas are *both* blank. We next diagram the particular premise. This premise says that there is at least one P which is an M. But where do we put the asterisk? It could go in either the $\overline{S}MP$ area or the SMP area. Since we lack sufficient information, we put it on the line bordering the two possible areas. Thus:

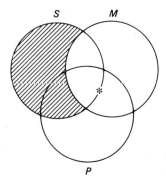

But in this case the conclusion, namely that there is at least one S which is a P, is *not* unequivocally diagramed, for the P in question *could* be an S or it might *not* be an S. Hence the premises do *not* entail the conclusion; and the argument is invalid.

Consider, finally, the argument:

All M is P.
All S is M.
_____
Some S is P.

Since we have given only the form of the argument, we cannot say for sure whether or not the two universal premises have existential import. Let us assume that they do not. We then diagram them:

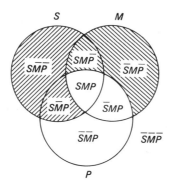

But the conclusion asserts that there is at least one *S* which is *P*, and this does carry existential import. However, since the diagram reveals no asterisk, the argument is invalid.

With the same argument, let us now assume that the universal premises do have existential import. Again, the major premise indicated that we shade out *MP̄* (which includes *SMP̄* and *S̄MP̄*), indicating that there can be no *S*'s which are not *P*'s; but in addition, we must put an asterisk in the *M* areas. However, it is not clear whether the asterisk should be put in the *SMP* area or in the *S̄MP* area. As before, let us tentatively put the asterisk on the line bordering the two possible areas.

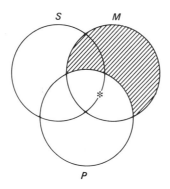

It may be that its location in the *P* area will be irrelevant or that the minor will rule out one or another of the possibilities. We then diagram the minor. This premise, "All *S* is *M*," rules out the possibility of there being any *S*'s which are not *M*'s, so *SM̄* is shaded in.

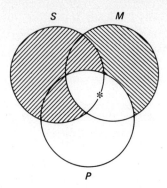

But the minor *also* has existential import (by assumption); hence it also asserts that there are S's. So we must put another asterisk on the diagram. Since the major premise rules out the $SM\bar{P}$ area, we must put it in the SMP area.

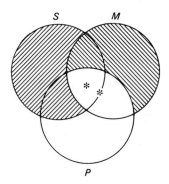

Now, however, the premises *do* entail the conclusion, namely that there is at least one S which is a P. Hence, assuming existential import for the universals, the argument is valid. (Notice that in this case, we required that only the minor carry existential import for the S term.)

In each of the valid arguments exhibited, we needed to diagram both premises before we could be sure that the conclusion followed. This means that the premises *when taken together* entailed the conclusion. In the last example the major premise alone did not entail the conclusion since the asterisk could have been in the S area, in which case it would not be true that there was at least one S which was a P. Similarly, the minor premise alone did not entail the conclusion, since without the other premise, the asterisk could have been in the $\bar{P}$ area.

EXERCISES

A Use Venn diagrams to test for validity of each of the following. Assume that the universal statements lack existential import.

1 All bouzouki players drink ouzo and ouzo drinkers are invariably diabetics. Hence, bouzouki players are diabetics.
2 The yellow-bellied sapsucker is a bird and it is a seedeater; so, some birds are seedeaters.
3 Every object freely falling near the earth falls at 32 feet per second squared. Every object which falls at 32 feet per second squared falls 16 feet in 1 second. Therefore, any object which free falls near the earth for 1 second falls 16 feet.
4 Every object falling near the earth falls at 32 feet per second squared, but there are no objects falling near the earth which are in free fall. Hence, no object falling at 32 feet per second squared is in free fall.
5 Gases expand when heated; oxygen is gas; so some oxygen expands when heated.

B Provide Venn diagram proofs for the exercises on p. 163 above.

Nonstandard-Form Syllogisms and Singular Statements

We noted earlier that we often encounter syllogisms which are not in standard form. In ordinary language the conclusion is sometimes stated first and sometimes the minor premise is stated first. If we have three and only three terms, this arrangement causes no trouble since we can always rearrange the statements and put them into standard form; if we choose, we can attack them directly. But sometimes, it is not even clear that we have three and only three terms. For example,

> Not all strangers are welcome in the Ozarks, because revenue agents are never received with open arms by mountain people; and occasionally, a stranger in the Ozarks works for the government agency which collects taxes from distillers.

This is quite clearly an argument. Moreover, the conclusion is "Not all strangers are welcome in the Ozarks." But it appears that we have more than three terms. By judicious translation, however, we can restate this argument as a categorical syllogism with just three terms. We begin with the conclusion. "Not all strangers are welcome in the Ozarks" becomes "Some strangers are not welcome in the Ozarks."

The second statement, "Revenue agents are never received with open arms by mountain people," might become, "All revenue agents are unwelcome by mountain people"; that is, if we don't receive someone cordially, we may say that they are not welcome. And since we know that the people of the Ozarks live in the mountains, we can make this "unwelcome in the Ozarks." Now, we can rid ourselves of the complement "unwelcome" by obverting, so that the statement becomes "No revenue agents are welcome in the Ozarks."

The last statement, "Occasionally, a stranger in the Ozarks works for the government agency which collects taxes from distillers," apparently needs much reworking. The "occasionally" looks like a time parameter, but the sense of it seems to be, "Some strangers in the Ozarks . . . ." Since we know what a revenue agent does, we are entitled to identify "works for the government agency which collects taxes from distillers" with the term "revenue agent." This statement then becomes "Some strangers are revenue agents." We now can put the argument into standard form:

No revenue agents are welcome in the Ozarks.
Some strangers (in the Ozarks) are revenue agents.

Some strangers (in the Ozarks) are not welcome in
   the Ozarks.

Singular Terms Frequently we encounter arguments of this sort:

No presidents of the United States were Mormons;
Lyndon Johnson was a President, so he was not a Mormon.

The minor premise, "Lyndon Johnson was President," and the conclusion, "He was not a Mormon," are what are called **singular statements.** How are we to treat statements of this sort? In traditional logic, singular statements are treated as *universals, either affirmative or negative.* Thus we would say that the statement "Lyndon Johnson was President" is an **A**-form categorical, and "He was not a Mormon" is an **E**-form categorical. This can be defended in the following way: "Lyndon Johnson was President" becomes "Every object identical to Lyndon Johnson is some President." This is awkward, to be sure, but it logically captures the force of the original and is comparable to any **A** statement, with the exception that there is only one object identical to Lyndon Johnson, namely, Lyndon Johnson himself. Similarly (eliminating the pronoun), "Lyndon Johnson was not a Mormon" becomes "Every object identical to Lyndon Johnson is distinct from every Mormon." Since singular statements refer to individuals, they will be treated as having existential import.

EXERCISES

A Put the following into standard form and check for validity. Use both rules and Venn diagrams. Make decisions for yourself as to whether the universals carry existential import. For syllogisms with two universal premises which *lack* existential import, remember that a fifth rule must be added to our list of four.

   1 It should be evident that not all unwise policies are unjust to all the parties who may be affected by them. This feature, to be sure, is not something we should be especially ready to congratulate ourselves upon. On the other hand, it must be conceded that no just policy — confining ourselves to those persons who are affected by such policies — fails to be in the best interest of all. At least this much, then, seems clear: There are policies which are in the best interests of all and are at the same time wise.

2 The falsity of the bizarre thesis that there are no material objects may be amply demonstrated by the following two considerations: First, if something existed before there were sentient beings, then it was not nonmaterial; second, the best geological evidence well supports the claim that there were objects which did exist long before sentient creatures made an appearance.

3 Of course, social problems are complex, but it could hardly be denied that many complex problems may be understood. For example, molecules are complex and today we know a great deal about them. Thus social problems, like molecules and other complex phenomena, may be brought within the province of intelligibility.

4 There is not one member of the entire United States Senate who would quarrel with the right of independent nations to seek their own destiny. Yet not all the members of that august body agree with our present foreign policy. Why is this so? What can the reason be? The answer to that I will leave to you. But one thing certainly follows: it is that some of those who agree with our present foreign policy are not among those who quarrel with the right of independent nations.

5 Campus leaders always have decent grades; otherwise they wouldn't be students long enough to be leaders. Indeed, they generally work hard, and are socially conscious and energetic. Nonetheless, all the rabble-rousers, demagogues, and leftist agitators on campuses become campus leaders. Hence, there are students with decent grades who are rabble-rousers and the like.

B Each of the following arguments contain singular statements. Check for validity. Use any method.

6 Only students are eligible. Harry is a student; therefore he is eligible.

7 There are no popular jazz groups. The Oscar Peterson trio is a jazz group; hence, it is not popular.

8 If a group plays rock-and-roll, then it is loved by everyone. Herman's Hermits are loved by everyone; hence they play rock-and-roll.

9 If a musician wants to eat, then he doesn't play classical music; Van Cliburn is a musician who wants to eat; therefore, he doesn't play classical music.

10 No composer lacks musical talent. Harry Truman was not a composer; thus, he lacked musical talent.

Enthymemes

Just as we cannot always readily identify the various terms of a syllogism expressed in everyday language, so can we not always readily identify its three statements. For, more often than not, in everyday discourse syllogisms are expressed elliptically; that is, certain statements which are taken for granted are not even expressed. A syllogism with a suppressed statement, whether it be one of the premises or the conclusion, is called an *enthymeme*. If the major premise is suppressed, the enthymeme is called *first order;* if the minor premise is suppressed, the enthymeme is called *second order;* if the conclusion is suppressed, the enthymeme is called *third order.* For example, consider this argument:

> Freshmen can't be expected to know their way
> around—after all, they haven't been on campus long.

Here, the conclusion, "Freshmen can't be expected to know their way around," is supported by only one premise. But presumably a premise is suppressed. Filling in suppressed premises, however, is sometimes a risky business, for exactly how the suppressed premise should be put is not obvious. Consider this version: (1) "All people who have been on campus a long time are expected to know their way around." This seems plausible; but if this were the suppressed premise, the argument would be *invalid.* Consider it:

> All (people who have been on campus a long time)
>   are (expected to know their way around).
> No (freshman) is (a person who has been on
>   campus a long time).
> _____
> No (freshman) is (a person who is expected to
>   know his or her way around).

This argument is of the form **AEE**-1, which is invalid because it breaks Rule 2; the predicate term, "people who are expected to know their way around," is undistributed in the premise and distributed in the conclusion.

But perhaps (1) was not the suppressed premise. Perhaps what was intended is this: (2) "People who haven't been on campus a long time are not expected to know their way around." (2) is *not* equivalent to (1) but it *is* equivalent to (3): "All people who are expected to know their way around are people who have been on campus a long time." Statement (3) is in fact the *contrapositive* of (2). If we take (3) as the suppressed premise, the argument is valid (since reversing the order of the terms distributes the term "people who are expected to know their way around"). That is, the form becomes **AEE**-2, which is valid.

As we have already noticed several times, sometimes what we are saying is not altogether clear. In the arguments of everyday life, when enthymemes are offered, try to determine precisely the nature of the suppressed premise, for, as we have seen, this premise is significant for evaluating the argument. Indeed, for almost *any* enthymeme, one can always find a premise which makes the argument valid, but the problem is, was this the premise intended?

EXERCISES

For each of the following enthymemes, supply the premise or the conclusion which makes the argument valid:

1. New Hercules cleaner is stronger than dirt; that is why it is so effective in your wash.
2. The policy is effective; it does what it sets out to do.
3. Since blunders are forgivable, murder also is.
4. Americans, it is widely suspected, are always in a hurry without knowing where they are going. It must be because they have fast cars.
5. We must defend the institution of property. No freedom is possible without it.
6. Where there is garlic in the air, there are no werewolves; I see no werewolves, hence?
7. Tautaise is a good swimmer, so she must be Hawaiian.
8. Linguine is fattening, since macaroni always is.
9. Despite popular opinion, or common prejudice, apple pie does not make you sterile. Indeed, while cream pies might, no fruit pie makes you sterile.
10. Raw fish is nourishing; it has protein.

ADDENDUM A

THE CLASS CALCULUS AND THE LOGIC OF SETS

So-called "modern logic" has had a continuous development from the early nineteenth century. In 1847, the mathematician George Boole made a significant contribution with his "algebra," which was the basis for this development. Work by W. S. Jevons, Venn, C. S. Peirce, and E. Schroeder brought the "algebra of classes" to its present form. We shall briefly note some of its features and show how the analysis in the text may be interpreted as Boolean algebra.

Instead of the capital letters F, G, etc., representing terms, we will use small letters a, b, etc., to represent classes taken in extension. Thus, while previously the term "man" was said to be true of men, we will think of it as the class name for the *class of men*. Such a class can then be symbolized by a. $a = b$ will mean that a and b are classes composed of identically the same members; that is, the denotations of the expressions a and b are identical. $a \times b$, or more briefly, ab, will represent what is common to a and to b. Thus if a is interpreted as the class of men and b as the class of Greeks, then ab represents the class of Greek men. ab is the class of things which are both a and b. ab may also be written as $a \cap b$, where $\cap$ is the symbol for the *intersection* of classes.

O represents the null class, or the class of no members, and 1 can then be defined as the class of all things which are not members of the null class. The numeral 1 therefore represents the *universe of discourse* or the class which contains every entity in the system. Finally, for any class a, $-a$, or equivalently $\bar{a}$, is the complement of the class named a. It is the class of all things which are not members of a. With this symbolism, each of the four categoricals are easily expressed:

All a is b	becomes	$a\bar{b} = O$, or the class $a\bar{b}$ is empty.
No a is b	becomes	$ab = O$, or the class ab is empty.
Some a is b	becomes	$ab \neq O$, or the class ab is not empty.
Some a is not b	becomes	$a\bar{b} \neq O$, or the class $a\bar{b}$ is not empty.

This interpretation suits the Venn diagrams perfectly. The circles represent classes in extension. The **A** and **E** forms are true hypotheticals since they do not affirm the existence of members of classes. The **I** and **O** forms do affirm existence by explicitly noting that the class is not empty, or has members. On the assumption of the hypothetical point of view, all the valid inferences previously discussed hold when we construe the term "variables" as "variables for class names." For example, "All Greeks are men" is now understood to mean that the class of those things which are both Greeks and non-men is empty. Thus while its obverse, "No Greeks are non-men," evidently is entailed, the converse by limitation is not.

However, there would be little point to this interpretation of classical logic if that is all that could be done with the class logic. Indeed, by means of suitable definitions, the analysis so far generated may easily be enlarged. Thus $a + b$, to be read as "the class a or the class b or both," may be introduced by definition. $a + b$ is defined as $-(\bar{a}\bar{b})$. That is, the class of those entities which are either a or b or both is identical to the complement of the class of those things which are neither a nor b. For example, consider the class of entities which are either men or animals or both. If a represents the class of men and b the class of animals, then $\bar{a}\bar{b}$ represents the class of non-men, non-animals. $\bar{a}\bar{b}$ therefore contains chairs, pencils, trees, etc.; it does *not* contain Socrates, since he is a man (and animal); nor does it contain Moby Dick, since he is an animal. Hence, if anything is *not* a non-man, non-animal, it must be either a man or an animal or both. $a + b$ may also be symbolized as $a \cup b$, where $\cup$ is the symbol for the *union* of classes.

Suppose now that we have the formula $a + b = O$. This states that there is nothing which is either an a or a b. On a Venn diagram:

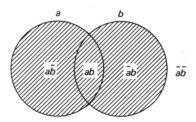

Similarly, $ab + \bar{a}b = 1$ asserts that if there is anything at all, it is either ab or $\bar{a}$. But that is tantamount to saying that $\bar{b} = O$.

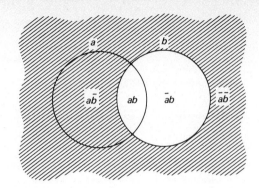

Notice that the areas outside the circles must also be shaded out. If there are no members of b, there can be no members of $a\bar{b}$ or $\bar{a}\bar{b}$ either.

Finally, $a \subset b$, to be read as "a is included in b," may be introduced by definition. "$a \subset b$ if and only if $ab = a$." Since $ab = a$ asserts that the class ab is identical in membership to the class named by a, anything which is an a must also be a b, though not conversely. Hence, a is included in b. **A**-form categoricals, for example, "All Frenchmen are Europeans," may be understood as asserting that the class of Frenchmen is included in the class of Europeans.

Given these interpretations and the new notation, a wide variety of relations may be stated. (In an axiomatic development of the calculus some of these would appear as axioms and the remainder could be deduced as theorems.)

1 $a \times a = a$, or $a \cap a = a$
2 $a \times b = b \times a$ or $a \cap b = b \cap a$
   $\times$ is commutative.
3 $a + b = b + a$ or $a \cup b = b \cup a$
   $+$ is commutative.
4 $a \times (b \times c) = (\mathbf{a} \times b) \times c$ or $\mathbf{a} \cap (b \cap c) = (a \cap b) \cap c$
   $\times$ is associative. (A corresponding law shows that $+$ is also associative.)
5 $a + O = a$ or $a \cup O = a$
6 $a \times O = O$ or $a \cap O = O$
   That is, the null class is included in every class.
7 $a + (b \times c) = (a + b) \times (a + c)$
   or
   $a \cap (b \cup c) = (a \cup b) \cap (a \cup c)$
   $+$ is distributable through $\times$.
8 $a + \bar{a} = 1$ or $a \cup \bar{a} = 1$
   The union of a class with its complement is identical to the universe.
9 $a \times \bar{a} = O$, or $a \cap \bar{a} = O$
10 $-(a + b) = \bar{a}\bar{b}$ or $-(a \cup b) = \bar{a} \cap \bar{b}$
11 $-(a \times b) = \bar{a} + \bar{b}$ or $-(a \cap b) = \bar{a} \cup \bar{b}$
12 $a = b$ is equivalent to the pair, $a \subset b$ and $b \subset a$.
13 $a \subset b$ is equivalent to $\bar{b} \subset \bar{a}$.
14 If $a \subset b$ and $b \subset c$, then $a \subset c$.

That is, $\subset$ is transitive. Relation 14 is called the *principle of the syllogism*.

15 $(ab) \subset (a + b)$ or $(a \cap b) \subset (a \cup b)$
The class ab is included in the class of a or b.

Some of these undoubtedly look familiar. Indeed, the close relation between the class calculus and the statement calculus may be seen. The letters a, b, etc., may be interpreted as statement variables. If we then add the principle: "For any element a, either $a = O$ or $a = 1$," we have the logic of truth functions. Addition of this principle has the effect of giving any element two values, either O or 1. But O can be read as false and 1 as true. Hence, for example, $a + b = -(\bar{a}\bar{b})$ becomes the equivalence $(p \vee q) \equiv -(\bar{p}\bar{q})$. And since $a \subset b$ asserts that $ab = a$, $a\bar{b}$ must be empty, or $a\bar{b} = O$. But $a\bar{b} = O$ now means that it is false that $a\bar{b}$. Hence, $a \subset b = -(a\bar{b})$ corresponds to the equivalence $(p \supset q) \equiv -(p\bar{q})$. By means of this interpretation, every tautology of the statement calculus will have a corresponding law in the logic of classes. For example, Identities 10 and 11 above correspond to DeMorgan's theorems in the statement calculus.

Certain odd syllogistic arguments may be formalized in our new notation and checked by Venn diagram. For example:

All doctors are either dedicated or rich.
Some doctors are not rich.
_____
Some dedicated people are not rich.

Reading a as the class of doctors, b as the class of dedicated people, and c as the class of rich people, we have:

$$a - (b + c) = O$$
$$a\bar{c} \qquad \neq O$$
$$\overline{b\bar{c} \qquad \neq O}$$

"All doctors are either dedicated or rich" asserts that the class composed of non-rich, non-dedicated doctors is empty. That is, by Identity 10, $a - (b + c) = a\bar{b}\bar{c}$. Hence $a\bar{b}\bar{c}$ is empty. This may be directly diagramed:

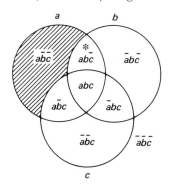

The minor premise asserts that the $a\bar{c}$ class is not empty, so an asterisk (*) is entered in it. The conclusion may then be read off.

Consider next this argument:

Everything is mind or matter.
Bodies are not minds.
_____

Bodies are material.

The major premise asserts that whatever is in the universe is either in the class of minds, represented by b, or in the class of material things, represented by a. Hence we have $a + b = 1$. But this is equivalent to asserting $-(a+b) = O$. That is, since $1 = -O$ by definition $[a + b = 1] = [-(a + b) = O]$. But again, since by 10 above, $-(a + b)$ is identical to $\bar{a}\bar{b}$, we know that there are no members of $\bar{a}\bar{b}$. We put this directly on the Venn diagram:

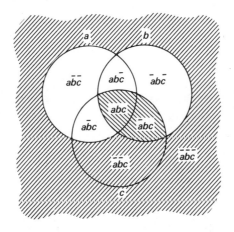

Notice that *everything* outside the a and b circles is shaded out. If there are no members of $\bar{a}\bar{b}$, there are no members of $\bar{a}\bar{b}c$ or of $\bar{a}\bar{b}\bar{c}$! The minor is then diagramed, it being an **E**-form statement. The conclusion is then read off.

From here one may also exhibit some elementary notions in the logic of sets.

We can represent a set with double braces; thus,

{1,2,3}

is the set comprised of the numbers 1, 2, and 3.

Sets may also be defined by properties; thus,

{x|Fx}

may be taken to mean "the set of x's (where x represents any sort of object) such that Fx, where F represents some property, e.g., being a natural number, or a rational man, etc." F thus functions exactly as do terms in traditional logic.

Sets may also be defined in terms of their membership, but for this we need a new symbol. We introduce ϵ (Greek letter epsilon) as an abbreviation for the English "is a member of" or "belongs to." We may then write

$$\{x|x \ \epsilon \ a\}$$

and read this as "the set of all x's such that $x \ \epsilon \ a$," or, more fully, "the set of all x's such that x is a member of a." But of course this set is the set a (or, in our previous formulation, the class a).

Each of the formulas on the preceding pages may be defined in terms of our new notation. Thus,

$$a \cap b = \{x|x \ \epsilon \ a \text{ and } x \ \epsilon \ b\}$$

The intersection of the classes a and b is the set of all x's such that x is a member of a and x is a member of b. And,

$$a \cup b = \{x|x \ \epsilon \ a \text{ or } x \ \epsilon \ b\}$$

The union of the classes (sets) a and b is the set of all x's such that x is a member of a or x is a member of b. And,

$$a \subset b = \{x| \text{ if } x \ \epsilon \ a \text{ then } x \ \epsilon \ b\}$$

and finally,

$$a = b = \{x|x \ \epsilon \ a \text{ if and only if } x \ \epsilon \ b\}$$

NINE

QUANTIFICATION: I

The task of logic is to serve as a spiritual hygiene, cautioning men against the disease of intellectual confusion.

Rudolf Carnap

Strictly speaking, the treatment of traditional logic constituted an "introduction" to quantification, for it was there that we first employed "quantifiers" in the analysis of argument. Modern symbolic logic, however, offers a far more comprehensive theory of quantification, and it is this to which we shall turn our attention. Analogous to the designation *statement calculus* (discussed in Chapters 5 and 6), the name frequently given to this mode of analysis is the *predicate calculus*. Its feature is the way it *combines* the term or "predicate" analysis of traditional logic with the statement analysis of the logic of truth functions. What results is a powerful instrument of analysis which can handle truth-functional arguments, categorical syllogisms, and much else besides. Almost everything that has been discussed thus far will be brought into use in the present discussion. But first we shall need some new symbolism.

The Existential Quantifier

As before, we shall have two sorts of quantifiers, corresponding to the universal and particular quantifiers of classical logic. We introduce first the **existential quantifier** and its symbol ($\exists$ x). ($\exists$ x) corresponds to the words "there is some x such that . . . ." Let us use our new symbol in a statement: (∃ x)(x is a dance and x is Greek). This says, "There is something x such that x is a dance and x is Greek," or, eliminating the x, "There is something such that it is a dance and it is Greek." In this rendering, the variable x has been replaced by the equally indefinite "it." Indeed, the two serve the same purpose: they are indefinite references. Other English versions of (∃ x)(x is a dance and x is Greek) are appropriate. For example:

1 Some dances are Greek. (This is, of course, our old friend the **I** form.)
There are dances which are Greek.
There are Greek dances.
Something is a Greek dance.
Greek dances exist.

Notice that (∃ x) does correspond to "some" as we used it before. "Some" asserts existence; so does (∃ x). But our new symbolism is not simply another way to say old things, for, as we shall see, it will allow us to say many new things as well. Let us reexamine the statement "(∃ x)(x is a dance and x is Greek)." After the quantifier, we find the sentence "x is a dance and x is Greek." This sentence and ones like it will be called **open sentences.** The name is descriptive: they are open because x is indefinite. x is exactly like "it" when we do not know to what "it" refers. Open sentences are *not* statements, since they cannot be said to be either true or false. We cannot say that "x is a dance" is true or that it is false, because we do not know what, if anything, x refers to. Compare "it is a dance" when we do not know to what "it" refers.

But like *terms*, open sentences are *true of* or *false of* various things. The open sentence "x is a dance" is true of all and only dances; it is false of elephants, tables, Socrates, etc.[1] In this respect the open sentence is analogous to the term "dance." Earlier, we gave considerable latitude to terms; we shall, in the same way, give considerable latitude to open sentences. For example, "The man who gave x a watch was x's best friend" is an open sentence. It is true of something (presumably some person) who was given a watch by his best friend, and it is not true of an elephant, a table, or the moon.

Open sentences are comparable to terms in yet another important respect, namely, they may become part of a quantified statement. As the terms "dance" and "Greek" enter into the *quantified statement* "Some dances are Greek," so too do the open sentences "x is a dance" and "x is Greek" enter the quantified statement "(∃ x)(x is a dance and x is Greek)." Existentially quantified sentences *are* statements, for they assert that "there is something such that . . . ," and such claims are either true or false.

By themselves, open sentences, like terms, cannot be used to make statements, but when open sentences are quantified, they *always* make a statement. Hence, the open sentence

---

[1] More technically, for some values of the variable x, the statement resulting from the substitution in the open sentence is true; for other substitutions it is false.

1 x swims

becomes the statement.

2 (∃ x)(x swims)

which asserts that something swims.

Notice that it does not say what swims, but that does not matter. Either something swims or nothing swims; hence "(∃ x)(x swims)" is either true or false and is a genuine statement. Sentence 2 is called the *existential quantification* of 1.

Open sentences contain **free variables,** while quantified statements do not. The x in "x is a dance" is a free variable since we are not sure of what, if anything, it names and since the sentence does not assert that there is anything which can be named by x. The x in "(∃ x)(x is a dance)," however, is *bound* by the quantifier. Accordingly, it is called a **bound variable.** The x still does not name anything in particular, but the whole statement *does* assert that there is something which could be named by x. Hence it is a statement.

The open sentence "x is a dance and x is Greek" is easily seen to be a *compound* of two open sentences with "and" conjoining them. Here we can use some of our old symbolism: the curl (~) for negation; the dot (·) for conjunction; the wedge (v) for alternation; the horseshoe (⊃) for "if . . . then"; and the triple bar (≡) for "if and only if." All of these connectives can be employed to construct open sentences and to compound quantified statements. Thus, each of the following are open sentences:

1 ~ (x is a whale)
2 x is foolish v x is wise
3 x flies ⊃ x has wings
4 x is a triangle ≡ x has three sides
5 ~ (x goes) ⊃ (x will be late · x will be punished)

By this means we can build up infinitely complex open sentences, each of which could be then made into statements by quantifying them.

Similarly, our connectives can be used to compound statements, as

1 (∃ x)(x is a dance) v (∃ x)(x is Greek)
2 (∃ x)(x is white · x is a whale) ⊃ (∃ x)(x is white)

Scope of the Quantifiers Up to this point we have used parentheses to mark off the quantifier and to group the open sentences. In all the quantified statements so far considered, we put a set of parentheses around the whole open sentence. This indicated that the *scope* of the quantifier extended to the end. But consider these two cases:

1 Something is square and is round.

2 Something is square and something is round.

Case 1 is patently false since nothing could be *both* round and square. But 2 is true. How can these two be distinguished with our notation? Thus:

1' (∃ x)(x is square and x is round)

2' (∃ x)(x is square) · (∃ x) · (x is round)

In 1' the *scope* of the quantifier extends to the end of the sentence. This has the effect of saying that there is something — the quantifier does this — and *that* something is square *and* round. Sentence 2', however, has the scope of the first quantifier stopped by the parentheses. The first quantifier of 2' says that there is something and *that* something is round. The second quantifier says that there is something and *that* something is square. Thus 2 does not claim that the something named by the first quantifier is the *same* something as that named by the second quantifier. In 1, however, it must be the same something.

Scope is important since we can easily change the meaning by failing to mark off the range of the quantifiers. For example:

1 (∃ x)(x is a dance) · (∃ x)(x is Greek)   *AND*

does not mean the same thing as

2 (∃ x)(x is a dance and x is Greek)   *BOTH*

Statement 1 means "There is something which is a dance *and* there is something which is Greek"; 2 means "There is something which is *both* a dance and is Greek."

The Universal Quantifier

We now introduce the other quantifier. It is called the **universal quantifier,** (x), and is read as "each thing x is such that . . . ." As before, this quantifier can be used to make statements out of open sentences. For example, "(x)(x has mass)" asserts each thing is such that it has mass, or "Everything has mass." (x) closely corresponds to the universal quantifier of traditional logic. This can be seen in this statement: (x)(x is whale ⊃ x is a mammal), which says, "Each thing x is such that if x is a whale, then x is a mammal," or, eliminating the x, "Each thing is such that if it is a whale, then it is a mammal," or, more briefly, "All whales are mammals." This is the familiar **A**-form statement.

Scope is again important.

1 Everything is possible and some things are difficult

becomes

(x)(x is possible) · (∃x)(x is difficult)

2 Everything is possible but difficult

becomes

(x)(x is possible · x is difficult)

Statement 1 asserts that everything is possible but allows that some things which are possible are *not* difficult. On the other hand, 2 says that everything is possible and everything is difficult.

Open Formulas and Closed Formulas

We need one more notational device, which may now be introduced. In the traditional analysis, the letters *S, M*, etc., stood in place of terms. In an analogous manner, we can use the formulas *Fx, Gx, Sx*, etc., to stand in place of *open sentences*. Thus, for example, *Fx* can be used to stand in place of "x is a whale," "x swims," "x has wings," or "The man who gave x a watch was x's best friend." Each of these open sentences may be thought of as *interpreting Fx*. They give it meaning. Thus the *statement formula* (x)(Fx ⊃ Gx) makes no factual claim. We must first interpret *Fx* and *Gx*. We do this by providing an open sentence. For example, *Fx* might be "x is a whale." *Gx* might be "x is a mammal." Now the statement formula (x)(Fx ⊃ Gx) becomes the statement "For each x, if x is a whale, then x is a mammal," or "All whales are mammals." This device will serve the *same* purpose which formalization did before. For now the formula (x)(Fx ⊃ Gx) is the *form of all* **A***-form statements*. By interpreting *Fx* and *Gx* in various ways, we can generate an infinite number of statements, each of which will share the same logical features.

Expressions like *Fx, Gx*, and *all truth-functional compounds of them* will be called *open formulas*. Thus, ~*Fx, Fx* ⊃ *Gx*, and ~(*Fx* v *Gx*) are open formulas. For each such formula, we can supply an open sentence which will interpret it. Thus ~*Fx* may be interpreted by any of the following open sentences:

1 ~(x is a whale)
2 ~(x swims)
3 ~(x has wings)
4 ~(the man who gave x a watch is x's best friend)

Fx ⊃ *Gx* may be interpreted by any of the following open sentences:

1 x is a whale ⊃ x is a mammal
2 x flies ⊃ x has wings
3 the man who gave x a watch is x's best friend ⊃ x is lucky

When we *quantify* an open sentence we get a statement; when we quantify an *open formula* we get a statement formula, or, to maintain the symmetry, a *closed formula*. Closed formulas, or statement formulas, are our main concern here, just as they were in previous chapters. The logic of truth functions allowed us to analyze the statement "If it rains, then it pours" as the statement formula *p* ⊃ *q*, where *p* and *q* stood for statements. Classical logic allowed us to analyze the statement "Whales are mammals" as the statement formula "All *S* are *P*," where *S* and *P* stood for terms. The present analysis allows us to analyze the statement "All politicians who are rich are youthful" as the statement formula (*x*)(*Fx* · *Gx* ⊃ *Hx*), where *Fx*, *Gx*, and *Hx* stand for open sentences.

The Four Categorical Forms

To see how this method of analysis works, let us put into form each of the four categoricals of traditional logic. As we have seen, "All *F* are *G*" becomes (*x*) (*Fx* ⊃ *Gx*). This makes explicit the hypothetical viewpoint of our earlier discussion, namely, that universal statements do not presuppose existence. For this formula does not say there are *x*'s which are *F*; it only says, *if* there are *x*'s which are *F*, *then* they are *G*. But the **I** form of statement, as we have seen, does assert existence. Thus, though there is a tendency for beginners to parallel the form of the **I** to the **A**, this is a mistake. "Some *F* are *G*" has no hypothetical features about it. It asserts (∃ *x*)(*Fx* · *Gx*), or "There is some *x* such that *x* is *both F and G*."

The **E** form of statement, "No *F* are *G*," is again interpreted as a hypothetical. It becomes (*x*)(*Fx* ⊃ ~*Gx*), which says, "For each *x*, if *x* is *F*, then *x* is *not* a *G*." The **O**, "Some *F* are not *G*," which does assert existence, becomes (∃ *x*)(*Fx* · ~*Gx*), or "There is an *x* such that *x* is *F* and *x* is *not G*."

EXERCISES

Render each of the following as *closed sentences* (open sentences which are quantified). Then express them as *closed formulas* by replacing the open sentences with open formulas.

Fx x is a whale

1 All aardvarks are callipygianous.
2 No reptiles are viviparous.
3 Some Hawaiians are swimmers.
4 Some elephants are not friendly.
5 Not all insects bite.
6 Every trapezoid is four-sided.
7 There are tiny football players.

8 There are no innocent coeds.

9 Everywhere he goes, I go.

10 Fish got to swim.

The Truth-Functional Character of Open Formulas

It is an interesting and useful feature of all open formulas that they can be treated as truth-functions. Thus, for example, $(Fx \supset Gx) \equiv (\sim Fx \vee Gx)$ is a tautology. Why this is so can best be seen by considering a simple case, that of $Fx \supset Fx$. The open formula Fx is not a statement form; hence, even if interpreted, it cannot be said to be either true or false. But, as we noted, it could be said to be true *of* or false *of* objects. Obviously, whether or not Fx is true of or false of (say) an elephant will depend upon what Fx is interpreted as. But the formula $Fx \supset Fx$ must come out true of *anything;* since for *any* object x, *regardless* of how Fx is interpreted, if Fx is intrepreted as true of it, then $Fx \supset Fx$ must be true by truth of the consequent. On the other hand, if x is selected so that Fx is false of it, then $Fx \supset Fx$ is *still* true of it by the *falsity* of the antecedent. By comparison, the formula $Fx \supset Gx$ is not a tautology, since it is easy to interpret Fx so that it is true of some object x and to interpret Gx so that it is false of that object. In general, if under all interpretations an open formula is true of everything, then it is a tautology. Similarly, if under all interpretations an open formula is false of everything, it is a contradiction. Indeed, all open formulas behave just like truth-functional formulas. This means that all the entailments and equivalences of Chapters 5 and 6 can be brought to bear upon open formulas, and this, as we shall see, is quite important.

More Complex Formulas   Our present method of analysis allows us to treat statements which are far more complex than the usual categorical forms. Indeed, having available the truth-functional connectives makes possible full formalization of statements like this: "Some rich uncles are not generous." This becomes, "($\exists$ x) [x is an uncle $\cdot$ x is rich $\cdot \sim$(x is generous)]," which in turn becomes ($\exists$ x) $(Fx \cdot Gx \cdot \sim Hx)$. As before, we may need parentheses and brackets, etc., to unambiguously group our sentences. For this purpose the same conventions which applied before can easily be adopted. To illustrate further, consider this example:

1   If anything is expensive and hard to find, then buying it is neither wise nor necessary

becomes:

2   (x)[(x is expensive $\cdot$ x is hard to find) $\supset \sim$(buying x is wise v buying x is necessary)]

or, finally,

3 $(x)[(Fx \cdot Gx) \supset \sim (Hx \text{ v } Ix)]$

This rendering has several equivalent formulations. If we use DeMorgan's theorem on the consequent, for example, we get

4 $(x)[(Fx \cdot Gx) \supset (\sim Hx \sim Ix)]$

The advantage of our new notation is obvious. In traditional logic, 1 could have been rendered as:

5 No expensive, hard-to-find things are wise necessary things.

But then this would have to be formalized as:

6 No S is P

and we would have lost the internal structure of the terms.

With our new notation, we should strive to reveal as much of the structure of the sentence as possible. This will allow us much greater clarity and deductive power.

EXERCISES

Each of the following statements are complex. Render each of them as closed sentences (open sentences which are quantified). Then express them as closed formulas. Make explicit as much of the structure as you can. (Several equivalent formulations are possible.)

1. All politicians are either rich or youthful.
2. Some delicious berries are poisonous.
3. There are no infants who are ugly, who are not loved, or who are pleasant.
4. A few garrulous poets are not dirty-minded.
5. Anything which makes Charlie happy is either food, drink, or sleep.
6. Spiders are horrible and snakes are disgusting.
7. Some spiders eat insects while all of them have eight legs.
8. Either all cows ruminate or most cowboys do.
9. A figure is a triangle if and only if it has three sides and lies in a plane.
10. Fuzzy teddy bears are fuzzy.
11. A pussy cat with bad manners and a mean disposition does not make a good pet.
12. Little boys who are either mean or inconsiderate are not loved by pussy cats.
13. There are some who love their pets but who don't care well for them.

14 Some angry lions are either neurotic or have notions of oppression.

15 If politicians are wise, then circles are squares.

Singular Sentences and Names

We shall employ the small English letters *a*, *b*, *c*, etc., as **names** for particular objects. Thus, just as the word "Socrates" names Socrates, the small letter *a* will be used to name some particular object. Indeed, for our purposes the letters *a*, *b*, etc., may be thought of as akin to proper names which unambiguously identify particular objects. Of course, ordinarily we don't name chairs, trees, etc., but our "names" could be used to name some particular chair. We then can construct sentences like *Fa*, *Fb*, *Gb*, etc. Let us call sentences of this sort **singular sentences.** Like any formula, singular sentences can be interpreted. *Fa*, for example, could be interpreted as "*a* is a chair," *Gb* as "*b* is mortal," etc. Since we are using the letters *a*, *b*, etc., to name particular objects, when we interpret singular sentences, we get **singular statements.** They are singular because the name refers to one and only one object; they are statements because they are either true or false. For example, in "*b* is mortal," since the symbol *b* purports to name some object, either that object is mortal or it is not; hence the statement is true or false. As "Socrates is a man" is a singular statement, so is "*b* is a man." Indeed, *either* statement could be formalized as *Fb*, or *Gb*, etc. In what follows we shall find several important uses for the notion of a singular sentence.

Some Important Logical Equivalences   The first use to which we can put singular sentences is in proving some important logical equivalences which employ quantifiers. Suppose that we limit the universe to a finite set of objects, designated *a*, *b*, *c*, . . . , *h*.[2] We then can expand the universal quantification $(x)Fx$ into a long conjunction; thus, $Fa \cdot Fb \cdot Fc \ldots Fh$. This is so because $(x)Fx$ says "Everything is an *F*"; but since *a*, *b*, . . . , *h* (by assumption) is everything, then $(x)Fx$ is tantamount to saying, "*a* is an *F*," and "*b* is an *F*," . . . , and "*h* is an *F*," which is compressed as $Fa \cdot Fb \ldots Fh$. *Fa*, etc., is called an *instance* of the universal formula $(x)Fx$. Similarly, the existential quantification $(\exists x)Fx$ becomes an alternation, $Fa \lor Fb \lor Fc \lor \ldots Fh$, for $(\exists x)Fx$ says "Something is an *F*." But, again, since *a*, *b*, *c*, . . . , *h* (by assumption) constitute everything, *either* "*a* is an *F*" *or* "*b* is an *F*" . . . *or* "*h* is an *F*."

Notice that if we wanted to limit our universe in the way we have done, we could eliminate the quantifiers and say everything in our expanded form as truth-functions. Thus, for example, in such a limited universe,

1 $(x)(Fx \supset Gx)$

---

[2] As throughout, where no confusion is likely, an italicized letter or formula is an abbreviation for its name.

is equivalent to

    2 $(Fa \supset Ga)(Fb \supset Gb)(Fc \supset Gc) \ldots (Fh \supset Gh)$

Also,

    3 $(\exists x)(Fx \cdot Gx)$

is equivalent to

    4 $(Fa \cdot Ga) \lor (Fb \cdot Gb) \lor (Fc \cdot Gc) \ldots \lor (Fh \cdot Gh)$

Though we can use the device just introduced to clarify many interesting features of our analysis, for most problems, unfortunately, we cannot list each of the objects in the universe. Indeed, for many problems the relevant universe comprises an infinite number of objects. Hence, the quantifiers will be useful, indeed indispensable, symbols.

Relation between (x) and ($\exists$ x)

There is an intimate relation between the universal quantifier (x) and the existential quantifier $(\exists x)$. $(\exists x)Fx$ says "There are F," or "F exists." Suppose that we deny this, thus: $\sim(\exists x)Fx$. This means, "It is not the case that there are F," or "There are no F," which is the same thing as saying that everything is non-F, or that each thing is such that it is not an F. Hence $\sim(\exists x)Fx$ is equivalent to "$(x)\sim Fx$." Or, more generally:

    1 $\sim(\exists x)\phi x \equiv (x)\sim\phi x$

The Greek letter ϕ here represents any open formula containing x. Thus, $\sim(\exists x), (Fx \supset Gx)$ is equivalent (by 1) to $(x)\sim(Fx \supset Gx)$.

Similarly, $\sim(x)Fx$ says "It is not the case that everything is F" or "not everything is F," or "There are x's which are not F." Hence $\sim(x)Fx$ is equivalent to $(\exists x)\sim Fx$. Or, more generally:

    2 $\sim(x)\phi x \equiv (\exists x)\sim\phi x$

By the same line of argument, we could eliminate the use of either the universal quantifier or the existential quantifier by defining one in terms of the other. Thus:

    3 $(x)\phi x \equiv \sim(\exists x)\sim\phi x$
    4 $(\exists x)\phi x \equiv \sim(x)\sim\phi x$

"Everything is an *F*" is equivalent to asserting that it is false that there is anything which is not an *F*. Similarly, to say, "There are *F*" is equivalent to asserting that it is false that each thing is not an *F*. Again, if we think of the universe as limited to a finite set of objects, these equivalences become applications of DeMorgan's laws.

Consider ~(∃ x)Fx and (x) ~ Fx. ~(∃ x)Fx becomes ~(Fa v Fb . . . v Fh), which by DeMorgan's law is equivalent to ~ Fa · ~ Fb . . . ~ Fh; (x) ~ Fx becomes ~ Fa · ~ Fb . . . ~ Fh.

However, we must be careful when using negation signs with quantifiers. While (∃ x) ~~Fx is equivalent to (∃ x)Fx by double negation, ~(∃ x) ~Fx is *not* equivalent to (∃ x)Fx. ~(∃ x) ~Fx says *everything* is *F*; (∃ x)Fx says that *something* is *F*. Similarly, we must distinguish ~(x)Fx from (x) ~Fx. ~(x)Fx asserts that *something* is not *F*; (x) ~Fx asserts that *everything* is not *F*. In general, the curl in *front* of a quantifier serves to deny the statement which follows it. Thus, ~(x)Fx is best thought of as ~[(x)Fx]. The expression within the bracket is first expanded; then truth-functions suffice. By contrast, a curl *after* the quantifier operates on the open formula which follows it.

EXERCISES

Assume a universe limited to the objects *a, b, . . . , h*. Expand the following quantified formulas to provide their equivalences. Thus, (x)(Fx v Gx) becomes (Fa v Ga)(Fb v Gb) . . . (Fh v Gh).

1 (x)(Fx ≡ Gx)	**2** (∃ x)(Fx · ~Gx)
3 ~(x)(Fx ⊃ Gx)	**4** (∃ x) ~(Fx ⊃ Gx)
5 (x) ~(~Fx · ~Gx)	**6** (x)[Fx ⊃ (Gx ≡ Hx)]
7 (∃ x)Fx · (x)Gx	**8** (∃ x)Fx v (∃ x)Gx
9 ~[(x)(Fx ⊃ Gx) · (∃ x)Fx]	**10** (x)(Fx ≡ Gx) · ~(∃ x)Fx

Proof of Invalidity

The apparatus so far generated has had the worthwhile purpose of forcing us to get clear about the logical features of quantified statements in English. But we can also use our analysis to produce some methods for checking the validity and invalidity of arguments which use quantifiers. In this section we reintroduce some methods for proving invalidity. In the next chapter we will offer a method for proving validity.

In the last chapter we employed a method called *refutation by logical analogy*. This method involved reducing an argument to its form and then finding interpretations of its terms which showed that the premises could be true and the conclusion false. If we could do this, we would prove an argument invalid. This same approach can be utilized with the statement formulas of the present discussion. However, instead of interpreting terms, we shall now interpret open formulas. As before, this method *does* require ingenuity and is not a proof of validity, since if we cannot find an interpretation in which the premises are true and the conclusion false, it *may* be that the argument is valid, but it *also* may be that we have not yet found the right interpretation. Consider this argument:

> Every conservative is either a Republican or a patriot; some patriots are Republicans who are misled; hence there are misled conservatives.

In closed sentences, this becomes

> $(x)[x$ is a conservative $\supset (x$ is a Republican v x is a patriot)]
> $(\exists x)(x$ is a patriot $\cdot$ x is a Republican $\cdot$ x is misled)
> _____
> $(\exists x)(x$ is a conservative $\cdot$ x is misled)

In closed formulas, it becomes

> $(x)[Cx \supset (Rx$ v $Px)]$
> $(\exists x)(Px \cdot Rx \cdot Mx)$
> _____
> $(\exists x)(Cx \cdot Mx)$

Can we interpret Cx, Rx, Px, and Mx so as to make the premises true and the conclusion false? If we read Cx as "x is round," Rx as "x has shape," Px as "x is a figure," and Mx as "x is square," and put these interpretations back into closed sentences, we have:

> $(x)[x$ is round $\supset (x$ has shape v x is figure)]
> $(\exists x)(x$ is a figure $\cdot$ x has shape $\cdot$ x is square)
> _____
> $(\exists x)(x$ is round $\cdot$ x is square)

Clearly the premises "If anything is round, then it has shape or is a figure" and "There are square figures with shape" are true. But the conclusion is patently false, "There are round squares!" Hence the form of the argument is invalid; and so is the original argument. This method can always be used to prove invalidity.

However, we may understand "interpret" in another sense. Instead of finding an open sentence for (say) Fx in the formula $(x)Fx$, we can restrict the universe to a finite set of objects and provide singular *sentences* as interpretations of the *closed* formula $(x)Fx$. Thus, if the universe had only one member, $(x)Fx$ would be equivalent to Fa. If it had two members, $(x)Fx$ would be equivalent to $Fa \cdot Fb$, and so on for any finite number. Now, since arguments using quantifiers are valid *if and only if* they are valid, no matter how many objects there are in the universe, we can prove an argument invalid if we can provide a universe with at least one member in which the premises of the argument are true and the conclusion false. For example:

> Communists and socialists are advocates of economic planning. Liberals

frequently advocate economic planning; hence some liberals are either communists or socialists.

In closed sentences this becomes:

(x)[(x is a communist or x is a socialist) ⊃ x advocates economic planning]
(∃ x)(x is a liberal · x advocates economic planning)
_____
(∃ x)[x is a liberal · (x is a communist v x is a socialist)]

which in turn becomes:

(x)[(Cx v Sx) ⊃ Ax]
(∃ x)(Lx · Ax)
_____
(∃ x)[Lx · (Cx v Sx)]

First notice especially the translation of the first premise. It does *not* say (x)[(Cx · Sx) ⊃ Ax], for this would mean "All communists *who are* socialists advocate economic planning."

The proof of invalidity is short. Assume the universe limited to one member. The argument then becomes:

(Ca v Sa) ⊃ Aa
La · Aa
_____
∴ La · (Ca v Sa)

But since Ca, Sa, La, etc., may be treated just as p, q, r, etc., we may use the methods of Chapter 5 to determine invalidity. Thus, by a shortened truth table, we have

[(Ca v Sa) ⊃ Aa] · (La · Aa) ⊃ La · (Ca v Sa)

But when Ca and Sa are interpreted as false and all the rest as true, the formula is not a tautology; hence the argument is invalid.

The difficulty with this method of disproof is that some invalid arguments may be valid in a one-member universe, or two, etc. Accordingly, if assuming one member does not prove invalidity, we must go on to try more members. If the argument is invalid, however, *some* definite universe can be provided which will prove invalidity.

Though we have finished with the preceding argument, let us see how it would have looked if we had assumed two members in the universe:

[(Ca v Sa) ⊃ Aa] · [(Cb v Sb) ⊃ Ab]
(La · Aa) v (Lb · Ab)
_____
∴ [La · (Ca v Sa)] v [Lb · (Cb v Sb)]

Remember, since the first premise was universally quantified, it expands as a *conjunction;* the second premise and the conclusion were existentially quantified, so they expanded as *alternations.* For highly involved forms of this sort, the shortened truth table is the most expeditious method of proof.

EXERCISES

A   Prove the invalidity of the following argument forms by assuming a finite universe, expanding, and using truth-functional methods. If convenient, use the quantifier equivalences of p. 195.

1   (x)(Fx ⊃ Gx)
    (x)(Fx ⊃ Hx)
    ∴ (x)(Gx ⊃ Hx)

2   (x)(Fx ⊃ ~Gx)
    (∃ x)(Fx · ~Hx)
    ∴ (∃ x)(Gx · ~Hx)

3   (∃ x)(Fx · Gx)
    (∃ x)(Gx · Hx)
    ∴ (∃ x)(Fx · Hx)

4   (x)[Fx ⊃ (Gx v Hx)]
    (∃ x)Gx
    ∴ (∃ x)Hx

5   (∃ x)(Fx ≡ Gx)
    (∃ x)Fx
    ∴ (∃ x) ~Gx

6   (x) ~(Fx ⊃ Gx)
    (x)Fx
    ∴ (∃ x)Gx

7   ~(∃ x)(Fx ⊃ ~Gx)
    (x)Fx
    ∴ (x) ~ Gx

8   (x)[Fx ⊃ (Gx · Hx)]
    (x)(Fx ⊃ Jx)
    ∴ (x)[(Gx · Hx) ⊃ Jx]

9   (x)(Fx v Gx)
    ~(∃ x)(Fx · ~Hx)
    ∴ ~(∃ x) ~Hx

10   ~(x) ~Fx
     (x)(Gx ⊃ Fx)
     ∴ (∃ x)Gx

B   Use either of the foregoing techniques to prove the following arguments invalid.

11   Everything which has carbohydrates and fats is unhealthful; hence everything which has either a carbohydrate or fat is unhealthful (Cx, Fx, Ux).

12   There are no folk singers who are impoverished musicians and there are folk singers who are not musicians; hence some folk singers are not impoverished (Fx, Ix, Mx).

13   Some obscure and confused thinkers are philosophers; every sincere and intelligent person is a philosopher; so, there are intelligent people who are confused (Ox, Cx, Px, Sx, Ix).

14   There are sincere and intelligent people who are not philosophers; so there are philosophers who are not intelligent (Sx, Ix, Px).

15   Birds do it; bees do it; everything which likes it does it; hence birds and bees like it.

TEN

QUANTIFICATION: II

*Of that which receives precise
formulation in mathematical logic, an
important part is already vaguely
present as a basic ingredient of daily
discourse.*

Willard V. O. Quine

In the preceding chapter we introduced the basic symbolism of quantification and considered several methods for proving the invalidity of arguments which use quantifiers. In this chapter we shall be concerned primarily with various methods for proving the validity of such arguments.

Proof of Validity

The method of proof for quantified formulas will utilize the equivalences listed on p. 195 above, the truth-functional rules of inference which were used in Chapter 6, and special quantification rules which need to be introduced. We will then be in a position to employ the method of deduction which was used in Chapter 6 for quantified formulas.

The Rule of Universal Instantiation   Earlier we employed the notion of an *instance*. We said that sentences like *Fa, Fb*, etc., were instances of the universally quantified formula (x)Fx.   Thus, if (x)Fx is true, then each of its instances is true. Similarly, if (x)(Fx ⊃ Gx) is interpreted as true, then *Fa ⊃ Ga* and *Fb ⊃ Gb* are true.   In general, *from any universally quantified formula we may infer any instance of it*.   This is the **rule of universal instantiation.**

Indeed, if as before we think of a, b, etc., as names of particular objects, the letters x, y, and z may be used as variables to represent *indeterminate objects*. Accordingly, we may count Fx or Fy also as an instance of (x)Fx. That is, if (x)Fx is true, i.e., if everything is F, then any indefinite object in the universe, x or y, must also be F. The rule of universal instantiation will be abbreviated as "**UI**" and may be stated in a more general form as follows:

> **UI**: (u)φu entails φi (where u represents any variable, x, y, etc., and i represents any individual symbol, either names, a, b, etc., or variables, x, y, etc.).

UI allows us to drop a universal quantifier, but in formulating this rule, we assume that when the universal quantifier (u) is dropped, the variables thus freed in φu are replaced throughout φi with but one name or variable. If they are not, we get an erroneous proof. For example, the following is a misuse of **UI**:

```
*   1   (x)(Fx ⊃ Gx)
*   2   Fa ⊃ Gb          1, UI Erroneous
```

Line 1 says, "If anything is F, then *it* is G," where "it" refers to the thing which is F. By contrast, line 2 says, "If a is F, then b is G," where a and b are different things. The premise hardly guarantees the conclusion. Similarly, the foregoing notational convention will disallow Fx ⊃ Gy as an instance of (x)(Fx ⊃ Gx).[1]

The rule of **UI** allows us to infer Fx v Gx from (x)(Fx v Gx) and (Fy · Gy) ≡ Hy from (x)[(Fx · Gx) ≡ Hx]. However, it does not allow any inference from (x)Fx ⊃ (x)Gx, for this formula is not a universally quantified formula but a *compound* whose parts are universally quantified. The φu in our rule may be any open formula, but the (u) in front must extend its scope to the end of the expression. Again, while ∼(x)Fx looks like a universally quantified formula, it is not. In asserting that it is false that everything is F, we are asserting that something is not F, and this is an existential claim. Accordingly, we cannot use **UI** for expressions of the form ∼(u) . . . .

To see how **UI** is used, consider this simple argument:

> All men need food, warmth, and shelter;
> John is a man; hence John needs food.

This becomes:

> (x)[x is a man ⊃ (x needs food · x needs warmth · x needs shelter)]
> (a is a man)
> _____
> ∴ (a needs food)

---

[1] In general quantification theory, stronger restrictions are required for each of the four quantificational rules stated in this chapter. (See Chapter 11.)

or, in full formalization:

$$(x)[(Mx \supset (Fx \cdot Wx \cdot Sx)]$$
$$Ma$$

$$\therefore Fa$$

We assert the premises and asterisk them, and we write the conclusion along-side the premises:

$$* \begin{cases} 1 & (x)[Mx \supset (Fx \cdot Wx \cdot Sx)] \\ 2 & Ma \qquad /\therefore Fa \end{cases}$$

For line 3 we use **UI** on line 1:

$$* \quad 3 \quad Ma \supset (Fa \cdot Wa \cdot Sa) \qquad \textbf{1, UI}$$

We now can use the truth-functional rules of Chapter 6:

$$* \quad 4 \quad Fa \cdot Wa \cdot Sa \qquad \textbf{2 and 3}, \text{ Modus Ponens.}$$
$$* \quad 5 \quad Fa \qquad \textbf{4}, \text{ Simplification}$$

This proves that lines 1 and 2 entail line 5, since *Fa* was deduced from lines 1 and 2. Line 5 still carries an asterisk.

We can also utilize conditional proofs and *reductio ad absurdum* proofs with our new rule. Consider this argument:

Economists are neither prophets nor wizards; hence if John Kenneth Galbraith is an economist, he is not a prophet.

or,

$$(x)[x \text{ is an economist} \supset \sim(x \text{ is a prophet} \lor x \text{ is a wizard})]$$

$$\therefore a \text{ is an economist} \supset \sim(a \text{ is a prophet})$$

The proof is as follows:

$$* \quad 1 \quad (x)[Ex \supset \sim(Px \lor Wx)] \qquad /\therefore Ea \supset \sim Pa$$
$$** \quad 2 \quad Ea$$
$$** \quad 3 \quad Ea \supset \sim(Pa \lor Wa) \qquad \textbf{1, UI}$$
$$** \quad 4 \quad \sim(Pa \lor Wa) \qquad \textbf{2 and 3}, \text{ Modus Ponens}$$
$$** \quad 5 \quad \sim Pa \cdot \sim Wa \qquad \textbf{4}, \text{ DeMorgan}$$
$$** \quad 6 \quad \sim Pa \qquad \textbf{5}, \text{ Simplification}$$
$$* \quad 7 \quad Ea \supset \sim Pa \qquad \textbf{2 and 6}, \text{ Conditionalization}$$

The Rule of Existential Generalization   Suppose that we have some singular sentence, such as *Fa*, or some open formula, such as *Fx*.   Since *a* is a name and purports to name something, if it is true, there is something which is an *F*.   Similarly, if *Fx* is true of something, there is something which is *F*.   But this entitles us to infer from *Fa* or from *Fx* the existential quantification (∃ x)Fx.   We shall call this the **rule of existential generalization** and designate it **EG**.   Stated explicitly, this rule is: *From any open formula or singular sentence we may infer its existential quantification.*   Thus, from *Fa · Ga* we may infer (∃ x)(Fx · Gx); from *Fb v Gb* we may infer (∃ y)(Fy v Gy); and from ∼ *Fx* we may infer (∃ x) ∼ *Fx*.
   EG may be stated in a more general form as follows:

EG: φi entails (∃ u)φu (where, as before, *i* represents any individual symbol, either *a*, *b*, etc., or *x*, *y*, etc., and *u* represents any variable).

To see how **EG** is used, consider this argument:

Everything is possible but difficult; therefore, some things are possible.

or,

$$\frac{(x)(x \text{ is possible} \cdot x \text{ is difficult})}{\therefore (\exists x)(x \text{ is possible})}$$

*	1	(x)(Fx · Gx)	/∴ (∃ x)Fx
*	2	Fx · Gx	**1, UI**
*	3	Fx	2, Simplification
*	4	(∃ x)Fx	3, **EG**

This proves that (x)(Fx · Gx) entails (∃ x)Fx.[2]   In this proof, when we instantiated line 1, we deduced the instance *Fx · Gx*, using *x* as an indeterminate individual. In this case we didn't need to name any particular individual; it was enough that whatever object we chose, it was *F*.
   We assume, as we did when considering **UI**, that when we *add* an existential quantifier, the variables or names quantified are the same variables or names throughout φi.   If they are not, we get an erroneous proof.   The following is thus a misuse of **EG**:

*	1	Fa · Gb	
*	2	(∃ x)(Fx · Gx)	**1, EG** *Erroneous*

Interpret *Fa* as "a is round," and *Gb* as "b is square."
   We can also treat arguments with quantifiers mixed with pure truth functions. For example:

---

[2] We assume throughout that the universe is not empty.

If the Dean doesn't forbid, every student is eligible; Alphonse is a student and the Dean has given his OK; so some student is eligible.

This becomes:

$$
\begin{array}{lll}
* \quad \left\{ \begin{array}{ll} 1 & \sim p \supset (x)(Sx \supset Ex) \\ 2 & Sa \cdot \sim p \end{array} \right. & & /\therefore (\exists x)(Sx \cdot Ex) \\
* \quad 3 & \sim p \cdot Sa & \text{2, Commutation} \\
* \quad 4 & \sim p & \text{3, Simplification} \\
* \quad 5 & (x)(Sx \supset Ex) & \text{1 and 4, Modus Ponens} \\
* \quad 6 & Sa \supset Ea & \text{5, UI} \\
* \quad 7 & Sa & \text{2, Simplification} \\
* \quad 8 & Ea & \text{6 and 7, Modus Ponens} \\
* \quad 9 & Sa \cdot Ea & \text{7 and 8, Conjunction} \\
* \quad 10 & (\exists x)(Sx \cdot Ex) & \text{9, EG}
\end{array}
$$

For the following argument we can employ a *reductio ad absurdum*:

Everything has mass; therefore something has mass or energy.

Or:

$(x)Fx \qquad /\therefore (\exists x)(Fx \lor Gx)$

In the *reductio ad absurdum* proof we assume the contradictory of the conclusion as an added premise and attempt to deduce a contradiction. If P entails Q, then $P \cdot \sim Q$ is a contradiction; hence if we can deduce a contradiction, we know that P entails Q. The proof is as follows:

$$
\begin{array}{llll}
* & 1 & (x)Fx & /\therefore (\exists x)(Fx \lor Gx) \\
** & 2 & \sim (\exists x)(Fx \lor Gx) & \\
** & 3 & (x) \sim (Fx \lor Gx) & \text{2, Equivalence I (p. 195)} \\
** & 4 & (x)(\sim Fx \cdot \sim Gx) & \text{3, DeMorgan's Law} \\
** & 5 & \sim Fx \cdot \sim Gx & \text{4, UI} \\
** & 6 & \sim Fx & \text{5, Simplification} \\
** & 7 & Fx & \text{1, UI} \\
** & 8 & Fx \cdot \sim Fx & \text{6 and 7, RAA}
\end{array}
$$

In this proof we utilized one of the equivalences on p. 195. The proof also illustrates instantiating formulas with negation signs either before or after the quantifier. When this situation occurs, it is *always* best to use the equivalences on p. 195 and truth-functional formulas *before* instantiating to put the negation signs entirely *within* the sentence following the quantifier.

By judicious use of these equivalences it will always be possible either to eliminate negation signs altogether, for example by replacing ~(∃ x) ~ with (x), or to move the negation sign so that it operates on the sentence following the quantifier. From this position, truth-functional equivalences will suffice to bring it within the sentence.

EXERCISES

A Prove the validity of the following. None of these is mixed with pure truth-functions, and none requires either conditional proof or *reductio ad absurdum*. If necessary, use **UI**, **EG**, truth-functional inferences, and the quantification equivalences.

1   If Alphonse is going, everybody is; but if Alphonse doesn't go, then neither will Harry. Harry is going, so everybody is. (*Fa* = Alphonse is going; *Fx* = x is going; *Fb* = Harry is going.) (Notice that this argument is truth-functionally valid. That is, its validity does not depend upon the meaning or use of quantifiers.)

2   Nobody loves Sam and Bobbie is somebody, so Bobbie doesn't love Sam. [Symbolize: (x)[(x is a person ⊃ ~(x loves Sam)]; (a is a person); ∴ ~(a loves Sam).]

3   Every karate expert practices zen; Shizuo Nakamura is a karate expert; hence there are zen practicers. (*Fx* = x is a karate expert; *Gx* = x practices zen; etc.)

4   Moby Dick is a whale only if there are white whales; if there are white whales, then whales are fictitious; Moby Dick is a whale; hence, he is not a whale unless he is fictitious. (*Fx* = x is a whale; *Gx* = x is white; *Hx* = x is fictitious, etc.)

5   There are souls, or there are minds, only if everything is spiritual. But since some things are not spiritual, it follows that there are things which are not souls and not minds. (*Fx* = x is a soul; *Gx* = x is a mind; *Hx* = x is spiritual.) (In this example the use of the quantification equivalences will be important.)

B Prove the following. If necessary or convenient, use conditional proof and *reductio ad absurdum*.

6   Fortune tellers are never Gypsies, so if Tomara is a fortune teller, she is not a Gypsy. (*Fx* = x is fortune teller; *Gx* = x is Gypsy, etc.)

7   Nothing is impossible; hence something is possible.

8   Either Ronald Reagan is a conservative, or everything is goofy; but there are some things which are not goofy; so Ronald Reagan is a conservative. (*Fx* = x is a conservative; *Gx* = x is goofy, etc.)

9   Unhappy beings are either ill-fed or ill-housed; if anything is ill-fed it ought to be on welfare; Leo the lion is unhappy but well-housed; therefore Leo the lion ought to be on welfare. (*Fx* = x is unhappy; *Gx* = x is ill-fed; *Hx* = x is ill-housed; *Jx* = x ought to be on welfare.)

10   If today is Monday and the Mets are in last place, then New Yorkers

are all sad. Mayor Beame is a New Yorker and today is Monday, so, if the Mets are in last place, he is sad. (p = today is Monday; q = the Mets are in last place; $Fx = x$ is a New Yorker; $Gx = x$ is sad.)

11 Whoever dances a belly dance has good stomach muscles and is not Greek. Aphrodite belly dances, so she is not Greek. ($Fx = x$ belly dances; $Gx = x$ has good stomach muscles; $Hx = x$ is Greek, etc.)

12 Everything is ultimately spiritual; hence there are things which are spiritual or there are things which are material.

13 Movie stars are affable only if affable people make good politicians; but movie stars are affable; hence, if Ronald Reagan is a movie star, he is a good politician. ($Fx = x$ is a movie star; $Gx = x$ is affable; $Hx = x$ is a good politician, etc.)

14 If there are bald German Shepherds, then the Mets will win the pennant or I will eat my hat; I will neither eat my hat nor will the Mets win the pennant; hence it is false that there are bald German Shepherds.

15 Hippies are cute and cute people are tolerable. But tolerable people are not guilty of subversion. Larry is a hippie, so how can you say that he is guilty of subversion?

The Rule of Existential Instantiation The method of proof so far generated enables us to treat a wide range of arguments not amenable to either truth-functions or to the classical analysis of terms. It also enables us to treat many of the syllogistic forms. But there remain many valid arguments which still escape us. For example, all valid arguments with universally quantified conclusions cannot yet be proved. In this section and the next we shall introduce two new rules which will greatly improve our apparatus.

The first new rule is called the **rule of existential instantiation,** which, unlike either **UI** or **EG**, is *not* perfectly general. That is, its use as a rule of inference must be restricted. Let us state it and then see how it works and why it must be restricted: *From an existential quantification we may infer an instance of it, provided that the variable freed is not free in any previous line of the proof.* Or, more formally,

EI: ($\exists$ $u)\phi u$ entails ϕw *provided that* w is a variable which does not occur free in any previous line of the proof.

Suppose we have an existential quantification ($\exists$ $x)Fx$. Since this would be true if and only if it has at least one true substitution instance, we may infer any *one* of its instances. That is, *either Fa or Fb or Fc* . . . is true. There can be no assurance that every instance is true, nor can we say *which* is true. **EI** says that we can select any one as true. We indicate this by representing the one selected as perhaps Fx. We use x (or y) here to indicate that it is some indeterminate something which is F, but we don't know which one. Moreover, to help us remember that our inference is tentative—that for purposes of the proof we are identifying the true instance as *Fx*—we write *x* alongside **EI** in our justification. Let us see how **EI** works in a valid proof.

All golfers are athletes; some golfers are over forty years old; hence there are athletes who are over forty years old.

$$
\begin{aligned}
* \quad & \begin{cases} 1 & (x)(Gx \supset Ax) \\ 2 & (\exists x)(Gx \cdot Fx) \end{cases} & /\therefore\ (\exists x)(Fx \cdot Ax) \\
* \quad & 3 \quad Gx \cdot Fx & \textbf{2, EI } x \\
* \quad & 4 \quad Gx & \textbf{3, Simplification} \\
* \quad & 5 \quad Gx \supset Ax & \textbf{1, UI} \\
* \quad & 6 \quad Ax & \textbf{4 and 5, Modus Ponens} \\
* \quad & 7 \quad Fx \cdot Gx & \textbf{3, Commutation} \\
* \quad & 8 \quad Fx \cdot & \textbf{7, Simplification} \\
* \quad & 9 \quad Fx \cdot Ax & \textbf{8 and 6, Conjunction} \\
* \quad & 10 \quad (\exists x)(Fx \cdot Ax) & \textbf{9, EG}
\end{aligned}
$$

When we used **EI** for line 3, we decided to call that over-forty-year-old golfer *x*, and we wrote *x* alongside **EI**. We then used **UI** on premise 1. Since it is perfectly general, we instantiated to $Gx \supset Ax$. We then moved easily to line 9, which asserts that there is something named *x* which is both *F* and *A*. But $Fx \cdot Ax$ couldn't stand as a conclusion. The *x* in line 3 represents *some* determinate golfer, but we can't say who. We assumed for purposes of the proof that it was *x*; hence the deduction is not quite complete. Line 10, the **EG** of line 9, rids us of the assumption by making explicit that we proved only that *something* is both an athlete and over forty.[3]

In using **EI**, as with **UI**, the same notational conventions hold. That is, when the existential quantifier ($\exists u$) is dropped, the variables freed in ϕu are to be replaced by identical variables throughout ϕw. Again, if they are not, we get an erroneous proof. So, the following is an improper use of **EI**:

$$
\begin{aligned}
* \quad & 1 \quad (\exists x)(Fx \lor Gx) \\
* \quad & 2 \quad Fx \lor Gy & \textbf{1, EI } \textit{Erroneous}
\end{aligned}
$$

To understand the proviso that the instantiated variable be a variable which does *not* occur free in a previous line of the proof, let us consider this invalid argument:

There are Mormons who swim in the Great Salt Lake; there are Mormons who don't. Hence, there is a Mormon who both swims in the Great Salt Lake and who doesn't.

This is obviously invalid, but our *misuse* of **EI** makes it appear valid.

---

[3] Formally, $(\exists x)Fx \supset Fy$ is not a tautology, but $(\exists y)[(\exists x)Fx \supset Fy]$ is.

$$
\begin{array}{lll}
{}_* \left\{
\begin{array}{ll}
1 & (\exists x)(Mx \cdot Sx) \\
2 & (\exists x)(Mx \sim Sx)
\end{array}
\right. & / \therefore (\exists x)(Mx \cdot Sx \cdot \sim Sx) \\
{}_*\ \ 3 & Mx \cdot Sx & 1,\ \textbf{EI}\ x \\
{}_*\ \ 4 & Mx \cdot \sim Sx & 2,\ \textbf{EI}\ \textit{Erroneous} \\
{}_*\ \ 5 & \sim Sx & 4,\ \text{Simplification and Commutation} \\
{}_*\ \ 6 & Mx \cdot Sx \cdot \sim Sx & 3\ \text{and}\ 5,\ \text{Conjunction} \\
{}_*\ \ 7 & (\exists x)(Mx \cdot Sx \cdot \sim Sx) & 6,\ \textbf{EG}
\end{array}
$$

The trouble here is fairly obvious. The truth of premise 1 guarantees that there is some particular Mormon who swims in the Great Salt Lake—call him Joe—and the truth of premise 2 assures us that there is some Mormon who does not—call him Sam. But in instantiating we have illicitly assumed that the *same* Mormon is an instance of both premises. The premises surely do not guarantee that. If we had obeyed the proviso, the difficulty would have been prevented, for the proviso says that a variable freed through **EI** cannot be free in any previous line of the proof. The device of "flagging" the variable (of writing it alongside **EI** in the justification) should also help here.[4]

In the deduction regarding golfers (above), an important strategy might have been noticed. Since **UI** is not limited, we can infer any instance through its use. Consequently, when we want to use both **EI** and **UI**, we should always use **EI** *first*. We then can use the unrestricted **UI** to infer whatever variable we freed with the use of **EI**.

The Rule of Universal Generalization   We have seen that while **EG** permits us to add an existential quantifier, we have not as yet considered any means which would permit us to add a universal quantifier. And yet for some proofs the need to do so is required. Consider, for example, this argument form:

$$
\begin{array}{l}
(x)(Fx \supset Gx) \\
(x)(Gx \supset Hx) \\
\hline
\therefore (x)(Fx \supset Hx)
\end{array}
$$

It is obviously valid. (Indeed, it is the quantified version of **AAA**-1.) How can we prove it valid?

$$
\begin{array}{lll}
{}_* \left\{
\begin{array}{ll}
1 & (x)(Fx \supset Gx) \\
2 & (x)(Gx \supset Hx)
\end{array}
\right. & / \therefore (x)(Fx \supset Hx) \\
{}_*\ \ 3 & Fx \supset Gx & 1,\ \textbf{UI} \\
{}_*\ \ 4 & Gx \supset Hx & 2,\ \textbf{UI} \\
{}_*\ \ 5 & Fx \supset Hx & 3\ \text{and}\ \textbf{4},\ \text{Hypothetical Syllogism}
\end{array}
$$

But here we are stopped, for we have no rule which allows us to *add* a uni-

---

[4] The terminology of "flagging" and much of the discussion in this chapter is indebted to W. V. Quine. See his *Methods of Logic,* revised edition (New York: Holt, Rinehart and Winston, 1959).

versal quantifier. **EG** would allow us to say, for line 6, $(\exists x)(Fx \supset Hx)$, but this is not what we want. However, from line 5, $Fx \supset Hx$, we surely have a right to infer $(x)(Fx \supset Hx)$. Let us consider why. The $Fx \supset Gx$ of line 3 and the $Gx \supset Hx$ of line 4 are radically unlike instances derived with the use of **EI**, for unlike them, the x of $Fx \supset Gx$ and of $Gx \supset Hx$ does not represent anything in particular. In the strictest sense,

$Fx \supset Gx$ is an *arbitrary instance* of $(x)(Fx \supset Gx)$

and

$Gx \supset Hx$ is an *arbitrary instance* of $(x)(Gx \supset Hx)$.

Hence what was established as true of $Fx \supset Hx$ (line 5) is true of all x's, or $(x)(Fx \supset Hx)$ is true.

The legitimacy of this move may be compared to statements of this sort: "A male student is not allowed in the girls' dormitory." Since the expression "a male student" refers to *any* male student, we can say that *all* male students are forbidden.

When we infer that what is true of some arbitrary something is true of all such things, we are using what is called **universal generalization,** or **UG. UG** is frequently used in mathematics. For example, when something is established as true of some arbitrary triangle and we then conclude that what is true of this triangle is true of all triangles, we use **UG**. The proof is valid only if what is established does not depend upon some special characteristics of the triangle in question. For example, if the proof depends upon the triangle's being isosceles, then we cannot infer that what is true of it is true of all triangles—though, of course, it may be true of all isosceles triangles.

UG may be roughly stated as follows: *From an arbitrary instance we may infer its universal generalization.* But to guard against erroneous uses of **UG**, we state it more exactly:

UG: ϕw entails $(u)\phi u$ *provided that* (1) w is a free variable, (2) w is not flagged in any previous line, and (3) w is not free in an assumed premise within whose scope ϕw occurs.

To be clear about what these restrictions mean, let us look at some proofs with erroneous uses of **UG**. Consider, first, this argument:

Each and every planet is in revolution around the sun; Mars is a planet; so everything is in revolution around the sun.

$$
*\begin{cases} 1 & (x)(Px \supset Rx) \\ 2 & Pa \end{cases} \qquad /\therefore (x)Rx
$$
$$
*\ \ 3 \quad Pa \supset Ra \qquad \textbf{1, UI}
$$

*	4	Ra	2 and 3, Modus Ponens
*	5	$(x)Rx$	4, **UG** *Erroneous*

The inference from line 4 to line 5 by **UG** is invalid because a is not a free variable. So, while we have proved that it is true that Mars (named by a) is in revolution around the sun (it is R), it by no means follows that what is true of it is true of everything. By restricting the use of **UG** to free variables (and thereby excluding names), we block this sort of invalid inference.

But this means that we must be careful with our use of names and variables. If we had (wrongly) formalized "Mars is a planet" as Px, then line 4 would read Rx, which would look like an arbitrary instance. However, in this context x still names Mars and only Mars. For our rules to be helpful to us, we must always use the letters a, b, etc., as names for particular objects, and x, y, etc., for variables representing indeterminate "somethings."

Closely related to the foregoing is the second proviso in our formulation of **UG**, the proviso which prevents us from using **UG** on flagged variables. In using **EI**, as we saw, we free variables, but the open formulas derived with the use of **EI** are not arbitrary instances in the required sense. They represent some one particular thing and thus are like singular sentences containing names, even though the object represented by x or y is indeterminate and the name is ambiguous. Attention to the rules would prevent an illicit deduction like the following:

*	1	$(\exists x)Fx$	$/\therefore (x)Fx$
*	2	Fx	1, **EI** x
*	3	$(x)Fx$	2, **UG** *Erroneous*

Finally, the third proviso in the use of **UG** says that ϕw entails $(u)\phi u$ provided that w is not free in an assumed premise within whose scope ϕw occurs. Ignoring this proviso can yield the following:

*	1	$(x)(Fx \supset Fx)$	
**	2	Fy	
**	3	$(x)Fx$	2, **UG** *Erroneous*
*	4	$Fy \supset (x)Fx$	2 and 4, Conditionalization
*	5	$(y)[Fy \supset (x)Fx]$	4, **UG**

Interpreting Fx as "x is red," the premise is the tautology "Everything red is red," but the conclusion asserts the falsehood "If anything is red, then everything is red." The third proviso blocks the inference from line 2 to line 3 because the variable to be generalized upon—in this case y—was free in an assumed premise (premise 2) within the scope of the line where **UG** was to be used (in this case line 3). That is, the **UG** wrongly occurred on a line which carried a double asterisk.

The following use of **UG** with conditional proof, however, is correct:

```
*    1   (x)(Fx ⊃ Gx · Hx)      /∴ (x)(Fx ⊃ Gx)
**   2   Fx
**   3   Fx ⊃ Gx · Hx           1, UI
**   4   Gx · Hx                2 and 3, Modus Ponens
**   5   Gx                     4, Simplification
*    6   Fx ⊃ Gx                2 and 5, Conditionalization
*    7   (x)(Fx ⊃ Gx)           6, UG
```

Up to this point at least, the informal justifications for the quantifier rules and their use have, hopefully, been in touch with our ordinary intuitions. But this third proviso for using **UG** may be nonintuitive. Why, one may wonder, does invalidity ever ensue from generalizing on lines within the scope of assumed premises where the variables generalized on are free in those premises? The answer is that such formulas are not necessarily arbitrary instances in the required sense. That is, it is one thing to use **UG** on some open formula where lines in the proof guarantee that the instance is arbitrary in the required sense, but it is quite another to *assume* that it is. Whatever the best explanation may be, however, the best justification for the proviso is that without it, we could go from true premises to false conclusions; and in valid inferences, as we know, this is not possible. Perhaps all this says something about our intuitions.

SOME EXAMPLES

In this section we shall simply offer a series of valid proofs. They should be studied so as to get acquainted with various strategies in using the rules at our disposal.

A
```
*    1   (x)Fx                  /∴ ~(∃ x) ~Fx
**   2   (∃ x) ~Fx
**   3   ~Fx                    2, EI x
*    4   (∃ x) ~Fx ⊃ ~Fx        2 and 3, Conditionalization
*    5   Fx                     1, UI
*    6   ~~Fx                   5, D.N.
*    7   ~(∃ x) ~Fx             4 and 6, Modus Ponens
```
B
```
*    1   (∃ x)(p v Fx)          /∴ p v (∃ x)Fx
*    2   p v Fx                 1, EI x
**   3   Fx
**   4   (∃ x)Fx                3, EG
*    5   Fx ⊃ (∃ x)Fx           3 and 4, Conditionalization
*    6   ~p ⊃ Fx                2, Imp.
*    7   ~p ⊃ (∃ x)Fx           5 and 6, H.S.
*    8   p v (∃ x)Fx            7, Imp.
```

C

* $\begin{cases} \textbf{1} & (x)[Gx \supset (Fx \lor Hx)] \\ \textbf{2} & (\exists x)(Gx \cdot \sim Hx) \end{cases}$ $/\therefore (\exists x)(Fx \cdot \sim Hx)$

*   **3** $Gx \cdot \sim Hx$ 2, **EI** x
*   **4** $Gx \supset (Fx \lor Hx)$ 1, **UI**
*   **5** Gx 3, Simplification
*   **6** $Fx \lor Hx$ 4 and 5, Modus Ponens
*   **7** $\sim Hx \cdot Gx$ 3, Commutation
*   **8** $\sim Hx$ 7, Simplification
*   **9** $Hx \lor Fx$ 6, Commutation
*   **10** Fx 8 and 9, D.S.
*   **11** $Fx \cdot \sim Hx$ 10 and 8, Conjunction
*   **12** $(\exists x)(Fx \cdot \sim Hx)$ 11, **EG**

D

* $\begin{cases} \textbf{1} & (\exists x)(Fx \lor Gx) \\ \textbf{2} & \sim(\exists x)Gx \end{cases}$ $/\therefore (\exists x)Fx$

**   **3** $\sim(\exists x)Fx$
**   **4** $Fx \lor Gx$ 1, **EI** x
**   **5** $(x)\sim Gx$ 2, Equivalence
**   **6** $(x)\sim Fx$ 3, Equivalence
**   **7** $\sim Fx$ 6, **UI**
**   **8** Gx 4 and 7, D.S.
**   **9** $\sim Gx$ 5, **UI**
** **10** $Gx \cdot \sim Gx$ 8 and 9, **RAA**

E

* $\begin{cases} \textbf{1} & (x)(Fx \supset Gx) \\ \textbf{2} & (x)(Gx \cdot Hx \supset Jx) \\ \textbf{3} & \sim(\exists x)\sim Fx \end{cases}$ $/\therefore (x)(Hx \supset Jx)$

*   **4** $(x)Fx$ 3, Equivalence
*   **5** Fx 4, **UI**
*   **6** $Fx \supset Gx$ 1, **UI**
*   **7** Gx 5 and 6, Modus Ponens
*   **8** $(Gx \cdot Hx) \supset Jx$ 2, **UI**
*   **9** $Gx \supset (Hx \supset Jx)$ 8, Exp.
*   **10** $Hx \supset Jx$ 7 and 9, Modus Ponens
*   **11** $(x)(Hx \supset Jx)$ 10, **UG**

EXERCISES

Prove each of the following:

1.   * $\begin{cases} \textbf{1} & (x)(Fx \supset Gx) \\ \textbf{2} & (\exists x)Fx \end{cases}$ $/\therefore (\exists x)Gx$

2.   * $\begin{cases} \textbf{1} & (x)(Fx \equiv Gx) \\ \textbf{2} & (x)(Gx \supset \sim Ix) \end{cases}$ $/\therefore (x)(Fx \supset \sim Ix)$

3   *$\begin{cases} 1 & (\exists x)(Fx \cdot Gx \cdot Hx) \\ 2 & (x)[(Fx \cdot Gx) \supset \sim Ix] \qquad /\therefore (\exists x)(Hx \cdot \sim Ix) \end{cases}$

4   *$\begin{cases} 1 & (\exists x)(Fx \lor Gx) \\ 2 & (x) \sim Fx \qquad /\therefore (\exists x)Gx \end{cases}$

5   *$\begin{cases} 1 & (x)(Fx \supset Hx) \\ 2 & (\exists x)(\sim Hx \cdot \sim Ix) \qquad /\therefore \sim (x)(Fx \lor Ix) \end{cases}$

6   *$\begin{cases} 1 & (\exists x)[(Fx \cdot Gx) \lor Hx] \\ 2 & (x)(Fx \supset \sim Jx) \\ 3 & \sim(\exists x)Hx \qquad /\therefore (\exists x)(Gx \cdot \sim Jx) \end{cases}$

7   *$\begin{cases} 1 & \sim(\exists x)(Fx \cdot \sim Gx) \\ 2 & (x) \sim (Gx \cdot Hx) \\ 3 & (\exists x)(Fx \cdot \sim Ix) \qquad /\therefore (\exists x) \sim Hx \lor (\exists x)Ix \end{cases}$

8   *$\begin{cases} 1 & (\exists x)(Fx \cdot Gx) \supset (p \supset q) \\ 2 & (x)(Hx) \cdot p \\ 3 & \sim q \lor \sim(\exists x)Hx \qquad /\therefore \sim(\exists x)(Fx \cdot Gx) \end{cases}$

9   *$\begin{cases} 1 & (x)(Fx \supset Hx) \\ 2 & Ha \supset p \\ 3 & Fa \qquad /\therefore p \end{cases}$

10   *$\begin{cases} 1 & \sim(\exists x) \sim (Fx \supset Gx) \\ 2 & \sim(Ga \lor Ha) \\ 3 & (x)[\sim(Fx \cdot Ix) \supset \sim Jx] \qquad /\therefore (\exists x) \sim Jx \end{cases}$

11   There are no sailors who get seasick on aircraft carriers, but there are sailors who get seasick on LSDs and destroyers. Hence, some sailors who get sick on destroyers do not get sick on carriers. ($Fx = x$ is a sailor; $Gx = x$ gets seasick on aircraft carriers; $Hx = x$ gets sick on LSDs; $Jx = x$ gets sick on destroyers.)

12   Ryan is Irish or he doesn't like potatoes. Irishmen invariably drink beer and eat cornbeef and cabbage on St. Patrick's Day. Ryan does like potatoes; so, he drinks beer on St. Patrick's Day. ($Fx = x$ is Irish; $Gx = x$ likes potatoes; $Hx = x$ drinks beer; $Jx = x$ eats cornbeef and cabbage on St. Patrick's Day.)

13   A male cannot enter the girls' dormitory unless a proctor is available. Last Tuesday, some male students were in the dorm. Hence a proctor must have been available. ($Fx = x$ is a male; $Gx = x$ enters the girls' dormitory; $p = $ a proctor is available; $Hx = x$ is a student.)

14   Cigarette smokers may end up with cancer and alcoholics may ruin their livers and get *delirium tremens*. So, if you are both a cigarette smoker and an alcoholic, you may end up with cancer, a ruined liver, and *delirium tremens*. ($Fx = x$ smokes cigarettes; $Gx = x$ may end up with cancer; $Hx = x$ is an alcoholic; $Jx = x$ may ruin his liver; $Kx = x$ may get *delirium tremens*.)

15 Professors may be either just or merciful, and sympathetic professors are not just. Hence if anyone is a professor, then if he is sympathetic, he is merciful. ($Fx = x$ is a professor; $Gx = x$ is just; $Hx = x$ is merciful; $Jx = x$ is sympathetic.)

16 Either gambling is immoral or it is unnecessary. A lottery is a form of gambling. But since nothing which promotes good is immoral and some lotteries do promote good, there are lotteries which are unnecessary. ($Fx = x$ is gambling; $Gx = x$ is moral; $Hx = x$ is necessary; $Jx = x$ is a lottery; $Kx = x$ promotes good.)

17 A person is authoritarian if and only if he is militant. Tyrants are all Janus-faced. Each and every militant is neurotic, and if anyone is Janus-faced, then he is successful. Since there are authoritarians who are tyrants, there are successful neurotics. ($Fx = x$ is authoritarian; $Gx = x$ is militant; $Hx = x$ is a tyrant; $Jx = x$ is Janus-faced; $Kx = x$ is neurotic; $Lx = x$ is successful.)

18 If God exists, then something is neither false nor evil. Everything which is either true or good is beautiful. There is a God who is merciful and just. Hence there is beauty. ($Fx = x$ is God; $Gx = x$ is false; $Hx = x$ is evil; $Jx = x$ is beautiful; $Kx = x$ is merciful; $Lx = x$ is just.)

19 Something is beautiful only if love is beautiful; something is tragic only if all beautiful things are tragic. Something is both beautiful and tragic; hence love is tragic. ($Fx = x$ is beautiful; $Gx = x$ is love; $Hx = x$ is tragic.)

20 Mini-boppers who major in philosophy are Fulbright Fellows, and only students with good grades are Fulbright Fellows. Still, if there are students with good grades who are not gorgeous, then no students with good grades are boys. So, there are some Fulbright Fellows who are not gorgeous only if there are no mini-boppers who are boys and philosophy majors. ($Fx = x$ is a mini-bopper; $Gx = x$ majors in philosophy; $Hx = x$ is a Fulbright Fellow; $Jx = x$ is a student with good grades; $Kx = x$ is gorgeous; $Lx = x$ is a boy.)

ELEVEN

QUANTIFICATION: III

> *If, by examining the simplest cases, we can . . . extract . . . what is universally valid in them, may we not thus arrive at general methods for . . . establishing principles which will be applicable also in more complicated cases?*
>
> Gottlob Frege

The apparatus generated so far is quite powerful and enables us to treat a wide variety of arguments. But there are still some fairly straightforward sorts of deductions which we cannot prove with the tools presently available to us. And for purposes beyond the analysis of everyday deductive argument—for example, in discussions of the foundations of mathematics—a still more powerful apparatus is needed and is available. In this chapter we shall introduce an enrichment of our apparatus.[1]

Relational Predicates

Up to this point we have been restricted to statements which do not involve relations. Thus "Sam is friendly" became *Fa*, and "Whales are mammals" became $(x)(Fx \supset Gx)$. In these cases the predicate letters *F*, *G*, etc., represented properties or characteristics. But we can use them as well to express relations. Thus "Sam is friendlier than Sally" becomes *Fab*, where *a* names Sam, *b* names Sally,

---

[1] We try here, as in the foregoing, to keep the discussion as intuitive and uncomplicated as possible. But doing so involves a sacrifice of rigor, which, hopefully, does not significantly reduce the usefulness of the discussion.

and *F* represents the relational term "is friendlier than." Similarly, "Sam loves Sally" becomes *Lab*, with *L* representing the relational term "loves." Note that consistency in the formalization is crucial: If *a* names Sam, *b* names Sally, and *L* represents "loves," then *Lab* is not the same as *Lba*, for the latter asserts that Sally loves Sam. Keeping *a* for Sam and *b* for Sally, *Lba* would be appropriate for "Sam loves Sally" only if *L* represented "is loved by."

The device of open sentences will serve us well here, for we can use open sentences to interpret open formulas which involve relations. In the open formula *Fxy*, *F* represents a relational term between the variables *x* and *y*, and *Fxy* may be interpreted with any of the following open sentences:

x loves y.
x is taller than y.
x is soluble in y.
x belongs to y.

But we need not restrict ourselves to dyadic relations, that is, relations involving just two components. We can, if we wish, employ triadic and polyadic relations as well. For example, *Fxyz* may be interpreted by "x is between y and z," and *Fxyzw* might be "x pays y to z for w."

Moreover, we can also introduce more than one quantifier. Interpreting *Fxy* as "x is soluble in y," we have:

1 (∃ x)(∃ y)Fxy   symbolizes   Something is soluble in something.
2 (x)(y)Fxy   symbolizes   Everything is soluble in everything.
3 (∃ x)(y)Fxy   symbolizes   Something is soluble in everything.
4 (y)(∃ x)Fxy   symbolizes   For each thing, something is soluble in it.
5 (x)(∃ y)Fxy   symbolizes   Everything is soluble in something.

In 1 and 2 the order of the quantifiers is irrelevant. (∃ x)(∃ y)Fxy is equivalent to (∃ y)(∃ x)Fxy, and this is so because they both say "There is something such that there is something it is soluble in." As before, the variables x, y, etc., are serving as place markers. In 2, (x)(y)Fxy and (y)(x)Fxy both assert that each thing is such that each thing is soluble in it. Note that 2 doesn't mean only that everything dissolves everything *else*, for "everything" includes *everything*, including itself. If we want to, we can say that everything is soluble in itself (which is different from saying that everything is soluble in everything). "Everything is soluble in itself" looks like this: (x)Fxx, with Fxx interpreted as "x is soluble in x."

In 3 and 4 the order of quantifiers is highly relevant, and it is crucial that we discriminate between the two. Statement 3, (∃ x)(y)Fxy, says that there is some one thing (at least) such that it is soluble in everything. By contrast, 4, (y)(∃ x)Fxy, says that for anything you pick there is something which is soluble in it. For example, if you pick water, then perhaps it is sugar which is soluble in it; if you pick nitric acid, perhaps the x is silver, and so on—for anything there is. More generally, 4 says that once any object y is fixed upon, there is some object *x* forthcoming such that *Fxy*. By contrast, 3, (∃ *x*)(*y*)*Fxy*, says that there is some object *x* such that for *that* fixed object, it stands in the relation *F* to all things.

The device of limiting the universe can be used to great advantage in seeing the difference between 3 and 4. Statement 3, (∃ *x*)(*y*)*Fxy*, which is properly understood to be an existentially quantified formula with another quantifier within its scope, is seen more graphically as (∃ *x*)[(*y*)*Fxy*]. Similarly, 4 is to be understood as a universally quantified formula with an existential quantifier within its scope, that is, as (*y*)[(∃ *x*)*Fxy*].

Assume a universe comprised of but two objects, *a* and *b*. We eliminate first the outside quantifier, which in 3 is the existential quantifier. Thus (∃ *x*)[(*y*)*Fxy*] becomes first the alternation:

   3' (*y*)*Fay* ∨ (*y*)*Fby*   *EI*

(∃ *x*)(*y*)*Fxy* asserts that there is something such that it stands in relation *F* to everything. In a two-member universe 3' asserts what is equivalent, namely, that *either a* stands in relation *F* to everything *or b* stands in relation *F* to everything. But since everything is just *a* and *b*, 3' becomes, finally:

   3" (*Faa* · *Fab*) ∨ (*Fba* · *Fbb*)   *UNI* *UI*

That is, *either a* stands in relation *F* to itself *and* to *b* (the only things there are being *a* and *b*) *or b* stands in relation *F* to *a* and to itself.

By contrast, in 4, (*y*)(∃ *x*)*Fxy*, the universal quantification becomes a *conjunction:*

   4' (∃ *x*)*Fxa* · (∃ *x*)*Fxb*   *UI*

Or, finally:

   4" (*Faa* ∨ *Fba*) · (*Fab* ∨ *Fbb*)   *EI*

If we make *Faa* and *Fbb* true and *Fba* and *Fab* false, 4 comes out true and 3 false. Hence 4 does not entail 3, and hence they are not equivalent.

Similarly, though it is by no means a proof, we can see that the order of quantifiers in 1 and 2 above is irrelevant. Consider each version of 2:

   (*x*)[(*y*)*Fxy*]   becomes   (*y*)*Fay* · (*y*)*Fby*

which becomes

   Faa · *Fab* · *Fba* · *Fbb*

Reversing the order of the universal quantifiers, we have

$(y)[(x)Fxy]$ which becomes $(x)Fxa \cdot (x)Fxb$

which becomes

$Faa \cdot Fba \cdot Fab \cdot Fbb$

Finally, 4, $(y)(\exists x)Fxy$, must also be distinguished from 5, $(x)(\exists y)Fxy$, which, reading as before, Fxy as "x is soluble in y," means "Everything is soluble in some-thing (or other)." Formula 5 is *not* the same as 4, "For each thing, there is some-thing which is soluble in it." For, while both 4 and 5 are universally quantified formulas with an existential formula within the scope of the universal quantifier, the *order* of the variables quantified makes a difference (assuming, of course, a consistent reading of Fxy in both formulas). Formula 4 says that for every y you choose there is something x which is soluble *in it*. By contrast, 5 says that for every x you pick, there is something y *which x is soluble in*.

EXERCISES

A   Limit the universe to two members and expand the following:
1   $(\exists x)(\exists y)Fxy$ 2 $(x)Fxx$ 3 $(x)(\exists y)Fxy$
4   $(x)(y)(Fx \supset Gy)$ 5 $(\exists x)[Fx \cdot (y)Gxy]$

B   Interpreting Fxy as "x is larger than y," put the following into plain English:
6   $(\exists x)(y)Fxy$ 7 $(x)(\exists y)Fxy$ 8 $(\exists x)(y)(Fxy \equiv Fxx)$

Negation and Multiple Quantifiers

We saw in Chapter 9 that quantifiers with negation tend to cause trouble. Things are not improved with multiple quantifiers. Unfortunately, quantified expres-sions are often misleading in English. Here attention to what is being said is crucial, and quantificational analysis is (or should be) an aid to clear thinking. Through its use, we can grasp with precision what is often vague in ordinary dis-course. Compare:

6   Nothing is soluble in itself

and

7   Not all things are soluble in themselves

Though these must be distinguished, they are sometimes confused. Reading "Fxx" as "x is soluble in x," 6 becomes

6′ $\sim$($\exists$ x)Fxx

and 7 becomes

7′ $\sim$(x)Fxx

As always, a curl operating in front of an expression serves to deny the entire expression which follows it. Thus $\sim$[($\exists$ x)Fxx] says *"It is false that* something is soluble in itself," which is the contradictory of "Something is soluble in itself." Accordingly, $\sim$($\exists$ x)Fxx precisely says "Nothing is soluble in itself."

Formula 7, $\sim$[(x)Fxx], says *"It is false that* everything is soluble in itself," which is the contradictory of "Everything is soluble in itself," or "Something is *not* soluble in itself." Consider then the following more complex pair:

8 Nothing is soluble in anything.

and

9 Nothing is soluble in everything.

Statements 8 and 9 parallel 6 and 7, even though the use of "anything" and "everything" is deceptive.

Consider first what 8 and 9 say: 8 says that there is nothing in the world which you can get to dissolve, no matter what you put it in, and 9 asserts the much weaker claim that for each thing, there is something in which it *won't* dissolve. Statement 8 becomes

8′ (x)(y)$\sim$Fxy

and 9 becomes

9′ $\sim$($\exists$ x)(y)Fxy

Let us first look more closely at 9′. It says "It is false that there is something x such that for each and every y, x is soluble in y." The first part of the expression, "It is false that there is something . . ." corresponds exactly to $\sim$($\exists$ x) and says "There is nothing . . ." or, more briefly, "Nothing is . . . ." The second quantifier, then, is universal; so, "Nothing is soluble in *everything*."

Moreover, $\sim$($\exists$ x)(y)Fxy is equivalent to (x)$\sim$(y)Fxy via quantifier equivalence, and this is equivalent to (x)($\exists$ y)$\sim$Fxy via another quantifier equivalence.

(x)($\exists$ y)$\sim$Fxy reads as "For each (and every) thing x you pick, there is something y, such that x is not soluble in y." Contrast this, then, with 8′, (x)(y)$\sim$Fxy, which says "For each thing x you pick, (and) for any thing y you pick, x is not soluble in y." The following are equivalent to 8′:

$(x) \sim (\exists\ y)Fxy$ and $\sim (\exists\ x)(\exists\ y)Fxy$

$(x) \sim (y)Fxy$ reads, "For each thing x, it is false that there is something y such that x is soluble in y." Likely, it is the most intuitive version. $\sim (\exists\ x)(\exists\ y)Fxy$ is "It is false that there is something x such that x is soluble in some y," or, better, "Nothing is soluble in anything." Here, the difference between "everything" and "anything," as in "I won't give you everything" versus "I won't give you anything," is all the difference in the world.

Limiting the universe brings out the contrast between 8' and 9' quite dramatically:

$(x)(y) \sim Fxy$ becomes $(y) \sim Fay \cdot (y) \sim Fby$

which becomes

$\sim Faa \cdot \sim Fab \cdot \sim Fba \cdot \sim Fbb$

By contrast, 9', $\sim (\exists\ x)(y)Fxy$, must be treated as being of the form $\sim (\ .\ .\ .)$. It becomes:

$\sim [(y)Fay \vee (y)Fby]$
$\sim [(Faa \cdot Fab) \vee (Fba \cdot Fbb)]$
$\sim (Faa \cdot Fab) \cdot \sim (Fba \cdot Fbb)$
$(\sim Faa \vee \sim Fab) \cdot (\sim Fba \vee \sim Fbb)$

EXERCISES

A Limit the universe to two members and expand:
1 $\sim (\exists\ x)(y)Fxy$ 2 $\sim (y)(\exists\ x)Fxy$
3 $(x)(\exists\ y) \sim Fxy$ 4 $(x) \sim (y)Fxy$
Do the expansions of 3 and 4 convince you that they are equivalent? Why?

B Reading Fxy as "x is larger than y," put the following into standard English (or as close to standard English as you can).
5 $(\exists\ x)Fxx \supset \sim (\exists\ x)Fxx$ 6 $(x)Fxx \supset \sim (x)Fxx$
7 $\sim (\exists\ x)(y)Fxy$ 8 $(x) \sim (\exists\ y)Fxy$

Multiple Quantification and Ordinary English

When relations and several quantifiers are involved, it is not always easy to go from ordinary English to the symbolism, even though, as before, the effort to do so is an excellent way to force clarity of thought and expression. In this section we shall examine closely a few very common forms of expression using two quantifiers.

The best way to begin is to think, as before, of any quantified statement as either universally or existentially quantified and to get that quantifier out first. Use open sentences. Then deal with the internal structure of the sentence.

1 Pollution kills fish.

In this sentence there are no explicit quantifiers, so they must be supplied. The implicit quantifier most readily supplied is the main quantifier, which in this case is universal.

   (x)(x is pollution ⊃ x kills fish)

The question now is, does the sentence say, "There are fish killed by whatever is polluting" or does it say, "*Every* fish is killed by whatever is polluting"? Likely it says the former. Hence,

   (x)[x is pollution ⊃ (∃ y)(y is fish · Kxy)]

Finally, then,

   (x)[Px ⊃ (∃ y)(Fy · Kxy)]

2 There's a pitcher who can strike out any hitter.
     (∃ x)(x is a pitcher · x can strike out any hitter)
     (∃ x)[x is a pitcher · (y)(y is a hitter ⊃ x can strike out y)]
     (∃ x)[Px · (y)(Hy ⊃ Sxy)]

These are not the only correct formalizations of the two preceding examples, but they are the formalizations which seem most direct and intuitive. Moreover, they bring out the close relation of the two to our old friends, the **A** form and **I** form categoricals. Where the main quantifier is universal, as in 1, the main break—as we might expect—is a horseshoe. Where the quantifier out front is existential, as in 2, the main break, as in the **I** form, is the dot of conjunction. And this is true even of the internal structure of the two statements. For example, within the scope of the universal quantifier of 1 is an existential quantifier, and within it, the main break is a dot.

3 Nobody loves a fool.
     (x)[x is a person ⊃ ~(x loves a fool)]
     (x)[x is a person ⊃ ~(∃ y)(y is a fool · x loves y)]
     (x)[Px ⊃ ~(∃ y)(Fy · Lxy)]

   Someone might say here, "But doesn't 'a fool' refer to *any* fool and hence shouldn't the quantifier be universal?" But it is, since, as we saw earlier, ~(∃ y)(. . .) is equivalent to a universally quantified formula. Consider this version of 3 with the curl in a different place.

$$(x)[Px \supset (y)(Fy \supset \sim Lxy)]$$

The two versions of 3 are equivalent. To illustrate the general point of alternative, but equivalent, formulations, let us see how one may be deduced from the other.

* 1 $(x)[Px \supset \sim(\exists y)(Fy \cdot Lxy)]$
* 2 $(x)[Px \supset (y)\sim(Fy \cdot Lxy)]$ 1, Quantifier Equivalence
* 3 $(x)[Px \supset (y)(\sim Fy \vee \sim Lxy)]$ 2, DeMorgan
* 4 $(x)[Px \supset (y)(Fy \supset \sim Lxy)]$ 3, Implication

or

* 1 $(x)[Px \supset \sim(\exists y)(Fy \cdot Lxy)$
* 2 $(x)[\sim Px \vee \sim(\exists y)(Fx \cdot Lxy)$ 1, Implication
* 3 $(x)\sim[Px \cdot (\exists y)(Fx \cdot Lxy)$ 2, DeMorgan
* 4 $\sim(\exists x)[Px \cdot (\exists y)(Fx \cdot Lxy)]$ 3, Quantifier Equivalence

4   Some people are not helped by money.
$(\exists x)(x$ is a person $\cdot$ x is not helped by money)
$(\exists x)[x$ is a person $\cdot \sim(x$ is helped by money)]
$(\exists x)[x$ is a person $\cdot \sim(\exists y)(y$ is money $\cdot$ x is helped by y)]
$(\exists x)[Px \cdot \sim(\exists y)(My \cdot Hxy)]$

or, alternatively,

$$(\exists x)[Px \cdot (y)(My \supset \sim Hxy)]$$

or, alternatively,

$$\sim(x)[Px \supset (\exists y)(My \cdot Hxy)]$$

which is a fairly straightforward rendition of "Not all persons are helped by money." Note here the relation between our familiar **O** form and the contradictory of the **A** form.

5   Aircraft which have no wings sometimes have horizontally mounted propellers.

This sentence requires three quantifiers.

$(\exists x)(x$ is an aircraft $\cdot$ x has no wings $\cdot$ x has horizontally mounted propellers)
$(\exists x)[x$ is an aircraft $\cdot \sim(\exists y)(y$ is a wing $\cdot$ x has y) $\cdot (\exists z)(z$ is a horizontally mounted propeller $\cdot$ x has z)]
$(\exists x)['Ax \cdot \sim(\exists y)(Wy \cdot Hxy) \cdot (\exists z)(Pz \cdot Hxz)]$

In this sentence, "sometimes" is not serving as a temporal parameter. Rather, it makes clear that only some aircraft lacking wings are being spoken about.

6 People always need people.

Likely, this becomes,

> (x)(x is a person ⊃ x always needs some person)
> (x)[x is a person ⊃ (y)(y is a time ⊃ x needs some person at y)]
> (x){x is a person ⊃ (y)[y is a time ⊃ (∃ z)(z is a person · x needs z at y)]}
> (x){Px ⊃ (y)[Ty ⊃ (∃ z)(Pz · Nxzy)]}

EXERCISES

Using quantifiers and relational predicates where appropriate, put the following into symbols. Use open sentences first.

1 Everything is identical with something.
2 Something is identical with something.
3 Everything is identical with itself.
4 Nothing is identical with everything.
5 There is a restroom in every subway.
6 No subways have restaurants.
7 Every misfortune causes some unhappiness.
8 There are no people who are not bothered by noise.
9 Everybody adores Elizabeth, but Elizabeth doesn't adore anybody.
10 Everybody loves somebody sometime.
11 If Andy helps Bette, then someone helps someone.
12 If every student is helped by every student, then each student is helped by himself.
13 Andy grows tomatoes and onions.
14 People have faith only if they have love.
15 Someone who will befriend an enemy has a great soul.

Proofs Involving Relations

To prove arguments involving relations, the apparatus of Chapter 10 can be used, but we need to add further provisos to the quantification rules. Accordingly, the revised rules are as follows:

UI: (u)φu entails φi *provided that,* if i is a variable, then it must occur free in φi in all places that u occurs free in φu.

This proviso blocks the following erroneous use of **UI:**

```
*   1   (x)(∃ y)Fxy
*   2   (∃ y)Fyy        1, UI Erroneous
```

Assume it is true that for anything you pick x there will be something forthcoming y which stands in relation F to it; but from this it doesn't follow that there is something which stands in relation F to itself. For example, interpret F as "larger than." In this example, φu is everything following the universal quantifier, (x) of line 1. In (∃ y)Fxy, then, x is u and is free. But in φi, which is (∃ y)Fyy, the variable y is i, and y is bound in both of its occurrences by the quantifier (∃ y).

> **EG**: φi entails (∃ u)φu *provided that* if i is a variable then for every u free in φu, the same i is free in φi.

This proviso prevents the following invalid inference:

```
*   1   (x)(∃ y)Fxy
*   2   (∃ y)Fxy        1, UI
*   3   Fxy             2, EI y
*   4   (∃ x)Fxx        3, EG Erroneous
```

The inference from line 1 to line 4 is invalid on the same grounds as those in the previous example. Here the trouble is that the **EG** caught both y and the free x of line 3. But there is no guarantee that the something tentatively named y is the same something which x represents. The proviso prevents us from capturing two (or more) different variables with one use of **EG**.

The following uses of **EG**, however, are correct:

```
*   1   (x)(y)Fxy
*   2   (y)Fxy          1, UI
*   3   Fxx             2, UI
*   4   (∃ x)Fxx        3, EG
```

and

```
*   1   (x)Fxx
*   2   Fxx             1, UI
*   3   (∃ y)Fxy        2, EG
*   4   (x)(∃ y)Fxy     3, UG
```

> **EI**: (∃ u)φu entails φw *provided that* (1) w is a variable which does not occur in any previous line and (2) w occurs free in φw in all places that u occurs free in φu.

Proviso (2) serves the same purpose as the similar proviso of **UI** (above). When we instantiate, either with **UI** or **EI**, we want to prevent the instantiating variable from being captured by another quantifier. Thus, this inference is invalid:

```
*  1   (∃ x)(y)Fxy
*  2   (y)Fyy            1, EI Erroneous
```

A fourth proviso needs to be added to **UG**, which now reads:

UG: ϕw entails $(u)\phi u$ *provided that* (1) w is a free variable, (2) w is not flagged in any previous line, (3) w is not free in an assumed premise within whose scope ϕw occurs, and (4) w is not free in a line obtained by **EI**.

Proviso (4) blocks this invalid inference:

```
*  1   (y)(∃ x)Fxy
*  2   (∃ x)Fxy         1, UI
*  3   Fxy              2, EI x
*  4   (y)Fxy           3, UG Erroneous
*  5   (∃ x)(y)Fxy      4, EG
```

In this case w is y and y is free in line 3, the line obtained from 2 by **EI**. Notice that y is not the variable instantiated by **EI**; yet our rule makes the inference to line 4 invalid, even though the free y was the consequence of the correct use of **UI**. Nonetheless, it was shown earlier that $(y)(\exists x)Fxy$ could be interpreted as true when $(\exists x)(y)Fxy$ was false. Hence the inference from line 1 to line 5 must be invalid. Here again, it may be hard to see why. The answer would seem to be this: Line 1 says that for any y there is some x forthcoming which stands in relation F to it. But by the time we get to line 3, the identity of the x may depend upon *which* y was selected. Thus, Fxy need not hold for *any* y whatever, and hence the use of **UG** on the free y is invalid.

Intuitions notwithstanding, the inference needs to be blocked and proviso (4) accomplishes this — without doing violence to proper uses of **UG**.

SOME EXAMPLES

A Whoever harms anyone harms himself. Andrew harmed Bette; so Andrew harmed himself.

To symbolize this argument, we conveniently limit the "universe of discourse" to persons. That is, instead of letting (x) read as "each thing x," we restrict the objects to persons and let (x) read "each person x." Thus, $(x)(\exists y)Fxy$ can be interpreted as "Everyone harms someone" or "Everyone loves someone." Using obvious predicate letters, then, the argument will look like this:

$$\ast \begin{cases} 1 & (x)(y)(Hxy \supset Hxx) \\ 2 & Hab \qquad /\therefore Haa \end{cases}$$

And the proof proceeds easily:

$\ast$	**3**	$(y)(Hay \supset Haa)$	**1, UI**
$\ast$	**4**	$Hab \supset Haa$	**3, UI**
$\ast$	**5**	Haa	**2** and **4**, Modus Ponens

B   There is somebody whom everybody loves; hence everybody loves somebody.

This becomes:

$\ast$	**1**	$(\exists y)(x)Lxy$	$/\therefore (x)(\exists y)Lxy$
$\ast$	**2**	$(x)Fxy$	**1, EI** y
$\ast$	**3**	Fxy	**2, UI**
$\ast$	**4**	$(\exists y)Fxy$	**3, EG**
$\ast$	**5**	$(x)(\exists y)Fxy$	**4, UG**

C   Some cats eat anything which is nutritious.   No cat eats greasy french fries; hence french fries which are greasy are not nutritious.

$\ast$	$\begin{cases} 1 \\ 2 \end{cases}$	$(\exists x)[Cx \cdot (y)(Ny \supset Exy)]$ $(x)[Cx \supset (y)(Fy \cdot Gy \supset \sim Exy)]$	$/\therefore (x)(Fx \cdot Gx \supset \sim Nx)$
$\ast$	**3**	$Cz \cdot (y)(Ny \supset Ezy)$	**1, EI** z
$\ast$	**4**	Cz	**3**, Simplification
$\ast$	**5**	$Cz \supset (y)(Fy \cdot Gy \supset \sim Ezy)$	**2, UI**
$\ast$	**6**	$(y)(Fy \cdot Gy \supset \sim Ezy)$	**4** and **5**, Modus Ponens
$\ast$	**7**	$Fy \cdot Gy \supset \sim Ezy$	**6, UI**
$\ast$	**8**	$(y)(Ny \supset Ezy) \cdot Cz$	**3**, Commutation
$\ast$	**9**	$(y)(Ny \supset Ezy)$	**8**, Simplification
$\ast$	**10**	$Ny \supset Ezy$	**9, UI**
$\ast$	**11**	$\sim Ezy \supset \sim Ny$	**10**, Trans.
$\ast$	**12**	$Fy \cdot Gy \supset \sim Ny$	**7** and **11**, H.S.
$\ast$	**13**	$(x)(Fx \cdot Gx \supset \sim Nx)$	**12, UG**

When we used **EI** to derive line 3, we instantiated to z so as not to run afoul needlessly of our rule for the use of **UG**.

D   All suffering is evil; hence whatever causes suffering causes evil.

$\ast$	**1**	$(x)(Sx \supset Ex)$	$/\therefore (y)[(\exists x)(Sx \cdot Cyx) \supset (\exists x)(Ex \cdot Cyx)]$
$\ast\ast$	**2**	$(\exists x)(Sx \cdot Cyx)$	
$\ast\ast$	**3**	$Sz \cdot Cyz$	**2, EI** z

**	4	$Sz \supset Ez$	1, UI
**	5	Sz	3, Simplification
**	6	Ez	4 and 5, Modus Ponens
**	7	$Cyz \cdot Sz$	3, Commutation
**	8	Cyz	7, Simplification
**	9	$Ez \cdot Cyz$	6 and 8, Conjunction
**	10	$(\exists x)(Ex \cdot Cyx)$	9, EG
*	11	$(\exists x)(Sx \cdot Cyx) \supset (\exists x)(Ex \cdot Cyx)$	2 and 10, Conditionalization
*	12	$(y)[(\exists x)(Sx \cdot Cyx) \supset (\exists x)(Ex \cdot Cyx)]$	11, UG

EXERCISES

Provide a proof for each of the following:

1   *   **1** $(x)(y)(Fx \supset Gxy)$ $/\therefore (x)(\exists y)(Fx \supset Gxy)$

2   *   **1** $(x)(y)Fxy$ $/\therefore (\exists x)(y)Fxy$

3   *   **1** $(\exists x)(\exists y)(Fx \cdot Gxy)$ $/\therefore (\exists x)Fx$

4   * $\begin{cases} 1 & (x)(y)(Fxy \equiv Gx) \\ 2 & Ga \end{cases}$ $/\therefore Faa$

5   * $\begin{cases} 1 & (x)(Fx \supset Gx) \\ 2 & (x)[(\exists y)(Hxy \supset Fx)] \\ 3 & \sim(\exists x)Gx \end{cases}$ $/\therefore (\exists x)(\exists y) \sim Hxy$

6   *   **1** $(\exists x)[Fx \cdot (y)(Gy \supset Hxy)]$ $/\therefore (\exists x)[Fx \cdot (Ga \supset Hxa)]$

7   *   **1** $(y)(\exists x)(Fx \supset Gy)$ $/\therefore (x)Fx \supset (x)Gx$

8   *   **1** $(x)(y)(Fxy \supset \sim Fyx)$ $/\therefore (x) \sim Fxx$

9   It is false that everyone frustrates everyone; hence there is someone who doesn't frustrate someone else.

10   It is false that someone frustrates everyone; hence there is someone who doesn't frustrate someone else.

11   Nobody frustrates anybody; hence no one frustrates himself.

12   When a person cheats someone, he ought to recompense her. Andrew cheated Bette, so he ought to recompense her.

13   Everything in the Louvre is a work of art. If one does a work of art, one is a genius. There are things in the Louvre done by people who are not well known. Hence, there are geniuses who are not well known. ($Lx = x$ is in the Louvre; $Wx = x$ is a work of art; $Px = x$ is a person; $Dyx = y$ does x; $Gy = y$ is a person; $Wy = y$ is well known.)

14   Everyone is frightened at some time or another. Anytime you are frightened, you tend to act irrationally. There are times, accordingly, when anyone tends to act irrationally. ($Px = x$ is a person; $Ty = y$ is a time; $Fxy = x$ is frightened at y; $Gxy = x$ tends to act irrationally at y.)

15 If there is a barber in the town, then he is required to shave all and only those citizens who don't shave themselves. But if he does, there is no barber in the town.

Some Properties of Relations

The familiar argument, "Andrew is taller than Bette and Bette is taller than Charles, so Andrew is taller than Charles," is valid, but how do we prove it valid? Arguments like these are best seen as *enthymemes* with a suppressed premise: "If x is taller than y, and y is taller than z, then x is taller than z," or, put more simply, the relation "taller than" is *transitive*. Indeed, we can define a transitive relation as follows:

1 $(x)(y)(z)[(Fxy \cdot Fyz) \supset Fxz]$

That is, for any interpretation of F, if 1 is true, then the relation Fxy is transitive. Other examples of transitive relations include "heavier than," "older than," "north of," and many others. Ordinarily, of course, the fact that some relation is transitive is left unsaid in argument, and of course, it is reasonably left unsaid. Yet if necessary, the missing premise can be supplied.

In addition to transitivity there are other important properties of relations which can be defined with quantifiers. Here are some others:

2 $(x)(y)(Fxy \supset Fyx)$

This defines a *symmetrical* relation, e.g., "next to" and "married to."

3 $(x)(y)(Fxy \supset \sim Fyx)$

This defines an *asymmetrical* relation, e.g., "older than" and "south of."

4 $(x)(y)(z)[(Fxy \cdot Fyz) \supset \sim Fxz]$

This defines an *intransitive* relation, e.g., "mother of."

5 $(x)Fxx$

This defines a *totally reflexive* relation. Such relations are rare, but examples include the important relation of identity. *Total reflexivity* is distinguished from *reflexivity*, which is defined variously. Here we define it as:

6 $(x)(y)[Fxy \supset (Fxx \cdot Fyy)]$

Examples of reflexivity include "is the same age as" and "has the same nationality as."

Some relations lack *all* these properties. They are not transitive or intransitive, symmetrical or asymmetrical, etc. A much-used example is "loves." If x loves y, and y loves z, x may or may not love z; if x loves y, y may or may not love x. And while there are those who love themselves but not others and those who love others but not themselves, "loves" would seem to be neither reflexive nor irreflexive.[2]

These features of relations are of interest in their own right, and of course, transitivity and symmetry in particular play important roles in ordinary deductive argument. And it is not hard to prove arguments of the sort with which we began this section—once we supply the missing premise. Thus the argument in question ("Andrew is taller than Bette, etc.") would look like this:

$$
\begin{array}{lll}
* & \left\{
\begin{array}{ll}
\mathbf{1} & Tab \cdot Tbc \\
\mathbf{2} & (x)(y)(z)[(Txy \cdot Tyz) \supset Txz] \quad /\therefore Tac \\
\end{array}
\right. \\
* & \mathbf{3} \quad (y)(z)[(Tay \cdot Tyz) \supset Taz] \quad \mathbf{2, UI} \\
* & \mathbf{4} \quad (z)[(Tab \cdot Tbz) \supset Taz] \quad \mathbf{3, UI} \\
* & \mathbf{5} \quad (Tab \cdot Tbc) \supset Tac \quad \mathbf{4, UI} \\
* & \mathbf{6} \quad Tac \quad \mathbf{1} \text{ and } \mathbf{5}, \text{ Modus Ponens} \\
\end{array}
$$

EXERCISES

Determine whether the following relations are transitive, intransitive, symmetrical, asymmetrical, reflexive, totally reflexive, or none of these. Some relations may have more than one property.

1	west of	**2**	brother of
3	sibling of	**4**	darker than
5	equal to	**6**	belongs to
7	is the same color as	**8**	weighs twice as much as
9	father of	**10**	respects

---

[2] It is, of course, not obviously true that there are those who love themselves, but not others and those who love others but not themselves!

PART THREE

INDUCTION AND INFORMAL FALLACY

TWELVE

INDUCTION

*As absolute certainty is seldom obtainable
in human affairs, reason requires that
men form their opinion of the truth on
the superior number of probabilities on
one side or the other.*

Paraphrased from Lord Mansfield

Differences between Deduction and Induction

Our examination of deduction has provided tools and concepts with which we
can treat a wide range of important arguments. Indeed, deduction is indispensable to thinking, reasoning, problem solving, decision making, science, and
mathematics. But, as we saw earlier, not all inferences and not all arguments
are deductive. In fact, it is probably fair to say that most of the arguments we
encounter in our daily activity are inductions rather than deductions. Moreover,
induction is absolutely indispensable for arriving at all our knowledge of the
universe as it is. Before we see why this is so, let us recapitulate and expand
upon the crucial differences between deduction and induction.

Unlike the premises of deductions, the premises of inductive arguments do
not entail, or necessarily imply, their conclusions. If we call the premises of
inductive arguments *evidence statements* or simply the evidence, then we can
say that in inductions the evidence is not complete. That is, the conclusions
of inductions *go beyond* the evidence. Therefore, if the evidence statements are
true, the conclusion is not necessarily true; it is *at best probable* on the evidence.
For example, suppose that you just turned the ignition key of your 1957 Ford
convertible. The starter turns the engine over, but the car doesn't start. What is

the first thing you might do? You might check the gas gauge. Why do this? You made an induction which could be put into this form:

> 1 Whenever my car is out of gas, it does not start;
> my car does not start;
> _____
> so, probably, my car is out of gas.

In this case, we know that the premises are true, but still we cannot say that *necessarily* the car is out of gas. (It might not start because the fuel pump is clogged or for many other different reasons.) Indeed, examining the *form* of the argument shows it to be an example of the *formal* fallacy of affirming the consequent. That is, the form is invalid. Still, we would want to say that the premises do provide some support for asserting that the car is out of gas. Why is this so? Since it cannot be a matter of form, the answer must lie elsewhere. Quite simply, the *correctness* (*not* validity) of this particular argument derives from the fact that we know something about cars. Specifically, we know that though there are many reasons why cars do not start, one of the common reasons is that they are out of gas. Thus there is a "connection" between the evidence and the conclusion. To be sure, we would not be astonished if we discovered plenty of gas in the tank; the failure of the car to start could also be due to the carburetor, the plugs, the coil, etc. Still, the inference to "Probably, my car is out of gas" is not arbitrary or ill-conceived. It is reasonable. The premises do "support" or tend to "confirm" the conclusion. Such arguments, as indicated earlier, we shall call *correct*.

Now compare this incorrect argument:

> 2 Whenever I wear orange overshoes, my car does not start;
> my car does not start;
> _____
> so, probably, I'm wearing orange overshoes.

This argument is inane, but notice why. Even assuming the premises to be true (and this is certainly possible, especially if I *never* wear orange overshoes), we still would not reasonably suppose that the conclusion is true. And we would not, for we have no reason to believe that there is any connection whatever between the wearing of orange overshoes and cars not starting. To be sure, the world could have been different, and there might have been a connection between such phenomena, but so far as is known there is not. Indeed, this sort of *incorrect* induction accounts for a great many fallacies, myths, and superstitions.[1] In sum, arguments are either valid or invalid; if they are valid, they are deductions; if they are invalid, they are inductions and may be either correct or incorrect.

But correctness, like validity, depends upon the *relation* between premises

[1] See the discussion of inductive fallacies, below, Chapter 15.

and conclusion. In deductions, we called the relation *entailment,* or necessary implication. Thus we have:

DEDUCTION

Premises $\begin{Bmatrix} \text{entail or} \\ \text{necessarily imply} \end{Bmatrix}$ conclusion

In *correct* inductions, though the relation of entailment does not obtain (by definition), we call the relation between premises and conclusion the *relation of confirmation, support,* or *warrant.*[2]
    This relationship can be schematized thus:

INDUCTION

Premises (evidence) $\begin{Bmatrix} \text{confirm} \\ \text{support} \\ \text{warrant} \end{Bmatrix}$ conclusion

In what follows, the three expressions "confirm," "support," and "warrant" will be used interchangeably. The tests for entailment discussed in Part One will not do as tests for the relation of confirmation, since *all* the tests for entailment depended upon the condition that if the premises entail the conclusion, the premises cannot be true and the conclusion false. In inductions, however, the premises can be true and the conclusion false. Our problem, then, will be to see how we can evaluate inductions as being correct or incorrect.
    Suppose now that you were back in the driver's seat of that 1957 Ford, but instead of checking the gas gauge (or the color of your overshoes), you immediately stepped out of the car, dropped the engine, and began a systematic check of the parts responsible for compression. Again, your actions would reflect a belief arrived at by induction. We might put the resulting argument this way:

3 Whenever there is inadequate engine compression, my car does not start; my car does not start;

---

so, probably, there is inadequate compression.

This argument is identical in form to Arguments 1 and 2 above; and, again, if the premises were true, what could be inferred? We said that 2 was incorrect — that we could not reasonably infer its conclusion. But what of 3? As 3 stands, the premises do provide *some* evidence for asserting that there is inadequate engine compression, but saying that this is *probably* so seems too strong. Intuitively, we would judge that the probability that there is inadequate compression is less than the probability that the car is out of gas. This judgment could be illustrated by stating the two arguments in this way:

---

[2] Modern writers call this the *relational concept of confirmation.*

1' Many instances of cars not starting are instances
    when they are out of gas;
    the car will not start;
    _____

    so, . . . it is out of gas.

3' A few instances of cars not starting are instances
    when there is inadequate compression;
    the car will not start;
    _____

    so, . . . there is inadequate compression.

The question then is, what word or words should we fill in for the dots in the conclusions? Notice first that in *neither* can we put the word "necessarily," for that is much too strong. Remember, we could say "so, necessarily, . . ." only if the arguments were deductions. But in order to be deductions, the arguments would have to contain the premise "*All* instances of cars not starting are instances of . . . ." The premises in question do not say this, however. Rather, they are *statistical* statements, which occur frequently in inductions and which will subsequently be examined. For the present let us note that on the basis of the two sets of evidence statements, the probability that the car is out of gas is higher than the probability that there are compression problems. In other words, the evidence statements of the two arguments may be compared with respect to their conclusions. Let us call each conclusion a *hypothesis*, by which we mean a proposed or tentative explanation. Since our two conclusions may be easily understood as being proposed explanations of why the car is not starting, they may be called hypotheses. If we call "The car is out of gas" H_1 and "There is inadequate compression" H_3, then the evidence of Argument 1' supports, warrants, or confirms H_1 more than the evidence of Argument 3' supports, warrants, or confirms H_3.[3]

Now consider deductions with respect to the relation between evidence and conclusion. It would not make sense to say that the premises of one valid argument "entail" its conclusion more than the premises of some *other* valid argument entail its conclusion. All valid arguments are on a par; they each entail, or provide conclusive evidence, for their conclusions. The fact that inductions may sometimes be compared as to their relative probability is important for the methodology of science and for ordinary situations where we are faced with alternative proposals, explanations, and decisions. When we say "This is the best explanation" or "This is the most satisfactory proposal," we are making a comparison whose soundness depends upon how accurately we are estimating the relative confirmation of two or more hypotheses.

Because we frequently can compare inductions, it does not follow, however, that we can say precisely how much more one hypothesis is confirmed over another. Usually we must be content with rather rough qualitative estimates.

_____

[3] Modern writers refer to this feature as the *comparative concept of confirmation*.

Secondly, hypotheses may be so different in kind and subject that they cannot be properly compared at all. For example, there is evidence that confirms the hypothesis that smoking is related to lung cancer and there is evidence that confirms the hypothesis that man descended from Australopithecines. Which hypothesis is better confirmed? That would be a hard question to answer.

Another feature of inductions which is illustrated by Examples 1' and 3' is that correctness is also a function of the relation between the evidence statements and the force of the conclusion. The force of a conclusion depends upon the qualifying expression, also called **modal qualifier,** which can precede it, such as "necessarily" (in deductions), "probably," "very probably," "possibly," etc. Such expressions attach to the conclusions; in "probably *p*," this means "*p* is probable *with respect to the evidence.*"[4] If the conclusion to Argument 3', for example, had been prefaced with the word "necessarily," yielding "So, *necessarily,* there is inadequate compression," we would say that the argument is *in*correct. That is, the evidence does not warrant that claim. To make the argument correct, we would need to make the force of the conclusion compatible with the evidence. If we made the conclusion "*Quite probably,* there is inadequate compression," it still would not be supported by the evidence. The only claim that would be warranted would be "So, *possibly,* there is inadequate compression." One might offer here a kind of rule: The difficulty of constructing a correct argument is directly proportional to the force of the conclusion. As conclusions are made "stronger," the evidence must more nearly approximate completeness. Of course, deciding on the force of the conclusion with respect to any set of evidence statements is not at all an easy matter, and no precise rules are available. Indeed, some writers confess that it is simply a matter of "judgment" (by which they mean something rather subjective) and that is *all* that can be said. In the sections which follow, however, we shall seek certain guidelines for making this decision.

In some inductive arguments, we can replace the vague modal qualifiers with precise quantitative expressions.[5] Suppose we had a statistic compiled by the American Automobile Association that 64 percent of the times when cars fail to start they are out of gas. We could then produce this inductive argument:

1"   64 percent of the instances when cars do not start, they are out of gas; my car does not start;
_____
so, the probability that my car is out of gas is .64.

In this case, having a numerical statistic to appeal to enables us to assign a *numerical* probability to our inference. There are dangers and difficulties in the use of statistics, however, which are discussed in the next chapter.

There is one last important feature of all inductions, called the *requirement*

---

[4] This notion is more fully discussed in the chapter on probability.

[5] The attempt to substitute precise quantitative expressions for the vaguer qualitative modal qualifiers takes one into what is called by modern writers the *quantitative concept of confirmation.*

of total evidence.   This requirement means that in constructing or appraising inductive arguments, we must take into account all the *known* relevant evidence. To illustrate the importance of this requirement, recall the situation in which we have just turned our ignition key and the car does not start.   What are the relevant factors?

We know that there are many things which could cause the engine to fail, among them being no gas, a deficient coil, faulty spark plugs, a clogged fuel line or carburetor, a defective distributor, faulty compression, etc.   We are fairly confident that the day of the week, the color of the car, the apparel of the operator, the intended destination, etc., are each irrelevant.   The decision as to what is relevant or not is a product of what may be termed *background knowledge.* These beliefs are themselves warranted by induction.   For example, the evidence of past experience and our knowledge of auto mechanics, combustion, etc., support our belief that color is irrelevant and that gasoline is relevant.   This background knowledge forms a fabric of interconnected beliefs regarding the problem at hand, and to spell out each item of the fabric would be difficult.   Moreover, some items are supported by high inductive warrant, while others are not.   Finally, we must account for those factors which may be indirectly but not obviously relevant.   Should we, for example, consider the season of the year?   Reflection shows that temperature is relevant since we know inductively that sometimes a very cold temperature is sufficient to prevent a car from starting.   Is there something about the history of this *particular* car which needs to be considered?   A history of ignition defects, for example, would bear on the problem.   It should be clear by now that our original arguments were far from complete as stated.   For example, Argument 1':

Many instances of cars not starting are instances when they are out of gas; my car does not start;

therefore, probably, my car is out of gas.

would be correct *only* if the temperature on that day were *not* far below zero, if that particular car did *not* have a history of ignition defects, etc.   If we ignored these factors, we would be making an unwarranted inference, for we would have not taken into account all the *known* relevant evidence.   Thus, to appraise an argument as correct or to make a correct inductive inference, we must differentiate between all the relevant evidence and all the *known* relevant evidence.   This is so because inductions are *context-dependent.*   That is, we must appraise them in terms of the evidence available at a concrete time and place.   Thus, the argument:

4   The earth appears to be flat;

so, probably, the earth is flat.

is correct in the context of a primitive race of men.   All the background knowledge available to (say) Neanderthal man would adequately support that conclusion. For us, however, there is much relevant evidence which leads us to a contrary conclusion. Neanderthal man did not have telescopes, Newtonian physics, airplanes, and space vehicles. Although all this evidence is relevant to the conclusion, it was not *known* to Neanderthal man and hence could not be known to be relevant. If we remember that correctness, like validity, depends upon the relation between premises (evidence) and conclusion, we should not be puzzled here. To say that an argument is correct is not to say that its conclusion is true; it is to say only that the evidence does support, warrant, or confirm the conclusion. The observational (or empirical) evidence available to Neanderthal man did confirm as probable the hypothesis that the earth is flat. Hence, though the conclusion is (almost certainly) false, the argument in that context was correct.

By comparison with the appraisal of correctness, the appraisal of *validity* is much easier because in deductions the requirement of total evidence is automatically satisfied. If an argument is valid, then the premises constitute complete evidence for the conclusion. Adding new evidence (so long as it is not contradictory) cannot alter the validity of the argument. Thus, by comparison, deductions are *context-independent*. A valid argument was, is, and always will be valid.

It should be emphasized that although inductions are context-dependent, as indicated, it does not follow that they are "subjective," in the sense of being "personal," "whimsical," "capricious," or "arbitrary." In the first place, the correctness of any given inductive argument stems from the *objective* relation between the known relevant evidence statements and its conclusion. Hence, any two impartial evaluations of the argument would be the same. Secondly, in any given context there is a certain amount of relevant evidence which could be produced. That is, to make a correct induction, *any* impartial inquirer must account for all the evidence which would have been available to any *other* inquirer in the *same* context. Thus the correctness of early *homo sapiens'* inference regarding the flatness of the earth is not a matter of their unique ignorance but of the fact that in their context no contrary evidence was available to them or anyone else. Similarly, if today someone offered us Induction 1' on a day in which the temperature was far below zero, we would agree that the argument was incorrect since it ignored relevant evidence which was available. At the same time, it must be noted that scientific breakthroughs and significant new discoveries frequently result when some factor considered irrelevant is shown to be relevant, and vice versa. Louis Pasteur's researches into fermentation and disease, for example, showed that microorganisms, theretofore considered irrelevant, were relevant; and Galileo's researches into free-falling bodies showed that the weight of an object, theretofore considered relevant, was irrelevant. Thus, we cannot be sure in *any* context that *all* the relevant evidence has been accounted for. Still, in induction we must try to account for all the *known* relevant evidence. Going back to our example with the car, since temperature is known to be relevant, an induction which ignored it would not be correct. Only to the extent to which we can approach the ideal of accounting for *all* the relevant evidence can we have confidence in the truth of our inductions. This means, of course, that all inductions are·subject to revision in the light of new evidence.

At this point, let us summarize the chief features of inductions as compared with deductions. Understanding the differences between the two helps considerably in appraising inductive arguments.

1   Inductions, unlike deductions, cannot be appraised by virtue of their form. Formally, they are all nonvalid; hence, appraisal depends upon extraformal or nonformal considerations.

2   The conclusions of inductions are only probable, never certain. Since no inductions are valid, new words of logical appraisal are needed. The words we will use for this purpose are "correct" and "incorrect." Thus, an argument is correct if the evidence statements confirm, warrant, or support the conclusion; incorrect, if they do not.

3   Inductions as well as deductions are appraised by considering the objective relation between premise and conclusion. In deductions the relation is called *entailment*; in inductions it is called the *relation of support, warrant,* or *confirmation*

4   The degree of warrant, support, or confirmation depends upon the completeness of evidence and the force of the conclusion. In deductions, conclusions always have the force of necessity with respect to their evidence since the evidence is always complete. In inductions, the conclusions never have the force of necessity since the evidence is never complete; inductive conclusions can only be expressed in varying degrees of probability.

5   Inductions may be compared as to their degree of probability, but deductions may not be, since their conclusions are always certain with respect to their premises.

6   In some inductions the degree of warrant, support, or confirmation may be represented quantitatively, or numerically, although usually it is expressed qualitatively by means of expressions like "probably," "possibly," etc.

7   Appraising inductions involves what was called the *requirement of total evidence,* which means that all possible known relevant evidence must be taken into account. In appraising deductions this requirement is automatically satisfied.

8   Inductions are context-dependent since their correctness depends upon the evidence available at a particular time and place, or context.

9   While deductions are "self-contained," complete, and hence context-independent, inductions are always subject to revision in the light of new evidence, or new contexts.

In the first paragraph of this chapter we noted that induction is absolutely indispensable for arriving at *all* our knowledge of the universe as it is. Let us see now why this is so. If, for example, you were asked to justify the true statement "All whales are viviparous," you might produce the following deduction:

1   All whales are mammals;
  all mammals are viviparous;

  ∴ all whales are viviparous.

Since this argument is valid and since in valid arguments the conclusion follows, it would appear that we have proved that, necessarily, all whales are viviparous. Actually, however, the argument proves that all whales are viviparous only if the premises themselves are true. Now how can we establish that? Well, we might offer another deduction:

2   All whales have four-chambered hearts;
  all animals with four-chambered hearts are mammals;

  ∴ all whales are mammals.

This establishes the truth of the first premise of Argument 1, but again *only if* the premises of Argument 2 are true. Now, again, how do we establish them? Evidently we could continue this process for some time, but *eventually* we would be forced to make an induction. Somewhere along the way we must begin to look at whales or mammals or animals with four-chambered hearts, etc. Somewhere along the way we shall be forced to offer an argument like this:

3 $Whale_1$ has a four-chambered heart;
  $whale_2$ has a four-chambered heart;
  ⋮
  $whale_n$ has a four-chambered heart;

  so, probably, all whales have four-chambered hearts.

This type of induction, called a *generalization,* is frequently taken to be the paradigm, or model, or induction. That it is an induction can readily be seen by noting that no matter how many whales the subscript n represents, the number will be finite. But the conclusion goes beyond the evidence in asserting that *all* whales have four-chambered hearts, including those which have not yet been inspected! Thus it is possible for the conclusion to be false and the premises, true.

Nor would it do to say that if we found a whale or a collection of whales which did not have four-chambered hearts, they would not *by definition* be whales; for that would reduce the statement "All whales have four-chambered hearts" to a tautology. And tautologies tell us nothing about the world; this particular tautology would only indicate how we have decided to use the word "whale." Indeed, if we did find an animal or a collection of animals which otherwise seemed to be whales but did not have four-chambered hearts, there is no telling what scientists would do, for the statement "All whales have four-chambered hearts" is very well confirmed. That is, *on the evidence* it is reasonably taken as true. Still, until *all* the whales can be counted, past, present, and future (an impossibility), the statement "All whales have four-chambered hearts" must be accepted inductively.

By the same token, all empirical statements, or statements about the world in which we live, ultimately rest on inductions. Consider even the trivial claim that this page is made of paper. What evidence justifies that claim? Someone might say, "It looks like paper, it feels like paper, it tears like paper, it burns like paper; hence it is paper." But does the conclusion follow *necessarily*? Could not all the premises be true and yet the conclusion false? Yes, this is possible, and since it is possible, the argument is an induction. To be sure, the probability that this page is made of paper is very high, or close to certainty, for there is no evidence that it is not. Still, "almost certain" is not the same as "certain." Some skeptical philosophers have made much of this feature which characterizes all knowledge of factual matters, but it need not cause us much concern. After all, from a practical standpoint very near to certainty is all we generally ever need.

EXERCISES

Which of the following arguments are correct? Which are incorrect? Which are difficult to appraise?

1. It has been raining all day; so probably, the fairways will be wet.
2. Each of the eggs on the table came from the same container; the first three tasted were fresh; so, probably, the rest are fresh.
3. Each of a dozen eggs on the table came from the same container; the first eleven we cracked were fresh; so, necessarily, the twelfth is fresh.
4. Mars is a planet; Earth is a planet. Earth has life; hence, Mars probably has life.
5. She accepted my invitation to go to the dance; so surely she loves me.
6. Since most orangutans are unfriendly, we can expect that orangutan to be unfriendly.
7. Generally, we have an early spring in this part of the country; so we can count on having one this year.
8. It looks like soap, it feels like soap, it tastes like soap; so it's soap.
9. Sixty-seven percent of the students on this campus have cars; so Alphonse, a student on this campus, most likely has a car.
10. A front has been moving easterly at a rate of 10 knots, bringing with it wet snow and rain. Since it was in the Ohio Valley last night, the western parts of New York State can expect snow and rain by tonight.

Species of Inductions

For purposes of study, it is convenient to distinguish several species or "forms" of inductions. The three types which we shall discuss are important not only because they are very common, but because they point up many of the pitfalls of induction. These three types are known as **enumerative induction** (or **generalization**), **inductive analogy**, and **eliminative induction** (or **causal reasoning**). We do not mean to imply, of course, that these three are the *only* species of inductions. Indeed, since correct inductions must account for all the relevant evidence (the requirement of total evidence), we can hardly hope to exhaust all the possibilities, especially where a rich diversification of evidence statements is involved. Hence the "forms" of induction which will be described here are only skeletons of certain important types. Moreover, we shall not be concerned with the question of whether or not the three types can somehow be assimilated into one type. Some writers have taken one or another to be primary and have argued that the others can be understood as subspecies of the primary type. Others have made sharp distinctions between them. Our discussion will make only those distinctions which seem important in getting correct inductions.

Enumerative Induction, or Generalization In all of science, especially in the study of animal behavior, there are many examples of enumerative induction. A typical one involves the study of the fiddler crab, a small beach-dwelling crab with a greatly outsized claw. A. S. Pearse spent years watching him, in places as diverse as the Eastern seaboard of the United States, Manila Bay, and the mangrove swamps of Colombia. After carefully observing thirteen different species, Pearse discovered that all fiddler crabs dig burrows in the sand or mud and that when the tide is flowing, they retreat into their burrows and plug up the openings. Pearse also discovered that most fiddler crabs remain within two yards of the burrow. Pearse's inferences were a form of enumerative induction, shown as follows:

> a_1 is a fiddler crab and when the tide flows, he enters his burrow and closes it.
> a_2 is a fiddler crab and when the tide flows, he enters his burrow and closes it.
> $\vdots$
> a_n is a fiddler crab and when the tide flows, he enters his burrow and closes it.
> _____
> Probably all fiddler crabs enter their burrows when the tide flows and close them.

Or, more generally:

> a_1 is an S and P.
> a_2 is an S and P.
> $\vdots$
> a_n is an S and P.
> _____
> Probably all S's are P's.

As before, a represents individuals, "S" and "P" stand for terms. The subscript n represents some finite number. Such inferences are inductions because the conclusions *go beyond* the evidence statements; the inductions are called *enumerative inductions* because the premises enumerate, or list, each of the particular individuals and make some claim about them; they are called *generalizations* because they generalize in going from statements about the observed individuals to a statement about *all* such individuals. Inductions of this sort must be sharply distinguished from what are paradoxically called *perfect inductions,* which are not inductions at all in our sense of the word. The premises of "perfect inductions" enumerate a set of individuals and assert something as true about each individual, but their conclusions do *not* go beyond the evidence. For example:

> a_1 has been observed to be a fiddler crab and has an oversized claw.
> a_2 has been observed to be a fiddler crab and has an oversized claw.
> $\vdots$
> a_n has been observed to be a fiddler crab and has an oversized claw.
> _____
> Therefore, all observed instances of fiddler crabs have oversized claws.

Since the conclusion follows necessarily from the evidence, this argument is not an induction at all. There is all the difference in the world between (1) "All observed instances of fiddler crabs have oversized claws" and (2) "All fiddler crabs have oversized claws." (1) simply summarizes the premises in a single statement; (2) makes a claim about all *possible* fiddler crabs — past, present, and future, observed and *un*observed. Therefore, a "perfect induction" is in fact a deduction.

Not all inductive generalizations have conclusions which assert something as being true of each and every S. Frequently, we can conclude from enumeration that something is true of some determinate portion of the S's. Such inductions are statistical. For example, if in observing fiddler crabs we noticed that most of them never travel more than two yards from their burrows, we could schematize the argument as follows:

> Most of the observed a's which are fiddler crabs
>   remain within two yards of their burrows.
> _____
> Therefore, probably, most fiddler crabs remain within
>   two yards of their burrows.

Or, more generally,

> Most of the observed a's which are S's are P's.
> _____
> Therefore, probably, most S's are P's.

Notice that although the conclusion does not assert that "All S's are P's," we still have an induction, since the conclusion goes beyond the evidence. We are saying that on the evidence some percentage of the observed S's are P's and the same *percentage* holds for *all* S's, both the observed *and* the unobserved. This type of inference can be better seen by enumerating the full set of observed instances. Thus, if in our study we observed 1,167 fiddler crabs for a period of one week or longer and if of that number 984 remained within two yards of their burrow, our argument could then have taken this form:

.84 of the observed a's which are S's are P's.
_____
Therefore, probably, .84 of *all* S's are P's.

This argument is still a generalization, for its conclusion asserts that whenever we are likely to find fiddler crabs, along the Massachusetts coast, Manila Bay, or the mangrove swamps of Colombia, we should expect to find approximately 84 percent of them remaining within two yards of their burrows. In this (fictitious) study, our conclusion would be based upon a sample of 1,167 fiddler crabs. To be sure, there are some special problems concerning the use of statistics, which will be covered in the next chapter. But in all enumerative inductions, both statistical and nonstatistical, several important factors must be considered, for not all arguments of the form so far discussed are correct. Although some are quite forceful, others are practically worthless. To be able to determine which are which, the following factors must be taken into account:

1   The respects in which the individuals have been observed to be *alike* must be known. This is called the *positive analogy*. Our induction, of course, depends upon the fact that each individual has been observed to be both an S and a P, but we must know what other characteristics the individuals have in common. For example, if all the crabs we observed were of one species and lived in one geographical area, the induction would be considerably weakened since we could not reasonably consider the set of observed instances to be a *representative sample* of the fiddler crab population. It might be that *only* that species of fiddler crab under study exhibited the specified behavior characteristic. Or, if we looked only at crabs found on the Massachusetts coastline, it might be that only those crabs behaved in a given way. Pearse's investigation, on the other hand, took this factor into account, for, as we said, he studied twelve different species in a variety of locations. In general, the more alike the exhibited characteristics are, excluding, of course, the fact that each is an S and a P, the less representative is the sample, and hence the lower the probability of the conclusion. To take another case, if we wish to predict how the voters of the United States will vote in a national election, we will have to pick a sample as varied as possible, selecting subjects from different economic and educational levels, religious backgrounds, geographical locations, occupations, sex, etc.

2   For reasons already indicated, the extent to which the individuals of the observed sample *differ* from one another must be known. This is called

the *negative analogy*. As we noted, Pearse attempted to account for this factor in his study not only by observing different species in different locations but also by observing them in different seasons, at different times of the day, etc. It is interesting to note here that the sole fact that a set of individuals shares many characteristics does not entail the conclusion that they differ in few, or conversely. It is entirely possible that individuals which are alike in many ways are also unlike in many ways. Take human beings, for example. Thus, the two factors of similarity and dissimilarity are independent of one another. Which one should be given greater weight in an induction would depend mainly on which characteristics were deemed relevant. If, for example, independent evidence indicates that the color of hair is not relevant to voting behavior, the fact that the individuals of a sample poll had different hair color would not strengthen or weaken the induction. Similarly, if independent evidence indicates that height does not affect voting behavior, the fact that all the individuals in the sample happened to be under six feet tall would not affect the induction. These last considerations suggest the factor which is perhaps the most important but about which the least can be said, namely, relevance.

3   The relevance of S to P must be considered. In general, relevance is determined by considering independent evidence as to whether or not a uniform connection between S and P probably exists. Can we reasonably expect, for example, that a behavior trait like burrowing into sand and closing the opening is a trait uniformly associated with fiddler crabs? To arrive at an answer to this question we must consider a whole fabric of knowledge. Thus, we might ask, are behavior traits usually associated with various types of animals? We know that most species of birds have characteristic behavior traits with respect to their nesting habits, and we know that wood mice, chipmunks, and other burrowing animals display behavior traits which resemble those of the fiddler crab under study. Each of these bits of evidence and many more besides would be a part of the independent evidence which might be used to determine the relevance of S to P. Adducing such evidence would depend upon what was called (in the previous section) *background knowledge*, which, as we noted then, can rarely be spelled out precisely or in great detail.

At times, however, we can state enough of the background knowledge to give high warrant to our generalization. Suppose, for example, that a chemist has discovered a new element, which she calls "mestosperos." In heating a sample of it, she finds that it melts at 476°C. She then concludes that all mestosperos melts at 476°C. The induction here is based on one instance:

a_1, a piece of mestosperos, melted at 476°C.
_____
Therefore, probably, all mestosperos melts at 476°C.

Again, the "all" refers to the mestosperos that she has not tested and to all the mestosperos which will be subjected to heat in the future. But this induction—though based upon one instance—is a correct one. This is so because there is a wide range of independent evidence that *any* pure sample of a given element—whether zinc, copper, gold, etc.—has the same melting point as any other pure sample of that element. Thus, supporting the induction about mestosperos is not only the one observed instance but also all the previous inductions which have established the more general "all" statement that all elements of the same atomic structure will have the same specific melting point. Moreover, this statement is in turn supported in the fabric of our knowledge by a well-developed atomic theory. Hence, in this case we are quite confident that a melting point of 476°C will be uniformly connected to our fictitious new element.

In this connection it might be pointed out that in the physical sciences one or two cases may be enough to warrant designating generalizations as "almost certain," whereas in the social sciences a great many cases are usually required to establish a generalization with a much lower degree of probability. Further reflection as to why this is so reveals that the cases used in the physical sciences are homogeneous, whereas in the social sciences they are heterogeneous. Since one molecule of water or one atom of mestosperos or whatever is like any other molecule of water or atom of mestosperos or whatever, one case in this area is just about completely representative of the whole, so that what is found to be true of one can almost surely be said to be true of all. In the social sciences, on the other hand, the cases generally are much more complex and heterogeneous. Although individuals may be called "workers" or "voters" or "students" because of a few salient characteristics which they have in common, such individuals probably differ in more ways than they are alike. Hence in these areas the problem of picking a representative sample in order to generalize about the whole becomes extremely difficult.

By way of contrast with the generalization concerning the melting point of mestosperos, consider the popular generalization "All redheads are bad-tempered" (or even "Most redheads are bad-tempered"). Such a generalization lacks the independent evidence we have been discussing. Even if conditions one and two above were met, we would strongly be inclined to believe that the connection was "accidental"—that color of hair was *not* relevant to disposition.

The example of an induction from one instance leads us to a fourth factor.

4   Generally, the larger the number of observed instances the greater the probability of the conclusion. But as we have just indicated, a large number of observed instances is neither necessary nor sufficient for the correctness of an induction. And in some areas, like physical science, a small number can actually yield a conclusion with a much higher de-

gree of probability than can a large number in an area like human behavior. Moreover, where there is considerable independent evidence
supporting relevance, as in the case of our fictitious element mestosperos,
enumerative inductions need very few instances to be quite correct. On
the other hand, having many instances does not guarantee a correct induction, especially if conditions one, two, or three above are not satisfied. To be sure, increasing the instances generally increases the number
of differences between individuals (factor 2), although this does not
necessarily improve the sample. Thus if, after interviewing the operators
of cars at the George Washington Bridge, one inferred that all New
Yorkers drive cars, the inference would not be improved by interviewing
1,000, 2,000, or 10,000 people.

To sum up, each of these four factors are important in making correct generalizations; and, although they do not constitute an ironclad
set of rules for correctness, keeping them in mind can help to prevent
many incorrect enumerative inductions.

EXERCISES

A Suppose that on a recent visit to a small village in southern France, a
village named "Fromage," you noticed that the first six Fromagians whom you
met ate cheese with white wine. You therefore concluded that most Fromagians
eat cheese with white wine. Would this inference be made stronger or weaker
by the following alterations? Why?

1 The six Fromagians were members of the same family.
2 The six Fromagians were members of the same economic and social
class.
3 We observed 100 Fromagians eating cheese with white wine.
4 The six Fromagians were all Catholic and we saw them on Friday.
5 We remembered seeing many residents of the Côte d'Azur eating cheese
with white wine.
6 The six Fromagians were all Catholic and they were observed on different days of the week.
7 Instead, we concluded that most Frenchmen ate cheese with white
wine.
8 We remembered seeing many Parisians eating cheese with white wine.
9 We saw one Fromagian who ate cheese with red wine.
10 We saw one Fromagian who ate snails with white wine.

B Suppose that you have been doing some psychological testing with
white rats. A maze has been constructed with a female rat at the end. Four
males have been run through the maze and each has found its way to the female.
You therefore conclude that any rat will find its way to the female. Would this
inference be made stronger or weaker by the following considerations? Why?

11 All four rats had been previously conditioned in the maze.
12 The first two rats had been deprived of food for two days.

13 The first three rats had been isolated from females for one week.

14 The rats were arbitrarily selected from a cage containing seventy-five rats.

15 Only one of the four rats had been previously conditioned in this maze.

16 The conclusion is weakened to read: Any white rat will find its way to the female.

17 The rats were each one month old.

18 Seventy-five male rats were run through the maze and each found its way to the female.

19 The four rats were males who were isolated from females for two weeks.

20 The conclusion is weakened to read: All male rats when suitably conditioned will find their way to the female if they have been isolated from females for one week or longer.

Inductive Analogy An *analogy* is a relation of likeness between two things, such that one or more characteristics of one thing resemble one or more characteristics of another. Thus, societies have been compared to organisms, the flow of electricity to the flow of water, the collision of atoms to the collision of billiard balls, etc. *Similes* and *metaphors* are figurative uses of analogies. To speak figuratively is to employ words and phrases in nonformal ways. Poetry frequently employs figurative language, especially metaphors and similes. For example:

Errors, like straws, upon the surface flow.

The intention of this line is not to assert that literally an error is like a straw. Rather, the line draws attention, in an imaginative way, to how errors are perpetuated by superficial thinking. Similes may be distinguished from metaphors. A simile is an explicit comparison, as exemplified by the line above. A metaphor *suggests* or *implies* a comparison, as for example, "The ship plowed the water," or "She fired a volley of oaths."

Analogies, similes, and metaphors are frequently used nonargumentatively as illustrations or descriptions. In what follows we shall be interested only in inductive analogies, or analogies which are used to establish conclusions. Hence we must distinguish inductive analogies from illustrative or descriptive analogies. The metaphor "She fired a volley of oaths" makes an implicit comparison between a manner of speech and the firing of guns. But there is no argument (in our technical sense), since no conclusion has been drawn and no inference made. The line is best understood as a vivid way to describe her utterances. In class, instructors frequently use analogies to clarify a point. In explaining how current moves in a circuit, for instance, a physics teacher might appeal to the analogy of water moving in a pipe. But so long as he draws no inference from this analogy, no argument is involved. The analogy is purely illustrative. On the other hand, the argument from analogy, or inductive analogy, does draw a conclusion from premises. If the physics teacher in our last example concluded that electricity will not freely flow upward because water does not, he would be using an inductive analogy (however faulty it might be). Or consider the famous "argument from design," used by certain philosophers in the eighteenth century to prove the existence of God:

> Look round the world, contemplate the whole and every part of it: you will find it to be nothing but one great machine. . . . The curious adapting of means to ends, throughout all nature, resembles exactly, though it much exceeds, the productions of human contrivance — of human design, thought, wisdom and intelligence. Since therefore the effects resemble each other, we are led to infer, by all the rules of analogy, that the causes also resemble and that the Author of nature is somewhat similar to the mind of man, though possessed of much larger faculties. . . .[6]

In this inductive analogy the speaker (Cleanthes in Hume's famous *Dialogues*) argues, on the basis of a comparison between the universe and a great machine, that since the machine requires an intelligent creator, so, too, does the universe require an intelligent creator. The form of the argument may be rendered thus:

a has characteristics C_1, C_2, C_3, C_4.
b has characteristics C_1, C_2, C_3.
_____
So, probably, b has characteristic C_4.

In this case a stands for some great machine which has a set of observed characteristics, for example, the purposeful arrangement of parts. C_4 represents the property which all objects having C_1 through C_3 also have, namely, that of being intelligently designed. Since b is *like* a in having C_1 through C_3, it is inferred that (*like* a) b also has an intelligent designer.

The analogical argument is frequently put to more mundane uses. Suppose that from a carton of eggs, all of which were white and graded extralarge, you cracked three and found that each one was fresh. You might then infer that the next egg cracked will also be fresh. This argument from analogy would have a form quite similar to that of our previous example:

a, b, c, have characteristics $C_1, C_2, C_3, C_4, C_5, C_6$.
d has characteristics C_1, C_2, C_3, C_4, and C_5.
_____
So, probably, d has characteristic C_6.

Again, a, b, c represent individuals. C_1 through C_5 represent a set of observed characteristics shared by a, b, c, and d — for example, their shape, size, color, weight, and the fact that they came from the same carton. C_6 represents the property of being fresh. Inductive analogy is related to enumerative induction, particularly insofar as both depend upon drawing an inference based upon sets of characteristics which are shared by individuals and characteristics which are

[6] David Hume, *Dialogues Concerning Natural Religion* (New York: Hafner Publishing Company, 1948), p. 7.

not shared. In both types of argument, we must infer from our observed sample *which* characteristics are connected. But a difference between the two is that in inductive analogy the conclusion is a *singular statement,* while in enumerative induction the conclusion is a *generalization,* either universal or statistical.

Again, not all arguments from analogy are correct; indeed, many of those daily encountered are *not* correct. Most people, it seems, are prone to thinking analogically,[7] and great caution must be exercised when using this form of argument. Each of the four tests applied to enumerative induction apply to inductive analogy, though the first two are applied differently.

1   The respects in which the individuals in the analogy have been observed to be alike must be known. In the argument from design, for instance, we would have to consider to what extent the universe may be compared to a machine. Is the positive analogy strong or weak? If the universe resembles a machine in many ways (if many of its characteristics are indeed like those of a machine), then the argument would be *stronger.* (Notice, by comparison, that in enumerative induction, given a strong positive analogy the argument would be *weaker.*) In the *Dialogues Concerning Natural Religion,* Hume subjects this particular analogy to penetrating criticism and argues that the analogy is thin indeed. He suggests (in the person of Philo) that one might as well argue that the universe is an animal or a vegetable! Similarly, to what extent can the three cracked eggs be compared to the fourth uncracked egg? If a great many characteristics are shared, then, other things being equal, we can reasonably expect the individuals being compared to share the inferred property.

2   The extent to which the individuals compared in the analogy *differ* from one another must be known. Again, if they differ in very many respects, then, other things being equal, the probability that they will share the inferred characteristic is diminished. (Again, notice by comparison that a large negative analogy *increases* the probability of the enumerative induction.) If we know, for example, that that fourth egg came from a *different* carton, then the probability that it will be fresh would be greatly reduced.

3   Relevance must be considered; that is, we must consider whether or not the characteristics upon which the comparison has been made are relevant to the inferred property. As Hume remarks: "Nothing so like as eggs; yet no one, on account of their apparent similarity, expects the same taste and relish in all of them." Hume's point is well taken; the fact that four eggs all *look* alike is little reason to believe that they will *taste* alike, for color, shape, and size are not properties relevant to taste. On the other hand, knowing that they came from the same box would increase the probability that the fourth egg will be fresh since we have reason to believe that in packing eggs, the packers fill the cartons from

---

[7] This is not surprising, for in one sense analogy or comparison underlies all reasoning processes.

the same day's supply. Again, to determine relevance requires background knowledge, in this case a knowledge of eggs, how they are checked, packed, distributed, etc.

4 Generally, the larger the number of observed instances the greater the probability. This factor, however, is subject to the same limitations noted earlier. In our egg example, if we crack eleven eggs instead of three and find them all to be fresh, the probability that the twelfth is also fresh will be quite high.

EXERCISES

Determine which of the following selections contain inductive analogies and which contain analogies for explanation or vividness. Appraise the inductive analogies by applying the tests discussed here.

1   "Then you should say what you mean," said the March Hare.
   "I do," Alice hastily replied; "at least—at least I mean what I say—that's the same thing, you know."
   "Not the same thing a bit!" said the Hatter. "Why, you might just as well say that 'I see what I eat' is the same as 'I eat what I see'!"
   "You might just as well say," added the March Hare, "that 'I like what I get' is the same thing as 'I get what I like'!"
   "You might just as well say," added the Dormouse, which seemed to be talking in its sleep, "that 'I breathe when I sleep' is the same thing as 'I sleep when I breathe'!"
                               Lewis Carroll, *Alice in Wonderland*

2 When a squid injects its ink into the water to confuse an enemy or its potential prey, it is obfuscating—that is, clouding the water in order to prevent clear sight. Many editorial writers act like the frightened squid. They confuse and cloud, obfuscate, by introducing issues which are not germane to the question being discussed.
       Curtis Bradford and Hazel Moritz, *The Communication of Ideas*

3 Much of the revulsion against the use of atomic weapons arises because the very newness makes it seem more horrible. A careful cataloguing of the injuries resulting from the use of the automobile would also be impressive but any proposal to outlaw the automobile would be considered ridiculous.
                               R. E. Lapp, *Must We Hide?*

4 Concerning the illegal faking of football injuries to get a time-out, the sports writer Whitney Martin once wrote: "Efforts have been made to defend the faking of injuries by pointing out it has been done hundreds of times, which is the same as saying a speeder isn't guilty of exceeding the speed limit because others do it and get by with it."

5 The difference between a composition that is not planned and one that

is well planned is the difference between a pile of stones and a house made of stone. A pile of stones has no organization; it is a mere heap, a little chaos. A stone house has organization; the stones have been put into place according to a design; they are parts of a whole.

Donald Davidson, *American Composition and Rhetoric*

6 Gentlemen, I want you to suppose a case for a moment. Suppose that all the property you were worth was in gold, and you had put it in the hands of Blondin, the famous rope walker, to carry across the Niagara Falls on a tight rope. Would you shake the rope while he was passing over it, or keep shouting to him, "Blondin, stoop a little more! Go a little faster!" No, I am sure you would not. You would hold your breath as well as your tongue, and keep your hands off until he was safely over. Now the government is in the same position. It is carrying an immense weight across a stormy ocean. Untold treasures are in its hands. It is doing the best it can. Don't badger it! Just keep still, and it will get you safely over.

Abraham Lincoln

7 Running a government is like running a ship; we need a strong hand at the helm.

Thomas Carlyle

8 In arguing that the cure of mental illness should be stressed rather than the exact diagnosis of it, Dr. William Menninger, the well-known psychiatrist, once stated: "One does not have to know the cause of a fire to put it out."

9 A Monarchy is a merchantman which sails well, but will sometimes strike on rock, and go to bottom; a republic is a raft which will never sink, but then your feet are always in the water.

Fisher Ames

10 Speaking of Federal appropriations to the States, James M. Beck, Solicitor General under President Harding, compared them "to that tragedy on the ocean seas when the Titanic was struck by a submerged ice floe. After the collision, which was hardly felt by the steamer at the time, the great liner at first seemed to be intact and unhurt and continued to move. But a death wound had been inflicted under the surface of the water. . . . The power of appropriation is such an ice floe . . . and has inflicted a similar fatal wound to the good ship Constitution."

As quoted by Lindsay Rogers, "Speaking of Books: Metaphors"[8]

Eliminative Induction: Mill's Methods   Eliminative induction is a type of induction also known as causal reasoning. To illustrate it, let us recall the problem introduced at the beginning of the chapter: Our 1957 Ford will not start, and we are

[8] *The New York Times Book Review*, July 9, 1967, sec. 7, p. 2.

interested in determining why. As we saw, we might begin by posing several hypotheses which would account for this fact, such as the car is out of gas, the ignition is poor, the carburetor is not functioning, the engine compression is inadequate, etc. By eliminating some of these, we reason that we can narrow the possibilities and thereby approach the truth. We proceed to check the gas gauge; it reads full, a finding supported by a check of the tank. The plugs are in good condition, as are the coil and the carburetor. So we conclude that it is probably the compression. Such a process illustrates eliminative induction.

The principle here is this: If $H_1, H_2, \ldots, H_n$ constitute a set of hypotheses, each of which would account for some fact (in this case the failure of the car to start), and if $H_1, H_2, \ldots$ is *not* the correct hypothesis, then probably H_j is. Notice that we must say probably H_j is correct since we have no way of knowing if the set of hypotheses originally proposed constitutes a *complete* set. It is entirely conceivable that we have overlooked the one hypothesis which in fact does account for the failure of the car to start. In eliminative induction this situation always exists, since the set of hypotheses which might be produced is, theoretically, infinite, although practically the state of our knowledge limits the possibilities. Again, the possibilities which are actually chosen would depend upon background knowledge.

Of course, if we could be sure that our set of hypotheses was complete, then, by elimination, we could establish with *certainty* the correct hypothesis. But then we would have a deduction, not an induction. Eliminative induction, however, does utilize deduction in the elimination. When we concluded, for example, that the failure of the car to start was not the lack of gas (here H_1 is "The car is out of gas"), we reasoned thus:

> If the car is out of gas, the tank will be empty.
> The tank is not empty.
> _____
> Therefore, necessarily, the car is not out of gas.

This is a deduction; indeed, it is an example of the valid argument form which we called *modus tollens*. Hence, the elimination or disconfirmation of possible hypotheses can always be construed as an example of modus tollens. Similarly, universally quantified hypotheses, "All S is P," or, in modern notation, $(x)(Sx \supset Px)$, are proved false by finding one individual which is S and not-P. Notice that the universal conclusions of enumerative inductions are for this reason *deductively disconfirmed* by finding one individual, $a_1, a_2, \ldots$, etc., which is S and not-P.[9] This feature is sometimes referred to as the *asymmetry of confirmation and disconfirmation*. That is, one individual which is S and not-P is sufficient (deductively) to *disconfirm*, while many individuals which are both S and P does not assure confirmation. Eliminative induction utilizes this asymmetry in seeking to eliminate hypotheses from among alternatives. The process, however, is still essentially inductive since we can never be sure that we have eliminated all but one of the alternatives.

[9] Statistical generalizations are not so easy to disconfirm. See the next chapter.

John Stuart Mill's famous methods of experimental inquiry are perhaps best understood as methods of elimination. Mill emphasized the use of the methods in investigating causes and effects. We shall instead introduce the clearer and wider notions of necessary and sufficient conditions.[10]

Necessary and Sufficient Conditions   *A is a sufficient condition for B, if whenever A occurs (or is present), B occurs (or is present).*   If we adopt the symbol for the material conditional, then we have: $A \supset B$, where $A \supset B$ will be read as "Whenever A, B" or "If A, then B."[11]   Thus, if it is true that whenever a person is shot in the heart, the person dies, then getting shot in the heart is a sufficient condition for dying.   Similarly, if it is true that if there is life on Mars, then there is oxygen on Mars, we can say that the presence of life on Mars is a sufficient condition for there being oxygen on Mars.   Notice that only the first example would normally be understood as a "cause."   But both examples satisfy our definition of a sufficient condition.

   A is a necessary condition for B, if whenever A is absent (or does not occur), then B is absent (or does not occur).   Symbolically we have $\sim A \supset \sim B$: "If it is not the case that A (or A is absent), then it is not the case that B (or B is absent)."   For example, oxygen is a necessary condition for life as we know it; that is, if oxygen is absent, then life is absent.   Similarly, having a passing average is necessary for earning a degree, and raising the temperature of a substance to its kindling temperature is necessary for its combustion.   Again, only the *last* example would normally be understood as a "cause," yet all the examples satisfy our definition.

   As the examples show, the notion of "cause" is not clear; sometimes it means sufficient condition and sometimes it means necessary condition.   Generally, what we will call "the cause" will be some condition (sufficient or necessary) which strikes us as important or as constituting a significant difference in a given situation.   Thus, for example, we normally would not consider the presence of oxygen a "cause" for a fire, since it is always present.   Yet it is as necessary a condition for combustion as raising the temperature of the combustible material to kindling temperature.[12]

   We may now readily define necessary and sufficient condition: *A is a necessary and sufficient condition for B means* $(A \supset B) \cdot (\sim A \supset \sim B)$.   For example,

---

[10] Mill's discussion, which appeared originally in his *A System of Logic*, first edition, 1843, has been much maligned and misunderstood.   While we do not wish to compound the misrepresentation, our discussion will not be restricted to his treatment but will contain several points of departure.

[11] We are adopting and *adapting* $\supset$ here, since, while previously it was used as a connective between statements, it now represents a connection between conditions.

[12] Analysis of "causes" in terms of necessary and sufficient conditions is helpful but at best only a partial analysis.   Most would want to add that if A causes B, A must be temporally prior, spatially contiguous, and, in some sense, efficacious in bringing about B.   As Hume showed, this last feature seems unanalyzable (or even meaningless), since all we ever observe is constant conjunction.

   It is worth emphasizing here, however, that whatever constitutes the full explication of "cause," the notions of necessary and sufficient conditions are extremely helpful in inquiry.

being a three-sided plane figure is necessary and sufficient for something being a triangle. Notice further the relations which obtain between sufficient and necessary conditions:

1 If A is sufficient for B, then B is necessary for A; and if B is necessary for A, then A is sufficient for B:

$$(A \supset B) \equiv (\sim B \supset \sim A)$$

Thus, if the presence of life as we know it is sufficient for the presence of oxygen, then the presence of oxygen is necessary for the presence of life, and conversely.

2 Each of the following are equivalent statements:
    a The presence of A is sufficient for the presence of B;
    b The absence of B is sufficient for the absence of A;
    c The presence of B is necessary for the presence of A;
    d The absence of A is necessary for the absence of B.

All are logically equivalent to $A \supset B$. They can be tested intuitively by reading A as "life as we know it," and B as "oxygen." Statement **d** seems counterintuitive, but this is so because we would rarely use this version.

EXERCISES

Given that paying your parking tickets is necessary for graduation, determine whether the following are true or false:
    1 If you graduate, then you will have paid your parking tickets.
    2 Not paying your parking tickets is sufficient for not graduating.
    3 If you don't graduate, then, necessarily, you didn't pay your parking tickets.
    4 Either you don't graduate or you pay your parking tickets.
    5 If you pay your parking tickets, then necessarily you graduate.

The Method of Agreement Suppose that you are interested in determining which factors are responsible for alcoholic fermentation and you have selected a wide variety of fermented liquids, including various sorts of wine, beer, vinegar, and cider. Under microscopic examination you find that each of these fermented liquids has a characteristically shaped microorganism[13] (which is yeast, or *Mycoderma aceti*). You conclude that this microorganism is the "cause" of the fermentation. This simple experiment reveals the logic of Mill's method of agreement. Since in each of the fermented samples there was, presumably, only one

---

[13] This example is suggested by the work of Louis Pasteur, whose various researches reveal illuminating applications of the methods.
    It should be noted that it was known before Pasteur's researches that yeast was responsible for fermentation. But according to the then prevailing view, yeast was only a catalytic chemical substance. Pasteur argued that yeast (and other microorganisms) were living things.

factor in agreement, that factor is inferred to be the "cause." As Mill put his "canon":

> If two or more instances of the phenomenon under investigation have only one circumstance in common, the circumstance in which alone all the instances agree is the cause (or effect) of the given phenomenon.

Although this method is certainly useful and efficacious, notice that it does not "prove" that yeast causes alcoholic fermentation. There are two main reasons why: (1) We must assume that *one and only one* factor is in agreement; (2) we must assume that our analysis of the possible alternatives is complete. But neither of these assumptions can be met. In our present example there are many other factors which are common to all cases of fermentation. Not only is sugar always present, but so are certain other conditions, such as temperature, degree of dilution, etc., which our microscopic analysis would not have revealed. Moreover, many other factors which are probably present are deemed to be *irrelevant*, such as the source, location, type of container, manner of handling, and season of the year. And other factors considered irrelevant, such as the position of the moon or the presence of kitchen odors, are conceivably relevant. To begin our experiment, however, we *assumed* both that these factors were not operative and that the cause might be found by microscopic analysis of the liquids. The need for these assumptions emphasizes the role of an initial hypothesis in the use of the method. Without some prior idea or educated guess as to where to look and as to how to carry out our analysis, we simply could not have even begun.[14] In the chapter which follows, we shall look more thoroughly into what the "invention" of hypotheses involves and into their role in inquiry.

If we schematized the method of agreement, it might look like this:

1 $A\ B\ C\ D(x_1, x_2, \ldots) \rightarrow E(y_1, y_2, \ldots)$
2 $A\ B\ F\ G(x_1, x_2, \ldots) \rightarrow E(y_1, y_2, \ldots)$
3 $A\ G\ C\ K(x_1, x_2, \ldots) \rightarrow E(y_1, y_2, \ldots)$
   $\therefore A \qquad\qquad\qquad \rightarrow E$

In terms of our example the capital letters A, B, C, D, F, etc., would represent the factors which are hypothetically responsible for fermentation, and the capital letter E would represent fermentation. But since there are many other factors present which are not taken into account by our experiment, we use small letters (x_1, x_2, y_1, etc.) to represent them and put them within parentheses. Then, since A is the only factor known to be in agreement, or common to all cases, we conclude that A is a possible determining condition of E.

We say "determining condition" instead of "cause" since we are now in a better position to see what the method of agreement actually does. Though it

---

[14] Mill tended to overrate his methods, especially in thinking that they were methods of *proof.* Although he also says that they are methods of discovery, he recognized the need for hypotheses.

does not prove that *A* is the cause of *E*, *it does eliminate certain factors as not being necessary conditions for E.* Thus, if *B* were a necessary condition for *E*, *E* could not have occurred in the absence of *B*. In line three, *E* does occur in *B*'s absence; hence *B* cannot be necessary for *E*. Similarly *C*, *D*, *F*, *G*, and *K* are *eliminated* as necessary conditions,[15] which leaves us with *A* as being the only possible factor in our experiment which is a *possible* necessary condition. "Possible" is the most we can say of it, for, even though it has not yet been eliminated, the experiment does not, and cannot, positively confirm it to be a necessary condition. In some other experiment, we might find that alcoholic fermentation occurred in the *absence* of yeast. That this could happen may easily be seen. Perhaps it is not the yeast as such which is necessary, but some ingredient in the yeast also present in some other substance which causes fermentation. Notice, finally, that the method of agreement cannot eliminate conditions as not being *sufficient.* Indeed, each of the factors represented by capital letters might be sufficient for fermentation.[16]

The method of agreement has many various applications. Suppose, for example, that in investigating head injuries in automobile crashes, we discover that in every case where the passenger's head collided with the windshield he was not wearing a seat belt. We conclude that not wearing a seat belt is a possible necessary condition for sustaining a head injury resulting from impact with the windshield.

The Method of Difference In 1858, while on vacation at his summer home in Arbois, France, Pasteur had the opportunity to submit a variety of the regional wines, both spoiled and unspoiled, to microscopic examination. In each of the spoiled wines he found microorganisms which were absent in the unspoiled wines. This finding led him to the conclusion that the "diseases" of fermentation were caused by microorganisms differing from the yeast bacteria. This procedure illustrates the method of difference, which Mill stated as follows:

> If an instance in which the phenomenon under investigation occurs and an instance in which it does not occur have every circumstance in common save one, that one occurring only in the former, the circumstance in which alone the two instances differ is the effect, or the cause, or an indispensable part of the cause of the phenomenon.

Schematically,

[15] The elimination is deductive. Compare above, p. 254.

[16] This raises the question of the so-called "plurality of causes," or preferably "plurality of sufficient conditions." However, we have good reason to suppose that if (say) *B* is sufficient for *E* and *K* is sufficient for *E*, *E* in fact is *not* the same, though it may be called by the same name, in this case "fermentation." That is, different "causes" of "fermentation" lead to different *sorts* of fermentation. Similarly, a bullet in the heart is sufficient for death and so, too, is decapitation, but the sort of death is quite different. Although from a practical view *death* is regarded as a *single* occurrence, it is an abstraction which varies in different contexts and requires analysis.

$$1 \quad A \ B \ C \ D(x_1, x_2, \ldots) \rightarrow E(y_1, y_2, \ldots)$$
$$2 \quad \bar{A} \ B \ C \ D(x_1, x_2, \ldots) \rightarrow \bar{E}(y_1, y_2, \ldots)$$
$$\therefore \ A \qquad\qquad\qquad \rightarrow E$$

Here the bar over the letters indicates the absence of what the letters A and E stand for. As before, in using this method, we must make assumptions: (1) We must assume that *one and only one* factor is different in the positive case (where E occurs) and in the negative case; and (2) we must assume that our analysis of the factors is complete. Again, in practice these two assumptions cannot be fully realized. Undoubtedly, the wines examined had differences other than the presence of different microorganisms, some of which were not revealed by Pasteur's analysis. A chemical analysis, for example, would have brought them out. Moreover, many of these factors and probably others were ruled out at the outset of the experiment. As previously suggested, they were ruled out by Pasteur's initial hypothesis, namely that the "cause" was something which could be discovered by microscopic analysis.

The method of difference, however, unlike the method of agreement, *does eliminate conditions as not being sufficient.* For if B, for example, were sufficient for E, then in the presence of B, E should have occurred. Since it did not, B is not sufficient for E. Similar considerations apply to C and D in our illustration. Hence, A remains as the only possible sufficient condition of E. Again we say "possible" since it might be that E would *not* occur in A's presence. This can be seen by noticing it is A and B when taken *conjointly* which is sufficient, or perhaps E was occasioned by one of the unknown x's in line 1. By contrast with the method of agreement, the method of difference sheds no light on the necessity of conditions, but this is a very important inductive method with wide applications in science and ordinary life. Its correct use, however, usually requires carefully controlled test conditions, although we often unwittingly and correctly use the method without such conditions. As Mill noted, "When a man is shot through the heart, it is by this method that we know it was the gunshot that killed him, for he was in the fullness of life immediately before, all circumstances being the same except the wound."

The Joint Method of Agreement and Difference   The joint method has frequently been thought to be nothing more than a combination of the methods of agreement and difference. But it is not.[17] As Mill states it:

> If two or more instances in which the phenomenon occurs have only one circumstance in common, while two or more instances in which it does not occur have nothing in common save the absence of that circumstance, the circumstance in which alone the two sets of instances differ is the effect, or the cause, or an indispensable part of the cause, of the phenomenon.

---

[17] Mill makes this point quite clear, and it is puzzling why so many have thought otherwise.

Schematically,

$$
\begin{array}{llll}
\textbf{1} & A\ B\ C\ D(x_1,\ x_2,\ \ldots) & \rightarrow & E(y_1,\ y_2,\ \ldots) \\
\textbf{2} & A\ B\ H\ G(x_1,\ x_2,\ \ldots) & \rightarrow & E(y_1,\ y_2,\ \ldots) \\
\textbf{3} & A\ G\ J\ L(x_1,\ x_2,\ \ldots) & \rightarrow & E(y_1,\ y_2,\ \ldots) \\
\textbf{4} & \bar{A}\ G\ M\ N(x_1,\ x_2,\ \ldots) & \rightarrow & \bar{E}(y_1,\ y_2,\ \ldots) \\
\textbf{5} & \bar{A}\ O\ C\ R(x_1,\ x_2,\ \ldots) & \rightarrow & \bar{E}(y_1,\ y_2,\ \ldots) \\
\therefore & A & \rightarrow & E
\end{array}
$$

Lines 1, 2, and 3 may be taken as the method of agreement, but no combination of lines will provide the method of difference. Indeed, as Mills points out, the joint method can frequently be used where the method of difference could not have been. This is especially true where it is not possible to control test conditions, as, for example, in certain research in the social sciences. To illustrate, suppose that we were interested in determining which factors are responsible for juvenile delinquency. After interviewing a wide variety of youths, both those who have been convicted of juvenile crimes and those who have not, we find that the delinquents are hostile to their parents (A in our schema) and the non-delinquents are not. Hence, we infer that hostility to parents is a determining factor. Perhaps all the test cases differ widely in their socioeconomic backgrounds, a fact which would rule out our being able to use the method of difference. Moreover, the delinquents might have *several* characteristics in common. If so, then we could not have even used the method of agreement. In our schema, this would mean that B (say) was found in lines 1, 2, *and* 3. In this case, there would be grounds for inferring that A was a possible determining factor, either by itself or perhaps in conjunction with B. Further research might then be directed toward checking these possibilities.

Although the joint method has extremely important uses, it does not, as we have suggested, combine the virtues of the other two methods. In many ways it combines their vices. Like the other methods, it requires the intelligent use of an hypothesis in order to get started. Thus assumptions as to relevance must still be made, and, as before, the adequacy of the analysis is always subject to doubt. But like other methods it does eliminate. In our illustration, for example, C, H, and G are eliminated as being not necessary conditions, G, M, and R are eliminated as being not sufficient. A fuller discussion of some of the pitfalls to which arguments of this type are vulnerable appears in Chapter 15.

The Method of Concomitant Variations This method, which seems a variant of the method of difference, was formulated by Mills as follows:

> Whatever phenomenon varies in any manner whenever another phenomenon varies in some particular manner, is either a cause or an effect of that phenomenon, or is connected with it through some fact of causation.

Examples of the method are very common: The more money a family earns, the more it spends for recreation; the higher the interest rates go, the less building occurs; the more rain that falls, the better the crops grow. As one factor varies, the other varies concomitantly. It should be noted, however, that such variations, or correlations, are not necessarily causal though they may suggest some type of causal relationship. Some correlations, as we shall see a little later, can be wholly accidental.

The Method of Residues   Although Mill thought otherwise, this method is also a variation of the method of difference. Mill described it thus:

> Subduct from any phenomenon such part as is known by previous inductions to be the effect of certain antecedents, and the residue of the phenomenon is the effect of the remaining antecedents.

Schematically,

$$A \longrightarrow E_1 \quad \text{(Known)}$$
$$A + X \rightarrow E_1 + E_2$$
$$\therefore X \rightarrow E_2$$

The method may be illustrated by the Curies' discovery of radium. When they found that a specimen of pitchblende was far more radioactive than its uranium content could account for, they concluded that the pitchblende contained some theretofore unknown substance which was causing the increased radioactivity. This presumably led to their discovery of radium.

EXERCISES

A   In the following cases, determine (a) which of Mill's methods are used and (b) what conclusion is reached and how probable it is.

1   Knowing that anthrax bacteria do not develop in temperatures of 44°C and higher, Pasteur set about to discover why birds were immune to these bacteria, which killed mice, sheep, guinea pigs, and other animals. Inoculating a hen with anthrax, he put its feet in 25°C water, whereupon its body temperature went down to 37°C and it died within twenty-four hours. He did the same thing to another hen, but this time when the disease was at its peak, he removed the hen, wrapped it in wool, and put it in an oven at a temperature of its original body heat. The hen recovered and its blood showed no trace of anthrax. Pasteur concluded that birds are immune because of their warm blood, which is 42°C, the difference of two degrees being compensated for by their general resistance.

2   It seems that economic conditions have a direct bearing on health. As former Senator Paul Douglas pointed out, "The Detroit Housing Commission reports that the pneumonia death rate is 3 times greater in the

slum area than elsewhere; infant mortality 6 times that of normal neighborhoods; the tuberculosis death rate is 10½ times greater in the slums."

3   For the years 1948 to 1957, the average price earnings ratio of Dow-Jones industrial stocks was 11.1. For the years 1958 to 1967, the average was 18.6. Alfred L. Malabre Jr. of *The Wall Street Journal* (August 29, 1967) points out:

In 1948–57, U. S. joblessness was below 5% of the labor force in 7 of the 10 years. The unemployment rate even dipped below the 3% mark one year and never reached 6%. In the second ten years, unemployment exceeded 5% of the labor force seven times, nearly 7% in two years, and dropped below 4% only once — not surprisingly in 1966, the year that the price-earnings ratio plunged. Thus, a relative scarcity of manpower, as indicated by a low unemployment rate, has seemed to go hand-in-hand with low price-earning ratios, while ratios have been high in years that a high unemployment rate indicated relatively free availability of men for industry to hire.

4   In a certain textile plant in Philadelphia absenteeism and labor turnover in the mule-spinning department were excessive — 250 percent per year compared to 5 percent for the other departments. Although wages were increased and bonuses offered, the excessive absenteeism and labor turnover continued. It was then decided on the basis of certain physical examinations to give the men regular rest periods throughout the day. After a year of this system there was no labor turnover at all. It seems evident that the rest periods caused the big improvement.

5   Doctors at the University of Georgia Medical School, in examining eleven patients suffering from keratitis, a form of blindness, found that all had a vitamin deficiency of riboflavin. When the eleven were put on a diet rich in riboflavin, their sight became normal.

6   To prove that pellagra was not caused by microbes, Goldberger injected himself and his assistants with the blood of pellagra victims and even ate small portions of their excreta. Aside from a certain temporary discomfort, there were no ill effects.

7   In North Carolina in 1954, the year that radar systems for clocking automobiles were instituted, there was a 19 percent reduction in the rate of automobile accidents and fatalities. The state subsequently decided to institute more systems.

8   On Friday night a certain inveterate partygoer drank a large quantity of scotch and soda and later felt queasy. The next afternoon he drank bourbon and soda and later felt queasy. That night he drank rye and soda and later felt queasy. On Sunday night he drank gin and soda and later felt queasy. He concluded that drinking soda made him feel queasy.

9   From 1920 to 1960 the Dow-Jones industrial stock average rose 609 percent. During that same period the average gain in total post office

revenues, the daily average of local telephone calls in the Bell system, and the number of bachelor degrees conferred on male college students was 614 percent. Since this correlation is too high to be coincidence, it must be concluded that all these factors are causally interrelated.

B Given the following model schema of Mill's joint method, what can be inferred? Answer true, false, or unknown.

$ABCD \rightarrow E$

$ABFG \rightarrow E$

$AGHJ \rightarrow E$

$KGHN \rightarrow \bar{E}$

$KHNO \rightarrow \bar{E}$

10	A is sufficient for E	**T**	**F**	**U**
11	A is necessary for E	**T**	**F**	**U**
12	G is not sufficient for E	**T**	**F**	**U**
13	H is not sufficient for E	**T**	**F**	**U**
14	H is not necessary for E	**T**	**F**	**U**
15	B is sufficient for E	**T**	**F**	**U**
16	GH is not necessary for E	**T**	**T**	**U**
17	$KGNO$ is necessary for E	**T**	**F**	**U**
18	E is not sufficient for A	**T**	**F**	**U**
19	E is not necessary for G	**T**	**F**	**U**

THIRTEEN

PROBABILITY

There is no more common error than to assume that, because prolonged and accurate mathematical calculations have been made, the application of the result to some fact of nature is absolutely certain.

Alfred North Whitehead

Three Senses of "Probable"

In the last chapter we made considerable use of expressions like "probably," "quite probably," "possibly," etc. Indeed, we needed them to describe inductive arguments. However, though it may not be immediately apparent, there are several different concepts of probability which need to be differentiated. For our purposes we shall distinguish between three different senses, each of which is important to inductive logic.

Probability as Degree of Confirmation In the last chapter we discussed what has been called **probability as degree of confirmation.** This means that when we say "It is probable that *p*" (where *p* is some statement) or "Probably, *p*," we are saying that *p is probable relative to, or with respect to, a given body of knowledge.* This sense of "probable" is central to inductive logic, for induction is concerned with the relation of support, warrant, or confirmation of a conclusion (or hypothesis) with respect to the evidence. When we say, for example, "Probably, the car is out of gas," we are saying in an elliptical way "On the basis of the relevant evidence, it is probable that the car is out of gas," or "On the evidence, we may inductively infer that the car is out of gas." Similarly, when we say "Darwin's hypothesis is highly probable," we are saying, "Given the body of evidence E, Darwin's hypothesis H is highly probable." Notice that in each case, we are talking about the probability of a *statement* with respect to a *body of statements*, each of which expresses the relevant evidence.

Thus though we often speak of the probability of a statement, statements in themselves are neither probable nor improbable. Statements are either true or false, though we may not know whether they are true or whether they are false. When we call them *probable* or *improbable*, however, we do so only with respect to evidence statements. And for this reason the degree of probability (in this sense) varies with the context, or available evidence. In some contexts, where less evidence is available, the probability will be less; in other contexts, where more evidence is available, the probability will be greater. For example, the statement "The earth is flat" is either true or false and by itself is neither probable nor improbable. But when Neanderthal man said, "It is probable that the earth is flat" his statement could be taken to mean "It is probable relative to the evidence now available."

This sense of *probable* has frequently been called *rational credibility, degree of belief*, or *degree of reasonable expectation*. These expressions are acceptable but misleading, for they suggest that probability in this sense is subjective since "belief," "expectation," or "credibility" are psychological manifestations. But as we have seen, probability as degree of confirmation is concerned with the objective relation between a statement (the conclusion) and a body of evidence statements. Indeed, many people believe things that they ought not to believe; that is, their beliefs rest on *incorrect* inductions.

Probability as Relative Frequency   The second important concept of probability is called **probability as relative frequency,** or **statistical probability.** Suppose it is asserted that the probability of recovering from a streptococcus infection is very high if suitable dosages of penicillin have been administered. What is being asserted? What we are saying is that with respect to the total cases of streptococcus infections treated with penicillin, most of the persons who have been administered penicillin have recovered. That is, given a certain class of cases, a large subclass has recovered. Thus, this sense of probability refers to classes of cases or classes of outcomes in which something is true of some portion of the class. That is why this sense of probability is called *relative frequency*. In our example, the frequency of recoveries is high relative to the total class of infections treated with penicillin. Similarly, this sense is statistical since it is based on a statistic which in this case involves an enumeration of patients who were treated and recovered as compared to all those who had the infection and were not treated.

So as to keep our senses of probability straight, let us call probability as degree of confirmation *probability$_1$* and probability as relative frequency, *probability$_2$*. By comparison, then, probability$_1$ refers to the probability of a statement with respect to other statements; probability$_2$ refers to the probability of a class of outcomes with respect to another class of outcomes. Thus while probability$_1$ is concerned with the logical relation between statements, probability$_2$ is factual and empirical and is based upon the actual happenings in the world. Because of this, statistics of various sorts are the data from which statistical probabilities arise. If an insurance company, for example, charges a higher premium for drivers under twenty-five years of age, they justify this by appealing to statistical probabilities. They might maintain that the proportion of accidents is higher among youthful drivers than among older drivers. Here they compare total accidents with the relative frequencies of accidents involving drivers under twenty-five with accidents involving drivers over twenty-five. They then conclude that the probability of accidents occurring with drivers under twenty-five is higher. This sense of probability is clearly that of probability$_2$.

Although a book of this kind is not the place to discuss in detail statistical techniques, some of the pitfalls resulting from a misapplication of statistical probability may be avoided by keeping in mind the following points:

1   Statistical numbers give us information about the characteristics of a class of items or events, that is, about items taken as a collection. They do not supply information about any one item in the class. Thus, though we may have a statistic which says that 86 percent of the patients treated with penicillin for streptococcus infection recovered, we cannot say whether or not any one patient who was treated recovered or will recover. Similarly though the probability$_2$ of accidents of drivers under twenty-five years of age is higher than that of drivers over twenty-five years of age, Willy, a teenage driver, may never have had an accident while his father, Harry, has had several. As we shall see later on, the error of attributing to individuals a characteristic of the class or set to which they belong is called the *fallacy of division*. This error is illustrated by the argument that since the cost of living index rose by 5 percent last week, housewives are now paying more for meat. Since the index represents an average of many commodities, there is no way of knowing what happened to the price of meat. Other items, like clothing and transportation, might have caused the index to go up while the price of meat might have remained unchanged or even gone down.

2   Statistical probabilities, without independent evidence, cannot be understood as providing invariable relations within the class. Even if the relative frequency of recoveries of streptococcus treated with penicillin remains around 86 percent over a period of years, we cannot infer that 86 percent *must* recover. Perhaps next year 94 percent will recover or perhaps only 43 percent will recover. For though we now know a great deal about the causes of such infections and in general how penicillin affects the disease, certain unknown factors or factors not under control may produce a worse result, or, indeed, the discovery of new knowledge may lead to eliminating the disease altogether.

The attempt to forecast graphically or mathematically what will happen on the basis of statistics concerning the past is called *extrapolation*. If done with caution, this procedure can yield valuable results — that is, if the prediction does not go too far into the future and if proper allowances are made for changing conditions. But if one blithely assumes that all present conditions will prevail in the future, extrapolation can give rise to absurd conclusions. One frequently hears, for example, that based on the present rate of growth, the world population 200 years hence will be such that only one square foot of space will be available for each person. What is overlooked in this prediction is that present conditions would undoubtedly not continue to prevail in the face of such growth. Famine, pestilence, war, etc., would undoubtedly take their toll. An amusing example of false extrapolation appears in this satirical selection by Mark Twain from *Life on the Mississippi:*

In the space of 176 years the Lower Mississippi has shortened itself 242 miles. That is an average of a trifle over one mile and a third per year. Therefore, any calm person, who is not blind or idiotic, can see that in the Old Oolithic Silurian Period, just a million years ago next November, the Lower Mississippi River was upwards of one million three hundred thousand miles long, and stuck out over the Gulf of Mexico like a fishing-rod. And by the same token any person can see that 742 years from now the Lower Mississippi will be only a mile and three quarters long, and Cairo and New Orleans will have joined their streets together, and be plodding comfortably along under a single mayor and a mutual board of aldermen. There is something fascinating about science. One gets such wholesale returns of conjecture out of such a trifling investment of fact.

3 High statistical correlations, without independent evidence, are not sufficient to infer a causal connection. One might produce a statistic, for example, which showed that 96 percent of the persons who have two or fewer children earn more than $10,000 a year. From this one could not infer that earning $10,000 or more *causes* people to have fewer than two children or conversely. There may be some sort of complex connection between the two facts—for example, both may be the product of background, education, etc.—but then again the connection may be merely accidental. High correlations sometimes result simply from the mathematical properties of the two groups or sometimes from the special characteristics of a unique situation. For example, in an unpublished study of Dr. George Marshall of the Brookings Institution, cited by Morris R. Cohen, it is revealed that variations in the membership of the International Association of Machinists from 1912 to 1920 are almost identical with those in the death rate of the State of Hyderabad, India, from 1911 to 1919. Also revealed is the fact that the rapid rise of college enrollments from 1920 to 1931 closely parallels the rise in the number of inmates in insane asylums during the same period. One would hardly conclude that such correlations are causally connected (although conceivably some students might want to take issue with the authors on the second example). On the other hand, of course, high statistical correlations do frequently indicate causal connections. But even then, such connections must be established independently of the statistical fact of high relative frequency. Such research may take many different forms. For example, high statistical probabilities have been produced regarding cigarette smoking and lung cancer. Supporting this statistic there is now a body of independent evidence on the physical effects of nicotine and the effects of tobacco tar on the skins of mice, and research as to the nature of cancer. Moreover, independent statistical studies have been made which show low relative frequencies regarding other possible causes of lung cancer, such as relative frequencies between city dwellers subject to air pollution and noncity dwellers and the rate of lung cancer.

4 Since most relative frequencies are based on a sample of the total population, such statistics are vulnerable to a wide variety of sampling errors. Though statisticians have developed many methods to minimize this difficulty, it is ever present. Suppose, for example, someone went to the telephone book to get a list of names and then established that all the people he interviewed had telephones! Obviously his sample would be bad. Almost any list of names might have been better to establish the relative frequency of persons with telephones. But which list would *assure* him of a fair sample? A list of doctors would be equally bad because we know that doctors need telephones for their practice. How about a list of people on welfare?

In general, then, the sample must be representative of the whole group both quantitatively and qualitatively. Technically such a sample is known as a *random sample,* in the sense that it represents a cross section of the whole. It is not random in the sense that it is selected haphazardly, without design, or on the basis of pure chance. On the contrary, much thought must be given to how and where the sample is to be drawn, as is evidenced by the following description of the sampling method used by one of the most successful practitioners of polling, the American Institute of Public Opinion, which conducts the Gallup polls:

Statisticians have repeatedly demonstrated that a few thousand voters correctly selected will reflect faithfully the views of an electorate of millions of voters. The secret is in the cross section — in the way voters for the sample are selected. To be a reliable indicator of public opinion the sample must include views of members of all political parties, and of rich and poor, old and young, men and women, farmers and city dwellers, persons of all religious faiths — in short, voters of all types from every state in the land. Moreover the sample must include these types numerically in approximately the same population. It must, in effect, select a miniature electorate that is representative of the views of the larger whole.[1]

A dramatic illustration of what can happen when a *loaded,* or un-

---

[1] *The New Science of Public Opinion* (Princeton, N. J.: American Institute of Public Opinion), p. 1.

representative, sample, is selected is the now famous *Literary Digest* presidential poll of 1936 which predicted a substantial victory for Alfred Landon, who in fact received only 8 electoral votes to Franklin Roosevelt's 523 votes. Although the magazine (which shortly thereafter went out of business) polled over 2 million people—in contrast with the 25,000 or so now polled by Gallup—it restricted its sample to people listed in telephone directories and hence neglected many classes of people who (because of the depression) could not afford telephones at that time.

5 Statistical numbers are frequently the basis for illicit comparisons. For example, suppose one argued that there were more criminal assaults in the United States in 1975 than in 1900 as evidenced by the fewer convictions recorded in 1900. This comparison would be misleading unless we were sure that "criminal assault" was defined in 1975 the same as it was in 1900, that law enforcement was as efficient then as now, and that the methods of collecting and recording such data were the same then as now. For it is entirely possible that what constitutes "criminal assault" now is much less restrictive in meaning than it was (and hence more crimes are now included in this category), that law enforcement in 1900 was relatively quite poor (and hence many crimes went undetected), and that many convictions in 1900 either were not recorded at all or were so recorded as to make them obscure to statistical analysis. Similar considerations apply to comparisons of "income," "national wealth," "infant mortality," "poverty," "divorce," "health," "mental illness," and a great many other important factors. To compare the average teacher's income in 1947, for example, with that in 1975 without taking into account the increased cost of living during that period would be to make a misleading comparison.

All this is not to say that statistics are always misleading, useless, or unimportant. On the contrary, the use of statistics has greatly enhanced our ability to make warranted inductions. Indeed, they have become indispensable to many areas of inquiry. But they can be misused, as we have seen, and being aware of how can help us to use them correctly.

EXERCISES

Evaluate each of the following inductions which rest on statistical premises. State clearly how the statistic has been illicitly employed.

1 Instructor: 7 percent of the class earned an A; 22 percent earned a B, 54 percent earned a C, and the remainder failed.
Student: Hooray, I passed.

2 In 1950, 24 percent of the population was at the poverty level. Today, through a variety of programs and incentives, and a flourishing economy, only 18 percent of the population is at the poverty level. We have made great strides in the elimination of poverty.

3 Eighty-three percent of the teenagers who come from broken homes have at least one encounter with a juvenile court; hence juvenile delinquency is caused by the broken home.

4 Examination of the records of the students going to Garden City High School shows that 77 percent of the graduating seniors go on to some form of higher education. We may conclude that Long Island high schools may be compared favorably with high schools across the country.

5 The suicide rate in the United States has remained almost the same for the past forty years and this despite dramatic changes in the social conditions, including an era of boom, a depression, war, and postwar recovery. Hence we are forced to the conclusion that there are reciprocal and compensatory forces which determine the suicide rate and place it in the category of one of the regularities of nature.

6 In 1946 the number of deaths due to railroads was 4,712. This certainly seems to refute the claim of the railroads that their mode of travel is the safest. (What factors have been overlooked in this argument which would alter the conclusion? Clue: This figure includes people killed at railroad crossings.)

7 When a certain doctor was asked what chance the patient had of pulling through the operation, the doctor replied, "An excellent chance. After all, statistics at this hospital show that although only one out of three comes through this operation successfully, so far this year out of twenty-three such operations seven have survived. So the chances of survival for this next one are just about perfect."

8 When asked what his average rate of speed was on a 60-mile trip, John replied, "I drove the first 30 miles at an average of 60 miles an hour and the second 30 at an average of 30 miles an hour, so I guess my overall average was 45 miles an hour."

9 After receiving a number of reports that some of the soldiers were not getting enough to eat, a certain general questioned his quartermaster, who defended himself by reporting that the average food consumption per soldier during the campaign in question was more than adequate.

10 In the first eighty years since the mile has been a competitive event, the record went down from 4:44.3 to 4:01.4. At this rate, it seems safe to predict that by the year 2000, the record will be around 3:40.

Formal or Mathematical Probability

A third sense of probability—one which is often confused with the other two senses—is that of formal, or mathematical, probability. This concept, which goes back to Pascal, Jacob Bernoulli, and Laplace and which is a branch of pure mathematics, probably arose in connection with questions of probability in gaming, including roulette, dice, cards, and the like. According to this concept, probabilities are determined a priori, or prior to (and hence independently of) any examination of test data, by means of the so-called *calculus of probabilities*. The probability of tossing an ace with a die (singular for "dice"), for example, is defined as the ratio of the number of favorable alternatives to the number of all possible alternatives (that is, the favorable plus the unfavorable). Or, symbolically, the probability is expressed by the formula $F/(F + U)$.

This formula will always yield a fraction whose values will range between 0 and 1. A probability of zero means that the alternative is impossible, that the event cannot occur; a probability of 1 means that the alternative, or event, must, of necessity, occur. This definition of probability, it should be noted, assumes that the alternatives under consideration are equiprobable, that is, that no one alternative is favored over any of the others. In our case with the die, this assumption means that the die is not "loaded" but is "fair" and that each side has the same chance of coming up. Now, using the formula to determine the probability of an ace appearing on any one given roll, since only one side has an ace (or a single dot), the number of favorable alternatives is 1; and since a die has 6 sides, the total number of alternatives is 6. Hence, the mathematical probability of tossing an ace (or any one of the other five numbers for that matter) on a single roll is 1/6. Note that this probability is, was, and *always* will be 1/6, since it is arrived independently of any actual throwing of the die.

On the other hand, the *statistical* probability of an ace appearing would be based upon a set of actual tosses of the particular die. This means that after every toss the probability would vary and also that after, say, 100 tosses it might diverge widely from the a priori probability. To be sure, *if* our assumptions are being met, namely that the die does have 6 equiprobable sides and the tosses are fair, then we would reasonably expect *after a long series of trials* that the ratio of aces to total tosses would approximate 1/6. The qualification "after a long series of trials" is crucial here but unfortunately not easy to define. When we speak of statistical probability (probability$_2$), we must accept the facts as they occur. If (say) after 20 tosses, we have obtained only 2 aces, the statistical probability at that time is 1/10 and not 1/6. What will occur on the next 20 tosses or 100 tosses or even 500 tosses cannot be determined in advance, for in saying that the probability$_2$ will approximate 1/6 after a long series of trials we do not commit ourselves to that probability after *any* finite number of tosses. But, again, the *formal* probability (probability$_3$) is unaffected by any data which we may obtain. It remains 1/6 for each toss no matter what the actual results have been.

Failure to keep this distinction between a priori and statistical probabilities in mind often results in what is called the *gambler's fallacy*. Suppose that in an actual game with a die (presumably fair), an ace has not appeared after 30 straight tosses. The natural tendency would be to assume that on the next toss, the probability of an ace coming up would be much *greater* than 1/6. But this is incorrect, for if indeed the die is fair, the formal probability would still be, by definition, 1/6 and would remain so. If, on the other hand, we are speaking statistically, then 1/6 is the probability after a long series of trials, but this implies nothing about what the probability would be after 40, 60, 100, or 10,000 tosses — that is, after any finite number. Finally, if the die were *not* fair, then on the basis of data so far accumulated the probability of tossing an ace would be much *less* than 1/6. Indeed, the statistical evidence would suggest that the die is *not* fair, and at this juncture a wise dice player would insist on a change of dice.

This is not to say that the calculus of probability cannot be used to formulate probability hypotheses about actual events. It can be so used if we can make the necessary *material* assumptions. These material assumptions are not part of the formal system but must be made when we apply the formal system to the real world. Mathematicians need only worry about deducing the consequences of their assumptions. Put another way, they need only concern themselves with "ideal dice" just as they do with "ideal triangles." Thus, for example, Euclidean triangles are plane figures composed of three straight lines. That is how they are defined in pure geometry. It follows necessarily that for such triangles the sum of their angles equals 180 degrees. But engineers work with real triangles which may or may not be coincident with abstract Euclidean ideals. Thus, they are not surprised when, in measuring the angles of a triangular fitting, they discover that the angles are equal to more than 180 degrees. Rather they assume that their fitting is not a perfect Euclidean triangle or that their instruments are incorrect. In short, the material assumptions regarding triangles might not be realized. So, too, with dice, coins, roulette tables, and the like. These real objects may not satisfy the conditions stipulated by the formal calculus. To satisfy these conditions the following material assumptions must be made before formal probability can be applied:

1   The number of favorable and unfavorable alternatives must be determined.
2   The alternatives must be equiprobable.
3   The events must be independent. That is, the occurrence of one must not be affected by the occurrence of another.

Thus we see why it is that formal, or mathematical, probability can be used to determine gaming probabilities, for in situations of this kind, we are generally willing to make the necessary material assumptions. The probability, for example, of cutting the ace of spades in a shuffled bridge deck is 1/52, since there is 1 ace of spades in the pack of 52 cards (Assumption 1); and 52 alternatives which the shuffling makes equiprobable (Assumption 2). Similarly, the probability of tossing two consecutive heads with a fair coin is 1/4, since there is one favorable combination out of a total of four possible combinations, namely *HH*, *HT*, *TH*, and *TT*. The assumptions here are: (1) there are only two alternatives for each toss; (2) the alternatives are equiprobable; and (3) the probability of the second toss is unaffected by the results of the first toss.

Unfortunately the need for making these material assumptions seriously limits the definition of probability in terms of the calculus, mainly because we must assign probabilities to outcomes about which we generally have no way of marking off equiprobable alternatives.

Theorems of the Calculus

Despite its limitations, the calculus is a useful device for determining a priori probabilities which can then be employed as hypotheses; and since we can calculate probabilities from given probabilities, we shall briefly discuss four important theorems of the calculus.

The Probability of Exclusive and Non-Exclusive Events   Suppose that we wanted the probability of rolling either an ace or a two with one die.   Since we now have 2 favorable alternatives (either the one or the two), the probability is 2/6 or 1/3. The theorem for disjunctive events would also have yielded this answer.

> In general, if a and b are two **strictly alternative** or **mutually exclusive** events, then the probability of a or b, $P(a \text{ or } b)$, is equal to the probability of a $P(a)$, plus the probability of b, $P(b)$; or $P(a \text{ or } b) = P(a) + P(b)$.

> In applying this theorem, one must keep in mind that the events must be mutually exclusive.   If someone asked for the probability of tossing a head on the first toss of a coin or a head on the second toss, it would be a mistake to argue that the probability would be $1/2 + 1/2$, or 1, since the events are *not* exclusive.   That is, a head on the first toss does not rule out the possibility of a head on the second toss.   Inspection of the alternatives, *HH*, *HT*, *TH*, *TT*, shows the probability to be 3/4, not 1.   However, a theorem for *non*-exclusive events may be derived.

> In general, if a and b are two **non-exclusive** events, then the probability of a or b **and possibly both,** $P(a \text{ v } b)$, is equal to the probability of a, $P(a)$, plus the probability of b, $P(b)$, minus the probability of a and b, $P(ab)$; or $P(a \text{ v } b) = P(a) + P(b) - P(ab)$.

> This formula would yield the correct answer.

Probability of Non-Occurrence of Events   We saw that the probability of tossing "heads" with a single toss of a coin was 1/2, since there are but two alternatives and one is favorable.   Evidently, then, the probability of tossing a head *or* a tail is $1/2 + 1/2$ or 1.   If so, the probability of *not* tossing a head is $1 - 1/2$ or 1/2. This easily-arrived-at result is generalized as follows:

> Since the probability that some event a will occur is $P(a)$, the probability that it will **not occur** is $1 - P(a)$ or, $P(\text{not-}a) = 1 - P(a)$.

Thus, given a die, suppose that we wanted the probability of not rolling an ace. Since the probability of rolling an ace is 1/6, our theorem says, $P(\text{not-ace}) = 1 - P(\text{ace}) = 1 - 1/6 = 5/6$.   With a little more work, of course, we could have reached this result by applying the theorem for disjunctive events, since $P(\text{not-ace}) = P(2) + P(3) + P(4) + P(5) + P(6)$ or $1/6 + 1/6 + 1/6 + 1/6 + 1/6$.

The Probability of a Joint Occurrence   Earlier we noted that the probability of tossing two consecutive heads was 1/4, for, as we saw, there are four possible combinations, *HH, HT, TH,* and *TT,* only one of which is favorable. Again, notice that the estimate of 1/4 is predicted *before* any tosses are made. If we have already tossed a head and *then* we ask about the probability of tossing *another* one, this probability would be 1/2, or the probability of tossing a head on any one independent toss of the coin. Here we are concerned with the probability of the complex event: the *joint occurrence* of two independent events. The calculus shows that the probability of the joint occurrence (the compound or conjunction of two events) is equal to the *product* of the probabilities of the two independent events.

> In general, if *a* and *b* are two independent events, the probability of their **joint occurrence,** *P(ab),* is equal to the probability of *a, P(a)* times the probability of *b, P(b);* or *P(ab) = P(a) × P(b).*

Thus the probability of tossing three consecutive heads is 1/8 or 1/2 × 1/2 × 1/2. We can see that this is so by enumerating the total alternatives and seeing how many are favorable. Thus:

H	*H*	*H*
H	*H*	*T*
H	*T*	*H*
H	*T*	*T*
T	*H*	*H*
T	*H*	*T*
T	*T*	*H*
T	*T*	*T*

Since only the first combination is favorable and there are eight total combinations, by our definition, *F/(F + U),* the probability is 1/8, or exactly what the theorem for joint occurrence predicted. Similarly, the probability of rolling boxcars (two sixes with two dice) is 1/36, or 1/6 × 1/6.

In computing the probabilities of complex events, however, one must be careful that all of the alternatives are enumerated. For example, the probability of rolling seven with two dice is 1/6 and the theorem for joint events cannot be directly employed. To compute this probability it is easier to enumerate the alternatives and employ *F/(F + U).* Thus:

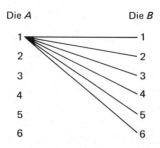

Each die has 6 sides, as represented by our numbers. Side 1 of *A* may fall with each of the 6 sides of *B*, side 2 of *A* may fall with each of the 6 sides of *B*, etc. In all, there are 36 alternatives. Which are favorable? There are 6 ways to make seven: A1-B6, A2-B5, A3-B4, A4-B3, A5-B2, A6-B1. And that is all of them. Hence the probability of rolling a seven on any one roll is 6/36, or 1/6.

We can use the theorem for joint occurrences along with the previous theorem to determine the probability of tossing *at least* one head in four consecutive tosses of a coin. This is the same as *not* tossing four consecutive tails. The probability of tossing four consecutive tails is $(1/2)^4$ or 1/16. Hence the probability of at least one head in four tosses is $1 - 1/16$ or 15/16.

Conditional Probability   Up to this point we have been speaking of the probabilities of the joint occurrence of events which were independent, that is, where the occurrence or non-occurrence of one event had no effect on the probability of a second event. But sometimes we want the probability of joint occurrences when the events are *not* independent. For example, what is the probability of drawing 2 hearts from a deck of 52 cards in two consecutive draws? For this to occur, one must draw a heart on the first draw *and* a heart on the second. Since there are 13 hearts, the probability of a heart on draw one is 13/52. But then we must draw again, assuming that a heart has been drawn. On condition that this has occurred, the probability on the second draw is 12/51, not 13/52, since we assume one less heart and one less card in the deck. The probability of their *joint* occurrence is then 13/52 × 12/51.

In general, where the events *a* and *b* are not independent, the probability of their joint occurrence *P(a and b)* is equal to the probability of *a*, *P(a)*, times the probability of *b*, given *a*; or $P(ab) = P(a) \times P(b)$, given *a*.

EXERCISES

   A   Determine the formal probability of each of the following:
   1   Tossing five consecutive heads
   2   Rolling "hard eight" (four and four) with two dice
   3   Rolling either an ace, a three, or a six with one die
   4   Tossing at least one tail in five tosses of a coin
   5   Rolling an even number or a number less than three with one die
   6   Guessing ten correct answers in a true-false test with ten questions
   7   Guessing the correct answers to five questions in a multiple-choice exam when there are four choices to each question
   8   Rolling anything but boxcars (two sixes) with two dice
   9   Rolling anything but seven with two dice
   10   Drawing the ace of spades from a bridge deck

   B   Given that an urn contains six black balls and four red balls, determine the following:
   11   The probability of drawing two red balls in succession
   12   The probability of drawing first a red ball and then a black ball

13 The probability of drawing two red balls on one draw

14 The probability of drawing at least one black ball in three drawings

15 Is the probability of being dealt thirteen spades higher, lower, or the same as being dealt the following hand: A*s*, J*d*, 10*h*, 4*c*, 9*c*, Q*c*, 7*h*, A*h*, 2*s*, 5*d*, 8*d*, 10*s*, Q*h*? Why? (*c* = clubs; *d* = diamonds; *h* = hearts; *s* = spades.)

16 Four players have been dealt five cards from a standard pack. What is the probability that the first card you pick up is the ace of diamonds? What is the probability that the first card the player on your left picks up is the ace of diamonds?

17 A player in a poker game has been dealt Q*h*, Q*d*, 10*s*, 5*d*, and 9*c*. He discards the ten, five, and nine and draws two cards. What is the probability that he will draw a third queen? Does it make any difference that fifteen cards are already in the hands of three other players? What is the probability that he will make four queens?

18 What is the probability of drawing to an outside straight? (You have four cards in serial order and can fill on either end.)

19 A player is dealt 4*s*, 7*s*, 8*s*, 9*s*, 10*d*. She could discard the four and draw for a straight or discard the ten and draw for a flush. (A flush consists of five cards of the same suit.) She determines that she can win with either a flush or a straight. What should she do?

20 (For bridge players only.) You have the ace, king, and jack of a suit but are missing the queen. Under what conditions is the finesse a better risk than playing the ace and king off the top?

Relations of Three Senses of Probability

Although the three senses of probability differ significantly, they also have something in common; and this common attribute enables us to use them in conjunction. In this section we shall examine that attribute and see how it can be used to develop inductive arguments.

Since all three concepts of probability have a common mathematical characteristic, we can explicate probability as degree of confirmation (probability$_1$) and probability as relative frequency (probability$_2$) so that they satisfy the basic principles of mathematical probability (probability$_3$). For convenience let us introduce the following notation: Let c be "confirmed," H be "hypothesis," e be "evidence," and r be a probability number. Then the formula

$$c(H, e) = r$$

means that the hypothesis H is confirmed (warranted or supported) on evidence e to the degree r. This is the sense of probability$_1$. Remember, H and e refer to statements. Now let O be a certain kind of outcome or event, R, the total class of results of a certain kind, and p, the probability$_2$.

$$p(O, R) = r$$

means that the probability$_2$, or relative frequency, of result O relative to R is the probability number r. For example, O might represent 1,075 cases of persons with streptococcus treated with penicillin who recovered and R might represent the total number of persons with the infection who were treated, say 1,142. Then the probability$_2$ of recovering would be 1,075/1,142, or r would be equal to .94.

We can now see that the two concepts satisfy the basic principles of formal or mathematical probability:

1   The possible numerical values of both probabilities (the value of r in each case) range from O to 1 inclusive:

$$O \leq c(H, e) \leq 1$$
$$O \leq p(O, R) \leq 1$$

Thus, for example, if e bears no logical relevance to H, then $c(H, e)$ is zero, or the probability of H on e is zero. Similarly, if the evidence e *entails* H, then the probability of H on e is 1. In this case, which is the *limiting* case, we have a deduction. In all others we have an induction or a probability of less than 1. Similarly, if *none* of the patients treated with penicillin recovered, then since zero divided by anything is zero, $p(O, R)$ would be zero. If, on the other hand, all the patients recovered, the probability would be 1.

2   The probability that two independent hypotheses are both true on the evidence is equal to the product of their respective probabilities; the probability that two independent outcomes will occur is equal to the product of their respective probabilities:

If H_1, H_2 are two independent hypotheses (the truth of H_1 being independent of the truth or falsity of H_2), then

$$c(H_1 \text{ and } H_2, e) = c(H_1, e) \times c(H_2, e)$$

If O_1, O_2 are two independent outcomes (the outcome of O_1 not affecting the outcome of O_2), then

$$p(O_1 \text{ and } O_2, R) = p(O_1, R) \times p(O_2, R)$$

These, of course, constitute an application of the theorem for conjunctive events in formal probability. Accordingly, if the probability that H_1 is true is .67 and the probability that H_2 is true is .83, then the probability that both are true is .556 (.67 $\times$ .83). It should be noticed that since we can only infrequently assign probability numbers to degree of confirmation, this application is not of great practical importance. However, if in some given test situation we employ two hypotheses, each of which independently has a relatively high degree of confirmation, we should not be surprised that the probability of both being true is considerably less than the probability of either one being true. Thus, even when not speaking quantitatively, suppose that there is much evidence for believing that a certain stock on the New York Exchange will go up and that some horse will win at Aqueduct. We would expect the probability$_1$ of *both* the stock going up and the horse winning to be less than either taken individually.

Applying the theorem to relative frequencies is very common. For example, suppose the probability$_2$ of a woman living to sixty-five years is .81 and the probability of a man living to sixty-five is .76. If these two persons were born in the same year and were to marry, the probability$_2$ that they will celebrate each other's birthday at sixty-five would be .615, or the product of two respective probabilities. Going further, suppose the probability$_2$ of a marriage not ending in divorce is .84. Then the probability that the couple mentioned above will celebrate their sixty-fifth birthday together is equal to the probability that they will both be alive at sixty-five (or .615) multiplied by the probability that they will not be divorced (or .84). This joint probability (.615 × .84) is .516.

3   The probability that either one of two contradictory hypotheses is true is 1; the probability that either one of two contradictory outcomes will occur is 1:

$$c(H \text{ or not } H, e) = 1$$
$$p(O \text{ or not-}O, R) = 1$$

That is, it is logically certain that either H or not-H is true, and either O or not O must occur. (It is important to notice that the theorem applies *only* to contradictories.) Thus the probability$_1$ that there is life on Mars or that there is not life on Mars is 1. But the probability$_1$ that light is a wave or that light is a particle is *not* 1, since these two hypotheses are not contradictory but *contrary*. Since contrary hypotheses can *both be false*, the probability$_1$ that either is true is not 1. Similarly, the probability$_2$ that a person will earn $1 million or not earn $1 million is 1, but the probability that the person will earn $5,000 or $25,000 is not 1. There is a theorem, however, which can be applied to contrary hypotheses and to outcomes which are mutually exclusive but not exhaustive.

4   The probability that either of several *contrary* hypotheses is true is equal to the sum of their respective probabilities; the probability that either of several mutually exclusive outcomes will occur is equal to the sum of their respective probabilities:

If $H_1, H_2, \ldots, H_n$ are contrary hypotheses, then

$$c(H_1 \text{ or } H_2 \ldots \text{ or } H_n, e) = c(H_1, e) + c(H_2, e) + \ldots + c(H_n, e)$$

If $O_1, O_2, \ldots, O_n$ are mutually exclusive outcomes, then,

$$p(O_1 \text{ or } O_2 \ldots \text{ or } O_n, R) = p(O_1,R) + p(O_2,R) + \ldots + p(O_n,R)$$

For example, let us assume that the probability$_1$ that light is a wave is .46 and the probability$_1$ that light is a particle is .39; then the probability that light is either a wave or a particle is .85. This example is unrealistic in that, as we have said, it is difficult to assign quantitative measures to probability$_1$. Notice also that the sum of a set of contrary hypotheses can never exceed 1. Unfortunately, since the set of logically possible contrary hypotheses is, strictly speaking, infinite, we can never establish as certain any one of the set. This feature bears on our discussion of eliminative induction.

Regarding probability$_2$, in using this theorem we must be sure that the outcomes are mutually exclusive. Thus, if the probability$_2$ of a male living to sixty-five is .76 and that of a female living to sixty-five is .81, the probability of either living to sixty-five is *not* 1.57. Since both out-bility$_2$ of earning \$5,000 is .62, the probability$_2$ of earning \$10,000 is .22, and the probability$_2$ of earning \$25,000 is .13, then the probability$_2$ of earning either \$5,000, \$10,000, or \$25,000 is .97, or the sum of the respective probabilities; this is so because these three outcomes *are* mutually exclusive, which is to say that if one occurs the other two can-*not* occur.

A theorem is also available for determining the probability$_1$ of sub-contrary hypotheses and the probability$_2$ of non-exclusive independent outcomes.

5 The probability that either of several subcontrary hypotheses is true is equal to the sum of their respective probabilities minus the product of their joint probability; the probability of either of several non-exclusive outcomes is equal to the sum of their respective probabilities minus the product of their joint probability:

If $H_1, H_2, \ldots, H_n$ are subcontrary hypotheses, then

$$c(H_1 \text{ or } H_2 \ldots \text{ or } H_n, e) = c(H_1,e) + c(H_2,e) + \ldots + c(H_n,e) - c(H_1 \text{ and } H_2 \ldots \text{ and } H_n, e)$$

If $O_1, O_2, \ldots, O_n$ are non-exclusive outcomes, then

$$p(O_1 \text{ or } O_2 \ldots \text{ or } O_n, R) = p(O_1,R) + p(O_2,R) + \ldots + p(O_n,R) - p(O_1 \text{ and } O_2 \ldots \text{ and } O_n, R)$$

Again, since we can rarely assign a quantitative measure for the probability$_1$ of a hypothesis, this application of the theorem is not prac-tically important. The theorem for non-exclusive outcomes, however, is very useful. The example concerning the mortality rates of males and females is illustrative. If the probability$_2$ of a male living to sixty-five is .76 and that of a female .81, then the probability that either a male or a female will live to sixty-five is .76 plus .81 (or 1.57) minus .76 times .81 (or .65), the result being .92 (or 1.57 − .65).

This discussion shows how the calculus of probability may be applied to the concepts of probability$_1$ and probability$_2$. But it is important to emphasize that in making this application two conditions must be met. First, to use the theorems, we must have the initial probabilities of joint outcomes, contrary hypotheses, etc. In the case of probability as degree of confirmation, or probability$_1$, this condition is not easy to meet. In the paragraphs which follow, we will show how the concept of probability as relative frequency can sometimes be used to provide quantitative measures of confirmation. Secondly, to apply the theorems, we must make appropriate material assumptions. To know which theorem to use, we must know if the outcomes are independent, exclusive, or non-exclusive and if the hypotheses are independent, contradictory, contrary, etc. This information is not provided by the calculus but depends upon our knowledge of logic and of the world.

In sum, formal probability serves two roles in inductive argument. First, we can use it at times to generate hypotheses. If, for example, we were asked for the probability of tossing seven with a pair of dice, we would know that the a priori probability is 1/6. This hypothesis could then be tested by appeal to relative frequencies. Thus, a priori probabilities are valuable heuristically; that is, they can lead us in some direction and thereby guide our inquiry. The heuristic role of assumptions such as the material assumptions required to apply formal probabilities is not to be underestimated, for such assumptions have led to many important discoveries, especially in theoretical physics. Secondly, the theorems of formal probability enable us to calculate probabilities, *provided* that other probabilities are given or known. Thus, given the statistical probabilities on divorce and death rates, we can calculate new probabilities by means of the theorem for conjunctive events.

Probability$_1$, or probability as degree of confirmation, and probability$_2$, or probability as relative frequency, can also be used together in inductive argument. For example, suppose we were asked whether or not we believed that Mabel and Joe, a married couple, would be divorced. Our answer might take the form of an argument like this:

The probability that any married couple will not be
   divorced is greater than .50.
Joe and Mabel are a married couple.
_____

Therefore, it is probable that Joe and Mary will not
   be divorced.

The first premise is a probability$_2$ statement, but taken together the two premises confirm as probable that Joe and Mary will not be divorced. The "probable" in the conclusion cannot be a statistical probability, for it qualifies the relation of confirmation, which is a relation between the statements comprising the premises and conclusion. Thus, in this example, the two senses are used together. The information provided by the premises, one of which is statistical, confirms the conclusion. If the exact statistic were provided, we would have this:

The probability that any married couple will not be divorced is .84.
Joe and Mabel are a married couple.
_____

Therefore, the probability that Joe and Mabel will not be divorced is .84.

This information has enabled us to assign a *quantitative* measure to the degree of confirmation, a measure which was based upon the statistic of the first premise. More formally we would have:

$p(O, R) = r$
i is a case of R.
_____

i is a case of O with probability r.

Since H is "i is a case of O," e is "i is a case of R," and $p(O, R) = r$, we would have:

$c(H, e) = r$

This example, incidentally, underscores once more how common this type of reasoning is in everyday life. As we have said repeatedly, as human beings we are far more concerned with the probabilities of inductive reasoning than with the certainties of deductive inference.

EXERCISES

Based on the data contained in the accompanying table, answer the following questions:

1 What is the probability that "Eggs" McDermott, who was convicted of embezzlement in 1965, was a first offender?
2 What is the probability that Eggs had been a juvenile delinquent?
3 What is the probability that "Sleepy" Sleeper, who was convicted of income tax evasion in 1965, was a first offender *or* was previously convicted of some adult felony?
4 What is the probability that Sleepy was *not* a juvenile delinquent?

5 What is the probability that "Snails" White and his wife "Swivel Hips" White, who were convicted of armed robbery in 1965, had no previous convictions?

6 What is the probability that "Fat Jack" Thomas, convicted in 1965 of possession of narcotics, was previously a juvenile delinquent or guilty of some adult misdemeanor? (He could have been convicted of both.)

7 What is the probability that "Boston" Kathleen and her husband, "Peter the Fox," who were convicted of forging securities, were first-time losers or were juvenile delinquents?

8 What is the probability that Demetrius, "The Greek," who was convicted of auto theft in 1965, had a previous conviction for auto theft (an adult felony) or for a misdemeanor?

9 What is the probability that Jack Armstrong, who had previous convictions for adult felonies, misdemeanors, and juvenile delinquency, was convicted under the Selective Service Act in 1965?

Court Commitments to Bureau of Prisons: 1965
(adapted from Department of Justice, Bureau of Statistics)

Offense	With Known Most Serious Previous Commitments				Without Known Previous Commitments
	% of Total Committed	Adult Felony	Juvenile	Misdemeanor	
All offenses	62.4	42.0	9.8	10.6	37.6
Drugs	62.4	42.4	6.8	13.2	37.6
Embezzlement	13.5	7.9	0	5.6	86.5
Income tax	23.2	17.0	1.4	4.8	76.8
Larceny-theft, transportation (autos, etc.)	75.5	47.0	16.6	11.9	24.5
Selective Service Act	11.6	2.3	2.3	7.0	88.4
Robbery	65.3	47.0	8.0	10.3	34.7
Securities forged, false and transported	77.6	65.0	5.4	7.2	22.4

FOURTEEN

INFORMAL FALLACIES: I

Our disputants put me in mind of the
skuttle fish, that when he is unable to
extricate himself, blackens all the water
about him, till he becomes invisible.

Joseph Addison

The Nature of Fallacies

In this chapter we shall deal with common errors of reasoning, which, because
they are so common, are usually classified and discussed in a book of this kind.
Every argument, it may be recalled, has the form "This is true since that is true"
or "That is true; therefore, this is true." By a *fallacy* we shall mean an argument
which is incorrect, that is, one in which the premises, even if true, would neither
entail nor warrant the conclusion. In this sense, a "fallacy," a "fallacious argument," and an "incorrect argument" are synonymous. It should be noted that
an argument may not be fallacious in our sense and yet be unsound, since by
sound we mean a correct (or valid) argument with *true premises*. Here, as before, we are concerned with the *relation* between premises and conclusion and
not with the truth of the premises. In general, to determine if a fallacy has been
committed, we may ask: "If the premises *were* true, could we justifiably infer
the conclusion?"

It should be noted that the term "fallacy" has been used in other senses than
the one used here. In ordinary usage it sometimes refers to a false belief, but
since this meaning does not involve an argument, it is not related to ours. Then,

too, some writers on logic restrict the meaning of "fallacy" to an incorrect argument which *appears* to be correct. Unfortunately, what "appears to be correct" is too subjective a criterion and hence not very useful. To be sure, many fallacies are deceptive, for otherwise we would not find it very profitable to discuss them. But the significant feature of fallacious arguments is not that they seem to be correct but that they can be seen to be incorrect. And, hopefully, in studying why this is so, we shall be deceived less frequently. Most fallacies are probably unintentional, being due to carelessness, ignorance, indolence, or wishful thinking. Some, however, are intentional and are used to deceive the unwary. In either case, an uncritical acceptance of such arguments is imprudent and can be dangerous. Or, as Aristotle put it, "If it is a disgrace to a man when he cannot defend himself in a bodily way, it would be odd not to think him disgraced when he cannot defend himself with reason."

Theoretically the number of ways in which an argument may be incorrect is infinite; practically, however, certain errors seem to recur regularly and thus lend themselves to classification and study. Many errors have already been discussed, namely those which result from a failure to conform to the rules of deductive inference. These, as we have seen, are known as *formal* fallacies, since the concern of formal logic is exclusively the form, or structure, of an argument rather than its content. In the discussion which follows we shall be concerned with errors pertaining to other than the form of the argument — errors which are therefore designated as *informal fallacies*.

Before we begin, however, it should be stressed that many of the errors which appear in arguments are complex or very subtle and that a relatively simplified discussion of them, as this must be at times, provides no sure key to their detection. As we indicated earlier, an awareness of faulty reasoning must be cultivated diligently over a long period of time. To develop a sensitivity to informal fallacies requires not only intensive study of certain principles but also the constant application of them. It should be noted also that, although the fallacies discussed here have been put into separate and rather neat categories, in reality they are by no means always so clear-cut or recognizable. Indeed, many of them, as we shall see, can be explained in more than one way and could justifiably be put into different categories from those we have chosen. For this reason there is no one acceptable or agreed-upon classification, even among logicians. Finally, when encountered in real-life situations, most arguments, as we have seen, are embedded in superfluous rhetoric and we must dig them out before we can analyze them. For purposes of study we have used fairly clear-cut examples in the discussion which follows, but, in keeping with our overall aim, we have tried to include more realistic, and thus frequently ambiguous, examples in the exercises.

Although this classification is by no means the only possible one, we have chosen to classify informal fallacies as *verbal fallacies, begging the question, unwarranted assumptions, fallacies of neglected aspect, irrelevancies, inconsistencies,* and *questionable evidence*. This classification covers all of the common fallacies as well as many of the uncommon ones.

In general, verbal, or linguistic, fallacies are fallacies because of some misuse, or confusion in the *meaning,* of the words, phrases, or sentences used in arguments. Question-begging fallacies all assume what is to be proved by the argument, and hence they prove nothing. The premise sets of arguments with unwarranted assumptions include various sorts of unwarranted assumptions, which when made explicit show the argument to be incorrect. Fallacies of neglected aspect — sometimes called fallacies of insufficient evidence — have premise sets which are not adequate for their conclusions. The fallacies of irrelevance all employ premises which are logically irrelevant to their conclusions. Fallacies of inconsistency have contradictory premise sets or conclusions which contradict their premises. And the fallacies of questionable evidence appeal to dubious or unreliable evidence statements. Each of these will be explained, clarified, and illustrated in what follows. Let us begin with the verbal, or linguistic, fallacies.

Verbal Fallacies

Verbal fallacies are deceptive because they often seem to conform to the rules of valid inference. However, a careful examination reveals that the argument appears to be valid because a word or a phrase has been misused. Either a word or a phrase has been used in two different senses or its meaning has been distorted by improper emphasis, wrenching it out of its context, or ignoring certain particulars which are unstated but implied. Typical among verbal fallacies are the following:

1   Equivocation   This error consists of using a word or a phrase in two different senses in the same argument. A popular classroom example is exhibited by the argument:

>   Nothing is better than a good grade.
>   A bad grade is better than nothing.
>   Therefore, a bad grade is better than a good grade.

Here the argument appears to be valid, but since "nothing" is used in two different senses, we have four terms and no middle term.

It should be noted that the fallacy of equivocation can occur only in an argument. In expressions like "Boys will be boys," and "Business is business," there is no fallacy, for there is no argument.[1] In the fallacy of equivocation a word or expression shifts its meaning in the course of the argument and this meaning shift gives the argument its initial plausibility. For example:

We are told that to discriminate against women in employment is wrong.

---

[1] Moreover, the shift in meaning is not disguised as it is in equivocal arguments; however, such disguise is not a criterion in evaluating an argument, though it makes the fallacy harder to detect.

Yet we must discriminate. We discriminate when we say that a woman couldn't be a bridge builder or a longshoreman. They simply lack the necessary strength for these tasks. We discriminate when we require college degrees or special training. Hence, it makes no sense to say that discrimination against women is wrong.

The word "discriminate" is being used here in two different senses. When it is said that it is wrong to discriminate against women in employment, "discriminate" means something like "treating unequally simply because of some arbitrary and irrelevant difference." In its other sense, "discriminate" means "selecting on the basis of certain abilities or skills."

The best way to answer an argument which contains an equivocation is to do what we have done here, that is, to name the word or phrase which has shifted in meaning and to point out its several meanings.

2 The Fallacy of Accident This fallacy, also known as a *dicto simpliciter ad dictum secundum quid,* consists of overlooking certain qualifications of a generalization or principle not spelled out but generally understood and then misapplying the generalization. A timely illustration of this fallacy is the argument commonly offered in opposition to the passage of the Dodd bill, which would outlaw the sale of firearms through the mail. Such a bill, it is claimed, would be unconstitutional, since the Constitution states that the people have a right "to keep and bear arms." However, this principle is not quite so broad as is commonly interpreted. It contains certain qualifications which those who invoke this principle conveniently overlook. According to the Supreme Court,[2] for example, this right "to keep and bear arms" is conditioned by the statement that "a well-regulated militia is necessary to the security of a free state." In other words, the special circumstances under which the people have a right "to keep and bear arms" are overlooked, and shipping guns through the mail would not be covered by the principle when properly qualified.

Closely related fallacies are those which indiscriminately apply overly broad definitions to cases not intended to be covered by them. For example, the argument: "Stealing is a means of getting money wrongfully; so advertisers who make misleading claims and get money wrongfully may be called thieves." Here "stealing" is defined so broadly as to include activities not legally regarded as stealing — such as embezzling, making fraudulent claims, etc. Though making misleading claims is wrong, it is not stealing — at least not as defined by law.

Another aspect of this fallacy, known as the *converse fallacy of accident,* is the error of refuting an unqualified generalization by means of exceptional cases. Although exceptions do invalidate rules, as we know, here the rule is misinterpreted — again by making it broader than it was intended to be. For example, one may argue, "If a doctor is justified in deceiving a sick person and if there is no harm in telling children about Santa Claus, then we must reject the maxim

[2] *United States v. Miller,* 307 U.S. 174 (1939).

that lying is wrong." Here an unqualified principle "lying is wrong" is attacked by citing exceptional cases. However, the speaker ignores such qualifications as "in most circumstances" or "except where human life may be lost," which are generally intended though not explicitly stated whenever such principles are appealed to.

In one sense, then, the fallacy of accident and its converse is a "straw man" argument, in this case a form of irrelevancy which consists of applying or attacking a nonexistent principle. It occurs when one ignores exceptional circumstances and certain qualifications usually implied whenever generalizations are used. To answer such arguments one should properly qualify the generalization, principle, or definition used and point out that with such qualifications there is no relationship between the evidence and conclusion.

3　The Fallacy of Composition　This fallacy occurs when the premises assert something about the parts of some whole and the conclusion asserts that what is true of the parts necessarily is true of the whole. Thus, one argues, "Every man on the National League All Star team is superior to his counterpart on the American League team; hence the National League team is superior." In this case what is true of each member of a team is not necessarily true of the team. Notice that some inferences from part to whole are not fallacious. It is not fallacious, e.g., to argue: "Every part of this motor is made of steel; so the motor is made of steel" or "Each member of the class wanted a final exam, hence, the class wanted a final exam." The fallacy of composition is usually included under the verbal fallacies since it mistakenly supposes that a term which meaningfully and correctly applies to a part applies equally correctly to its whole. The fallacy also could easily be classified under the general heading of "neglected aspect," for the reasoning ignores the relationship between parts—how they may affect or interact among each other. In the example given here, individual players, though they may be excellent as individuals or even as members of their own team, may not function well together as a team made up of relative strangers.

4　The Fallacy of Division　This fallacy is the converse of the error of composition and consists of concluding that what is true or characteristic of the whole is necessarily true or characteristic of the parts or elements which constitute the whole. Thus the premises assert something as true of a whole, and the conclusion asserts that it is also true of its parts. For example, one concludes that if Congress passes a poor bill, each member of Congress exercised poor judgment. But this, of course, doesn't follow; many members may have opposed the bill but were outvoted.

This type of error is commonly committed when averages are applied to the individual units which compose them. A humorous classroom example is the argument "Since one out of every four children born in the world is Chinese, Mrs. Jones, who is due to have her fourth child next week, can expect it to be Chinese." Once again, the answer to such arguments is to point out that what is true of the whole is not necessarily true of the part. As we have seen, parts may combine and interact with other parts and result in a whole completely unlike any of the parts which compose it.

Begging the Question

The fallacies discussed in this section might be called "illusions of proof" because they only appear to be proving something when in fact they do nothing of the kind. This illusion of "proof" is accomplished by assuming the truth of what is ostensibly being proved. However, assuming something to be true is very much different from proving it. Fallacies of begging the question, also called *petitio principii*, take several different forms, the most characteristic of which are the following:

1 Circular Arguments In its simplest form, a circular argument consists of two statements: "*p* is true because *p* is true." But if it appeared as baldly as this, its triviality would be immediately apparent. In actuality the form is disguised by rephrasing the evidence statement. Thus we get, for example, "Capital punishment for murderers is justified because there are good reasons to put to death those who have committed murder." If we pause to reflect on the reason given here to justify capital punishment for murderers, we see that no reason at all has been given; the statement to be proved has merely been restated, and the so-called argument boils down to "Capital punishment for murderers is justified because capital punishment for murders is justified."

In another common form of this fallacy, the conclusion and the initial assumption of it are separated by another statement. An example of this is the following argument: "If men are to survive, they must be fit — indeed, only the fittest survive. And we can verify this by simply looking around and seeing who have survived. Obviously, they have survived because they are fit." Here the fallacy takes the form:

Since *p* is true (since men survive), *q* is true (they are fit).
Since *q* is true (since they are fit), *p* is true (they survive).

The fallacy of circular reasoning becomes more difficult to detect when there are several intervening links in the argument chain, or when many premises are offered and the assumed conclusion is masked by complexity. For example, consider this form:

Since *p* is true, *q* is true;
since *q* is true, *r* is true;
since *r* is true, *s* is true;
but since *s* is true, *p* is true.

Here a lengthy argument is developed to show that *p* is true. But *p* has not been proved true since it was a premise for the initial link in the argument. Indeed, if we accept the truth of p as premise, then the remainder of the "argument" is unnecessary. On the other hand, we cannot prove that p is true by offering evidence which includes the assumption that it is true. Here is an argument of this form:

> Since free speech is vital to a democracy like ours, we can criticize current government policies — and even the President. If we don't like what is happening in Laos or Cambodia, we can say so. This right to dissent and to criticize — basically the right to discuss, debate, and exchange ideas — enables us to arrive at more intelligent decisions than we would ordinarily make. And, of course, it follows from this that we can govern ourselves more intelligently than those in authoritarian states, like Spain or Albania, who have little or no say about the policies which govern them. There seems to be little doubt that people who govern themselves intelligently will choose a liberal democratic form of government, such as ours or England's. Thus, we must have the right of free expression, the right to have our views compete with others in the open marketplace of ideas.

Reduced to essentials, this argument says:

> Since p (free speech is needed), therefore, q (we can criticize);
> since q (we can criticize), therefore r (we can decide intelligently);
> since r (we can decide, etc.), therefore s (we can govern intelligently);
> since s (we can govern etc.), therefore t (we choose democracy);
> since t (we choose democracy), therefore p (free speech is needed).

Circular arguments are attacked simply by pointing out that the conclusion has been assumed as true.[3]

2 Question-Begging Expressions This type of begging the question consists of using certain terms or rhetorical constructions which assume the truth of what one is trying to prove or the truth of a relevant statement which should be proved and not assumed. The lawyer, for example, who declares to the jury, "You cannot let this man go free because your sister or your wife may be his next victim," commits this fallacy, for the statement assumes that the man had previous victims and is thus guilty — which is precisely what must be proved. Other variations of this fallacy are seen in such an example as "Now let's consider some

---

[3] Arguments in a circle, it may be noted, are always deductively valid, since it is impossible for the premises to be true and the conclusion false. This is impossible, for the conclusion *is* one of the premises. Strictly speaking, the fallacy of arguing in a circle is not a fallacy according to our definition of a fallacy, since *petitio's* are valid. However, because the conclusion is assumed, the argument is spurious; indeed, in a sense they are nonarguments.

It has been maintained that all deductions, in particular the syllogism, are in fact *petitio's*. But one must distinguish between a premise set which entails its conclusion and a premise set which *includes* its conclusion.

disadvantages of the immoral policy of legalized gambling; etc., etc."[4] In this case, calling a policy "immoral" is an assumption which must first be proved.

3 The Loaded Question Often we find question-begging assumptions creeping into questions, the most common type being called the *loaded question* or *complex question.* For example, in the question "Do you still cheat on examinations?" "still" assumes that the person being questioned used to cheat; and even if he or she says "No" to the question, he or she is tacitly admitting this. Such a question is really two questions: "Did you ever cheat on examinations?" and "If so, do you still cheat?" This type of question is reminiscent of the one still asked of government employees: "Are you now or have you ever been a member of a subversive organization?" Actually there are two questions here, which, in the interest of clear thinking, should be phrased as such.

4 The Suggestive Question A more subtle, and perhaps insidious, form of the question-begging question is the *suggestive question,* often encountered in speeches on controversial subjects. Such questions are actually assertions, that is, unsupported statements or assumed conclusions. For example, "How likely is it that Russia would *agree* to such provisions?" or "Won't this program place a great burden on the taxpayers?" From the tone of voice in which such questions are usually asked, the first one really means "Russia *won't* agree to such provisions" and the second, "The program would place a great burden on the taxpayers." But neither assertion is supported; each is assumed to be true.

5 Question-Begging Epithets Another form of question-begging suggestion is the common attempt to persuade by the confident manner, specifically by the use of such terms as "obviously," "certainly," "surely," "it is clearly evident," "there's no question that," and "of course." Such expressions of confidence are designed to allay doubts and to inculcate belief. But even when one tries to prove what one is saying, such terms are usually unwarranted, for the conclusions dealt with in discourse on controversial subjects ordinarily do not lend themselves to the type of conclusive proof suggested by such terms. Thus their use in such discourse usually constitutes an assumption of what one is trying to prove.

6 Fallacy of the Impromptu Definition Sometimes one will begin a discussion reasonably enough and, only when challenged, will counter by shifting ground and assuming one's original position by means of a definition. In effect, one establishes an impregnable position—i.e., one which automatically precludes the use of contrary evidence—by means of an impromptu definition. Thus one might initially claim, "A good Christian attends church regularly," intend-

---

[4] The "etc., etc." represent "reasons," which are really not needed to illustrate the point of the example but which are needed if we are talking about arguments. As the example stands without the "etc., etc.," it is not an argument but a statement.

ing this to be an empirical generalization about good Christians. But when a second party contends that many good Christians don't attend church regularly, one counters that such people can't be called "good Christians" because regular church attendance is part of the definition of a "good Christian." Thus, what started out to be a factual statement about certain kinds of people is rendered impervious to disproof by being interpreted as a definitional statement, that is, a statement about a word or a concept.

To avoid fruitless controversy, one should ask beforehand what kind of statement the speaker has in mind. With regard to our last example, is the speaker saying that regular church attendance is one of the defining characteristics of a "good Christian," or assuming that we know the definition of a "good Christian" and saying that good Christians *also* attend church regularly? In order to discuss the statement, we must know what the speaker means by it. If we were to dispute the first interpretation, we would be questioning the verbal usage of the phrase "a good Christian," and an appropriate rejoinder might be, "I don't believe that dictionaries, ecclesiastical authorities, or most people interpret the phrase 'a good Christian' as you have done." If we were disputing the second interpretation, we might reply, "How about Smith and Jones and Brown? They're all good Christians but don't attend church regularly." As can be seen, this fallacy could as easily be classified as a form of ground shifting or even equivocation.

Unwarranted Assumptions

The fallacies discussed below are characterized by unwarranted assumptions resulting usually from an imperfect understanding of certain principles or from a failure to make careful and proper distinctions. These assumptions are often quite deceptive because they either are partly true or in some contexts may be wholly true. The fallacy consists in assuming that the principle involved is always true or completely true regardless of the context. By thus overlooking significant factors, such fallacies are often closely related to those discussed in the section called "fallacies of neglected aspect."

Although certain principles underlie all rational discourse — the laws of identity, excluded middle, noncontradiction, implication, etc. — the following fallacies all contain misleading or dubious assumptions.

1 Appeal to Ignorance This fallacy, also called *argumentum ad ignoratiam*, consists of assuming that the absence of proof or the inability to prove a statement constitutes proof that its contradictory is true. Examples are: "Since we can't prove that mental telepathy doesn't exist, there must be something to it" or "Since the advocates of economic aid cannot show where this program has made friends for the United States in Pakistan, we can only conclude that it hasn't made any." Absence of proof, however, is usually not the same as proof. Only evidence can constitute proof or disproof. The inability to prove that Hitler died in a bunker in Berlin does not prove that he is living. To show this we would need some concrete evidence.

A seeming exception to this principle is found in law, where it is held that in the absence of evidence to the contrary, every person is presumed to be innocent. But even this presumption of innocence is not without some foundation, since experience has shown that most people are innocent of any serious wrongdoing when there is no evidence to the contrary. And, of course, when there is, the presumption is rebuttable. Similarly, in debates on a controversial policy, such as one might hear in Congress, failure to prove that the existing policy is inadequate or that the proposed new policy would be significantly advantageous would favor the retention of the status quo. But, again, there are reasons for such a presumption, one being that it is generally imprudent to risk an extreme change for no apparent reason.

In one other context does absence of proof constitute proof, namely, when an unsuccessful search has been made to find proof of a contradictory proposition. As we saw with causal relationships, for example, when a given factor is known to be absent, we may assume that it cannot be part of the cause. Thus, if we get a rash and have not eaten strawberries, we may assume that the rash was not caused by eating strawberries. Here again, however, our conclusion is based not on ignorance but on the knowledge that we have not eaten strawberries. Similarly, if we eat strawberries and do not get a rash, we may conclude that we are not allergic to strawberries. But this conclusion, too, is based not on ignorance but on the knowledge that a rash has not occurred. In the same way scientists try to find facts that will disprove their hypothesis, and only when they cannot find any do they permit themselves to have confidence in their hypothesis. But once again this confidence has been justified by a diligent search, which, though negative in its findings, still constitutes positive evidence that the conclusion may be true. And so, as with all arguments, we must know when and how to make the proper distinctions; not to draw a conclusion can sometimes be as illogical as drawing a false one.

By contrast, consider this argument by Richard Nixon: ". . . Mr. Sparkman and Mr. Stevenson should come before the American people, as I have, and make a complete financial statement as to their financial history, and if they don't, it will be an admission that they have something to hide." In sum, Mr. Nixon argued that if Mr. Sparkman and Mr. Stevenson didn't prove their honesty, we would have to assume they were dishonest. Not only is this a fallacy of *argumentum ad ignoratiam* but it also violates the American legal principle that a person is presumed honest until proved dishonest. Here Mr. Nixon assumed the opposite, that a person may be presumed dishonest until proved honest. (Perhaps politicians have reasons for thinking the rule should not apply to them.) This fallacy is also encountered frequently in discussions of a controversial policy, when it is argued that since the advocates of the new policy cannot prove that it has worked, we must assume that it cannot work. Once again, positive proof — not lack of proof — is needed to prove the latter.

2 Confusing Necessary and Sufficient Conditions An unwarranted assumption often made in the sphere of eliminative induction is that a necessary condition is also a sufficient one. While this assumption is sometimes true, more often it is not. A good diet, for example, may be a necessary condition for maintaining good health, but this factor alone is not sufficient. One also needs fresh air, exercise, rest, etc. The confusion here probably stems from the fact that although a good diet is necessary but not sufficient to produce good health, the absence of a good diet is sufficient to produce poor health. Similarly, studying before an examination may be necessary to ensure a good grade, though, as most students know, not sufficient by itself. One must also have intelligence, the ability to write coherently, etc. The fallacy often appears in political speeches when the speaker, after condemning the opposition's policy, concludes that his own should be adopted. However, showing that one policy is ineffective is not a sufficient reason for claiming that a new one will be effective. In most cases one must demonstrate this fact.

3 The Assumption of Irreversible Order Still another related fallacy is the unwarranted assumption that there is an irreversible order between events or factors, that if event or factor *a* affects event or factor *b*, event or factor *b* cannot affect event or factor *a*. This assumption, however, overlooks the possibility of mutual, or reciprocal, relationships. Thus, does ignorance lead to poverty, or does poverty lead to ignorance? Or do both mutually affect one another? Does an educational system affect civic attitudes or do civic attitudes affect an educational system? Or is there a reciprocal relationship here? The assumption is frequently encountered in economics where reciprocal relations are common. Thus, one economist will argue that surpluses affect unemployment, and another, that unemployment affects surpluses. Or one economist will argue that increasing consumer consumption will ultimately increase production, while another will argue that increasing production will ultimately increase consumer consumption. Which, then, is more fundamental, increasing consumer consumption or increasing production? In other areas it is argued that environment is more basic than heredity and vice versa, that experience is more basic than reason and vice versa, and so on. In most disputes of this kind, neither party is probably right, since the factors involved mutually affect one another.

4 Argument of the Beard This fallacy derives its name from the ancient Greek philosophers who were fond of propounding such puzzles as how many hairs constitute a beard: 1, 10, 50, 500, 1,000?[5] The fallacy itself takes several forms. In one form, it falsely assumes that small differences are always unimportant, as

---

[5] The answer is that there is no exact number, for "beard" is a vague term, which means that it cannot be quantified or precisely defined, except arbitrarily. And the reason it cannot be is that its referent is by nature not clear-cut. Similar terms are "crowded," "warm," "usurer," and "mature." Calling such terms "vague," incidentally, doesn't mean that they are meaningless or useless. On the contrary, they are quite useful. See Chapter 1.

does the student trying to enroll in a class that's already filled who argues, "Just one more will make no difference." Now while it is true that one more, or a small quantity, is often insignificant, there are times when it may be very significant, like the proverbial straw which (when added to many others) broke the camel's back. Marshal Tito of Yugoslavia probably used this fallacy facetiously when he remarked, "There really isn't very much difference between the political systems of America and Yugoslavia; after all, America has two major political parties and Yugoslavia one, a difference of only one party." A dramatic illustration of how important 1 can be is a recent election result on Long Island, New York, where both candidates[6] for the position of district court judge received exactly 53,371 votes—an amazing result, to be sure, but still a tie which only one vote could have broken.

Another form of this fallacy assumes that since small differences are unimportant, such as differences of degree, all differences—particularly of degree—are, practically speaking, indistinguishable from one another. Water heated to 89°C, for example, cannot be differentiated from water heated to 90°C. And since no sharp distinctions can be made between 90 and 91°C, 91 and 92°C, 92 and 93°C, and so on, it is concluded that no distinction can be made between 89 and 93°C, and, finally, that since no distinction can be made anywhere along the line, no distinctions at all on a continuum are meaningful. There is no stopping-off point or line that can be drawn since all differences are connected by intermediary degrees on a continuum. In effect, then, it is absurdly concluded that even extremes, or contraries, are alike—hot is the same as cold, black is the same as white, smart is the same as stupid.[7] Now, of course, this isn't so. Even though a sharp line cannot be drawn between contiguous, or overlapping, categories like "hot" and "warm," they are still significantly different from one another, let alone "hot" and "cold." The inability to draw sharp distinctions in certain contexts does not mean that no distinction at all can be made, as this fallacy assumes.

The assumption is made in such arguments as the following: "I am against the two-thirds rule. If you require a two-third's rule, why not a three-fourth's rule, or a 99 percent rule? Indeed, why not go all the way as in totalitarian countries and require everyone to vote yes?" And: "If we provide medical care for the aged, we may as well provide it for the whole population. In fact, the state may as well go ahead and guarantee food and lodging for everyone. It's just a matter of degree." In both cases the speaker goes from one extreme to the other, claiming there is no difference between the two extremes because "It's all just a matter of degree," which the speaker has assumed is unimportant. In answer, one should point out that the proposed course of action is significantly different from the extreme to which it has been extended, that a distinction can be made, and that the suggestion that it cannot be is merely an unwarranted assumption.

---

[6] The candidates, Julius R. Lippman and Frank X. Altimari, both became judges subsequently.

[7] It may be recalled that in George Orwell's *1984*, the state kept people in subjection by getting them to believe such slogans as "War is peace" and "Freedom is slavery."

5 All or Nothing Fallacy This fallacy, also called the *black or white fallacy*, although closely related to the previous fallacy, differs subtly from it. Where the former assumes that there is no important difference between contraries connected on a continuum, this fallacy treats certain contradictories as though they were contraries. To review briefly the difference between contradictory and contrary statements, consider the following groups of statements:

A: John is rich.
B: John is not rich.
C: John is poor.

A: Strontium 90 poses a great threat to human life.
B: Strontium 90 does not pose a great threat to human life.
C: Strontium 90 poses no threat to human life.

Note that statements A and B in each group, if taken as a pair, are contradictory, while statements A and C are contrary. In the first pair of contradictories, John is either rich or not rich, one or the other, but he doesn't necessarily have to be either rich or poor; he can be somewhere in between. Similarly, in the second pair, strontium 90 either poses a great threat or it doesn't. If it does, then statements B and C of this group are necessarily false. If it does not, statement A is necessarily false, but nothing can be assumed about the truth or falsity of statement C, for strontium 90 may pose a medium threat, a small threat, or no threat.[8]

The failure to differentiate between contradiction and contrariety is a source of much confused thinking and fallacious argument. The fallacy under discussion, for example, erroneously assumes that certain contradictories are really contraries. We meet it in an argument like the following: "Either the Chinese are free or they are not. And if not, then they are really enslaved." So subtle is this fallacy that it almost escapes detection. On the surface it appears sound, for it legitimately assumes a pair of contradictory alternatives as a premise. In the conclusion, however, it assumes contrary alternatives; in this case it assumes that something is either absolutely free or absolutely not free, or enslaved. But such an assumption, of course, is unwarranted, for there are many degrees between these two extremes.

The fallacy is more easily recognized when the premise assumes contrary alternatives and treats them as though they were contradictory, that is, as exclusive and exhaustive. In this form it is generally referred to as the *fallacy of false alternatives* and is seen in an argument like the following: "We must either fight Russia or appease her. Since history has shown that appeasement fails, we have no choice but to fight." Here the alternatives, to fight or to appease, are clearly not contradictories but contraries and thus do not exhaust all the possibilities. If one were to claim, "We must either fight Russia or seek some peaceful means of working out our differences with her"—i.e., fight or not fight—at least this

---

[8] For a fuller discussion of contradiction and contrariety, refer back to pp. 146–147.

premise would be sound, for the alternatives would be mutually exclusive and exhaustive.

To take another example: "Either the Soviet Union is ahead of the United States in the development of fusion power, or the United States is ahead of the Soviet Union. That's why they refuse to work jointly on this project, for one or the other would be giving up an advantage if it did." Here, of course, the premise overlooks a third possibility—that both countries are about equal.

Occasionally one encounters a premise in which the alternatives aren't even related—that is, both may be true or both false. For example, "John was either naive or dishonest to have done what he did." Actually, he may have been both or neither.

In answering this type of fallacy, one need merely point out other alternatives than those offered or assumed.

6 Misuse of Contradictory Alternatives This fallacy falsely assumes that no two alternatives are exclusive and exhaustive, even contradictory ones. Thus, it falsely assumes that a premise may not assume such alternatives as "Either Truman was the thirty-third President of the United States or he was not," but must contain additional alternatives. Premises with only two alternatives, whether contradictory or contrary, are condemned as being *two-valued* in contradistinction to the more desirable *multivalued*. We have seen, however, that the assumption of contradictory alternatives as a premise is legitimate, as illustrated in the argument: "Either Jones was in Chicago on June 1 or he wasn't. And since we know that he wasn't, he couldn't have personally committed the crime." Thus, to assume that the use of only two alternatives is always fallacious is itself a fallacious assumption (which probably stems from a desire to avoid the more common fallacy of false alternatives).

This fallacy generally appears as a form of refutation. Thus, we might hear:

Jones argues that if liberal arts colleges are to be worthy of the name, they must permit freedom of inquiry. And if a college doesn't permit such inquiry but insists on indoctrinating its students, it should not be called a liberal arts college. Unfortunately, however, Jones presents us with only two alternatives and is therefore guilty of oversimplifying the issue.

Now while it is true that our hypothetical Jones has presented only two alternatives as his premise—either permit freedom of inquiry or not permit it—these alternatives are exhaustive (there are no others) and exclusive (both are not possible at the same time). Hence the premise is legitimate, even if there were some doubt about the rest of the argument. The obvious rejoinder to this type of fallacy is simply to ask, "What other alternatives could you offer?"

In passing, it is worth noting that if the law of the excluded middle, "Every proposition is either true or false," were invalid, it would be impossible to deny or to contradict any statement. Indeed, it would be impossible for anyone to deny the principle, for in order to deny it, he would have to use it. When one says, "*P* is false," one means that one's statement contradicts the statement "*P* is true." And here there are only two alternatives: either *P* is true or *P* is not true. Thus it is impossible to deny the principle of denial without using that principle.

EXERCISES

Explain the fallacy, if any, in the following arguments:

1 The costly practice of giving away stamps in supermarkets should be stopped, for the consumers don't really benefit and they're a nuisance.

2 An electrician is usually a man, so a good electrician is usually a good man.

3 Don Quixote concluded that he was plagued by a sorcerer who foiled his attempts at chivalrous feats by changing castles into windmills and watermills, and a horde of armed men into a flock of sheep as soon as he got close to them. When he sent Sancho Panza with a message of devotion for his lady love, who turned out to be a coarse shepherdess, Don Quixote concluded that this was but another manifestation of the sorcerer's power.

4 Since there is no conclusive proof that certain people don't have extra-sensory perception, we can only conclude that they do have it.

5 We are told that a harmonious world community is a precondition for world government. But actually the reverse is true; a unified political system, by reducing misunderstanding, would lead to a better world community.

6 We should legalize gambling because we can't stop it. It is an integral part of living; a man gambles everytime he crosses the street or takes a wife.

7 Since negotiation would be a peaceful means of settling our differences with Castro, we may conclude that a refusal to negotiate will result in increasing tensions.

8 All people tend to think of things in terms of good and bad, black and white, hot and cold, God and Satan, rich and poor. . . . There is no middle ground between black and white; it is *all* or *none*. This is what is meant, of course, by the "excluded middle" of Aristotelian logic.

S. I. Hayakawa, "The Meaning of Semantics"[9]

9 One who lies or tells the truth by compulsion or by necessity is not truly a free agent. But everyone must either lie or tell the truth. Therefore, insofar as lying or telling the truth is concerned, no one is really a free agent.

10 Since it is wrong to betray a friend, John should not have told the police

[9] *New Republic* (August 2, 1939).

that his friend Bill pushed the little boy off the roof because the latter refused to give him his money.

11 Since whooping cranes are rapidly disappearing, this whooping crane may be said to be rapidly disappearing.

12 Whatever the Koran affirms is true because it was written by Mahomet, God's prophet. And we know that he was God's prophet because the Koran says so.

13 We must either deny freedom of speech to all critics of government or give the communists a free hand in destroying the government. Since the latter course is unthinkable, we must pursue the former.

14 Universities like Ohio State, Minnesota, and NYU all have enrollments of over 30,000 students. Thus the classes must be large and the students cannot receive much individual attention.

15 One man is telling another that a bull had chased him up a tree.
". . . Sure enough, it was just as I had dreaded; he started in to climb the tree —"
"What, the bull?"
"Of course — who else?"
"But a bull can't climb a tree."
"He can't, can't he? Since you know so much about it, did you ever see a bull try?"

Mark Twain, *Roughing It*

16 If the peoples of the world could arrive at some mutual understanding, the chances of war would be lessened. Thus we need a universal language, for this would enable the people of different countries to understand each other.

17 Since it is wrong to take a life, the captain of the lifeboat should have let the two men in the water climb aboard even if it meant sinking the boat with the other eighteen aboard.

18 In a recent book on psychiatry and crime, Professor S. L. Halleck declares that "for every zealot who heralds psychiatric concepts and treatments as the only answer to the crime problem, there is a critic who believes that psychiatric contributions to criminology are unscientific and misleading. A realistic assessment of the value of psychiatric criminology must lie somewhere between these two extrems.[10]"

19 The *New Testament* tells us: "For whosoever shall keep the whole law, and yet offend in one point, he is guilty of all."

20 Modern education is becoming highly mechanized and impersonal. For example, IBM machines now register student grades.

21 Logic teacher, after explaining a difficult principle: "Now with this explanation, the principle should be clear. Those who didn't get it were probably not paying very close attention. Are there any questions?"

[10] *Psychiatry and the Dilemma* (New York: Harper and Row with Hoeber Medical Books, 1967).

22 A change is a change, whether it is extreme or gradual. Since you cannot really draw the line anywhere, the difference between the two is merely academic.

23 Good football teams are needed to pay the salaries of first-class coaches and to pay off the mortgages on large stadiums. And without large stadiums and first-class coaches, you can't have good football teams.

24 It is fruitless to discuss the Point Four program of aid to underdeveloped nations, since "underdeveloped" can't be precisely defined.

25 A mob is no worse than the individuals that make it up because a mob is just a large group of individuals.

26 Impartiality is not taking sides in a dispute. Yet the commission sided with the company and fined the union. How can it claim to be impartial, and how can we respect a biased judge?

27 The state is supposed to protect every person's property. Therefore, evicting a person from the person's home, tearing it down, and building a road over it is clearly an abrogation of the state's responsibility.

28 Since great works of art are scarce, *Hamlet,* which is a great work of art, is scarce.

29 Whoever obeys laws submits to a governing will. Since nature obeys laws, she submits to a governing will, which can only be God's will.

30 "What is good for General Motors is good for the country."

31 Since lying is wrong, the manager of the theater erred when he told the patrons that the star was ill and the performance canceled when he knew that the theater was on fire.

FIFTEEN

INFORMAL FALLACIES: II

*There is no expedient to which a man
will not resort to avoid the real labor of
thinking.*

Sir Joshua Reynolds

Having considered three main categories of fallacies in the last chapter — verbal
fallacies, begging the question, and unwarranted assumptions — we conclude our
discussion here with fallacies of neglected aspect, irrelevancies, inconsistencies,
and questionable evidence.

Fallacies of Neglected Aspect

In the fallacies of neglected aspect, conclusions are usually supported by relevant
facts or evidence, but neglected or missing are relevant facts which, if introduced,
would weaken or create doubt about the conclusions. Hence these fallacies
might also be called *fallacies of insufficient evidence.* They are perhaps best
illustrated by the arguments of advertisers, lawyers, politicians, and debaters
who present only evidence favorable to their side but conveniently suppress the
unfavorable. This type of error is amusingly illustrated by the testimony of the
night watchman who, in testifying for the railroad company for which he worked,
swore that on the night of the accident he had frantically waved his lantern for
several minutes to signal the on-coming train but who neglected to mention that
his lantern wasn't lighted. Common fallacies of neglected aspect are the following.

1 Hasty Generalization This error consists of generalizing on the basis of either too few cases or unrepresentative ones. When a man argues, for example, that women drivers should be relieved of their licenses because of three stories in the paper last week about women being involved in auto accidents, he is guilty of picking both an insufficient and an unrepresentative number of cases (as well as overlooking important causal factors). The hasty generalization based on too few cases is much easier to recognize than that based on unrepresentative cases. The latter is illustrated by the following argument: "Senator McClelland's committee received 40,000 letters protesting various abuses in unions. It seemed clear that most workers are dissatisfied with unions." Although 40,000 ordinarily represents a sufficiently large sampling, in this instance it is not a fair or representative one (such as might be obtained by a careful selection), for only those union members who were dissatisfied would be inclined to write. The eighteen or so million other members who didn't write were apparently satisfied. So, if anything, the evidence would seem to justify the opposite conclusion, namely, that most workers seem to be satisfied with unions.

Another argument containing unrepresentative cases is the following: "As a result of a poll of 300 adults interviewed on the street between 7 and 9 P.M., we may conclude that about three-quarters of the poeple of Centerville prefer movies to television." Again, although the number interviewed seems adequate for the purpose, a little reflection will reveal that the cases are not representative. Those who prefer television to movies would probably be at home watching television at the time of the interviews, whereas those who prefer movies would probably be going to them and hence be on the street and available for the interviews. Since those who prefer movies would more likely be among those interviewed, the sample would be *loaded*.

2 False Analogy An analogy, as we have seen, is a comparison, which lies perhaps at the root of all inductive reasoning. We buy Bellow's new book, believing that it will be good because we thought his last one was. We put on rubbers when it rains because we know from past experience that when we don't, we get our feet wet and tend to catch cold. But when we overlook significant differences in making such comparisons, we get questionable conclusions and are guilty of reasoning from a *false analogy*.

In general, the greater the differences between the two components of an analogy, the more differences will be overlooked, and the greater the danger of error. There are more differences between a bucking bronco and a ship in a storm, for example, than between two automobiles of the same model manufactured by the same company. Hence, any conclusion drawn from a comparison of the first two is likely to be less dependable than one drawn from a comparison of the second two. A fairly well-known example of a dubious conclusion derived from comparing two very unlike things was the German historian Spengler's conclusion derived from an analogy between a plant and a civilization. Since both are born, grow, flourish, grow weak or strong, well or ill, and since a plant eventually dies, Spengler concluded that Western civilization will eventually decline and disappear. Overlooked in this argument, however, is the significant difference between the two which bears on the conclusion. Whereas a plant is subject to the processes of all organic matter, a civilization is not organic matter — it embodies concepts, art forms, ethical codes, and ways of living which are not necessarily subject to the same processes of deterioration.

3 Slanting Rational argumentation requires that we present our evidence as fairly and as completely as possible. The courts take cognizance of this principle when they require a witness to swear to "tell the truth, the whole truth, and nothing but the truth." To deliberately suppress unfavorable evidence (as did our night watchman) is both unreasonable and unscrupulous. The fallacy of presenting only evidence that is favorable to one's position and suppressing the unfavorable is called *slanting*. Newspapers, advertisers, lawyers, and public relations experts are often guilty of this fallacy. The advertiser, for example, tells us that the Paragon refrigerator contains 8 cubic feet of storage space, including a special storage compartment for eggs and butter, has a deep-freeze unit which can hold 50 pounds of meat, runs on a rugged expertly designed motor, and costs but a few pennies a day to operate. But he neglects to tell us that it costs $75 more than any other 8-cubic-foot refrigerator on the market or that its outer covering of enamel tends to crack and chip because the manufacturer, in pursuit of profits, has skimped on the painting.

The fallacy of slanting is seen in an argument like the following: "The Soviet Union is becoming quite democratic. New members of the High Presidium are now chosen by a majority vote of the old members." You will probably recognize this fallacy as a first cousin to the fallacy of composition. Thus, in answer, it could be pointed out that what is true of one aspect of the Soviet system is not necessarily true of the system as a whole. None of the facts which have a bearing on whether or not a system is democratic — free elections, guarantee of civil rights, etc. — are mentioned in the argument.

4 Post Hoc Fallacy From the Latin expression *post hoc, ergo propter hoc* — literally, "after this, therefore because of this" — this fallacy assumes that a chronological sequence of events is a causal one. Now while chronology seems to characterize causal relationships, that is, the effect follows the cause (we get a stomachache after overeating and not vice versa), chronology is only *one* sign of such a relationship and not sufficient by itself to warrant a conclusion that one exists. Simply because the Super Chief leaves for Chicago an hour after another train has left for Miami, we may not conclude that these events are causally related. Or take the argument: "In the last hundred years wars have become bloodier and bloodier. During the same period we discern a gradual decrease in the steadfastness of man's religious faith. Thus we may conclude that this decline in religious faith has resulted in bloodier wars." This conclusion may be true, but then again it may not be. The point is, no conclusion is justified because too many factors have been overlooked in the argument for it to be sound — growth of nationalism, competition for markets and raw materials, imperialism, ideological differences, advances in weaponry, etc.

Many *post hoc* arguments are actually the result of coincidence. A man walks under a ladder and later trips; so he attributes his accident to his having walked under the ladder. Thus are generated many of our superstitions, which are basically *post hoc* arguments. Also, many *post hoc* arguments result from confusing cause and effect. The ancient Egyptians, for example, worshipped the ibis because at a certain time each year shortly after these birds migrated to the banks of the Nile river, the river would overflow its banks and irrigate the land. Thus, the birds were credited with magical powers, when in fact both their migration and the overflow of the river were effects of a common cause, the change of season. In the same vein, one reads essays which credit an extensive vocabulary as being responsible for success in the business world, since certain studies show that the most successful executives also have the most extensive vocabularies. Overlooked, however, is the possibility that both phenomena may be due to an alert mind or even to an interaction between the two, with a large vocabulary contributing to success and success in turn contributing to a large vocabulary.

Another manifestation of what medieval logicians called *non causa pro causa*, or "taking as a cause what is not a cause," is the fallacy referred to as *fallacia accidentis*, i.e., making "an unqualified judgment of a thing on the basis of an accidental characteristic." To quote the author of the *Port Royal Logic*, "This fallacy is . . . committed by those who attribute to eloquence all the ill effects it works when abused or to medicine all the faults of ignorant doctors."[1] The fallacy is worth mentioning because it is committed so often by those who advocate new programs or want to reject current ones. To ask, for example, for the discontinuance of an economic aid program to Burma because the current program is being misadministered would be to commit *fallacia accidentis*, since presumably it is not the program itself that is the cause of any problem but rather its administrators. Hence, the reasonable approach would be to ask for the removal of the latter rather than the former.

Irrelevancies

As we have seen, one of the claims made by a sound argument is that the evidence is relevant to the conclusion. Arguments containing irrelevant evidence are therefore fallacious. To argue, for example, that the press is freer now than it used to be because more papers are sold now than twenty years ago is to give a reason which has no bearing whatever on the conclusion. Another common type of irrelevancy is the straw-man argument, that is, one which refutes a point never really presented. Errors of irrelevancy, or "slipping away from the point," are theoretically of infinite variety, though for purposes of study the following may be taken as being fairly typical:

[1] Antoine Arnauld, *The Art of Thinking (Port Royal Logic)*, 1662, translated by James Dickhoff and Patricia James (New York: Bobbs-Merrill, 1964), p. 259.

1 Irrelevant Reason The fallacy, also called *irrelevant conclusion* or *ignoratio elenchi,* consists of offering evidence which is irrelevant to the stated conclusion though the evidence may support or even prove some vaguely similar or quite different, though unstated, conclusion. For example, "We had no moral right to be in Vietnam since there was no stable government there, guerilla tactics are difficult to cope with, and we were risking an all-out nuclear war with Red China." In this case the evidence statements offer some very good reasons for asserting the conclusion that the Vietnamese war would be long, costly, and dangerous. But they have little to do with whether or not the United States had a moral or legal right to be engaged in such a war. To establish the stated conclusion, that the United States had no moral right to be in Vietnam, would involve evidence regarding the relevant international laws, our commitments, and so on. Or take this example: "Some educators claim that coeducation often leads to distractions which interfere with a student's work in class, but reliable tests show that there is very little difference in mental ability between boys and girls." Needless to say, the reason given here has nothing whatever to do with whether or not students are distracted by members of the opposite sex.

2 Genetic Fallacies In general, genetic fallacies consist of attacking the source rather than what is at issue, namely, that which has been produced by the source. To argue, for example, "A compulsory national health insurance plan should be rejected because we would be borrowing the idea from countries that don't have as good a system of health service or as fine a health record as ours in the United States", would be to attack an irrelevant feature of the plan, namely its source. If this were a valid attack, we would be committed to the position of never borrowing anything from anyone worse off than we. If a prison inmate discovered a cure for cancer or a cheap substitute for gasoline, we would have to reject it because of its source. The late Senator McKellar committed this fallacy (and possibly one or two others) when he contended that David Lilienthal could not be trusted to be the head of the Atomic Energy Commission because his parents were born in Hungary, a country which subsequently became communist. Another version of this fallacy is the argument that Caryl Chessman's books must be poor because their author was convicted of, and executed for, a heinous crime. Overlooked, of course, is the real issue: "Do his books have any literary merit?"

Perhaps the commonest manifestation of the genetic fallacy is the *argumentum ad hominem* (literally, the argument directed against the man), which attacks a person's character rather than the person's argument. Whether a person is industrious or lazy, rich or poor, married or single, discreet or indiscreet has no bearing on the argument that person advances. In other words, an argument must stand or fall on its own merits. For example, to reject an argument for dealing with the oil shortage because the person advancing it is homosexual is an *ad hominem* attack, for a person's sexual orientation is not the issue. The person's argument is.

As is often the case with fallacies, however, certain distinctions must be made here. If someone is reporting something that he or she has observed or experienced, it is legitimate to ascertain that person's credibility as a witness by considering certain aspects of his or her character. If, for instance, one is known to be a chronic liar or a convicted perjurer, it is prudent to have reservations about whether he is now telling the truth, even though he may be. To voice such a doubt under these circumstances would not be considered an *ad hominem* attack. Also, when a presumed expert gives an opinion without backing it up, it is legitimate to inquire into his or her ability or qualifications to make such a judgment and also into his or her motivation for doing so. If it can be shown that he or she is not truly qualified in the area of the judgment or that he or she stands to profit in some way by having his or her judgment believed, it is legitimate to point out such facts, since they bear on the reliability — i.e., the ability and willingness to speak the truth — of the one whose word we are asked to take. (For a fuller discussion of unqualified and biased testimony, see p. 312.)

A subtle though common form of the *ad hominem* attack is to psychoanalyze people with whom one disagrees or to explain their arguments away as the effect of some psychological quirk, to suggest that the arguments are the product of emotionally disturbed minds. The underlying principle here may be described as "Don't take issue with your opponent's argument; psychoanalyze him." Thus, when Schopenhauer criticized women for being too dependent, many women (rather than come to grips with his argument) replied that he must have been a disappointed lover or that he had a very unhappy childhood. More recently, when a high school student refused to accept an award from the American Legion, the commander of the local post declared, "A lot of people who weren't in military service don't like the Legion — probably because they can't qualify for it." The suggestion here is that jealousy must motivate opposition to the Legion, and how can jealous people think clearly?

Another familiar variation of the *ad hominem* attack is the *tu quoque* fallacy, which literally means "you're another." What happens here is an exchange of name-calling which has nothing to do with the issue at hand. When a woman criticizes her husband for baking a soggy cake and he replies, "Can you do any better?" he is commiting the *tu quoque* fallacy, for the issue is not whether the wife can bake but whether the husband can. This type of diversion usually works, since most people feel compelled to defend themselves when they are criticized. To take another example, consider the following exchange:

> **A:** The draft is needed because the United States has certain military commitments to fulfill and because she must be ready at all times for threats of aggression.

> **B:** The real reason you favor the draft is that you're too old to be drafted.

> **A:** By the same token, young man, the reason you oppose it is that you're afraid of being drafted.

Here both parties are guilty of *ad hominem* attacks. When B suggests that A is a coward, A replies, "You're another." Lost, of course, in this exchange of insults is the original issue of whether or not the draft is needed.

3 Irrelevant Function or Goals This error consists of criticizing a policy or a program because it does not achieve certain goals it was never intended to achieve. To criticize the Marshall Plan because it did not bring about the downfall of Russia or to criticize mathematics because it does not lend itself to experimental verification illustrates this kind of irrelevancy. By the same reasoning, one could as well reject social security because it does not produce clean air or combat the traffic problem.

4 Irrelevant Emotional Appeals This fallacy is known variously as *argumentum ad misericordiam* (appeal to pity), *argumentum ad populum* (appeal to the mob), *argumentum ad verecundiam* (appeal to tradition), *argumentum ad baculum* (appeal to force), appeal to pride, appeal to vanity, and appeal to fear. Advertisers, high-pressure salespersons, demagogues, and others who use irrelevant emotional appeals to inculcate belief or to get a proposal acted upon know that strong feelings tend to short-circuit the thinking process. Such appeals not only provide strong motives for believing or acting but also divert attention from weak or unreasonable claims. Essentially, all irrelevant emotional appeals try to get us to respond to certain statements or proposals by arousing in us feelings of approval or disapproval. Such feelings, however, have no bearing on the truth or falsity of a given claim; only the available evidence has. Since the emotional appeals in question present something other than evidence to support a claim, they are classed as irrelevancies.

Practically all irrelevant emotional appeals employ a transfer technique; that is, they try to associate that which most people approve of with the idea they want accepted, and to associate that which most people disapprove of with the idea they want rejected. More often than not they employ highly emotive terms for this purpose, terms bound up with strong feelings — usually of hate, fear, or love. On the hate side are words like "Communist," "Red," "left-winger," "right-winger," "reactionary," and "anarchist"; and on the love side are words like "our Founding Fathers," "the American flag," "this great land," "our noble heritage," and "God." A good example of this technique is contained in the following excerpt from a speech delivered to a Southern jury by the late Matt Murphy, who was acting as defense counsel for a man being tried for murder:

> And this white woman who got killed? White woman? Where's that N.A.A.C.P. card? I thought I'd never see the day when Communists and niggers and white niggers and Jews were flying under the banner of the United Nations flag, not the American flag we fought for. . . . I'm proud to be a white man and I'm proud that I stand up on my feet for white supremacy. Not black supremacy; not the mixing and mongrelization of races . . . not the Zionists that run that bunch of niggers. The white people are not gonna run before them. And when white people join up to 'em they become white niggers. . . .[2]

In this obscene appeal the speaker is trying to get the jurors to transfer their fav-

[2] *Life Magazine,* May 21, 1965, p. 35.

orable feelings for white supremacy to the man he is defending and at the same time to transfer their unfavorable feelings for the civil rights movement to those responsible for his client's plight. All this, however, is obviously irrelevant since it has no bearing on the guilt or innocence of the man being tried.

In the same way TV commercials sell shampoo by associating it with a thrilling sexual experience, ketchup by associating it with the strains of a symphony, and practically all other products—whether automobiles, beer, lawnmowers, or mouthwashes—by associating them with beautiful girls, usually partially clad. In his book *The Hidden Persuaders* Vance Packard quotes an advertising executive as saying, with regard to soap, which is sold not just to make women clean but beautiful, "The women are buying a promise. . . . The cosmetic manufacturers are not selling lanolin, they are selling hope. . . . We no longer buy oranges, we buy vitality. We do not buy just an auto, we buy prestige."[3]

On the political scene, speakers vie with each other in quoting Lincoln, the Bible, the Constitution and in identifying themselves with American heroes of the past as well as with their audience, whatever its makeup—whether farmers, plumbers, factory workers, school teachers, or what have you. This latter technique, labeled by some as "plain folks," is illustrated by the following introductory remarks of a campaign speech by a presidential candidate: "I am a farm boy myself. My folks were farmers, and I spent some of the happiest years of my life on our farm in Wisconsin." The suggestion behind such appeals is "I am one of you, so it follows (!) that I must have your best interests at heart. Therefore, you can believe what I say, especially when I tell you, you ought to vote for me."

One of the commonest types of emotional appeals is called *argumentum ad misericordiam,* or the appeal to sympathy or pity. This is the appeal that the lawyer uses when he introduces the accused's wife and children, the appeal that students use when they ask to be excused from an assignment or to be given a passing grade because of some personal misfortune. The fact that the accused has a wife and many children, however, is irrelevant to whether or not he is guilty, though it might have a bearing on the punishment to be meted out *if* the relevant facts show that he is guilty. Similarly, the draft plight of the failing student is not relevant to the grade he *earned* in the course—if grades we must have —though his plight is very relevant to the *need* he has for the passing grade. In other words, all attempts to persuade by appealing to emotions or accepted values like compassion are not necessarily irrelevant. Such attempts are irrelevant when there is no connection between the proposition we are being asked to accept and the feelings or values which are being appealed to.

Another common emotional appeal is known as *argumentum ad populum,* or the appeal to the mob—usually to its feelings of hate, anger, fear, and greed. This is the appeal that Marc Antony uses when speaking to the Roman populace and vividly describing Caesar's wounds and blood-splattered toga, when he tells

[3] (New York: Pocket Books, 1963), p. 60.

them how generous Caesar has been to them in his will — all of which is irrelevant to the question of Brutus's culpability, which is really what he wants them to accept and act on.

Still another kind of emotional appeal is that known as *argumentum ad baculum,* or the appeal to force or threats. Thus a recent newspaper editorial warns that the Ford administration had better do something about Cambodia or it will lose the editor's support. Sometimes the appeal is more direct as when parents threaten their children with a licking or with cutting off their allowance in order to control their behavior — all of which is irrelevant to the merit or demerit of what is being proposed.

The next several fallacies which we will discuss may be summed up as straw-man arguments, for instead of dealing with the point at issue, they deal with a different one. The lawyer, for example, who should be considering the innocence or guilt of the defendant but who sets out to prove that the crime committed was a serious one is guilty of this type of fallacy.

5 Extension This error consists of extending or exaggerating the opposition's point, usually for the purpose of making it easier to attack. The answer given, however, is irrelevant since it does not come to grips with the original point. To illustrate: "The advocates of technology maintain that a machine civilization will eliminate many of our economic ills, but frankly I can't see where technology will make us all wealthy overnight; for etc., etc." Here the speaker goes on to prove that technology won't make us all wealthy overnight — which is not too difficult to show — rather than answer the opposition's point that technology will eliminate many of our economic ills, a much more modest position than the one set up as a straw man for attack.

6 Oversimplification or Distortion This error resembles the previous one in that the speaker misrepresents the argument he is answering by leaving out significant portions of it so that he can answer it more easily. Darwin's theory of evolution, for example, is often oversimplified to mean "Man is descended from monkeys." To see how oversimplification works, consider this exchange:

A: To sum up, unemployment compensation benefits are low, there is chronic misadministration of the program, states vie with each other in keeping benefits low, and agricultural interests, which have no stake in the program, control most legislatures.

B: We are told that there is chronic misadministration of the unemployment compensation program, but is this a reason for making a drastic change? Why not go in with a broom and simply clean it up?

Here B conveniently ignores three of A's points and chooses to answer only one, giving the impression all the while that he has answered them all.

7 Diversion This error consists of shifting to a more tenable position by diverting attention away from the main point. It is illustrated by the following exchange:

A: That India disagrees with the United States over its policy of nonrecognition of Communist China is evidenced by the fact that India's late Prime Minister Nehru characterized American policy as "the root cause of all international troubles during the past four years."

B: I fail to see A's reasoning, for Communist China was the main cause of troubles in the Far East, not the United States. Who intervened in Indo-China? Who invaded Korea and Tibet? And who started a war with India? Certainly not the United States.

Though perhaps difficult to recognize at first glance, the fallacy can be seen when the conclusions of both arguments are juxtaposed:

A: India disagrees with the United States.

B: Communist China was the main cause of troubles in the Far East.

Thus it can be seen that B diverts from the issue of whether India disagrees with the United States to the issue of who caused the troubles in the Far East. But his answer is irrelevant to A's contention.

8 Attack on a Minor Point This error, commonly committed by debaters, consists of answering a minor point and evading the main one. It is illustrated by the exchange which occurs when a mathematics teacher draws a circle on the board and says, "Now, let's consider the characteristics of this circle," to which a student objects, "But that's not a perfect circle." It also appears in an exchange like the following:

A: In a speech delivered at the University of California at Los Angeles, in April, 1964, Adlai Stevenson declared: "If we turn in upon ourselves, allow our self-styled patriots to entice us into the supposed security of an impossible isolation, we shall be back in the jungle of rampant nationalisms . . . and irreconcilable conflicts which . . . would—literally—send everybody to final destruction."

B: But Stevenson's speech was delivered at the University of California at Berkeley, not Los Angeles.

The important issue, of course, is what Stevenson said, not where he said it. Pointing out minor inaccuracies is permissible only when one does so in an aside, or parenthetical remark, and then turns to the main issue.

Inconsistencies

An important characteristic of rational argumentation is consistency; that is, not only must the premises of an argument be compatible with the conclusion drawn from them (rather than contradictory or contrary), but the conclusion in turn must be compatible with other conclusions one tries to establish. Although insane people see nothing wrong in deliberately contradicting themselves, sane people as a rule do not consciously do so. They do not say, in one breath, that the earth is round and, in the next, that it is not round; they do not claim that they attended a certain college and also that they never attended that college. Sometimes in the heat of a discussion, however, they will unwittingly contradict themselves. Or, owing to carelessness they will do so, like the author of a recent book, who wrote, "Kierkegaard does not stand alone in his unique use of the word 'ethical.' " Since "unique" means that he does stand alone, the author is saying that Kierkegaard both stands alone and does not stand alone. Such errors are undoubtedly due to carelessness, for what the author probably meant was "unusual" instead of "unique." Often we are unwittingly guilty of inconsistency, as when we use a construction like "John was taller than any member of his class." What this says literally is an impossibility since, being a member of his class, John would have to be taller than himself. This type of error is easily corrected, however, simply by inserting the word "other" after "any." Recently a newspaper columnist reported that Yogi Berra, in speaking of a certain restaurant, had remarked, "The place is so crowded that nobody goes there anymore." No doubt Mr. Berra had in mind some meaning other than what this statement literally conveys, and his intended meaning would probably be easy to get at.

The error of inconsistency is not so easily rectified, however, when in a discussion one advances two arguments whose conclusions or premises contradict each other. Again, one generally doesn't do this deliberately and is usually unaware of it when he or she does. Still, the effect is very damaging when the inconsistency is pointed out, since one of the claims *must* be false.

Some of the more typical inconsistencies found in argument are the following:

1 Contradictory Premises or Assumptions Very few inconsistent arguments appear on the surface to be inconsistent, for obvious inconsistencies are readily recognized and avoided. It is only when we draw out the implications of certain arguments or when we examine their underlying (and often unstated) premises that the inconsistency appears. Two common reasons for opposing a national health insurance program, for example, are the following. (1) Most people do not seek needed medical care because of fear, habit, religious belief, degree of education, etc. Cost is *not* a factor. That is, the underlying assumption here is, *Most people do not make medical decisions on economic grounds.* (2) With medical care available to everyone, most people would take advantage of the program. Those with minor ailments, as well as malingerers and hypochondriacs, would overburden our medical facilities and deprive those of care who most needed it.   In other words, the assumption here is: *Most people do make medical decisions on economic grounds.*   For the reader's convenience, the underlying assumptions of both arguments have been italicized and are readily seen to be contradictory.

To illustrate how easily one can fall into a contradiction, recently a speaker advocating the abolishment of the jury system argued that a judge's verdict is more reliable than that of twelve untrained jurors.   In the question period following his speech, someone raised the objection that a verdict by twelve is more representative of the people, to which the speaker replied, "That's not necessarily true, for it has been found by means of questionnaires that in practically all cases judges would have reached the same verdict given by the juries."   "If that's so," countered the questioner, "how can you say that a judge's verdict is more reliable than a jury's?"   Clearly, the speaker had contradicted himself.

2   The Fallacy of Special Pleading[4]   Another variation of inconsistency is the fallacy of special pleading, which consists of attacking an opposing argument by applying a principle that is equally damaging to one's own position or of defending a position by applying a principle which also supports the opposing position. The contradiction consists in implying that a principle is true for the opposition but not for oneself, or vice versa.   However, a principle cannot be true for one and false for another; it is either true for both or false for both.   The fallacy is illustrated by the rich man who argues that being poor is a virtue, because it stimulates ambition, but a virtue that the rich man himself wants no part of, or by the couple who oppose free education but favor scholarships for their own children. In a televison debate on whether or not the voting age should be lowered to eighteen, the opponent of the proposal that it be lowered argued that many eighteen-year-olds have little knowledge of current affairs and would therefore make poor voters.   When it was pointed out to him that many twenty-one-year-olds also have little knowledge of current affairs but are still permitted to vote, he replied: "No system is perfect; we have to take the bad along with the good." However, if this principle were applied to his first argument, it would destroy it, for it would justify letting eighteen-year-olds vote even if many of them did have little knowledge of current affairs.   In his own words, "No system is perfect; we have to take the bad along with the good."   Thus the principle was a two-edged sword cutting in both directions.

Another familiar example is that of the speaker who advocates electing the President by a direct vote of the people because under the present system candidates concentrate on the large states and neglect the small ones.   Unless it could be shown that under the plan advocated the significance of carrying large states (and hence the need for devoting more campaign time to them) would be diminished, the argument would be self-defeating.   It is, of course, conceivable that what the speaker meant in the first place was that at present candidates concentrate on large states where the vote is likely to be close and that they therefore

[4] Some writers give this designation to the fallacy which we have discussed here as slanting.

spend much time and money to influence a relatively small number of votes in those states and comparatively little time and money to influence a much larger number of votes in a state not considered important. But if this, indeed, is the point, it is generally not made clear, and the argument as it stands is vulnerable to the charge of special pleading. The lesson to be derived here is, to avoid being vulnerable to the charge of arguing fallaciously, one should take pains to express one's arguments as clearly and as accurately as possible.

Thus, special pleading can prove to be self-defeating—that is, what is advocated can be turned upon the one advocating it. Several examples of this fallacy were introduced in the section dealing with unwarranted assumptions. Indeed, a most convincing proof that an assumption is false is the fact that it can be reduced to nonsense by its own provisions. The philosophers, for example, who contend that "not" is not a meaningful concept or those who declare that "all generalizations are false" contradict themselves by using the very concept which they are rejecting. The complete skeptic who denies the possibility of one's attaining any reliable knowledge is vulnerable to the same attack, for he must reject his very own utterance if he applies his principle to it.

Questionable Testimony

An important criterion of evidence is reliability, for clearly a sound conclusion cannot be drawn from evidence that is untrue or suspected of being unreliable. Unfortunately, people in high places have been known to express opinions on matters about which they are unqualified or opinions which were motivated by personal gain rather than by the desire to speak the truth as they know it. Since many arguments depend for their probative force upon expert testimony, we must be alert to the fallacies of unqualified and biased testimony.

1 Unqualified Source This error consists of quoting the judgment of someone who is not truly an expert in the field to which the judgment pertains. To qualify as an expert requires special training, experience, and demonstrated competence or ability in a given field. The fact that someone reports on political affairs does not make that person an expert in the field of politics. And, of course, the fact that someone may be an expert in one field does not make that person an expert in another. This fallacy is seen in an argument like the following: "I don't think much of that painting, for as Edward Thompson, a leading economist, has declared, 'Representational art is worthless. It does nothing the camera does not do or cannot do as well.' " Now Edward Thompson, though an economist, may have some interesting ideas about art, but they are worth no more than those of any other intelligent layman.

Another reason for disqualifying a source might be that it is outdated. The fact that Thomas Jefferson advocated free trade would not by itself be a good reason for advocating it today, since economic conditions are very much different today than they were 200 years ago when Jefferson made his recommendation.

2 Biased Testimony This error consists of citing as an expert one who is obviously motivated by self-interest, i.e., either money, power, prestige, or position. To cite the views of Wellington Koo, former Nationalist Chinese Ambassador to the UN, as being authoritative on a question involving Communist China's admission to the UN is to commit this fallacy. All paid testimonials must likewise be ruled out as unacceptable reasons for believing anything. On the other hand, testimony which is prejudicial to the individual quoted may be rated as especially reliable, since people do not usually say things to hurt themselves unless their integrity compels them to. If, for example, an American doctor expressed a favorable judgment of England's state-run medical program, his testimony would carry special weight inasmuch as he would be expected to say just the opposite.

3 Lifting Out of Context This error consists of omitting significant portions of a quotation and conveying a meaning not intended by the person quoted. Usually the portions omitted are qualifying phrases, although sometimes whole sentences are omitted. Instead of reporting that a reviewer wrote, "The scintillating dialogue of the play from which this movie was made is completely gone, and the overall effect is about as richly rewarding as getting knocked down by a truck," the advertisement in front of the movie house will quote from the review the following: "Scintillating dialogue . . . richly rewarding. . . ." This, then, is the fallacy of lifting out of context. By this means, one can quote the Bible to support the Devil, for in the Bible there appears the phrase "There is no God." The full quotation, however, is "The fool has said in his heart, 'There is no God.' "

Conclusion In concluding this discussion, it cannot be overemphasized that much practice and a constant awareness are prerequisites to recognizing and handling fallacies. Two stumbling blocks, in this regard, are: (1) We are frequently so emotionally involved in what is being discussed that we cannot be properly objective, and (2) most fallacies resemble sound arguments up to a point. Moreover, many people believe what they want to believe — what is comforting or emotionally satisfying to them to believe — or they are disarmed by a prior belief in certain conclusions. Until we recognize such shortcomings in ourselves, natural as they are, we will continue to overlook fallacious arguments, to base our actions on dubious beliefs, and to suffer the consequences of such folly. As Voltaire once shrewdly remarked, "Men will continue to commit atrocities as long as they continue to believe absurdities."

EXERCISES

Explain the fallacy, if any, in the following arguments:

> 1 Wall Street exerts more influence over skirt lengths than the Paris fashion houses. According to Fay Roberson, a research analyst for Harris, Uphan and Company, Inc., "Fashion seems very sensitive to

economic conditions. In times of prosperity, skirt lengths go up. When the market goes down, so do skirts." For the skeptics Miss Roberson contrasts today's miniskirts with the ankle-length skirts of 1897, and notes that the stock market has gone up 2,100 percent in value since women hid their ankles.

2 In order to avoid a conflict of interest the late Senator Edward Long declared that he always referred federal cases to other lawyers. When questioned about the American Bar Association's canon that it is unethical for a lawyer to accept a fee merely for "finding" a case, Senator Long insisted that he earned his fees by doing part of the work on the federal cases which he referred to other lawyers.

3 Activist groups are disrupting administrative procedures at our universities. At the University of California recently hundreds of students joined riots and picket groups.

4 A tax rebate is justified, for no less a distinguished senator than the late Senator Kerr of Oklahoma, who himself owned many oil wells, declared that there should be a liberal tax rebate for those engaged in the risky business of drilling for oil.

5 Congressman Jones's proposal for a compulsory health insurance program for all citizens cannot be taken lightly. After all, the congressman has donated considerable sums of money to charity and has the reputation of being a true humanitarian.

6 The United States should resume diplomatic relations with Cuba. Trade relationships should begin. And by all means, a cultural exchange program should be initiated. To be ignorant of one's enemy is as ridiculous as not knowing the difference between the red and green of a traffic light.

7 While addressing a group of farmers during his first campaign for the Senate, a certain senator is reported to have said of the man he subsequently defeated: "Are you aware that my opponent is known all over Washington as a shameless extrovert? Not only that, but this man is reliably reported to have practiced nepotism with his sister-in-law, and he has a sister who was once a thespian in wicked New York. He matriculated with coeds at the University, and it is an established fact that before his marriage, he habitually practiced celibacy."

8 If we compare the total number of fatalities, we must conclude that train travel is safer than air travel.

9 There was only one catch and that was Catch—22, which specified that a concern for one's own safety in the face of dangers that were real and immediate was the process of a rational mind. Orr was crazy and could be grounded. All he had to do was ask; and as soon as he did, he would no longer be crazy and would have to fly more missions. Orr would be crazy to fly more missions and sane if he didn't, but if he was sane he had to fly them. If he flew them he was crazy and didn't have to; but if he didn't want to he was sane and had to.

Joseph Heller, Catch—22.

10   Instead of shortening life, participation in sports promotes longevity. The life span of Harvard crewmen during the last fifty years is an average of 6.3 years above that of people at large throughout the country.

11   The late Ely Culbertson, one of the world's outstanding bridge players, once declared that the United Nations as presently constituted has serious defects. I don't think the opinion of a man of his caliber should be taken lightly.

12   The TVA can hardly be called a success, considering that it has not eliminated unemployment in the state of Tennessee.

13   Man is a product of his environment, as most sociologists agree; then how can it be said, as some historians claim, that man shapes the course of history and creates his own milieu?

14   Practicing physicians very often look up cases in their medical books, and lawyers in their lawbooks. Therefore, when students take a difficult examination, they should be given their textbooks.

15   Speaker advocating replacing the jury system with a panel of judges: "At present there are long delays before a case comes to trial. These are due in large part to a shortage of judges and courtrooms; etc., etc."

16   A recent survey shows that college dropouts are on the whole much heavier smokers than those who stay in college. Is there any doubt that smoking has a harmful effect on grades?

17   *The Valley of the Dolls* must be good. It's been on the bestseller lists for many weeks.

18   **A:** American prestige in Asia is high. (A cites selected pieces of evidence.)

    B: American prestige in Asia is low. (B cites several pieces of contrary evidence.)

    A: Well, you can't deny that American prestige in Asia is rising. (A now proceeds to support this point.)

19   The advocates of a bill to abolish capital punishment in New York State recently argued: (a) that the death penalty is not an effective deterrent to murder and (b) that the state has no right to play God by taking a human life. They advocated, and subsequently passed, a bill outlawing capital punishment "except when a law enforcement officer was killed while on duty or when a life convict committed a murder in prison while escaping."

20   Here's how Jim Seiler explains that a 1,200-home sample can provide ratings for 40 million TV sets: "If you're testing soup, one teaspoonful tells you how a 10-gallon vat would taste. If you have a 30-gallon vat, you don't have to taste three teaspoonfuls."

21   If you want to lose your faith in democracy, visit the Senate chamber some day and see how inattentive some of the senators are while one of their associates makes a speech.

22   That Truman's policies dealing with the Korean war were wrong is attested to by the late General MacArthur's criticism of them.

23   Activist groups should be banned from college campuses. They dress outrageously and some of the students are homosexuals.

24   When Carl Sandburg's poem "Chicago" first appeared in the March 1914 issue of *Poetry Magazine,* the editor of *Dial* wrote: "The typographical arrangement for this jargon creates a suspicion that it is intended to be taken as some form of poetry, and the suspicion is confirmed by the fact that it stands in the forefront of the latest issues of a futile little periodical described as 'a magazine of verse.' . . . We think that such an effusion as the one now under consideration is nothing less than an impudent affront to the poetry-loving public."

25   Student arguing against legalized off-track betting: "Legalized betting exploits the weaknesses of people, and it is immoral for the state to benefit from such weaknesses." When asked what system he supported, he replied, "The present system, where people must go to the track in order to bet."

26   We are told that modesty is a good thing, but I can't see where proclaiming oneself to be inferior helps anyone's character.

27   For a man who is supposed to be a champion of democracy, Lincoln said, "You can fool all of the people some of the time." This doesn't sound as though he had much faith in the people.

28   The difficulty is not that Kierkegaard's term "ethical" is ambiguous but rather that it has a double meaning.

29   What is taught in school should depend entirely on what the students are interested in. Teaching is like selling, with the teacher being the seller and the student the buyer. If nothing is learned, then nothing is taught, just as if nothing is bought, then nothing is sold. So, just as buyers determine what is to be sold, pupils should determine what is to be taught.

30   **A:**   Despite recent increases in many states, unemployment compensation benefits are still too low.

   B: But the unemployment compensation program is flexible. States can increase the benefits. Not long ago, thirty-two states did.

31   World War I erupted when Archduke Ferdinand was assassinated at Sarajevo. How, then, can it be denied that his murder caused the war?

32   Mickey Spillane's and Ian Fleming's books must be good. They sell in the millions.

33   Advocates opposing a public work program for the unemployed argued that the new proposal represented no significant change from the status quo. Thus the new program was not needed. Moreover, they contended, this program would be unworkable and disadvantageous.

34   **A:**   American prestige in Asia is low, especially in view of our policies in Vietnam and Cambodia.

   B: I don't think so. I believe that American policies are slowly but surely being understood, and our prestige is rising.

35   The late Wilfred Funk was fond of pointing out that the *Literary Digest*

1936 presidential poll which predicted a victory for Landon was no worse than the Gallup poll of 1948 which predicted a victory for Dewey. "It would seem to me that they made pretty much the same mistakes," he was reported to have said.

36 In a test made of several thousand school children it was found that in about 90 percent of the cases the children with appreciably bigger feet wrote better than those with smaller feet. When this test was performed in several other cities, the same result occurred. For some strange reason the size of a person's feet evidently affects the person's handwriting.

A Case Study

To suggest how easily fallacies can creep into argument, we shall now consider a short speech which might have been made in opposition to a proposal for compulsory government health insurance for all citizens. For our purposes the speech will contain more fallacies than speeches of this type usually contain, although the reader will have little difficulty in recognizing the breed. Following the speech we shall offer a brief analysis of it.

DEFENDING THE AMERICAN WAY OF LIFE

(1) As a true American, I wish to speak for something which is near and dear to the hearts of all Americans. I wish to speak against something as foreign to these shores as communism, socialism, totalitarianism, and other foreign "ism's," except of course Americanism. I speak of the Administration's "medicare bill," better called "socialized medicine."

(2) First, let me say that the advocates of this bill are as confused on this issue as they were last year when they led the fight to get a more liberal trade policy with communist countries. These men apparently do not realize that our concern should be for the best interests of our country and not with the interests of those who would destroy our country. Either they do not realize this or their motives are seriously suspect. Either they do not realize that socialized medicine would not serve the nation's interests or they are representing a minority vested interest. Moreover, this proposal emanated from the closed chambers of the President's hired economic advisers. It was the brain child of those ivory-towered eggheads whose motives are also anything but clear.

(3) What, then, is wrong with socialized medicine? Little imagination is needed to see that this measure would commit us to the complete takeover by government of everything traditionally reserved for the individual. As the late great Senator Robert A. Taft—a true American—warned, "If we are going to give medical care free to all people, why not provide them with free transportation, free food, free housing and clothing, all at the expense of the taxpayer. . . . Socialization is just a question of degree, and we cannot move much farther in that direction unless we do wish a completely socialistic state." In a word, if medicare is sound, then a government-sponsored, -financed, and -controlled program is sound for every—I repeat every—aspect of our life. But this principle must be rejected. As Americans, freedom must be our watchword. And since freedom means *no* control, *no* regulation, *no* restraint, gov-

ernment programs like medicare are obviously contrary to the American concept of freedom.

(4) Let me say further that unlike the pseudo-Americans who want to socialize this country, I believe that socialized medicine would be an insult to true Americans. For true Americans don't want any handouts. They want to stand on their own two feet. They're willing to meet their obligations. They're willing to work and to pay for their own medical bills. As convincing proof of this, the AMA has advertised that it will give free medical care to anyone who wants it, and practically no one responds to these ads. So what I am saying here is, it is perfectly clear that such a program is not needed or wanted.

(5) Finally, we need only look to England to see what effects socialized medicine would have here — to see how it would lower the quality of medical care. For as Dr. Lull of the AMA reminds us, the record in Great Britain shows that governmentally dominated medical systems burden doctors with much red tape and paper work, thus robbing them of the valuable time needed for careful diagnosis and treatment of patients. Not to mention all the freeloaders, hypochondriacs, and malingerers, who daily crowd the hospitals and doctors' offices and thus take away valuable beds and time from those who are really sick. In other words, socialized medicine is not only unnecessary but it would positively be undesirable.

(6) It should be clear by now that it would not accomplish the utopia claimed for it. Indeed, what proof do we have that it would make everyone healthy overnight? Since there is no conclusive proof, we can only conclude that it would be a dismal failure.

(7) Finally, though socialized medicine might help a few, it doesn't follow that it would help the nation. But even if it hurt one — and surely it would hurt a great many more — then it would hurt the nation.

Analysis of the Speech

Paragraph 1: As a true American, I wish to speak for something which is near and dear to the hearts of all Americans. I wish to speak against something as foreign to these shores as communism, socialism, totalitarianism, and other foreign "ism's" except of course Americanism. I speak of the Administration's "medicare bill," better called "socialized medicine."

Comment: The speaker uses highly emotional and suggestive language to prejudice his audience against the bill — before he offers any relevant argument. If he can convince them that he is "a true American" and if he can get them to associate the bill with "communism, socialism, totalitarianism, and other foreign ism's," his battle is better than half won. Calling the bill "socialized medicine" is a form of question-begging, since this term has unfavorable connotations in our society — heightened here by associating it with something quite unrelated, namely communism and totalitarianism. The tone of the second paragraph is also directed toward this end, but the paragraph contains other fallacies as well.

Paragraph 2: First, let me say that the advocates of this bill are as confused on this issue as they were last year when they led the fight to get a more liberal trade policy with communist countries.

Comment: This is a pure *ad hominem* attack. The passage seeks to discredit the opposition by calling them "confused," though it makes no effort to show that the *policy* is confused. But the policy is what is at issue and not the intellectual capacities of its advocates. Of course, one might show that they are confused by showing that what they advocate is confused, but the speaker fails to do this. Moreover, introducing the trade issue is irrelevant unless it is shown how it is relevant. In this irrelevant diversion the speaker also assumes without warrant that a policy in our best interests is necessarily contrary to the best interests of other countries, and conversely. But this need not be so; a policy can be in the best interests of all concerned.

> *Paragraph 2* (continued): These men apparently do not realize that our concern should be for the best interests of our country and not with the interests of those who would destroy our country. Either they do not realize this or their motives are seriously suspect. Either they do not realize that socialized medicine would not serve the nation's interests or they are representing a minority vested interest.

Comment: Here we have more *ad hominem* attack, this time by impugning the motives of the opposition. Even if their motives were suspect—unwarrantedly assumed here as one of two alternatives (or the fallacy of false alternatives)—the policy is what is at issue. One might legitimately be cautious of a policy advocated by persons with questionable motives if it were shown (and not assumed) that their motives were questionable. But one cannot reject a policy on these grounds, since the policy might still be sound.

> *Paragraph 2* (continued): Moreover, this proposal emanated from the closed chambers of the President's hired economic advisers. It was the brain child of those ivory-towered eggheads whose motives are also anything but clear.

Comment: This is a form of the genetic fallacy. The speaker hopes to establish that the policy is wrong because it was formulated in "closed chambers" by "hired" advisers. These terms, of course, are emotionally loaded, implying secrecy, collusion, and undemocratic methods. Similarly, the epithet "ivory-towered" suggests an impractical or unrealistic plan, and the term "eggheads" (with unclear motives) suggests something both too sophisticated and sinister for the average person. All of these suggestions are also unsupported and hence beg the question.

> *Paragraph 3:* Little imagination is needed to see that this measure would commit us to the complete takeover by government of everything traditionally reserved for the individual. . . . "Socialization is just a question of degree, and we cannot move much farther in that direction unless we do wish a completely socialistic state." In a word, if medicare is sound, then a government-sponsored, -financed, and -controlled program is sound for every . . . aspect of our life.

Comment: This kind of argument is more common than one would like to believe. We have called it the *argument of the beard,* one which obscures distinctions and differences. Here it is argued that there is no difference between a compulsory health insurance program, socialized medicine, and complete socialism in all areas. And, since most Americans would reject the latter, they should reject the former. But between black and white, compulsory education and a Lenin five-year plan, there are significant differences; and distinctions can be made even if they aren't always sharp ones.

Paragraph 3 (continued): As Americans, freedom must be our watchword. And since freedom means *no* control, *no* regulation, *no* restraint, government programs like medicare are obviously contrary to the American concept of freedom.

Comment: The speaker may be quite correct in saying that "freedom is our watchword," but the sense of freedom expressed in that slogan is hardly the sense of which he than speaks. His sense—"*no* control, *no* regulation, *no* restraint"—suggests licentiousness. To be sure, a compulsory health insurance program would not be compatible with his sense of freedom, but it doesn't follow that it would be "contrary to the American concept of freedom"—let alone "obviously," a question-begging term used to persuade by suggesting more confidence in the conclusion than is warranted.

Paragraph 4: . . . unlike the pseudo-Americans who want to socialize this country, I believe that socialized medicine would be an insult to true Americans. For true Americans don't want any handouts. . . . As convincing proof of this, the AMA has advertised that it will give free medical care to anyone who wants it, and practically no one responds to these ads. . . . It is perfectly clear that such a program is not needed or wanted.

Comment: This passage begins with another *ad hominem* remark, "pseudo-Americans," and a misrepresentation by extension, or exaggeration, of the opposition view, "who want to socialize this country." The plan makes no such claim. The speaker then makes his first real attempt to argue reasonably, by presenting a conclusion supported by relevant evidence. The evidence, however, is too vague to warrant the conclusion that the program is not needed or wanted. We are not told where the ads appeared, how often they appeared, the kind of aid they offered, or what the phrase "practically no one" stands for. And yet this type of evidence is claimed to make the conclusion "perfectly clear"—another attempt to persuade by the confident manner.

Paragraph 5: Finally, we need only look to England to see what effects socialized medicine would have here—to see how it would lower the quality of medical care. For as Dr. Lull of the AMA reminds us, the record in Great Britain shows that governmentally dominated medical systems burden doctors with much red tape and paper work, thus robbing them of the valuable time needed for careful diagnosis and treatment of patients.

Comment: Again the speaker tries to argue reasonably, this time by means of an analogy with the British plan. But the analogy is a poor one, for the British plan differs in many important respects from the American plan— in the reimbursement of physicians, to cite only one—not to mention significant economic, social, medical, and other differences between the two countries. Moreover, the testimony of Dr. Lull of the AMA concerning the British plan is biased, since the AMA has long been on record as opposing any plan of state-supported medicine. (If Dr. Lull had had kind words to say about the British program, this would be most effective testimony, since we would expect him to say just what he did say.)

> *Paragraph 5* (continued): Not to mention all the freeloaders, hypochondriacs, and malingerers who daily crowd the hospitals and doctors' offices and thus take away valuable beds and time from those who are really sick.

Comment: Here we have a basic contradiction of the point concerning the AMA's offer of free care and the people's refusal to take advantage of it. The implication of the latter point is that people are not motivated by economic considerations, that they are willing to pay for their own care and hence would not avail themselves of free care. But the implication of the "freeloader" argument is that people are motivated by economic considerations, that they would take excessive advantage of free care if it were offered and would thus burden the doctors and hospitals. Ironically, the only two partially reasonable arguments in the speech contradict each other. In passing, the term "positively" represents another attempt to persuade by the confident manner.

> *Paragraph 6:* It should be clear by now that it would not accomplish the utopia claimed for it. Indeed, what proof do we have that it would make everyone healthy overnight? Since there is no conclusive proof, we can only conclude that it would be a dismal failure.

Comment: The first sentence is another example of extension, or straw-man argument, for the advocates of compulsory health insurance have never claimed that it would "accomplish utopia." The second sentence is more of the same, for they have never claimed it "would make everyone healthy overnight." The third sentence compounds the fallacy by being an *argumentum ad ignoratiam* coupled with a false alternative. Absence of proof that the plan would work is no reason to conclude that it would not. To prove this, one would have to present some kind of concrete evidence. On top of all this, the unwarranted assumption itself is extended to a false alternative, "a dismal failure." Even if a plan didn't work, we may not assume that it is a dismal failure. Finally, the word "conclusive" is used illegitimately for no policy of this type can be "proved conclusively." If it could be, it would not be controversial.

> *Paragraph 7:* Finally, though socialized medicine might help a few, it doesn't follow that it would help the nation. But even if it hurt one — and surely it would hurt a great many more — then it would hurt the nation.

Comment: The speaker avoids the fallacy of composition when he correctly claims that because it might help some, the conclusion doesn't follow that it would help the nation. But, ironically, in the next breath he commits this very fallacy by arguing that if it hurt one, it would hurt the nation. Finally, notice again the unwarranted confident manner suggested by the word "surely."

PART FOUR

APPLIED LOGIC

SIXTEEN

SCIENTIFIC METHOD

Please observe, gentlemen, how facts which at first seem improbable will, even on scant explanation, drop the cloak which has hidden them and stand forth in naked and simple beauty.

Galileo

A great deal has been written about "science" by scientists, historians, philosophers, journalists, theologians, and many others. With different perspectives and goals, these writers often express different views about the nature of science. Some speak about mathematics as an "exact science," others about a "scientific philosophy," and still others about the "religion of science," "scientific thinking," and the "horrors wrought by science." Some dispute vigorously whether sociology or psychoanalysis is a science, whether psychology is a "natural science" or a "social science," whether we can have a "scientific ethic," whether science can somehow save us, or whether science robs human beings of their dignity. Moreover, the word "science" itself and its linguistic variants is frequently used with little discrimination in ordinary language. Thus, we hear advertisements which tell us about a cigarette's "scientific filter" or about the "scientific" combination of ingredients ("like a doctor's prescription") in a headache remedy. What follows is not intended to provide answers to all the many questions which might be raised regarding "science." Rather, we shall concentrate on science as embodying a *method* and try to clarify those elements which constitute scientific method. In the concluding sections of this chapter, we shall sketch a few of the outstanding features of the well-developed sciences.

Scientific Method

The requirement that assertions be *warranted* may be taken as the distinctive feature of what is called *scientific method*. Broadly conceived, scientific method is the persistent critique of argument in the light of evidence and in accordance with the canons of logic. Accordingly, everything that has been said in previous chapters bears on scientific method. Indeed, one may say that scientific method is *applied logic*. Although scientific method has been used very successfully in science, its use need not be limited to that area. Rather, if understood as applied logic, it may be used in coping with the problems of everyday life.

Scientific inquiry, like all inquiry, begins with a problem. If there is no problem to be solved, no perplexity or doubt to be overcome, we do not inquire. Indeed, Charles Sanders Peirce (1839–1914) defined inquiry as "the struggle to attain a state of belief." The sorts of "problems," "puzzles," "perplexities," and "doubts" which generate inquiry are many and various. They range from puzzlement as to the nature of a DNA molecule to satisfaction of what John Dewey (1859–1952) called a "felt need." But in each case we seek solutions, and in so doing we inquire.

Peirce described four *methods of inquiry*.[1] The first he called the method of tenacity, which involves simply adopting the first convenient solution which comes along and then clinging to it with the tenacity of a bulldog. Peirce noted that "the social impulse" is against this method, for "the man who adopts it will find that other men think differently from him, and it will be apt to occur to him, in some saner moment, that their opinions are quite as good as his own, and this will shake confidence in his belief." The second method, called the method of authority, utilizes some authority—an institution or individual—to establish what is to be accepted. Peirce sarcastically observed that this method, while "successful" in fixing belief, is limited insofar as men can "put two and two together." The third method Peirce called the a priori method, which involves accepting that which is "agreeable to reason," or more narrowly, that which is "self-evident." This method, said Peirce, "makes of inquiry something similar to the development of taste; but taste, unfortunately, is always more or less a matter of fashion." Peirce's fourth method, the method of science, is the only one which can give us any confidence in our solutions, for it alone is self-corrective.

To illustrate this method, let us return to our car which does not start. Here the "problem" is clear: "Why is the car not starting?" We begin to inquire. Could it be the gas? Could it be the ignition? Could it be the carburetor? Each of these suggestions constitutes a possible solution to the problem. Technically, we call them *hypotheses*, the implications of which we develop. If the car is out of gas, then the tank will be empty. We check the facts. The tank has plenty of gas. We reason that our difficulty is not due to lack of gasoline. One hypothesis has been tested and disconfirmed. Perhaps it is the ignition? If it is the ignition,

---

[1] C. S. Peirce, "The Fixation of Belief," originally published in *Popular Science Monthly*, 1877, and reprinted in many places.

then it might be the spark plugs. If it is the plugs, then one, two, or all of them will not spark. We test them. Each functions properly. But other factors could cause an ignition breakdown. We further explore consequences. This procedure illustrates an application of scientific method. In our inquiry, the possible solutions, or hypotheses, are constantly being checked against the facts. If there is a way to solve the problem, this method will give us the maximum assurance that the hypothesis which leads to a solution is the true one. To be sure, it may not be, but by contrast, the other methods can give us *no* confidence in our solution, for they are not self-corrective. Tenacious acceptance of convenient answers, blind acceptance of authority, and unchecked intuition may yield solutions, but there is *no* way to determine if they are true. If we want warranted beliefs, the only safe way to get them is through logic, or the scientific method.

Similar examples could be recounted almost without number from both science and everyday life, but our commonplace example embodies all of the salient features of the method. First, there is the problem to be solved, the puzzlement to be overcome. Second, there is the formulation of a hypothesis or hypotheses. Third, there is an elaboration of the consequences of the hypothesis. Fourth, there is the testing of hypotheses against the facts. Finally, there is the acceptance or rejection of a hypothesis, depending upon whether or not it has been confirmed or disconfirmed.

Schematically, the method may be represented as follows:

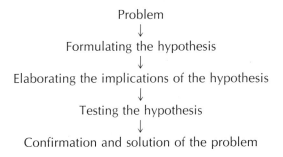

Problem
↓
Formulating the hypothesis
↓
Elaborating the implications of the hypothesis
↓
Testing the hypothesis
↓
Confirmation and solution of the problem

Now let us look more closely at these various stages of inquiry.

The Problem   It is important to remember that inquiry begins with a problem, for, as was emphasized in the discussion of induction, context is important. There are several reasons why. In the first place, what constitutes a "problem" will vary from place to place, from time to time, and from inquirer to inquirer. Many of the "problems" of other times and places are simply not problems for us, either because they have been satisfactorily solved or because, for various reasons, they do not concern us. Sometimes, a single inquirer will see a problem in a situation where others do not. And sometimes that inquirer's struggle will result in an innovation or scientific breakthrough. For the average person, it takes some unusual, personal, and generally unpleasant circumstance to generate a problem—for example, failure in school, lack of money, being fired from a job, or a sudden illness. For the advanced or highly sophisticated inquirer, on the other hand, circumstances which are generally taken for granted by most people can raise problems. For years lamps had swayed back and forth on their long chains from the Cathedral of Pisa but only Galileo thought them worth studying and from them discovered the principle of the isochronism of the pendulum. More recently Einstein was led to ask: "What happens to a ray of light shining into an elevator when the elevator suddenly descends?" Though this is a daily occurrence, only Einstein seemed to be interested in it. For many generations men have known of moldy bread, but only Sir Alexander Fleming thought mold an interesting enough phenomenon to study it carefully, and his study of mold led to the discovery of penicillin. And countless millions see plants growing every day, but, generally, only botanists think of asking why plants seem to respond to sunlight. Alfred North Whitehead summed it up well when he said, "It requires a very unusual mind to undertake the analysis of the obvious." For such reasons, it is not easy to say which problems are significant and worthy of inquiry.[2] It must be observed, however, that what constitutes a problem is not a logical or methodological question but one which falls properly into the areas of psychology, sociology, and history.

Secondly, and more importantly, in realizing that problems are context-dependent, we must remember that what constitutes background knowledge is also context-dependent. Since the formulation of hypotheses (stage two) in response to specific problems depends heavily on background knowledge, this formulation is restricted by that knowledge. Not that background knowledge *logically determines hypotheses* or *logically rules out* any; but it does make certain hypotheses more available than others and, what is more important, tends to make them more dependable. In Aristotle's world, for example, to formulate the principle of inertia[3] in response to certain problems of motion would have been a prodigious feat. Even Galileo, for all his comparatively modern sophistication, did not fully relinquish the belief that "natural motion" was circular.[4] Similarly, while today certain problems seem almost irresolvable because we cannot "hit upon" the correct hypotheses, history suggests that these hypotheses will seem obvious to future generations.

Since background knowledge is relative, what may be acceptable as a confirmed hypothesis varies. A hypothesis rejected in one context because it doesn't "fit" the known facts may be accepted in a later context. As new knowledge is uncovered, old problems are often reconsidered and solved in the light of that knowledge. To the ancient Greeks, for example, the available evidence sup-

---

[2] A currently important dispute, especially among social scientists, is over whether social science has neglected significant problems in its endeavor to be "scientific." Some argue that social scientists frequently fit problems to available techniques rather than find techniques for coping with important problems.

[3] A body in motion tends to remain in motion in a straight line to infinity.

[4] Significantly, René Descartes, Pierre Gassendi, and Isaac Newton, each influenced by Galileo, did formulate and accept forms of the principle of inertia — and in the *same* century.

ported the view of a stationary earth; in the sixteenth century there was much new evidence which supported Copernicanism and the concept of a moving earth.

Finally, what may be a good solution in one context may be inadequate in another, owing to different circumstances — different needs, values, and so on. Thomas Hobbes's solution, for example, to the problem of securing individual rights was rejected by John Locke and others because of differing views concerning the role of government.[5] The context of inquiry implies that viable solutions are not infinite and that those which are accepted are not fixed or permanent, either because of new knowledge, changing needs, or both. This point is important for understanding the use of scientific method.

Formulating Hypotheses In the last section we noted that the formulation of hypotheses is somehow a function of background knowledge. However, this does not mean that there is a "method" for formulating hypotheses, for there is no clear-cut procedure or rule which can be followed in formulating them. Those formulated depend upon many factors besides one's knowledge of the subject matter. Although the "wild guesses" of an ill-informed individual are more likely to be disconfirmed than not, sometimes such guesses lead to important new discoveries. In such cases the guesses were good because they were confirmed.

But experience indicates that workable hypotheses rarely, if ever, come full-blown like Athena from the head of Zeus. As we said earlier, extant knowledge poses certain limits, even if they are ill-defined. At the same time, no hypothesis, logically speaking, is inconceivable, although practically speaking, the set at any time and place is finite. Moreover, while being well informed is neither a necessary nor a sufficient condition for producing the right hypothesis, it undoubtedly improves one's chances of doing so. Galileo, Newton, Pasteur, Lavoisier, Maxwell, and Einstein were all innovators, but they were also scientists who knew their subject matter thoroughly.

The Role of Hypotheses Hypotheses direct inquiry. Without them there could be no inquiry, for we would not know where to begin or where to look. Some writers have mistakenly supposed that scientific method involves *first* an unprejudiced "gathering of the facts," and *then* the formulation of hypotheses. But without a hypothesis to guide us, *which* facts would we gather? If the car didn't start, would we gather data on baseball scores, current dance rages, the position of the moon? Indeed, the number of available "facts" is infinite; so even if we wanted to gather them *all*, we could not. Fortunately, however, we are interested in only the *relevant* facts. To rule out data on baseball scores, dance rages, and astronomical phenomena as irrelevant to auto mechanics is to *presuppose* some hypothesis as to what is relevant. And this will always be so. As Charles Darwin put it, ". . . observation must be for or against some view, if it is to be of any service. . . ." We cannot just observe at random; we observe what we think

---

[5] The example here is complex, but there is little doubt that ill-defined wants and aims often play a significant role in determining the acceptability of a proposed solution.

is relevant, and what we think is relevant is predicated upon some hypothesis. Once a possible solution to a particular problem is thought of, we can begin to gather facts which either support or undermine it. This step in turn leads us either to accept, reformulate, or reject the hypothesis altogether.

Now let us see in more detail how hypotheses direct inquiry and how elaborating them leads to confirmation or disconfirmation.

Elaborating and Confirming Hypotheses Like many observers before him, Aristotle was puzzled by the phenomenon of motion. Led by the belief that some uniform relation could be found in all cases of moving bodies, he arrived at the hypothesis that the "speed" of a moving object was proportional to the "force" exerted upon it, divided by the "resistance."[6] This hypothesis is characteristic of all scientific hypotheses in that it brings order to an otherwise isolated set of factors. Aristotle's hypothesis links together in a "lawlike" relation three common factors of all moving bodies, their speed, their force, and the resistance. Indeed, all the "laws" of science share in this characteristic: They uniformaly associate apparently isolated factors or events.[7]

Moreover, Aristotle's hypothesis, which came to be called Aristotle's Law of Motion, satisfied the requirement that it be testable. In fact, it seems to account quite adequately for most of the situations which we familiarly encounter. If, for example, we take two objects of the same weight and on the same surface and exert more force on one than on the other, it will move faster. Similarly, given two objects of the same weight, we know that if the resistance on one is less, say, than it is on ice, then it will move faster. Further commonplace instances in which the hypothesis holds can easily be produced. Thus, Aristotle's hypothesis checks out with "the facts."

But like any hypothesis, it leads to further implications. For example, if two objects of the same size and weight are dropped from the same height, one through water and the other through oil, the former should move faster. This prediction is also confirmable. What we are doing here is quite clear. We are elaborating the hypothesis by deducing its implications. In its simplest form, this only means applying the rule of universal instantiation. That is, if the speed of *all* moving bodies is proportional to force divided by resistance, then the speed of any one moving body should be proportional to its force divided by its resistance. The deduced implications are then tested. As each implication of the hypothesis is tested and confirmed, then, other things being equal, the probability that the hypothesis is true increases.

Compare this principle with that of increasing the instances in enumerative induction, and note also the logic involved. If we call the hypothesis H and the implications deduced from it $I_1, I_2, \ldots, I_n$, then we have this form of argument:

---

[6] In symbols, $S \cong \frac{F}{R}$. Strictly speaking, Aristotle did not express his law of motion in this way. The use of equations, itself a significant procedure, was not common until the seventeenth century.

We are indebted for this example to I. B. Cohen's discussion in *The Birth of a New Physics* (New York: Anchor Books, Doubleday & Company, Inc., 1960).

[7] See below, p. 337.

$$\begin{array}{ll} \text{If } H \text{, then } I. & \text{or} \qquad H \supset I \\ \underline{I.} & \qquad\quad \underline{I} \\ \text{So, probably } H. & \qquad \therefore H \end{array}$$

Since this argument commits the formal fallacy of affirming the consequent, even if the premises were true (which in fact they are) it would not necessarily follow that the conclusion is true. All we can say is that on the evidence the conclusion is to some degree probable.

As formulated, Aristotle's hypothesis is somewhat vague. What, for example, is the "force" referred to in the original equation, especially as it is exerted upon bodies which are dropped? Aristotle argued, again from a commonsense point of view, that the force of falling objects was a product of their weight. Thus, heavy bodies exert more force than light bodies. But this hypothesis in conjunction with the original one implies that heavier bodies should fall faster than lighter ones when the resistance is the same for both. This implication can easily be tested. If two bodies of unequal weight but of the same size and shape (to keep resistance the same) are dropped from the same height, then the heavier body should fall faster. Indeed, if it were twice as heavy as the other, it should fall twice as fast. What actually occurs, however, is that the difference in speed is not perceptible.[8] (So far as is known, this experiment was first performed by John the Grammarian in the sixth century and later by Simon Stevin and Galileo in the sixteenth century.) But this result deductively falsifies the hypothesis:

$$\begin{array}{ll} \text{If } H \text{, then } I. & \text{or} \qquad H \supset I \\ \underline{\text{Not } I.} & \qquad\quad \underline{\sim I} \\ \text{So, necessarily, not-}H. & \qquad \therefore \sim H \end{array}$$

Or so it would appear. But the matter is not that simple, for as we noted, in order to deduce I from H, we also had to assume that more force is exerted on heavier falling objects than on lighter ones. This auxiliary assumption — call it A — was essential in deducing I.[9] Thus we did not simply test H, but H in conjunction with A:

[8] Since "speed" is distance divided by time, the heavier body should hit the ground perceptibly sooner. Actually, there is a small difference, which elementary physics texts sometimes ignore.

[9] If speed is directly proportional to force and inversely proportional to resistance, and force (of falling bodies) is directly proportional to weight, then, necessarily, speed is directly proportional to weight and inversely proportional to resistance. Symbolically:

$$S \propto \frac{F}{R}$$
$$\underline{F \propto W}$$
$$\therefore S \propto \frac{W}{R}$$

Now if R is constant and W_2 is twice W_1, then when W_2 is substituted for W_1, S will be twice as great as it was.

$$\begin{array}{ll} \text{If } H \text{ and } A, \text{ then } I. & \text{or} \qquad (H \cdot A) \supset I \\ \text{Not-}I. & \underline{\qquad \sim I \qquad} \\ \hline \text{So, necessarily either} & \therefore \ \sim H \lor \sim A \\ \text{not-}H \text{ or not-}A. \end{array}$$

That is, our test refuted *either* the original hypothesis *or* the assumption essential to deducing *I*, or both. But it does not tell us which. Although something is undoubtedly wrong, several options are nevertheless available: We could reject Aristotle's Law of Motion, as Galileo did; we could argue that *A* is false; we could argue that *H* does not *apply* to objects in free fall; or finally, we could reject both *H* and *A*. Commonsense evidence suggests that *A* is correct—that more "force" is exerted on heavier bodies in free fall. Indeed, until the time of Galileo, who offered a *better* hypothesis, it was generally held that Aristotle's law was correct but that it simply did not apply to objects in free fall. Galileo, as you may remember, distinguished speed from acceleration and argued that weight is *irrelevant*. Thus, he concluded that the correct relation is between the *distance* in free fall and the *time squared*.

This somewhat oversimplified recital reveals a variety of key features concerning the role of hypotheses in scientific method.

1 In seeking to show that every moving body is subject to the same laws, Aristotle's hypothesis brought order to the problematic nature of motion. For him the "problem" was solved, though future inquirers felt compelled to reopen the problem and subsequently to reject his solution. The point here is, *all hypotheses are vulnerable in this way.*

2 Aristotle's hypothesis directed inquiry into the common features of force, resistance, speed, and weight and at the same time mistakenly led him away from other considerations, which Galileo and others later examined. But the point here is, like *all hypotheses, this hypothesis directed inquiry.*

3 The hypothesis was tested by deductively elaborating its implications. *Such testing applies to all hypotheses.* Sometimes, this step goes unnoticed, especially when the elaboration is simply a matter of deducing particular instances from a generalization. Usually, however, it is more complex.

4 *The elaboration of hypotheses involves the use of auxiliary assumptions, or auxiliary hypotheses.* Sometimes the auxiliary assumptions are beyond dispute, but sometimes they are not. Consider again the car which was out of gas. You will recall that in elaborating the hypothesis that the car was out of gas, we reasoned that if it were, the tank would be empty. Here the auxiliary hypothesis took the form of an implicit conditional: "If the car is out of gas, then the tank will be empty." On this assumption *and* on the assumption that the car was out of gas, we *deduced* that the tank would be empty. When we saw that it was not, we

rejected the hypothesis that it was out of gas. But notice that, logically, we could also have rejected the *conditional* as false and thus preserved our original hypothesis.[10] In this case we did not, however, since we had good reason to believe that the auxiliary assumption (the conditional statement) was not false.

A famous historical example of the use of auxiliary hypotheses in a full-blown scientific theory concerns the dispute between Isaac Newton and Christian Huygens on the nature of light. Newton argued that light is a particle emitted from the light source and that such particles may be described by his laws of motion. From these and some other assumptions, he deduced a set of laws on reflection and refraction and proceeded to test them and thus confirm his *corpuscular theory*. Huygens, however, argued that light was a wave which was propagated much like the ripples created on a still pond by a stone thrown into it. This *wave theory* can also be elaborated to imply the laws of reflection and refraction. Which hypothesis, then, is correct? Arago deduced an implication from Newton's set of assumptions that light would travel faster in water than in air. When this was tested, it turned out to be false. Arago supposed that he had refuted Newton's claim that light is a particle. But, indeed, what he had refuted was the *set of assumptions* necessary to deduce the statement that light travels faster in water than in air. Subsequent research revised the corpuscular theory of Newton by altering some of the auxiliary assumptions, and today the nature of light remains an unsolved dilemma of modern physics.

5   *A hypothesis will ordinarily be accepted as confirmed when it successfully solves the problem for which it was posed and when competing hypotheses are either not as substantially confirmed or simply not available.* This feature emphasizes the *comparative* nature of confirmation. Faced with several possible solutions, we must judge which is the most confirmed. The factors discussed in the chapter on induction are pertinent here, as well as some others.

In general, we must consider the quantity, variety, and precision of the evidence. The *quantity* of evidence refers to the number of tested implications of the hypothesis. If H_1 has more tested implications than H_2, then, other things being equal, H_1 is more probable than H_2. The *variety* of evidence refers to the extent to which the evidence is heterogeneous or disparate. With generalizations it is, as we saw, a question of the type of sample. With other hypotheses, it is more a matter of the extent to which the hypothesis can account for apparently disconnected facts. The *precision* of evidence refers to the *quality* of the evidence. In other words, is the evidence itself well substantiated or is it probably spurious? In discussing Mill's methods we saw the importance of controlled test conditions. The test of a hypothesis may not be a true test at all if

---

[10] The conditional is $P \supset Q$. But P and $\sim Q$ may both be true if $P \supset Q$ is false.

many factors have been ignored and the experiment is poorly designed. Courtroom procedure clearly recognizes the importance of precision of evidence by insisting on many different rules of evidence, such as the inadmissibility of hearsay evidence.

Besides the quantity, variety, and precision of the evidence, a fourth factor is *fruitfulness*—that is, the number of new predictions a hypothesis leads to. Although several competing hypotheses may account for most of the available facts, that which leads to some new fact or successful prediction may be considered more probable than the others. Newton's hypothesis, for example, was designed to account for the elliptical orbit of the planets and succeeded in doing so. But his hypothesis also implies that acceleration in free fall should vary with latitude, a fact unknown to Galileo. When this implication was checked, it proved to be true. Similarly, on the basis of Newtonian and Copernican theory, the French astronomer Leverrier predicted that a theretofore undiscovered body must be causing the planet Uranus to deviate from what should have been its orbit. When he turned his telescope to the predicted location of this body, he discovered the planet Neptune.

A fifth factor important in evaluating a hypothesis is *simplicity*, which is to say that if two different hypotheses both explain the same set of facts, the simpler one is usually regarded as the more acceptable or more probable. Though we cannot define "simplicity" precisely, we can indicate its meaning in a general way. Since a hypothesis is a supposition about the nature or cause of some happening, the fewer the factors involved in this supposition the simpler the hypothesis is. If detectives, for example, discovered strange footprints of the kind usually made by a lame person leading up to and from one of the windows of a room where a theft had occurred, they could explain this phenomenon by the hypothesis that the thief was a stranger who was lame. But they could also explain it by the hypothesis that the owner of the house, in order to collect the insurance, had really committed the theft but, in order to throw the police off the trail, had managed to entice a lame person onto the grounds and got him to walk up to the window. The former hypothesis, however, is simpler and more acceptable, for it involves fewer assumptions or auxiliary hypotheses and thus raises fewer questions and does not involve elaborate explanations for which there is little evidence. From this example it can be seen that simplicity is not only an esthetic criterion but one of probability. The more factors or events which must be supposed—the more auxiliary hypotheses which must be introduced to support the main hypothesis—the lower the probability of the main hypothesis. Hence, all other factors being equal, the simpler the hypothesis the more probable it is.

Finally, when there are *no* competing hypotheses to solve a problem or explain certain facts, then the hypothesis which has been accepted will usually continue to be accepted until a more satisfactory hypothesis is offered. It was long known, for example, that certain implications of Aristotle's laws did not hold, but until Galileo proposed an alternative hypothesis which was more satisfactory, Aristotle's hypothesis was not rejected. Many other examples from the history of science illustrate this point, as do those from our everyday experience. Accepted solutions are not readily rejected when alternative solutions are not available. In this respect the scientific attitude is "conservative," being unwilling to abandon workable solutions until better ones come along.

There are other aspects of the conservative nature of scientific method; for example, alternative and possibly *more* satisfactory hypotheses will carry the burden of proof. A new hypothesis regarding some domain of inquiry will inevitably conflict with some of our previous beliefs regarding this domain. To accept the new hypothesis thus means that we will have to reject some of our old beliefs, at least in their current form. A dramatic example is Copernicanism. To accept the heliostatic hypothesis required rejection of most of Aristotelian mechanics. Consider, for example, the implications of the view that our earth is hurtling through space and that it rotates on its axis once in every 24 hours. On the Aristotelian view, the earth is stationary in space. An object thrown straight up should come straight down. But if the earth is rotating at approximately 1,500 feet per second, then during (say) a 4-second interval in which an object is thrown upward and falls back down, the earth will have moved some 6,000 feet from the point from which the object was thrown. How is it possible, then, that objects thrown straight up do come down close to where they are thrown? The reluctance to reject the intuitively sensible Aristotelian physics was indeed rational. Accordingly, the advocates of Copernicanism had the burden of proving their theory.[11]

To be sure, not all new hypotheses are revolutionary, nor may it be said that their displacement of currently accepted hypotheses can always be characterized as scientific revolutions. But in general we may say that, other things being equal, the less a new hypothesis requires rejection of already held beliefs, the more plausible the hypothesis. Or, put the other way around, the greater the challenge to existing beliefs, the greater the burden of acceptability.[12]

The criteria mentioned here for evaluating hypotheses — the quantity, variety, and precision of the supporting evidence as well as the fruitfulness, simplicity, and plausibility of the hypotheses — are not unrelated to one another. Indeed, they generally stand in an uneasy tension with respect to each other. Of two hypotheses, one may be simpler than the other but have less evidence to support it. Or, one may be more fruitful than another but require the rejection of more

---

[11] This accords with the principle "He who asserts must prove." A parallel may be seen with our judicial system. Whoever brings a charge, whether an individual or the state, must prove it. Otherwise, the charge is dismissed. For discussion of the example above, see I. B. Cohen, op. cit., and Thomas S. Kuhn, *The Copernican Revolution* (New York: Vintage Books, 1957). For discussion of the host of complex issues regarding scientific revolutions, see Kuhn, *The Structure of Scientific Revolutions*, 2nd ed., enlarged (Chicago: University of Chicago Press, 1970).

[12] Less "rational" reasons also play a role in explaining the conservative nature of science as an institution. Thus, political, bureaucratic, and sociological factors are an inherent part of the institutionalization of science. Consider, e.g., the role of the church in earlier times and, more recently, the role of government funding. These issues are too complex for discussion here. But see C. W. Mills, *The Sociological Imagination* (New York: Oxford University Press, 1959), chaps. 4 and 5.

beliefs. Or, again, one may have more evidence to support it than another, but the evidence may be less precise or less heterogeneous. Thus, when applying the foregoing criteria, we have no clear-cut rules to guide us. As several recent writers in the philosophy of science have persuasively argued, the scientific process is "under-determined by rule" in *all* of its stages.[13] That is to say, insight, judgment, and sensitivity enter both the process of discovery (the formulation of hypotheses) *and* the process of confirmation (the elaboration and testing of hypotheses). In short, there are no infallible rules to guarantee a consensus regarding the results of inquiry.

This does not mean, however, that scientific inquiry is either mystical or arbitrary. The criteria previously mentioned — the nature of the evidence, fruitfulness, simplicity, etc. — are used because they maximize one's chances for success.

One final feature of scientific method requires mention. Scientific inquiry is peculiarly *public* in that hypotheses are subject to the tribunal not only of experience but also of the community of inquirers. Scientific method is thus a deliberative, critical, and social process whose purpose is to frame hypotheses that can stand the test of further deliberation and criticism by subsequent inquirers. In this sense, scientific method is "liberal," both because the process is open and public and because *every* hypothesis is constantly vulnerable to being reformulated or rejected altogether.

As we have emphasized, the use of scientific method is not confined to scientific problems, although their solution is a model for inquiry. In the chapter which follows we shall give special attention to the application of scientific method to problems in decision and policymaking. But before doing so, we shall offer some introductory remarks on the nature and role of laws and theories in science.

The Nature of Scientific Laws

Scientific hypotheses can become scientific laws or theories. If a hypothesis is of the kind which asserts a relation of uniform association, when confirmed and made a part of the body of knowledge of some science, it is usually called a *law*. Hence, laws are universal statements which assert an invariant association between events, properties, or phenomena. Most laws can be expressed as simple **A**-form categoricals, "All A is B," or, in modern symbolism, $(x)(Fx \supset Gx)$. For example, "All sugar is soluble in water." "All bodies freely falling near the earth fall at $\frac{1}{2} gt^2$," "All mammals require oxygen," and so on. Other laws are statistical and assert a uniform relation of a statistical nature, such as "The probability that an atom of radium will decay within 1,620 years is $\frac{1}{2}$." Such statements are

[13] See, e.g., Kuhn, op. cit.; Michael Polanyi, *Personal Knowledge* (Chicago: University of Chicago Press, 1958); and N. R. Hanson, *Patterns of Discovery* (Cambridge: Cambridge University Press, 1958).

still universal in that it is asserted, as in our example, that *all* atoms of radium behave in a specified way.

While a scientific law must be a universal statement and be confirmed, these conditions alone are not generally considered to be sufficient. That is, some universal statements, for example, "All the students at Smart College are honor students," would not be considered laws. Such statements, sometimes called *accidental generalizations,* are not laws, *not* because they refer to a finite class of entities (in our case, the students at Smart College) but because they could not be used to support subjunctive conditionals. We could not say "If x (some person) *were* a student at Smart College, then x *would* be an honor student." Compare this statement with one which *is* considered a law, "All the planets revolve around the sun in elliptical orbits." This statement also refers to a finite class (in this case, the nine planets), but it *would* support the subjunctive conditional, "If x were a planet in the solar system, then x would revolve around the sun in an elliptical orbit." Thus, to be considered a law, a statement must not only be universal and confirmed but must also support subjunctive conditionals.[14]

The Importance of Laws   Laws are important because with them we can order our experience. We can make intelligible what was chaotic, disordered, and unintelligible. In short, with laws we can "explain." By making connections among the fragments of experience, laws organize them into meaningful patterns. Sometimes this process is so rudimentary that it goes unnoticed. Common sense, for example, makes distinctions between different kinds of things: copper is different from silver, flounders are different from mackerel, oak is different from elm, and so on. But each of these commonsense distinctions, discovered long before "science" emerged as a discipline, involves laws. Why is this so? In encountering the world, people found that certain sets of properties are invariably associated. Thus, that which we now call "copper" is brownish in color, malleable, a good conductor of heat, and resistant to rust. All things having these properties were the same and were called by the same name, "copper"; and a portion of experience was thereby organized. But other things in experience could now be marked off from copper. Fish and trees were fundamentally different; silver was also different but not so different, for we discovered that copper and silver share significant properties. Hence, we called them "metals." And so on.

Our experience became more and more intelligible as new "laws" were discovered. Notice that such classification does involve laws since we are saying that properties $P_1, P_2, P_3, \ldots, P_n$ are invariably associated and that all entities which have those properties in common are things of a certain kind. Indeed, all empirical concepts implicitly involve laws, for each of them denotes regularities and uniform associations. What would it mean to say that "iron rusts" if the words "iron" and "rust" did not themselves represent the invariable association of properties in experience? As Norman Campbell has put it, "Laws are both the

---

[14] See the remarks of Chapter 4, pp. 76ff.

raw material and the finished product. Science begins from laws, and on them bases new laws."[15] The law "All iron rusts" was based upon the laws that there are certain sets of properties which are invariably associated and shared by all that is called "iron," and that there are properties invariably associated and shared by all that is called "rust." But then experience confuses us. What we customarily call iron does not rust on some particular occasion. Why? Perhaps it is not iron after all? Perhaps it merely looked like iron? Or perhaps other conditions need to be satisfied? Perhaps iron rusts only when exposed to damp air? Thus, to *reorder* our experience we are prompted to make new distinctions. Frequently we offer new hypotheses which distinguish the apparently similar. Iron, for example, is distinguished from aluminum, uranium from plutonium, and so on. Sometimes the apparently dissimilar is seen to be the same in certain important respects. For example, rats, chipmunks, and squirrels are rodents; whales, dogs, and human beings are mammals. And sometimes we must mark off more carefully the specific conditions under which things occur in our experience.

Each of these steps reflects the development of laws, and each serves to make experience more coherent and intelligible. These same features characterize the more sophisticated stages of science. The technical terms of science—for example, force, mass, potential difference, propensity to consume, oxidation, and so on—depend upon laws which formulate new facts to be expressed in giving order to experience. Thus, "oxidation" had no meaning before Black, Priestley, Cavendish, Scheele, and Lavoisier showed that "air" was composed of *different* gases and that "dephlogisticated air" (oxygen) was necessary for combustion, oxidation, and respiration. With this discovery, the commonplace occurrences in ordinary experience of fire, rust, and breathing were made intelligible by being brought under a lawlike relation. Hence, if we are asked why some particular material did not burn or why some particular iron bar did not rust or why some animal died, we might explain these events by pointing out that oxygen was not present.

Schematically,

All instances where there is life,
   there is respiration.
All instances where there is respiration, ⎱ Statements of law
   there is oxygen.
The animal was deprived of oxygen. } Statement of condition
_____
Therefore, the animal died. ⎱ Statement expressing event to be explained (or predicted)

The explanation here takes the form of a deductive argument. If the event has occurred, we explain it by appealing to the law statements and conditions. If

[15] *What Is Science?* (New York: Dover Publications, Inc., 1952), p. 40.

the event has not occurred, then by means of the same statements we may predict that it will occur.

This simple model, usually called the *covering-law model of explanation*, is extremely helpful and revealing, even though it would be a mistake to suppose that all adequate (or proper) scientific explanations may be cast into the form of deductive arguments containing lawlike statements as part of their premises.[16]

The Nature and Role of Scientific Theories

Hypotheses may not only become laws; they may also become *scientific theories*. By "theory" we shall mean a set of systematically related statements which when taken together are testable and serve to explain and predict. We speak, therefore, of the kinetic theory of gases, the theory of evolution, Keynesian theory, and the theory of relativity. Each of these theories differs from laws in being sets of statements or *systems* of statements. Generally, theories are used to explain the uniformities expressed by laws and for this reason often use what are known as "theoretical terms," such as electron, nucleus, and quantum jump.

An important feature of scientific theories is that they organize bodies of knowledge. As laws express invariant relations between the apparently isolated events of experience and thereby order these events, theories go one step further; they provide an understanding of the uniformities of experience by linking together the statements of invariable relations under broad theoretical principles. Newtonian theory, for example, showed that the regularities which characterize events as diverse as falling bodies, projectile motion, the revolution of the planets, the movements of the tides, the equatorial bulge, and the precession of the equinoxes could be understood in terms of the same set of theoretical principles. Similarly, the atomic theory formulated by Dalton to account for the chemical discoveries of Priestley, Cavendish, and Lavoisier has led to the more comprehensive quantum theory. With the latter we see that there is a unity of all matter and that the ways in which many different physical phenomena undergo change and transformation may be understood by the same theoretical principles.

The nature of scientific theories has been a subject of considerable con-

---

[16] The covering-law reconstruction of scientific explanation has systematically been argued for by C. G. Hempel in his many articles, as well as in a more recent book, *Aspects of Scientific Explanation and Other Essays in the Philosophy of Science* (New York: The Free Press, 1965).

Hempel distinguishes between *deductive-nomological* explanation, in which the argument form is deductive, and *statistical* explanation, which takes the form of inductive argument. He also distinguishes various forms of explanatory *incompleteness*, including *partial explanation*, and what he calls an *explanation sketch*. Explanations in history and the social sciences typically are "incomplete" in Hempel's sense, but it is moot as to whether this makes them less adequate (and less "scientific") or whether the covering-law model may not be entirely appropriate in these domains. The issues here are too complex for discussion in this chapter.

troversy in recent years, and a thorough examination of this subject would take a book at least the size of this one. Here we can only touch upon some of the least controversial elements. In what follows we shall sketch a miniature economic theory. This sketch is not intended to be a complete economic theory or to reveal all of the complexities or issues of scientific theory construction.[17] Rather, it is intended only to illustrate certain features of some scientific theories and to show how deductive techniques play a role in the organization of knowledge. The "theory" we shall use for this purpose is the following:

1 If the liquidity preference remains constant and the supply of money increases, then the rate of interest falls and the marginal efficiency of capital decreases.
2 If the rate of interest falls and the marginal efficiency of capital decreases, then aggregate investment increases.
3 Aggregate investment increases if and only if aggregate saving increases.
4 If aggregate investment increases, then the best opportunities for investment are used up and the marginal efficiency of capital decreases.

That theories may sometimes be organized deductively can be seen by using the language of the statement calculus (Chapters 4 to 6) to express their basic statements. (The language of mathematics usually serves this purpose.) In terms of our sample theory, substituting letter variables for its constituent statements reveals its formal structure. Thus:

1 $pq \supset rt$
2 $rt \supset w$
3 $w \equiv s$
4 $w \supset ut$

where p = liquidity preference remains constant
q = supply of money increases
r = rate of interest falls
s = aggregate saving increases
t = marginal efficiency of capital decreases
u = best opportunities for investment are used up
w = aggregate investment increases

The logic at our disposal shows that from this theory many implications may be deduced, some of which are as follows:

---

[17] Nor is the "theory" intended to be "true" or to be a vindication of the often exaggerated claims of formalist defenses of economic theory construction. For a critique, see Benjamin Ward, *What's Wrong with Economics?* (New York: Basic Books, 1972), especially chap. 10. For an excellent review of problems and issues in theory construction in the biological sciences, see David Hull, *Philosophy of Biological Science* (Englewood Cliffs, N.J.: Prentice-Hall, 1974).

$T_1 : pq \supset r$ (From 1)

$T_2 : p \supset (q \supset t)$ (From 1)

$T_3 : pq \supset w$ (From 1 and 2)

$T_4 : pq \supset s$ (From T_3 and 3)

$T_5 : rt \supset s$ (From 2 and 3)

$T_6 : rt \supset ut$ (From 2 and 4)

$T_7 : r \supset (t \supset u)$ (From T_6)

$T_8 : \sim u \supset \sim(rt)$ (From T_6)

$T_9 : \sim(rt) \supset \sim(pq)$ (From 1)

$T_{10}: pq \supset u$ (From T_8 and T_9)

$T_{11}: (w \lor rt) \supset ut$ (From T_6 and 4)

$T_{12}: s \supset ut$ (From 3 and 4)

$T_{13}: pq \supset ut$ (From 1 and T_6)

$T_{14}: (t \supset \sim u) \supset (p \supset \sim q)$ (From T_{13})

$T_{15}: s \supset u$ (From T_{12})

Each of these "theorems" may be considered "laws" which were deduced from the initial assumptions. By thus drawing out the implications of a theory, a significant systematization is effected. Our theory shows that apparently unconnected phenomena may be brought under a few basic principles. The theory also leads to the discovery of new uniformities. Thus, Theorem T_{10}, $pq \supset u$, asserts: "If liquidity preference remains constant and the supply of money increases, then best opportunities for investment are used up. Theorem T_{12}, $s \supset ut$, shows that savings, s, determine both best opportunities for investment, u, and the marginal efficiency of capital, t. Theorem T_5, in turn, shows that the rate of interest, r, and the marginal efficiency of capital, t, determine savings, s.

Moreover, the theory *explains* many diverse phenomena. Suppose that we wondered why, during some period, aggregate saving increased. We might note that during that period, while liquidity preference remained constant, the supply of money was increased, say by government fiscal policy. In arriving at this explanation, we would be appealing to Theorem T_4, $pq \supset s$. But in accordance with the basic assumptions of the theory, statements 1 through 4, we should have expected this, since we know that liquidity preference and the supply of money affect the interest rate and the marginal efficiency of capital. These in turn determine investment, which affects savings. In short, appealing to the law expressed in Theorem T_4 and to the particular conditions enabled us to explain the particular event; and appealing to the *theory* enabled us to explain the law.

Finally, confirming a theory is accomplished by testing its many implications, or by testing each of its theorems. If the theory is "true," then its logical implications must be true. By testing these implications, we *indirectly* confirm the theory. Notice, however, that as before, establishing the theorems as true does not necessarily *prove* that the theory is true, for again we are confirming by means of the formal fallacy of affirming the consequent. Logically, we could produce many other theories from which we could deduce these theorems. But if we could deduce *only the very same* implications from another theory, that theory would really not be a different theory; it would be the very same one. Thus, when competing theories are being considered, they must show *some* differences in their testable implications.

On the other hand, if one or several of the testable implications of a theory prove to be false, then we may conclude that the theory *taken as a whole* is false, but we may not conclude that some particular assumption or set of assumptions is false. Any or all of these components could be rephrased or modified to make the theory compatible with the testable data. Compare the earlier discussion of the corpuscular and wave theories of light. Because scientific theories may be amended to account for new facts, it is extremely desirable, though not always possible, that the assumptions of the theory be fully spelled out.

A valid criticism of certain theories is that they are so loosely formulated that they are compatible with *any* possible data. When this happens, the theory loses its scientific value since there is no possible way to falsify it. If it cannot be falsified, it can prove anything, and, paradoxically, if it can prove anything, it proves nothing and hence is worthless. This is true not only of theories which are very loosely formulated but also of theories which contain contradictory assumptions. For, as we saw earlier, an argument with contradictory premises can prove any conclusion and hence proves none. To illustrate a theory which is formulated in a way which makes it impossible to refute, we can turn to Freud's theory of dreams. Freud believed that all dreams are wish fulfillments. When a woman patient (the "cleverest of all" his dreamers) told him about a dream—spending the holidays with her mother-in-law in the country—so disagreeable that it was apparently not a wish fulfillment, Freud observed, "The dream showed that I was wrong. *Thus it was her wish that I might be wrong, and her dream showed that wish fulfilled.*" (Italics Freud's.)[18] In other words, all dreams, by definition really, are wish fulfillments, even those which do not appear to be. Now either all dreams appear to be wish fulfillments or some do not appear to be. (There are no other alternatives.) The former are easily explained (and thus prove Freud right), while the latter are explained as fulfilling a wish to prove Freud wrong (and thus also prove him right). So, in either case Freud's theory must be right; it cannot be proved wrong. Any empirical data offered in opposition to it must (in accordance with Freud's stipulation, or definition) support it.

We have frequently stated that scientific statements must be testable. And, if they are to explain the phenomena of experience, they must link up with our experience. Many laws of science meet this requirement quite easily, for they establish relations between entities and processes which are more or less available to "direct" experience. When we say, for example, that all whales are mammals, the terms "whales" and "mammals" refer to entities commonly recognizable in experience. Similarly, the parameters of Boyle's law—temperature, mass, volume, and pressure—are measurable quantities; and hence the statement, "The pressure of a fixed mass of gas at constant temperature is inversely

---

[18] Sigmund Freud, *The Interpretation of Dreams,* translated and edited by James Strachey (New York: Basic Books, 1955), p. 151.

proportional to its volume," is one which is testable "directly" in experience. However, when we make reference to entities like electrons and DNA molecules, to processes like electron jumps, and to such phenomena as the random behavior of the molecules in a gas, it is not immediately clear to what we are referring. But in seeking to explain the phenomena of "direct" experience, theories characteristically appeal to entities and processes not immediately accessible. This was true even of our miniature economic theory.

Although the problem of formulating theories which are explanatory and testable is more complex than this introductory account suggests, two more comments may be made. First, any distinction which we might make between entities and processes accessible to direct experience and those not directly accessible would be imprecise or vague. Hence a distinction between so-called "theoretical terms" and "observation terms" is also vague. Although there is a clear difference between (say) the status of the term "electron" and that of "whale," many different useful and important scientific terms do not readily fall into either one of these two widely divergent categories, for example, "mass," "vacuum tube," "soluble," "anxiety," and "liquidity preference." Although we can measure mass, our measurements themselves presuppose a wide variety of physical laws and theoretical assumptions. Mass itself is not something directly experienced. For example, we might measure mass by means of a beam balance, but the beam balance itself presupposes the principle of the lever. Nor do we "directly experience" vacuum tubes, for to call an object a "vacuum tube" also presupposes a host of physical theories. Thus it would appear that the transition from what we consider theoretical to what we consider observational is gradual and, to a great extent, depends upon the current state of knowledge. The distinction, however, may be made *contextually*. That is, in providing empirical content to the terms of a theory, we appeal to terms which are antecedently available, or which can be understood independently of the theory in question. "Pressure," for example, a term which is antecedently understood, is linked to the random impacts of molecules of a gas in a chamber. "Liquidity preference" is linked to a demand schedule between interest and supply of money, and so on. In this way, the meaning of theoretical concepts is partially provided by considering them in the large network of concepts which are antecedently understood and connected to the fabric of experience.

Secondly, as a body of laws is gradually built up, the concepts which enter into them become linked in various ways to each other as well as to those concepts which were antecedently available. Thus the term "mass" appears in very many laws in science, each of which provides a partial explication of the term in a complex fabric of concepts. To come to understand what mass means is to come to understand the body of laws in which the term occurs. And here lies the systematic power of key scientific concepts. As C. G. Hempel has put it:

"The concepts of science are the knots in a network of systematic relationships in which laws and theoretical principles form the threads. . . . The more threads converge upon, or issue from, a conceptual knot, the stronger will be its systematic role, or its systematic import."[19]

This brief account of scientific method is intended to whet the reader's appetite, to encourage the reader to examine more thoroughly the nature of science. Although only a few become scientists, everyone should be concerned with understanding the nature of scientific method, its great potentialities, as well as its limitations.

EXERCISES

Comment on the following passages as they relate to the ideas discussed in this chapter.

1   Science is built up of facts, as a house is built up of stones; but an accumulation of facts is no more a science than a heap of stones is a house.

Henri Poincaré

2   Wrong hypotheses, rightly worked from, have produced more useful results than unguided observation.

Augustus DeMorgan

3   [E]very conceivable case could be interpreted in the light of Adler's theory, or equally of Freud's. . . . I could not think of any human behavior which could not be interpreted in terms of either theory. It was precisely this fact—that they always fitted, that they were always confirmed—which in the eyes of their admirers constituted the strongest argument in favour of these theories. It began to dawn on me that this apparent strength was in fact their weakness.

Karl R. Popper[20]

4   There is a tradition of opposition between adherents of induction and deduction. In my view it would be just as sensible for the two ends of a worm to quarrel.

Alfred North Whitehead

5   A more real danger, because most people do not know that it exists, is the belief that a working hypothesis must be right if it describes the facts accurately.

Wilder D. Bancroft

[19] C. G. Hempel, *Philosophy of Natural Science* (New York: Prentice-Hall, 1966), p. 94.

Recent studies in the philosophy of science have shown convincingly that a strict empiricism, as typified by the views found in the earlier writings of Rudolf Carnap and P. W. Bridgman, is untenable. While the positivist insistence that all scientific statements be testable has led to a much clearer understanding of theory construction and confirmation in science, it is now generally agreed that a full specification of empirical concepts and the elimination of theoretical concepts through explicit or operational definition is neither possible nor desirable.

[20] *Conjectures and Refutations* (London: Routledge and Kegan Paul, 1963), pp. 35–36.

6 The progress of science lies in the continual discovery of more and more comprehensive formulae, by aid of which we can classify the relationships and sequence of more and more extensive groups of phenomena. The earlier formulae are not necessarily wrong; they are merely replaced by others which in briefer language describe more facts.

Karl Pearson[21]

7 When one of the professors at the California Institute of Technology asked Albert Einstein how he came to formulate his famous theory, he is said to have replied, "By refusing to accept an axiom."

Harold Larrabee

8 It is still true that the natural scientist seeks the enduring laws afforded by most of his subject matter, while the social scientist must seek truths which may become obsolete while he is finding them.

Richard T. Ely

9 Look for precision in each class of things just so far as the nature of the subject permits.

Aristotle

10 Seek simplicity but distrust it.

Alfred North Whitehead

11 In the following selection point out the various stages of inquiry: the problem, hypothesis or hypotheses, background knowledge used, auxiliary assumptions, consequences deduced and tested, conclusion. Estimate the probability of the conclusion.

I already knew that poisoning with carbon monoxide makes the blood scarlet in the whole circulatory system. I had to make hypotheses, and establish a preconceived idea about my first observation so as to go ahead. Now, reflecting on the fact of scarlet blood, I tried to interpret it by my earlier knowledge as to the cause of the color of blood. Whereupon all the following reflections presented themselves to my mind. The scarlet color, said I, is peculiar to arterial blood and connected with the presence of a large proportion of oxygen, while dark coloring belongs with absence of oxygen and presence of a larger proportion of carbonic acid; so the idea occurred to me that carbon monoxide, by keeping venous blood scarlet, might perhaps have prevented the oxygen from changing into carbonic acid in the capillaries. Yet it seemed hard to understand how that could be the cause of death. But still keeping on with my inner preconceived reasoning, I added: If that is true, blood taken from the veins of animals poisoned with carbon monoxide should be like arterial blood in containing oxygen; we must see if that is the fact.

Following this reasoning, based on interpretation of my observation, I tried an experiment to verify my hypothesis as to the persistence of oxygen in the venous blood. I passed a current of hydrogen through scarlet venous blood

[21] *Grammar of Science* (New York: Everyman Library, Dutton, 1937), p. 85.

taken from an animal poisoned with carbon monoxide, but I could not liberate the oxygen as usual. I tried to do the same with arterial blood; I had no greater success. My preconceived idea was therefore false. But the impossibility of getting oxygen from the blood of a dog poisoned with carbon monoxide was a second observation which suggested a fresh hypothesis. What could have become of the oxygen in the blood? It had not changed into carbonic acid, because I had not set free large quantities of that gas in passing a current of hydrogen through the blood of the poisoned animals. Moreover, that hypothesis was contrary to the color of the blood. I exhausted myself in conjectures about how carbon monoxide could cause the oxygen to disappear from the blood; and as gases displace one another I naturally thought that the carbon monoxide might have displaced the oxygen and driven it out of the blood. To learn this, I decided to vary my experimentation by putting the blood in artificial conditions that would allow me to recover the displaced oxygen. So I studied the action of carbon monoxide on blood experimentally. For this purpose I took a certain amount of arterial blood from a healthy animal; I put this blood on the mercury in an inverted test tube containing carbon monoxide; I then shook the whole thing so as to poison the blood sheltered from contact with the outer air. Then, after an interval, I examined whether the air in the test-tube in contact with the poisoned blood had been changed, and I noted that the air thus in contact with the blood had been remarkably enriched with oxygen, while the proportion of carbon monoxide was lessened. Repeated in the same conditions, these experiments taught me that what had occurred was an exchange, volume by volume, between the carbon monoxide and the oxygen of the blood. But the carbon monoxide, in displacing the oxygen that it had repelled from the blood, remained chemically combined in the blood and could no longer be displaced either by oxygen or by other gases. So that death came through death of the molecules of blood or in other words by stopping their exercise of a physiological property essential to life. . . .

Experimental analysis, here, has reached its goal. This is one of the cases, rare in physiology, which I am happy to be able to quote. Here the immediate cause of the phenomenon of poisoning is found and is translated into a theory which accounts for all the facts and at the same time includes all the observations and experiments. Formulated as follows, the theory posits the main facts from which all the rest are deduced: Carbon monoxide combines more intimately than oxygen with the hemoglobin in a molecule of blood. It has quite recently been proved that carbon monoxide forms a definite combination with hemoglobin. So that the molecule of blood, as if petrified by the stability of the combination, loses its vital properties. Hence everything is logically deduced: because of its property of more intimate combination, carbon monoxide drives out of the blood the oxygen essential to life; the molecules of blood become inert, and the animal dies, with symptoms of hemorrhage, from true paralysis of the molecules.

But when a theory is sound and indeed shows the real and definite physico-chemical cause of phenomena, it not only includes the observed facts but predicts others and leads to rational applications that are logical consequences of the theory. Here again we meet this criterion. In fact, if carbon monoxide has the property of driving out oxygen by taking its place in combining with a molecule of blood, we should be able to use the gas to analyze the gases in blood, and especially for determining oxygen. From my experiments I deduced this application which has been generally adopted to-day. Applications of this property of carbon monoxide have been made in legal medicine for finding the coloring matter of blood; and from the physiological facts described above we may also already deduce results connected with hygiene, experimental pathology, and notably with the mechanism of certain forms of anemia.

Claude Bernard[22]

12 For the following facts, formulate several different hypotheses; indicate the kind of background knowledge that would be helpful and any auxiliary assumptions which might be needed. Give your reasons for what you think is the best hypothesis and indicate a possible testable consequence for it.

The Mysterious Disappearance of Judge Crater

Shortly after 9 o'clock in the evening, August 6, 1930, N. Y. State Supreme Court Judge Joseph F. Crater stepped into a taxi in front of a restaurant at 332 W. 45th, waved goodbye to two friends with whom he had just had dinner, and settled back as the cab pulled into traffic. He was 41 years old at the time and has never been seen since. A quarter of a million dollars has been spent to track him down and he has been reported seen, at one time or another, in just about every state and foreign country, but he is still missing.

Concerning Crater's public life, after graduating from Lafayette College he attended Columbia University Law School, received his law degree, and set up practice in downtown New York. Hard-working and ambitious, he became involved in politics and, within a few years, became president of a Tammany-dominated upper West Side Democratic Club. In 1916 a client, Stella Mance Wheeler, retained him as her divorce lawyer. On March 16, 1917, seven days after her divorce became final, she married Crater, and they were apparently a devoted couple.

Shortly after his marriage, Crater attracted the attention of Robert F. Wagner, Sr., then a New York State Supreme Court Judge himself, and from 1920 until 1927, when Wagner was elected to the U. S. Senate, Crater served as his secretary. When Wagner went to Washington, Crater returned to private practice. In early May of 1930, owing largely to his Tammany connections, he was named to fill an unexpired term on the State Supreme Court. Presumably he was to receive the Democratic nomination (almost tantamount at that time to election) in the fall for a full fourteen-year term.

Concerning his private life, he was a familiar figure on Broadway, where he was known as "Goodtime Joe." He often went to night clubs in the company of Ziegfeld chorus girls, and for seven years before his disappearance had been supporting an attractive divorcee in a midtown apartment. After his disappearance it was learned that he had been involved in a somewhat shady real-estate deal, and there was some evidence that he may have paid Tammany $22,500 (a year's salary) for his judgeship.

[22] *An Introduction to the Study of Experimental Medicine,* translated by Henry Copley Greene (New York: Abelard-Schuman, Inc., 1949), pp. 159–162.

In mid-July, 1930, Judge Crater and his wife went to spend the rest of the summer at their country home at Belgrade Lakes, Maine. On the morning of Sunday, August 3, he received a call from New York and told his wife that he had to return to the city at once. "I've got to straighten those fellows out," he said, and promised to return to Maine on August 9. On Monday, August 4, he was seen entering the Craters' New York apartment at 40 Fifth Avenue. For the next two days he apparently did nothing out of the ordinary. On Wednesday morning, however, the day he disappeared, he showed up at the County Courthouse and had his assistant, Joseph Mara, go to the bank and cash two checks for him totaling $5,150. After receiving the money from Mara, he locked himself in his chambers and stayed there for almost two hours. A little after noon he came out, carrying two locked briefcases. He asked Mara to help him carry them, and the two went by taxi to the judge's apartment, where the briefcases were left in the study. As his assistant left, the judge said to him, "I'm going up to Westchester for a swim."

He was next seen early that same evening at the Arrow Theatre Ticket Agency on Broadway, where he bought one ticket for "Dancing Partners," a comedy which had opened the night before. The agent didn't have a ticket at the time but promised to leave one at the box office. Crater was wearing the suit and hat he wore when he disappeared, but he had left behind in his apartment all the items he normally carried which had identifying monograms—a card case, a fountain pen, a watch and chain.

Judge Crater was next seen at about 8 o'clock, when he entered the West 45th restaurant, where he met two friends—William Klein, a lawyer for the Shuberts, and Sally Lou Ritz, a Follies girl. At their invitation he joined them for dinner, and on the sidewalk at about 9:15 it was to them that he waved. He then disappeared.

When ten days had passed and Mrs. Crater hadn't heard from her husband, she sent the family chauffeur to New York to investigate. The chauffeur spoke to several of the judge's friends, who told him that, though they hadn't seen the judge, they were sure everything was all right. Nothing was done until August 25, the day the court opened—almost three weeks after his disappearance—when his fellow judges became alarmed and started their own search. When this failed, they notified the police, who took over the case on September 3, almost a month after the judge had disappeared.

In the course of their investigation, the police searched the Craters' apartment. Nothing unusual was found, except that the two locked briefcases were not there. A check of the judge's safe deposit box revealed that it was empty. In October, a grand jury investigation was ordered, and after three months and 975 pages of testimony, the jury had no idea of what had happened to the judge. Its final report said: "The evidence is insufficient to warrant any expression of opinion as to whether Crater is alive or dead, or as to whether he absented himself voluntarily, or is a sufferer from a disease in the nature of amnesia, or the victim of a crime."

Mrs. Crater remained in Maine. Then on Jan. 20, 1931, she returned to the Fifth Avenue apartment and there in a bureau drawer which had been empty when the police had searched it, she found three folders. In them were a number of checks, a packet of stocks and bonds, Judge Crater's three life insurance policies, and a long note written by the judge himself. The undated note contained no personal information but listed his debts and assets. It looked like a final financial statement. At the end the judge had written, "I am very weary." Among the checks was one made out by Judge Crater himself and dated August 30, 1930—more than three weeks after his disappearance.

As the years passed, reports were received that he was prospecting for gold in California, that he was an amnesia victim in a Missouri hospital, that he had been seen on a steamer in the Adriatic.[23]

13 In the following passage, what is being explained and what hypothesis or hypotheses are used to explain it? Indicate the nature of each hypothesis and any tests used to confirm or disconfirm it.

A mystery of considerable interest is presented by the high light levels recorded near the limb of the planet in the first picture. Where we expected to find a black sky the sky was more than half as bright as the planet! The other pictures also show evidence of "fogging," as if the Martian atmosphere were enormously brighter and more extended than anyone had expected.

Our first thought was that the fogging represented some kind of defect in the optical system. We wondered, for example, if the surface of the telescope mirror could have been pitted by the impact of meteoritic dust, but this seems to be ruled out by the fact that the meteorite detector, fully exposed outside the spacecraft, received only a few hundred hits. We have also considered the possibility that volatile substances from the foam cushions used to protect the Vidicon tube might have whitened the black inside surface of the telescope tube and created internal reflections. We found, however, that we could not duplicate the fogging even by inserting white cardboard baffles in place of the black ones in the optical system.

Finally, we considered the possibility that the nickel compound that provides the top coat on the telescope mirror before it receives final polishing might have blistered after long exposure to the vacuum of space. We simulated blisters by putting drops of glue on a mirror but were still unable to duplicate the fogging seen in the Mariner IV pictures. We have tentatively decided that the cause of the fogging is really on Mars. Recent models of the Martian atmosphere seem to suggest that tiny crystals of frozen carbon dioxide are present at all times, even at great heights. Whatever the cause of the fogging in July, 1965, it must have extended to at least 100 kilometers above the surface of the planet and therefore it may be distinguishable from the earth with careful observation.

Robert B. Leighton[24]

14 In the following inductive arguments state the main point at issue and evaluate the evidence adduced to support it. Assuming the facts are true, rate the probability of the conclusion.

[23] Adapted from Tom Meehan, "Case No. 13595, *New York Times Magazine,* August 7, 1960, pp. 27–28.

[24] "Photographs from Mariner IV," *Scientific American,* 214 (April, 1966), p. 68.

a Most baseball fans have accepted the view that Abner Doubleday invented baseball at Cooperstown, New York, in 1839. This view stems from a 1907 committee report of six public-spirited men. The committee, however, based its findings on scant evidence — a letter written by an elderly mining engineer named Abner Graves, who said that he had been a pupil with Doubleday at Green's Select School in Cooperstown. Graves claimed that Doubleday had outlined in the dirt a sketch of a diamond-shaped baseball field and had made a memorandum of rules similar to those used today. Much evidence has since been uncovered to disprove this claim. Robert W. Henderson of the New York Public Library has disclosed that in 1839, Doubleday, rather than attending Green's, was a second-year cadet at West Point and not eligible for furlough. From 1836 to 1838 he had been a practicing civil engineer and could not have been attending Green's. Henderson also points out that several books on sports published before 1839 contained diamond diagrams and rules on how to play the game called "base ball." The name itself was well known before Doubleday was born. Apparently baseball did not have any single one inventor. The game simply grew, developing during the eighteenth century from "rounders" to "town ball" to "baseball."

b Cancer, stomach, and heart specialists have found that the habitual use of tobacco has destructive effects upon the body. In 1938, Dr. Raymond Pearl, of Johns Hopkins University, studied the case histories of over 6,000 white males and found that "smoking is associated with a definite impairment of longevity." Toxicologists list some thirty substances taken into the lungs with each inhale of smoke from a cigarette. Twelve of these substances are acids, while the rest are composed of arsenic, alcohol, and ammonia. Nicotine, a potent poison found in cigarettes, has been found to cause detrimental effects to the nervous system, heart, blood vessels, and digestive tract. It may cause nervous excitability, tobacco heart, high blood pressure, indigestion, and irritations to the mouth and throat. Recently scientists have reported producing cancer in mice by coating their skin with a concentration of tars from cigarette smoke. Dr. William Lieb, author of *Safer Smoking* and research adviser to a major tobacco company for ten years, states, "Tobacco contains as nice a collection of poisons as you will find anywhere in one small package. The least you can do, out of respect for the only body you will ever have, is to use these poisons, if use them you must, in moderation."

15 Using the criteria discussed in this chapter, indicate what, if anything, is wrong with the following theories or explanations:

a According to the Irish philosopher, Bishop George Berkeley, the physical world, the world of matter, does not exist independently of our perception. What are commonly regarded as physical objects are actually collections of ideas in a mind; that is, all we can know of objects is our sensations of them. Thus Berkeley equated objects with the appearances of them and these in turn he equated with the sensations or perceptions which a thinking being received. A desk, for example, existed only insofar as it was experienced by a mind. It did not exist, according to Berkeley, if it were not so experienced. To counter common criticisms (What happens to "objects" when we aren't experiencing them? and How does one account for the fact that separate minds seem to have very similar experiences about particular objects?) Berkeley postulated the existence of some other and greater mind than the finite human one, a mind which not only receives all sensations at all times but which also forces us to receive certain groups of sensations which make up our experience. This universal mind which constantly perceives is God's. In Berkeley's words, "[A]ll the choir of heaven and furniture of the earth, in a word all those bodies which compose the mighty frame of the world, have not any subsistence without a mind, . . . their *being* (*esse*) is to be perceived or known; . . . consequently so long as they are not actually perceived by me, or do not exist in my mind or that of any other *created spirits*, they must either have no existence at all, *or else subsist in the mind of some eternal spirit.*"

b   In an essay, "Gravity and Ventilation," Roger Babson discusses a topic in which he has long been interested. When a young man, Babson became ill with tuberculosis and was advised by his doctor to remain in the West where he had gone to convalesce; he chose instead to return to his home in Wellesley Hills, Massachusetts. To insure an abundance of fresh air, he refused to close any of his windows. During the freezing winter he wore a coat with an electric heating pad in back and his valiant secretary did her typing by wearing mittens and hitting the keys with rubber hammers. Babson got well and has been a fresh-air fiend ever since. He thinks children should be trained to enjoy fresh air flowing against their faces from a fan, and that air from pine woods has 'chemical and/or electrical qualities' of great medicinal value. His essay suggests that gravity should be used to clear bad air from a building by giving a slight slope to all the floors and having air outlets at the lower end of the room. Apparently this drains off the bad air in the way a sloping roof drains water. Such a house has actually been built in New Boston, with floors sloping a half-inch to the foot.

Martin Gardner[25]

---

[25] *Fads and Fallacies in the Name of Science* (New York: Dover Publications, 1957), p. 97.

SEVENTEEN

DECISION MAKING

*When all has been said in favor of
skepticism, it remains clear that men
must act, that some acts are better
than others, and that some basis of
discrimination must be used.*

Columbia Associates

Warranted Decisions

In the Introduction of this book, we observed that most of our actions involve
beliefs. In the course of a day we may turn off the alarm clock, dress, eat, catch
a bus, go to class, and so on. Although many of these acts are habitual—that is,
performed without conscious deliberation—even these involve beliefs. We believe that the alarm is ringing, that the bus is due at 10:10, and that food is
nourishing. If we are rational, even in our habits, these beliefs can be supported
by reasons. Insofar as rationality commits us to the persistent critique of beliefs,
opinions, and practices in the light of reasons, a habit, like the activity of which
it is a manifestation, is subject to rational criticism. If a habit presupposes beliefs
which are not warranted, then it itself is unwarranted. Logic, therefore, has a role
to play even at the level of habitual activity, a role which will be more fully delineated in the subsequent discussion.

Perhaps we should note here that it would be wrong to suppose that everything we did should be guided by conscious deliberation. Imagine for a moment
the implications of such a doctrine. Before we reached over to turn off the alarm,
we would first need to establish by inductive argument that the alarm is ringing,
that the probability of its going off when we reset the button is very high, that there

are good reasons for turning it off, and so on. All this is quite far fetched, but it does show that many commonplace activities are fortunately guided by habit. If this were not so, we would accomplish very little during the course of a day or of a lifetime. But, again, this does not mean that all habits are, or should be, irrational. Some habits, unfortunately, survive long after their warrant has evaporated, and some—our "bad habits"—have no warrant at all.

On the other hand, many activities do require conscious deliberation. When they do, there is, what may be called, the need for a decision. A *decision*, roughly, is a conscious choice to act in some way; it is intentional and deliberate. (Since there is a continuum between activities which are called "habits" and those which result from conscious choice, the distinction is not a sharp one.) In this chapter we shall consider the kind of inquiry which precedes deliberate action. Like scientific method, it is the kind of inquiry which starts from a problem, but unlike scientific inquiry it is directed toward making a conscious choice. Habit may get you to the bus stop in the morning. But if you miss the bus, then inquiry starts, for now action must be guided by a decision: should you walk, wait for the next bus, catch a subway, or perhaps return home to bed? Some decision must be made, for whatever action is taken involves a decision.

Decisions range from the trivial to the monumental. Perhaps a decision to return home after missing the bus is relatively trivial, but perhaps it is not. A decision to get married is usually very important. Many factors determine the "importance" of a decision, but the chief factor is the kind of consequences which follow from it. As a rule, those decisions which effect a radical departure from the status quo are considered significant. In any event, all rational decisions, whether considered important or not, have certain factors in common which enable us to call such decisions "warranted." Briefly, a **warranted decision** means a decision for which "good reasons" can be produced. Explicating what is meant by good reasons will be the main task of this chapter, and, as we shall see, this will involve all the considerations of logic thus far discussed as well as some special ones. A warranted decision should not be confused with a "right" decision. We cannot tell if a decision is right until *after* we have acted—that is, we cannot tell if it will achieve what we seek—but we can tell if a decision is warranted *before* we act. By way of analogy, we can determine the correctness of an argument even if we cannot be sure that its conclusion is true, since correctness depends upon the relation between evidence and conclusion. So can we determine if a decision is warranted, since its warrant depends upon the relation between it, its alternatives, and its supporting "reasons." Thus though we cannot be assured in advance of acting that a decision is "right," we can be assured in advance that it is warranted. In discussing the characteristics of a warranted decision, we shall pursue this analogy between reasons for belief and reasons for decisions to act. To repeat, we shall be able to appropriate much from our previous discussions but we shall also need to consider certain complexities which are distinctive to decision making.

Before moving on, let us make one last preliminary comment. We shall construe decisions broadly enough so as to include those which are called policy decisions, that is, those which usually involve many people or, at the very least, a group of people. Thus a decision to go to war or to institute a compulsory health insurance program is a policy decision, while a personal decision to see a dentist is not. Like all decisions, however, policy decisions are subject to the same criteria of warrant, and thus what may be said about any warranted decision applies to them.

A Popular Conception of Rational Decision Making Despite certain basic weaknesses which have often been pointed out, a popular conception of rational decision making embraces the following points. First, we must define the problem. Second, we must determine the end sought, for otherwise there would be no point in acting. That is, a rational decision is one for which the end has been clearly ascertained. Third, having defined the problem and ascertained the end, we can now judge which means will most effectively achieve the desired end. Thus, a rational person decides to go to college because that person has determined that this is the best means for enabling him or her to achieve the desired goal. Additional elements of this view include a consideration of "real," or "ultimate" ends, since some ends are in fact but intermediate means to the "real" end; and the acknowledgment that since ends sometimes conflict, rational choice involves adjudicating between conflicting ends either by establishing relative priorities or by seeking means to maximize ends. According to this conception, then, rational decisions involve five basic steps:

1 Defining the problem
2 Clearly stating the ultimate end or ends
3 Providing a set of alternatives as means to the end
4 Attaching a set of consequences to each of the alternatives
5 Deciding which alternative of the set is the best means to the end

A *completely* rational decision would be based upon a comprehensive survey of *all* the alternatives and would require consideration of the *full* set of consequences of each alternative.

The reason this view is so popular is undoubtedly that it contains certain elements of truth. Rational people do indeed act for some purpose, or to achieve some end, or else they would not be rational. Moreover, it would seem that before they can formulate alternatives they must be clear about the problem. And presumably rationality would demand that they canvass all the alternative means for satisfying their ends. Presumably, also, they must explore the full set of consequences, since if they do not, those which are ignored might very well frustrate their achieving the expected end. To be sure, the proponents of this view of rational decision making admit that it is an ideal which is rarely, if ever, achieved but that this should not prevent us from trying to achieve it. Other proponents contend that since such an ideal can never be fully realized and since we must act in any case, we should, in the words of William James, let our "passional" nature take over; that is, since we cannot act on completely rational grounds, we must act on the basis of certain emotional or "irrational" drives.

Another reason why this view is popular is that it harmonizes with certain preconceptions about the nature of facts and values, and lends itself to the neat (but oversimplified) categories of common sense. Thus the highly complex problem of rational decision making is reduced to something quite simple and almost mechanical: "Facts" and "values" are held to be distinctively different. "Ends" are equated with values, and values are preferences or desires and hence not subject to rational criticism. "Means" are equated with facts, for they are prediction statements which depend upon the regularities establishable by scientific method. And scientific method applies only to means but has nothing whatever to say about ends. Hence, rational decision making is restricted to appraising the means to some end.

Although this view provides certain insights into rational decision making, in certain crucial respects it is false, in others it is oversimplified. To understand why, we will need to discuss more fully the notions of ends and means, and facts and values. Let us consider first ends and means.

Problems with Ends and Means   As John Dewey pointed out,[1] means and ends form an existential continuum. That is, as human experience is a complex network of relations, so too are means and ends parts of a complex network. Indeed, the distinction between the two is significant only because it provides some perspective from which to understand experience. Means and ends may be construed as a continuum for three main reasons. First, no end is solely an end, for other consequences follow from it; second, no means is solely a means, for it is also an end; and, third, no means achieves only one specially selected end, for other consequences follow from it. To illustrate, from one perspective, going to college is an end, but from another, it is a means to getting an education. At the same time, it may be a means of staying out of the army, spending a great deal of money, and being independent, all of which are consequences, whether sought for or not. Indeed, going to college may be a means of much else besides, including consequences which we would ordinarily not even think of, such as getting to meet the dean, having your picture in a yearbook, delaying a career in business, living in a dormitory or fraternity house, and even flunking out! Moreover, to think of college solely as a means to one, two, or even all of these ends suggests that it is like taking vitamin pills—that is, something "instrumental" but not in itself very valuable.

But this is a strange view, since going to college, like *everything* else we do, is part of the larger fabric of total experience which we call life. Indeed, even if we accepted the vitamin pill view of college as being *merely* a means, what indeed would be *the* end—education, general enrichment, making money, or what? If we considered it to be making money, could this not in turn be considered a

---

[1] As will be evident, the chapter owes much to the work of John Dewey.

means to success? If so, would success be *the* end? Thus, it may be seen that what we call life consists of a *plurality* of activities, aims, and goals, and that thinking in terms of sharp separations of means and ends is neither easy nor always helpful. Indeed, if we confined ourselves to the vitamin pill view—that means are only instrumental but never valuable in themselves—*everything* would be a means to some "ultimate end" and we would forever be living in the future and never enjoying the present.

Let us say, as have certain philosophers, that the ultimate end is "happiness." Now as decision makers we decide that everything we do will be done ultimately because it is the means to happiness. But happiness itself is complex and may be manifested in many concrete situations of life. If we fail to recognize this fact, then life will be one long taking of vitamin pills for an end which never seems to occur. Since all we will ever be preoccupied with is the means, ironically we will never achieve the very end we seek. As Dewey pointed out, happiness, like all the "ends of life" is not something which can be attained apart from the activities of life. Happiness, like health, success, and justice, must be viewed *adverbially*. That is, we can live happily, healthfully, successfully. We can *be* happy in this or that activity, but these ends are not separable from the sum total of our "ongoing experience."

In this regard, consider the popular view that ends can be formulated independently of the concrete situations in which decisions are made. But happiness, health, or success viewed abstractly do not help decision making. Since actions are concrete and specific, decisions on what actions to take must be concrete and specific. We cannot act to achieve happiness in general; we can only decide to act in a certain way in a specific concrete situation. But this means that in one situation one end may dominate, while in another it may not, for ends are plural, specific, and changing to meet specific changing situations, problems, and aims. In one situation, for example, we may forego the claims of "health" to get a job done and thus miss some sleep or a meal because we consider getting the job done more important. In another situation we may forego "happiness" to meet an obligation, please a friend, or safeguard our health. Thus, to consider means and ends in the abstract or apart from specific contexts is an unrealistic and barren exercise. Rather than acting on the basis of some general means to some general end, we must act in particular situations and do our best to evaluate all of the complex consequences of our acts.

The foregoing remarks are not intended to deny that as human beings we have goals, aims, and "ends-in-view." They deny only that these ends-in-view can be isolated from their existential framework. An end-in-view may be differentiated from the total set of consequences which follow from actions as the specially selected consequence of the total set. It may even be the dominating feature of the total set, but this does not mean that it alone occurs. Territorial integrity, for instance, may be an end-in-view which can be preserved by war; but war also brings death, suffering, sacrifice, economic disorder, and social chaos.

Similarly, because ends and means form a continuum, it does not follow that we cannot distinguish *immediate* goods from *instrumental* or *mediate* goods. Esthetic enjoyment, for example, may be understood as an immediate good and taking medicine an instrumental good. That is, taking medicine is not valued for its own sake, but is valued as a means to attaining health. But this shows that means, like ends, have values and disvalues attached to them. A decision to take medicine would involve weighing the *total* value to be accrued. By contrast, some means have a disvalue so high that they are ruled out as means.

Acts and Consequences   Some of the misleading connotations of means and ends would disappear if we spoke instead of "acts" and "consequences." In what follows, therefore, we shall adopt this latter terminology. After all, acts stem from decisions, and decision making does involve evaluating the consequences of alternative courses of action. However, we should not think of an act as the means and of consequences as the end, although this would still be an improvement since it recognizes that more than one end results from any act.

Unfortunately, the distinction between acts and their consequences is also not perfectly clear. Consider a classical example from ethics. Suppose that the children of a cancer-inflicted mother decided to tell her that the disease is not cancer lest the truth would do more harm than good. In this situation, what is the act and what are the consequences? From one point of view, telling a lie was the act and relieving a parent's anxiety, the intended consequence. From another point of view, the act was lying *to a person with cancer*. Are there two different acts here or two different descriptions of the same act? Obviously the latter. But the description makes considerable difference in our understanding. Also, by selecting different features of the total situation, we could generate many different descriptions, each of which would slant our understanding in various ways. At some point, the description of the total situation would begin to include features marked off as consequences. Indeed, where do the consequences begin and end? When the children finish talking? When the parent's reaction becomes evident? The next day or the next month? Similarly, by considering different features in the total situation we can generate many different consequences, such as the parent was relieved, the children felt conscience-stricken, the brother who was opposed to lying from the beginning became annoyed with his sister, and so on. And suppose that the parent suspected that a lie was told and became even more miserable. Would her misery be a consequence of the lie which was told or of other circumstances which attended the lying? Would her misery be a consequence of her suspicion and her suspicion a consequence of something else? Again, the web of relations is so complex that neither the act nor the consequences can be easily identified.

However, to bring some order out of such complexity requires our making some distinctions. Indeed, to understand anything at all, we must select or abstract certain features from the total situation and devise categories for them. In this respect, the distinction between acts and consequences is less misleading and more illuminating than that between means and ends. Still, we must remember that even this distinction is vulnerable, which means that in describing any act and its consequences we might omit those very features which, as they bear on our decision, are significant. In our hypothetical example, ignoring the difference between lying in a court of law and lying to a cancer-inflicted mother would be disastrous.[2] Not considering why the lie is told, the attitude of the parent, or the feelings of the kin might also be disastrous. But since even the most careful analysis must be incomplete, we are *always* liable to omit features which may turn our decisions into catastrophes.[3] This is a human limitation, and, as such, is not remedial. It also underscores another shortcoming of the popular conception of decision making. In presuming that a rational decision requires that all the consequences of each alternative be examined, this conception postulates an unrealizable ideal and, in so doing, misleads us into thinking we can do that which we cannot. It also misleads us into thinking that "rational" decisions can never go wrong; but a rational decision is a warranted decision, and warranted decisions can go wrong. Just as scientists rationally and legitimately accept *false* hypotheses, so must we be prepared to accept the disappointment of a fully warranted decision that goes wrong. But just as science so often succeeds in finding the "truth," so may we hope, by being rational, for "right" decisions. Before we can grasp the features of rational decision making, however, we must also examine the popular distinction between facts and values.

Facts and Values Although to explicate fully the various notions of "a fact" and "a value" would not be easy, the salient feature of the distinction seems clear enough. For purposes of further clarity, however, when we speak of facts and values, properly we should speak of *statements of fact* and *value judgments*. A statement of fact, then, is an empirical statement about which universal agreement is possible. Usually such agreement is obtainable by what we called scientific method; hence, the statements of science may be considered typical. Thus, "Sugar is water-soluble," "If the interest rate increases, then generally inflation occurs," "A molecule of water is composed of two atoms of hydrogen and one atom of oxygen" are statements of fact. Such statements are confirmed independently of our desires, attitudes, preferences, or wishes. Value judgments, on

---

[2] Ordinary language, of course, makes a distinction between white lies and lies, just as courts of law make a distinction between murder and manslaughter. Such distinctions bear on the problem of identifying acts and indicate that context is all-important.

Kant's moral philosophy is often and perhaps rightly understood as being inflexible — as being predicated upon unconditional absolutes. But his categorical imperative — "Act only according to that maxim by which you can at the same time will that it should become a universal law" — allows for much flexibility by construing "maxims" in different ways. Thus the maxim "Tell lies" cannot be universalized, but the maxim "Tell lies when life is endangered" might easily be universalized. In his *Lectures on Ethics*, Kant, of course, resists this move.

[3] This feature of decisions constitutes one of the most persuasive arguments against *utilitarian* ethical perspectives. Again, Kant's position may be taken as typical. For him, morality cannot be empirical, since, among other reasons, empirical judgments are fallible. "Prudence" may indeed require "a good understanding," but "morality" requires a "good will," which is good in itself and not dependent upon contingent factors.

This is not the place to discuss these issues, since we not concerned here with the nature of a "moral" decision (as distinct from a "rational" one).

the other hand, are typically claims about what is of worth—for instance, what is good, beautiful, or just. In most circumstances the following would be examples: "*West Side Story* was a good musical," "The *David* of Michelangelo is a beautiful sculpture." "The laws punishing bigamy are just," "A government policy should aim at maximizing equality," "Success is not so important as health." These examples suggest that value judgments are not and cannot be universally agreed upon because desires, attitudes, preferences, and wishes—considered subjective or *relative*—lie at their root. For example, the judgment "Success is not so important as health" would crucially depend upon how we evaluated success and health. Since such evaluations are relative to different persons, times, and cultures, value judgments are considered to be unlike factual statements, which if true are true for everyone, at all times and in all places.

We need hardly point out the importance of this distinction for decision making; since decisions, essentially, do involve aims, purposes, and desires, they involve values. Hence, any account of decision making must come to grips with the nature and role of values in the making of warranted decisions.

In discussing the popular conception of decision making, we noted that separating means and ends was correlated with separating facts and values. According to that view, means are expressed as factual statements, while ends are expressed as value judgments. As we saw, however, no neat division of means and ends is possible; and for the same reason neither is a neat division of facts and values possible. Some of the difficulties of making a sharp distinction can be illustrated by just briefly examining the complexities of presumed value judgments. Consider the form of the sentence "x is good." Although this appears to represent a value judgment, most would agree that there are contexts in which it is not. For instance, suppose you were a peach packer who was asked why you put a particular peach in some crate. You might reply, "My job is to pack into crates only those peaches which are ripe, smooth, large, and unbruised. This peach is a good peach; so it goes into the crate." In this instance, the word "good" would be used to denote the factual characteristics of being ripe, smooth, large, and unbruised. But if this were so, then the sentence "This peach is good" would be testable in the usual ways and would be a statement of fact. Such a use of what are commonly regarded as *value words,* like "good," "just," "right," and "valuable," is not uncommon. Of course, when used in this way, they presuppose some agreement on what the factual content of the word is, but this agreement can often be arrived at.

To take another example, someone might object that a certain action will lead to gross injustice, where the latter roughly means that those affected by the action will suffer arbitrary inequalities. Although the *full* meaning of "injustice" and similar concepts cannot be specified, they have a common core of meaning which can be grasped, particularly by those exposed to similar biological, psychological, social, and cultural influences. Thus, most people in our society would agree that good peaches are ripe, smooth, large, and unbruised and that justice involves eliminating arbitrary inequalities. Of course, among those who agree that justice means eliminating arbitrary inequalities, there might now be fundamental differences as to the meaning of arbitrary inequalities. And still others might insist that justice involves emphasizing rather than eliminating arbitrary inequalities. Although disagreements of this kind reveal fundamental differences in moral attitudes, it would be wrong to think that such disagreements are not subject to rational criticism. In a moment we shall try to show why they are.

In other contexts "x is good" might be used to mean that something satisfies some purpose or function. A physician, for example, might prescribe a remedy for a skin disease and remark, "This compound is quite good." Here the sentence would mean that the remedy will effectively cure the disease: it is good *for* skin diseases. Again, statements conveying such meanings are confirmable and factual. In still another context, we might refer to one of various alternatives as "the better" or "the best," meaning simply that this one alternative would more effectively solve the problem at hand. The problem, for example, might be where to place a bridge for which a particular amount of money is available. From an engineering standpoint, one location might be much better than three others under consideration. In such contexts "values" need not enter at all despite our use of what seem to be evaluative statements. In other contexts, of course, such as where the alternatives involve conflicting aims or purposes, values do enter.

In still other contexts "x is good" does express an attitude or a feeling. For example, "The play was good," might mean something like "I enjoyed the play" or "I liked the play." When used in this way, such expressions are factual assertions about our preferences.[4] This does not mean, of course, that it is a factual assertion about the *play*; rather it is a factual assertion about an *attitude toward* the play. Interpreted in this way, the two assertions "The play was good" and "The play was not good" as expressed by two different people would not be contradictory, for two different people obviously can have different attitudes about the same thing. (In effect, one person would be saying, "I liked the play," while the other would be saying, "I did not like the play," both of which statements could be true.) But even here it might be possible to bring to bear a rational criticism, for usually the expression of feelings of like and dislike are predicated on reasons, which, when explored, are often seen to contain a mixture of factual presuppositions and broad evaluative considerations. Thus, reasons for liking the play might be its witty dialogue, its fast pace, and the insight it reveals into the psychology of adolescents. Reasons for disliking the play might be its superficial characterization, its lack of a coherent plot, and its forced ending. But all of these reasons are of a factual nature and presuppose certain norms for plays, and are thus subject to rational discussion.

Finally, "x is good" might also be used to convey approval, which is not quite the same thing as liking something. Sometimes we may not *like* x, but still

[4] As to whether or not such expressions are confirmable in the usual sense is a moot question, for ordinarily when someone states that he or she feels a certain way, we have no other recourse but to take that person's word. Hence, the ancient Romans were wont to say, *"De gustibus non est disputandum"* ("Concerning taste, there is no dispute").

say it is good because we approve of it. For instance, one might say, "This is a good piece of legislation, although personally I find it repugnant." Here the speaker would be approving of the law, although the reasons for approval could not be equated to those for "liking" it. Similarly, we may approve of spanking children, even if we don't like doing it or seeing others do it, because we think perhaps it is something which benefits children. Understood in this way, "x is good" would have the force of "x ought to be done" or "x ought to be valued." Thus, "This piece of legislation is good" could mean "We ought to vote for this piece of legislation." "Success is not so important as health" might mean "We ought to aim for health rather than for success." Such judgments are often called *normative judgments,* for they *prescribe norms* to be followed. And here again, normative judgments are subject to rational criticism. In advocating spanking, for example (even though we may not like it personally), we might be saying that it discourages children from being antisocial, a statement which is subject to empirical confirmation (or disconfirmation).

Adding to the difficulty of ascertaining the character of sentences like "x is good" is that they often combine many of the elements just discussed and are used for several different purposes simultaneously, that is, to convey facts, express feelings, state attitudes, elicit responses, persuade, and even direct.

Besides these difficulties which arise when we try to draw a sharp distinction between facts and values, there are other problems we must consider before we can arrive at a clear understanding of how value judgments are subject to rational criticism.

Consider once again the popular conception. Let us suppose that to make a rational decision one first establishes one's aims and goals. These will constitute a set of values. Let us also suppose that these values can be arranged in terms of priorities. Having a car, for example, would be good, but so would having the necessary money for the down payment. Perhaps having the car is better than having the money. Being in debt is not good, nor is robbing a bank. After having established our list of relevant values, presumably we then need only to establish all the relevant facts. We have money for a down payment but will need more. If we buy the car, then we will spend the money we have and be forced to get more. We can get the money if we borrow it, work for it, or rob a bank. If we borrow it, then . . . , etc. Presumably the decision maker then considers all the facts as they affect his or her predetermined values. Convincing as this picture may seem, let us see what is wrong with it.

As with the separation of means from ends, it supposes that facts can be considered independently of values and values independently of facts. But the two are interwoven in several important ways. First, facts bear on, influence, and in some cases determine values. For instance, the fact that a car is needed bears on the worth of having it. Without this need, which presumably could be supported by appealing to evidence, having a car would not be at all valuable. Nor would it help to say that the need itself brings in value considerations. To illustrate, we need the car because of the value we place on having this job which requires the use of a car. Yet, it is a fact that the job does require a car. But it might as well be insisted that the value is not in having the car but in having the job. However, is the car only of instrumental value, as this argument suggests? Moreover, why is the job a value? Isn't it a fact that we want the job because it is a "good" job (descriptive, evaluative, which?) and because of other needs which are related to having the job? Obviously, one could keep this up indefinitely until we arrived at some ostensible "ultimate" value. But, as before, we are now caught in an unending chase where *nothing* is of value except the abstract ultimate value. In reality, however, each of the facts is value-laden and each of the values is fact-imbedded in a complex and unclear network of relations. This is why, when we considered the fact that buying a car required additional money, we were immediately led to the implications of borrowing, working, or stealing. Each of these implications in turn gains its significance from a network of facts concerning, for example, our attitudes, our relations with others and with the community, the gravity of the need, the effects on our health, and other aspects deemed important.

Second, as inquiry progresses and new facts are uncovered, we gain new insights into the attending values. In considering various alternatives and their implications, we discover perhaps that the need for a car was more apparent than real. This, in turn, would affect the value to be placed upon having it. Finally, in actual situations of inquiry few of us, if any, would be able to state clearly and unequivocally the relevant values. This is so mainly because such values depend upon the particular problem being faced and the peculiar features of the situation which has prompted the inquiry—features which are largely factual in nature. Thus it is that even though one may announce that "health," "wealth," "honor," and "happiness" are values, until they are located in concrete contexts, their particular manifestation, implementation, and importance can neither be stated nor appraised. But this is to say again that facts are an essential part of determining values. As the features of a particular situation change, so too do our needs, wants, preferences, and goals. As these latter change, so too do the relevant values. In short, values do not spring from a vacuum, nor are they simply given. Rather, they are imbedded in existing situations. Thus, decisions involve the continual contemplation of the facts and the values as they bear upon each other.

Once we recognize the close interplay between facts and values, we can then see how value judgments are subject to rational criticism.

In the first place, insofar as facts bear on, influence, and in some cases determine values, a rational criticism of the latter must include a consideration of the relevant facts. Since desires, needs, preferences, and goals have a basis in the facts of human experience, biological, psychological, sociological, and anthropological data are relevant to appraisal. To take an obvious case, if human beings did not require food, warmth, friendship, and security, these would be doubtful values. Even though such values are fairly general, there is still much room for diversity in how these values are manifested; and here again factual knowledge can shed light. Japanese eat raw fish, Italians like tomatoes, and Mexicans like hot food, but they all find in food a value.

Secondly, as we observed, a particular set of values is part of a larger network of relations between facts and *other* values. Thus they must be appraised in terms of their bearing on the total picture. A man who obstinately clung to his judgment that health or wealth, success or salvation, were supremely valuable despite all relevant facts and conflicting values would rightly be considered a fanatic, regardless of the worth of his cause or the courage of his convictions. But to call him a "fanatic" would be to say that he has closed his mind to the complexity and fluidity of life's many situations and problems.

In this connection the criterion of logical consistency is relevant to critical appraisal. Since values must be appraised in terms of a larger framework, value judgments are vulnerable to inconsistency. Thus someone may assert that the use of narcotics is good and in another breath assert that he values his health. But clearly one cannot have both. This is a factual and logical point and not an evaluation. Such inconsistencies in appraisal are often difficult to detect mainly because the implications of our judgments are not well-developed. As Plato observed, all too often outspoken defenders of ethical subjectivism and relativism catch themselves in contradictions which pass the unwary eye unnoticed. But this only means that the test of consistency is more difficult regarding evaluations, not that it is any less important.

One might interject that even if we grant that evaluations may be rationally criticized as to their logical consistency, and that facts are relevant to *understanding* human values, evaluations cannot be *justified* as statements of fact can. Whereas factual statements can be confirmed or falsified by methods which permit universal agreement, value judgments cannot be. To see how much weight such an objection carries, let us return to our simple decision problem. Suppose it were maintained that having a car is valuable. How could this claim be justified? To justify any claim, one must produce reasons. If one could do so here, then to that extent at least logical criteria would be relevant. One might offer as a reason that a need for a car exists, a need which could in turn be supported by showing how a car would enhance opportunities for a particular job. One might also indicate that the necessary funds were available and that, so far as could be known, negligible sacrifice would be involved. In most cases, this would be an adequate justification: the claim would be well supported by the evidence. But, logically, the justification (or argument) would be incomplete. For, though it might go unnoticed, presupposed is an *evaluative* premise that enhancing job opportunities where negligible sacrifice is involved is generally a good thing. Here the difficulty arises, for if *this* premise were challenged, how could we justify it? It is significant to note that this premise would probably not be challenged, since it is one which is widely accepted. But since it can always be challenged, the logical point remains. At this juncture we would have to broaden the argument and produce another one of the same type—one which would involve those considerations relevant to the principle that enhancing job opportunities is generally good. But as before, we would now become involved with still another value premise which could be challenged. Logically, we could be driven to a point where no new argument would be possible.

It should be emphasized, however, that this logical feature of justification is *always* present, not only in arguments involving values but also in other arguments. Indeed, when ultimate grounds are called for, because they are by definition "ultimate," no additional grounds can be provided. Thus, if we were called upon to defend the claim that the sun will rise tomorrow we could produce past experience, and Copernican theory and all its supporting evidence, but we could do no more. Such evidence would suffice, and any demand for more evidence would be considered unreasonable.[5] In a sense, the same is true of arguments involving values. At some point most of us would agree that no further justification is necessary. There still remains, however, one difference between the two types of arguments. Insofar as someone may have fundamentally different value premises from our own, there is no *logical* way to prove that person wrong. A suicide club, for example, may reject *all* the values shared by most people, in which case no argument in favor of relatively trivial values like having a car or of more crucial values like maintaining life would have any impact. Such a club would probably have to reject either all, or almost all, the values commonly held; and if they did not, they would undoubtedly be guilty of the kind of logical inconsistency previously alluded to.[6] Although this difficulty should not be underestimated, neither should it be exaggerated. In most contexts the ultimate justification is not required. But what is required is a serious effort to see problems in all their complexity and to have the available facts. Even though fundamental differences may and do exist, given enough time the facts have a way of eventually forcing resolutions. In passing, it is surprising how many apparently fundamental value disagreements are due to an inadequate appraisal of the facts or to a hidden inconsistency. Such disagreements range from those concerning Nazi elitism, which was predicated on a host of pseudo-facts, to those concerning economic policy, the rights of minority groups, and the "justice" of particular wars. Of course, not all important issues can be resolved by assiduously applying the data of science and the canons of logic, but until more serious efforts are made to do so, we shall not know how many can be.

Although the issue raised here is far more complex than this account may suggest, enough has been said to provide a point of departure for rational decision making. In the next section we shall try to combine the various elements discussed thus far into a strategy for decision.

---

[5] A parallel problem in many respects is the so-called "problem of induction," which has perplexed philosophers since at least the time of Hume. What is the logical basis for believing that the sun will rise tomorrow? Doesn't any justification presuppose that the future will be like the past? But how could we justify this? Surely not inductively, for we are asking for the *ultimate* ground of all induction, and to assume that ground in the process of proving it would be circular reasoning.

[6] By the same token, a person might decide to reject the canons of logic as a dependable instrument of knowledge and rely upon mysticism, intuition, or some other irrational procedure. To attempt to argue rationally with such individuals is fruitless since they do not accept the postulates upon which logic is based. But, then, neither can they justify their position by producing reasons, for if they were to do so they would be using what they had rejected. In actuality, those who do reject reason are not troubled by such inconsistencies and are content, simply, to reason badly.

A More Realistic Account of Rational Decision Making

We are now in a better position to present a more realistic account of rational decision making. In doing so, we shall outline the various stages, discuss each one, and compare it with that of the popular conception. We shall also emphasize the important role of logical criteria and methods discussed in earlier chapters.

For purposes of analysis, the various stages may be stated as follows:

1 The Problem As indicated in our discussion of scientific method, inquiry begins with a problem and is aimed at making a decision. Decisions are always made in answer to a particular problem. That is to say, we do not make decisions unless some feature of the situation calls our attention to the need for a choice. Because decisions are located in contexts, not only is our inquiry a response to specific features, but it must also begin with them. Though this may seem obvious, problem-solving is not helped by saying that the problem would not have arisen had we acted differently; the conditions as given constitute our point of departure. Thus a foreign policy decision on Vietnam made in May, 1962, would take into account different facts than one made in May, 1975.

2 Formulating Proposals Just as scientific inquiry in general requires the formulation of hypotheses, so too does inquiry aimed at decisions. These hypotheses take the form of suggested alternatives, proposals, or alternative policies. Without them we would not know which facts and values were relevant to the solution of our problem. They direct inquiry, just as in scientific investigations. We cannot define the problem first because the context of the problem can be defined in many different ways. At one extreme it could include the total situation of the universe in all of its ramifications; at the other, it could be restricted to only one or two variables. But once we have proposals, we can begin to specify the particular context we are interested in and the relevant facts and values. As inquiry progresses, this context can be enlarged or restricted in accordance with the facts and values which emerge as relevant to our decision. Thus, it is impractical to require that we first define the problem completely before we formulate proposals. As we saw, in decision making *the* problem is rarely only *one* problem. Usually, there is a nest of problems which emerge as inquiry progresses. Take the very simple example of a car that constantly has trouble starting. It is this particular feature of the situation which generates inquiry and demands a decision. The problem here seems very clear: the car is undependable, annoying, bothersome, and so on. Now if this were the only problem, the solution would be clear: abandon the car and replace it with a new one. We would now have a proposal. But further analysis shows that having an undependable car is not the only problem, nor is replacing it the only possible solution; for as soon as we consider our first proposal, new problems arise. Where do we get the money? We might work for it, but that in turn raises problems, such as, can we work and at the same time maintain our B average?

We might sell our books or pawn our watch. But again, new problems arise. Indeed, the problem is defined *only* when we see it in all of its ramifications. And we cannot see it in all of its ramifications until we have proposed several alternatives whose consequences usually involve several auxiliary alternatives. Then, when the implications of each alternative have been clarified—then and only then—can we say that the problem has been defined. Ironically, irrational decisions often spring from hastily thinking that the problem is clear, for then we act imprudently and involve ourselves in problems more difficult to solve than the original one.

Like scientific hypotheses, the alternatives to a given problem are not infinite in number. Like the scientific inquirer, the rational decision maker has a store of knowledge, habits, and frames of reference which narrow down his choices.

Several implications follow from this:

1 Only a certain set of alternatives will be *meaningful*. As William James put it, some hypotheses are "dead." Suppose we were troubled about holding on to religious beliefs with which we were reared. For many of us in the West, becoming Buddhists or Taoists or Hindus would not be viable alternatives. This does not mean, of course, that such religions are unattractive. It only means that for most of us our frame of reference, habits, and dispositions preclude them as genuine alternatives; for us they simply lack probative force, or are not serious candidates. This, of course, would not be true for a Japanese who, being part of a different context, would have a different frame of reference. Similarly, an American youth who was having problems in school and whose father was a professional man would not likely consider quitting to become a chimney sweep.

2 Many conceivable alternatives will not be seriously considered because implementing them is either impossible or only remotely possible. We would not consider an alternative, for instance, which required our being in two places at once or one which required our suddenly becoming rich or talented. In framing a foreign policy we would not consider an alternative which required that the Chinese abandon communism or one which required that the Arabs give foreign aid to Israel. Though we might wish that these were real possibilities, no rational decision maker would entertain them for long.

3 Many possible alternatives will not be considered because of limited knowledge. Just as an automobile mechanic has much more knowledge than the average person from which to generate hypotheses regarding the failure of an engine to start, so do the rest of us have special knowledge which aids us in framing proposals. On the other hand, if we lack certain knowledge, certain proposals will not occur to us. For example, if we did not know that it is possible to borrow money against an insurance policy at a lesser rate of interest than that of a commercial loan, this alternative would not be available to us. If we did not know that

we were eligible for a scholarship, we would not consider this possibility. The more knowledge we have the better and the more effectively we can seek out the relevant possibilities. But no decision maker can ever know that he or she has considered them all; for to know this would require omniscience.

4 Finally, some alternatives will not be considered because they are obviously incompatible with a meaningful solution, or because they would obviously produce more harm than good. Suicide, for example, is always a conceivable alternative, but few of us would consider it as an answer to our problems. Similarly, annihilating all communists would be a solution to ending the cold war, but no rational decision maker would consider it.

All of the foregoing considerations show that the naive demand to consider all possible alternatives is untenable, for, in effect, it is impossible and unnecessary. It is impossible because it requires omniscience and people are not omniscient. It is unnecessary because the most that we require is that only the *relevant, possible,* and *meaningful* alternatives be considered. As to which alternatives will be relevant, possible, and meaningful, this will vary with the context. Like the formulation of hypotheses, the formulation of alternatives belongs to the context of discovery. There are no infallible rules to guide us, but an awareness of the factors involved is the first step toward finding viable alternatives.

It must, however, be emphasized that while the popular conception demands too much, it is correct in seeing that the failure to consider *one* relevant, possible, and meaningful alternative is sufficient to make the decision *un*warranted. For example, suppose that Sam was being pressed to become engaged to either Shirley or Isabella. Though he is not too eager for either, he decides on Isabella and has a calamitous engagement. Sam quite obviously failed to consider a *third* alternative: not becoming engaged to either. Thus, the first step in making a decision warranted demands that *all* the relevant, possible, and meaningful alternatives be considered.

3 Elaborating the Alternatives   This step parallels the elaboration of a hypothesis. But instead of speaking of implications (as we do with a hypothesis), we shall speak of the consequences of various alternatives or proposals. As the acceptability of hypotheses depends upon the result of testing their implications, the *warrant* of a decision depends also upon *evaluating the consequences* of each alternative. However, there are certain distinctions between the two which must be noted:

First, the consequences will always be *probable*. For example, if I elope now, what consequences can I expect? If I take this job, what would be the consequences? If the United States were to widen trade relations with China what would occur? How well we explore consequences depends upon our ability to frame *warranted prediction statements*. What is the probability that my parents will be unhappy? What is the probability that this job will improve my opportunities? What are the probabilities that relations between China and the United States would be improved? Since the answers to these questions depend upon evidence, making warranted decisions depends heavily upon our ability to make prediction statements of warranted probability. At this juncture all the discussion of the previous pages is relevant. Indeed, a thorough understanding of the features, problems, and criteria of deduction, induction, and scientific method is the most necessary ingredient in arriving at warranted decisions. The main task of this text has been to provide a basis for such an understanding. A decision which rests upon inconsistencies, ill-supported beliefs, irrelevancies, and misunderstandings is a decision which cannot hope to gain warrant.

Secondly, consequences are interwoven. They do not develop in a straight line, as exemplified by this type of schema:

$$A \longrightarrow B \longrightarrow C \longrightarrow D \longrightarrow etc.$$

Rather, they are usually much more complex and are better exemplified by this schema:

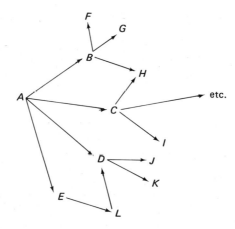

Here act A leads to (at least) B–F, which in turn are interconnected in a complex network of factors. Just as means and ends form an existential continuum, as we saw earlier, so do acts and consequences, and hence our analysis of the consequences is vulnerable to being incomplete. Moreover, not only are the consequences which we mark off probable at best, but they constantly overlap and interconnect and thus cannot be wholly isolated from the network of which they are a part. Fairly accurate predictions can sometimes be made of relatively immediate consequences, but rarely of more remote consequences. To illustrate, we might be able to predict quite adequately that if we cut an exam, then we risk failing the exam. And if we fail the exam, then the probability of receiving an F in the course would be high. And an F in the course would very likely result in probation. But at some point the consequences would become obscure. Sometimes even immediate consequences may be obscure. The manifold consequences of a decision to directly intercede in the Middle East, for example, would not be very clear.

As a rule, the consequences of "important" decisions — that is, those which mark a radical departure from the status quo — are relatively more obscure than those of decisions which entail minor changes. Thus, getting married, moving across the country, or changing one's career would be important personal decisions, while going to war, instituting a full-scale government plan for medical care, or nationalizing the oil industry would be important policy decisions affecting many people.

Although a major change of the status quo involves more risk, more uncertainty, and more readjustments than a minor change, failure to make a major change because of an emotional attachment to what actually exists is a form of irrationalism. That people inherently oppose a major change under normal circumstances is a well-founded generalization, but this intrinsic conservatism is irrelevant (logically) to the question of whether a major change is desirable. What is relevant, however, is that a major change generally involves major consequences. Thus there must be good evidence for thinking that significant advantages would accrue from the change and that these would not be offset by significant disadvantages. When one is offered a new position 3,000 miles away from home, for example, there should be compelling reasons to make such a move. If the only difference between the new position and the old were a $200-increase in annual salary, it would be imprudent to move unless one could also reasonably expect significant improvements in other facets of living — climate, friends, recreation, etc.

The advocate of a new policy, like the scientist with a new hypothesis, has a burden of *proof*. Two factors seem to interact to make up this burden or to constitute a presumption for retaining the status quo. First, the status quo is generally *known* to be functioning, however imperfectly, whereas one can only *predict* what will happen with the new policy. Since the status quo is almost never a total failure,[7] the presumption for retaining it varies with its degree of failure. And, of course, the degree of failure itself is a moot point. Second, the presumption will also vary with the nature of the policy advocated and its susceptibility to being proved as a viable policy. If one were advocating the erection of a new school, for example, there would be less of a presumption in favor of the status quo than if one were advocating that the United States should join the European Economic Community (EEC). This is so because it would be appreciably easier to show that a school with the appropriate specifications could be built than it would be to anticipate all the consequences of the United States joining

---

[7] Only under extraordinary circumstances does it become clear that an extant policy has failed almost totally. The economic catastrophe of the 1930s might be cited as a case in point. During those years the feeling was widely prevalent that the economic system was radically disordered. Then, if ever in American history, a quite clear presumption lay in favor of the advocates of change, justifying Franklin Roosevelt's assertion, "The country needs, the country demands, bold experimentation."

the EEC.   There would be, in short, less left to doubt about the former policy than about the latter.

These two factors then (first, that the status quo has been somewhat—and determinably—successful and second, that the policy advocated can hardly be presented in such a way as to eliminate all doubt that it will be successful) seem to interact to constitute a burden of *proof,* which must be carried before a major change of the status quo can be logically justified.   As with all scientific hypotheses, however, the presumption for retaining the status quo is always—in the parlance of the courts—rebuttable.

Third, the number of consequences of any alternative which can be practically explored is restricted.   This is contrary to the popular conception which holds that the *full* set of consequences be explored.   The number is restricted, however, largely because of the inherent complexity of the task.   Lacking omniscience, as we inquire we must make *auxiliary decisions* as to what consequences can be fruitfully considered.   One might almost say that a certain criterion of "importance" is presupposed, although it is not easy to say in advance what is important and sometimes what is omitted is more important than what is included.   But this is not to say that auxiliary decisions as to what will be considered are arbitrary, if by "arbitrary" is meant irrational or unwarranted. That such decisions are not arbitrary may be seen by some of the factors which guide them, namely:

1   Excluded from consideration is the remote, poorly understood, or intangible.   Since every decision is part of a larger network of relationships, in one sense every decision affects *everything*.   But no one could reasonably be expected to take into account everything.   Obviously a line must be drawn somewhere.   That "somewhere" generally depends on the ability to make warranted predictions.   Changing jobs, for example, might conceivably lead to meeting someone who invites you to a party, where you meet someone else who recommends that you talk to someone else; and *that* conversation opens up golden opportunities.   But no rational decision could be based upon such remote possibilities.   On the other hand, long-run consequences cannot be totally ignored or deemphasized in decision making.   The determining factor as to which consequences, long-run or short-run, should be considered is the available knowledge for making reasonably warranted predictions.   Of course, anything *could* happen, but we should consider only what might happen.

Some decisions might also involve a poorly understood complexity. For example, there is some evidence that family ties are affected by the type of dwelling in which a family resides.   But whatever this connection may be, it is so poorly understood that one might reasonably omit it from consideration in deciding what kind of dwelling to buy or rent.

Finally, some intangible value might be involved, such as an ill-defined notion of equality as it bears upon the location of a new highway. But unless we could explicate this notion and see its connection to the decision, it would be an *imponderable*. The word "imponderable" is revealing, meaning not *capable* of being weighed. But if something is not capable of being weighed or assessed, then it is not worthy of consideration. The determining factor as to what is or is not imponderable is available knowledge.

2 Also excluded from consideration is that which our previous knowledge leads us to believe is irrelevant. In deciding whether or not to change jobs, for example, we would not consider the effects of this decision upon real estate values, the weather, prospects for peace, or the composition of the Senate. We would have no reason to believe that the consequences of our decision would in any way affect such factors. Of course, we might be wrong, but if we did not know this, then the decision to exclude such factors from consideration would be reasonable.

3 Lastly, excluded from consideration are those consequences deemed relatively insignificant. Thus a decision made to save a life would exclude from consideration such consequences as getting one's clothes wet, missing a meal, making one's mate unhappy, breaking a law, or possibly even endangering one's own safety. Some of these consequences might be initially considered but would not be elaborated because of their relative unimportance. As before, such omissions would involve auxiliary decisions as to the relative worth of various values, and of course, the worth assessed would vary with the context. Getting one's clothes wet, for example, might be considered an important consequence if one were deciding whether or not to go fishing in the rain, but it would be considered trivial if one were deciding on whether or not to rescue a drowning person.

Although no sharp line can be drawn between what may be considered significant and insignificant, this does not mean that no distinction at all can be made or that auxiliary decisions as to relative importance are arbitrary. At the very least, a rational decision as to relative importance requires justification. In deciding on a policy in the interests of national security, for example, one might decide that the effects on certain freedoms are relatively unimportant and may thus be excluded from consideration. But this judgment could be questioned, and if it were, one would have to explain how any policy could be considered consistent if it undermined the very thing it was designed to protect. Insofar as facts and values are intimately related and insofar as the logical criteria of consistency, inductive warrant, and deductive validity are involved, such judgments are subject to rational criticism.

All the foregoing considerations suggest that the ideal set up by the popular conception of decision making is not attainable. While having the *full* set of consequences of any act would be desirable, human limitations prevent us. Indeed, insofar as the consequences of our acts flow into the yet unfilled future, and insofar as the universe is "open" to infinite possibilities, not even omniscience would guarantee *right* decisions. But omniscience is not required for warranted decisions, since the latter require that auxiliary decisions as to what should be considered be themselves warranted. If a remote or poorly understood consequence were ignored, this would be warranted. Or if a consequence which obscurely affects an intangible value or one known to be irrelevant were omitted, this would be warranted. Or, finally, if a consequence involving certain values deemed relatively unimportant were omitted, this too would be warranted. Of course, we could always be wrong. The remote, poorly understood, intangible, presumably irrelevant, and presumably unimportant might return to haunt us, but this would be a failure of our finitude, not of our method.

4 Evaluating the Proposals   Insofar as means and ends, acts and consequences, and facts and values are intermixed, the evaluation of alternatives occurs throughout the decision-making process. It stops only when the decision has been made and the act performed. In general, however, evaluation involves considering the merits of various alternatives insofar as their complexity permits. Such evaluation usually entails careful consideration of costs and liabilities as weighed against assets and values, in short, the possible disadvantages versus the possible advantages. It also involves making comparative judgments, that is, weighing one alternative against another. Rarely is any alternative *perfect,* but usually there is a *best* alternative. Although there are no clear-cut or easy rules for determining it, this much seems clear: We cannot state unequivocally what the ultimate ends are and then weigh the various means for efficiency. Nor can we gather all the facts and then appraise them as they bear on our values. As we saw earlier, no neat separation between ends and means or between facts and values is possible. Rather, once the alternatives have been elaborated and we have made warranted auxiliary decisions as to what to omit and what to include, then we must make a decision in terms of the total situation, evaluating as best we can the merits and demerits of the various alternatives.

5 Testing the Decision   Ultimately the testing of a decision can come only when it is put into action. And herein lies a crucial difference between proposals and scientific hypotheses. Scientific hypotheses may be tested, corrected, tested, rejected, and retested again. The self-corrective nature of the scientific method provides the maximum assurance that *eventually* the truth will out. But decisions have no such saving grace. A decision is *right* (not necessarily warranted) if it *works*. But we cannot know for sure if it will work until we try it. In a sense, of course, alternatives may be tested in the imagination, particularly by appeal to analogies. For example, a decision to wear rubbers when it is raining might be tested imaginatively by recalling the consequences of a past decision not to wear rubbers — that is, getting one's feet wet and ultimately catching a cold. Similarly, a policy decision to raise taxes might be tested imaginatively by recalling the consequences of a similar decision made in the past. Here, of course, such testing would be subject to all the pitfalls of reasoning by analogy, particularly the danger of overlooking significant differences in the situations being compared. This type of testing goes on in the stages in which we elaborate our proposals. But at this juncture the consequences are all probabilities. What actually does happen is no longer probable, it is actual. And it is the actualities with which we must live.

EXERCISES

A   The following passages contain different views on the nature of value judgments. Which views seem to be in accord with those expressed in this chapter and which do not? Comment briefly on the implications of each view.

1   Men do not desire the good because it is good; it is good because men desire it.

Baruch Spinoza

2   Advocates of death point out, with a lamentable degree of truth, that reason is a very feeble force in human affairs.

Bertrand Russell

3   If I say "stealing is wrong," I produce a sentence which has no factual meaning — that is, expresses no proposition which can be either true or false. . . . Another man may disagree with me about the wrongness of stealing, in the sense that he may not have the same feelings about stealing as I have. . . . But he cannot, strictly speaking, contradict me. . . . There is plainly no sense in asking which of us is in the right. For neither of us is asserting a genuine proposition.

Alfred J. Ayer[8]

4   "Good" is one of those unnumberable objects of thought which are themselves incapable of definition, because they are the ultimate terms by reference to which whatever *is* capable of definition must be defined.

George E. Moore[9]

5   Spiritual progress up to today has come about through the achievements of thought.

Albert Schweitzer

6   Traditional interest theories hold that ethical statements are descriptive of the existing state of interest — that they simply *give information* about interests. . . . Doubtless there is always *some* element of description in ethical judgments, but this is by no means all. Their major use is not to indicate facts, but to *create an influence*. Instead of merely describ-

---

[8] *Language, Truth and Logic,* 2d ed. (New York: Dover Publishing, Inc., 1952), pp. 107–108.

[9] *Principia Ethica* (Cambridge: Cambridge University Press, 1903), p. 9.

ing people's interests, they *change* or *intensify* them. They recommend an interest in an object, rather than state that the interest already exists.

Charles L. Stevenson[10]

7   You may identify the words *meaningful* and *physical* by an arbitrary definition or resolution. But the difference between what is ordinarily meant by *meaning* and *physical existence* cannot be thereby wiped out.

Morris Cohen[11]

8   Acts are not right or wrong in themselves but are so or not relative to the degree of resistance they offer to socially approved endeavor, or retardation. Since these social objectives change, morality is relative and adjustable to the changed conditions.

J. P. Lichtenberger[12]

9   Verily, awake or dreaming, to be ignorant of what is right and what is wrong, of what is good and what is bad, cannot escape from being blameful, not even if the entire mob were to applaud it.

Plato

10   It is certainly undesirable for men of science to restrict their thinking to what is and will be, leaving to propagandists and reformers and talkers the decisions about what ought to be. . . . Can science avoid trying what impartial curiosity and honest work can accomplish in this field of controversy and prejudice?

E. L. Thorndike[13]

B   Discuss various interpretations of the meaning of value terms or value judgments. (Besides those mentioned in the text, several others are contained in the last question.)

C   What criteria would you use for evaluating the following? Try to be specific.

1 Diesel locomotives	2 Grand opera in English
3 The Fifth Amendment	4 A course in logic
5 This book	6 One of your professors
7 Advertising	8 Government subsidies for higher
9 Capital punishment	education
10 Standardized tests	11 The present Supreme Court

D   Consider some decision you recently made and reconstruct the reasoning used in arriving at it. Was your decision warranted or not? Explain.

---

[10] "The Emotive Meaning of Ethical Terms," *Mind* (1937), pp. 18–19.

[11] *A Preface to Logic* (New York: Meridian Books, Inc., 1958), p. 76.

[12] *Divorce* (New York: Whittlesey House; McGraw-Hill, 1931).

[13] "Science and Values," *Science,* (Jan. 3, 1936).

E Find an example of an argument (at least a paragraph long) in the letters to the editor section of a newspaper or magazine, the editorial page of your local newspaper, or some article or book. Analyze the argument as it relates to facts and values, acts and consequences, and evaluate the reasonableness of the conclusions drawn.

ANSWERS TO SELECTED EXERCISES

Answers are provided to every third question of each exercise. Thus, beginning with one, answers are provided to 1, 4, 7, 10, 13, 16, etc.)

Chapter One

Pp. 8–9
A (The following conditions are obviously not the only ones which could be cited.)
1　**a**　There is some person named "Sam" who is the addressee of the utterance.
　　b　"Sam" refers to Sam.
　　c　It is indeed raining.
4　**a**　There is some person named "Sam" who is the addressee of the utterance.
　　b　"Sam" refers to Sam.
　　c　Sam has just graduated from high school.
　　d　Sam has distinguished himself in high school by being either an outstanding athlete or an outstanding student.
　　e　As a result of his prowess (athletic or academic), Sam has been awarded a scholarship to a college he would like to attend.
　　f　"What great news!" is an expression of happiness and congratulations.
7　As a question; as an utterance of disapproval — you know the homework isn't done and are displeased; as an expression of feelings of surprise or dismay — with emphasis on "your," you saw the person doing *some* homework, supposed it was the person's own, discovered it wasn't.
10　As an appraisal within the framework of consensually accepted criteria; as an expression of your pleasure; as a recommendation to see the play.

P. 12
1　Collective, general.　　**4**　Polar, general.　　**7**　Relative, general.　　**10**　Mass.
13　Relative, general.　　**16**　Polar, abstract.　　**19**　Abstract.

P. 14

1 This view overlooks the fact that a word in one context may have an entirely different meaning when used in a different context. The word "good" is apparently such a word. When applied to food, e.g., it may mean something very much different from what it means when applied to a house. Hence, it is untrue to say that various things which are called "good" necessarily share some characteristic.

P. 17

A 1 Complimentary: firm, determined; pejorative: obstinate, pigheaded, stubborn
4 Complimentary: self-reliant, independent, resolute; perorative: self-centered, know-it-all
B The program,
> {though not spelled out in every trivial detail, marked a significant change.}
> {which was muddled and confused in some of its aspects, was revolutionary.}

It appealed mainly to
> {liberals and progressives as well as to those who believe in an equitable distribution of the country's wealth.}
> {communists and isolationists}

A key feature of the program was that
> {it substantially reduced the funds for military aid to foreign countries.}
> {it threw a roadblock in the way of funding programs which provide friendly countries with military assistance.}

Pp. 20–21

A 1 Contrary to what this view implies, vague terms are not meaningless. Though they can't be *precisely* defined, they can be defined in a manner which allows for an intelligent discussion.
4 The degree of specificity of the terms used is not a criterion of whether or not some body of knowledge is scientific. Moreover, open texture characterizes "gold," "mass," etc.
7 "More" could mean (a) additional or (b) a comparison.
10 "Desirable" could have two meanings: (a) that which *is* desired; (b) that which *should be* desired.

Chapter Two

Pp. 25–27

1 Starts out as a question of fact: Who built the first cotton mill in New England? However, Lida defends herself by redefining "first cotton mill" as "first cotton mill to use power looms" and thus reduces the issue to a verbal one.
4 Factual and verbal. Factual issue: how many are really unemployed? Verbal issue: how are the "unemployed" to be defined?
7 Factual and verbal. Factual: are most of the paintings done in simply one or two colors? Verbal: what is the meaning of "inferior"? What criteria are to be used?

Pp. 31–32

C 16 Too broad. **19** poetic. **22** Too broad. **25** Poetic. **28** Okay.

Pp. 38–39

D **1** Real, genus and difference, genetic. **4** By synonym, lexical. **7** Real, theoretical, genus and difference, functional. **10** Stipulative, precising.

Chapter Three

Pp. 41–42

1 Question. **4** Statement. **7** Supposition or stipulation. **10** Statement.
13 Statement.

Pp. 48–50

1 Nonargument
4 Argument:
   You can't legislate, etc.
   ∴ An FEPC law will be unworkable.
7 Statement
10 Argument:
   Our imports amounted to 3 percent of GNP.
   ∴ If we lowered trade barriers, etc., there would be no dollar gap.
13 Argument:
   Mr. Blumenthal came out strongly, etc., and the next day he was removed, etc.
   ∴ (Implied) Mr. Blumenthal was removed for his views.
16 Nonargument, though a conclusion is suggested.

Pp. 57–58

1 Deductive. **4** Deductive. **7** Inductive, correct. **10** Inductive, incorrect.
13 Inductive, incorrect.

Chapter Four

P. 68

1 Rome was built in a day. **4** ——. **7** A bat is a bird. **10** This is equivalent to "It is false that no athlete is well paid."

P. 71

1 $p \cdot q$, no loss of meaning. **4** Not formalizable as $p \cdot q$ unless rendered as "Richard married Elizabeth *and* Elizabeth married Richard." **7** Not formal. **10** $p \cdot q$, no loss.

Pp. 72–73

1 $p \lor q$. **4** $p \lor q$. **7** Exclusive. **10** Exclusive. **13** $p \lor q$.

P. 79

1 ——. **4** ——. **7** $q \supset p$. **10** $p \supset q$. **13** $q \supset p$.

P. 80

1 $p \equiv q$.

P. 84

1 $p \supset (q \supset r)$ or $(p \supset q) \supset r$.   **4** $p \equiv (q \vee r)$ or $(p \equiv q) \vee r$.   **7** Not ambiguous.
10 Not ambiguous.   **13** Ambiguous: either $pq \vee r$ or $p(q \vee r)$.

Chapter Five

P. 90

1 $(p \vee q) \cdot pq$

    T   T T
    T   F F
    T   F F
    F   F F

4 $\sim(p \vee q)$

    F   T
    F   T
    F   T
    T   F

7 $pq \supset \sim(pq)$

    T   F   F
    F   T   T
    F   T   T
    F   T   T

10 $pq \vee [\sim p \supset (p \equiv \sim q)]$

    T T   F   T   F
    F T   T   T   T
    F T   F   T   T
    F F   T   F   F

P. 94

1 Invalid.   **4** Valid.   **7** Valid.   **10** Invalid.

P. 99

1 Contingency.   **4** Tautology.   **7** Tautology.   **10** Contingency.

Pp. 103–104

1 Valid.   **4** Invalid.   **7** Valid.   **10** Invalid.   **13** Contingency.

Pp. 108–109

1 Inconsistent.   **4** Inconsistent.

Chapter Six

P. 112

1 ——.   **4** ——.   **7** Equivalent.   **10** ——.

Pp. 119–121

   1   *4 $\sim s$ 3, Simp.
        *5 p 2&4, DS
        *6 $q \supset r$ 1&5, MP
   4   *4 p 3, Simp.

	*5	$p \lor q$	**4**, Add.
	*6	r	**1**&**5**, MP
	*7	$r \lor q$	**6**, Add.
	*8	$p \supset (s \supset t)$	**2**&**7**, MP
	*9	$s \supset t$	**4**&**8**, MP
7	*4	$\sim p$	**2**, Simp.
	*5	$q \supset r$	**1**&**4**, DS
	*6	q	**3**, Simp.
	*7	r	**5**&**6**, MP
10	*5	$(p \supset qr)(s \supset t)$	**1**&**2**, Conj.
	*6	$qr \lor t$	**5**&**3**, CD
	*7	t	**6**&**4**, DS

13
$*\begin{cases} \mathbf{1} & (p \lor q) \supset r \\ \mathbf{2} & r \supset \sim s \\ \mathbf{3} & \sim s \supset t \\ \mathbf{4} & ps \qquad /\therefore t \end{cases}$

*	5	p	**4**, Simp.
*	6	$p \lor q$	**5**, Add.
*	7	r	**1**&**6**, MP
*	8	$\sim s$	**2**&**7**, MP
*	9	t	**3**&**8**, MP

P. 123

1	*3	$\sim q \sim r$	**2**, Dem.
	*4	$\sim q$	**3**, Simp.
	*5	$\sim p$	**1**&**4**, MT
4	*4	$\sim r \lor \sim s$	**3**, Add.
	*5	$\sim (rs)$	**4**, DeM.
	*6	$\sim q$	**5**&**2**, MT
	*7	$(p \supset q)(q \supset p)$	**1**, Equiv.
	*8	$p \supset q$	**7**, Simp.
	*9	$\sim p$	**6**&**8**, MT

P. 124

1	* 4	$\sim t$	**3**, Simp.
	* 5	$\sim r$	**2**&**4**, MT
	* 6	$\sim r \lor \sim s$	**5**, Add.
	* 7	$\sim (rs)$	**6**, DeM.
	* 8	$\sim (p \lor q)$	**6**&**1**, MT
	* 9	$\sim p \sim q$	**8**, DeM.
	*10	$\sim p$	**9**, Simp.
4	* 4	$s \lor t$	**3**, Add.
	* 5	pq	**2**&**4**, MP
	* 6	qp	**5**, Com.
	* 7	q	**6**, Simp.
	* 8	$q \lor \sim p$	**7**, Add.
	* 9	$\sim p \lor q$	**8**, Com.
	*10	$p \supset q$	**9**, Imp.
	*11	r	**1**&**10**, MP

7   * 5   ~t v ~u   3, Imp.
       * 6   (~t ⊃ ~q)(~u ⊃ ~s)   2, Trans.
       * 7   ~q v ~s   5&6, CD
       * 8   (~q ⊃ ~p)(~s ⊃ ~r)   1, Trans.
       * 9   ~p v ~r   7&8, CD
       *10   ~r v ~p   9, Com.
       *11   r ⊃ ~p   10, Imp.
       *12   p ⊃ ~p   4&11, HS
       *13   ~p v ~p   12, Imp.
       *14   ~p   13, Taut.
10   * 5   s ⊃ p   2, Imp.
       * 6   p   4&5, MP
       * 7   q ⊃ r   1&6, MP
       * 8   tu   3&7, MP
       * 9   ut   8, Com.
       *10   u   9, Simp.
       *11   u v m   10, Add.

Pp. 129–130

1   **3   p
       **4   q   3&1, MP
       **5   ~~q   4, DN
       **6   ~~r   2&5, MT
       **7   r   6, DN
       *8   p ⊃ r   3&7, Cond.
4   ** 3   p
       ** 4   q ⊃ r   3&1, MP
       *** 5   q
       *** 6   r ⊃ s   2&5, MP
       *** 7   r   4&5, MP
       *** 8   s   6&7, MP
       ** 9   q ⊃ s   5&8, Cond.
       *10   p ⊃ (q ⊃ s)   3&9, Cond.
7   *{ 1   (p ⊃ q)(r ⊃ q)
         { 2   s ⊃ (r v p)   /∴ s ⊃ q
       ** 3   s
       ** 4   r v p   2&3, MP
       ** 5   p v r   4, Com.
       ** 6   q v q   1&5, CD
       ** 7   q   6, Taut.
       * 8   s ⊃ q   3&7, Cond.
10   { 1   (p ⊃ q)(r ⊃ s)
     *{ 2   (q v s) ⊃ ~t
      { 3   w ⊃ h
      { 4   p v r v w   /∴ t ⊃ h
       ** 5   t
       ** 6   ~~t   5, DN
       ** 7   ~(q v s)   2&6, MT

** 8	~q ~s	7, DeM.
** 9	~q	8, Simp.
**10	p ⊃ q	1, Simp.
**11	~p	9&10, MT
**12	p ∨ (r ∨ w)	4, Assoc.
**13	r ∨ w	11&12, DS
**14	~s~q	8, Com.
**15	~s	14, Simp.
**16	(r ⊃ s)(p ⊃ q)	1, Com.
**17	r ⊃ s	16, Simp.
**18	~r	15&17, MT
**19	w	13&18, DS
**20	h	3&19, MP
*21	t ⊃ h	5&20, Cond.

Pp. 133–134

1
**3	p	
**4	q	1&3, MP
**5	~q~r	2, DeM.
**6	~q	5, Simp.
**7	~qq	6&4, Conj.

4
** 4	~(s ∨ r)	
** 5	~s~r	4, DeM.
** 6	~s	5, Simp.
** 7	r ∨ p	6&3, MP
** 8	~r~s	5, Com.
** 9	~r	8, Simp.
**10	p	7&9, DS
**11	q	2&10, MP
**12	q ⊃ r	1&10, MP
**13	r	11&12, MP
**14	r~r	13&9, Conj.

7
*{ 1	p ⊃ q	
2	q ⊃ r~s	
3	r ⊃ s	/∴ ~p
4	p ⊃ r~s	1&2, HS
5	~r ∨ s	3, Imp.
6	~~~r ∨ ~~s	5, DN
7	~(~~~r~s)	6, DeM.
8	~(r~s)	7, DN
9	~p	4&8, MT

10
*{ 1	p ⊃ q	
2	q ⊃ r	
3	s ⊃ ~r	
4	~s ⊃ ~t	
5	~t ⊃ ~q	
6	s ∨ ~s	/∴ ~p
** 7	p	

** **8**	q	**1&7**, MP
** **9**	r	**2&8**, MP
***10**	$\sim\sim r$	**9**, DN
***11**	$\sim s$	**3&10**, MT
***12**	$\sim t$	**4&11**, MP
***13**	$\sim q$	**5&12**, MP
14	$q\sim q$	**8&13**, Conj.

13
* **1** $p \vee qr$
* **2** $p \supset (s \supset t)$
* **3** $\sim p \supset u$
* **4** $s\sim r$ $/\therefore t \vee u$

** **5**	$\sim t$	
** **6**	$ps \supset t$	**2**, Exp.
** **7**	$\sim(ps)$	**5&6**, MT
** **8**	$\sim p \vee \sim s$	**7**, DeM.
** **9**	$p \supset \sim s$	**8**, Imp.
***10**	s	**4**, Simp.
***11**	$\sim\sim s$	**10**, DN
***12**	$\sim p$	**11&9**, MT
***13**	u	**12&3**, MP
*14	$\sim t \supset u$	**5&13**, Cond.
*15	$t \vee u$	**14**, Imp.

Chapter Seven

Pp. 142–143

1 All persons are hated by Smith.   **4** All students who miss this question are students who deserve to flunk.   **7** All who love only glory are brave.   **10** Some dancing is not vulgar.   **13** All who know her are those who love her.   **16** All dead fleas are good fleas.   **19** No men are men who can live on bread alone.   **22** Some brave hearts are hearts which are asleep in the deep.   **25** No callipygian aardvarks are frigorific beings.

Pp. 145–146

	QUALITY	QUANTITY	DISTRIBUTED	UNDISTRIBUTED	**A E I O**
1	Affirmative	Universal	non-S	P	**A**
4	Affirmative	Universal	S	P	**A**
7	Affirmative	Particular	$\cdots$	S & P	**I**
10	Negative	Particular	P	S	**O**
13	Affirmative	Particular	$\cdots$	non-S & non-P	**I**

P. 149

1	**a** T.	**b** F.	**c** T.	**d** F.
	a F.	**b** ?.	**c** ?.	**d** T.
4	**a** T.	**b** F.	**c** ?.	**d** ?.
	a F.	**b** T.	**c** F.	**d** T.

Note: ? = undertermined.

Pp. 153–154

1 Some Indians are sitar players.   **4** No persons who are humane are indifferent.
7 Some beverages are not nonintoxicants.   **10** All visitors are welcome.   **13** True;
implicant of contrapositive.   **16** False; contrary of obverse.   **19** False.

Chapter Eight

P. 157

1 All people are lovers of lovers.
  No pugilists are lovers of lovers.

∴ No pugilists are people.
  AEE-2

4 Some barbiturates are not habit-forming.
  All barbiturates are narcotics.

∴ Some narcotics are not habit-forming.
  OAO-3

P. 159

	ORIGINAL	FORM	REFUTATION BY LOGICAL ANALOGY
1	All advocates are friends.	All *A* are *B*.	All dogs are mammals.
	No employers are advocates.	No *C* are *A*.	No cats are dogs.
	∴ No employers are friends. (Illicit major.)	No *C* are *B*.	No cats are mammals.
4	All supporters are Legionnaires.	All *A* are *B*.	All collies are dogs.
	All Legionnaires are veterans.	All *B* are *C*.	All dogs are mammals.
	∴ All veterans are supporters. (Illicit minor.)	All *C* are *A*.	All mammals are collies.

P. 163
A   1 Valid.   **4** Valid.   **B   1** Valid.   **4** Invalid; two negative premises.

Pp. 169–170

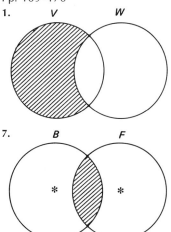

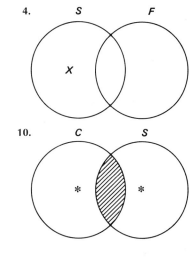

Pp. 174–175

1. *AAA*-1
Valid

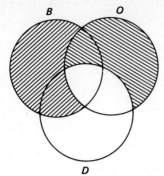

4. *EAE*-A
Invalid (illicit minor)

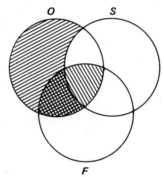

Pp. 176–177

1 To obtain three terms, use contrapositive of the major premise and obvert minor premise. This yields:

Some just policies are not wise.
All just policies are in the best interest of all.
_____
∴ Some policies in the best interest of all are wise.

Invalid: one negative premise, affirmative conclusion.

4 No senators are quarrelers.
Some senators are not agreers.
_____
∴ Some agreers are not quarrelers.

Invalid: two negative premises. Obverting the premises and taking the contrapositive of the conclusion would still yield three terms, but there would be a negative conclusion and two affirmative premises.

7 Valid.   **10** Invalid; both premises negative.

P. 179

1 Major premise: Any cleaner that is stronger than dirt is effective.   **4** Minor premise;

We must all defend freedom.   **7**   Major premise: All good swimmers are Hawaiian.
10   Major premise: Anything with protein is nourishing.

Chapter Nine

Pp. 191–192
  1 $(x)(x$ is an aardvark $\supset x$ is callipygian); $(x)(Fx \supset Gx)$
  4 $(\exists x)[x$ is an elephant $\cdot \sim(x$ is friend$)]$; $(\exists x)(Fx \cdot \sim Gx)$
  7 $(\exists x)(x$ is tiny $\cdot x$ plays football); $(\exists x)(Fx \cdot Gx)$
  10 $(x)(x$ is a fish $\supset x$ has got to swim); $(x)(Fx \supset Gx)$

Pp. 193–194
  1 $(x)[x$ is a politician $\supset (x$ is rich v x is youthful$)]$; $(x)[Fx \supset (Gx \text{ v } Hx)]$
  4 $(\exists x)[x$ is garrulous $\cdot x$ is a poet $\cdot \sim(x$ is dirty-minded$)]$; $(\exists x)(Fx \cdot Gx \cdot \sim Hx)$
  7 $(\exists x)(x$ is a spider $\cdot x$ eats insects$) \cdot (x)(x$ is a spider $\supset x$ has eight legs); $(\exists x)(Fx \cdot Gx) \cdot (x)$
          $(Fx \supset Hx)$
  10 $(x)(x$ is fuzzy $\cdot x$ is a teddy bear $\supset x$ is fuzzy); $(x)(Fx \cdot Gx \supset Fx)$
  13 $(\exists x)[x$ loves their pets $\cdot \sim(x$ cares well for their pets$)]$; $(\exists x)(Fx \cdot \sim Gx)$

P. 196
  1 $(Fa \equiv Ga) \cdot (Fb \equiv Gb) \cdots (Fh \equiv Gh)$
  4 $\sim(Fa \supset Ga) \text{ v} \sim(Fb \supset Gb) \text{ v} \cdots \sim(Fh \supset Gh)$
  7 $(Fa \text{ v } Fb \text{ v} \cdots Fh) \cdot Ga \cdot Gb \cdots Gh$
  10 $(Fa \equiv Ga)(Fb \equiv Gb) \cdots (Fh \equiv Gh) \cdot \sim[Fa \text{ v } Fb \text{ v} \cdots Fh]$

P. 199
     T F   F F   T   F
  1 $(Fa \supset Ga)(Fa \supset Ha) \supset (Ga \supset Ha)$
     T   T F F
  4 $[Fa \supset (Ga \text{ v } Ha)] \cdot Ga \supset Ha$
   T T   FT T F   FT
  7 $\sim(Fa \supset \sim Ga)Fa \supset \sim Ga$
   T F   F F
  10 $Fa(Ga \supset Fa) \supset Ga$
  13 $(\exists x)(Ox \cdot Cx \cdot Px) \cdot (x)(Sx \cdot Ix \supset Px)$ $/\therefore (\exists x)(Ix \cdot Cx)$
     T   T   T   T   F F   T
          $(Oa \cdot Ca \cdot Pa)(Sa \cdot Ia \supset Pa) \supset Ia \cdot Ca$

Chapter Ten

Pp. 205–206
  1   ⎧ **1** $Fa \supset (x)Fx$
          *⎨ **2** $\sim Fa \supset \sim Fb$
          ⎩ **3** Fb $/\therefore (x)Fx$
          * **4** $Fb \supset Fa$ 2, Trans.
          * **5** Fa 3&**4**, MP
          * **6** $(x)Fx$ 1&**5**, MP

4 ⎧ **1** $Fa \supset (\exists x)(Fx \cdot Gx)$
 * ⎨ **2** $(\exists x)(Fx \cdot Gx) \supset (x)(Fx \supset Hx)$
  ⎩ **3** Fa /∴ $Fa \supset Ha$
 * **4** $(\exists x)(Fx \cdot Gx)$ **1**&**3**, MP
 * **5** $(x)(Fx \supset Hx)$ **2**&**4**, MP
 * **6** $Fa \supset Ha$ **5**, UI

7 * **1** $\sim(\exists x)\sim Fx$ /∴ $(\exists x)Fx$
 * **2** $(x)Fx$ **1**, Quant. Eq.
 * **3** Fx **2, UI**
 * **4** $(\exists x)(Fx)$ **3**, EG

10 ⎧ **1** $pq \supset (x)(Fx \supset Gx)$
  * ⎨ **2** $Fa \cdot p$ /∴ $q \supset Ga$
 ** **3** q
 ** **4** $p \cdot Fa$ **2**, Comm.
 ** **5** p **4**, Simp.
 ** **6** pq **3**&**6**, Conj.
 ** **7** $(x)(Fx \supset Gx)$ **1**&**6**, MP
 ** **8** $Fa \supset Ga$ **7, UI**
 ** **9** Fa **2**, Simp.
 ****10** Ga **8**&**9**, MP
 ***11** $q \supset Ga$ **3**&**8**, Cond.

13 ⎧ **1** $(x)(Fx \supset Gx) \supset (x)(Gx \supset Hx)$
  * ⎨ **2** $(x)(Fx \supset Gx)$ /∴ $Fa \supset Ha$
 * **3** $(x)(Gx \supset Hx)$ **1**&**2**, MP
 * **4** $Ga \supset Ha$ **3**, UI
 * **5** $Fa \supset Ga$ **2**, UI
 * **6** $Fa \supset Ha$ **4**&**5**, HS

Pp. 212–214

1 * **3** Fx **2, EI** x
 * **4** $Fx \supset Gx$ **1, UI**
 * **5** Gx **3**&**4**, MP
 * **6** $(\exists x)Gx$ **5, EG**

4 * **3** $Fx \lor Gx$ **1, EI** x
 * **4** $\sim Fx$ **2, UI**
 * **5** Gx **3**&**4**, DS
 * **6** $(\exists x)Gx$ **5, EG**

7 * **4** $Fx \cdot \sim Ix$ **3, EI** x
 * **5** $(x)\sim(Fx \cdot \sim Gx)$ **1**, Quant. Eq.
 * **6** $(x)(\sim Fx \lor Gx)$ **5**, DeM.
 * **7** $\sim Fx \lor Gx$ **6, UI**
 * **8** Fx **4**, Simp.
 * **9** Gx **7**&**8**, MP & Imp.
 ***10** $(x)(\sim Gx \lor \sim Hx)$ **2**, DeM.
 ***11** $(x)(Gx \supset \sim Hx)$ **10**, Imp.
 ***12** $Gx \supset \sim Hx$ **11, UI**
 ***13** $\sim Hx$ **9**&**12**, MP
 ***14** $(\exists x)\sim Hx$ **13, EG**
 ***15** $(\exists x)\sim Hx \lor (\exists x)Ix$ **14**, Add.

10	* 4	$(x)(Fx \supset Gx)$	**1**, Quant. Eq.
	* 5	$Fa \supset Ga$	**4, UI**
	* 6	$\sim Ga \cdot \sim Ha$	**2**, DeM.
	* 7	$\sim Ga$	**6**, Simp.
	* 8	$\sim Fa$	**5&7**, MT
	* 9	$\sim Fa \lor \sim Ia$	**8**, Add.
	*10	$\sim(Fa \cdot Ia)$	**9**, DeM.
	*11	$\sim(Fa \cdot Ia) \supset \sim Ja$	**3, UI**
	*12	$\sim Ja$	**10&11**, MP
	*13	$(\exists x)\sim Jx$	**12**, EG

13	*⎰ 1	$(x)(Fx \cdot Gx \supset p)$	
	⎱ 2	$(\exists x)(Fx \cdot Gx \cdot Hx)$	
	* 3	$Fx \cdot Gx \cdot Hx$	**2, EI** x
	* 4	$Fx \cdot Gx \supset P$	**1, UI**
	* 5	$Fx \cdot Gx$	**3**, Simp.
	* 6	P	**4&5**, MP

16	⎧ 1	$(x)(Fx \supset \sim Gx) \lor (x)(Fx \supset \sim Hx)$	
	*⎪ 2	$(x)(Jx \supset Fx)$	
	⎨ 3	$(x)(Kx \supset Gx)$	
	⎩ 4	$(\exists x)(Jx \cdot Kx)$	$/\therefore (\exists x)(Jx \cdot \sim Hx)$
	* 5	$Jx \cdot Kx$	**4, EI** x
	* 6	$Jx \supset Fx$	**2, UI**
	* 7	$Kx \supset Gx$	**3, UI**
	* 8	Jx	**5**, Simp.
	* 9	Fx	**6&8**, MP
	*10	$Kx \cdot Jx$	**5**, Comm.
	*11	Kx	**10**, Simp.
	*12	Gx	**7&11**, MP
	*13	$Fx \cdot Gx$	**9&12**, Conj.
	*14	$(\exists x)(Fx \cdot Gx)$	**13, EG**
	*15	$\sim(x)\sim(Fx \cdot Gx)$	**14**, Quant. Eq.
	*16	$\sim(x)(\sim Fx \lor \sim Gx)$	**15**, DeM.
	*17	$\sim(x)(Fx \supset \sim Gx)$	**16**, Imp.
	*18	$(x)(Fx \supset \sim Hx)$	**1&17**, DS
	*19	$Fx \supset \sim Hx$	**18, UI**
	*20	$\sim Hx$	**9&19**, MP
	*21	$Jx \cdot \sim Hx$	**8&20**, Conj.
	*22	$(\exists x)(Jx \cdot \sim Hx)$	**21, EG**

19	⎧ 1	$(\exists x)Fx \supset (x)(Gx \supset Fx)$	
	*⎨ 2	$(\exists x)Hx \supset (x)(Fx \supset Hx)$	
	⎩ 3	$(\exists x)(Fx \cdot Hx)$	$/\therefore (x)(Gx \supset Hx)$
	* 4	$Fx \cdot Hx$	**3, EI** x
	* 5	Fx	**4**, Simp.
	* 6	$Hx \cdot Fx$	**4**, Comm.
	* 7	Hx	**6**, Simp.
	* 8	$(\exists x)Fx$	**5, EG**
	* 9	$(\exists x)Hx$	**7, EG**
	*10	$(x)(Gx \supset Fx)$	**1&8**, MP
	*11	$(x)(Fx \supset Hx)$	**2&9**, MP

*12	$Gy \supset Fy$	10, UI
*13	$Fy \supset Hy$	11, UI
*14	$Gy \supset Hy$	12&13, HS
*15	$(x)(Gx \supset Hx)$	14, UG

Chapter Eleven

P. 218

1 $(\exists x)(\exists y)Fxy$ becomes $(\exists y)Fay \lor (\exists y)Fby$ becomes $Faa \lor Fab \lor Fba \lor Fbb$. **4** $(x)(y)(Fx \supset Gy)$ becomes $(y)(Fa \supset Gy) \cdot (y)(Fb \supset Gy)$ becomes $[Fa \supset (Ga \cdot Gb)] \cdot [(Fb) \supset (Ga \cdot Gb)]$.

B 7 Everything is larger than something.

P. 220

1 $\sim(\exists x)(y)Fxy$ becomes $\sim[(y)Fay \lor (y)Fby]$ becomes $\sim[(Faa \cdot Fab) \lor (Fba \cdot Fbb)]$. **4** $(x)\sim(y)Fxy$ becomes $\sim(y)Fay \cdot \sim(y)Fby$ becomes $\sim[(Faa \cdot Fab)] \cdot \sim[(Fba \cdot Fbb)]$ becomes $(\sim Faa \lor \sim Fab) \cdot (\sim Fba \lor \sim Fbb)$. **7** Nothing is larger than everything.

P. 223

1 $(x)(\exists y)Fxy$. **4** $\sim(\exists x)(y)Fxy$.
7 $(x)[Mx \supset (\exists y)(Ux \cdot Cxy)]$.
10 $(x)(y)[(x$ is a person $\cdot y$ is a person$) \supset (\exists z)(z$ is a time $\cdot x$ loves y at $z)]$, or finally, $(x)(y)[(Px \cdot Py) \supset (\exists z)(Tz \cdot Lxyz)]$.
13. $(\exists x)(\exists y)(Tx \cdot Oy \cdot Gax \cdot Gay)$.

P. 227

1
*1	$(x)(y)(Fx \supset Gxy)$	$/\therefore (x)(\exists y)(Fx \supset Gxy)$
*2	$(y)(Fx \supset Gxy)$	1, UI
*3	$Fx \supset Gxy$	2, UI
*4	$(\exists y)(Fx \supset Gxy)$	3, EG
*5	$(x)(\exists y)(Fx \supset Gxy)$	4, UG

4
*{1	$(x)(y)(Fxy \equiv Gx)$	
{2	Ga	$/\therefore Faa$
* 3	$(y)(Fay \equiv Ga)$	1, UI
* 4	$Faa \equiv Ga$	3, UI
* 5	$(Faa \supset Ga) \cdot (Ga \supset Faa)$	4, Equiv.
* 6	$(Ga \supset Faa) \cdot (Faa \supset Ga)$	5, Comm.
* 7	$Ga \supset Faa$	6, Simp.
* 8	Faa	2&7, MP

7
*1	$(y)(\exists x)(Fx \supset Gy)$	$/\therefore (x)Fx \supset (x)Gx$
*2	$(\exists x)(Fx \supset Gy)$	1, UI
*3	$Fx \supset Gy$	2, EI x
**4	$(x)Fx$	
**5	Fx	4, UI
**6	Gy	3&5, MP
**7	$(x)Gx$	6, UG
*8	$(x)Fx \supset (x)Gx$	4&7, Cond.

Restricting the universe to people:

10   1 $\sim(\exists x)(y)Fxy$ $/\therefore (\exists x)(\exists y)\sim Fxy$
      2 $(x)\sim(y)Fxy$ 1, Equiv.
      3 $(x)(\exists y)\sim Fxy$ 3, Equiv.
      4 $(\exists y)\sim Fxy$ **3, UI**
      5 $(\exists x)(\exists y)\sim Fxy$ **4, EG**

13   ⎧ 1 $(x)(Lx \supset Wx)$
    *⎨ 2 $(x)\{Wx \supset (y)[Py \supset (Dyx \supset Gy)]$
     ⎩ 3 $(\exists x)[Lx \cdot (\exists y)(Py \cdot Dyx \cdot \sim Ky)]$ $/\therefore (\exists x)(Gx \cdot \sim Kx)$
   * 4 $Lz \cdot (\exists y)(Py \cdot Dyz \cdot \sim Ky)$ 3, EI z
   * 5 $(\exists y)(Py \cdot Dyz \cdot \sim Ky) \cdot Lz$ 4, Comm.
   * 6 $(\exists y)(Py \cdot Dyz \cdot \sim Ky)$ 5, Simp.
   * 7 $Py \cdot Dyz \cdot \sim Ky$ **6, EL y**
   * 8 Lz 4, Simp.
   * 9 $Lz \supset Wz$ **1, UI**
   *10 Wz 8&9, MP
   *11 $Wz \supset (y)[Py \supset (Dyz \supset Gy)]$ **2, UI**
   *12 $(y)[Py \supset (Dyz \supset Gy)]$ 10&11, MP
   *13 $Py \supset (Dyz \supset Gy)$ **12, UI**
   *14 Py 7, Simp.
   *15 $Dyz \supset Gy$ 13&14, MP
   *16 $Dyz \cdot Py \cdot \sim Ky$ 7, Comm.
   *17 Dyz 16, Simp.
   *18 Gy 15&17, MP
   *19 $\sim Ky \cdot Py \cdot Dyz$ 7, Comm.
   *20 $\sim Ky$ 19, Simp.
   *21 $Gy \cdot \sim Ky$ 18, Conj.
   *22 $(\exists x)(Gx \cdot \sim Kx)$ **21, EG**

P. 229
1 Transitive, asymmetrical.   **4** Transitive, asymmetrical.   **7** Transitive, symmetrical, reflexive.   **10** None.

Chapter Twelve

P.242
1 Correct.   **4** Incorrect.   **7** "Count on" tends to be ambiguous; correct if interpreted as "very probably" rather than as "certainly."   **10** Correct.

P. 248
1 Weaker.   **4** Weaker.   **7** Weaker.   **10** Weaker.   **13** Weaker.
16 Stronger.   **19** Weaker.

Pp. 252–253
1 Inductive analogy; sound.   **4** Inductive analogy; sound.   **7** Inductive analogy; weak; a ship is subject to the elements and hence running it often requires quick decisions; this is not so, usually, of running a government.   **10** Inductive analogy; weak; no reason is given for the analogy drawn; the latter is just assumed.

P. 256
1 True. **4.** True.

Pp. 261–262
1 Difference; conclusion: birds are immune to anthrax because of their warm blood; very probable. **4** Difference; conclusion: high turnover in physically strenuous jobs is due to inadequate rest periods; very probable. **7** Difference; conclusion: radar systems cause a reduction in the rate of automobile accidents and fatalities; possible.
10 U. **13** T. **16** T. **19** T.

Chapter Thirteen

Pp. 269–270
1 Because the majority passed, one cannot infer that any particular individual passed, even if, as in this case, the probability is high.
4 A poor sample for the generalization, since Garden City, L.I., is an affluent community.
7 It doesn't follow that because the last two operations were failures the next will be a success. More relevant would be knowledge about which physicians performed the previous twenty-three operations.
10 The extrapolation assumes that there are no inherent physical limits on the ability of humans to run a mile.

Pp. 275–276
1 $(1/2)^5$. **4** $1 - (1/2)^5$. **7** $(1/4)^5$. **10** 1/52. **13** $4/10 \times 3/9$.
16 1/52; 1/52. **19** Probability of straight: 2/47; of flush: 9/47.

Pp. 281–282
1 .865. **4** 1.00 .014 − .986. **7** .224 + .054 = .278.

Chapter Fourteen

Pp. 297–299
1 Begging the question; "costly" is assumed.
4 *Ad ignoratiam.*
7 *Ad ignoratiam.* Also related to the formal fallacy of denying the antecedent.
10 Accident; the principle "It is wrong to betray a friend" is usually qualified.
13 False alternatives; there are many others besides those which are mentioned.
16 Equivocation on "understand."
19 Fallacy of the beard; no distinction is made between polar opposites.
22 Fallacy of the beard; no distinction is made between polar opposites.
25 Composition; what is true of the part (individuals) is not necessarily true of the whole (a mob).
28 Division.

Chapter Fifteen

Pp. 313–317
1 False cause; here correlation is mistaken for causation.
4 Biased source.
7 Irrelevant emotional appeals.
10 Hasty generalization; Harvard crewmen don't constitute a representative sample.
13 Overlooks possibility of reciprocal causation.
16 Assumes a correlation is a causal relationship; much more evidence would be needed to establish such a conclusion.
19 Contradictory assumptions: state can't take like (only God can), but the state can take life (under certain circumstances).
22 Biased source; the two were in conflict.
25 Inconsistency, or special pleading; first he condemns legalized betting but then recommends one form of it.
28 Inconsistency. The speaker says that the term "ethical" both has and does not have a double meaning.
31 Confusing necessary with sufficient conditions. The argument overlooks all the other conditions which led to war.
34 Diversion. *A's* point is that American prestige in Asia is low. *B* answers that American prestige is rising. It could be rising and still be low.

THE WORKBOOK: PROGRESS TESTS

Language and Meaning

Progress Test 1 (Chapter One)
Indicate whether the following are true or false; use T for true, F for false.

1 Language is a system of symbols which are meaningful in virtue of the ways they are used by members of a linguistic community. _____

2 Because speaking and writing are things we do, they involve both purposes and a social context. _____

3 In saying something we perform a linguistic act, but our linguistic acts may be taken as having different purposes. _____

4 Whether the force of a given speech act is a request or a command depends solely upon the form of the sentence used. _____

5 There are just three functions or purposes of discourse. _____

6 A given linguistic act cannot serve different purposes simultaneously. _____

7 The perlocutionary effects of an utterance are the effects which are brought about by the utterance. _____

8 There is no important difference between what we intend in saying something, what we do in saying something, and what the effects are of our saying something. _____

9 Informing is not the same as convincing just as expressing is not the same as persuading. _____

10 Only nouns are terms. _____

11 Singular terms are used to refer to a single person, place, thing, or event. _____

12 Demonstratives and pronouns, such as "this" or "it," can never function as singular terms. _____

13 General terms are indifferently true of any member of the class defined by the term. _____

14 "Taller than" is an absolute term. _____

15 "The tallest man in the world" is both a singular term and a collective term. _____

16 A term is used distributively when something is predicated of the unit or class taken as a whole. _____

17 In "Humility is a virtue" "humility" is an abstract term. _____

18 The connotation of a term consists of all those objects of which the term is true. _____

19 "Connotation," "sense," and "extension" are often used interchangeably. _____

20 The denotation of a term is the conventional criterion of application of a term. _____

21 If a term is correctly to apply to different things, then those things must have at least one feature in common. _____

22 If two terms have different senses or connotations, they must have different denotations. _____

23 Efforts to persuade and influence often depend as much upon the choice of words with different connotations as upon the facts. _____

24 Where settling questions of meaning depends primarily upon linguistic facts, settling questions of fact depends primarily upon existential facts. _____

25 The failure to express ourselves clearly invariably results from the inherent vagueness of some terms. _____

26 "Open texture" is an important type of ambiguity. _____

27 Like ambiguity, the vagueness of terms is always an obstacle to communication. _____

28 A word may have several different meanings and yet be unambiguous in the contexts in which it occurs. _____

29 Polar-opposite terms are inherently vague and hence rarely serve any useful purpose. _____

30 Context is important in preventing ambiguity of reference. _____

Terms, Connotation, and Vagueness

Progress Test 2 (Chapter One)
Use the appropriate letter to identify the items in the first column. Note that each letter may be used more than once.

1	beehive	**a**	general term	_____
2	Senator Muskie	**b**	singular term	_____
3	ketchup	**c**	relative term	_____
4	redness	**d**	collective term	_____
5	aunt of	**e**	mass term	_____
6	the broken bicycle	**f**	abstract term	_____
7	regiment	**g**	polar term	_____
8	school			_____
9	dark			_____
10	grove			_____
11	connotation	**h**	x, y, and z are all called A even	_____
12	denotation		though they have no one feature	_____
13	family resemblance		in common.	_____
14	open texture	**i**	an expression which makes sense	_____
15	intension		to apply to a thing	_____
16	extension	**j**	may be understood in several ways	_____
17	sense	**k**	the objects of which a term is true	_____
18	term	**i**	absence of definite boundaries	_____
19	vague	**m**	the conventional criterion of	_____
20	ambiguous		application	_____
		n	the possibility of vagueness	_____

Definition

Progress Test 3 (Chapter Two)
Indicate whether the following are true or false; use T for true, F for false.

1 Many disputes are due to a misunderstanding of the force of an utterance. _____

2 A dispute over the meaning of a term is customarily called a factual dispute as opposed to a verbal dispute. _____

3 Even if two parties agreed on the meaning of "religion," it would still be possible for them to disagree on whether the term applied in a given case. _____

4 Lexical definitions are useful in increasing our vocabulary, clarifying the meanings of words of which we are unsure, and settling disputes over meaning. _____

5 Stipulative definitions, like lexical definitions, are basically reports or descriptions of how a word is actually used in the language. _____

6 Connotative definitions are sometimes also called "analytic definitions." _____

7 In exact definitions the definiens includes the necessary and sufficient characteristics for correct application of the term. _____

8 In exact definitions the definiens is synonymous with the definiendum in the sense that the two are interchangeable in contexts without a change in meaning. _____

9 It is always possible to provide an exact definition of a word. _____

10 In a definition "automobile" means "vehicle used for transportation," the definiens is too broad. _____

11 It is logically impossible for the definiens of a definition to be *both* too broad and too narrow. _____

12 Defining "bachelor" as "unmarried male" violates the rule that the definiens should not be expressed negatively. _____

13 An inherent difficulty with definition by synonym is the problem of finding two words with the same connotation. _____

14 Ostensive definitions for the most part are useless. _____

15 Definition by example has the important feature of explicitly providing the connotation of words. _____

16 Definition by example has no important uses. _____

17 Stipulative definitions are proposals to use a word in a certain way. _____

18 The boundary between lexical and stipulative definitions is clear-cut. _____

19 Stipulative definitions are useful in settling disputes regarding the established meaning of words. _____

20 Precising definitions are useful in fixing the boundaries of the extension of vague terms. _____

21   In an operational definition nothing is ever stipulated or described.   _____

22   In stipulative definitions the stipulator has no restrictions in framing the definiens.   _____

23   Like lexical definitions, real definitions give the meanings of words in some language.   _____

24   Historically, the most important method of providing real definitions is definition by genus and differentia.   _____

25   The differentia may refer to parts or characteristics of the thing defined or to its function or origin.   _____

26   Evaluating a theoretical definition is tantamount to evaluating the theory in terms of which the definition is couched.   _____

27   Controversies over the nature of law, religion, justice, and the like are generally not disputes which can be settled by appeal to dictionary definitions of "law," "religion," etc.   _____

28   The definition "A polygon is a many-angled plane figure" could be explicated as a definition by genus and differentia.   _____

29   The definition "A polygon is a many-angled plane figure" is ambiguously either a connotative definition of the word "polygon" in English or a real definition of polygons.   _____

30   Whenever something lacks precisely determinable characteristics, one should insist on a definition of it which sets forth some precisely determinable characteristics.   _____

Rules for Sound Definitions

Progress Test 4 (Chapter Two)
Indicate which rules, if any, the following definitions violate. Use the following criteria and place the appropriate letters in the space provided:

a   Too broad   **b**   Too narrow
c   Circular   **d**   Too negative
e   Too figurative or poetical   **f**   Too technical

1   "Piety means prosecuting the wrongdoer who has committed murder or sacrilege or any other such crime."
Euthyphro, as quoted by Plato   _____

2   "A cynic is one who knows the price of everything and the value of nothing."
Oscar Wilde   _____

3   Man is a featherless biped.   _____

4   Being autonomous is having autonomy over one's decisions and actions.   _____

5   "To 'eat' is to perform successively (and successfully) the functions of mastication, humectation, and deglutination."
Ambrose Bierce   _____

6 A prudent man is one who does not take unnecessary chances and who is not extreme in his actions. _____

7 ". . . to define true madness,
What is't but to be nothing else but mad?"

Shakespeare, *Hamlet* _____

8 "A fanatic is a man who redoubles his efforts after he has forgotten his aim."

George Santayana _____

9 "What is pleasing to the gods is pious and what is not pleasing is impious."

Euthyphro, as quoted by Plato _____

10 A dormitory is an edifice used by college students as a residence away from home. _____

11 An effect is that which is produced by a cause, just as a cause is that which produces an effect. _____

12 A cow is a domesticated animal which gives milk. _____

13 "An idiot is a member of a large and powerful tribe whose influence in human affairs has always been dominant and controlling."

Ambrose Bierce _____

14 "A gentleman is a man whose principal ideas are not connected with his personal needs and his personal success."

William Butler Yeats _____

15 Democracy is that form of government which respects the civil rights of the people. _____

Types of Definitions

Progress Test 5 (Chapter Two)
Classify the following definitions, using the letters from the accompanying list.

a	Lexical	**b**	Stipulative
c	Real	**d**	By synonym
e	By example	**f**	By subclass
g	By ostension	**h**	Operational
i	Contextual	**j**	Precising
k	Theoretical	**l**	Persuasive
m	Connotative	**n**	Genetic
o	Functional	**p**	Genus and difference

Keep in mind that each definition will have at least two letters.

1 x lifts y when x moves y to a higher position. _____

2 A proposition is an expression in words or other symbols which are used to affirm or to deny something. _____

3 For the purpose of this course, a passing grade will be defined as a grade of 70 or over. _____

4 "Circle" means "a closed plane figure whose points are equidistant from the center." _____

5 "Prodigality" means "wastefulness." _____

6 "That is a salamander," said the ichthyologist, as he pointed to a small spotted lizard. _____

7 "Emotion" is exemplified by love, hate, fear, joy, and frustration. _____

8 "The true definition of each thing involves nothing and expresses nothing but the nature of the thing defined."

Spinoza, *Ethics* _____

9 A delta is a nearly flat plain formed by the alluvial deposit between diverging branches of the mouth of a river.

10 Wisdom consists in knowing not only facts but also their significance — how facts are interrelated, how they affect beliefs, and how they apply to people's lives. _____

11 The speed of an object is obtained by dividing the distance it covers by the time it takes to cover it. _____

12 We shall use the term "propaganda" to mean a discourse which attempts to persuade by illogical means and for the benefit of the persuader. _____

13 "Bird" denotes creatures like a swallow, oriole, or owl. _____

14 x jumps when x springs clear of the ground or some other support by a sudden muscular effort. _____

15 Studying is going over a certain body of material, making an effort to understand it, and learning it well enough so as to be able to recall it. _____

Sentences, Statements, and Arguments

Progress Test 6 (Chapter Three)

Write T for true or F for false after each of the following statements.

1 Statements are sentences which could be either true or false. _____

2 Any sentence may serve as the premise of an argument. _____

3 Not all statements are sentences. _____

4 Not all sentences are statements. _____

5 Arguments, like statements, are either true or false. _____

6 An argument is correct if the premises are all true. _____

7 For an argument to be correct, the premises must be true. _____

8 A sound argument is a correct argument with true premises. _____

9 An argument is not correct if the premises do not constitute sufficient grounds for the conclusion. _____

10 If an argument is sound, then its premises must be true. _____

11 If an argument is correct, then the premises must be true. _____

12 If an argument is valid, then if the premises are true, the conclusion must be true. _____

13 Valid arguments are by definition correct, and correct arguments are by definition valid. _____

14 In deductions, the premises entail the conclusion. _____

15 In deductions, the premises may be true or false. _____

16 All inductions are nonvalid, or invalid. _____

17 Inductions may be correct or incorrect. _____

18 An argument may be correct but not valid. _____

19 If *P* represents the premise set and *C* represents the conclusion, then in deductions, the relation between *P* and *C* is "*P* entails *C*." _____

20 In inductions, the premises may be false or true. _____

21 Words like "since" and "because" always indicate a premise of an argument. _____

22 "If it rains, the Mets won't play" is an example of a deductive argument. _____

23 "The Mets didn't play because it rained" is an example of an inductive argument. _____

24 "Sam is taller than Sally and Sally is taller than Harry; so Sam is taller than Harry" is an example of a deductive argument. _____

25 "The footprints in the clay matched Sam's; so Sam was the culprit" is an example of an inductive argument. _____

Statements

Progress Test 7 (Chapter Three)
Indicate which of the following are statements by putting S in the space provided.

1 Tomorrow is Tuesday. _____

2 Please try not to cause any trouble. _____

3 Tomatoes are classified as fruit. _____

4 Let's think this over carefully. _____

5 Why should they expect *us* to attend? _____

6 May all your days be fruitful. _____

7 We'll probably see a sharp decline in the GNP next year. _____

8 I ask the Lord my soul to keep. _____

9 I was told that the meeting was cancelled. _____

10 I'll not take "no" for an answer. _____

11 Unfortunately, the steak was overdone. _____

12   Twelve is larger than a baker's dozen.   _____
13   I now pronounce you man and wife.   _____
14   All mimsy were the borogoves, and the momraths outgrabe.   _____
15   I'll wager that the series doesn't last six games.   _____
16   Do you call *that* clear thinking?   _____
17   The square root of 9 is 3.   _____
18   In case of rain, take along an umbrella.   _____
19   $E = mc^2$ _____
20   How about doing me a little favor?   _____
21   Do we get stronger by doing nothing?   _____
22   If you love me, then marry me.   _____
23   Help, I'm drowning.   _____
24   Blue ran tomorrow.   _____
25   If you're a good boy, I promise to take you to the circus.   _____
26   Can anyone convince him?   _____
27   A friend in need is a friend indeed.   _____
28   If it comforts you, we're both mistaken.   _____
29   Dog is man's best friend.   _____
30   To my dear sister I leave my automobile.   _____

Arguments

Progress Test 8 (Chapter Three)
Indicate which of the following are arguments by putting A in the space provided.

1   Leonardo was a student of Verrocchio.   It is reasonable to suppose that some of his techniques resemble Verrocchio's.   _____
2   The word "carnal" comes from a Greek word meaning "flesh." In Western culture, the word "flesh" has frequently connoted something unclean.   _____
3   Since iodine is an antiseptic, it is used for cuts and bruises.   _____
4   It *must* have rained.   This grass isn't wet just from the dew.   _____
5   If dreams are wish fulfillments, then what are hallucinations?   _____
6   There is a big difference between the British and American forms of government.   In the British parliamentary system there is no strong executive branch and no real checks on the legislature.   _____
7   Spaghetti vongole is my favorite spaghetti dish, but carbonara comes a close second.   _____
8   Erroneous beliefs are not uncommon.   For years many believed that people walked upside down at the antipodes.   _____
9   Every symptom can be treated by treating its cause.   So, if you're allergic to milk chocolate, why do you eat it?   _____
10   If $x^2 - 9 = 0$, then x must equal 3.   _____

In the space provided, write the subject and last word of the conclusions contained in the following arguments. Note that some of the selections contain more than one conclusion.

11 Good works do not make a good man, but a good man does good works. Bad works do not make a bad man, but a bad man does bad works. Thus it is always necessary that the substance or person should be good before any good works can be done, and that good works should follow and proceed from a good person. As Christ says: "A good tree cannot bring forth evil fruit, neither can a corrupt tree bring forth good fruit."

Martin Luther, *On Christian Liberty* _____

_____

12 No man is allowed to be judge in his own cause, because his interest would certainly bias his judgment, and, not improbably, corrupt his integrity. With equal, nay with greater reason, a body of men are unfit to be both judges and parties at the same time; yet what are many of the most important acts of legislation, but so many judicial decisions, not indeed, concerning the rights of single persons, but concerning the rights of large bodies of citizens?

James Madison, *Federalist, No. X* _____

_____

_____

13 Had we but world enough, and time,
This coyness, Lady, were no crime. . . .
But at my back I always hear
Time's winged chariot hurrying near; . . .
Now, therefore, while the youthful hue
Sits on thy skin like morning dew, ...
Now let us sport us while we may,
And now, like amorous birds of prey,
Rather at once our time devour
Than languish in his slow-chapped power.

Andrew Marvell, "To His Coy Mistress" _____

_____

14 Notwithstanding the tendency of wages to conform to their natural rate, their market rate may, in an improving society, for an indefinite period, be constantly above it; for no sooner may the impulse which an increased capital gives to a new demand for labor be obeyed, than another increase of capital may produce the same effect; and thus, if the increase of capital be gradual and constant, the demand for labor may give a continued stimulus to an increase of people.

David Ricardo, *Principles of Political Economy and Taxation* _____

_____

15 It has been thought a considerable advance towards establishing the principle of freedom to say that government is a compact between those who govern and those who are governed; but this cannot be true, because it is putting the effect before the cause; for as man must have existed before governments existed, there necessarily was a time when governments did not exist.

Thomas Paine, *The Rights of Man* _____

_____

16 Men have various dispositions, which are different from, and diametrically opposed to, one another. There is one man who is irascible, and is continually angry; while there is another who is of a calm disposition and does not get angry at all; and even if he gets angry, his wrath is mild, and this only happens once in several years. There is one man who is exceedingly haughty, while there is another who is exceedingly meek. There is one man who is voluptuous, whose soul can never be satisfied with indulging in pleasures; while there is another whose heart is so pure, that he desires not even the bare necessities which the body requires.

Moses Maimonides, *Mishneh Torah* _____

_____

17 I observe that many of our complex ideas never had impressions that corresponded to them, and that many of our complex impressions never are exactly copied in ideas. I can imagine to myself such a city as the New Jerusalem, whose pavement is gold and walls are rubies, though I never saw any such. I have seen Paris; but shall I affirm I can form such an idea of that city as will perfectly represent all its streets and houses in their real and just proportions? I perceive, therefore, that though there is in general a great resemblance betwixt our complex impressions and ideas, yet the rule is not universally true that they are exact copies of each other.

David Hume, "On the Origin
of Our Ideas" _____

_____

18 "Nature cannot distinguish the just from the unjust," must by no means be admitted. For though man is indeed an animal, he is an uncommon animal, differing much more from all other animals than they differ from one another; this is evidenced in many actions peculiar to the human species. Among the attributes peculiar to man is the desire for society . . . for communion with his fellow-man . . . for a tranquil association and one suited to the quality of his intellect. . . . Therefore, the statement that by nature every animal is impelled to seek only its own advantage cannot be conceded in this general form.

Hugo Grotius, *On the Law of
Peace and War* _____

_____

Inductive and Deductive Arguments

Progress Test 9 (Chapter Three)
Write I for inductive argument or D for deductive argument after each of the following arguments.

1 Boswell's last two books were mysteries; so his next one will probably be a mystery. _____

2 There are no gold mountains; so there is no gold mountain in Tibet. _____

3 Since $A = 6b^3$, when $b = 2$, $A = 48$. _____

4 The sprinklers were on; so someone must have been home. _____

5 French is spoken in Montreal, and Montreal is in Canada; so French is spoken in Canada. _____

6 If John is being honored at commencement, he will be notified. Since he hasn't heard anything, we can only assume he isn't being honored.

7 Independent thinkers are often misunderstood. Emerson was often misunderstood, and so was Hegel, Mill, Heidegger, and Plato. _____

8 He was born in New Orleans; so he's a native-born American. _____

9 Henry has difficulty reading. I never see him touch a book, and he's been taught by the new phonetic method, which has been giving students a lot of trouble. _____

10 Trains which don't stop at this station are express trains; so that last train must have been an express since it didn't stop. _____

11 Steve is the brother of Bob, and Bob is the brother of Michael; so Steve is the brother of Michael. _____

12 Fire is possible only if oxygen is present. Since oxygen is present, there's always the possibility of fire. _____

13 Khruschev was a good friend of capitalism; he liked football and he liked to come to New York. _____

14 How can we take the word of a man who says he is against integration when he speaks in the South and for integration when he speaks in the North? _____

15 In the event of rain, the game was to be cancelled. I hear it's just been cancelled; so it must be raining. _____

16 If a child has measles, a characteristic spotting effect is visible. This child has the characteristic spots; so she has measles. _____

17 My last Ford was a great car. Since this one is also a Ford, it will be a great car. _____

18 If the plane stopped in Chicago, it will be late. It stopped in Chicago; hence it will be late. _____

19 A great many people like spaghetti; so, likely, Sam does. _____

20 Jack was the sole owner of the tavern; so he had no partners. _____

Statement Connectives

Progress Test 10 (Chapter Four)
In the following pairs of statements, each a statement may be symbolized as ~p. Indicate whether the b statement is a correct representation of p. If it is, place a check (✔) in the space provided.

1 **a** It is inconceivable that interest rates would go so high.
   b It is conceivable that interest rates would go so high.   _____

2 **a** It's not true that steam engines are cleaner than diesels.
   b Steam engines are cleaner than diesels.   _____

3 **a** She was not cooperative.
   b She was uncooperative.   _____

4 **a** Newspaper comics aren't really funny.
   b Newspaper comics are really funny.   _____

5 **a** Some students did not fail the exam.
   b Some students did fail the exam.   _____

Check (✔) each of the following which may be formalized as p · q.

6 Though I hate to say it, I must.   _____
7 The Knicks were good as long as Willis Reed played center.   _____
8 Frazier is a great guard, but the Knicks have a weak bench.   _____
9 Johnson and Boswell were collaborators.   _____
10 A bushel of apples and a bushel of pears makes two bushels.   _____
11 While I respect his right to speak, I disagree with what he says.   _____
12 A good book is more interesting than a good film.   _____
13 She was lovely and bright as well.   _____
14 Parents are complaining; students are complaining.   _____
15 The Allies landed at Normandy and the invasion was under way.   _____
16 Four and three equals seven.   _____
17 Russia and the United States fought against Germany in World War II.   _____
18 The war between Athens and Sparta lasted thirty years.   _____
19 Sit down and be quiet.   _____
20 He came to this country in 1899 and became a wealthy man.   _____

In the following, identify those which clearly indicate the exclusive use of "or." Use I for inclusive, E for exclusive.

21 Holmes was intuitive or very clever.   _____
22 The car was driven by the mayor or his chauffeur.   _____
23 Paris is in France or Kentucky.   _____
24 Either Hitler is dead or you can't believe the papers.   _____
25 You will be admitted with a ticket or an invitation.   _____

26 Either the carburetor or the fuel pump was clogged. _____

27 His lone escort was Mary or Susan. _____

28 The door is closed on windy or on rainy days. _____

29 Either Route 115 passes through Wilkes-Barre or Route 73 does. _____

30 Either they love each other or enjoy each other's company. _____

31 His accent was either acquired or was an affectation. _____

32 A walrus is either a denizen of the deep or a mammal. _____

33 A headache can be caused by tension or eyestrain. _____

34 The plane fell into the sea or hit a mountain peak. _____

35 It always pays to be prudent or conscientious. _____

If possible, symbolize each of the following as $p \supset q$. Take the first affirmative statement as p, the second as q.

36 In case of rain, the concert will be cancelled. _____

37 She won't tolerate brashness unless she loves you. _____

38 She loves you only if she tolerates your brashness. _____

39 She loves you, if she tolerates your brashness. _____

40 The South would have won the Civil War only if the North had not mobilized so quickly. _____

41 Unless you are prepared, you won't pass. _____

42 You should have many children only if you love children. _____

43 If sugar dissolves in water, then it is water-soluble. _____

44 He will sign only on condition that he gets a bonus. _____

45 Provided that you have paid your library bill, you will graduate. _____

Place a check (✔) after each of the following which may be symbolized as $p \equiv q$.

46 Koko is a poodle only if she is a dog. _____

47 If and only if you place in the top three will you win a prize. _____

48 The car will be ready if you decide to go. _____

49 X is a rectangle if and only if its angles are right angles. _____

50 Your tactic will work if and only if the others cooperate. _____

Statement Connectives: Summary

Progress Test 11 (Chapter Four)
Put each of the following into form, if possible. Take the first affirmative statement as p, the second as q.

1 Though the results are not conclusive, we have reason to believe that Mars does have an atmosphere. _____

2 We often tolerate incompetent teaching because we have no other alternative. _____

3 Isn't a summer sunset something to behold! _____

4 If beauty is in the eyes of the beholder, then what is beautiful to one may not be beautiful to another. _____

5 Neither our oceans nor our streams are free from pollution. _____

6 Jack and Jill went up the hill to fetch a pail of water. _____

7 Despite the fact that everyone has good intentions, it is not easy to say whether the outcome in each case will be successful. _____

8 Either there is little evidence that unconscious motivations exist or psychoanalysis is unsuccessful. _____

9 Certain claims made by ESP advocates would be credible only if much more data were available. _____

10 A strenuous effort is sometimes gratifying if it is well received. _____

11 Misstating facts is immoral if and only if there is a deliberate intention to do so. _____

12 Lying is never justified unless the circumstances are truly exceptional. _____

13 If we meet the deadline, then we'll celebrate. _____

14 Humpty-Dumpty sat on a wall; Humpty-Dumpty had a great fall. _____

15 In case of inclement weather, take a raincoat. _____

16 Studying is tolerable only if the subject isn't dull. _____

17 Capital punishment prevents rehabilitation and in some cases may actually encourage murder. _____

18 Students living in New York can go to either a community college or a state university. _____

19 I'll bet you the Derby winner doesn't win the Preakness. _____

20 Where there is no vision, the people perish. _____

Logical Punctuation

Progress Test 12 (Chapter Four)
In the following formulas, indicate the main connective if there is one.

1 $p \lor qr$ _____

2 $(p \lor q)(\sim q \supset r)$ _____

3 $[(\sim pq) \lor (q \supset r)] \supset p$ _____

4 $\sim [(p \equiv q)(r \supset s) \sim (r \lor p)]$ _____

5 $[\sim (p \supset q) \lor (\sim pq)] \supset (p \equiv q)$ _____

6 $\sim p \lor (q \lor r \lor s)$ _____

7 $[(p \lor q) \supset (qr)] \lor r$ _____

8 $(p \lor \sim q \lor \sim r)s$ _____

9 pqr _____

10 $(pq \supset r) \equiv (r \lor s)$ _____

Express the following in the symbolism. Take the first affirmative statement as p, the second as q, etc.

11 Either the Flyers or the Rockets will win and the fans will be happy.

_____

12 The Flyers will win or the Islanders and Canadians will be surprised.

_____

13 If Seaver or Matlack is pitching, then the Mets have a chance. _____
14 Either Seaver is pitching or if Matlack is, then the Mets have a chance.

_____

15 Seaver will pitch and either Milner is playing first base or if Staub is, then Jones is in the outfield. _____
16 Jones will be in the outfield and Matlack is pitching or if Staub is at first base, then Millan plays second. _____
17 If either Jones is in the outfield and Matlack is pitching or Staub is at first base, then Millan plays second. _____
18 It is not the case that Jones plays first base or that Seaver is in the outfield. _____
19 Kranepool doesn't play regularly and Tate is a pitcher. _____
20 If it is false that Jones plays first base and Seaver is an outfielder, then Matlack or Tate is a pitcher. _____

Truth Functions

Progress Test 13 (Chapter Five)
Answer the following questions. Use T for true, F for false.

1 What is the truth value of $p \vee q$ when p is true? _____
2 What is the truth value of $p \supset q$ when q is true? _____
3 What is the truth value of pq when p is false? _____
4 What is the truth value of $p \supset (q \vee r)$ when p is false? _____
5 What is the truth value of $(pq) \supset (p \vee q)$ when q is false? _____
6 What is the truth value of $p \vee (q \supset r) \vee (pq \supset \sim r)$ when p is false? _____
7 Under what condition is a conjunction of statements true? _____
8 Under what condition is an alternation of statements false? _____
9 Under what condition is a biconditional false? _____
10 Under what condition is a conditional false? _____

Given that p, q, and r are true and that s, t, and u are false, indicate the truth value of the following. Use T for true, F for false.

11 $p \vee (qs)$ _____
12 $(p \supset q)s$ _____
13 $(p \vee r)(s \vee t)$ _____
14 $p \equiv t$ _____

15 $s \supset (p \supset q)$ _____

16 $\sim p \supset (s \equiv t)$ _____

17 $\sim(p \vee q)r$ _____

18 $pq \vee rt \vee ps$ _____

19 $[(p \supset r)(s \vee t) \vee q] \supset p$ _____

20 $(pq \vee rt) \sim (tu) \vee (s \supset p)$ _____

Truth Tables

Progress Test 14 (Chapter Five)
Write T for true and F for false in the spaces after each statement.

1   A truth table gives the truth value of a formula under all interpretations of its variables.   _____

2   If a formula is false under all interpretations of its variables, it is a contradiction.

3   If P entails Q, then $P \supset Q$ is a tautology.   _____

4   If "P, therefore Q" is valid, then $P \supset Q$ is a contingency.   _____

5   In the shortened truth-table method for determining validity, one should try to make the consequent true and the antecedent false.   _____

6   To determine the truth value of a contingency, one must know the truth values of the statement variables.   _____

7   Tautologies can tell us nothing about the world.   _____

8   To determine the truth value of contradictions, we need to appeal to the facts of the world.   _____

9   We need to know whether the statement "Today is Monday," is true or is false before we can determine whether "If today is Monday, then today is not Monday" is true or is false.   _____

10   If the antecedent of a material conditional is false, then the conditional is false.   _____

11   If a set of statements is consistent, then it is impossible for the conjunction of statements to be true.   _____

12 $\sim p \supset p$ is a contradiction.   _____

13   If "P, therefore Q" is valid, then $P \cdot \sim Q$ is a contradiction.   _____

14   If a set of statements is inconsistent, then their conjunction is a contingency.   _____

15   From an inconsistent premise set, one may deduce any statement whatever.   _____

16 $\sim pp \supset q$ is a contradiction.   _____

17   If the antecedent of a conditional is necessarily false, then the conditional is necessarily true.   _____

18   If P, Q, R entail S, then $P \cdot Q \cdot R \cdot \sim S$ is a contradiction.   _____

19   To determine whether a formula which is a biconditional is a tautology, find one case in which it comes out true.   _____

20 To determine whether a formula is not a tautology, find one case in which it comes out false. _____

Truth Tables

Progress Test 15 (Chapter Five)
In the following truth tables, some truth values have been omitted. Fill them in and write your answers in the appropriate spaces provided. For illustration, table 1 has been completed.

			b		a			a	b
1	p	q	(p v q)	⊃	pq			a	b
	T	T	T	T	T			T	T
	T	F	T	F	F			F	F
	F	T	T	F	F			F	F
	F	F	F	T	F			F	T

				b		a			a	b
2	p	q	p	v	(pq	≡	~q)		a	b
	T	T	T	___	T	___	FT		___	___
	T	F	T	___	F	___	TF		___	___
	F	T	F	___	F	___	FT		___	___
	F	F	F	___	F	___	TF		___	___

				b		a			a	b
3	p	q	(q ⊃ p)	⊃	(q	⊃	~p)		a	b
	T	T	T T T	___	T	___	FT		___	___
	T	F	F T T	___	F	___	FT		___	___
	F	T	T F F	___	T	___	TF		___	___
	F	F	F T F	___	F	___	TF		___	___

				b		a			a	b
4	p	q	~	[(p v pq)	≡	(~q ⊃ p)]			a	b
	T	T	___	T T T	___	FT T T			___	___
	T	F	___	T T F	___	TF T T			___	___
	F	T	___	F F F	___	FT T F			___	___
	F	F	___	F F F	___	TF F F			___	___

				a	b			a	b
5	p	q	r	(p ⊃ q)	⊃	[(r v p) ≡ (~r v p)]		a	b
	T	T	T	___	___	T T FT T T		___	___
	T	T	F	___	___	T T TF T T		___	___
	T	F	T	___	___	T T FT T T		___	___
	T	F	F	___	___	T T TF T T		___	___
	F	T	T	___	___	T F FT F F		___	___
	F	T	F	___	___	F F TF T F		___	___
	F	F	T	___	___	T F FT F F		___	___
	F	F	F	___	___	F F TF T F		___	___

As above, some truth values are missing from the following truth tables. Fill them in so as to determine whether the formula is a tautology, a contradiction, or a contingency. Write your answer in the spaces provided.

6

p	q	pq	∨	~q
T	T	T	_____	FT
T	F	F	_____	TF
F	T	F	_____	FT
F	F	F	_____	TF

_____

7

p	q	(p ⊃ ~q)	≡	pq
T	T	T F FT	_____	T
T	F	T T TF	_____	F
F	T	F T FT	_____	F
F	F	F T TF	_____	F

_____

8

			a		b	
p	q	(~p	≡	q)	⊃	(p ∨ q)
T	T	FT	_____	T	_____	T
T	F	FT	_____	F	_____	T
F	T	TF	_____	T	_____	T
F	F	TF	_____	F	_____	F

_____

9

		e		d		c	b	a
p	q	~	{pq	∨	[(p ≡ q)	∨	~	(pq)]}
T	T	_____	T	_____	T	_____	_____	_____
T	F	_____	F	_____	F	_____	_____	_____
F	T	_____	F	_____	F	_____	_____	_____
F	F	_____	F	_____	T	_____	_____	_____

_____

10

				b		c	a	
p	q	r	(p ≡ q)		(q ⊃ r)	⊃	(~p	∨	r)
T	T	T	T	T	T	_____	F	_____	T
T	T	F	T	F	F	_____	F	_____	F
T	F	T	F	_____	T	_____	F	_____	T
T	F	F	F	_____	T	_____	F	_____	F
F	T	T	F	_____	T	_____	T	_____	T
F	T	F	F	_____	F	_____	T	_____	F
F	F	T	T	_____	T	_____	T	_____	T
F	F	F	T	_____	T	_____	T	_____	F

_____

Validity: I

Progress Test 16 (Chapter Five)
In the following exercises, steps have been omitted. Fill them in so that you may determine whether the argument is valid or invalid. Write your answer in the space provided.

1 If detergents are not polluters, then shampoos are; but shampoos aren't polluters, so it must be that detergents are. (p = detergents are polluters; q = shampoos are polluters.)

	1st premise	2d premise	con-clusion
$\sim p \supset q$	$\sim p \quad \supset \quad q$	$\sim q$	____
$\sim q$	FT ____ T	FT	____
$\therefore$ ____	FT ____ F	TF	____
	TF ____ T	FT	____
	TF ____ F	TF	____ _____

2 Pie eaters tend to be overweight or pies are not fattening. As with cake, ice cream, and most good things, pies are fattening, so pie eaters tend to be overweight. (p = pie eaters tend to be overweight; q = pies are fattening.)

	1st premise	2d premise	con-clusion
$p \vee \sim q$	$p \quad \vee \quad \sim q$	____	p
____	T T FT	____	T
$\therefore p$ ____	T T TF	____	T
	F F FT	____	F
	F T TF	____	F _____

3 If and only if Shirl has an M.D. degree does she practice medicine. She practices medicine or she has an M.D. degree. Hence she has an M.D. degree.

	1st premise	2d premise	con-clusion
____	_____	$p \quad \vee \quad q$	p
$p \vee q$	_____	T T T	T
$\therefore p$	_____	T T F	T
	_____	F T T	F
	_____	F F F	F _____

4 Sam will go only if Harry goes. But if Harry goes, then Edith won't. So, Sam won't go unless Edith does. (p = Sam goes; q = Harry goes; r = Edith goes.)

	p	q	r	1st premise $p \supset q$	2d premise $q \supset \sim r$	con- clusion $p \supset r$
$p \supset q$	T	T	T	T		
$q \supset \sim r$	T	T	F	T		
$\therefore p \supset r$	T	F	T	F		
	T	F	F	F		
	F	T	T	T		
	F	T	F	T		
	F	F	T	T		
	F	F	F	T		_____

Progress Test 17 (Chapter Five)

In each of the following shortened truth tables, truth values have been omitted. Fill them in so as to show whether the formula is a tautology or not. Indicate the tautologies by writing "taut" in the space provided.

  T   F

1 $[(p \supset q)p] \supset q$ _____

      TF   F

2 $[(p \vee q)\sim p] \supset q$ _____

   F T F   F

3 $[(p \equiv q)\sim q] \supset p$ _____

  T   T   T

4 $p \supset (pq \vee \sim qp)$ _____

  F   F T F   F

5 $(p \supset q)(\sim q \supset r)(s \equiv p) \supset s$ _____

  F   T F   F

6 $(p \supset q)(\sim q \supset s)(s \vee p) \supset p$ _____

   F F F   T   F F F

7 $[(p \vee qs) \supset (t \supset u)] \sim (u \vee s) \supset (p \vee q)$ _____

            F T   TF T TT   FF

8 $(pr \vee pq)(r \supset t)(\sim t \supset pq) \supset rt$ _____

                    F

9 $(p \supset qr)(s \vee t) \supset \sim qt$ _____

10 $[(pr \vee q) \supset (r \equiv t)] \sim (r \vee q) \supset \sim (pt)$ _____

Proofs

Progress Test 18 (Chapter Six)
In each of the following proofs, justifications and occasional lines have been omitted. Fill in the missing lines and put the justifications in the spaces provided. (All nineteen rules may be used.)

1
    1   $p \supset (q \supset r)$
 * 2 $r \supset s$
    3   pq $/\therefore s$
 * 4 $pq \supset r$ _____
 * 5   _____
 * 6 s _____

2
 * 1 $(p \supset q)(q \supset p)$
    2   $\sim q(r \supset ps)$ $/\therefore r$
 * 3 $p \supset q$ _____
 * 4 $\sim q$ _____
 * 5   _____
 * 6 $\sim p \vee \sim s$ _____
 * 7 $\sim (ps)$ _____
 * 8 $(r \supset ps)\sim q$ _____
 * 9   _____
*10 $\sim r$ _____

3
    1   $p \supset q$
 * 2 $r \supset s$
    3   $(p \vee r)\sim q$ $/\therefore s$
 * 4   _____
 * 5 $p \vee r$ _____
 * 6 $q \vee s$ _____
 * 7 $\sim q(p \vee r)$ _____
 * 8   _____
 * 9 s _____

4
 * 1 $pq \supset r$
    2   $\sim p \supset s$ $/\therefore q \supset (r \vee s)$
 * 3 $p \supset (q \supset r)$ _____
 * 4 $\sim (q \supset r) \supset \sim p$ _____
 * 5   _____
 * 6 $(q \supset r) \vee s$ _____
 * 7 $\sim q \vee r \vee s$ _____
 * 8 $\sim q \vee (r \vee s)$ _____
 * 9   _____

5
 * 1 $p \supset (\sim q \supset \sim r)$
    2   $q \supset s$ $/\therefore p \supset (q \supset s)$
** 3 p _____
** 4 $\sim q \supset \sim r$ _____

```
 **  5    _____
 **  6    r ⊃ s                  _____
  *  7    p ⊃ (r ⊃ s)            _____
6    ⎧ 1    p ∨ qr
   * ⎨ 2    ~s ≡ t
     ⎩ 3    q ⊃ (r ⊃ s)    /∴ t ⊃ p
  *  4    (~s ⊃ t)(t ⊃ ~s)       _____
  *  5    (t ⊃ ~s)(~s ⊃ t)       _____
  *  6    t ⊃ ~s                 _____
 **  7    t                      _____
 **  8                           _____
 **  9    qr ⊃ s                 _____
 **10                            _____
 **11    qr ∨ p                  _____
 **12    p                       _____
  *13    t ⊃ p                   _____
7    ⎧ 1    ~(p~q)
   * ⎨ 2    (q ⊃ r)(p ∨ ~s)
     ⎩ 3    s      /∴ r
 **  4    ~r                     _____
 **  5    q ⊃ r                  _____
 **  6                           _____
 **  7    ~p ∨ ~~q               _____
 **  8    ~p ∨ q                 _____
 **  9                           _____
 **10    ~p                      _____
 **11    (p ∨ ~s)(q ⊃ r)         _____
 **12    p ∨ ~s                  _____
 **13    ~s ∨ p                  _____
 **14                            _____
 **15    p                       _____
 **16    p · ~p                  _____
8    ⎧ 1    pq ⊃ r
   * ⎨ 2    r ⊃ s
     ⎩ 3    q~s      /∴ ~p
 **  4    p                      _____
 **  5    p ⊃ (q ⊃ r)            _____
 **  6                           _____
 **  7                           _____
 **  8    r                      _____
 **  9                           _____
 **10    ~sq                     _____
 **11                            _____
 **12    s · ~s                  _____
```

9 $\begin{cases} \textbf{1} & p \supset q \\ *\textbf{2} & \sim(r \sim s)) \\ \textbf{3} & q \supset \sim s \qquad /\therefore p \supset \sim r \end{cases}$

** **4** _____

** **5** q _____

** **6** $\sim s$ _____

** **7** _____

** **8** _____

** **9** $r \supset s$ _____

**10 _____

11 _____

10 $\begin{cases} *\textbf{1} & (p \supset q)(r \supset s) \\ \textbf{2} & q \supset \sim s \qquad /\therefore p \supset \sim r \end{cases}$

* **3** _____

* **4** $p \supset \sim s$ _____

* **5** $(r \supset s)(p \supset q)$ _____

* **6** _____

* **7** _____

.* **8** _____

Standard-Form Categorical Statements

Progress Test 19 (Chapter Seven)
Using the letters A, E, I, O, indicate what each of the following would be translated into and write the subject of each translated statement.

1   A man without a purpose in life is like a ship without a sail.
____ _____

2   One should never trust a chronic liar.
____ _____

3   Not all novels are interesting.   ____ _____
4   Some lotus eaters are also people who daydream.
____ _____

5   Every teenager likes rock music.   ____ _____
6   There are no swarthy Scandinavians.
____ _____

7   The girl who asked the question was a college student.
____ _____

8   Only men are priests.   ____ _____
9 A few bridge players are friendly. ____ _____
10   He who dislikes others dislikes himself.
____ _____

11   Pomegranates are usually delicious.
____ _____

12 None but Americans tip in European restaurants.

_____ _____

13 Worthwhile tasks are always arduous.

_____ _____

14 There are people who work hard but manage to relax.

_____ _____

15 None of the people attending the concert were inattentive.

_____ _____

16 Not everything which tastes good is nutritious.

_____ _____

17 One can't race at Indianapolis unless he qualifies.

_____ _____

18 If anything is a square, then it has four right angles.

_____ _____

19 All except season ticket holders have to wait in line.

_____ _____

20 Conflicting views characterize all public debates.

_____ _____

21 I met a million-dollar baby in a five-and-ten-cent store.

_____ _____

22 You make me happy when skies are gray.

_____ _____

23 Everybody loves somebody.   _____ _____
24 Good things don't always come in small packages.

_____ _____

25 An unkempt and likeable fellow was singing songs.

_____ _____

Progress Test 20 (Chapter Seven)
**Indicate whether b is a correct translation of a.   Check only those which
are correct.**

1 a He who hesitates is lost.
   b All lost people are hesitaters.   _____
2 a Not all cookies are fattening.
   b Some cookies are not fattening.   _____
3 a There are no meat-eating goats.
   b Some goats are not meat eaters.   _____
4 a Only the diligent are rewarded.
   b All who are rewarded are diligent.   _____
5 a I had lunch with Harold.
   b Some time that I had lunch was a time I had lunch with
     Harold.   _____
6 a When it rains, it pours.
   b All times when it pours are times when it rains.   _____

7   a   The man in the trench coat is not a detective.
    b   No men in trench coats are detectives.   _____
8   a   Blessed are the meek.
    b   All who are meek are blessed.   _____
9   a   Some children are never cranky.
    b   No times are times when some children are cranky. _____
10 a   Almost all the apples were ripe.
    b   Some apples are not apples which were ripe.   _____
11 a   Everything which is edible is not healthful.
    b   Some things which are healthful are not edible. _____
12 a   A porpoise is a mammal.
    b   Some porpoise is a mammal.   _____
13 a   Some professors are never relaxed.
    b   Some professors are professors who are never relaxed. _____
14 a   None but heroes are honored.
    b   All heroes are honored.   _____
15 a   It is not the case that good deeds are forgotten.
    b   No good deeds are forgotten.   _____

The Immediate Inferences

Progress Test 21 (Chapter Seven)
Check only those where b is a correct conversion of a.

1   a   All hockey players have broken noses.
    b   Some hockey players have broken noses.   _____
2   a   Trapezoids are all four-sided.
    b   Some four-sided figures are trapezoids.   _____
3   a   No VW's are made in Italy.
    b   None of the Italian-made vehicles are VW's.   _____
4   a   Not all triangles are equilateral.
    b   Some equilaterals are not triangles.   _____
5   a   Some plane figures are rhomboids.
    b   Some rhomboids are plane figures.   _____

Check only those where b is a correct obversion of a.

6   a   All neurotics are abnormal.
    b   No neurotics are normal.   _____
7   a   Some eleven-year-olds are mature.
    b   Some eleven-year-olds are not immature.   _____
8   a   Some choices are voluntary.
    b   No choices are involuntary.   _____
9   a   Not all people are honest.
    b   Some people are dishonest.   _____

10 a   An unmarried male is sometimes insecure.
     b   An unmarried male is never secure.   _____
11 a   No Freudians are behaviorists.
     b   All Freudians are non-behaviorists.   _____
12 a   Some behavior is not conditioned.
     b   Some behavior is unconditioned.   _____
13 a   There are no happy neurotics.
     b   No happy person is non-neurotic.   _____
14 a   Everyone was unpleasant.
     b   No one was pleasant.   _____
15 a   Some schizophrenics are impotent.
     b   Some potent persons are not schizophrenics.   _____

Check only those where b is a correct contrapositive of a.

16 a   All employees are eligible.
     b   All ineligible persons are non-employees.   _____
17 a   Some bikinis are immodest.
     b   Some immodest garments are non-bikinis.   _____
18 a   No resident is assessed.
     b   All assessed persons are non-residents.   _____
19 a   All those who are unemployed are without income.
     b   All those who have income are employed.   _____
20 a   Some hard workers are not richly rewarded.
     b   Some who are non-richly rewarded are non-hard workers.   _____

Truth Relations

Progress Test 22 (Chapter Seven)
Assuming a is true, indicate the truth value of b. Then, assuming a is false, indicate the truth value of b. Use T for true, F for false, and ? for undetermined.

1	a	Some *S* is not *P*.	T	F
	b	All *S* is *P*.	___	___
2	a	Some *S* is not *P*.	T	F
	b	Some *S* is *P*.	___	___
3	a	No *S* is *P*.	T	F
	b	Some *S* is not *P*.	___	___
4	a	Some *S* is *P*.	T	F
	b	No *S* is *P*.	___	___
5	a	No *S* is *P*.	T	F
	b	Some *S* is *P*.	___	___
6	a	Some *S* is *P*.	T	F
	b	Some *S* is not *P*.	___	___

7	a	No S is P.	T	F
	b	All S is P.		
8	a	All S is P.	T	F
	b	Some S is not P.		
9	a	All S is P.	T	F
	b	Some S is P.		
10	a	All S is P.	T	F
	b	No S is P.		
11	a	Spaghetti is fattening.	T	F
	b	Some spaghetti is not fattening.		
12	a	Eclipses are predictable.	T	F
	b	Eclipses are not predictable.		
13	a	The Fiat is made in Italy.	T	F
	b	Some Fiats are made in Italy.		
14	a	Some hockey players have broken noses.	T	F
	b	Some hockey players do not have broken noses.		
15	a	There are American mountains which are higher than the Alps.	T	F
	b	Some American mountains are not higher than the Alps.		
16	a	No carpets are made in Finland.	T	F
	b	Some carpets are not made in Finland.		
17	a	There are no churches with artwork like that found in Italian churches.	T	F
	b	Every church has artwork like that found in Italian churches.		
18	a	Not all compact cars are economical.	T	F
	b	All compact cars are economical.		
19	a	Students never study for exams.	T	F
	b	Students always study for exams.		
20	a	There is no camera like the Instamatic.	T	F
	b	Some cameras are like the Instamatic.		

Progress Test 23 (Chapter Seven)
Using the following code: 1, contradictory; 2, contrary; 3, subcontrary; 4, implicant; 5, subimplicant; 6, equivalent; and 7, independent — indicate the relationship that b holds to a in the following pairs.

1 a Only politicians are self-seeking.
   b No politicians are self-seeking.   _____

2 a My car is always dependable.
   b Sometimes my car is dependable.   _____

3 a None but the foolhardy take chances.
   b The foolhardy do anything but take chances. _____

4 a Not all tobacco is Cuban.
   b There is Cuban tobacco.   _____

5   **a**   A country without free elections is not a democracy.

      b   A democracy is not a country without free elections. _____

6   **a**   A social philosophy is always an outgrowth of political and economic conditions.

      b   Social philosophies are sometimes an outgrowth of political and economic conditions. _____

7   **a**   Everything he writes is challenging.

      b   Once in a while he writes something which is not challenging. _____

8   **a**   Poems are not all rhymed.

      b   Poems are never rhymed. _____

9   **a**   Only the fittest survive.

      b   No; only the survivors are fit. _____

10   **a**   A whale is a fish.

      b   It is not true that a whale is a fish. _____

11   **a**   Any one who likes Bach is a music lover.

      b   No one who likes Bach is a music lover. _____

12   **a**   There are students here from Canada.

      b   There are no students here from Canada. _____

13   **a**   Sangria is a Spanish wine.

      b   Sangria isn't always a Spanish wine. _____

14   **a**   Some fish is broiled.

      b   Some fish is not broiled. _____

15   **a**   Italian guides are always polite.

      b   There are polite Italian guides. _____

16   **a**   Not every painting is successful.

      b   Some paintings are successful. _____

17   **a**   There aren't any Italian dishes which use curry.

      b   Some Italian dishes do not use curry. _____

18   **a**   Only fresh fish is used in Sashimi.

      b   Fresh fish is never used in Sashimi. _____

19   **a**   Szechuan cooking is spicy.

      b   Some Szechuan cooking is not spicy. _____

20   **a**   American cars come equipped with heaters.

      b   Some American cars come equipped with heaters. _____

21   **a**   Everything he did was meaningless.

      b   He did nothing which was meaningful. _____

22   **a**   Some points are indisputable.

      b   Some points can be argued. _____

23   **a**   There are no non-sinkable rafts.

      b   No rafts are sinkable. _____

24   **a**   Only latecomers are penalized.

      b   Some who come on time are penalized. _____

25   **a**   Fathers are not consistent.
       b   All fathers are inconsistent.   _____
26   **a**   Some sounds are inaudible to human ears.
       b   There are sounds which are not audible to human ears.   _____
27   **a**   Every tulip is a flower.
       b   Flowers are all tulips.   _____
28   **a**   An uninformed action is never productive.
       b   All actions which are productive are informed.   _____
29   **a**   Some non-Frenchman is a non-Asian.
       b   Some Asian is a Frenchman.   _____
30   **a**   There are a few sincere teachers.
       b   All non-teachers are insincere.   _____

Progress Test 24 (Chapter Seven)

Assuming the first statement to be true, indicate what can be inferred about the remaining statements in each of the following sets. Then, assuming the first statement to be false, do the same. Use T for true, F for false, and ? for undetermined.

1   **a**   Everyone present was responsible.   T   F
       b   No one present was responsible.   ____   ____
       c   Some who were present were responsible.   ____   ____
       d   Some who were present were not responsible.   ____   ____
2   **a**   There are no cantankerous Geishas.   I   F
       b   Some Geishas are cantankerous.   ____   ____
       c   Geishas are cantankerous.   ____   ____
       d   Geishas are not all cantankerous.   ____   ____
3   **a**   Some places where it is foggy are beautiful.   T   F
       b   Foggy places are never beautiful.   ____   ____
       c   If a place is foggy, then it is beautiful.   ____   ____
       d   There are foggy places which are not beautiful.   ____   ____
4   **a**   There are times when patience is not expected.   T   F
       b   Patience is always to be expected.   ____   ____
       c   One should never expect patience.   ____   ____
       d   Sometimes patience is to be expected.   ____   ____

If "Some investments are unwise" is false, what can be inferred about the following?

5   **a**   Some investments are not wise.   _____
       b   All investments are unwise.   _____
       c   Investments are always wise.   _____
       d   All unwise things are investments.   _____
       e   There are wise investments.   _____
       f   If anything is wise, then it is an investment.   _____

g No non-wise thing is a non-investment. _____
h Not all investments are unwise. _____
i Only investments are unwise. _____
j Some investments are not unwise. _____

Standard-Form Categorical Syllogisms

Progress Test 25 (Chapter Eight)
Indicate the mood and figure of the following. Then, of the four rules of the syllogism listed:

1. **The middle term must be distributed at least once.**
2. **A term distributed in the conclusion must be distributed in the premise in which it appears.**
3. **At least one premise must be affirmative.**
4. **If the conclusion is negative, then one premise must be negative, and if one premise is negative, then the conclusion must be negative.**

Indicate which one, if any, is violated. If the form is valid, write V.

	Mood and figure	Rule violation	Valid or invalid
1 No *M* is *P*; therefore, some *P* are *G*, since some *M* are *G*.	_____	_____	_____
2 All *H* is *F*; that is because all *F* are *G* and all *G* are *H*.	_____	_____	_____
3 All *W* are *M*, since many *C* are not *W* and no *C* is *M*.	_____	_____	_____
4 Some *K* is *L*; for some *K* are *G*, and all *L* are *G*.	_____	_____	_____
5 All *H* are *R* and some *R* are *L*; therefore, all *H* are *L*.	_____	_____	_____
6 Because some *K* is not *L*, and since no *J* is *L*, it follows that some *K* is not *J*.	_____	_____	_____
7 All *L* are *D*, since some *L* are *R* and all *R* are *D*.	_____	_____	_____
8 Some *S* is *P*, since all *S* is *M* and some *P* is *M*.	_____	_____	_____
9 No *I* is *N*, and all *N* are *D*; therefore, no *I* is *D*.	_____	_____	_____
10 No *M* is *P*; some *S* is *M*; so some *S* is not *P*.	_____	_____	_____
11 Everything which is worthwhile is worth striving for; but some things			

which are profitable are not worth striving for; hence some worthwhile things are not profitable (W, S, P).   ____ ____ ____

12   Not all lawsuits are justified; each divorce case is a lawsuit; so some divorce cases are not justified (L, J, D).   ____ ____ ____

13   A triangle with one 90-degree angle is a right triangle; right triangles are never isosceles; hence isosceles triangles never have a 90-degree angle (T, R, I).   ____ ____ ____

14   To grade fairly, one must grade according to a student's performance; to grade fairly, one must judge dispassionately; hence a grade based on a student's performance is one which was judged dispassionately (G, P, D).

____ ____ ____

15   Trees are never pruned in the spring; not all trees are deciduous; hence deciduous trees are not pruned in the spring (T, P, D).

____ ____ ____

16   All roads lead to Nome; any road which leads to Nome doesn't lead to Paris; so, some roads don't lead to Paris (R, N, P).   ____ ____ ____

17   If anything is admired, then good deeds are; if anything is remembered, then good deeds are; therefore, there are admired things which are remembered (A, G, R).   ____ ____ ____

18   You can't ignore economic danger signals with impunity; there are obvious economic danger signals; so there are obvious signals which can be ignored with impunity (E, I, O).   ____ ____ ____

19   Whenever the Dow Jones averages fall, the brokers become despondent; only when the Dow Jones averages fall is the price-earnings ratio affected; hence, if the brokers become despondent, the price-earnings ratio is affected (F, D, R).   ____ ____ ____

20   Not all syllogisms are invalid; a syllogism is invalid if it has two negative premises; hence some syllogisms have two negative premises (S, I, T).

____ ____ ____

Venn Diagrams

Progress Test 26 (Chapter Eight)
Assuming the hypothetical viewpoint, determine the validity of the following by means of Venn diagrams.   Underneath each diagram, write V for valid or I for invalid.

1   If Joe Namath is out, everyone beats the Jets; when everyone beats the Jets, there are plenty of empty seats in Shea; so there are plenty of empty seats in Shea when Joe Namath is out (J, E, P).

2   Referees sometimes favor the home team, since referees are usually intimidated, and those who favor the home team are frequently intimidated (*R, F, I*).

3   A baseball manager is subject to considerable harassment; umpires are not always subject to considerable harassment; hence baseball managers are not umpires (*B, S, U*).

4   Some hockey players are belligerent; belligerent players are not very sportsmanlike; so there are hockey players who are not very sportsmanlike (*H, B, S*).

5   A pitcher who can hit is valuable to a team; pitchers who can hit can't play regularly; so if a player is valuable to a team, he can play regularly (*P, V, R*).

6   Nobody notices the contribution of the lineman; everybody notices the star halfback; accordingly, those who notice the contribution of the lineman do not notice the star halfback (*P, C, S*).

7   Football players are always tough; so, since there are tough people who like to sing, some football players like to sing (*F, T, S*).

8   Only golfers wear colorful shirts; hence a golfer who wears colorful shirts has to be an exhibitionist, since golfers are exhibitionists (*G, C, E*).

9   No mathematician has squared the circle; only mathematicians worry about squaring circles; hence, some circle squarer doesn't worry about squaring circles (M, S, W).

10 Ice skaters train diligently; those who train diligently take pride in their performance; consequently, there are ice skaters who take pride in their performance (I, T, P).

Assume existential import for the following.

11 The playoff game was exciting. Exciting games are never forgotten; hence, the playoff game won't be forgotten (P, E, F).

12 The jaguar is a dangerous predator; it has a beautiful coat and runs very fast; hence there are predators which have beautiful coats, run very fast, and are dangerous (J, P, B).

13 There are no nonfattening jelly beans; some things which make you fat are nonetheless nutritious; so jelly beans are nutritious (F, J, N).

14 If you live in Buffalo, you live in Erie County; everyone who lives in Buffalo must get accustomed to snow; therefore some residents of Erie County must get accustomed to snow (B, E, S).

15 Fire engines are always painted red; there are no fire engines which are painted blue; accordingly, some things which are painted red are not painted blue (F, R, B).

Enthymemes and Singular Statements

Progress Test 27 (Chapter Eight)
In each of the following supply either the premise or conclusion which would make the argument valid.

1 Every immature person is irresponsible, so John is quite mature.

_____

2 If a philosophy is not non-obscure, it is unintelligible; that is why Heidegger's philosophy is not intelligible. _____

3 He must be pretty glib; he comes from Ireland.

_____

4 Plagiarism is dishonest since it involves a deliberate misrepresentation.

_____

5 Divorce is not immoral, since any contract which may be broken by mutual consent is not immoral. _____

6 They were rabid Yankee fans; so they had season tickets.

_____

7 Not everyone can afford to go to college. That's why there are people without college degrees. _____

8 Not all valid arguments are sound, since sound arguments always have true premises. _____

9 Because no induction is formally valid, deductions are not inductions.

_____

10 Bill didn't have any partners; for he was the sole owner of the shop.

_____

Using Venn diagrams or rules, determine the validity of the following. Underneath each diagram, write V for valid or I for invalid.

11 Van Johnson is not the President of the United States; the President of the United States is not a movie actor; hence, Van Johnson is a movie actor (V, P, M).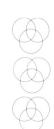

12 Some thrilling moments on the silver screen have been provided by Henry Fonda. Those moments provided by Fonda are popular with moviegoers. Among moviegoers, therefore, there are some popular and thrilling moments on the silver screen (T, H, P).

13 Not all existentialists are atheists; Sartre is an existentialist; thus, he is not an atheist (E, A, S).

14 Jack and Jill went up the hill to fetch a pail of water; so, since everyone who goes up a hill to fetch water comes down, so did they (J, W, C).

15 A bat is not a bird; Batman is not a bat; so, necessarily, Batman is not a bird (B, D, M).

Quantification

Write T for true and F for false.

1 Open sentences are statements. _____
2 A quantified open sentence is a statement. _____
3 The open formula $Fx \supset Fx$ is true of everything in the universe. _____
4 Open formulas may not be treated truth functionally. _____
5 If $(\exists x)Fx$ is true, then everything is F. _____
6 If $(x)Fx$ is true, then everything is F. _____
7 If $(x)Fx$ is true, then Fa, Fb, Fc, . . . (to infinity) is true. _____
8 In an infinite universe it is possible to prove that a statement of the form $(\exists x)Fx$ is false. _____
9 The formula $Fx \supset Gx$ is true of everything which is F. _____
10 The formula $Fx \cdot {\sim}Fx$ is true of everything. _____
11 If it is false that everything is F, then something is not F. _____
12 If it is false that something is not F, then everything is F. _____
13 If it is true that something is F, then everything is F. _____
14 If it is true that everything is F, then nothing is non-F. _____
15 In a finite universe, the quantifiers are logically superfluous. _____
16 In a universe of two members a and b, $(\exists x)Fx$ is equivalent to $Fa \cdot Fb$. _____
17 In a universe of two members a and b, $(x)Fx$ is equivalent to $Fa \vee Fb$. _____
18 ${\sim}(x)Fx$ is equivalent to ${\sim}(\exists x)Fx$. _____
19 The statements "Something is in space and time" and "Something is in space and something is in time" are equivalent. _____
20 $(\exists x)(Fx \cdot {\sim}Gx)$ is equivalent to $(\exists x){\sim}({\sim}Fx \vee Gx)$. _____
21 $(x)(Fx \supset Gx)$ is equivalent to $(x)(Fx \cdot {\sim}Gx)$. _____
22 $(\exists x)(Fx \cdot Gx)$ is equivalent to $(x)(Fx \supset Gx)$. _____
23 $(x)({\sim}Fx \vee Gx)$ is equivalent to ${\sim}(\exists x)(Fx \cdot Gx)$. _____
24 $(x)(Fx \equiv Gx)$ is equivalent to $(x)[(Fx \supset Gx) \cdot (Gx \supset Fx)]$. _____
25 ${\sim}(x)Fx$ is equivalent to $(x){\sim}Fx$. _____

Translations

Write the appropriate quantified formula in the space provided.

1 The dog is man's best friend. ($Fx = x$ is a dog; $Gx = x$ is man's best friend.) _____
2 A few El Greco's are in the Prado. ($Fx = x$ is an El Greco; $Gx = x$ is in the Prado.) _____

3 Sometimes I'm not hungry. (*Fx* = x is a time; *Gx* = I am hungry at x.)

_____

4 If it's ridiculous, then it's not splendid. (*Fx* = x is ridiculous; *Gx* = x is splendid.) _____

5 Everything is either in space or in time. (*Fx* = x is in space; *Gx* = x is in time.) _____

6 Everything is in space or everything is in time. _____

7 There are plumbers who are talented or gregarious. (*Fx* = x is a plumber; *Gx* = x is talented; *Hx* = x is gregarious.) _____

8 Not all American products are inexpensive. (*Fx* = x is an American product; *Gx* = x is expensive.) _____

9 If nothing is worthwhile, then nothing deserves our attention. (*Fx* = x is worthwhile; *Gx* = x deserves our attention.) _____

10 If something is worthwhile, then it deserves our attention.

_____

11 If there are fireplugs, dogs don't need trees. (*Fx* = x is a fireplug; *Gx* = x is a dog; *Hx* = x needs trees.) _____

12 Bullfighters and baseball players have either long sideburns or chew tobacco. (*Fx* = x is a bullfighter; *Gx* = x is a baseball player; *Hx* = x has long sideburns; *Jx* = x chews tobacco.) _____

13 There's no time like the present. _____

14 There are gamblers who are sinners and those who aren't. (*Fx* = x is a gambler; *Gx* = x is a sinner.) _____

15 Logicians are either smart alecks or they are not, and if they are smart alecks, who needs them? (*Fx* = x is a logician; *Gx* = x is a smart aleck; *Hx* = x is needed.) _____

The Restricted Universe

Progress Test 30 (Chapter Nine)
In the following exercises, steps and truth values have been omitted. Fill them in to determine whether in a limited universe formula a entails formula b. For illustration, the first item has been completed.

1 **a** (x)Fx
    b (x)(Fx · Gx)
    T T   T   T F   T
    Fa · Fb … Fh ⊃ Fa · Ga · Fb · Gb … Fh · Gh   No
            T   F   F

2 **a** (x)(Fx ⊃ Gx)
    b (x)Fx
    F   F   F
    (Fa ⊃ Ga)(Fb ⊃ Gb) … (Fh ⊃ Gh) ⊃ _____ _____
        T   T   T

3   **a** $(\exists x)Fx \lor (\exists x)Gx$
    b $(\exists x)(Fx \cdot Gx)$
    T   **F**   **F**   **F**
    $Fa \lor Fb \lor \dots Fh \lor Ga \lor Gb \lor \dots Gh \supset$ _____   _____
                   T

4   **a** $(x)(Fx \supset \sim Gx)$
    b $\sim(\exists x)Gx$
                                       F   T   T   T
    _____ $\supset \sim[Ga \lor Gb \lor \dots Gh]$ _____

5   **a** $(x)Fx \lor (\exists x)Gx$
    b $(\exists x)(Fx \cdot Gx)$
    _____ $\supset [(Fa \cdot Ga) \lor (Fb \cdot Gb) \lor \dots (Fh \cdot Gh)]$ _____

6   **a** $(\exists x)\sim(Fx \cdot Gx)$
    b $\sim(x)(Fx \supset \sim Gx)$
    T
    $\sim(Fa \cdot Ga) \lor \sim(Fb \cdot Gb) \lor \sim(Fh \cdot Gh) \supset$ _____   _____

7   **a** $\sim(x)Fx$
    b $(\exists x)Fx \supset \sim(\exists x)Gx$
    _____ $\supset [(Fa \lor Fb \lor \dots Fh) \supset \sim(Ga \lor Gb \lor \dots Gh)]$ _____

Proofs

Progress Test 31 (Chapter Ten)
In each of the following proofs justifications and occasional lines have been omitted. Fill in the missing lines and put the justifications in the spaces provided. (All nineteen rules plus all quantification rules may be used.)

1   * $\begin{cases} \textbf{1} & (x)(Fx \supset Gx) \\ \textbf{2} & (\exists x)Fx \qquad /\therefore (\exists x)Gx \end{cases}$
    * **3** Fx _____
    * **4** $Fx \supset Gx$ _____
    * **5**   _____
    * **6** $(\exists x)Gx$ _____

2   * $\begin{cases} \textbf{1} & (x)(Fx \equiv Gx) \\ \textbf{2} & (x)Gx \qquad /\therefore (x)Fx \end{cases}$
    * **3** $Fx \equiv Gx$ _____
    * **4** Gx _____
    * **5** $(Fx \supset Gx)(Gx \supset Fx)$ _____
    * **6** $(Gx \supset Fx)(Fx \supset Gx)$ _____
    * **7**   _____
    * **8**   _____
    * **9** $(x)Fx$ _____

3 *{1 $(x) \sim (Fx \cdot Gx)$
   {2 $\sim (x)(Gx \supset Hx)$ $/\therefore (x) \sim Fx$
 * 3 $(\exists x) \sim (Gx \supset Hx)$ _____
 * 4 $(\exists x) \sim (\sim Gx \lor Hx)$ _____
 * 5 $(\exists x)(\sim\sim Gx \cdot \sim Hx)$ _____
 * 6   _____
 * 7 $Gx \cdot \sim Hx$ _____
 * 8 $(x)(\sim Fx \lor \sim Gx)$ _____
 * 9 $\sim Fx \lor \sim Gx$ _____
 *10 $\sim Gx \lor \sim Fx$ _____
 *11   _____
 *12 Gx _____
 *13   _____
 *14 $(\exists x) \sim Fx$ _____

4 *{1 $(x)Fx \supset (\exists x)(Gx \cdot Hx)$
   {2 $(x)(Gx \supset \sim Hx)$ $/\therefore (\exists x) \sim Fx$
 ** 3 $\sim (\exists x) \sim Fx$ _____
 ** 4   _____
 ** 5 $(\exists x)(Gx \cdot Hx)$ _____
 ** 6 $Gx \cdot Hx$ _____
 ** 7 $Gx \supset \sim Hx$ _____
 ** 8   _____
 ** 9 $\sim Hx$ _____
 **10 $Hx \cdot Gx$ _____
 **11   _____
 **12 $Hx \cdot \sim Hx$ _____

5 *{1 $(x)(Fx \supset \sim Gx) \lor (\exists x)Hx$
   {2 $\sim (\exists x)(Hx \lor \sim Gx)$ $/\therefore (x) \sim Fx$
 * 3 $(x) \sim (Hx \lor \sim Gx)$
 * 4 $(x)(\sim Hx \cdot \sim\sim Gx)$ _____
 * 5 $(x)(\sim Hx \cdot Gx)$ _____
 * 6 $\sim Hx \cdot Gx$ _____
 * 7 $\sim Hx$ _____
 * 8   _____
 * 9 $\sim (\exists x)Hx$ _____
 *10 $(\exists x)Hx \lor (x)(Fx \supset \sim Gx)$ _____
 *11   _____
 *12 $Fx \supset \sim Gx$ _____
 *13 $Gx \cdot \sim Hx$ _____
 *14   _____
 *15 $\sim\sim Gx$ _____
 *16 $\sim Fx$ _____
 *17 $(x) \sim Fx$ _____

6   * 1   ($\exists$ x)(Fx $\supset$ p)   /∴ (x)Fx $\supset$ p
    ** 2   (x)Fx   _____
    ** 3   _____
    ** 4   _____
    ** 5   p   _____
    * 6   _____

Relational Predicates

Progress Test 32 (Chapter Eleven)
Indicate whether the following are true or false; use T for true and F for false.

    For items 1 through 8, interpret Fxy as "x is the cause of y."

1   (x)($\exists$ y)Fxy says "Something is the cause of everything."   _____
2   (y)($\exists$ x)Fxy says "Everything is caused by something."   _____
3   ($\exists$ x)($\exists$ y)Fxy says "There is something which is the cause of something."   _____
4   ~($\exists$ x)($\exists$ y)Fxy says "Nothing is the cause of anything."   _____
5   (x)(y)~Fxy says "Nothing is the cause of anything."   _____
6   ~($\exists$ x)(y)Fxy says "Nothing is the cause of anything."   _____
7   ~(x)(y)Fxy says "Something is not the cause of everything."   _____
8   ($\exists$ x)($\exists$ y)~Fxy says "Something is not the cause of something."   _____
9   (x)[Fx $\supset$ ($\exists$ y)(Gy · ~Hxy)] is equivalent to (x)[Fx $\supset$ ~(y)(Gy $\supset$ Hxy)].   _____
10   ~($\exists$ x)[Fx · ($\exists$ y)(Gy · Hxy)] is equivalent to (x)[Fx $\supset$ ~(y)(Gy · Hxy)].   _____

For items 11 through 15, assume a two-member universe:

11   (x)($\exists$ y)Fxy expands first to ($\exists$ y)Fay · ($\exists$ y)Fby.   _____
12   ($\exists$ x)(y) Fxy expands first to (y)Fay · (y)Fby.   _____
13   (x)(y)(z)Fxzy expands first to (y)(z)Fayz · (y)(z)Fbyz.   _____
14   ~(x)(y)Fxy expands to ~[(Faa v Fab) · (Fba v Fbb)].   _____
15   ~($\exists$ x)Fxx expands to ~Faa v ~Fbb.   _____
16   (x)[Fx $\supset$ ($\exists$ y)(Gy · Hxy)] entails, by **UI**, Fa $\supset$ ($\exists$ y)(Gy · Hay).   _____
17   (x)[Fx $\supset$ (y)(Gy $\supset$ ~Hxy)] entails, by **UI**, Fx $\supset$ (y)(Gy $\supset$ ~Hyy).   _____
18   Fa · ($\exists$ y)(Fx · Gxy) entails, by **EG**, ($\exists$ x)[Fx · ($\exists$ y)(Fx · Gxy)].   _____
19   ($\exists$ x)(Fx · Gxy) entails, by **EI**, Fx · Gxx.   _____
20   If (x)Fxa entails Fya by **UI**, then Fya entails, by **UG**, (y)(Fya).   _____

Relational Proofs

Progress Test 33 (Chapter Eleven)
In each of the following proofs, justifications and occasional lines have been omitted. Fill in the missing lines and put the justifications in the spaces provided.

1   * **1** $(\exists x)(y)Fxy$ $/\therefore (\exists x)Fxx$
    * **2** $(y)Fxy$ _____
    * **3** Fxx _____
    * **4** $(\exists x)Fxx$ _____

2   * **1** $(x)\sim(\exists x)Fxy$ $/\therefore (x)\sim Fxx$
    * **2** $\sim(\exists y)Fxy$ _____
    * **3** $(y)\sim Fxy$ _____
    * **4**   _____
    * **5** $(x)\sim Fxx$ _____

3   * **1** $(x)Fxx$ $/\therefore (\exists x)(\exists y)Fxy$
   ** **2** $\sim(\exists x)(\exists y)Fxy$ _____
   ** **3**   _____
   ** **4** $(x)(y)\sim Fxy$ _____
   ** **5** $(y)\sim Fxy$ _____
   ** **6** $\sim Fxx$ _____
   ** **7**   _____
   ** **8** $Fxx \cdot \sim Fxx$ _____

4   *$\{$**1** $(x)[Fx \supset (y)(Gy \supset Hxy)]$
    $\{$**2** $(\exists x)Gx$ $/\therefore (x)[Fx \supset (\exists y)(Gy \cdot Gyy)]$
    * **3** Gx _____
   ** **4** Fx _____
   ** **5** $Fx \supset (y)(Gy \supset Hxy)$ _____
   ** **6** $(y)(Gy \supset Hxy)$ _____
   ** **7** $Gx \supset Hxx$ _____
   ** **8** Hxx _____
   ** **9** $Gx \cdot Hxx$ _____
   10 $(\exists y)(Gy \cdot Hyy)$ _____
   *11 $Fx \supset (\exists y)(Gy \cdot Hyy)$ _____
   *12 $(x)[Fx \supset (\exists y)(Gy \cdot Hyy)]$ _____

5   * **1** $(x)(y)[Fxy \supset (\sim Fxx \cdot \sim Fyy)]$ $/\therefore (x)\sim Fxx$
    * **2** $(y)[Fxy \supset (\sim Fxx \cdot \sim Fyy)]$ _____
    * **3** $Fxx \supset (\sim Fxx \cdot \sim Fxx)$ _____
    * **4** $Fxx \supset \sim Fxx$ _____
    * **5** $\sim Fxx \vee \sim Fxx$ _____
    * **6**   _____
    * **7**   _____

Induction

Progress Test 34 (Chapter Twelve)
Indicate whether the following are true or false; use T for true, F for false.

1 The premises of correct inductive arguments entail their conclusions. _____

2 An argument is correct if the premises warrant, confirm, or support the conclusion. _____

3 Inductions, like deductions, can be appraised as correct or incorrect by virtue of their form. _____

4 Inductions are formally valid arguments. _____

5 In inductions, if the premises are true, then the conclusion must be true. _____

6 The expression "probably p" must be taken to mean that p is probable with respect to the evidence. _____

7 It makes sense to say that P_1 entails Q_1 more than P_2 entails Q_2. _____

8 In appraising and constructing inductive arguments we must account for all the known relevant evidence. _____

9 In inductions the modal qualifier "necessarily" can never attach to the conclusion. _____

10 Adding relevant evidence to the premise set of an inductive argument will generally alter the probability of the conclusion. _____

11 The premise sets of deductions are always incomplete. _____

12 It makes sense to say H_1 is better confirmed on evidence E_1 than H_2 on E_2. _____

13 In inductions the evidence is always complete. _____

14 The study of inductive logic enables one to decide unequivocally if evidence is relevant to some hypothesis. _____

15 An argument can be correct and have true premises and a false conclusion. _____

16 Evidence considered relevant to some hypothesis in one context may not be considered relevant to the same hypothesis in some other context. _____

17 There is no difference between the total relevant evidence and the total known relevant evidence. _____

18 An argument can be correct and yet have a false conclusion. _____

19 The degree of warrant, support, or confirmation depends upon the completeness of the evidence and the force of the conclusion. _____

20 Deductions are context-independent. _____

21 It is almost always possible to express the degree of confirmation in quantitative terms. _____

22 Inductions are like deductions in that both are subject to revision in the light of new experience. _____

23 The conclusions of inductions "go beyond" the evidence. _____

24 Inductions are context-independent. _____

25 Background knowledge plays no role in determining if evidence is relevant to a hypothesis. _____

Enumerative Induction

Progress Test 35 (Chapter Twelve)
Indicate whether the following are true or false; use T for true, F for false.

1 Enumerative inductions are also called "generalizations." _____

2 In enumerative inductions it is desirable to have a high positive analogy. _____

3 Perfect inductions are deductions. _____

4 In enumerative inductions it is desirable to have a high negative analogy. _____

5 In enumerative inductions it is impossible to have both a high negative and a high positive analogy. _____

6 The nature of the analogy determines if the sample is representative. _____

7 Decreasing the population of the sample is usually sufficient to increase the probability of the induction. _____

8 Increasing the differences between the individuals in the sample decreases the probability of the induction. _____

9 Determining what factors in the analogy are relevant is a function of background knowledge. _____

10 While similarities between individuals in the sample must be considered, only similarities relevant to the hypothesis in question are significant. _____

11 Analogies may be used both argumentatively and non-argumentatively. _____

12 In most inductive analogies the conclusion is a generalization; in most enumerative inductions the conclusion is a singular statement. _____

13 In inductive analogies it is desirable to have a high positive analogy. _____

14 In inductive analogies it is desirable to have a high negative analogy. _____

15 If two individuals differ in many ways, then other things being equal, they will probably differ in the inferred property. _____

16 The characteristics or properties shared by individuals may or may not be relevant to the inferred property. _____

17 Increasing the number of observed individuals always increases the probability of the inference. _____

18 Inductive analogies are never valid. _____
19 Inductive analogies are never correct. _____
20 Weakening the conclusion of an inductive analogy increases the probability of its correctness. _____

Progress Test 36 (Chapter Twelve)
Suppose that it is claimed that most union members are registered Democrats. On the basis of each of the following sets of evidence, indicate whether this generalization is (a) inconclusive, (b) probable, or (c) quite probable. Assume that total union membership is 1,000. Use the letters a, b, or c for your answers.

1 Of 100 union members interviewed, 60 were Democrats; 25 were members of Local 181, United Auto Workers (UAW), 25 were members of the United Federation of Teachers, and 50 represented various trades, including plumbers, electricians, steam fitters, etc. _____
2 Of 100 members interviewed, 60 were Democrats. All 100 were from Local 181, UAW. _____
3 Same as 1 above except that the survey was conducted by *Commonweal,* a Catholic publication, and confined to their subscribers. _____
4 Same as 1 above except that 25 persons were black. _____
5 Same as 1 above except that all 100 lived in traditionally Democratic Kings County. _____
6 Same as 1 above except that all those interviewed owned telephones, automobiles, and television sets. _____
7 Of 300 members interviewed, 180 were Democrats. All were members of Local 181, UAW. _____
8 Of 300 members interviewed 180 were Democrats. All were members of the UAW in various locals located in the Detroit area. _____
9 Of 300 members interviewed, 180 were Democrats. All were members of the UAW, but they represented locals in every geographic area.
10 Same as 9 above except that the 300 had incomes of less than $8,500 per annum. _____

Inductive Analogy

Progress Test 37 (Chapter Twelve)
Of the following analogies, distinguish between those used for explanation and those used for argument. Use E for explanation and A for argument. In the latter briefly point out any weaknesses, if any.

1 Scientists have no right to object to the further development of nuclear weapons on moral grounds. When you hire a carpenter to build some cabinets, you don't expect him to offer his opinion on the beauty or utility of the cabinets. You expect him to build them, and the same applies to scientists. _____

2 In a solid, the molecules can be pictured as a crowd of men all doing physical exercises—"the daily dozen"—without moving from the spot where they stand. . . . In a liquid the molecules can be pictured as a swarm of men gathered together in a hall at a crowded reception; they are tightly wedged, but each one works his way through the others, with many a push and apology. . . . For a gas we have to think of a large open space on which men are walking without looking where they are going; each man continues in a straight line until he bumps into something else, when he abruptly starts off again in a different direction.
E. N. da C. Andrade, *What Is the Atom?*[1] _____

3 One of the dreams that lulls us into this hopeful make-believe is the theory of the so-called atomic standoff. This is the argument that, when both we and the communists have plenty of atomic weapons, neither of us will use them. To gamble on such a miracle is like betting that two men armed with loaded pistols will merely wrestle until one of them is thrown to the ground and kicked to death.
Senator Stuart Symington _____

4 Prudent people have insurance policies against fire and theft. Why shouldn't we have an insurance policy against a nuclear blast by building fall-out shelters? _____

5 Wittgenstein used to compare thinking with swimming: just as in swimming our bodies have a natural tendency to float on the surface so that it requires great physical exertion to plunge to the bottom, so in thinking it requires great mental exertion to force our minds away from the superficial, down into the depth of a philosophical problem.
George Pitcher,
The Philosophy of Wittgenstein _____

6 No body can be healthful without exercise, neither natural body nor politic: and certainly, to a kingdom or estate, a just and honorable war is the true exercise. A civil war, indeed, is like the heat of a fever; but a foreign war is like the heat of exercise, and serveth to keep the body in health; for in a slothful peace, both courages will effeminate and manners corrupt.
Francis Bacon,
The True Greatness of Kingdoms _____

7 Every one who really thinks for himself is like a monarch. His position is undelegated and supreme. His judgments, like royal decrees, spring from his own sovereign power and proceed directly from himself. He acknowledges authority as little as a monarch admits a command; he subscribes to nothing but what he has himself authorized.
Arthur Schopenhauer,
The Art of Literature _____

[1] (New York: Harper, 1926).

8 For while it may be a sound policy not to invite the Soviet Union to enter into formal engagements—beyond her obligations under the UN charter—it cannot be sound policy not to be talking to the Soviet Union about the Middle East. That would be like deciding not to notice the elephant that has strolled into the dining room.

Walter Lippmann,
"Today and Tomorrow" _____

9 The government should get out of the business of supplying electric power by such projects as the TVA. It's not fair for the government to both regulate the industry and also compete with others in it. That's like the referee of a basketball game playing for one of the teams.

_____

10 But you will not abide the election of a Republican President! In that supposed event, you say, you will destroy the Union; and then, you say, the great crime of having destroyed it will be upon us! That is cool. A highwayman holds a pistol to my ear, and mutters through his teeth, "Stand and deliver, or I shall kill you, and then you will be a murderer!" To be sure, what the robber demanded of me—my money—was my own; and I had a clear right to keep it; but it was no more my own than my vote is my own; and the threat of death to me, to extort my vote, can scarcely be distinguished in principle.

Abraham Lincoln,
"Cooper Union Address" _____

Eliminative Induction

Progress Test 38 (Chapter Twelve)
Indicate whether the following are true or false; use T for true, F for false.

1 Statements of the form $(x)(Fx \supset Gx)$ or "All S is P" may be positively confirmed though they may not be positively disconfirmed. _____

2 If A is necessary for B, then when B is absent A is absent. _____

3 In eliminative induction, confirmation proceeds by eliminating competing hypotheses. _____

4 The disconfirmation of a hypothesis is inductive. _____

5 Confirmation and disconfirmation are symmetrical. _____

6 If A is necessary and sufficient for B, then A has occurred if and only if B has occurred. _____

7 If A is sufficient for B, then B is necessary for A. _____

8 If A is sufficient for B, then when A is absent, B is absent. _____

9 The method of agreement eliminates conditions as not sufficient. _____

10 If B is necessary for A, then A is sufficient for B. _____

11 The method of agreement requires that there be one and only one difference between the instances. _____

12 If *A* is sufficient for *B*, then *B* is sufficient for *A*. _____

13 The method of difference is a method which can conclusively establish causal relations. _____

14 The joint method, like the other inductive methods, is vulnerable to inadequate analysis of the relevant factors. _____

15 The method of difference eliminates conditions as not sufficient. _____

16 Causal relations are not to be identified with functional relations. _____

17 The method of residues is most clearly related to the method of agreement. _____

18 The method of concomitant variations eliminates conditions as not sufficient. _____

19 The method of difference, like the other inductive methods, presupposes a hypothesis to begin inquiry. _____

20 The joint method is nothing more than the method of agreement plus the method of difference. _____

For the last five questions, given that being eighteen years old is a necessary condition for voting, indicate whether the following are true or false.

21 If you are eighteen, then necessarily you can vote. _____
22 Not being eighteen years old is sufficient for not voting. _____
23 If you can't vote, then necessarily you are not eighteen. _____
24 If you vote, then you are eighteen. _____
25 Either you don't vote or you are eighteen. _____

Progress Test 39 (Chapter Twelve)
In the following arguments indicate which of Mill's methods are used and how probable the conclusion is based on the evidence given. Use the following keys for your answers: 1, method of agreement; 2, method of difference; 3, joint method; 4, method of residues; 5, concomitant variations; a, very probable; b, probable; c, inconclusive; d, unlikely; e, improbable.

1 When asked if certain comic books depicting violence had any effect on their actions, many juvenile delinquents have said "yes." In reply, the Comics Code Authority has pointed out that most children who read comic books which depict violence do not become juvenile delinquents, and it therefore concludes that such comic books exert very little influence upon the behavior of its youthful readers. _____

2 In studying British genius, Havelock Ellis found that most of the famous men whose lives he looked into were first-born children. He therefore concluded that certain environmental factors contributed significantly to the development of outstanding ability. _____

3 Several years ago 16 children died and 250 other persons were hospitalized in Tijuana as a result of poisoning. First, certain drug products were suspected of having become contaminated, but an investigation showed that many people who were unaffected had consumed these products. Then suspicion fell on the bread that the afflicted parties had been known to eat. An investigation revealed that parathion, a deadly pesticide used in Northern Mexico against the boll weevil, had been stored in a certain warehouse along with flour and sugar, which were distributed to about nine bakeries and used to make bread and sweet rolls. Mexican officials concluded that the insecticide had become mixed with the flour and sugar and was responsible for the poisonings. _____

4 Just before the Mayaguez incident a Harris poll showed the President's popularity to be at 39 percent. Two days after he sent in troops, a Harris poll showed his popularity to be at 48 percent. His action evidently made a favorable impression on the American people. _____

5 In his autobiography Lord Asquith relates an incident concerning a member of Parliament named Kinglake, whose speeches contained excellent content but whose voice was so poor that his speeches made little impact. One day he delivered a particularly brilliant speech, which as always was received apathetically. The next day the second Sir Robert Peel, after getting permission, concluded his own speech with the identical words of Kinglake's conclusion and received a standing ovation. Asquith concludes that Peel's delivery made all the difference. _____

6 Because of certain deviations in the predicted orbit of Uranus, Leverrier concluded that a theretofore undiscovered planet was exerting a pull on Uranus and causing the deviation. His conclusion subsequently led to the discovery of the planet Neptune. _____

7 To determine the effect of fluorinated water on teeth, the neighboring communities of Newburgh and Kingston, New York, conducted an experiment. For ten years the residents of Newburgh drank water containing 1 part sodium fluoride to 1 million parts of water while the residents of Kingston drank water containing little or no fluorine. Before the test began, 1,000 children in each community had their teeth carefully checked so that the control groups used had approximately the same number of cavities. After ten years it was found that the children of Newburgh had approximately 40 percent fewer cavities than those of Kingston. The result was attributed to the fluorine. _____

8 To test his vaccine against anthrax, Pasteur inoculated twenty-four sheep and then injected them and twenty-four other sheep with anthrax microbes. Two days later the vaccinated sheep were still healthy while the others were dead or dying. Pasteur was satisfied that his vaccine worked.

_____

Probability

Progress Test 40 (Chapter Thirteen)
Indicate whether the following are true or false; use T for true, F for false.

1 Probability as degree of confirmation is subjective in the sense that it depends upon what people in fact believe. _____

2 Statements in themselves are neither probable nor improbable; rather they are either true or false. _____

3 The expression "probably p" is explicated as "p is probable relative to a given body of knowledge." _____

4 Given that divorce rates have steadily increased since World War II, it follows that they will continue to increase. _____

5 Statistical probability refers to the probability of a class of outcomes with respect to another class of outcomes. _____

6 A causal connection may be inferred from statistical correlations of over .90. _____

7 Statistical probabilities give us information only about classes of items or events. _____

8 Given that 77 of every 100 cigarette smokers contract lung cancer, you may be a cigarette smoker and not contract cancer, though the probability that you will is better than 3 to 1. _____

9 While probability as degree of confirmation refers to the probability of a class of outcomes with respect to another class, probability as relative frequency refers to the probability of a statement with respect to other statements. _____

10 A good sample is best assured by selecting items on the basis of chance. _____

11 To employ formal probabilities, certain material assumptions must first be made. _____

12 If in a series of tosses of a coin, a head has not come up in 18 tosses, the formal probability of a head on the 19th toss is considerably greater than 1/2. _____

13 Formal, or mathematical, probabilities may be determined à priori. _____

14 In games of chance, it is generally assumed that the possible alternatives may be enumerated. _____

15 If in a series of tosses of a coin a head has not come up in 18 tosses, the probability as relative frequency of a head on the 19th toss is considerably greater than 1/2. _____

16 The probability of joint occurrence of two independent events is equal to the probability of the first event plus the probability of the second event. _____

17 To employ the theorem of *exclusive* events, if one of the events occurs, the others may or may not occur. _____

18 The formal probability of some event *F* is determined by dividing *F* by the total number of alternatives, each of which is assumed to be equiprobable. _____

19 If the formal probability of rolling an ace is 1/6, then the probability of not rolling an ace is 2/3. _____

20 The formal probability of an event may or may not be coincident with the statistical probability for the same event. _____

Statistics

Progress Test 41 (Chapter Thirteen)
State briefly how statistics have been misused in the following arguments.

1 Unions are much weaker than the corporations they negotiate with. The assets of all the major unions combined are less than the assets of one large corporation like IBM. _____

2 The claim that the white man mistreated or killed Indians in large numbers is greatly exaggerated. After all, the Indian population now is about the same as it was when Jamestown was settled. _____

3 The more a state spends on education, the more prosperous it becomes. For example, in New York State last year an average of $550 was spent per pupil and the average per capita income was $3,500; in Ohio an average of $420 was spent per pupil and the average per capita income was $2,600; and in South Carolina $300 was spent per pupil and the per capita income was $1,900. _____

4 In 1975 the inflation rate was about 6 percent. If it continues at that rate for 30 years, a house which now costs $30,000 will cost $176,400. In other words, practically no one will be able to afford a home of his own.

_____

5 We're frequently told about equality of the sexes in the Soviet Union, especially economic equality. But a look at recent statistics shows that the percentage of women in Russia who are doctors, lawyers, professors, and engineers is relatively small. _____

6 In an area where a high percentage of the families have an income of under $5,000 a year, it was found that 25 percent of all the families of the area owned their own cars, 62 percent owned washing machines, and 68 percent owned television sets. Thus, it would seem that having a so-called poverty-level income doesn't create too many hardships.

_____

7 As an example of the efficacy of polling, a poll of 83 people taken on the South Side of Chicago before the election showed that Daley was a big favorite to win, and he did. _____

8 Last year there were more arrests for drug offenses than for liquor offenses. The drug problem is apparently getting out of hand and calls for new legislation. _____

9 Although Adlai Stevenson was defeated for the Presidency, he must be considered one of the most popular candidates of all time, since he received more than twice as many votes as Grover Cleveland, a man who was elected to office twice. _____

10 More people die from polio vaccination than from polio. Hence such vaccinations should be stopped. (Assuming that 40 million people are annually vaccinated and 1 million are not, use hypothetical figures which would refute the suggestion that polio vaccinations are dangerous or don't prevent polio.) _____

The Calculus of Probability

Progress Test 42 (Chapter Thirteen)
Write the correct answer in the space provided. Suppose you have an ordinary deck of fifty-two cards. The cards have been honestly shuffled so that the fifty-two cards are equiprobable. You are to draw one card. What is the probability that you will draw:

1 The ace of hearts? _____
2 The queen of hearts? _____
3 The ace of hearts or the queen of hearts? _____
4 Any ace? _____
5 Any spade? _____
6 Any spade or any heart? _____
7 A card that is not a diamond? _____
8 A card that is not a diamond or a heart? _____
9 Any card but the ace of spades? _____
10 An ace or any non-heart? _____

You are now to draw 2 cards consecutively without replacing cards. What is the probability that you will draw:

11 Two aces? _____
12 Two spades? _____
13 Two face cards (king, queen, or jack)? _____
14 Two non-black cards? _____
15 The ace of spades and the ten of hearts? _____
16 The ace of spades and the king of spades? _____
17 Anything but the ace of spades? _____
18 Anything but the ace of spades and the king of hearts? _____
19 The ace of spades or the ace of diamonds on draw 1 *and* the king of spades on draw 2? _____
20 The ace of spades or the ace of diamonds on draw 1 *and* any king on draw 2? _____

Informal Fallacies: I

Progress Test 43 (Chapter Fourteen)
Classify and briefly explain the error, if any, in the following arguments.

1 The Constitution guarantees the right of association. Therefore, laws limiting the hours that women and children may work or laws preventing an employer from hiring on the basis of color or creed are clearly unconstitutional, since they prevent an employer from associating with employees of his choice. _____

2 In every marriage either the man or the woman must dominate. Since the responsibility of the family's economic well-being generally falls on the shoulders of the man and since men have traditionally fended for their families, it follows that the man, rather than the woman, should dominate in the home. _____

3 "You argue that a man cannot inquire about that which he knows or about that which he does not know; for if he knows, he has no need to inquire; and if not, he cannot; he does not know the very subject about which he is to inquire."

  Socrates (quoted by Plato) _____

4 "To allow every man unbounded freedom of speech must always be, on the whole, advantageous to the State; for it is highly conducive to the interests of the community that each individual should enjoy a liberty perfectly unlimited of expressing his sentiments."

  Richard Whately, *Elements of Logic* _____

5 When I complained about my grade being lowered because of excessive cuts, the instructor and I had a big argument. It seems clear that he's giving me a lower grade because we don't get along. _____

6 Since the average college graduate at the time of graduation is between twenty-one and twenty-two years of age, the fact that Joe Brown was twenty-five when he graduated suggests that he was not the best of students. _____

7 It would be inconsistent to condemn Joyce's *Ulysses* on the grounds that it treated sex openly and realistically and at the same time to condone certain portions of the Bible for doing the same thing. _____

8 The Constitution tells us that "all men are created equal," but this obviously isn't so; for some are born richer, smarter, stronger, and more gifted than others. _____

9 Medical records show that alcoholics tend to be undernourished—which only proves that a poor diet contributes to alcoholism.

_____

10 We must either fight Russia now or continue to appease her. Since history has shown that appeasement only emboldens dictators, we have no choice but to fight. _____

11 When questioned about someone in the State Department who he had claimed had Communist affiliations, the late Sen. Joseph McCarthy declared: "I do not have much information on this except the general statement of the agency that there is nothing in the files to disprove his Communist connections."[2]

12 I can't see where the United States has such a high standard of living. Have you ever seen the Chicago slums? _____

13 In families where the average number of children is two or fewer, the standard of living is higher than in those families having more than two children. The standard is appreciably lower on the average in those families with five or more children. Hence, birth control seems to lead to a higher standard of living. _____

14 You always say you enjoy jokes, and now when someone plays a little practical joke on you and happens to stain your suit, you get angry. That's not being very consistent. _____

15 If the United States agrees to a permanent international police force, she will be yielding her sovereignty in this area—in which case she may as well yield it completely, for a nation is either wholly sovereign or has no say over its affairs. _____

16 "Seeing that eye and hand and foot and every one of our members has some obvious function, must we not believe that in like manner a human being has a function over and above these particular functions?"
Aristotle, *Nichomachean Ethics* _____

17 Since there is no real proof that the universe is limited, we can only conclude that space is infinite. _____

18 More people go to church and to movies on Sunday than on any other day in the week. Religion somehow stimulates a desire for togetherness at the movies. _____

19 "Those who disagree with me when I say that mankind is corrupted prove that they are already corrupted."
Nietzsche _____

20 "You don't have to stretch your imagination very far to believe that if they can take the profit out of housing, the next logical step is to take the profit out of the manufacture of automobiles or whatever else you manufacture. You cannot stop with housing; public housing borders on socialized housing, which in turn borders on the complete socialization of industry."[3] _____

21 Berkeley just received an excellent rating—in fact, it's considered to be one of the best universities in the country. So it must have a first-rate law school. _____

[2] Quoted by Richard Rovere, *Senator Joe McCarthy* (New York: Harcourt Brace & World, 1958).

[3] Adapted from Edward R. Carr, "Is Private Enterprise Doing an Adequate Housing Job?", *Vital Speeches,* 14 (May 1, 1948), p. 438.

22 **A:** Sensible people don't smoke marijuana.

B: I know some people whom I'd call "sensible" — they're intelligent and highly responsible — who occasionally smoke.

A: These people aren't really sensible, for if they were, they wouldn't smoke. _____

23 Although everyone extols cooperation we pass antitrust laws against large corporations, which after all are only collections of individuals who cooperate in trying to make profits. _____

24 Since fluorine is used in the manufacture of certain rat poisons, how can anyone seriously advocate that it be put into our drinking water to prevent tooth decay? _____

25 Poe argued that only short poems can be good. When considering masterpieces like Milton's *Paradise Lost,* which is hardly a short poem, he stated that it was really a collection of short poems, which thus proved his point that only short poems can be good. _____

26 Since democracy is the best form of government, it should be preserved. To preserve it, we must be prepared to fight for such principles as freedom of speech and freedom of worship. Since such freedoms are worth fighting for, it is evident that democracy is the best type of government. _____

27 Every event must have a cause, for if it didn't, it would have to cause itself, which is impossible. And the reason it's impossible is that every thing has to be caused by something other than itself. _____

28 **A:** All our thoughts and actions are the product of subconscious irrational forces and our so-called reasoning mere rationalization.

B: That's ridiculous. I'm thinking now, my thought process is conscious and rational, and it tells me your theory is all wet.

A: Your very response — i.e., your defensiveness — is undoubtedly the product of a subconscious irrational force and hence a mere rationalization — which only proves my theory. _____

29 If one calls "Government! government!" not an Adam will answer. Hence there is no such thing as a government. There may be individual buildings and people working in them, but no government. _____

30 Some people worry that government control of industry will wreck the free enterprise system. But tariffs and quotas are a form of government control and have helped many infant industries. So government control isn't really harmful to industry. _____

Informal Fallacies: 2

Progress Test 44 (Chapter Fifteen)
Classify and briefly explain the error, if any, in the following arguments.

1 I don't see why the United States should continue its membership in NATO. Our being allied with Europe certainly hasn't helped solve the oil shortage in the United States. _____

2 There are exceptions to every rule. But this statement is itself a rule, so there must be exceptions to it. Hence, if the rule is true, it is also false. _____

3 The questions of whether the press is freer now than it used to be can be answered by looking at circulation figures over the past ten years. Since the average number of copies sold per person has steadily increased, the press is freer now than it used to be. _____

4 One could do worse than vote for McNight. He served his country well. He was a colonel in the Air Force, flew 46 missions, and was awarded the Distinguished Flying Cross. _____

5 "A government run by the people is as impossible as a theatre managed by the audience."

George Bernard Shaw _____

6 In the past five years insurance companies have paid out much more in claims than they have collected in premiums. Thus, a substantial increase in the premium rate is justified. _____

7 In a poll of several thousand people taken in five communities representing a cross section of all Long Island communities, 71 percent favored tax exemptions for college tuition. Apparently, the American people strongly favor such a policy. _____

8 Psychologists contend that the ability to solve math problems is one index of a person's intelligence. But I can't agree. I know some students who are good in math and yet are not very intelligent in other respects. _____

9 They say that free clinics of the type they have in England would reduce the drug problem here. But I don't see where such clinics have completely eliminated the drug problem in England. _____

10 "The law of contradiction affirms that *A* cannot both be *A* and not be *A*. . . . In the hands of some Aristotelians, [this law has] congealed into a mental fixation where an event must be either black or white, with no room for shades of gray. So interpreted, the law of contradiction says nothing can be both 'good' and 'bad,' both 'poisonous' and 'beneficial.' But such drugs as arsenic, belladonna, curare can be beneficial in small doses, though lethal in large. And what about a friend of mine who has an allergy for fresh eggs, and becomes deathly ill if he eats one?"

Stuart Chase[4] _____

---

[4] *Guide to Straight Thinking* (New York: Harper, 1956), pp. 16–17.

11 In a random poll of 500 people taken recently at Emporia, Kansas, 83 percent of those interviewed favor agricultural price supports. Clearly, the American people favor a continuation of the present policy. _____

12 "We face the loss of all the accumulated gains of our civilization and the things our ancestors risked much to win, if we do not band together and stop this silly, Communist-encouraged socialistic idea of statism, or the welfare state that will care for all of us from the cradle to the grave—even as we care for chickens in brooder houses."

Edward T. Miller[5] _____

13 The Soviet Union can hardly be considered a military threat in Europe, for evidently she could not depend on the support of Hungary in the event of a conflict with the West. _____

14 How bad can beef be? After all, the Meat Institute of America has said, "Beef is one of nature's priceless foods." _____

15 A recent survey shows that college dropouts are on the whole much heavier smokers than those who stay in college. Smoking apparently has a harmful effect on grades. _____

16 "The camel of government control now has his nose under the tent of free competitive industry and is crowding in. We will all have to watch him or he will take over the tent, and we will lose our economic freedom and with it all our other liberties."

Charles E. Wilson _____

17 By insisting on the right of the administration to determine eligibility, the chancellor now seeks to undermine the tenure system. Yet, when he was hired six years ago, he insisted on getting tenure as a professor in a non-existent department. _____

18 It's foolish to talk about a national preventive health insurance program. There will always be people around with infirmities and health problems. _____

19 **A:** The members of a fraternity have the right to decide with whom they want to associate. The ultimate decision must be theirs.

    B: Does that mean that the members of your fraternity don't want to associate with Hindus? I notice that no Hindu has ever been asked to join.

    A: Not at all. That regulation comes from the national chapter, which, after all, is entitled to set its own standards for admission. _____

20 Big business tends to be oligopolistic. As Senator O'Mahoney pointed out, "Three milling corporations produce 38 percent of all the flour consumed in the United States, and three meat-packing companies produce 43 percent of all processed meat." _____

---

[5] "Is the Administration's Move to Expand Social Security Sound?" *Congressional Digest*, 28 (December, 1949), p. 311.

21 We're always told that a good biology teacher is supposed to have a good grasp of biology. Mr. Smith surely knows his biology and yet is not a very good teacher. Perhaps the requirements for good teaching need to be reexamined. _____

22 Ezra Pound should not have been committed to St. Elizabeth's Hospital for the criminally insane. After all, he helped many young poets and writers, like Robert Frost and T. S. Eliot, get started. _____

23 I find it hard to put much faith in my doctor's arguments for cutting down on cigarettes when he's such a heavy smoker himself. _____

24 In 1941 the starting wage for a college instructor with little or no experience was around $1,700. Now, in 1976, it is around $11,500 a year — which shows how much better off the college teacher is today. _____

25 **A:** During past recessions, unemployment, according to a certain psychologist, brought increases in certain types of abnormal behavior, such as apathy, suicide, crime, even marital unhappiness.

B: We are led to believe that during recessions unemployed workers were running around murdering their wives. This is a gross exaggeration. _____

26 The Foreign Minister of India himself has declared that his country has a legal right to Kashmir. Such testimony cannot be lightly regarded.

_____

27 At present many professional boxers are exploited by their managers. Therefore, professional boxing should be abolished. _____

28 Among girls between the ages of seventeen and twenty-three the percentage of those who marry and don't go to college is much higher than the percentage of those who marry and do go to college. Therefore, we may conclude that the more education a girl has, the less chance she has of getting married. _____

29 Building armaments may be compared with buying a child a new toy. As soon as he gets it, he wants to play with it. By the same token, when a country gets new rockets, it wants to use them. _____

30 How can we have a high regard for a program of governmentally supported medical care? The idea originated in a country far less democratic and much less prosperous than ours. _____

31 What Mr. Brown's review reveals is a ranting, crude, racial hysteria that doesn't belong in this age. When he grows up, he can try reading my novel again. _____

32 Out of 250 hunting accidents which occurred in the Poconos last year, 225 involved men whereas only 25 involved teen-aged boys. It seems clear that, when hunting, boys are much more careful than men. _____

33 Recently the president of a certain Midwestern university was seen on television endorsing the Leopard, a new compact sportscar. Evidently the car has merit. _____

34 The student council claims that an honor system will help combat cheating. But considering the competitiveness of our society and the drive for grades, I don't see how any system is suddenly going to make all students honest. _____

35 A public works program for the unemployed is not needed since it would represent no significant change of the status quo, which is working satisfactorily. Moreover, such a program would be undesirable, for it would not provide the unemployed with the skills needed for long-term employment. _____

36 In the 1920s the Bell System employed around 200,000 people. Now it employs over 600,000. Thus, automation apparently does not cause unemployment. _____

Scientific Method

Progress Test 45 (Chapter Sixteen)
Indicate whether the following are true or false; use T for true, F for false.

1 Like all inquiry, scientific inquiry begins with a problem. _____

2 What constitutes a problem in scientific inquiry is a logical or methodological question. _____

3 Logical truths are validated a priori. _____

4 As far as the laws of mathematics refer to reality, they are certain; and as far as they do not refer to reality, they are not certain. _____

5 A scientific hypothesis could become a theory, but it could not become a law of science. _____

6 Common sense is continuous with scientific method. _____

7 Those who promulgate a new hypothesis have the burden of proof. _____

8 Laws may be roughly characterized as universal statements, which assert an invariant relation between events, properties, or phenomena. _____

9 It would generally be agreed that any well-confirmed universal statement is a law. _____

10 Laws order experience and thereby make it intelligible. _____

11 Concepts presuppose laws. _____

12 Though we can explain an event by appeal to laws, laws cannot be used to make predictions. _____

13 A scientific theory is an untestable explanation. _____

14 Theories provide an understanding of the uniformities of experience by linking together statements of invariant relations under broad theoretical principles. _____

15 Theories are confirmed indirectly by testing their implications. _____

16 If a theory has contradictory assumptions, it is impervious to testing. _____

17 If a theory cannot be falsified, then it cannot be confirmed. _____

18 The distinction between "theoretical terms" and "observation terms" is clear and precise. _____

19 All empirical concepts are open-textured. _____

20 While a theory must be testable in principle, it is sometimes hard to determine if it is. _____

Progress Test 46 (Chapter Sixteen)
Indicate whether the following are true or false; use T for true, F for false.

1 The formulation of hypotheses belongs to the context of confirmation. _____

2 A hypothesis is a tentative solution to a problem. _____

3 "Background knowledge" plays no role in formulating successful hypotheses. _____

4 Insofar as scientific method is applied logic, it may be employed only in scientific inquiry. _____

5 The context in which inquiry occurs logically implies what hypotheses will be suggested to the inquirer. _____

6 We "elaborate" a hypothesis by deducing its consequences. _____

7 Hypotheses are tested by testing their implications. _____

8 The first stage of scientific method is the unprejudiced gathering of the relevant facts. _____

9 Like the scientific method, the a priori method is self-corrective. _____

10 There is no "method" for formulating successful hypotheses. _____

11 The disconfirmation or falsification of a hypothesis is deductive. _____

12 In confirming an hypothesis, typically we employ formally valid arguments. _____

13 Hypotheses serve to direct inquiry. _____

14 If H entails I and I is true, then it follows necessarily that H is true. _____

15 A hypothesis which might be plausible in one context might be implausible in another context, even though the problem is the same. _____

16 If H in conjunction with A entails I and not-I is true, then it follows necessarily that H is not true. _____

17 In deductively elaborating hypotheses, we frequently employ unstated assumptions. _____

18 It is not important that the auxiliary assumptions requisite for deducing a test implication be made explicit. _____

19 Other things being equal, if H_1 has more tested implications than H_2, H_1 is more probable than H_2. _____

20 Other things being equal, if the evidence in favor of H_1 is more homogeneous than that in favor of H_2, then H_1 is more probable than H_2. _____

21 The precision of evidence refers to its variety. _____

22 If between several competing hypotheses, one leads to new predictions while the others do not, then it is to be preferred. _____

23 Simplicity is exclusively an esthetic and psychological criterion regarding the acceptability of a hypothesis. _____

24 Once a hypothesis becomes well established, it is no longer vulnerable to disconfirmation. _____

25 In most cases confirmation involves a judgment as to which of several competing hypotheses is best confirmed. _____

Rational Decision Making

Progress Test 47 (Chapter Seventeen)
Indicate whether the following are true or false; use T for true, F for false.

1 According to a popular conception of decision making, we must first decide upon our "real" or "ultimate" ends. _____

2 Though we cannot say for sure whether a belief is true, we can determine if there is warrant for believing it to be true. _____

3 If means and ends form an existential continuum, then we cannot distinguish "instrumental goods" from "immediate goods." _____

4 Unlike the distinction between means and ends, the distinction between acts and their consequences is perfectly clear. _____

5 There are "good reasons" for a warranted belief and there are "good reasons" for a warranted decision. _____

6 A warranted decision is always a "right" decision. _____

7 In describing and analyzing a proposed action and its consequences, we are always apt to overlook significant features. _____

8 In order to make a rational decision, one must consider possible alternatives and possible consequences of one's action. _____

9 Rational decisions are warranted decisions. _____

10 The consideration of means and ends apart from the specific contexts in which decisions occur is of considerable help in decision making. _____

11 Rational choice involves purposes or ends-in-view. _____

12 In most contexts it is easy to distinguish statements of fact from value judgments. _____

13 A popular conception of decision making holds that scientific method may be employed in determining both means and ends. _____

14 It is generally easy to make an absolute distinction between means and ends. _____

15 Rational decisions can go wrong; that is, they may turn out to be "wrong" decisions. _____

16 Criteria of logical consistency are not relevant to the appraisal of evaluations. _____

17 Sentences like "x is good" often serve several different purposes simultaneously. _____

18 Value words like "good," "just," and "beautiful" may be largely factual, or signify factual concepts, in some contexts. _____

19 In the process of justifying the grounds of an argument by adducing further grounds, ultimate grounds cannot be provided. _____

20 In rational decision making the "problem" is always defined before alternative solutions are posed. _____

21 In rational decision making, alternatives which are considered relevant, possible, and meaningful vary with the context. _____

22 An individual's store of knowledge, habits, and frames of reference have little bearing on the alternatives which will occur to him when he is trying to arrive at a rational decision. _____

23 There is no close interplay between "facts" and "values"; the distinction between the two is always sharp. _____

24 The rational criticism of values does not involve a consideration of the facts bearing on them. _____

25 Just as scientific inquiry requires the formulation of hypotheses, inquiry directed at action requires the formulation of proposals. _____

26 The full ramifications of a "problem" can be seen only after a series of alternative proposals has been offered. _____

27 Like scientific method which requires the elaboration of the implications of a hypothesis, rational decision making requires the elaboration of the possible consequences of an action. _____

28 The ability to frame warranted prediction statements is not important to rational decision making. _____

29 The study of logic and scientific method is of little help in making warranted prediction statements. _____

30 The more radical the departure from the status quo, the easier it is generally to determine consequences. _____

31 Since long-run consequences are relatively more obscure than short-run consequences, the long run should not be considered. _____

32 Auxiliary decisions are required to determine the range of consequences which can be fruitfully considered. _____

33 Since an action conceivably affects everything, a rational decision must take into account the possible effects upon everything. _____

34 Even though some of its consequences may be deemed unimportant, a decision might still be fully warranted. _____

35 Unfortunately, during the course of rational decision making, auxiliary decisions as to what will be considered must be arbitrary and incapable of justification.

36 If some imponderables were not considered, a decision could still be warranted.   _____

37 Since a decision not to act is also a decision, rational decision-making always involves making comparative judgments of alternatives.   _____

38 Like weighing evidence in induction, evaluating alternatives is not subject to precise rules.   _____

39 Though decisions may and should be tested in the imagination, the final test of a decision comes only in action.   _____

40 A rational person never acts on probabilities.   _____

ANSWERS TO PROGRESS TESTS

Test 1, p. 396

1 T.		**2** T.		**3** T.		**4** F.		**5** F.		**6** F.		**7** T.
8 F.		**9** T.		**10** F.		**11** T.		**12** F.		**13** T.		**14** F.
15 F.		**16** F.		**17** T.		**18** F.		**19** F.		**20** F.
21 F.		**22** F.		**23** T.		**24** T.		**25** F.		**26** F.
27 F.		**28** T.		**29** F.		**30** T.				

Test 2, p. 397

1 d, a.		**2** b.		**3** e, a.		**4** f, g.		**5** c, a.		**6** b.
7 d, a		**8** a, d		**9** a, g.		**10** d, a.		**11** m.		**12** k.
13 h.		**14** n.		**15** m.		**16** k.		**17** m.		**18** i.
19 l.		**20** j.							

Test 3, p. 398

1 T.		**2** F.		**3** T.		**4** T.		**5** F.		**6** T.		**7** T.
8 T.		**9** F.		**10** T.		**11** F.		**12** F.		**13** T.		**14** F.
15 F.		**16** F.		**17** T.		**18** F.		**19** F.		**20** T.
21 F.		**22** F.		**23** F.		**24** T.		**25** T.		**26** T.
27 T.		**28** T.		**29** T.		**30** F.				

Test 4, p. 399
1 b.   2 e.   3 a.   4 c.   5 f.   6 d.   7 c.
8 e.   9 a.   10 a, b   11 c.   12 a.   13 e.   14 d.
15 a, b.

Test 5, p. 400
1 i, a.   2 a, m; or c, p.   3 b, j.   4 a, m.   5 a, d.
6 a, g.   7 a, e.   8 c, k.   9 c, p, n.   10 c, k.   11 h, c.
12 b, m.   13 a, f.   14 i, a.   15 h, c.

Test 6, p. 401
1 T.   2 F.   3 F.   4 T.   5 F.   6 F.   7 F.
8 T.   9 T.   10 T.   11 F.   12 T.   13 F.   14 T.
15 T.   16 T.   17 T.   18 T.   19 T.   20 T.
21 F.   22 F.   23 F.   24 T.   25 T.

Test 7, p. 402
1, 3, 5, 7, 9, 10, 11, 12, 16, 17, 19, 27, 28, 29; in some contexts, **21, 25.**

Test 8, p. 403
1, 4, 6, 8, 9.   11 The substance . . . done; good works . . . person.
12 No man . . . cause; a body . . . time.   **13** Let us . . . power.   **14**
Market rate . . . it; increase . . . people.   **15** This . . . true; it . . . cause;
there . . . exist.   **16** Men . . . another.   **17** Many . . . them; many
. . . ideas; the rule . . . other.   **18** Nature . . . admitted; the statement
. . . form.

Test 9, p. 406
1 I.   2 D.   3 D.   4 I.   5 D.   6 D.   7 I.
8 D.   9 I.   10 D.   11 D.   12 I.   13 I.   14 I.
15 I.   16 I.   17 I.   18 D.   19 I.   20 D.

Test 10, p. 407
1, 2.   4 is ambiguous, for the context does not make it clear whether
a means "No newspaper comics are really funny" or "Some newspaper
comics are not really funny" and whether **b** means "All newspaper comics
are really funny" or "Some newspaper comics are really funny."   For **a**
and **b** to be contradictories **a** must be interpreted as "No newspaper comics
are really funny" and **b** as "Some newspaper comics are really funny."
   Statement connectives: **6, 8, 11, 13, 14, 15** (with a meaning loss), and
17. Regarding **20,** replacing "and" with "dot" entirely corrupts the sense
of the sentence.
   Statement connectives: v **22, 23, 27,** and **34** are "exclusive or."
   Statement connectives: ⊃ **36, 37, 38, 42, 43, 44,** and **45** can be symbolized as $p \supset q$. **39** and **41** are $q \supset p$, and **40** is contrary to fact.
   Statement connectives: ≡ **47, 49,** and **50** are $p \equiv q$.

Test 11, p. 408

1 $\sim p \cdot q$.   **2** p.   **3** p (could be argued this is not a statement).
4 $p \supset q$.   **5** $\sim p \cdot \sim q$.   **6** $p \cdot q$.   **7** $p \cdot \sim q$.   **8** $p \vee \sim q$.
9 $p \supset q$.   **10** $q \supset p$.   **11** $p \equiv q$.   **12** $p \supset q$.   **13** $p \supset q$.
14 $p \cdot q$.   **15** If "take a raincoat" is interpreted as "You should take a raincoat" or "It would be advisable for you to take a raincoat," then **15** would be symbolized as $p \supset q$.   **16** $p \supset \sim q$.   **17** $p \cdot q$.   **18** $p \vee q$.   **19** Not a statement.   **20** $p \supset q$.

Test 12, p. 409

1 $\vee$.   **2** $\cdot$.   **3** $\supset$.   **4** $\sim$.   **5** $\supset$.   **6** __.   **7** $\vee$.
8 $\cdot$.   **9** __.   **10** $\equiv$.   **11** $(p \vee q)r$.   **12** $p \vee qr$.   **13** $(p \vee q) \supset r$.   **14** $p \vee (q \supset r)$.   **15** $p[q \vee (r \supset s)]$.   **16** $pq \vee (r \supset s)$.
17 $(pq \vee r) \supset s$.   **18** $\sim (p \vee q)$.   **19** $\sim pq$.   **20** $\sim (pq) \supset (r \vee s)$.

Test 13, p. 410

1 T.   **2** T.   **3** F.   **4** T.   **5** T.   **6** T.   **7** If and only if p is true and q is true.   **8** If and only if both p is false and q is false.   **9** If and only if p and q have different truth values.   **10** If and only if p is true and q is false.   **11** T.   **12** F.   **13** F.
14 F.   **15** T.   **16** T.   **17** F.   **18** T.   **19** T.
20 T.

Test 14, p. 411

1 T.   **2** T.   **3** T.   **4** F.   **5** F.   **6** T.   **7** T.
8 F.   **9** T.   **10** F.   **11** F.   **12** F.   **13** T.   **14** F.
15 T.   **16** F.   **17** T.   **18** T.   **19** F.   **20** T.

Test 15, p. 412

1 Completed.   **2** **a,** FFTF; **b,** TTTF.   **3** **a,** FTTT; **b,** FTTT.   **4** **a,** TTFT; **b,** FFTF.   **5** **a,** TTFFTTTT; **b,** TTTTFFFF.   **6** TTFT; contingency.   **7** FFFF, contradiction.   **8** **a,** FTTF; **b,** TTTT; tautology.   **9** **a,** TFFF; **b,** FTTT; **c,** TTTT; **d,** TTTT; **e,** FFFF; contradiction.   **10** **a,** TFTFTTTT; **b,** TFFFFFTT; **c,** TTTTTTTT; tautology.

Test 16, p. 414

1 Valid (line 2).   **2** Valid (line 1).   **3** Valid (line 1).   **4** Invalid (line 2).

Test 17, p. 415

    T   F T   F
1 $[(p \supset q)p] \supset q$; tautology
    F T F T   F
3 $[(p \equiv q) \sim q] \supset p$
    F   T   T F T F   F
5 $(p \supset q)(\sim q \supset r)(s \equiv p) \supset s$

    F F T F   F
2 $[(p \vee q) \sim p] \supset q$; tautology
    T   T   T
4 $p \supset (pq \vee \sim qp)$; tautology
    F T   T T T T F   F
6 $(p \supset q)(\sim q \supset s)(s \vee p) \supset p$

                    F F F   T   **T F   F   F F F**
7 $[(p \lor qs) \supset (t \supset u)] \sim (u \lor s) \supset (p \lor q)$
                    TT F T   TF T TT   FF
8 $(pr \lor pq)(r \supset t)(\sim t \supset pq) \supset rt$
        F T   T T F   F
9 $(p \supset qr)(s \lor t) \supset \sim qt$
              TF F F   T F   T   T F   F   FTT
10 $[(pr \lor q) \supset (r \equiv t)] \sim (r \lor q) \supset \sim (pt)$

Test 18, p. 416

1 ***4** 1, exp.   ***5** r, 3&4, MP.   ***6** 2&5, MP.
2 ***3** 1, simp.   ***4** 2, simp.   ***5** $\sim p$, 3&4, MT.   ***6** 5, add.   ***7** DeM.   ***8** 2, com.   ***9** $r \supset ps$, 8, simp. ***10** 7&9, MT.
3 ***4** $(p \supset q)(r \supset s)$, 1&2, conj.   ***5** 3, simp.   ***6** 4&5, CD. ***7** 3, Com.   ***8** $\sim q$, 7, simp.   ***9** 6&8, DS.
4 ***3** 1, exp.   ***4** 3, trans.   ***5** $\sim (q \supset r) \supset s$, 2&4, HS. ***6** 5, imp.   ***7** 6, imp.   ***8** 7, assoc.   ***9** 8, imp.
5 ****3** assump.   ****4** 1&3, MP.   ****5** $r \supset q$, 4, trans.   ****6** 2&5, HS.   ***7** 3&6, cond.
6 ***4** 2, equi.   ***5** 4, com.   ***6** 5, simp.   ****7** assump. ****8** $\sim s$, 6&7, MP.   ****9** 3, exp.   ****10** $\sim (qr)$, 8&9, MT. ****11** 1, com.   ****12** 10&11, DS.   ***13** 7&12, cond.
7 ****4** assump.   ****5** 2, simp.   ****6** $\sim q$, 4&5, MT.   ****7** 1, DeM.   ****8** 7, DN.   ****9** $p \supset q$, 8, imp.   ****10** 6&9, MT. ****11** 2, com.   ****12** 11, simp.   ****13** 12, com.   ****14** $s \supset p$, 13, imp.   ****15** 3&14, MP.   ****16** 15&10, conj., **RAA.**
8 ****4** assump.   ****5** 1, exp.   ****6** $q \supset r$, 4&5, MP.   ****7** q, 3, simp.   ****8** 6&7, MP.   ****9** s, 2&8, MP.   ****10** 3, com.   ****11** $\sim s$, 10, simp.   ****12** 9&11, conj., **RAA.**
9 ****4** p, assump.   ****5** 1&4, MP.   ****6** 3&5, MP.   ****7** $\sim r \lor \sim \sim s$, 2, DeM.   ****8** $\sim r \lor s$, 7, DN.   ****9** 8, imp.   ****10** $\sim r$, 6&9, MT.   ***11** $p \supset \sim r$, 3&10, cond.
10 ***3** $p \supset q$, 1, simp.   ***4** 2&3, HS.   ***5** 1, com.   ***6** $r \supset s$, 5, simp.   ***7** $\sim s \supset \sim r$, 6, trans.   ***8** $p \supset \sim r$, 4&7, HS.

Test 19, p. 418

1 **A**, men (persons).   **2** **E**, liars or trusted people.   **3** **O**, novels. **4** **I**, eaters or daydreamers.   **5** **A**, teenagers.   **6** **E**, Scandinavians, etc.   **7** **I**, girl, etc.   **8** **A**, priests.   **9** **I**, players.   **10** **A**, all who dislike others.   **11** **A**, pomegranates or **I**, some times are times when.   **12** **A**, tippers.   **13** **A**, tasks.   **14** **I**, people. **15** **E**, people.   **16** **O**, things.   **17** **A**, racers.   **18** **A**, squares. **19** **A**, nonticket holders.   **20** **A**, debates.   **21** **I**, person who is a million-dollar baby.   **22** **A**, times when skies are gray.   **23** **A**, people.   **24** **O**, things.   **25** **I**, fellow.

Test 20, p. 419
2, 4, 5, 8, 9, and **13** are correct.

Test 21, p. 420
The following are correct: **2, 3, 5, 6, 7?, 9, 11, 12, 14, 16, 19.**

Test 22, p. 421
1 F, T.   **2** ?, T.   **3** T, ?.   **4** F, T.   **5** F, T.   **6** ?, T.
7 F, ?.   **8** F, T.   **9** T, ?.   **10** F, ?.   **11** F, T.   **12** F, ?.
13 T, ?.   **14** ?, T.   **15** ?, T.   **16** T, ?.   **17** F, ?.   **18**
F, T.   **19** F, ?.   **20** F, T.

Test 23, p. 422
1 Contrary.   **2** Implicant.   **3** Contrary(?).   **4** Subcontrary.
5 Equivalent.   **6** Implicant.   **7** Contradictory.   **8** Subimplicant.   **9** Independent.   **10** Contradictory.   **11** Contrary.
12 Contradictory.   **13** Contradictory.   **14** Subcontrary.   **15**
Implicant.   **16** Subcontrary.   **17** Implicant.   **18** Contrary.
19 Contradictory.   **20** Implicant.   **21** Equivalent.   **22** Subcontrary.   **23** Contrary.   **24** Contradictory.   **25** Equivalent.
26 Equivalent.   **27** Independent.   **28** Equivalent.   **29** Independent.   **30** Subimplicant.

Test 24, p. 424
1 **b,** F, ?; **c,** T, ?; **d,** F, T.   **2** **b,** F, T; **c,** F, ?; **d,** T, ?.   **3** **b,** F, T;
c, ?, F; **d,** ?, T.   **4** **b,** F, T; **c,** ?, F; **d,** ?, T.   **5** **a,** F; **b,** F; **c,** T; **d,** F;
e, T; **f,** ?; **g,** F; **h,** T; **i,** F; **j,** T.

Test 25, p. 425
1 **IEI**-3, 4.   **2** **AAA**-4, 2.   **3** **EOA**-3, 3.   **4** **AII**-2, 1.   **5**
IAA-1, 1.   **6** **EOO**-2, 3.   **7** **AIA**-1, 2.   **8** **IAI**-2, 1.   **9**
AEE-1, 2.   **10** **EIO**-1, V.   **11** **OAO**-2, 2.   **12** **OAO**-1, 1.
13 **AEE**-4, V.   **14** **AAA**-3, 2.   **15** **EOE**-3, 3.   **16** **EAO**-1, V.
17 **AAI**-2, 1.   **18** **EII**-3, 4.   **19** **AAA**-4, 2.   **20** **AOI**-2, 4.

Test 26, p. 426

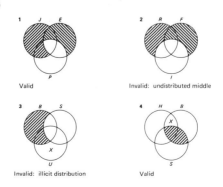

1 J E
   P
Valid

2 R F
   I
Invalid: undistributed middle

3 B S
   X
   U
Invalid: illicit distribution

4 H B
   X
   S
Valid

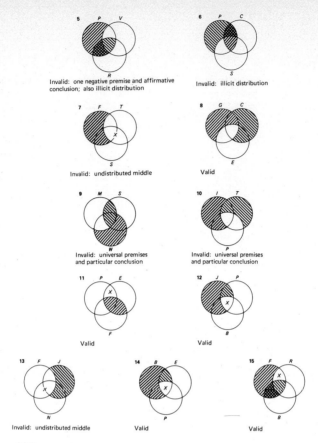

5 Invalid: one negative premise and affirmative conclusion; also illicit distribution

6 Invalid: illicit distribution

7 Invalid: undistributed middle

8 Valid

9 Invalid: universal premises and particular conclusion

10 Invalid: universal premises and particular conclusion

11 Valid

12 Valid

13 Invalid: undistributed middle

14 Valid

15 Valid

Test 27, p. 429

1 John is responsible.   **2** Heidegger's philosophy is obscure.   **3** All Irishmen are pretty glib.   **4** Whatever involves a deliberate misrepresentation is dishonest.   **5** Divorce is a contract which may be broken by mutual consent.   **6** All rabid Yankee fans have season tickets.   **7** All people with a college degree can afford college.   **8** Some valid arguments do not have true premises.   **9** All deductions are formally valid.   **10** Anyone who is the sole owner has no partners.

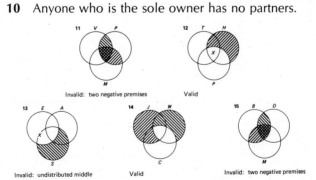

11 Invalid: two negative premises

12 Valid

13 Invalid: undistributed middle

14 Valid

15 Invalid: two negative premises

Test 28, p. 430

1	F.	2	T.	3	T.	4	F.	5	F.	6	T.	7	T.
8	F.	9	F.	10	F.	11	T.	12	T.	13	F.	14	T.
15	T.	16	F.	17	F.	18	F.	19	F.	20	T.	21	F.
22	F.	23	F.	24	T.	25	F.						

Test 29, p. 430

1 (x)(Fx ⊃ Gx). **2** (∃ x)(Fx · Gx). **3** (∃ x)(Fx · ~Gx). **4** (x)(Fx ⊃ ~Gx). **5** (x)(Fx ∨ Gx). **6** (x)Fx ∨ (x)Gx. **7** (∃ x)[Fx (Gx ∨ Hx)]. **8** ~(x)(Fx ⊃ ~Gx). **9** ~(∃ x)Fx ⊃ ~(∃ x)Gx. **10** (x)(Fx ⊃ Gx). **11** (∃ x)Fx ⊃ (x)(Gx ⊃ ~Hx). **12** (x)[(Fx ∨ Gx) ⊃ (Hx ∨ Jx)]. **13** ~(∃ x)Fx. **14** (∃ x)(Fx · Gx) · (∃ x)(Fx · ~Gx). **15** (x)[Fx ⊃ (Gx ∨ ~Gx)] · (x)[(Fx · Gx) ⊃ ~Hx]

Test 30, p. 431

    F   **T F**   **F**   **F**   **F**

2 Fa · Fb ... Fh, no. **3** FaGa ∨ FbGb ∨ ... FhGh, no. **4** (Fa ⊃

                                T T   **T**   **F**   **F**   **F**

~Ga)(Fb ⊃ ~Gb) ... (Fh ⊃ ~Gh), no. **5** FaFb ... Fh ∨ Ga ∨ Gb ∨ ... Gh,

         T F   **F**   **F**   **T F**

no. **6** ~[(Fa ⊃ ~Ga)(Fb ⊃ ~Gb) ... (Fh ⊃ ~Gh)], no. **7** ~[Fa ·

T   **T**

Fb ... Fh], no.

Test 31, p. 432

1 *3 2, **EI** x. *4 1, **UI.** *5 3&4, MP. *6 5, **EG.**

2 *3 1, **UI.** *4 2, **UI.** *5 3, equiv. *6 5, com. *7 Gx ⊃ Fx, 6, simp. *8 Fx, 4&7, MP. *9 8, **UG.**

3 *3 2, QE. *4 3, imp. *5 4, DeM. *6 (∃ x)(Gx · ~Hx), 5, DN. *7 6, **EI** x. *8 1, DeM. *9 8, **UI.** *10 9, com. *11 Gx ⊃ ~Fx, 10, imp. *12 7, simp. *13 ~Fx, 11&12, MP. *14 13, **EG.**

4 **3 assump. **4 (x)Fx, 3, QE. **5 1&4, MP. **6 5, **EI** x. **7 2, **UI.** **8 Gx, 6, simp. **9 7&8, MP. **10 6, com. **11 Hx, 10, simp. **12 9&11, conj., **RAA.**

5 *3 2, QE. *4 3, DeM. *5 4, DN. *6 5, **UI.** *7 6, simp. *8 (x)~Hx, 7, **UG.** *9 8, QE. *10 1, com. *11 (x)(Fx ⊃ ~Gx) 9&10, DS. *12 11, **UI.** *13 6, com. *14 Gx, 13, simp. *15 14, DN. *16 12&15, MT. *17 16, **UG.**

6 **2 assump. **3 Fx ⊃ p, 1, **EI** x. **4 Fx, 2, **UI.** **5 3&4, MP. *6 (x)Fx ⊃ p, 2&5, cond.

Test 32, p. 434

1 F.	2 T.	3 T.	4 T.	5 T.	6 F.	7 F.
8 T.	9 T.	10 F.	11 T.	12 F.	13 T.	14 F.
15 F.	16 T.	17 F.	18 F.	19 F.	20 T.	

Test 33, p. 435

1   *2 1, EI x.   *3 2, UI.   *4 3, EG.

2   *2 1, UI.   *3 2, QE.   *4 ~Fxx, 3, UI.   *5 4, UG.

3   **2 assump.   **3 $(x) \sim (\exists y)Fxy$, 2, QE.   **4 3, QE.   **5 4, UI.   **6 5, UI.   **7 Fxx, 1, UI.   **8 6&7, conj., RAA.

4   *3 2, EIx.   **4 assump.   **5 1, UI.   **6 4&5, MP.   **7 6, UI.   **8 3&7, MP   **9 3&8, conj.   **10 9, EG.   *11 3&10, cond.   *12 11, UG.

5   *2 1, UI.   *3 2, UI.   *4 3, taut.   *5 4, imp.   *6 ~Fxx, 5, taut.   *7 $(x) \sim Fxx$, 6, UG.

Test 34, p. 436

1 F.	2 T.	3 F.	4 F.	5 F.	6 T.	7 F.
8 T.	9 T.	10 T.	11 F.	12 T.	13 F.	14 F.
15 T.	16 T.	17 F.	18 T.	19 T.	20 T.	
21 F.	22 F.	23 T.	24 F.	25 F.		

Test 35, p. 437

1 T.	2 F.	3 T.	4 T.	5 F.	6 T.	7 F.
8 F.	9 T.	10 T.	11 T.	12 F.	13 T.	14 F.
15 T.	16 T.	17 F.	18 T.	19 F.	20 T.	

Test 36, p. 438

1 b.	2 a.	3 a.	4 a.	5 a.	6 b.	7 a or b.
8 b.	9 c.	10 b.				

Test 37, p. 438

1   A. It could be argued that a scientist does have a right to object since he may be seriously affected by his decision, whereas a carpenter generally is not.   2 E.   3 A. Since the consequences in each case would be radically different, atomic arsenals could conceivably constitute a deterrent to war.   4 A. Unlike most insurance policies, the insurance being advocated here would probably be of very little worth.   5 E.   6 A. The "exercise" advocated could destroy the body (politic), whereas healthful exercise doesn't generally have this effect.   7 E.   8 A. Although ignoring the elephant in the dining room illustrates the principle that one can't solve problems by ignoring them, this argument assumes that the United States has ignored the Soviet Union with respect to the Middle East. The argument also assumes that sitting down and talking is the way to recognize the Soviet Union's presence.   Both assumptions may be true, but they are not supported by any evidence (in this particular argument).

9   A. TVA was not designed to compete with private industry but to supply power when the latter refused to do so on the grounds that it would not be profitable to.   **10   A.** This appears to be a good example of refutation by logical analogy.

Test 38, p. 440

1 F.	2 F.	3 T.	4 F.	5 F.	6 T.	7 T.
8 F.	9 F.	10 T.	11 F.	12 F.	13 F.	14 T.
15 T.	16 T.	17 F.	18 T.	19 T.	20 F.	21 F.
22 T.	23 F.	24 T.	25 T.			

Test 39, p. 441

1   3, c. Problem: to determine the effect of reading comic books on juvenile delinquency.   Joint method: no factor can be a sufficient condition in whose presence the effect fails to appear.   Conclusion: comic books exert little influence upon the behavior of the children who read them.   This conclusion is unwarranted; the conclusion which is warranted is that reading comic books is not *the* cause, or *sufficient* by itself, to produce juvenile delinquency.   But this does not rule out the possibility that it is a contributing, or necessary, factor.

2   1, c. Problem: to determine factors affecting genius.   Method of agreement: most geniuses studied were first-born children.   Conclusion: not very dependable for most non-geniuses are also first-born children.

3   3, a, and 1, a. Problem: to determine the cause of poisoning.   Joint method (1): No factor can be the cause in whose presence the effect fails to appear; thus, certain drug products were eliminated as the cause because many of those who had consumed them were not poisoned.   Conclusion 1: highly probable.   Method of agreement 2: all who were poisoned ate bread and rolls made from the same flour and sugar stored in a warehouse in which parathion was also stored.   Conclusion 2, they died from parathion, highly probable.

4   2, b. Problem: to determine the cause of the increase in the President's popularity.   Method of difference: two situations are compared — the President's popularity before the Mayaguez incident and his popularity after it. It is assumed that all other significant factors in the two situations — economic, political, etc. — remained the same.   Conclusion: probable; other relevant factors, such as the state of the nation's economy (wholesale price index, level of unemployment, trade balance, etc.), may have been contributing factors.

5   2, b. Problem: to determine the effect of delivery on the reception of a speech.   Method of difference: the two situations were very much alike, the notable difference being in the way the speech was presented.   In one situation effective delivery was absent; in the other it was present.   Conclusion: the excellent reception of the speech was due to the delivery; probable, though Peel's reputation may have been a contributing factor.

6   4, a. Problem: to determine the cause of deviations in the orbit of

Uranus. Method of residues: the regular orbit due to solar attraction was known (or calculable). Conclusion: the deviation, or additional movement, was due to the attraction of another (theretofore unknown) heavenly body; confirmed by the discovery of Neptune and thus highly probable.

7   3, a. Problem: to determine the effect of fluorinated drinking water on teeth. Method: joint method of agreement and difference; the experiment included many children who had one important factor in common, fluorinated drinking water, and many children who had little in common except the absence of that same factor. Conclusion: moderate quantities of fluorine in drinking water reduce tooth decay; quite probable.

8   2, a. Problem: to determine the effect of a certain vaccine on anthrax. Method of difference: the only significant difference between the two sets of twenty-four sheep was the vaccination of one set and the non-vaccination of the other. Conclusion: Pasteur's vaccine was an antidote to anthrax; almost certainly true.

Test 40, p. 443

1	F.	2	T.	3	T.	4	F.	5	T.	6	F.	7	T.
8	T.	9	F.	10	F.	11	T.	12	F.	13	T.	14	T.
15	F.	16	F.	17	F.	18	T.	19	F.	20	T.		

Test 41, p. 444

1   The financial "assets" being compared are really not comparable. Moreover, such assets are not the most significant factor in determining how strong or weak unions are; their ability to bargain collectively and to strike are far more significant factors.

2   Since a comparison is being made, the growth of the white population since the settlement of Jamestown should have been considered.

3   Cause and effect may be, and probably are, confused. Though there may be a correlation, and even some type of causal relationship, between the two factors cited, it seems likely that the more prosperous a state becomes, the more it spends, and not vice versa.

4   Faulty extrapolation. The argument assumes that despite an overall inflation, the annual dollar income would remain the same for thirty years.

5   The percentage of professional women, like that of professional men, is relatively small in all countries and, taken by itself, reveals little about the comparative treatment of the sexes.

6   First, the argument assumes that what is true of the part is necessarily true of the whole (fallacy of composition). Also, the sample may be loaded in that the families represented may produce their own food, own their own farms, and pay little in taxes.

7   The poll is slanted, having been taken in a traditionally predominantly Democratic area. Also, the size of the poll is inadequate, *despite* the outcome. The outcome of such polls has little bearing on whether or not they were properly conducted.

8 This argument overlooks the fact that drinking is legal whereas taking narcotics without a prescription is not. Hence, one would expect many more arrests for drug offenses than for liquor offenses. Hence, the statistic in no way confirms the conclusion given.

9 Faulty analysis and comparison of statistics. Ignored are the total numbers voting in the various elections and the *percentage* of votes received by the various candidates. Since many more people voted in Stevenson's day than in Cleveland's, Stevenson's percentage of the total vote was much lower than that of Cleveland's.

10 As in 9, the percentage of fatalities in each situation is ignored. It is conceivable that 10 out of 40 million vaccinated died from vaccination, whereas 9 out of 1 million unvaccinated died. Such percentages would refute the suggestion that polio vaccinations are suspect.

Test 42, p. 445

1 $1/52$. **2** $1/52$. **3** $2/52$. **4** $4/52$. **5** $13/52$. **6** $26/52$. **7** $39/52$. **8** $26/52$. **9** $51/52$. **10** $40/52$. **11** $4/52 \times 3/51$. **12** $13/52 \times 12/51$. **13** $12/52 \times 11/51$. **14** $26/52 \times 25/51$. **15** $1/52 \times 1/51$. **16** $1/52 \times 1/51$. **17** $51/52 \times 50/51$. **18** $50/52 \times 49/51$. **19** $2/52 \times 1/51$. **20** $2/52 \times 4/51$.

Test 43, p. 446

1 Fallacy of accident. The right of association has implicit qualifications (as the Supreme Court subsequently ruled), as do all other rights guaranteed by the Constitution. Presumably association which results in the exploitation of women and children is proscribed, just as libelous remarks are forbidden despite the guarantee of freedom of speech.

2 False alternatives. Why assume that either the man or the woman must dominate? Why should anyone dominate?

3 Equivocation on the word "know." In one context it means "to have complete understanding of the subject" and in another it means "to be able to identify the type of subject of which one is ignorant."

4 Circular reasoning, or begging the question. Basically, the argument reduces to: "Complete freedom of speech is beneficial to the State, for complete freedom of speech is beneficial to the State," or "*p*, since *p*."

5 Confusing cause with effect. Apparently the grade led to their argument, and not vice versa.

6 Fallacy of division. What is true of the whole is not necessarily true of the part. It is conceivable that many of those in the twenty-one to twenty-two age group were mediocre students and that Brown, because of army service or economic hardship, had to delay his education. The fallacy can also be classified as slanting.

7 Sound argument. It *would be* inconsistent to say that a given principle is both sound and not sound.

8 Equivocation on the word "equal." As used in the Constitution it means "equal rights under the law," such as the right to vote, the right to a fair trial, etc. The reason given here apparently applies to a different meaning of "equal." Hence, the argument could also be classified as a form of irrelevancy.

9 Mistaking correlation for causation. The reverse might be true: alcoholism might contribute to a poor diet; or both may be the effects of a common cause, such as a neurotic or disordered personality.

10 False alternatives; we might try negotiating or other courses ignored in the argument.

11 Appeal to ignorance. Lack of evidence to disprove "Communist connections" does not prove Communist connections.

12 Fallacy of composition. What is true of the part (the Chicago slums) is not necessarily true of the whole (standard of living). Could also be called slanting since pertinent information is suppressed or ignored.

13 Mistaking correlation for causation or effect for cause. Rather than one factor (number of children) "causing" another (standard of living), the reverse may be true, or both may be the effects of a common cause. Or there might be some kind of interaction between the two.

14 Fallacy of accident. One can enjoy jokes, but there is usually a limit to what kind. "Practical" jokes of the type described here would not fall within the category initially mentioned.

15 Fallacy of the beard and false alternatives. First, there is the failure to differentiate between various degrees of sovereignty and then there is the assumption that only contrary alternatives exist, i.e., either complete sovereignty or no sovereignty at all. Obviously, there are many degrees between these two extremes which are ignored.

16 Fallacy of composition. The argument assumes that what is true of the part (eye, hand, foot) is necessarily true of the whole (a human being). Ironically, Aristotle was one of the first to identify this fallacy.

17 Appeal to ignorance. Lack of proof that the universe is limited does not constitute proof that it is unlimited, or infinite.

18 Mistaking effect for cause; both factors are evidently the product of the same condition—a day of leisure.

19 Circular reasoning, or begging the question. The question of whether mankind is corrupted is assumed, not proved. The argument is of the form "*p*, therefore *p*."

20 Fallacy of the beard, or the unwarranted assumption that distinctions cannot be made between contiguous categories. Here the speaker erroneously concludes that public housing is the same as complete socialism.

21 Fallacy of division. The argument unwarrantedly assumes that what is true of the whole (the university) is necessarily true of one of its parts (the law school). The latter, incidentally, happens to be excellent, but this is not established by the argument in question.

22 Fallacy of impromptu definition. At first, *A* apparently uses "sensible" in an empirical sense to describe certain people but, when questioned, falls back on a definition of "sensible" to refute B's objection. The argument can also be designated as ground shifting or begging the question, the latter since A assumes what he initially purports to prove.

23 Fallacy of accident. The generalization "cooperation is extolled" or "cooperation is desirable" is presumably qualified by certain types of cooperation, which do not include working together to take advantage of people. The fallacy might also be classified as a form of equivocation.

24 Slanting. The argument fails to consider the relative quantity of fluorine used in each process. A relatively large quantity is used in making rat poison, and an infinitesimally small quantity is used in drinking water. Could also be called the fallacy of division, since it assumes that what is true of large quantities of fluorine (when used to make rat poison) is necessarily true of very small quantities (when used in drinking water).

25 Fallacy of impromptu definition. Poe resorts to a questionable definition (that long poems are collections of short ones) to make his position irrefutable.

26 Circular reasoning of the form "Since p is true, q is true; since q is true, r is true; and since r is true, p is true." Rather than proving p (democracy is the best form of government), the argument assumes p as an initial premise.

27 Circular reasoning. The conclusion, every event must have a cause, is ultimately "proved" by the same proposition expressed in slightly different words ("everything has to be caused by something other than itself").

28 Begging the question, or assuming what one is trying to prove. Here A interprets B's response as evidence which supports A's initial contention. A could go on doing this indefinitely and thereby make his theory irrefutable, but in the process he wouldn't be proving anything; he would only be assuming the truth of his assertion. In effect, A establishes his position by definition rather than by empirical observation. From another perspective, the argument is also self-defeating, for if what A says is true, he condemns his very own theory as being a "mere rationalization" and hence something which cannot be taken very seriously.

29 Fallacy of composition. The argument assumes that what is true of certain components of a government, namely the people who work in the various agencies and who, of course, can speak, is necessarily true of government as a whole. The argument also makes the unwarranted assumption that all meaningful terms refer only to physical things.

30 Equivocation on "government control of industry." Though tariffs and quotas may be considered a form or aspect of government control, it is not the same kind of government control envisioned, say, by the nationalization of basic industries.

Test 44, p. 449
1 Irrelevant function. Membership in NATO was not designed to help solve the oil shortage problem in the United States.

2 "There are exceptions to every rule" is self-contradictory, for a rule, by definition, is always true and has no exceptions. This premise permits the absurd conclusion that "if the rule is true, it is also false." (Remember that contradictory premises are compatible with any conclusion.)

3 Irrelevancy. Circulation figures have no bearing whatever on the relative freedom of the press.

4 Irrelevancy. The candidate's military record has little bearing on his qualifications for the office.

5 Highly questionable analogy. Running a theater, besides being much simpler than running a government, calls for relatively quick and usually insignificant decisions, whereas running a government does not. The argument also assumes, rather than proves, that a theater cannot be managed — at least with respect to establishing major policies — by an audience.

6 Slanting. The argument ignores the fact that much money is collected from the investment of premiums, which together with the premiums usually total much more money than is paid out in claims.

7 Unsound generalization because of loaded sample. Although the number of people polled is impressive, they are not representative of "the American people." Coming from a very prosperous socioeconomic area, most very probably expect their children to attend college and hence would favor tax exemptions for college tuition.

8 Ground shifting. The argument attempts to prove that proficiency in math is not a sufficient condition of high intelligence, whereas the psychologists contend only that it is probably a necessary condition.

9 Extension. There is a significant difference between "reducing the drug problem" (which the opposition claims would result) and "completely eliminating the drug problem," which this argument claims would not occur.

10 Distortion. "*A* or not-*A*" does not mean "black or white" but "black or not-black." The argument confuses contradictory alternatives with contrary alternatives. Since it attacks the latter while presuming to attack the former, it could be called a straw-man argument.

11 Loaded sample and questionable generalization. The people of Emporia, Kansas (a farm state), could be expected to favor agricultural price supports. Such a sample, however, would not be representative of "the American people."

12 Irrelevant emotional appeals. Rather than give reasons for rejecting a particular program, the argument attempts to stir up the reader's feelings against the program by associating it with what he dislikes ("silly, Communist-encouraged socialistic idea of statism," "chickens in brooder houses," etc.) and associating the desired program (the status quo) with what he likes ("the things our ancestors risked much to win," "our civilization," etc.).

13 Slanting. Most of the significant factors which make a country "a military threat" are ignored — size of conventional forces, nuclear arsenal, productive capacity, certain raw materials, etc.

14 Biased source. The Meat Institute of America wants to sell beef.

15 Confusing cause with effect. Overlooked is the possibility that heavy smoking and poor grades both stem from a common source, namely, a certain type of personality.

16 Argument of the beard. It assumes that government regulation in one sector of the economy means total and complete control of the entire economy and ultimately the loss of all freedoms, economic and otherwise. In short, there is little difference between black and white.

17 *Ad hominem* attack. The chancellor's action when he was hired has little bearing on whether or not his current proposal is sound or unsound. Even if his current proposal were inconsistent with his previous action, this fact alone would still not constitute a valid criticism of the former, which is the real issue and should be judged on its own merits.

18 Irrelevant reason. The fact that people get sick has nothing to do with whether or not a national preventive health insurance program is needed. If anything, recurrent sickness might be a good reason for the opposite conclusion.

19 Self-contradiction, or inconsistency. On the one hand, *A* declares that the members should make their own decisions, and, on the other, she condones the making of decisions for them by someone else.

20 Hasty generalization. Sample is loaded, consisting of instances (and only two at that) in only one industry, the food industry.

21 A form of irrelevancy by ground shifting. Instead of refuting the point (as is implied) that a good grasp of biology is a necessary factor for one to be a good biology teacher, this argues that a good grasp of biology is not *sufficient* to make one a good biology teacher—a point not in contention.

22 Irrelevant reason. The fact that Pound helped young poets and writers has no bearing on whether or not he should have been committed. Incidentally, this very argument was advanced by certain prominent writers on Pound's behalf.

23 Genetic or *ad hominem* fallacy. The arguments for cutting down on cigarettes must be judged on their own merits and not in accordance with the personal habits of the individual advancing them.

24 Slanting, or misuse of statistics by comparing unlike entities—in this case the dollar amounts received by instructors as wages in two entirely different periods, 1941 and 1976. The argument is guilty of slanting because it ignores the relative purchasing power of the dollar in the two periods being compared.

25 Extension, or exaggeration. *A* never contended that "unemployed workers were running around murdering their wives." Ironically, it is *B* who exaggerates, not *A*.

26 Biased source. What else would the Foreign Minister of India say about Kashmir, a territory which India has claimed?

27 *Fallacia accidentis.* Since professional boxing per se is not responsible for the exploitation, no justification has been given for abolishing it. If anything, the evidence would justify abolishing managers or carefully supervising them.

28 Irrelevant conclusion. The evidence only proves that girls who marry young don't generally attend college (which is not surprising). It has no bearing on how education affects one's chances of getting married. Even if some type of correlation between education and marriage could be established—which is not the case here—this would not be sufficient to indicate a particular causal relationship between the two.

29 False analogy. The two components being compared, a country with newly acquired rockets and a child with a new toy, are so unlike with regard to motivations and potential consequences as to make any comment almost superfluous.

30 Genetic fallacy. Where a program originated is largely irrelevant to the question of whether or not it is any good.

31 Irrelevant emotional appeals combined with an *ad hominem* attack ("when he grows up, etc.").

32 Hasty generalization. The statistics given ignore the fact that many more men than boys go hunting and that what is significant is the *percentage* of accidents in each group, not the gross total.

33 Biased and unqualified source. The source is biased because he is paid to endorse the car and unqualified because he likely knows very little about cars.

34 Extension. The student council, whose argument is presumably being refuted here, never claimed that an honor system "is suddenly going to make all students honest." According to the speaker himself, its claim was much more modest.

35 Self-contradiction, or inconsistency. In the first reason given for rejecting the proposal, it is claimed that, in effect, the policy argued for already exists (it being the same as the status quo) and is working satisfactorily. In the second reason, it is claimed that the policy argued for would not work satisfactorily ("would be undesirable") for various reasons.

36 Slanting. The argument ignores the growth of the population since the 1920s and how many people might have been employed if automation had not been introduced. Conceivably, this figure could have been over a million.

Test 45, p. 452

1 T.	2 F.	3 T.	4 F.	5 F.	6 T.	7 T.
8 T.	9 F.	10 T.	11 T.	12 F.	13 F.	14 T.
15 T.	16 T.	17 T.	18 F.	19 T.	20 T.	

Test 46, p. 453

1 F.	2 T.	3 F.	4 F.	5 F.	6 T.	7 T.
8 F.	9 F.	10 T.	11 T.	12 F.	13 T.	14 F.

| 15 T. | 16 F. | 17 T. | 18 F. | 19 T. | 20 F. | 21 F. |
| 22 T. | 23 F. | 24 F. | 25 T. | | | |

Test 47, p. 454

1 T.	2 T.	3 F.	4 F.	5 T.	6 F.	7 T.
8 T.	9 T.	10 F.	11 T.	12 F.	13 F.	14 F.
15 T.	16 F.	17 T.	18 T.	19 T.	20 F.	21 T.
22 F.	23 F.	24 F.	25 T.	26 T.	27 T.	28 F.
29 F.	30 F.	31 F.	32 T.	33 F.	34 T.	35 F.
36 T.	37 T.	38 T.	39 T.	40 F.		

GLOSSARY

Accident, fallacy of: The error of applying a generalization to a case it was not intended to cover.

Addition: A deductive argument of the form "*P* entails *P* v *Q*."

Affirmative sentence: Any **A**-form or **I**-form statement. In the logic of truth-functions a simple affirmative statement is one which contains none of the five logical connectives.

Affirming the consequent, fallacy of: A formal fallacy exhibited by an argument with the form "If *p*, then *q*; *q*; therefore, *p*."

A-form statement: An affirmative universal statement; for example, "All men are mortal."

Agreement, method of: A form of eliminative induction whereby it is inferred, in the words of John Stuart Mill, that "if two or more instances of the phenomenon under investigation have only one circumstance in common, the circumstance in which alone all the instances agree is the cause (or effect) of the given phenomenon."

Alternation: Represented in the statement calculus by v. Inclusive sense: either . . . or, or both; exclusive sense: either . . . or but not both.

Alternatives, events or decisions: Alternatives are *mutually exclusive* if both cannot occur simultaneously. Alternatives are *exhaustive* if and only if the set of alternatives is complete.

Ambiguity: A word, an expression, or a sentence is ambiguous when it can readily be interpreted in two or more different ways.

Amphiboly: Ambiguity resulting from grammatical structure.

Analogy: A similarity of two things.

Analogy, argument from: An inductive argument in which a known similarity of two things in some respects is used as evidence for concluding that the two things are similar in other respects.   If the conclusion is unwarranted by the evidence, the argument is called a *false analogy.*

Analytic definition: See *connotative definition.*

Antecedent: In conditional statements of the form "If *p*, then *q*," statement *p* is called the antecedent.

A posteriori: Known only in experience or by appeal to the senses.

A priori: Known independently of experience or the evidence of the senses.

Argument: A set of statements in which some are used as premises to justify some conclusion.

Argument of the beard, fallacy of: The error of assuming that small differences are always insignificant.

Argumentum ad hominem, fallacy of: An irrelevant attack upon a man's character rather than upon his argument.   See *genetic fallacy.*

Argumentum ad ignoratiam (appeal to ignorance), fallacy of: The error of assuming that the absence of proof or the inability to prove a statement constitutes proof that its contradictory is true.

Argumentum ad misericordiam, ad populum, ad baculum, ad verecundian, fallacies of: The errors of appealing to pity, mob instincts, force, or tradition, rather than trying to prove a point.   Also called *irrelevant emotional appeals.*

Association: The principle that in a conjunction or disjunction, grouping doesn't matter.   Thus, $P \vee (Q \vee R)$ is equivalent to $(P \vee Q) \vee R$, and $P \cdot (Q \cdot R)$ is equivalent to $(P \cdot Q) \cdot R$.

Assumption: A statement treated as true.

Begging the question, fallacy of: An argument which assumes the truth of what it sets out to prove; a form of circular reasoning in which the conclusion is used as a premise to prove itself.

Biconditional sentence: Any sentence of the form "*p* if and only if *q*."   Also called *material biconditional.*

Boolean algebra: The systems of logic begun by George Boole (1815–1864) and developed by Jevons, Peirce, Schroeder, and others.   Also called *Boolean logic.*

Boolean functions: Generally this refers to so-called Boolean disjunctive normal forms, which are disjunctions of variables or conjuncts, for example, $pq \vee r \vee ps$.

Boolean interpretation of categorical forms: The universal affirmative "All *F* is *G*" and the universal negative "No *F* is *G*" are interpreted as conditionals: "If there are *F*'s, then they are *G*'s," etc.

Broadness: A connotative definition is too broad if the definiens is applicable to some things to which the definiendum is not.

Categorical statement: A statement with a subject-predicate form.   Compare **A**-, **E**-, **I**-, **O**-form statements.

Categorical syllogism: A syllogism consisting only of categorical statements.

Cause, causality, causal reasoning, causation: See *eliminative induction.*

Circular definition: A definition which uses the word being defined as part of the definition.

Circular reasoning, arguing in a circle: See *begging the question.*

Closed formula: Same as quantified open formula.   When interpreted by providing open sentences for their open formulas, closed formulas become statements. See *statement formula.*

Closed sentence: Quantified open sentence; a statement.

Collectively: A general or collective term is used collectively when something is predicated of the class or unit taken as a whole; for example, "Great works of art are relatively scarce."

Commutation: The principle that in a conjunction or a disjunction the order of the components doesn't matter. Thus, $P \vee Q$ is equivalent to $Q \vee P$, and PQ is equivalent to QP.

Complement: The complement of a term is its contradictory; e.g., the complement of the term *man* is *non-man.*

Composition, fallacy of: The error of assuming that what is true of the part is necessarily true of the whole. Compare *fallacy of division.*

Compound (or complex) statement: As used in logic, a statement consisting of two or more statements connected with the logical connectives of the statement calculus; e.g., "If it rains, we shall leave," which becomes "It rains $\supset$ we shall leave."

Conclusion: A statement which is either supported by premises or is claimed to be the consequence of them.

Concomitant variations, method of: A form of eliminative induction whereby it is inferred, in the words of John Stuart Mill, that "whatever phenomenon varies in any manner whenever another phenomenon varies in some particular manner is either a cause or an effect of that phenomenon, or is connected with it through some fact of causation."

Conditional proof: A mode of proof in which an added premise is assumed for purposes of the proof. However, before the proof is complete, the added premise must appear as the antecedent of a conditional with whatever was deduced with it as consequent.

Conditional statement: A statement having the form "If p, then q," where both p and q are statements. Also known as a *hypothetical* statement.

Conditional syllogism: See *hypothetical syllogism.*

Condition, necessary; condition, sufficient: A condition A is said to be necessary for condition B, if when A is absent (or does not occur), B is absent (or does not occur). A condition A is said to be sufficient for condition B, if when A is present (or occurs), B is present (or occurs). See *eliminative induction.*

Confirmation: A hypothesis is said to be confirmed when the consequences deduced from it are true, the hypothesis successfully answers the question it was formulated to answer, and competing hypotheses have been eliminated. See *hypotheses.*

Conjunction, logical: Expressed by $\cdot$, which is commutative and associative.

Connotation: The conventional criterion for applying a term.

Connotative definition: A definition in which the definiens is a report of the connotation of the definiendum; e.g., "bachelor" means "unmarried male."

Consequent: In conditional statements of the form "If p, then q," statement q is called the consequent.

Consistency: A set of statements is consistent if and only if it is possible for them all to be true.

Constant: A symbol which does not serve as a variable, for example, $\supset$, $\sim$, $\equiv$, etc. Individual constants, usually designated by small English letters, symbolize individuals; e.g., in "*a* is white," or *Fa*, *a* is an individual constant.

Context-dependent and context-independent arguments: All inductive arguments are context-dependent, for their correctness depends upon the evidence known at a given time, or in a given context. All deductive arguments are context-independent, for they are valid at all times, or in any context.

Contextual definition: A definition which defines a word by putting it into a context. For example, a contextual definition of "hard" would be "X is hard when it is solid and firm to the touch."

Contingent statement, attribute, or event: A statement, attribute, or event which is not necessary.

Contradiction: A statement which is logically false, e.g., "Some cats which are black are not cats."

Contradictory: Two statements are said to be contradictory when the truth of one entails the falsity of the other and the falsity of one entails the truth of the other.   For example, the statement forms "All A are B" and "Some A are not B" are contradictory.

Contrapositive: The contrapositive of a statement is its obverted converted obverse. For example, the contrapositive of the statement form "All A are B" is "All non-B are non-A"; the contrapositive of $p \supset q$ is $\sim q \supset \sim p$.

Contrary: Two statements are said to be contrary when the truth of one entails the falsity of the other; i.e., both cannot be true simultaneously though both can be false simultaneously.   For example, the statement forms "All A are B" and "No A are B" are contrary.

Converse: The converse of a statement is one in which the subject and predicate terms of the original statement have been reversed.   For example, the converse of the statement form "Some A are B" is "Some B are A."

Conversion: The process of converting a statement.

Copula: The verb which connects or links the subject and predicate of a statement having a *subject-predicate* form.

Correct argument: An argument in which the premises constitute sufficient grounds for asserting the conclusion.

Decision: A deliberate choice made in response to some problematic situation.

Decision procedure: Methods which in a finite number of steps yield unequivocal solutions.   The method of truth-tables is a decision procedure for determining the validity of arguments.

Deduction: See *deductive argument.*

Deductive argument: An argument in which the premises necessarily imply, or entail, the conclusion; the premises constitute conclusive evidence for the conclusion.

Definiendum: That which is defined.

Definiens: That part of a definition which gives the meaning of the definiendum.

Definition: Generally, an expression which gives the meaning of some word or other expression.   But see *real definition.*

Demonstration: A proof.   Premises are produced which entail that which is to be demonstrated.

Denotation: The denotation, or extension, of a term consists of all the objects to which the term applies.

Denying the antecedent, fallacy of: A formal fallacy exhibited by an argument with the form "If p, then q; not-p; therefore not-q."

Difference, method of: A form of eliminative induction whereby it is inferred, in the words of John Stuart Mill, that "if an instance in which the phenomenon under investigation occurs and an instance in which it does not occur have every circumstance in common save one, that one occurring only in the former, the circumstance in which alone the two instances differ is the effect, or the cause, or an indispensable part of the cause of the phenomenon."

Differentia: That part of the Aristotelian definition by genus and differentia which distinguishes one kind of thing from other kinds within the same genus, e.g., "Man is an animal (genus) that is rational (differentia)."

Dilemma: A compound syllogistic argument with the form "If *p*, then *q* and if *r*, then *s*; *p* or *r*; therefore, *q* or *s*," or some variation of it.

Disconfirmation: A hypothesis is said to be disconfirmed when a consequence deduced from it is proved false.   See *hypothesis*.

Distributed term: A term is distributed if it is preceded explicitly or implicitly by a universal quantifier.   In the sentence "No Spartans are cowards," both "Spartans" and "cowards" are distributed.

Distributivity: A general or collective term is used distributively when something is predicated of each of the several members of the class or unit, e.g., "Whales are mammals" or "The jury consisted of his neighbors."

Division, fallacy of: The error of assuming that what is true of a whole is necessarily true of its parts.   Compare *fallacy of composition*.

E-form statement: A negative universal statement, e.g., "No fish are mammals."

Eliminative induction: A form of induction in which confirmation proceeds by falsifying competing alternative hypotheses.

Emotional appeal, fallacy of: Appealing to the emotions of a listener rather than trying to prove the point at issue.   A form of irrelevancy.

Empirical data: Data obtained through the senses.

Entailment: *P* entails *Q* if *Q* is deducible from *P*.

Enthymeme: A syllogism with one of its three statements suppressed.

Enumerative induction: See *generalization*.

Equivalence: In general two propositions are equivalent if and only if *P* entails *Q* and *Q* entails *P*.

Equivocation, fallacy of: Using a term in two different senses in the same argument.

Evidence statement: A statement used in support of a conclusion.   Also called *premise* or *grounds*.

Exclusive disjunction: Any "or" sentence in which both components cannot be true, e.g., "Hitler is either living or dead."

Exclusive events: Those which cannot occur simultaneously.

Existential generalization, rule of: From any singular sentence or open sentence its existential quantification may be inferred.   For example, from *Fa* or *Fx* we may infer ($\exists$ x)*Fx*.   From "This chair is comfortable" we may infer "Something is comfortable."

Existential import: A statement is said to have existential import if it asserts (or presupposes) the existence of objects denoted by its terms.   The traditional interpretation of categorical statements gives existential import to all four forms.   The Boolean or hypothetical interpretation argues that only **I** and **O** forms have existential import.

Existential instantiation, the rule of: From an existential quantification any instance of it may be inferred, provided that the variable freed is not free in any previous line.   For example, from ($\exists$ x)*Fx*, we may infer *Fx* from "Something is red" we may infer "*x* is red."   However, before the deduction is complete, the open sentence must be requantified.

Existential quantification: An existentially quantified open formula or open sentence.

Existential quantifier: Corresponds to the words "There is some x such that . . .";
symbolized by (∃ x).

Extension: See *denotation*.

Extensional equivalence: Two predicates or formulas are extensionally equivalent if
they are true of the same objects.

Expression: Any word or symbol, or combination of words or symbols.

Fair sample: An enumeration of instances sufficiently representative for a sound generalization.

Fallacy: An incorrect argument, i.e., one in which the conclusion is not justified by
the evidence.

False alternatives, fallacy of: The error of assuming that all alternatives are mutually
exclusive and exhaustive.

Figure of a syllogism: The figure of a syllogism is determined by the position of its
middle term. Thus:

1	*M*	*P*	**2**	*P*	*M*	**3**	*M*	*P*	**4**	*P*	*M*
	S	*M*		*S*	*M*		*M*	*S*		*M*	*S*
	S	*P*		*S*	*P*		*S*	*P*		*S*	*P*

Form, logical: The form of statements and arguments.

Formal fallacy: Strictly, all formally non-valid arguments are formally fallacious; i.e.,
the form of the argument is not valid. Sometimes this designation is applied more
restrictively to formally non-valid arguments which *seem* valid.

Formula or statement form: A symbolic representation of the form of a statement.
For example, $p \supset q$ is a formula representing the statement "If it rains, we will leave."

Four terms, fallacy of: A categorical syllogism which is invalid because it has four
terms.

Free variable: A variable which in its context is not quantified. For example, in
(∃ x)Fx ⊃ Gx, the x following G is free. Open sentences contain free variables.

Generalization: A form of inductive argument in which the premises assert something
as true of a finite number of observed individuals and the conclusion asserts that
what is true of them is true of all such individuals. Also, the conclusion of such an
argument. Statistical generalizations conclude that what is true of some percentage
of observed individuals is true of the same percentage of all individuals.

Generalization, hasty: A fallacious argument whose conclusion is a generalization
based upon an inadequate or unrepresentative sample of observed instances.

Genetic fallacy: A fallacy of irrelevance in which a conclusion is rejected as false on
the grounds that its source is suspicious. Compare *argumentum ad hominem*.

Genus: Part of a definition by genus and differentia. For Aristotle, the genus marks
off a natural kind. See *differentia*.

Hypothesis: A tentative explanation or solution of a problem; a statement not yet confirmed or known to be true or false.

Hypothetical statement: A conditional statement.

Hypothetical syllogism: A syllogism whose premises are hypothetical statements.
The argument form "If *p*, then *q*; if *q* then *r*; therefore if *p* then *r*" represents a
hypothetical syllogism.

Hypothetical viewpoint: That viewpoint which regards **A**- and **E**-form statements as
conditionals. See *Boolean interpretation*.

I-form statements: An affirmative particular statement, e.g., "Some mammals are
viviparous."

Ignoratio elenchi: Fallacies of irrelevancy; irrelevant conclusion or reason.

Illicit process, fallacy of: A formal fallacy exhibited by a syllogistic argument in which a term is distributed in the conclusion but is undistributed in the premise in which it appears.

Immediate inference: A deductive inference whereby one categorical statement is derived from another.

Inconsistent statements: A set of statements is inconsistent if and only if it is impossible for them all to be true.

Independence: Two statements are independent if the truth or falsity of one has no bearing on the truth or falsity of the other.

Induction: See *inductive argument*.

Induction, enumerative: A species of induction in which it is inferred that what is true of a number of observed individuals is true of all such individuals.   Also called *generalization*.

Induction, perfect: A form of argument in which the premises assert that something is true about each of the observed individuals of a set and the conclusion asserts that what is true of each is true of all.   Since the resulting conclusion does not go beyond the evidence, the reasoning involved is deductive.

Inductive analogy: See *analogy*.

Inductive argument: An argument in which the premises provide some evidence, but not conclusive evidence, for the conclusion; that is, the premises do not necessarily imply the conclusion.

Inference: The mental act of moving from premises to conclusion.

Infinite regress: An argument whose premises depend upon other premises, which in turn depend upon other premises, and so on without end.

Intension: See *connotation*.

Invalid argument: An inductive argument.

Irrelevant conclusion: An incorrect argument whose conclusion is unrelated to the evidence.

Irrelevant function or goals, fallacy of: Attacking a policy, plan, or procedure for not achieving objectives it was not intended to achieve.

Joint method of agreement and difference: A form of eliminative induction whereby it is inferred, in the words of John Stuart Mill, that "if two or more instances in which the phenomenon occurs have only one circumstance in common, while two or more instances in which it does not occur have nothing in common save the absence of that circumstance, the circumstance in which alone the two sets of instances differ is the effect, or the cause, or an indispensable part of the cause, of the phenomenon."

Law: In science, a statement which expresses certain uniformities or regularities. Compare **A**-*form statement* and *universal statement*.

Lifting out of context, fallacy of: Misrepresenting the meaning of a quoted passage by leaving out significant words.

Logic: A study of the principles of inference and the evaluation of argument.

Logical equivalence: See *equivalence*.

Logical laws: Principles concerning logically true statements.   See *logical truth*.

Logical truth: Generally, a statement which is true by virtue of form alone.   For example, "If *p*, then *p*" is logically true.   More broadly, all analytic truths are logically true.

Major premise: In a syllogism, the premise containing the major term.

Major term: In a syllogism the predicate of the conclusion.

Metaphor: An implicit comparison between two things; e.g., "Life's but a walking shadow; a poor player, / that struts and frets his hour upon the stage, / And then is heard no more."

Middle term: The term which appears in both premises of a syllogism but not in the conclusion.

Mill's methods: Procedures for determining causal relations.   See also *eliminative induction.*

Minor premise: In a syllogism the premise containing the minor term.

Minor term: In a syllogism the subject of the conclusion.

Modal qualifier: A term which expresses the force of a conclusion with respect to the evidence, such as "possibly," "probably," "very probably," and "necessarily."

Modus ponens: A conditional argument of the form "$p \supset q$, p; therefore q."

Modus tollens: A conditional argument of the form "$p \supset q$, $\sim q$; therefore $\sim p$."

Mood (of a syllogism):   The mood of a syllogism is determined by the statement forms (**A, E, I, O**) of the premises and conclusion.

Narrow definition: A connotative definition is too narrow if the definiendum is applicable to some things to which the definiens is not.

Necessary truth: Any statement whose denial is a contradiction. For example, "All cats which are black are cats" is necessarily true, and "Some cats which are black are not cats" is necessarily false.

Negative analogy: In an inductive analogy, the negative analogy comprises those features in which the major components of the analogy are unlike or dissimilar.

Non-exclusive disjunction: An "or" sentence in which both components may be true, "He is wise or enterprising."

Non sequitur: Any argument whose premises do not justify the conclusion.

Obverse: The obverse of a statement is one in which the quality of the original statement is changed and the predicate term is replaced with its complement. For example, the obverse of the statement form "All A are B" is "No A are non-B."

Obversion: Process of obverting a statement.

Operational definition: A type of contextual definition in which the concept defined is said to be synonymous with a corresponding set of operations; e.g., "The length of x means placing a tape measure between the two extremities of x and calculating the distance covered."

Ostensive definition: A definition which consists of pointing to something denoted by the definiendum.

Positive analogy: In an inductive analogy, the positive analogy comprises those features in which the major components of the analogy are alike or similar.

Predicate: In classical logic, the term after the copula in a categorical statement. In modern discussions, it refers to all terms of various orders.

Premise: A statement in an argument which expresses the evidence or reasons for the conclusion.

Probability as degree of confirmation: Refers to the probability of a statement with respect to a body of evidence statements. For example, the probability that some hypothesis h is true must be judged in terms of the evidence statements relevant to its truth.

Probability, formal: Refers to the a priori probability, given certain material assumptions. For example, assuming a die has 6 equiprobable sides, the probability of rolling an ace is $F/(F + U)$, where F is 1 and U is 5, or 1/6.

Probability as relative frequency: Refers to the probability of an event with respect to a class of events. For example, the probability of some patient recovering from a disease is determined by the actual number of recoveries divided by the number of patients.

Proof: See *demonstration.*

Proposition: In logical writings, generally refers to that which is expressed by a sentence. Thus, *"Es regnet"* and "It is raining" are said to express the same proposition. Propositions are also characterized as sentences which are true or false. In this sense "proposition" is synonymous with "statement."

Propositional calculus: Contains only variables for statements and truth-functional modes of statement composition. Also called *sentential calculus* and the *logic of truth-functions.*

Propositional connective: Broadly speaking, any word or symbol which can be used to form a compound proposition. More frequently, it is used to refer to the connectives of the propositional or statement calculus, v, $\supset$, $\sim$, etc.

Quality: Refers to the negative or positive character of a subject-predicate statement.

Quantification theory: Species of logical analysis which combines the analysis of the logic of truth-functions with an analysis of the logical relations obtaining within a single (non-compounded) statement.

Quantifier: A word like "some" or "all" which indicates how many or how much.

Quantity: Refers to the quantifier which precedes the first term of categorical statements and which thus indicates whether a statement is universal or particular.

Real definition: A true statement about some object or concept which serves to distinguish and uniquely identify it; e.g., "Common salt is composed of sodium chloride."

Reasoning: The act of marshaling evidence, weighing it, and drawing a conclusion from it.

Reasons: Statements supporting a conclusion.

Reductio ad absurdum: An argument in which a statement p is proved by showing that if non-p were true, two mutually contradictory statements could be deduced.

Reduction: The process of showing that all valid syllogisms are equivalent to or implied by a first figure form.

Refutation by logical analogy: Exhibiting the fallaciousness of an argument by introducing one of the same form that is patently invalid.

Residues, method of: A form of eliminative induction; in the words of John Stuart Mill, "Subduct from any phenomenon such part as is known by previous inductions to be the effect of certain antecedents, and the residue of the phenomenon is the effect of the remaining antecedents."

Scientific method: The persistent critique of argument in the light of evidence and in accordance with the canons of logic.

Scope (of logical connectives), (of quantifiers): Concerned with the range or extent of the connective or quantifier within a statement form. For example, in $\sim(pq)$ the scope of $\sim$ extends to the end of the formula. In $(\exists x)Fx$ v $(x)Gx$, the scope of $\exists x$ extends to the parenthesis following Fx.

Simile: An explicit comparison between two things, usually containing the words "like" or "as," e.g., "My love is like a red, red rose."

Singular statement: A statement which asserts (or denies) something of one and only one thing. For example, "Socrates is bald" is a singular statement.

Singular term: A term which signifies one thing, e.g., proper names and general nouns preceded by the demonstrative "this."

Slanting, fallacy of: An argument which omits evidence that would affect the conclusion.

Sound argument: A correct argument with true premises.

Special pleading, fallacy of: A form of inconsistency in which a principle is accepted when applied to an opposing argument but rejected when applied to one's own argument, or rejected when applied to an opposing argument but accepted when applied to one's own argument.

Statement: A sentence which may be used to assert or to deny; a sentence which could be either true or false. Also called a *proposition*.

Statement calculus: See *truth-functions, logic of.*

Statement connectives: The symbols ∼, v, ·, ⊃, and ≡ as used in the statement calculus.

Statement formula: A symbolic representation of the form of a statement. For example, the statement "If it rains, we will get wet" may be represented by the formula $p \supset q$.

Stipulative definition: A proposal to use a word in a specific sort of way, e.g., "Let us define 'inherent' as 'structural.' "

Subcontrary: Two statements are said to be subcontrary when the falsity of one entails the truth of the other; i.e., both cannot be false simultaneously, though both can be true simultaneously. For example, the statement forms "Some A are B" and "Some A are not B" are subcontraries.

Substitution, principle of: If any part of a truth-functional expression is replaced by another of the same truth value, the truth value of the entire expression remains unchanged.

Syllogism: An argument consisting of two premises and a conclusion. See categorical syllogism.

Symbol: A conventional sign, which may be verbal or non-verbal. Verbal symbols are words; non-verbal symbols may be sign language or customary symbols, such as ≡, +, ∼, etc.

Tautologous statement or tautology: A statement which is necessarily true by virtue of its form or meaning, e.g., "All black cats are black" or "All bachelors are unmarried males."

Term: A word or phrase which it could make sense to apply to a thing.

Theory: A set of statements which is empirically testable and which deductively organizes laws.

Truth-function: A compound is a truth-function if its truth value depends only upon the truth value of its component parts. Thus, pq is truth-functional since its truth or falsity is determined only by the truth value of p and q.

Truth-functional compound: A compound whose truth value depends only upon the truth values of its component parts.

Truth-functions, logic of: Depends upon the analysis of compound statements in terms of truth relations. Also called the *statement calculus.*

Truth table: A diagram which shows the truth value of a compound statement for each combination of truth values of its component parts.

Truth value: The truth value of a statement is its truth or falsity, whichever the case may be.

Tu quoque, fallacy of: The error of responding to an *ad hominem* attack by using an *ad hominem* attack. See *Argumentum ad hominem.*

Undistributed middle, fallacy of: Formal fallacy exhibited by a syllogistic argument in which the middle term is undistributed in both premises.

Undistributed term: A term is undistributed if in its context it is preceded, explicitly or implicitly, by the quantifier "some." For example, in "Some men are rich" both "men" and "rich" are undistributed.

Universal generalization, rule of: From a formula its universal quantification may be inferred provided that the formula does not name some particular individual. For example, from the formula Fx we may infer $(x)Fx$ on condition that x in Fx is any arbitrary x.

Universal instantiation, rule of: From any universal quantification any of its instances may be inferred. For example, from the universally quantified statement "All dogs are mammals" it may be inferred that "This dog, Rover, is a mammal."

Universal quantifier: Corresponds to the words "Each thing x is such that. . . ." See *existential quantifier.*

Universal statement: A statement of subject-predicate form in which the subject has the quantifier "all" or "no" or its equivalent; e.g., **A**-form and **E**-form statements are universal statements.

Unqualified source, fallacy of: The error of using as evidence a source not qualified to know the truth.

Vagueness: A word is vague if its denotation is not precisely delimitable, as, e.g., the word "crowded."

Valid argument: An argument is said to be valid when the premises entail the conclusion; i.e., if the premises are true, the conclusion *must* be true. See *deductive argument.*

Variable: In logical studies a symbol which is used as a dummy for statements, terms, and objects.

Verbal dispute: A dispute caused (unwittingly as a rule) by a difference of opinion as to the meaning of certain words or concepts rather than as to what the facts are.

Warranted decision: A decision D is warranted if among the alternatives and on the evidence, D will most likely result in a satisfactory solution.

INDEX

A-form statement, 136—139, 182
Absolute terms, 10—11
Absorption, principle of, 121
Abstract objects, 12
Abstract terms, 11—12
Accident, fallacy and converse fallacy of, 286
Accidental connection, 247
Accidental generalization, 337
Action and beliefs, xiii—xv, 352—353
Acts and consequences, 357—358
Addison, Joseph, 283
Addition, principle of, 117
A dicto simpliciter ad dictum secundum quid, 286
Adler, Alfred, 344
Affirming the consequent, fallacy of, 92n., 234
Agreement and difference: joint method of, 259—260
    method of, 256—258
Ajdukiewicz, Kazimierz, 34
All-or-nothing fallacy, 295—296
Alston, William P., 4—5n., 7n., 17n.
Alternation, 72
Alternatives, 72
    contradictory, misuse of, 297
    in decision-making: auxiliary, 366
        best, 372
        elaborating, 367—372
        evaluating, criteria for, 366—367
        relevant, possible, and meaningful, 367
    equiprobable, 271—272
    false, fallacy of, 295
Altimari, Frank X., 294n.
Ambiguity, 17—20
    and amphiboly, 20
    and collective/distributive use of terms, 20
    and context, 19
    types of, 19—20
    and vagueness, 17—20
American Institute of Public Opinion, 268
Ames, Fisher, 253
Amphiboly, 20
Analogy: explanatory (illustrative), 249—250
    false, 301—302
    figurative use of, 249
    inductive, 249—252
        criteria for evaluating, 251—252
        negative and positive analogy in, 251
        relevance in, 251
        size of sample in, 252
    logical, refutation by, 157—159, 196—197
    negative: in enumerative induction, 245—246
        in inductive analogy, 251
    positive: in enumerative induction, 245
        in inductive analogy, 251
Analytic definition, 28
Analytic philosophy, 30n.
Analytic statement, 98
"And" and · , 68—71
Andrade, E.N. da C., 439
Apparent contradiction, 97
Appeal: to fear, pride, and vanity, 306
    to force, 308
    to ignorance, 291—292

Appeal: to the mob, 307—308
    to sympathy, 307
    to tradition, 306—307
Appraisal of argument, xiv—xv, 50—51
A priori probability (see Formal probability)
A priori truth, 96
Arago, Jean, 333
Arbiter linguae, 28
Arbitrary instance, 209
Arbitrary thing, 209
Argument, xv, 57
    analysis of, 42—46
    appraisal of, 50—51
    of the beard, 319
    circular, 288—289
    conclusion of, xiv, 42, 44, 52
    and conditional statement, 48
    correct, 50—52, 240
    deductive, 52—54, 59
    elementary forms of, 117
    elliptical, 43—44
        (See also Enthymeme)
    and explanation, 338—339
    formally valid, 55, 58
    incorrect, 50—51, 92—93
        (See also Fallacies)
    inductive, 52—54
    invalid, 54—57
    nondeductive, 52, 57
    nonvalid, 54—57
    one-premise, 55
    premises of, 42, 44, 52
    and reasoning, 42
    recognizing an, 44—47
    reductio ad absurdum, 131, 202, 204
    schema of, 43
    serial, 47
    simple, 43
    sound, 50—52
    and statements of motives and causes, 47—48
    subsidiary, 44—46
    valid, 54—57, 59
        (See also Validity)
    word clues in, 44
Argumentum ad baculum, 308
Argumentum ad hominem, 304—305, 318—320
Argumentum ad ignoratiam, 291—292, 321
Argumentum ad misericordiam, 307
Argumentum ad populum, 307—308
Argumentum ad verecundiam, 306—307
Aristotelian logic, 135
Aristotle, 3, 27, 32, 35, 36n., 38, 59, 63, 135, 144n., 151, 153n., 284, 328, 330—332, 334, 345
Aristotle's law of motion, 330—332, 334
Arithmetic and truth-functional logic, 95n.
Arnauld, Antoine, 303
Artificial language, 64
Asquith, Lord, 442
Association: and meaning, 16
    principle of, 121
Associative relation, 83, 116

Sheffer, Henry, 114*n.*
Shelley, Percy Bysshe, 18
Shortened truth table, 101−103, 198
Significant advantage, 369
Simile, 249
Simple affirmative statement, 65
Simple argument, 43
Simple conversion, 150−151
Simplicity of hypothesis, 334
Simplification, principle of, 117
Singular description, 10
Singular sentences and names, 194
Singular statement, 194, 251
  and nonstandard form syllogisms, 175−176
Singular terms, 9−10, 176
  and demonstratives, 10
  and possessives, 10
  and pronouns, 10
Size of sample: in enumerative induction, 247−248
  in inductive analogy, 252
Skolem, Thoralf, 108
Skolem's theorem, 108
Slanting, fallacy of, 302
Social context of speech acts, 4
Socrates, 30*n.,* 406
Sound argument, 50−52
Special pleading, fallacy of, 311−312
Specificity of language, 18
Speech acts, 3−4
  force and effects of, 5−8, 16
  perlocutionary effects of, 7−8
  social context of, 4
Spencer, Herbert, 32
Spengler, Oswald, 301
Spinoza, Baruch, 373, 401
Square of opposition: and implications of hypothetical
    viewpoint, 166−168
  traditional, 146−148
Squinting modifier, 20
Stamp, Josiah, 155
Standard form categorical syllogism, 155   156
Statement(s), 40−41, 51, 86
  A-form, 136−139
  analytic, 198
  of arithmetic, 95
  categorical form of, 135
    quality and quantity of, 143
  complex and compound, 59, 65
  conditional, 48
    generalized and contrary-to-fact, 76−77
  contingent, 94, 97−98
  contradictory, 146
  contrary, 147
  E-form, 136−137, 139−140
  elliptical, 70, 264
  empirical, and induction, 240−242
  evidence, 233
  "exceptive," 142
  of fact, 358
  I-form, 136−137, 140−141
  independent, 132
  O-form, 136−137, 141−142
  quantified, 137, 187
  simple affirmative, 65
  singular, and names, 194
  and statement forms, 67

Statement(s): statistical, 254*n.,* 265−269
  sub-contrary, 147
  synthetic, 98
  systems of, and theories, 339−344
Statement calculus, 59, 64
Statement connectives, 65−80
  · and "and," 68−71
  ≡ and "if and only if," 79−80
  ⊃ and "if . . . then," 73−78
  ~ and "not," 66−68
  v and "or," 71−72
Statement forms, 59, 66−67, 86
  and statements, 67
Statement-sentence distinction, 40−41
Statement variables, 86
Statistical correlation, 267−268
Statistical explanation, 339*n.*
Statistical fallacies, 266−269, 271−272
Statistical probability, 265
Statistical statement, 254*n.,* 265−269
Statistics: faulty analysis of, 269
  faulty comparison of, 269
Stebbing, L. Susan, 38
Stevenson, Adlai E., 309
Stevin, Simon, 331
Stipulative definition, 32−34
"Straw-man" argument, 303, 321
Strawson, P. F., 168*n.*
Strengthened moods of syllogism, 167
Stroke symbol (|), 114*n.*
Subaltern moods of syllogism, 167
Subclasses, definition by enumeration of, 30
Subcontraries, 147
Subcontrary hypotheses, probability of, 279
Subimplication, 148
Subject term, 143
Subjective connotation, 16
Subjunctive conditional, 337
Substitution instance, 117, 138
Successful communication, 8
Sufficient condition, 14, 25, 78, 255−256, 293
Suggestive question, 290
Support, relation of, 235, 240
Suppressed conclusion and premise, 178
Supreme Court, 286
Swinburne, Algernon Charles, 18
Syllogism: categorical (*see* Categorical syllogism)
  disjunctive, 117
  elliptical (*see* Enthymeme)
  figures of, 156
  hypothetical, 117
  moods of, 156
    strengthened, subaltern, and weakened, 167
  nonstandard form, and singular statements, 175−176
  odd, 183
  rules for, 159−163
  standard-form categorical, 155−156
  with universal premises, 167
Syllogistic forms, valid, memorization of, 159*n.*
Symbols, 58−60, 65, 114*n.,* 180−186, 189
Synonym, definition by, 29
Synthetic statement, 98

Tables, truth (*see* Truth tables)
Taft, Robert A., 317, 319
Tautologous biconditional, 111, 117*n.*

Verbal disputes, 22 – 25
Verbal fallacies, 285 – 288
Verification theory of meaning, 7n.
Voltaire, 313

Waisman, Friedrich, 18
Ward, Benjamin, 340n.
Warrant, relation of, 235, 240
Warranted decisions, 352 – 354
Warranted prediction statements, framing,
 367 – 368
Weakened moods of syllogism, 167

Wedge symbol (v), 65, 71 – 72
West, Mae, 19
Whately, Richard, 446
Whitehead, Alfred North, 85, 95n., 135, 264, 328,
 344 – 345
Wilde, Oscar, 399
Wilson, Charles E., 450
Wittgenstein, Ludwig, 13 – 14,
Word clues in argument, 44
Wordsworth, William, 30

Yeats, William Butler, 49, 400